ALL THE TINY MOMENTS BLAZING

ALL THE TINY MOMENTS BLAZING • A LITERARY GUIDE TO SUBURBAN LONDON •

GED POPE

REAKTION BOOKS

Published by Reaktion Books Ltd
Unit 32, Waterside
44–48 Wharf Road
London N1 7UX, UK

www.reaktionbooks.co.uk

First published 2020
Copyright © Ged Pope 2020

Printed and bound in Great Britain
by TJ International, Padstow, Cornwall

A catalogue record for this book is available from the British Library

ISBN 978 1 78914 307 2

CONTENTS

INTRODUCTION 7

1 'THE BASTARD SIDE' *Southeast London, I: From Deptford and New Cross to Greenwich, Woolwich, Blackheath, Charlton, Brockley and Lewisham* 13

2 'THE HOWLING DESERT' *Southeast London, II: From Camberwell to Peckham, Dulwich, Herne Hill and Forest Hill* 63

3 'A STRANGE FEELING IN THE AIR' *Outer Southeast London: From Sydenham to Penge, Crystal Palace and the Norwoods, South Norwood, Bromley, Chislehurst and Croydon* 105

4 'SO VERY GREY AND MEAN' *Southwest London: From Brixton to Clapham, Battersea, Wandsworth, Balham, Tooting and Streatham* 145

5 'UNCONGENIAL NEIGHBOURS' *Outer Southwest London: From Wimbledon to Putney, Mortlake, Richmond, Twickenham, Teddington, Kingston, Shepperton, Surbiton, New Malden and Worcester Park* 201

6 'REAL STABILITY' *West London: From Hammersmith to Chiswick, Brentford, Hounslow, Southall, Ealing, Shepherd's Bush and White City* 253

7 'FINE THINGS TO BE SEEN' *Northwest London: From Kensal Green to Neasden, Willesden, Kilburn, West Hampstead, Dollis Hill, Wembley, Harrow, Ruislip and the Outer Northwest* 291

8 'ASPIRING IN THE AIR' *North London: From Camden Town to Primrose Hill, Kentish Town, Holloway, Crouch End, Stoke Newington, Islington and Highbury* 321

9 'SO NEAR HEAVEN' *Hampstead and Highgate* 385

10 'IN ALL PLACES HIGH AND LOW' *Outer North London: Following the North Circular Road from Hendon to Finchley, Barnet and Friern Barnet, Cockfosters, Enfield, Palmers Green, Ponders End, Tottenham and Edmonton* 423

11 'THE ODOUR OF OLD STONE' *East London: From Dalston to Hackney, Walthamstow, Stratford and the Isle of Dogs* 451

12 'THE OVERLOOKED CITY' *Outer East London: From Barking to Ilford, Romford, Dagenham, Rainham and Purfleet* 487

REFERENCES 503
A READER'S GUIDE 546
ACKNOWLEDGEMENTS 559

INTRODUCTION

'It gets into your bones. You don't even realise it, until you're driving through it, watching all the things you've always known and leaving them behind. They're driving past the streets, the shops, the corners where they made themselves. Every ghost is out there, staring. Bad skin and sunken eyes, grinning madly at them from the past. It's in their bones. Bread and booze and concrete. The beauty of it. All the tiny moments blazing. Preachers, parents, workers. Empty-eyed romantics going nowhere.'
KATE TEMPEST, *The Bricks that Built the Houses* (2016)

Many of the numerous available guides to literary London offer us detailed explorations of the city centre. We get Shakespeare's Bankside, Evelyn Waugh's (or Bertie Wooster's) Mayfair, Pepys's City, Woolf's Westminster and Dickens's . . . well, take your pick – while the London suburbs, the places where most Londoners actually live, are mostly ignored. Aggrieved suburban readers might suppose that their neighbourhoods are being judged as more or less indistinguishable; deficient in history, lacking in any claim to either individuality or to a specific identity. Merely referring to 'the London suburbs' seemingly implies the false presumption that the entire zone is just one feature-less mass. The happy reality is that a huge number of books have been set in the London suburbs; a great expanse of literary treasures that deserve to be better regarded and, most importantly, more widely read.

This book will demonstrate that individual London suburbs do indeed have unique and specific identities, have a different 'feel' or quality, however difficult that might be to pin down exactly. As St John Adcock, in his lively 1926 miscellany *Wonderful London*, wisely counsels: 'to the experienced Londoner all these districts (Battersea, Clapham, Balham, Tooting etc.) are as distinct from one another as Wimbledon and Highgate.'[1] A morning in Forest Hill is not the same as an afternoon in Finsbury Park. Dulwich and Dalston are *not* identical, despite Will Self's creation of the limbo mirror-suburbs 'Dulburb' and 'Dulston'. Apart from being geographic mirror inversions of each other, Richmond and Rainham have nothing much in common.

These places have been written about variously and brilliantly. Even in the unlikeliest of London suburbs, interesting things *have* been seen, noted and, above all, written there. This needs emphasizing: the London suburbs have, for around two hundred years now, fired the creative literary imagination. There is indeed an extant alternative tradition of London suburban writing. Whether this is Samuel Johnson hiding away in bucolic pre-industrial Streatham, Vincent van Gogh walking the long route to work through Stockwell, Italo Svevo cheering on Charlton Athletic at The Valley or Angela Carter hymning the productive, joyful 'wrongness' of south-of-the-river Brixton, the suburbs have long been closely observed, keenly remembered and brilliantly imagined. London suburbs, after all, do have a place in literary London and, more widely, in British cultural geography.

Examining literary responses to specific London suburbs, and the ways in which particular suburbs have been created and recreated in literary work, can give us a much expanded view of the London imaginary. As many cultural geographers now argue, the many locations, urban or not, that we routinely perceive as just being unavoidably 'out there', as fixed, objective realities, are in many ways the product of some kind of cultural work and imaginative recreation. Nearly all the inhabited places on the globe are already rendered to us, to some extent, by the ways in which they have been interpreted and imagined. And literary work, of course, is one of the key ways in which certain places are given meaning.

So, for instance, many visitors see London through the prisms of Dickens's forbidding buildings, muddy streets and teeming crowds, Conan Doyle's (or is it Sherlock Holmes's?) slippery, foggy labyrinths or T. S. Eliot's London Bridge, with its shuffling undead commuters. The fictional, it seems, makes up a large part of any given place's perceived reality. Jonathan Raban, coining a handy phrase, calls this final version of personal and social place the 'Soft City'.[2] It is not just the city that is concrete, bricks and glass, but its stories, too. And these are infinitely malleable.

This works for the suburbs as well, for those places that are supposed not to have any history or tradition worth knowing. Writers have long realized that London suburban locations do have a particular character. This guide sets out to describe how writers, from the seventeenth century on, have responded to, and fictionally reimagined, London's peripheral zones.

We will see, for instance, how the devastation of southeast London's original pastoral identity is sensed, and mourned, by many writers dealing with the area: John Ruskin at Denmark Hill, Henry Williamson at Brockley and, above all, H. G. Wells in Bromley. Then we will see, in turn, as those same fields, lanes and rivers quickly disappeared under stretches of Victorian lower-middle-class terraces and semis, how writers became attuned to the lives of hard-working, aspirational, scrabbling clerks and their families, for whom all this 'desolation' presented, in fact, a new chance, the promise of a far better life.

We will see that Crystal Palace – or, formerly, Upper Norwood – was, in its mid-nineteenth-century heyday, rendered as quite the future of metropolitan living, much admired by Émile Zola, painted by Camille Pissarro and others, all marvelling at the startling modernity of spacious villas, new train stations and 'New Women' breezily cycling up and down the steep hills. This character of Victorian optimism then decays, the actual Palace building burns down, the area slowly traffic-choked and isolated, becoming the perfect setting for the grubby and flyblown in Lawrence Durrell's *The Black Book* (1938) and Angela Carter's *The Magic Toyshop* (1967).

Many of west London's suburban neighbourhoods, along the river and in and around the Great West Road (the A4), possibly because of this sense of being at the limits of London, the ends of London and the chance to escape the city's monstrous pull, have been coloured as zones of escape, transience or fantasy. Hammersmith alone is the site of Daniel Defoe's Moll Flanders's partial reinvention, of William Morris's startling vision of a utopian Britain in *News from Nowhere* (1890), and even the location of the bug itself in Richard Marsh's *fin de siècle* horror tale *The Beetle* (1897).

The selection of materials in the pages ahead is broad: including novels, short stories, diaries, poems, local guides, travelogues, memoir and biography. The guide is focused not so much on who lived where, but on how a wide range of observers and imaginative writers created a particular sense of that particular neighbourhood. Excerpts have been selected simply on the basis of which seems to best capture that place's character.

London's suburbs are vast in extent: from Croydon to Barnet, south to north, is around 20 miles. Purfleet to Hayes, from east to west, is nearly 30 miles. But while the vastness of London's suburban spread was, at first, in writing this guide, quite daunting, it turned out not to be too much of a problem. Most of the suburbs discussed below lie in that narrow band between about 3 and 6 miles out from Charing Cross: that is, out to where the famed 'Knowledge' of black cab drivers extends. Some of these places were clearly once 'classic' Victorian suburbs – Brixton, Neasden, Hackney – but are not suburban in that sense any more. Yet we can see that these places still retain a crucial suburban element – a question of commons, parks and open spaces, of streets of semis, villas and board schools, of thronged High Streets and Parades – that are very different to central London and very different to the 'Edgelands' even further out. These places feel like the suburbs.

Most of the locations discussed here, then, are part of that dough-nut of Victorian mass suburbia, built up from the 1860s, tracing a path, roughly, from Deptford, Peckham and Camberwell, Brixton, Clapham, Putney and Richmond in the south; across the river, to Hammersmith, Brentford, Acton; then up to Harlesden, Willesden and Kilburn; across to Camden, Kentish Town, north Islington, Highbury and Holloway; then east to Stoke Newington, with excursions up to Haringey, Tottenham and Walthamstow; back down to Hackney and Dalston, and finally, down to Stratford, the Lea Valley and Poplar.

Occasionally the guide goes further out to explore the southwest, as far as Surbiton and Kingston (even to Woking, to include the area where H. G. Wells's Martians kicked off their campaign for global domination). To outer northwest London, to Betjeman's 'Metroland'; to outer north London to include Barnet and Stevie Smith's Palmers Green; and to the outer suburbs in the east, Barking and Dagenham.

More exactly, the book is structured so that its twelve chapters explore fiction set in every one of the 32 London boroughs. Starting at the river in southeast London, at Greenwich and Woolwich, the book moves, clockwise, around Greater London, finishing in the far east, again on the Thames, at Rainham and Purfleet. To simplify things, suburban London is split into six key areas, starting with the inner suburbs: Southeast (two chapters), Southwest, West, Northwest, North and East London. Four additional chapters chart the outer suburbs. Hampstead and Highgate have their own chapter.

Each of the twelve chapters sweeps around its particular area, roughly following borough lines, but ignoring these if nearby districts seem to have a particular affinity. The material within each chapter is arranged almost entirely in chronological order so that it is easy to follow a particular suburb's evolution.

It soon became clear in working on the selection that many extracts are quite funny. In fact, many Victorian writers insisted that the suburbs were intrinsically comical. The two best-known London suburban fictions are both comedies. The Grossmith brothers' perennial favourite, *The Diary of a Nobody* (1888–9), features Holloway-based homebody Charles Pooter. The comedy here, a bit cruelly, lies precisely in the fact that Pooter has no idea at all that he is a comedic figure. Meanwhile Hanif Kureishi's novel of suburban escape, the Bromley-set *The Buddha of Suburbia* (1990), revels in suburban pretensions, snobberies and prejudice. Yet both novels present the London suburbs as being, as I hope you will find this guide affirms, places of energy, life, aspiration and fun.

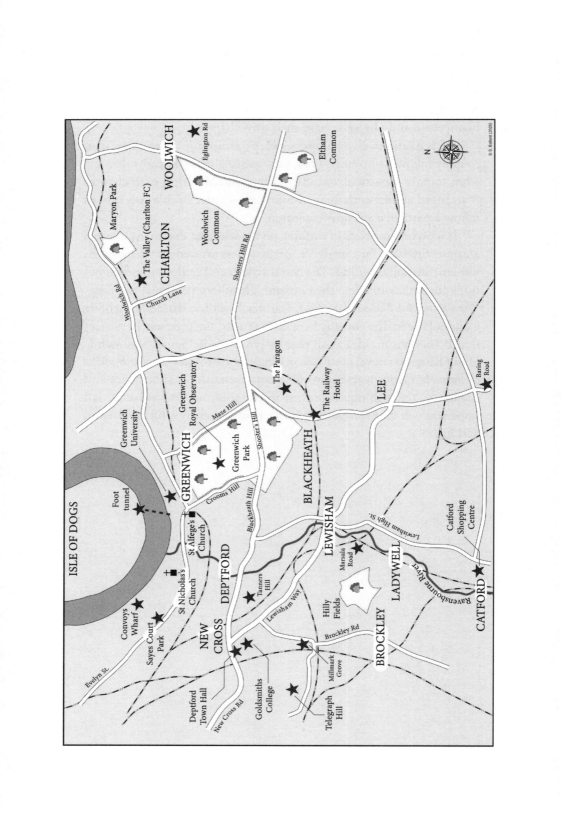

1 'THE BASTARD SIDE'

Southeast London, I: From Deptford and New Cross to
Greenwich, Woolwich, Blackheath, Charlton, Brockley
and Lewisham

South London – and southeast London in particular – has a
unique place in London suburban fiction and culture. 'Why is
London like Budapest?' opens Angela Carter's partly Brixton-set novel
Wise Children (1991): 'Because it is two cities divided by a river', comes
the answer. South London is frequently presented in much writing as
being the 'wrong side of the river' or 'the bastard side of Old Father
Thames'.[1] Here, in Carter's novel of doubles and duplications, twins
and reflections, south London is the unwanted reflection, the despised
and rejected other half, of the city proper.

For influential Victorian novelist and historian Walter Besant, the
place is defined by lack. In his popular history and guide *South London*
(1899), South London is a debased and empty wilderness, a fake. It
looks like a city but is not really a city at all:

> It is a city without a municipality, without a centre, without a
> civic history; it has no newspapers, magazines, or journals; it has
> no university; it has no colleges, apart from medicine; it has no
> intellectual, artistic, scientific, musical, literary centre – unless
> the Crystal Palace can be considered a centre; its residents have
> no local patriotism or enthusiasm – one cannot imagine a man
> proud of New Cross; it has no theatres, except of a very popular
> or humble kind; it has no clubs, it has no public buildings, it
> has no West End.[2]

This sense of the *wrongness* of south London is echoed in Harry
Williams's 1949 survey *South London*:

There is, in fact, something basically wrong about South London. Across 'the water' as the denizens of Bermondsey call the Thames, vigorous life is still to be found. Law, Government, Finance, Insurance, Shipping, Entertainment, Art Galleries, Museums, historical pageantry, these things are almost a monopoly of the northern bank . . . despite the fact that, as a town, it is barely one hundred and fifty years old, it is already moribund. It is a monument to mediocrity, bad taste, and lack of quality.[3]

South London is also, variously presented, as we shall see, as homogeneous, boring, flat, empty, insular, ugly, weird and – a common theme, this – highly destructive of what was once considered a beautiful and serene countryside. Besant catches this theme of suburban devastation well:

It is difficult, now that the whole country south of London has been covered with villas, roads, streets and shops, to understand how wonderful for loveliness it was until the builder seized upon it . . . All this beauty is gone and we have destroyed it; all this beauty has gone for ever and it cannot be replaced. And on the south there was so much more beauty than on the north. On the latter side of London there are the heights, with Hampstead, Highgate, and Hornsey and one row of villages; but there is little more. The country between Hatfield or St Albans and Hampstead is singularly dull and uninteresting; it is not until one reaches Hertford or Rickmansworth that we come once more into lovely country. But the loveliness of South London lay almost at the very doors of London; one could walk into it: the heaths were within an easy walk; and the loveliness of Surrey lay upon all.[4]

Jonathan Raban, in *Soft City* (1974), recalls how, in his younger years of exploring the capital, south London was a blank, off the map completely:

South of the river, I was lost, navigating by the *London A–Z* on cautious excursions to Clapham, Catford, Brixton and Battersea, each place intimately associated with a friend who, so far as I was concerned, might as well have chosen to live in

Sevenoaks or Guildford. But all of London north of the Thames felt like home to me.[5]

Deptford and New Cross

Around 3.5 miles south of London Bridge, along the key A2 traffic route out to Kent, along the Thames opposite the Isle of Dogs, Deptford is adjacent to Greenwich but in a different world altogether. New Cross is just along to the south and west. This area has long been the grubby, muddy industrial and commercial counterpart to celebrated 'Maritime' Greenwich. In riverside Deptford, originally a fishing village, Henry VIII built a huge naval dockyard, the area becoming an important victualing and repair yard. It was also the last safe stop for London-bound coaches in from Canterbury, a raw mix of stevedores, sailors, migrants, travellers, foreigners, outcasts and criminals. In the nineteenth century Deptford was a base for coal-yards, gas and chemical works and numerous sprawling workshops. Charlie Higson in *Happy Now* (1993) describes the dramatic shift from Greenwich to grubby Deptford:

> The drive from Blackheath to the printworks in New Cross usually took about ten minutes on a Saturday and as he drove westwards the surroundings grew more and more shabby and seedy. It was surprising how quickly elegant Greenwich and the Heath gave way to run-down Deptford and New Cross. The streets were dirtier, the buildings neglected, the people noticeably poorer-looking.[6]

Deptford is best known, in literary terms, as the place where Elizabethan playwright, poet and spy Christopher Marlowe was mysteriously murdered in a brawl in a tavern or rooming house over the settling of a bill (the famed 'reckoning'). Marlowe's remains lie unmarked somewhere in the churchyard of St Nicholas, Deptford (there is a memorial plaque). Marlowe's noirish death – a stab wound entering over the left eye – and his involvement with the shadowy and extensive Elizabethan spy network and criminal underworlds is the subject of Anthony Burgess's atmospheric reconstructive historical novel *A Dead Man in Deptford* (1993). Prominent here is the visceral filth and the murky double-dealing, violence and wordplay of Elizabethan London:

Cat or Kit, I said, and indeed about Kit there was something of the cat. He blinked his green eyes much, and evaded, as cats will, the straight gaze from fear of fearful aggression or of some shame of one order or another . . . He ate little but drank and vomited proportionally. He was given, when Sir Walter Stink, the Lord of Uppawaoc, brought the herb into fashion, to the rank tobacco of Barbados and filthy pipes that whistled and bubbled with brown juice . . . At first as at last he was a fair curser and ingenious in his blasphemies, as for example . . . by the stinking urine of John the Baptist, by the sour scant milk of God's putative mother the Jewish whore, by St Joseph's absent left ballock, by the sore buggered arses of the twelve apostles . . . and the like.[7]

In 1652 John Evelyn, diarist and gardener, and his wife, Mary Browne, moved back to Deptford from Paris, where, as Royalists, they had been nervously sitting out the Civil War. They returned to dilapidated Sayes Court, which had been in Browne's aristocratic family for generations:

9th March 1652. I went to Deptford where I made preparation for my settlement, no more intending to go out of England, but endeavour a settled life, either in this or some other place, there now being so little appearance of change for the better, all being entirely in the rebel's hands.[8]

Evelyn subsequently worked on improving the house and, especially, the gardens at Sayes Court:

this particular habitation and estate contiguous to it . . . very much suffering for want of some friend to rescue it out of the power of the usurpers, so as to preserve our interest, and take some care of my other concerns, by the advice and endeavour of my friends, I was advised to reside in it.[9]

Evelyn became an early horticulturalist (especially of trees, which he noted as crucial for building ships and hence national security) and Sayes Court eventually became celebrated for its garden, all 100 acres of it. Centuries later, in the 1880s, moves to preserve remnants of the garden led to the formation of a company with the aim of protecting 'the public interests in the open spaces of the country'. This became the National Trust.

A visit to Deptford is recorded by the antiquarian and historian Ralph Thoresby (1658–1725):

> We went by water to Deptford where another new church is built . . . and were very civilly treated at Mr Sherlock's (the minister) . . . he showed me some Roman coins, of Antoninus Pius, &c. and urns, dug up in the gardens . . . Discourse upon the Royal escape, occasioned another, of King Charles the First, which I had a mind to hear from the daughter of the party concerned . . . who told the history, with many circumstances, the chief whereof are that her mother, Mary Baily of Deptford, after she had been twelve years blind by the King's Evil, was miraculously cured by a handkerchief, dipped in the blood of King Charles the First.[10]

Deptford is the ideal setting for Paul Theroux's 1976 atmospheric novel *The Family Arsenal*. Here, shabby Deptford stands for a sense of national decay and exhaustion, of moral drift and political strife, set in that year's freakishly hot summer. We see how a disillusioned former American consul in Vietnam winds up living in a house in very down-at-heel Deptford at the centre of a pseudo-family of drifters, would-be terrorists and IRA activists, child criminals and slumming aristos. The novel is full of apocalyptic foreboding: 'this summer something dreadful was happening: a slump, or worse – an eruption.'[11] Teenage semi-criminal Brodie, 'envisioning bursting buildings', wills 'the wobbling pillars outward . . . with cart-wheeling men and spinning hats . . . dissolving to a sprinkle of dust'. Here the only way London can be made to mean something 'is by reducing it to shattered pieces'.[12] Aristocratic Lady Arrow, on a rare visit across London, crossing the Thames from Belgravia, eager for picturesque working-class poverty, experiences profound disappointment at Deptford Station:

> Lady Arrow got out of the taxi in Deptford High Street, looked around and felt cheated. Then she walked to assess it, to give it a name. No name occurred to her; she wondered if she had come to the right place. But she had: there were the signs. Deeply cheated, tricked by the map and her imagination. She

had wanted to like it and had prepared herself for a complicated riverfront slum with the kind of massive mirrored pubs she'd passed on the Old Kent Road, damp side lanes and blackened churches and brick-peaked Victorian schools contained by iron fences and locked gates; with a quaint decrepitude . . . a place where you could believe a poet might have been stabbed.[13]

Deptford here will not conform to Lady Arrow's expectation of picturesque dilapidation.

She had expected something different, not this. It was ugly, it was shabby – but not in any interesting sense. It was, sadly, indescribable. She had wanted to be startled by its grime, and the taxi ride across the vast grey sink of London had been long enough to suggest a real journey to a strange distant place. Deptford was only distant: characterless, without any colour, a dismal intermediate district, neither city nor suburb, boxed in by little shops and little brown terraces – many defaced with slanted obscure slogans – and very dusty . . . If anyone asked she would say Deptford was like the scar tissue of a badly healed wound. She was oppressed by the council estates, cheap towers of public housing draped in washing lines. All those people waiting; she could see many of them balancing on flimsy balconies, staring gravely down at her.[14]

Where Edwardian commentator Walter Besant argued that 'one cannot imagine a man proud of New Cross', Roy Porter, esteemed historian of Western medicine and theories of identity and selfhood, argues otherwise. At the start of *London: A Social History* (1994) Porter revisits and recalls his childhood in 1940s and '50s New Cross, a 'stable if shabby working-class community completely undiscovered by sociologists'. 'Nobody *liked* living in New Cross Gate,' Porter admits.[15] This was a strangulated world of grim austerity; food rationing, overcrowding and dirt, against a background of fog, gas lighting and tin baths. But, as Porter admits, 'there was much to be said for that kind of respectable working-class inner-city neighbourhood that is now pretty much a thing of the past'.[16] This was also a world of full and secure employment, benefits when needed, a loving extended family, and a knowable and reassuring community. There was also lots to do:

Who needed to travel far? There were plenty of things to do around home. The Gaumont, ABC and Astoria all lay within easy walking distance. There were municipal parks and swimming-baths. Millwall Football Club was only five minutes away at the Den, Cold Blow Lane; there were also greyhounds on Thursdays and Saturdays, and speedway on Wednesdays. In the summer there was the Oval, and that magical Surrey cricket team.[17]

Deptford and New Cross were rough yet slightly bohemian in the 1970s and '80s, the latter on account of Goldsmiths' College, especially its Fine Art course, which famously produced Damien Hirst. TAC Office Equipment on New Cross Road has a notice in the window that reads: 'WE SOLD A CHAIR TO DAMIEN HIRST'. New Cross crops up in Blur bassist Alex James's memoir of the Britpop years, *Bit of a Blur* (2007). James studied French at Goldsmiths and met two other band members there. They try to live, in south London, a bohemian-slacker life:

> There were a lot of people with no money in New Cross. On the other side of the A2 down Clifton Rise, past the cool off-licence, there was a largish park, all laid to grass. An endless game of cricket took place, all summer long . . . There was a pub in the park, the Dew Drop Inn. It stood as a monument to a more beautiful era, dwarfed now by the cold-blooded scale of dozens of modern high rises obscuring the horizon . . . It was the best pub in New Cross.[18]

They squat in a derelict block of flats next to Deptford Town Hall: 'We took over the flat, Flat 2, 302A New Cross Road, lying empty as the building was condemned. There was no heating . . . the kitchen had a collapsing rotten floor and was infested with slugs. They left their goo on the lino.'[19] This is perfect, and they host a party in the summer of their final year:

> There was a party at the flat. Large numbers arrived. Adam's girlfriend Raych set fire to a pile of debris behind the wall and it burnt dangerously out of control. Someone fell through the kitchen window. Damon climbed onto the roof of Deptford

Town Hall next door and changed the time on the big clock, which stayed at the same wrong time for several years. Dave locked himself in the bathroom. Graham passed out early on the sofa. My mum and dad arrived in the morning . . .[20]

Deptford is one of the key south London locations in Blake Morrison's sprawling 2007 state of the nation novel *South of the River*. The novel opens on the morning of Friday 2 May 1997, the day after Tony Blair's landslide election win. We follow the lives of a bunch of 'representative' Londoners for five years around the Millennium: small-businessman Jack (outer suburbs), council worker Anthea (Carshalton), middle-class professionals Libby and Nat (Clapham, probably) and local reporter Harry (Deptford). For frustrated writer and perennial metropolitan nearly-man Nat Raven, with Blair's win, things will now surely get better: 'It was no coincidence that the dawn celebrations had taken place south of the river, at the Royal Festival Hall. Lambeth, Southwark, Lewisham: the boroughs of south London were famously depressed, but under a new government the whole area would come up and Nat would come up with it.'[21]

Like Blair's promised new dawn, things don't quite turn out the way the deluded and complacent Nat imagines. It is the key black character in the novel, Deptford-based Harry, who is most attuned to the times, and to his south London location, at home there but also spitefully rejected:

> South of the river was tough at the best of times – the air more acrid, the concrete bleaker, the buildings dirtier, the street vibe more menacing than to the north. And today, under the high blue sky, the Old Kent Road seemed more than usually cluttered with gruesome memorabilia: bunches of flowers strung to lamp posts, yellow police signs appealing for witnesses . . . Arse end of London, people said. Arse end of Europe even. But it was the end Harry belonged to, the hole from which he had crawled.[22]

As a black man, Harry has good cause to take note of his surroundings. Out jogging in Deptford, on his way to his flat off Evelyn Street, he is casually racially abused by a car full of white youths: 'Two heads and eight fingers appeared from its rear window and it was the larger of

these heads – young, male Caucasian – that hurled the words. There
had been blacks in south London since the sixteenth century: Ignatius
Sancho, Olaudah Equiano and all the rest. And yet negritude still
surprised the natives: "we wasn't expecting a . . . *nigger*."'[23]

Harry is trapped between two worlds, between the 'ghetto' of
Peckham and gentrifying riverside Deptford:

> 'On the cusp of Greenwich,' the estate agent's blurb had said
> when he bought the place, but Harry wasn't fooled. Deptford
> was Deptford – had been since Christopher Marlowe had been
> stabbed in a brawl here four hundred years ago and always
> would be . . . There were schoolmates who would diss him for
> having bought a flat around here, indeed for buying a flat at
> all: gentrified Harry, the sell-out, in his uncle Tom cabin by the
> Thames – is Peckham not good enough for you, brother?[24]

A similar version of Deptford and Lewisham appears in spoken
word poet Kate Tempest's first novel *The Bricks that Built the Houses*
(2016). Following a William Blake epigraph ('They told me that the
night and day were all I could see; / They told me that I had five
senses to enclose me up'), this novel unfurls a scrappy, frenetic and
tense south London. We first see Leon, Becky and Harry at night in
a 'fourth-hand Ford Cortina', with a suitcase full of money, escaping
town forever. The townscape is both banal and transformative, an
estranging combination of the drab everyday with rare moments of
beauty: 'It's in their bones. Bread and Booze and concrete. The beauty
of it. All the tiny moments blazing. Preachers, parents, workers.
Empty-headed romantics going nowhere. Street lights and traffic
and bodies to bury and babies to make. A job. Just a job.'[25] At this
moment of leaving they are confronted with a vision of the reality of
what this place means:

> leaving the stress and shit food and endless misunderstandings.
> Leaving. The jobcentre, the classroom, the pub, the gym, the
> car park, the flat, the filth, the TV, the constant swiping of
> newsfeeds, the hoover, the toothbrush, the laptop bag . . . the
> queue for the cash machine, the cinema, the bowling alley,
> the phone shop, the guilt, the absolute nothingness that never
> stops chasing, the pain of seeing a person grow into a shadow

. . . It's all around you screaming paradise until there's nothing left to feel. Suck it up, gob it, double-drop it.[26]

The characters are all peripheral in some sense, makeshifts, 'shadows'; *everyone* in the novel is some kind of outsider struggling to stay afloat: Becky, occasional dancer forced to waitress and be a 'masseuse'; Pete, her depressed and aimless boyfriend; Harry (Harriet), Pete's sister, proficient and businesslike high-end drug-dealer, whose botched 'last big deal' is the reason they all have to leave quickly. This is a transitory city dominated by image, status and, above all, money: 'Money is killing us all.' These drifting twenty-somethings are forced to hustle, compete, and strive to become desperate entrepreneurs, urged to 'chase your talent', to invent and shift between numerous identities. Becky lives in a 'neat, friendly block behind Deptford High Street'; yet, beyond this, emptiness beckons: 'everybody has plants on their windowsills and the communal gardens are bright with tulips and bluebells. Beyond the gardens though, out on the street, the colour pales dramatically. Everything is pigeon grey and flecked with spit stains and dried-up chewing gum.'[27]

Pete, trapped and depressed, unable or unwilling to monetize his talents, finds it hardest to live here, in 'south London's shackles'. Walking south down to Honor Oak Park, Pete 'heads down the wide tree-lined street' towards Brockley and Ladywell Cemetery and encounters typical south London territory:

Snarling children. Smiling dogs . . . past the chip shop, the newsagent's, the off-licence, some girls on their bikes shouting at each other, the chicken shop, the barber's, three men in prayer robes . . . outside the Co-op, the jerk shop, the Good News Bakery, the funeral parlour, the block of flats, a man moving a fridge on two skateboards, the garage with the arsehole woman who works at the counter, the carwash, the kebab shop, the houses, their whitewashed walls and gravel drives, the pub, the other pub . . .[28]

Pete cannot make this work. He doesn't leave with the others.

New Cross features in A. L. Kennedy's novel *Serious Sweet* (2016). This features two isolated, unhappy and damaged Londoners, Meg Williams (who lives on Telegraph Hill, just south of New Cross Road, appearing here as 'the Hill') and Jon Sigurdsson, following them in the course of one very long day until, at the end, after endless interruptions and delays, they actually meet. We first meet Meg out on Telegraph Hill at '06:42' (chapter headings are times of the day – London as both ordered and ordering), looking out over the city, hoping the panoramic view will help her to make sense of it all. The Hill is the place where people go to 'check on the metropolis where it lay uncharacteristically prostrate at their feet'.[29] This chance to see London, and to keep an eye on it, cannot be passed up:

> even on an average day, the city needed watching, you shouldn't turn your back on it, because it was a sly old thing . . . By this point . . . the standard architectural landmarks were on offer: the complicated metallic cylinder rising up near Vauxhall, the vast stab of glass at London Bridge, the turbines rearing uneasily over Elephant and Castle, the shape of a well-turned banister marking Fitzrovia . . . each of the aids to navigation.[30]

London, from here, is a demonstration of the tyrannical power of spectacle:

> These were the self-conscious monuments of confident organisations and prominent men – everyone of less significance was forced to look at them and reflect. Insignificant people gave them nicknames purposely comparing this or that noble edifice to a pocket-sized object, a domestic item: mobile phone, cheese grater, gherkin. If you couldn't make them go away or prevent new ones appearing . . . then you could declare them ridiculous.[31]

Meg mocks and renames the cosily titled 'iconic' towers 'the Shinywank, the Spinywank, the Fatwank, the Flatwank . . .'. Yet where *this* London is unignorable and brashly confident, 'the Hill' offers a counterpoint, as it is itself human and sociable: 'In summer, when residents loitered outside in the early hours to smoke, paced on front paths and in gardens, leaned against doorways, sat on steps . . . slippers and nightgowns, quiet nods in passing, half-awake stares and faces still pillow-creased, soft.'[32]

At 05:25 the next morning (having met at last), Meg and Jon are on the Hill overlooking a waking city:

> She joins him and together they see and see and see the
> bright traces of the lives upon lives that are burning, floating
> unsupported in the thoughtless dark. She kisses his fingers and
> speaks to them: 'Down there I saw a kid have someone play
> a saxophone, only for him. And a man who caught a balloon
> instead of ignoring it. And two women who helped another
> woman when she was upset – this disabled woman on a train.
> They'll be there tonight, this morning. Or they'll have passed
> through and gone home, gone to wherever was next. But they'll
> still be who they are.'[33]

Greenwich

Greenwich, on the south bank of the Thames, about 4 miles down-stream and southeast from Tower Bridge (further of course if one takes the meandering river itself), is a curious anomaly. On the one hand, Greenwich can boast the former site of the rambling, Tudor Greenwich Palace (where Henry VIII, Mary I and Elizabeth I were born); Inigo Jones's highly influential cube, the Queen's House of 1616–35 and the Royal Park, both instigated by James I; the Royal Naval College, for-merly The Seamen's Hospital, started by Charles II and worked on by Christopher Wren and John Vanbrugh; and John Flamsteed's Royal Observatory, started in 1675. Greenwich became something of a resort in the eighteenth century (Vanbrugh built a bizarre folly-like Gothic castle on Maze Hill, next to the park), and then became the ideal loca-tion for grand Georgian villas, and later terraces, set among hills and winding lanes. This is heritage Greenwich, centre of British maritime power and royal patronage, symbolic centre of time and space, stately reminder of neoclassical ordered space.

Yet Greenwich was also an industrial and working suburb, with numerous Victorian terraces, housing estates and industrial infrastruc-ture, now disused. Greenwich was the destination of London's first passenger railway (from what would become London Bridge station), which was also the first elevated railway, built on an immense flying viaduct over the southeast London rooftops in 1837. Greenwich had a large working-class population and was also a centre of brewing, fishing, boat-building and fitting, with an arsenal (in nearby Woolwich) and numerous chemical works (especially in Deptford). A foot tunnel was built under the Thames that was designed to take workers over to the expanding Millwall and West India docks.

Samuel Pepys, as Clerk of the Acts to the Navy Board from 1660, was often down at Greenwich and clearly enjoyed overseeing the work at the busy shipyard in Deptford and his meditative walks along the riverbank. A diary entry for 22 April 1664 records: 'and so by water against tide, it being a little coole, to Greenewich and thence . . . walked with great pleasure of Woolwich, in my way staying several times to listen to the nightingales. I did much business and discovered a plain cheat, which in time I shall publish.'[34]

Not all his visits were so pleasant, however. He records a curious incident, on 30 June 1664:

> walked back from Woolwich to Greenwich all alone save with a man that had a cudgel in his hand; and though he told me that he laboured in the King's yard, and many other good arguments that he is an honest man, yet, God forgive me! I did doubt that he might knock me on the head behind with his club.[35]

Samuel Johnson stayed in Greenwich for a while in 1737, soon after arriving in London from his home town of Lichfield, and took lodgings in Church Street working on his tragedy *Irene*. He also composed his first major published work here, the long poem 'London'. This, very much in the Augustan fashion of the day, is a showy imitation of Roman poet Juvenal's Third Satire. Both poems have the same set-up: a friend of the poet (a certain Thales in Johnson's case) is leaving town for good, swapping traditional city vices ('Here Malice, Rapine, Accident, conspire, / And now a Rabble Rages, now a Fire') for country quiet, for refreshing honesty and decency. Thales takes his leave at the riverside in Greenwich, waiting for the ferry, the first part of a journey that will take him to Wales:

> On Thames's banks in silent thought we stood:
> Where Greenwich smiles upon the silver flood:
> Pleased with the seat which gave Eliza birth,
> We kneel, and kiss the consecrated earth.
> In pleasing dreams the blissful age renew,

And call Britannia's glories back to view;
Behold her cross triumphant on the main,
The guard of commerce, and the dread of Spain;
Ere masquerades debauch'd, excise oppress'd,
Or English honour grew a standing jest.
A transient Calm the happy Scenes bestow,
And for a Moment lull the Sense of Woe.
At length awaking, with contemptuous Frown,
Indignant Thales eyes the neighb'ring Town.[36]

Greenwich is far enough from London, and also suggestive of a greater, Elizabethan, age, to be able to offer a clear perspective on the capital, on its vices, stupidities and cruelty. Johnson's poem was read aloud by James Boswell, his admirer, friend and biographer, in Greenwich itself, as the pair took a leisurely trip downriver years later, in 1763. Boswell records the trip in his notoriously candid *London Journal*:

> When we got to Greenwich I felt great pleasure in being at the place which Mr Johnson celebrates in his *London: a Poem*. I had the poem in my pocket and read the passage on the banks of the Thames and literally 'kiss'd the consecrated earth'. Mr Johnson said that the building at Greenwich was too magnificent for a place of charity and too much detached to make a great whole . . . He said that he had country lodgings at Greenwich, and used to compose in the Park, particularly his *Irene*. We walked about, and then had a good dinner (which he liked very well) after which He run over the grand Scale of human knowledge, advised me to select some particular branch to excel in.[37]

A curious incident is also recorded of the return journey to town as Boswell, as often happened, is made to feel slightly inadequate:

> We stayed so long in Greenwich that our sail up the river in our return to London was by no means so pleasant as in the morning; for it was dusky and so cold that I shivered in the boat . . . Mr Johnson whose robust frame was not in the least affected scolded me, as if this had been a voluntary effeminacy, saying, 'Why do you shiver?'[38]

Ignatius Sancho, born either in West Africa or on a slave ship bound for the Spanish West Indies, arrived in Greenwich aged two, parentless, in 1731. Sancho would go on to become one of Britain's first prominent black figures, known then as 'the extraordinary Negro', eventually publishing and corresponding with key literary figures of the day (meeting Sterne and Johnson), becoming the first black Briton to vote, having his portrait done by Gainsborough (again, one of the first portraits of a black man to depict the sitter in a dignified or esteemed manner) and, eventually, opening a high-end grocery shop in Mayfair. His letters were published posthumously in 1782, prefaced with a brief biographic sketch by one Joseph Jekyll:

> At little more than two years old, his master brought him
> to England, and gave him to three maiden sisters, resident
> at Greenwich; whose prejudices had unhappily taught them,
> that African ignorance was the only security for his obedience,
> and that to enlarge the mind of their slave would go near to
> emancipate his person. The petulance of their disposition
> surnamed him 'Sancho', from a fancied resemblance to the
> 'Squire of Don Quixote.[39]

A chance meeting with a local aristocrat, the 2nd Duke of Montagu, gave him the chance to escape from this household slavery.

> The late Duke of Montagu lived on Blackheath: he accidentally
> saw the little Negro, and admired in him a native frankness
> of manner as yet unbroken by servitude, and unrefined by
> education – he brought him frequently home to the Duchess,
> indulged his turn for reading with presents of books, and
> strongly recommended to his mistresses the duty of cultivating
> a genius of such apparent fertility.[40]

Sancho's letters provide critical first-hand evidence of London life in the 1770s, up to an account of the Gordon Riots, 'the maddest times we were ever plagued with':

> June 6th 1780: There is at this present moment at least a
> hundred thousand poor, miserable, ragged rabble, from twelve
> to sixty years of age, with blue cockades in their hats – besides

half as many women and children – all parading the streets
– the bridge – the park – ready for any and every mischief. –
Gracious God! what's the matter now? I was obliged to leave
off – the shouts of the mob – the horrid clashing of swords
– and the clutter of a multitude in swiftest motion – drew
me to the door – when everyone in the street was employed
in shutting up shop. – It is now just five o'clock – the ballad-
singers are exhausting their musical talents – with the downfall
of Popery, S—h, and N—h. – Lord S—h narrowly escaped
with life about an hour since; – the mob seized his chariot
going to the house, broke his glasses, and, in struggling to get
his lordship out, they somehow have cut his face . . . This –
this – is liberty! genuine British liberty! – This instant about
two thousand liberty boys are swearing and swaggering by
with large sticks – thus armed in hopes of meeting with the
Irish chairmen and labourers – all the guards are out – and
all the horse; – the poor fellows are just worn out for want of
rest – having been on duty ever since Friday. – Thank heaven,
it rains; may it increase, so as to send these deluded wretches
safe to their homes, their families, and wives! About two this
afternoon, a large party took it into their heads to visit the King
and Queen, and entered the Park for that purpose – but found
the guard too numerous to be forced, and after some useless
attempts gave it up.[41]

The Greenwich Royal Observatory and Park of the 1760s feature
in Thomas Pynchon's compendious postmodern pastiche of the
eighteenth century *Mason & Dixon* (1997). This novel concerns
the scientific exploits (astronomical observations, land surveys, map-
making) of Charles Mason and Jeremiah Dixon, best known for
surveying disputed territory between Maryland and Pennsylvania (the
Mason–Dixon line, giving the name 'Dixie' for the U.S. South). Mason
here is an astronomer at Greenwich observatory – commissioned by
Charles II and built on a site chosen by Wren – and thus at the centre
of the scientific revolution. Greenwich in the novel is mysterious, dark
and strange, the terrain of the Gothic – madness, passion, the illogical
– as much as the scientific. This is the haunting scene in Greenwich
Park as two astronomers go for a walk:

Below them the lamps were coming on in the Taverns, the
wind was shaking the Plantation of bare Trees, the river ceasing
to reflect, as it began to absorb, the last light of the Day. They
were out in Greenwich Park, walking near Lord Chesterfield's
House – the Autumn was well advanced, the trees gone to Pen-
Strokes and Shadows in crippl'd Plexity, bath'd in the declining
light. A keen Wind flow'd about them. Down the Hill-side,
light in colours of the Hearth was transmitted by window panes
more and less optikally true. Hounds bark'd in the Forest.[42]

Similarly, Peter Ackroyd's 1985 novel *Hawksmoor* concerns an
early eighteenth-century architect, Nicholas Dyer, clearly a parallel
for Baroque architect Nicholas Hawksmoor, commissioned to build a
series of churches after the Great Fire; St Alfege, Greenwich, is one of
these. Yet Dyer is also a Satanist, a secret occultist whose church building involves a certain element of human sacrifice. Against Christopher
Wren's enlightened scientific optimism, Dyer – Hawksmoor – sees
London as evil, as 'that great and monstrous Pile'. 'Thus London',
Dyer says, 'grows more Monstrous, Straggling and out of all Shape:
in this Hive of Noise and Ignorance, Nat, we are tyed to the World
as to a sensible Carcasse and as we cross the stinking Body we call out
What News? or What's a clock?'[43]

This is not Wren's resurgent London, but the 'Capital City of
Afflictions'. In the nineteenth century, Greenwich, because of its ideal
location as distant from town but easily accessible by river and road,
was best known for its twice-yearly fair, held at Easter and Whitsun,
which was, quite predictably, abolished in 1857 for its extreme rowdi-
ness and tendency to become debauched. Dickens visits Greenwich
Fair in *Sketches by Boz* (1836), a motley collection of sketches, observations and stories describing the great surging spectacle London had
become. Greenwich Fair is a carnival, an uncontrollable reversal of
everyday normality:

if the Parks be the 'lungs of London', we wonder what
Greenwich Fair is – a periodical breaking out, we suppose, a
sort of spring-rash: a three days' fever, which cools the blood for
six months afterwards, and at the expiration of which, London
is restored to its old habits of plodding industry.[44]

Dickens, after describing the 'perpetual noise and bustle' of all approach roads to Greenwich, packed as they are with 'cabs, hackney-coaches, "shay"' carts, coal-waggons, stages, omnibuses, sociables, gigs, donkey-chaises', then gives his readers an eyewitness account of the extraordinary happenings at the fair, which largely involve rolling individuals down the park's steep hills.

> The chief place of resort in the day-time, after the public-houses, is the park, in which the principal amusement is to drag young ladies up the hill which leads to the Observatory, and then drag them down again, at the very top of their speed, greatly to the derangement of their curls and bonnet-caps, and much to the edification of lookers-on from below.[45]

As you move through the park, spectacle and sounds intensify:

> Five minutes' walking brings you to the fair; a scene calculated to awaken very different feelings. The entrance is occupied on either side by the vendors of gingerbread and toys: the stalls are gaily lighted up, the most attractive goods profusely disposed, and unbonneted young ladies, in their zeal for the interest of their employers, seize you by the coat, and use all the blandishments of 'Do, dear' – 'There's a love' – 'Don't be cross, now,' &c., to induce you to purchase half a pound of the real spice nuts, of which the majority of the regular fair-goers carry a pound or two as a present supply, tied up in a cotton pocket-handkerchief.[46]

Night falls, and things, naturally, get more extreme:

> Imagine yourself in an extremely dense crowd, which swings you to and fro, and in and out, and every way but the right one; add to this the screams of women, the shouts of boys, the clanging of gongs, the firing of pistols, the ringing of bells, the bellowings of speaking-trumpets, the squeaking of penny dittos, the noise of a dozen bands, with three drums in each, all playing different tunes at the same time, the hallooing of showmen, and an occasional roar from the wild-beast shows; and you are in the very centre and heart of the fair.[47]

Greenwich Fair's terrible reputation is also mentioned by William Makepeace Thackeray in his *Sketches and Travels in London* (1847–8), originally published in *Punch* and presented in the guise of a series of letters from wise, experienced Mr Brown to his nephew, Bob. There is a clear warning here to Bob, eager, newly rich, having 'completed academical studies' and 'about to commence a career in London': 'If I ever hear of you as a Casino haunter, a frequenter of Races and Greenwich Fairs, and such amusements, in questionable company, I give you my honour you shall benefit from no legacy of mine.'[48]

In the later nineteenth century Greenwich (and neighbouring Woolwich and Deptford) established themselves as centres of Britain's expanding maritime empire and of industry, and saw the rapid growth of shipping, dockyards, warehouses, related industries and workers' housing. Visiting French critic and historian Hippolyte Taine, recording his observations in his *Notes on England* (1872), is stunned by the dramatic spectacle of hundreds of ships' masts:

> One suddenly perceives an endless line of them. From Greenwich Park, where I ascended last year, the horizon is bounded with masts and ropes. The incalculable indistinct rigging stretches a spider web in a circle against the sky. This is certainly one of the great spectacles of our planet. To see a similar conglomeration of buildings, men, vessels, and business, it would be necessary to go to China.
>
> However, there is yet more. On the river further to the west into the city a tangled forest of yards, masts, and rigging rises. These are the vessels which arrive, depart or anchor. At first they gather in groups, then in long rows, then in a continuous heap, crowded together, massed against chimneys of houses and warehouse pulleys. All the tackle is worked by incessant, regular, gigantic labour. All is enveloped in a foggy smoke which is penetrated with the light of the sun, its golden rain sifted. Striking and unusual reflections balance in the undulations of brackish, tawny, half-green, half-violet water. It might be said that this was the heavy and smoky air of a large hothouse. Nothing is natural here.[49]

Henry James, in *English Hours*, also recalls the gritty and grubby reality of industrial Greenwich on a visit downriver from London Bridge in 1887:

Few European cities have a finer river than the Thames, but none certainly has expended more ingenuity in producing a sordid river-front. For miles and miles you see nothing but the sooty backs of warehouses; or perhaps they are the sooty faces . . . They stand massed together on the banks of the wide turbid stream, which is fortunately of too opaque a colour to reflect any image. A damp-looking dirty blackness is the usual tone. The river is almost black, and is covered with black barges; above the black housetops, from among the far-stretching docks and basins, rises a dusky wilderness of masts.[50]

On the same visit, James is amazed to see, at last, the real Greenwich Park and Observatory, uncannily familiar from their miniature reproduction in the corners of yellowing maps and charts on the walls of his old school. 'I used always to think of the joy it must be to roll at one's length down this curved incline', he recalls (oddly echoing Dickens's almost contemporary Greenwich Fair hill-rolling). However, the real view of the steep hill gives him second thoughts. The 'bank on which it would be so delightful not to be able to stop running' now fills him with fear. Now, middle-aged, it doesn't appeal: 'it made me feel terribly old to find that I was not even tempted to begin'.[51] We feel that this is the correct decision.

James's sense of Greenwich as a literal and symbolic global fulcrum ('the precise point from which the great globe is measured') is also central to Joseph Conrad's 1907 novel *The Secret Agent*. London is presented here as a fearful swamp: teeming, muddy, greasy and foggy, dark and exhausted: 'the vision of an enormous town presented itself, of a monstrous town more populous than some continents and in its man-made might as if indifferent to heaven's frowns and smiles; a cruel devourer of the world's light'.[52] The novel depicts an attempt by an anarchist group (instigated by Russia to provoke a crack-down on extremist groups) to blow up the Greenwich Royal Observatory. The Observatory is selected as the ideal target, as zero degrees longitude symbolizes here technological progress and international cooperation, and, of course, observation – seeing and controlling. This is an attempt to shatter reason itself; the coordinates of time and space: 'The attempt to blow up the Greenwich Observatory: a blood-stained inanity of so fatuous a kind that it is impossible to fathom its origin by any reasonable or even unreasonable process of thought.'[53]

Conrad based this central event on a real incident that happened in Greenwich Park, possibly Britain's first experience of an international terror attack. One day in February 1894, staff working at the Observatory heard a 'sharp and clear detonation, followed by a noise like a shell going through the air'. Running outside, they found a young man slumped on the winding path that leads up to the main building. His right hand had been blown off and there appeared to be a ghastly hole where his stomach should have been. Later, human bone fragments and body tissue were collected over a radius of more than 100 feet. The bomber turned out to be one Martial Bourdin, a 26-year-old French member of the London-based anarchist group Club Autonomie. He had stumbled on his way up the steep grassy hill to the Observatory, detonating his home-made nitroglycerin bomb. He lived for thirty minutes after being discovered. The Observatory was untouched.

Verloc, Conrad's titular secret agent, makes a similar mess. Cruelly exploiting the innocence and eagerness of his, probably autistic, stepbrother Stevie, Verloc persuades the boy to carry a bomb up the steep hill to the Observatory. Exact details of what happened next are not directly given to us in the novel: only odd fragments filter through. We overhear some anarchist gang members at a café trying to piece the news together: 'Bomb in Greenwich Park. There isn't much so far. Half-past eleven. Foggy morning. Effects of explosion felt as far as Romney Road and Park Place. Enormous hole in the ground under a tree filled with smashed roots and broken branches. That's all.'[54]

Later, we hear a local constable explain to the investigating officer, Chief Inspector Heat, what had happened:

> He had been the first man on the spot after the explosion. He mentioned the fact again. He had seen something like a heavy flash of lightning in the fog. At that time he was standing at the door of the King William Street Lodge talking to the keeper. The concussion made him tingle all over. He ran between the trees towards the Observatory. 'As fast as my legs would carry me', he repeated twice.[55]

We next see Heat at the local hospital mortuary, struggling to deal with the enormous reality of the human fragments on the table in front of him:

Not accustomed, as the doctors are, to examine closely the mangled remains of human beings, he had been shocked by the sight disclosed to his view when a waterproof sheet had been lifted off a table in a certain apartment of the hospital.

Another waterproof sheet was laid over that table in the manner of a tablecloth, with the corners turned up in a sort of mound – a heap of rags, scorched and blood-stained, half concealing what might have been an accumulation of raw material for a cannibal feast. It required considerable firmness of mind not to recoil before the sight . . .

Chief Inspector Heat, bending forward over the table in a gingerly and horrified manner, let him run on. The hospital porter and another man turned down the corners of the cloth and stepped aside. The Chief Inspector's eyes searched the gruesome details of that heap of mixed things, which seemed to have been collected in shambles and rag shops.

'You used a shovel,' he remarked, observing a sprinkling of small gravel, tiny bits of bark, and particles of splintered wood as fine as needles.[56]

Later, Heat interrogates Verloc, piecing together the crime, the victim:

'But tell me now how did you get away.'

'I was making for Chesterfield Walk . . . when I heard the bang. I started running then. Fog. I saw no one till I was past the end of George St. Don't think I met anyone till then.'

'So easy as that!' marvelled the voice of Chief Inspector Heat. 'The bang startled you, eh?'

'Yes; it came too soon.'[57]

Greenwich as still-working seaport and dock features in the murder mystery *The Worm of Death* (1961) by Cecil Day-Lewis, writing under his pseudonym Nicholas Blake. The Day-Lewis family (including young Daniel) lived at 6 Crooms Hill, and the house features here as the setting for the Loudron family, all seemingly respectable GPs, until the murder of domineering paterfamilias Piers Loudron. Amateur detective Nigel Strangeways, just outside the Trafalgar Tavern, sees the corpse being fished out of the river:

The launch stopped on the leeward side of the body, obscuring
Nigel's view. On its afterdeck, behind the cabin, two policemen
got busy, one with a boat hook, the other with a coil of rope.
Winds and tide swinging the launch round, Nigel was shortly
able to observe their catch. As it was hauled aboard, the rope
noosed beneath its arms, the torso stood up for a moment on the
water. Decay and long immersion had bloated the face almost out
of recognition . . . the swollen tongue protruded from blubber
lips in a grimace; the ruined eyes were smears of white. Only the
silver-white of hair and beard suggested that this could be the
remains of the elegant, vivacious Dr Piers Loudron.[58]

Greenwich here, in the early 1960s, is very much still a working
place. It is an atmospheric, fog-bound place, busy with noisy industry
and commercial shipping, drunken Dutch sailors and packed taverns,
clanking scrapyards and workshops, a working port, full of mysterious
river noises and the vivid tang of coal and grit:

> A smart black ship, with the label of the General Steam
> Navigation Company on its funnel, swept past toward the Pool
> of London . . . A Finnish tramp, its tall funnel heavily smoking,
> its hull rusty and patched, was moving in ballast down-river,
> the half-submerged screw sullenly thumping the water. A collier
> was unloading at the Greenwich power station, the clatter of
> whose conveyors could be distantly heard . . . To its right the
> oily waters smoothed over the place where the body of Dr Piers
> Loudron had been salvaged from the river. A quick-fire burst
> of riveting rattled across from a shipyard near the Trafalgar
> Tavern where lighters were being repaired. Away to the left,
> a piercing, blue-white eye opened – the dazzling flame of a
> welder's burner.[59]

South London often proves to be not at all the right kind of territory for Iain Sinclair's psychogeographic investigations or shamanic
divinations, though he makes quite a few attempts. In an account of a
walk taken across south London in summer 1994, recorded in *Liquid
City* (1999), Sinclair is not sure that this area even counts as London at
all. He records a strange meeting with a disorientated French tourist,
lost, just down the road from Greenwich in Shooter's Hill:

On the other shore, reborn, breakfasted, we bound like lambs
down Shooter's Hill. We're pushing it now, there's still plenty
of ground to cover and most of it unknown. We'll need to
stop, poke about, investigate the odd pub or bone-pit. I'm in
mid-stride, mid-monologue, when a deranged man (French)
grabs me by the sleeve. The Frenchness is not the source of his
derangement. There's something wrong with the landscape.
Nothing fits. His compass has gone haywire. 'Is this London?'
he demands, very politely. Up close he's excited rather than
mad. Not a runaway. It's just that he's been working a route
through undifferentiated suburbs for hours, without reward.
None of the landmarks – Tower Bridge, the Tower of London,
Harrods, the Virgin megastore – that would confirm, or justify,
his sense of metropolis.

But his question is a brute. '*Is* this London?' Not in my
book. London is whatever can be reached in a one-hour walk.
The rest is fictional.[60]

Sinclair gives directions for how to get to the proper London, the one
that tourists expect and want to see: '"Four miles," I reply. At a venture. "London." A reckless improvisation. "Straight on. Keep going.
Find a bridge and cross it."'[61]

Likewise, in *Lights Out for the Territory* (1997), a collection of
psychogeographic tramps through the 'secret history of London',
Sinclair's initial walk is from Hackney down to Greenwich University,
the aim to 'cut a crude V into the sprawl of the city', to physically etch
a sign into the landscape, to create meaning in a bewildering environment by an 'act of ambulant signmaking'. After leaving his home turf
of Hackney and passing through the Greenwich Foot Tunnel, Sinclair
records a familiar frisson: *this* place is not in his book:

Pleasantly disorientated: the south side of the river is much
more than a simple culture jump, it operates on an entirely
different pulse. The citizens of Greenwich have no choice, a
north-facing consciousness (the brass rule of zero longitude in
their spine): Canary Wharf as the inescapable point of focus.[62]

Sinclair cannot get his bearings here, nothing fits, and nothing can
be read:

It's beginning to fall apart. The University of *Greenwich*
isn't actually in Greenwich, that's a courtesy title. The gaff is
four hard miles downriver. But the University of Woolwich
doesn't have the same ring. (Even Arsenal Football Club found
Woolwich too low rent and relocated to Highbury.) The ascent
of Maze Hill – contemplated as we try to pull our spoons out of
our Sicilian coffee – is losing its appeal.[63]

Greenwich also features in Stewart Home's delirious satire of
obsessive Sinclairian psychogeographic-occultist 'magick', *Come
before Christ and Murder Love* (1997), featuring schizoid narrator
Philip Sloane, film director, and one K. L. Callan, aka the 'Magus'.
Reading like a crazed mashup of Richard Allen 1970s 'Skinhead' pulp
novels, arty erotica, Situationist theory and the esoteric excesses of
Sinclair, Ackroyd and co., the novel meanders around key London
psychogeographic honey-pots: Shoreditch, Brick Lane, Brixton and
Greenwich. Nothing, of course, is as it seems: the truth about these
overworked sites can only be found by deep reserves of esoteric research
and refined sensibility. Outside Greenwich's Hawksmoor church, St
Alfege, the narrator explains:

Archbishop Alfege was martyred by Danish invaders in 1012.
What actually happened . . . was that the Archbishop, like the
rest of the ruling class, was an active participant in the Old
Religion. The cleric's death was actually a carefully orchestrated
act of Ritual Human Sacrifice . . . believing as he did that this
bloody end would make him an incredibly powerful entity in
the spirit world.[64]

The novel goes on to give detailed accounts of banal trawls through
named Greenwich streets, which turn out to be just streets; and
nothing more.

In W. G. Sebald's final work, the genre-defying novel-cum-
memoir-cum-travelogue *Austerlitz* (2001), the unnamed narrator and
Jacques Austerlitz travel down to Greenwich from Liverpool Street's
Great Eastern Hotel:

Then we walked the rest of the way in silence, going on
downstream from Wapping and Shadwell to the quiet basins

which reflect the towering office blocks of the docklands area,
and so to the foot tunnel running under the bend in the river.
Over on the other side we climbed up through Greenwich
Park to the Royal Observatory, which had scarcely any visitors
apart from us on this cold day not long before Christmas. At
least, I do not remember meeting anyone during the hours
we spent there, both of us separately studying the ingenious
observational instruments and measuring devices, quadrants
and sextants, chronometers and regulators, displayed in the
glass cases . . . Time, said Austerlitz, in the observation room in
Greenwich, was by far the most artificial of all our inventions,
and in being bound to the planet turning on its own axis was
no less arbitrary than would be, say, a calculation based on the
growth of trees or the duration required for a piece of limestone
to disintegrate . . . If Newton thought, said Austerlitz, pointing
through the window and down to the curve of the water
around the Isle of Dogs glistening in the last of the daylight,
if Newton really thought that time was a river like the Thames,
then where is its source and into what sea does it finally flow?[65]

Ali Smith's 2011 novel *There but for the* has a Greenwich setting, and
uses the suburb's cultural status as a centre of time and space, along
with more recent concerns over property fetishism and gentrification,
to explore themes of how individuals are both embedded in specific
coordinates of time and space and also, dizzyingly, detached from them.
Greenwich in the novel appears as largely insubstantial and unreal: the
novel explores how we use language and narrative to try and give solidity
to the unstable coordinates of personal and historical time and space.

During an agonizing dinner party in a 'beautiful, perfectly done-
out, perfectly dulled house' in a nice part of gentrified Georgian
Greenwich, one mystery guest, a friend of a friend, one Miles Garth,
disappears upstairs to use the bathroom. He then slips into a spare room
– and doesn't come out again. This terrible infringement of middle-class
manners continues for days, then weeks and months. It becomes a
media spectacle, with press, TV and curious tourists all camped outside, looking on. The profound oddness of this event, a dinner-party
urban myth come to life, creates waves of confusion and disbelief and
stunned inaction. In an email explaining the situation, Genevieve Lee,
the host of the party, focuses on details about the house:

To cut a long short story Mr Garth has locked himself in our spare bedroom. I am only relieved the bedroom is ensuite. He will not leave the room. He is not just refusing to unlock the door and go to his own home, wherever that might be. He is refusing to speak to a single soul. It has now been ten days, and our unwanted tenant has only communicated by 1 piece of paper slipped under the bottom of the door. We are slipping flat packs of wafer paper-thin turkey and ham to him under the said door but are unable to provide him with anything more dimensional because of the size of the space between the said door and the floor. (Our spare room door, in fact all the upstairs doors in our house are believed 18th century although the house itself dates from the 1820s you can understand my concern and the hinges are on the inside side. I have reason to believe he has jammed one of our chairs under the c18th door handle too).[66]

This act of barricading oneself away from the world into one room creates a wider resonance. The everyday physical world, in Greenwich, is presented in the novel as alarmingly fluid: the narrative itself jumps between distinct temporal zones, slips backwards and forwards to different personal times, even between historical epochs. It switches between different voices and individual perspectives: characters them-selves are composed of a multitude of voices. The link between a specific time and distinct location untied, one series of recalled events startlingly shifts to another, and characters realize with a shock that they are in the world, here, now: 'Now she was walking up a hot summer street of beautiful buildings and shabby-chic houses trying to remember what Greenwich meant again, which was something to do with time', and 'Anna sat on a wall in Greenwich nearly forty years later in the summer of the year 2009 and looked down at her shoes.' For the characters in the novel there is no safe room to retire to. Greenwich is ideal for these kinds of explorations as it offers, in addition to the prime meridian as notional (yet symbolic, of course) centre of the world, the accretions of history: the palaces, the churches, the grand orderliness of the landscaped park and observatory. This restless mix of the inside and the outside, the personal and the his-torical, the present and the past can be seen as one character takes a walk in Greenwich Park:

> Mark walked through the park. He had forgotten how
> charming it was here . . . He looked down the slope at the
> trees in their rugged neatness, the paths that met and crossed
> themselves, so elegant the way they seemed both planned and
> random, elegant too, the white colonnades and all the grand
> old whitened buildings down at the foot of the park. The new
> business towers of the city shouldered each other beyond the
> river at the back of the view like a mirage, like superimposition.
> Greenwich. Then and now.[67]

The ways in which the non-coordinates of time and space are
stitched together through our cultural work – through language and
stories and imagination – are illustrated by the youngest character, the
insufferably precocious Brooke Bayoude. This nine-year-old is obsessed
with language, with puns, jokes and riddles, slips of the tongue, sayings,
songs and poems, and indiscriminately jumbles together in her lively
mind fictions, myths, snippets of history (especially Greenwich history,
such as the princesses Elizabeth and Mary in the Tudor palaces, martyred St Alfege and his talking frogs, and the Astronomers Royal at the
observatory). Brooke writes a story, a mishmash of the 'real' events of
the novel, and of half-certain history; she wants it to include everything:

> it's about a man who stays in the room and never leaves it but in
> that room he has, like, a bicycle and he cycles three thousand miles
> on it . . . he quite likes doing it and nobody is really making him do
> it. And though he doesn't ever leave the room, all the same he cycles
> through Greenwich when it is nothing but a forest, and he cycles
> up a mountain to the summit, where he learns how to breathe
> even though it is difficult to up there, then he cycles through time
> past the Queen who causes an uprising and burns London down,
> past all the people building it up again and past the Queen who is
> sheltering under the tree in the rain, and he gets off his bike and
> he takes his mac off and puts it over a puddle for her . . . Then
> he cycles so close to the window in a prison that he can hear the
> original frogs talking to the original St Alfege, Brooke said.[68]

The novel argues for fiction (as the prime meridian is a useful
fiction), for stories as the only way to contain the chaotic
multiplicity of the world. Brooke is in Greenwich Park at the end:

The Thames is brown and green today. It changes what it is every day. No: every minute. Every second. It is a different possible river every second, and imagine all the people under the water walking across to the other side and back to this side in the tunnel right now, because under the surface there is a whole other always happening. Brooke looks down at the water then up at the sky, which is blue with clouds today. Then the historic river flowing at her back, Brooke sits on the little bit of wall below the railing. She unfolds the piece of paper in her hands and she reads again the story written on it.[69]

Woolwich

Woolwich, a riverside suburb a mile downstream from Greenwich, is a great contrast. It has long been a centre of military and naval activity and for early industry. Although a small settlement existed here in Roman times, becoming a Saxon village, it expanded with the development of Henry VIII's naval dockyard in 1512, the Royal Arsenal in 1671 and the Military Academy in 1721. In turn, this military activity generated industrial growth: ceramics factories, glassworks, a brass foundry and munitions workshops. Woolwich, then, was a key site for the nation's emerging global military and trading empire. Both Francis Drake's naval and Martin Frobisher's exploratory ships launched from here.

The 2019 Booker Prize-winner Bernadine Evaristo's 1997 autobiographical novel-in-verse *Lara* is partly set in Woolwich in the 1960s and '70s and uses the suburb's past and riverside setting as an exploration of race and nation, cultural and national identity, belonging, and the nature of storytelling. *Lara* is subtitled 'the family is like water' and opens with a Yoruba proverb: 'However far the stream flows, it never forgets its source.' Lara herself is of mixed heritage and the verse-novel roams backwards and forwards in time, across continents and back over seven generations, to explore the complex network of Lara's ancestry: Irish Catholic, Yoruba in Brazil, German Protestants, white British. This complex intertwining of cultures and languages is like the restless, churning river itself as it flows from many different sources into one. Echoing Joseph Conrad here, downriver at Gravesend in *Heart of Darkness* (1899), Woolwich, indeed London itself, is seen as ever-changing, as transcultural, as part of many threads, including the submerged history of colonialism. This flowing and merging is also reflected in the writing, which uses multiple voices and perspectives, a non-rhyming couplet verse form with odd line breaks and shifts, stories within stories, fragments, slivers of memory and conversations.

We see the child Lara's first impressions of her home in Woolwich. It seems slightly unreal and will not come clearly into focus. It is presented as an odd, unrelated jumble of urban and pastoral, of dirt and imposing architecture:

No 173 Eglington Road, 'Atlántico', sits like a fat Victorian
doll's house on its own high land behind Nightingale Vale

Which rolls toward the wasteland of Woolwich Common.
Bland houses, shops, parks, and imposing army facades

fan up and down from the River Thames which sulks
Like a dirty industrial puddle by the old Arsenal . . .

Its garden slopes like an untended terraced field citizened
by two of apple, pear, sweet and sour cherry trees

A wood lurks at the bottom, home to foxes and owls.
next door slow nuns stoop, black bats in midsummer sun,

gathering fruit into baskets, offering us wild strawberries
while we pick cooking apples for their chunky jams

An alley skulks down the garden'd exposed right side;
a garage, plastered to Atlántico's torso, is an artificial limb;

huge Catholic windows stand watch over the distant Thames
which despatches mist and fog horns on grey mornings.

Sprawling, bedraggled, it is a wild mix of town and country.[70]

We see Lara, a child with a Nigerian father and a white British mother, at school in the 1970s, struggling to find a place, to explain herself to others, to assume a fixed identity:

'Where' you from La?' Susie suddenly asked
One lunch break on the playing field. 'Woolwich.'

'No, silly, where are you from, y'know, originally?'
'If you really must know I was born in Eltham, actually.'

'My dad says you must be from Jamaica,' Susie insisted.
'I'm not Jamaican. I'm English!' / 'Then why are you coloured?'

Lara's heart shuddered, she felt humiliated, so angry.
'Look, my father's Nigerian, my mother's English, all right?'

'Oh, so you're half-caste!' Lara tore at the grass in silence.
'Where's Nigeria, then, is it near Jamaica?' / 'It's in Africa.'[71]

For Iain Sinclair in *Lights Out for the Territory* Woolwich is pretty much the end of the line: 'Woolwich tips everything loose down towards the Thames. We're shepherded, wind-pitched, between charity shops. A Dieppe lacking the booze warehouse, but with its literary exiles in place . . . we're so far off the map that nobody has found it worthwhile to close down the free ferry.'[72] Desperate to make sense of it all, Sinclair tries to decode every scrap of graffiti he sees: 'THE MOONIE BOYS FRANKIE GOES TO HOLLYWOOD IS SHIT.' For Sinclair, baffled, defeated Woolwich is 'townscape in a liquidiser'.[73]

It is the sense of Woolwich as overlooked inferior sibling to touristy Greenwich that inspires Woolwich-born novelist Stella Duffy to write the Jonathan Swift-style 'Notes to Support Funding Application. Modestly Proposed to the Woolwich Tourist Board' in 2010. 'I was born in Woolwich and, as a child, Woolwich was a fairy ground to me,' Duffy records on her blog:

> It was right by the river, you could hear the ships at night (before the Thames barrier), I loved the common and the market, I loved Woolwich Common Nursery School, I couldn't wait to go to Mulgrave Primary like my big sister, and the view from our flat three floors up, of the setting sun behind the City, was stunning.[74]

The proposal then is to showcase Woolwich to the world for the duration of the 2012 Olympics, to create a cultural event, a multimedia tour, with drama and readings thrown in. This would, we are told, cater for the many tourists 'who regularly flock to visit Woolwich's famous sites over the summer months, and will also encourage them to visit the lesser known attractions – eg. Eltham Palace, Greenwich Park, the Maritime Museum, Observatory etc.' The tour, a 'Woolwich Promenade', would involve visits to Woolwich Market, Woolwich Library, Mulgrave Primary School, the row of shops on Ogilby Street, a block of 1960s council flats:

> We know 'our' Woolwich offers a truer insight into the heart of London, than for many of those for whom home is a 1930's semi, an Edwardian mansion block apartment, or modern river-view penthouse. If successful in this grant application we pledge, not only to endeavour to share this good fortune within the wider reaches of the borough itself, but also to reach still further in future. We hope to share Woolwich's privilege with those eking out a living in the Royal Borough of Kensington and Chelsea, the many suffering in Islington, and maybe even to those languishing in the outer reaches of Richmond upon Thames.[75]

Blackheath

Dramatically large-skied and kite-filled open heathland (especially if approached via the choked A2 uphill from Deptford), and just south of Greenwich, Blackheath had a decidedly forlorn aspect and a dangerous reputation until the end of the eighteenth century. Astride the main route from London to Canterbury, and then Dover, atop a long slow rise, Blackheath was ideal both as a rendezvous for rebellious or invading forces (invading Danes, Wat Tyler, Jack Cade) and also for highwaymen. Then Blackheath became one of the first proto-suburbs to attract the upper middle classes from increasingly crowded and virulent central London out to spacious semi-detached homes, purposely set in designed picturesque landscapes. This can be seen with the grand *rus in urbe* effect of the Regency crescent known as The Paragon, seven pairs of linked houses built in the 1790s.

Blackheath's dark, muddy, edge-of-things setting is brilliantly evoked (and works as a broader metaphor for international upheaval and chaos) in Dickens's account of a mail coach, 'one Friday night in November, one thousand seven hundred and seventy-five, lumbering up Shooter's Hill', just to the east of Blackheath Common, in the second chapter of *A Tale of Two Cities* (1859):

> It was the Dover road that lay, on a Friday night late in
> November, before the first of the persons with whom this history
> has business. The Dover road lay, as to him, beyond the Dover
> mail, as it lumbered up Shooter's Hill. He walked up hill in the
> mire by the side of the mail, as the rest of the passengers did;
> not because they had the least relish for walking exercise, under
> the circumstances, but because the hill, and the harness, and the
> mud, and the mail, were all so heavy, that the horses had three
> times already come to a stop, besides once drawing the coach
> across the road, with the mutinous intent of taking it back to
> Blackheath. Reins and whip and coachman and guard, however,
> in combination, had read that article of war which forbade
> a purpose otherwise strongly in favour of the argument, that
> some brute animals are endued with Reason; and the team had
> capitulated and returned to their duty . . .
> There was a steaming mist in all the hollows, and it had
> roamed in its forlornness up the hill, like an evil spirit, seek-
> ing rest and finding none. A clammy and intensely cold mist, it
> made its slow way through the air in ripples that visibly followed
> and overspread one another, as the waves of an unwholesome sea
> might do. It was dense enough to shut out everything from the
> light of the coach-lamps but these its own workings, and a few
> yards of road; and the reek of the labouring horses steamed into
> it, as if they had made it all.[76]

Blackheath reappears in *Our Mutual Friend* (1864–5). Bella Wilfer and John Harmon marry and move (temporarily, until Harmon's true identity can be revealed and a move to Cavendish Square effected) to suburban Blackheath. They live, according to Bella, in 'the charm-ingest of dolls' houses, de-lightfully furnished'.[77] Bella, previously very much a city creature, has to develop a more suburban mindset. Bella, we learn, 'was fast developing a genius for home'.[78] Dickens fa-cetiously presents her earnest and thorough domestic regime as though it were work: Bella, 'putting back hair with both hands, as if she were making the most business-like arrangements for going dramatically distracted, would enter on the household affairs of the day'. And, 'with all her dimples screwed into an expression of profound research', she studies the essential *Complete British Family Housewife*.[79]

Blackheath, approached from Greenwich Park, tends to appear unannounced. In 1877 Henry James, after opening a mysterious door in the enormous wall surrounding the park, was astonished: 'I . . . found myself, by a thrilling transition, upon Blackheath Common'. For James this is like stumbling across a fabled land: 'One had often heard, in vague, irrecoverable, anecdotic connections, of Blackheath: well, here it was – a great green, breezy place, where lads in corduroys were playing cricket.'[80]

Blackheath's village-like seclusion and domestic gentility, the sense perhaps of genteel facades hiding something else, makes it the perfect setting for Julian Symons's Victorian-set domestic murder mystery *The Blackheath Poisonings* (1979). Crime writer and scholar Symons has great fun here playing within the confines of the Victorian whodunit. In the 1840s entrepreneur Charles Mortimer moves his prospering toy company to Blackheath, which then 'counted almost as country but had a railway service that took travellers up to Charing Cross or Blackfriars in less than half an hour'. Here Mortimer indulges in his own suburban building mania, having two houses designed and built in two very typical suburban styles. First he builds Albert House, a forbidding Gothic pile on the edge of the heath made to look like a church, with a huge, dark, uncomfortable Great Hall. Down towards Lewisham he builds, slightly more modestly, Victoria Villa on a 'stunted Palladian plan', which turns out 'an impressive model of inconvenience'.[81] These solid houses are built for show, and characters in the novel are presented living in them as dramatis personae. In fact the outside world is only rarely referred to: glimpses of the local Blackheath pub, the Railway Hotel, a trip to the West End, a visit to a Greenwich chemist, who supplies the arsenic for the poisonings. Inspector Davis likes the area:

> He had several stations to look after but he had a particular feeling for the one at the bottom of Blackheath Hill, partly because he had been in charge of it as a sergeant, partly because of its closeness to the Heath. He liked Blackheath, feeling that it was a place where the nobs lived and that it was a mark of distinction to look after it. And Blackheath was also a place where, in spite of what was said about the dangers of the Heath at night, there was not much serious crime. Of course, there

had been the murder of the servant girl at Kidbrooke, but that was twenty years ago . . . and anyway Kidbrooke was not Blackheath.[82]

It is the inside that is the problem: crime lives indoors. These houses, shared by the extended Victorian families who are stuck with each other – huge yet cramped, multi-roomed yet entirely without privacy – are the ideal setting for the three cases of fatal poisonings. Everyone here has a double life, nobody is who they appear to be. Inspector Davis takes an instant dislike to the house: "'I don't like this kind of place, Charlie. Something wrong with it, it's not natural.' He thought this over. "Not normal, if you see what I mean. And Albert House, that's worse.'"[83]

Charlton

Just east of Greenwich, and just before Woolwich, is the easily over-looked and still vaguely village-like (with drinking fountain) Charlton. On his *A Tour through the Whole Island of Great Britain*, undertaken before 1722, Defoe was not much impressed with the troublesome locals:

> On the other side of the heath [Blackheath], north is Charleton, a village famous, or rather, infamous for the yearly collected rabble of mad-people, at Horn-Fair; the rudeness of which I cannot but think, is such as ought to be suppressed, and indeed in a civiliz'd well govern'd nation, it may well be said to be unsufferable. The mob indeed at that time take all kinds of liberties, and the women are especially impudent for that day; as if it was a day that justify'd the giving themselves a loose to all manner of indecency and immodesty, without any reproach, or without suffering the censure which such behaviour would deserve at another time . . . I rather recommend it to the public justices to be suppressed, as a nuisance and offence to all sober people.[84]

Charlton, ordinary and unpretentious, residential, semi-industrial and pocked with old quarries, was the unlikely temporary residence, on and off between 1903 and 1913, of Italian/Triestine modernist writer Italo Svevo (pseudonym of Ettore Schmitz). Mostly unsuccessful and unpublished in his own lifetime, Svevo, confidante of James Joyce in

Trieste (and partly the model for his twentieth-century everyman, Leopold Bloom), wrote the comic masterpiece *Zeno's Conscience*, self-published in 1923. Svevo, working for the family Veneziani marine paint business, was posted to Charlton and, though with mixed feelings about London and the English, seems to have enjoyed Charlton as an opportunity to escape the confines of class and suffocating family life back in Italy. For Svevo, Charlton represents freedom and the charm of simple, everyday pleasures: Svevo chats to the locals, gets on buses and trains, even goes down to The Valley to enthusiastically support Charlton Athletic (Svevo became well known for his lively and persistent chanting). An acquaintance from his Charlton days, Cyril Drucker, recalls that Svevo 'was never more content than when, having boarded a work-man's car, he engaged in honest communication with some shag-belching dock labourer'. In letters written home to his wife, Svevo describes life at 67 Charlton Church Lane:

> Church Lane is a steep street lined by small, brown English houses. Here the houses are all shops: dairies, butchers, tobacconists, newspaper sellers and even drapers. Typically, you can find just about everything here. The shop occupies three quarters of the house. Going into one of these houses one is amazed how you can have a kitchen, two bedrooms, a room to receive visitors – and the piano – in a space where we'd put an umbrella stand. But the poor home-owners are mountaineers; they have the kitchen and another room in the basement, a little room downstairs, then two upstairs and one more on the second. Church Lane becomes rather vulgar the further down you go. The houses only have a garden behind; in front is just the shop. Going up Church Lane the appearance of the houses is more refined; each has its own garden front and back. So I came to Charlton, my capital, where the proximity of the huge factories in Woolwich contaminate the environment and yet where I successfully manage to avoid all the 'gentlemen'.[85]

In *Lights Out for the Territory* Iain Sinclair also ends up at Charlton, at Maryon Park, slightly to the east of The Valley, searching for traces of the eerie park that featured prominently in Michelangelo Antonioni's Swinging Sixties art-house favourite, *Blow-up* (1966). This unsettling dissection of Mod London – fashion, rock 'n' roll, celebrity, youth, sex, photography – centres on a David Bailey-type celebrity photographer who may accidentally, he thinks, have photographed the body of a murder victim in said suburban park. The actual photo, blown up in his studio, offers inconclusive evidence of anything. Sinclair is searching for what he calls the 'patented weirdness of Maryon Park in Charlton': 'Maryon Park was the reason I came to Charlton in the first place: to see where Antonioni had filmed *Blow-Up*. In the Sixties the kick lay in finding it at all, the atmosphere was unique but the park didn't connect with any area of London that I knew.'[86]

What Maryon Park provides so well in the film, and for Sinclair, is a sense of a displaced uncanny. The park's unique atmosphere of familiar weirdness, of forlorn emptiness and subtle menace was only discovered by the film's makers after an exhausting London-wide search: 'Antonioni's moment of genius', Sinclair argues, 'was allowing himself to be found by Maryon Park'.[87] Antonioni sees London from the outside, as a visitor, and the suburban park brings out the strangeness of London that its inhabitants gradually fail to see. Maryon Park is perfect for Antonioni, who seeks the uncanny emptiness, a sense of disappearance and vacancy at the heart of the social:

> Coming into Maryon Park from Woolwich Road . . . is uncanny. It plays directly into the film, into the very specific sound of wind in the trees. (An effect that Antonioni had first exploited towards the end of *L'Avventura*.) Something you can't fake by rustling film stock in a bin. An amphitheatre, a wooded bowl with tennis courts at the centre, an old Chinaman in a white raincoat sitting on a green bench, a newspaper folded in his lap. Steep steps that run up to the tree-shaded lozenge of ground on which David Hemmings (as the photographer) sees Vanessa Redgrave setting up whatever it is that happens; the crime that is revealed (or created) when the film is developed, the contact sheet examined, and single frames are enlarged or distorted – until they develop their own momentum.[88]

Greenwich, in Paul Breen's football-themed 2014 novel *The Charlton Men* (the club at the centre of it all is Charlton Athletic, of course), functions both as a market of heritage and the past, and, in its position across the river from Canary Wharf, as a symbol of global finance, migration and placelessness. This contrasts strongly with working-class Charlton, here also being reluctantly transformed. Charlton-born Lance, just back from an army tour in Afghanistan, tries to explain this area's significance to the bemused Ulsterman newcomer Fergus, as the pair walk around a bewildering southeast London on the night of the 2011 riots (a matter of 'Hackney, Enfield and Croydon'). Fergus is confused, unable to orientate himself:

> Here in Greenwich, he had learnt that everything's old. Like the Old Royal Naval College, stationed on the riverside, directly behind them; a white stone fortress which seemed a fragment broken off a street in Rome or Athens and transported, like a ship inside a bottle, to the edge of the Thames.[89]

For Fergus, homesick, this all seems estranging:

> Greenwich's haunting greenery, armoured in moonlight, stood pristine as a watercolour from the 1800s. Tonight, as the Thames raced leathery-black and jewelled as a title belt, this wasn't the city of the 1800s, 1900s, any hundreds. Those had been swallowed up by the monstrous appetite of a 2011 AD dragon feeding off 3D TVs.[90]

Lance, who had grown up in 'in Charlton . . . in a brown-brick council house, with a whisky-bottle shaped garden', is also affected by the changing landscape, his family council estate house no longer his. Lance points out that Greenwich is 'cool', but 'it's not home'.[91] Home is eastward – Charlton. He explains to Fergus that these districts are not interchangeable but, on the contrary, unique, personally meaningful, that seemingly featureless inner and outer suburbs of London differ from each other. Charlton *is* distinct from Greenwich: 'might as well be a hundred miles . . . Greenwich is as different to Charlton, same as they're both different to Deptford, Lewisham or anywhere else in this part of the world'.[92]

Brockley

Just south of Deptford and New Cross and the A2 that leads out to Kent, Brockley was originally, like so much of pre-industrial south London, dominated by abundant market gardens. Industrialization began with the arrival of the Bermondsey–Croydon canal in 1809; this was superseded, filled in and built over, by the new railway in 1871. Numerous large villas were built, many by owners of thriving businesses in industrializing and commercial Bermondsey, New Cross and Deptford. Then, from the 1870s, lower-middle-class families moved in to new streets of terraces and semis.

Early twentieth-century, Greenwich-born popular journalist, pulp author and screenwriter Edgar Wallace (best remembered now for *Sanders of the River*, for completing the first rough screenplay of what would become *King Kong* (1933), and for his heroic literary output, made possible by dictating to a team of stenographers) lived for a time in Brockley. A sense of this suburb as quiet, respectable – in direct contrast to the fiendish criminal activities extant in central London – are well captured in his series of detective short stories *The Mind of Mr J. G. Reeder* (1925). Reeder is a former police officer now working for the Director of Public Prosecutions and lives very happily on Brockley Road: 'if there is one place in the world which is highly respectable and free from the footpads which infest wealthier neighbourhoods, it is Brockley Road.'[93] Here is his home, Daffodil House:

> On this bright Sunday morning, Mr Reeder, attired in a flowered dressing-gown, his feet encased in black velvet slippers, stood at the window of his house in Brockley Road and surveyed the deserted thoroughfare. The bell of a local church, which was accounted high, had rung for early mass, and there was nothing living in sight except a black cat that lay asleep in a patch of sunlight on the top step of the house opposite . . . From the half-moon of the window bay he regarded a section of the Lewisham High Road and as much of Tanners Hill as can been seen before it dips past the railway bridge into sheer Deptford.[94]

Reeder is oddly proud of Brockley and its environs. On a journey back from a West End theatre trip the ex-detective is keen to point out to his Brockley Road neighbour and romantic interest, Margaret Belman, some south London delights (Reeder, we hear, 'had an extraordinary knowledge of London's topography'):

> They crossed Westminster Bridge and bore left to the New Kent Road. Through the rain-blurred windows J. G. picked

up the familiar landmarks and offered a running commentary
upon them in the manner of a guide. Margaret had not realised
before that history was made in South London. 'There used
to be a gibbet here – this ugly-looking goods station was the
London terminus of the first railways – Queen Alexandra drove
from there when she came to be married – the thoroughfare
on the right after we pass the Canal bridge is curiously named
Bird-in-Bush Road . . .'[95]

Unfortunately, this pleasant guide to the gems of the Old Kent Road
is interrupted:

> A big car had drawn level with the cab, and the driver was
> shouting something to the cabman. Even the suspicious Mr
> Reeder suspected no more than an exchange of offensiveness,
> till the cab suddenly turned into the road he had been speaking
> about. The car had fallen behind, but now drew abreast.
> 'Probably the main road is up,' said J.G., and at that moment
> the cab slowed and stopped.
> He was reaching out for the handle when the door was
> pulled open violently and in the uncertain light Mr. Reeder saw
> a broad-shouldered man standing in the road.
> 'Alight quickly!'
> In the man's hand was a long, black Colt, and his face was
> covered from chin to forehead by a mask . . .
> 'Here – what's the game – you told me the New Cross Road
> was blocked.' It was the cabman talking.
> 'Here is a five – keep your mouth shut.'[96]

Between 1951 and 1969, Brockley-born Henry Williamson, of
Tarka the Otter fame, produced an enormous fifteen-volume family
saga (most of it autobiographical), 'A Chronicle of Ancient Sunlight'.
The series opens with *The Dark Lantern*, set in 1893, and presents
Brockley and Hilly Fields ('the Hill') as a pastoral paradise already
threatened by the creeping mass of suburbanizing London:

> Over the Hill at night shone the stars of heaven; but they were
> seldom observed by those walking there, for northward lay the
> city of London, with its street lights seen on a clear evening

winking away into the haze; while to the east and south of east
lay the high roads into Kent, the vegetable gardens of London,
marked by the diminishing gas-flares of the borough . . . Arable
farming was, towards the close of the nineteenth century, still
being carried on in the fields yet unbuilt upon south of the Hill.[97]

London is getting closer, and we see the 'extension of the county of
London into Kent', 'that distending and parvenu county . . . with
its suppression of farmland under the weight of its burnt subsoil'.[98]
Influenced by the Victorian naturalist Richard Jefferies, who also
recorded the transformation of London's suburban periphery and
noted the near-invisible perseverance of many plants and animals in
built-up areas (for more see the section on Surbiton in Chapter Five),
Williamson records the strange spaces of wild nature at the moment
when it is about to disappear for ever. London's polluting encroachment here is symbolized by the sighting, and loss, of the extremely
rare Camberwell Beauty butterfly, seen while the novel series's key
ancestor, Richard Maddison, is out collecting rare moths on dark
and densely wooded Hilly Fields, just to the east of Brockley. 'The
Hill', which is still undeveloped, 'the fields yet unbuilt', is presented
as magical and idyllic, with 'the cries of owls, the scents of lilac and
hawthorn blossom, the voices of nightingales'. Here the keen young
naturalist spies the butterfly: 'by Jove, it was – could it be – yes . . . it
was a Camberwell Beauty'. Maddison is then jumped by oiky youths,
drunk from a session at the Brockley Jack, including, we learn, a
'buck navvy', a coalman and 'a tom', and even a couple of prostitutes.
They glimpse Maddison, with his net, scrabbling in the dark: ''Ere,
cosh 'im all together, boys!' screams the coalman.[99] Maddison, with
the fine yeomanly vigour that Williamson so admired, easily beats off
the urbanized, and thus effete and cowardly, rowdies. Williamson,
in reality, had eagerly attended Nuremberg Rallies in the 1930s, was
sympathetic to Hitler and some Nazi aims, and became an associate
of Oswald Mosley.

Critic and novelist David Lodge offers a very Pooterish description of his 1930s Brockley childhood in his memoir *Quite a Good Time
to be Born* (2015). Ominously, Lodge humbly threatens that he will
'describe my parental home and other spaces in which I subsequently
lived, in some detail':

In 1936, when I was about one and a half, they bought a small house, with a mortgage of course, which apart from interruptions in wartime would be their home until they died, and mine until I married. It was in Brockley, a few miles east of Dulwich in the Borough of Deptford, where the first range of hills rises from the London plain south of the Thames. Its principal park is called Hilly Fields, and from another park, spread over the top of Telegraph Hill, on a fine day there is a panoramic view of London as far as the landmark buildings on the north bank of the Thames and beyond.[100]

Detailed, but not revealing in any way, Lodge continues:

Millmark Grove was something of an anomaly in its late Victorian architectural setting: just under a hundred houses with red-tiled roofs, timbered gables, casement windows and pebble-dashed facades, resembling millions of homes built in England between the wars, but terraced not semi-detached, in order to squeeze as many units as possible on to a sliver of land situated between a deep railway cutting and a main road that ran along the backs of grey, grimy Victorian terraced houses from Brockley Cross to New Cross.[101]

Lewisham

A mile or so southeast of New Cross and Deptford, around 6 miles from Charing Cross, down along the A20 (Lewisham Way), Lewisham's gradual evolution followed a typical pattern. Originally a small village established near the confluence of the tiny Quaggy and Ravensbourne rivers, it then became a popular, accessible proto-suburb in the seventeenth and eighteenth centuries (one of the new grander villas being inhabited by retired John Wesley), and then, after the coming of the railways in the 1840s, was gradually filled by long streets of sturdy middle-class villas. Much changed again in the 1960s and '70s as Lewisham became more urbanized and industrialized, with estates and tower blocks, new transport links (the DLR) and a shopping centre, and undergoing yet more change around 2000 with attempts for it to become, like Croydon or Bromley, a south London satellite town or 'Edge City' in its own right.

The once highly esteemed poet and novelist Walter de la Mare, born in Charlton in 1873, lived in Lewisham in the 1870s and '80s. De la Mare spent a long time in south London, moving to Beckenham and then Anerley, working in the City for Standard Oil for years, only moving out of south London altogether in 1924. His privileged middle-class childhood in a large house, the air of mystery of his extended family and home (a complicated multi-generational household of siblings, resident cousins and surrogate mothers), the freedom to roam and explore the mysterious and unchartered peripheral semi-rural zones of then new and semi-rural spots in Woolwich and Lewisham, all fed into his writing. De la Mare's world is one that children inhabit, one of both delight and fear, still untrammelled by reason and habit. Fellow south Londoner Angela Carter, in a preface to his best-known work *Memoirs of a Midget* (1921), suggests that de la Mare may be Britain's sole surrealist.

De la Mare wrote unsettling fables and fairy tales, the best-known being 'The Riddle' (1903), which opens: 'So these seven children, Ann and Matilda, James, William and Henry, Harriet and Dorothea, came to live with their grandmother'.[102] What happens here, in an unspecified South London suburban location, 'not a pretty house, but roomy, substantial, and square', is subtly unsettling. The children are clearly instructed by the grandmother *not* to go anywhere near the old oak chest that sits in the dark corner of one of the numerous empty rooms. Of course, one by one and sometimes in pairs, the children do precisely this: all climb inside the ornately carved trunk, lie down – and are never seen again. This is how Ann, the last of the children, meets her end:

> And in the dead of night she rose out of her bed in dream, and with eyes wide open yet seeing nothing of reality, moved silently through the vacant house. Past the room where her grandmother was snoring in brief, heavy slumber, she stepped lightly and surely, and down the wide staircase. And Vega the far-shining stood over against the window above the slate roof. Ann walked into the strange room beneath as if she were being guided by the hand towards the oak chest. There, just as if she were dreaming it was her bed, she laid herself down in the old rose silk, in the fragrant place. But it was so dark in the room that the movement of the lid was indistinguishable.[103]

This relationship between the expanding south London suburbs and children's writing continues with Lewisham- and Eltham-based novelist E. Nesbit, best remembered today for *The Railway Children* (1906). Nesbit lived at various addresses in the vicinity of Lewisham: first, on getting married in 1876, in Blackheath, but also in Lee, Grove Park, and Baring Road in Lewisham, before, finally, with growing success, moving to a large house in Eltham. A sharp awareness of the social distinction of address, incidentally, is keenly explored in her books. In Nesbit's first book for children, *The Story of the Treasure Seekers* (1899), for instance, the Bastables have come down in the world; the mother has died, the father is ill, and the family no longer have the large house, numerous servants and fine things of old. The children now live a threadbare life, without much adult supervision (the father is either dodging creditors or working all hours), in the distinctly lower-middle-class location of 150 Lewisham Road.

Nesbit's biographer, Julia Briggs, claims Nesbit as the first recognizable children's writer. Moving away from the late Victorian taste for stories that are either dreamlike fantasy (*Alice's Adventures in Wonderland*, *The Water Babies*), or morally instructive or sentimentalizing, Nesbit's children's books are based in recognizably contemporary, humdrum urban and suburban settings; but which are still exciting. These are the suburbs and suburban families, typically ones facing straitened economic circumstances or a family crisis, and full of familiar everyday sites and routines: commuting, shopping, neighbours, streets, parks, the emptiness and tedium of Sundays and holidays. In the Lewisham-set *The Story of the Treasure Seekers*, the narrator, fourteen-year-old Oswald, tells us how the action he describes is set in a very real location, not at all like the fabulous places of traditional fairy tale or fantasy, which he dismisses:

> There are some things I must tell before I begin to tell about
> the treasure-seeking, because I have read books myself, and
> I know how beastly it is when a story begins, "'Alas!' said
> Hildegarde with a deep sigh, "we must look our last on this
> ancestral home'" – and then someone else says something – and
> you don't know for pages and pages where the home is, or who
> Hildegarde is, or anything about it. Our ancestral home is in
> the Lewisham Road. It is semi-detached and has a garden, not

a large one. We are the Bastables. There are six of us besides Father. Our Mother is dead.[104]

The Bastables roam southeast London, play games and invent and explore strange new worlds, all gleaned from everyday popular stories and genres, but here applied to classic suburban terrain: hunting for lost 'treasure' in back gardens, detecting 'criminals' by bothering and spying on 'mysterious' neighbours, finding entire 'lost worlds' on the other side of a fence, meeting sad princesses in Greenwich Park, taking exciting trips into London to seek help from enigmatic respected adults. Above all, the kids are usefully employed trying to make a bit of money, to cling on to their precarious situation, and so we witness various get-rich-quick schemes and desperate entrepreneurial ploys: using divining rods, entering poetry competitions, selling sherry, attempted kidnapping . . .

In the next instalment of the Bastable series, *The Wouldbegoods* (1901), the family have escaped Lewisham and have moved upmarket to The Red House, up the road in tonier Blackheath:

> We *were* the Treasure Seekers, and we sought it high and low, and quite regularly, because we particularly wanted to find it. And at last we did not find it, but we were found by a good, kind Indian uncle, who helped father with his business, so that father was able to take us all to live in a jolly big red house on Blackheath, instead of in the Lewisham Road, where we lived when we were only poor but honest Treasure Seekers. When we were poor but honest we always used to think that if only father had plenty of business, and we did not have to go short of pocket-money and wear shabby clothes (I don't mind this myself, but the girls do), we should be quite happy and very, very good.[105]

Oswald, of course, is keenly aware of the value of property and what this means:

> And when we were taken to the beautiful big Blackheath house we thought now all would be well, because it was a house with vineries and fineries, and gas and water, and shrubberies and stabling, and replete with every modern convenience, like it

says in Dyer & Hilton's list of Eligible House Property. I read all about it, and I have copied the words quite right.[106]

In Betty Miller's 1935 novel of British anti-Semitism *Farewell Leicester Square* (published in 1941), Alec Berman, having escaped a claustrophobic Jewish family in Brighton, is lodging in Lewisham. Here he is leaving the Lewisham Public Baths, going home to Marsala Road, Ladywell.

He emerged at last through the turnstile into the noisy evening streets. The trams were keening their way along Lewisham High Street, swaying slightly as they went, top-heavy vessels, with masts aslant. He paused for a while to admire their oncoming grandeur; sailing up: to savour once again the peculiar quality of that diapason, swelling, metallic, which he found so disturbing when he lay awake in his room at night, eyes listening through the darkness . . . he looked about him. Daylight still persisted but dusk was imminent: about to fall. The voices of the children playing alongside the small banks of the Quaggy had something of the remote sad quality he always associated in his mind with summer evenings. As if to shake off this intangible nostalgia, he glanced up at the rise of Vicar's Hill in front of him, where, half way up, on the left-hand side, Ladywell Film Studios occupied a site between Hilly Fields and what had once been a bird sanctuary . . .

He turned a familiar corner: and Marsala Road was before him in the wan evening light. He walked down that road of small grey two-storied houses: semi-detached, all of them: coupled, like Siamese twins. They had, each one, a ground-floor bow window draped with Nottingham lace curtains in the aperture of which stood a glossy drooping aspidistra engulfed in a china pot. That of number fifty-eight had instead a number of other plants; searing red geraniums, white-rayed marguerites, an astonishing variety of ferns; all crowded behind the glass, so that the small window had about it something of the beauty of the baroque and humble beauty of the wayside shrine. Alec opened the low iron gate and heard its familiar plaint at his back as he reached the front door two yards away. Whi-i-ine . . . clang! That meant heads raised inquisitively within the house; in the houses on either side. Who was it this time? Oh, young Mr Berman, Mrs Stepney's lodger. *Been to the baths by the look of him.*[107]

The varied experiences of living on one of the massive post-war council estates in the late 1970s and the 1980s is captured by Tony Parker in his monumental oral history *The People of Providence* (1983). Here Parker records and reproduces, without comment, the words of about forty inhabitants of a housing estate in southeast London (including children, a police constable, pensioners, a clergyman, teachers, the unemployed, a Justice of the Peace, squatters, recently arrived migrants), who live variously in 'The Towers', 'The Flats', 'The Posh Part', 'The Prefabs' and so on. Individuals' experiences of the estate, of course, vary widely:

> I think the thing that's struck me most of all about living on the estate . . . [is] about all the people being nice and friendly . . . I think most people do enjoy living here on Providence . . . To me living here is perfect and I can't imagine living anywhere else.[108]

> You won't need me to tell you about how bad it is, you'll have seen a lot of it yourself. People pissing in the lifts, kids writing on the walls, and those big blocks across the road . . . My God, what places to put people to live.[109]

> Ever since I have been here, which is getting on for twenty years now, from my neighbours I have never experienced anything but courtesy and friendliness. They do not invite me into their homes but that is the English way.[110]

The mid-1970s had seen much neo-Nazi activity in New Cross and Lewisham, the National Front securing more council seats in one Lewisham council ward election than the Labour Party. A far-right march that was permitted to go ahead on Saturday 13 August 1977 was patrolled by 2,500 police officers and then intercepted by around 4,000 anti-fascist protesters. The police lost control and, after the neo-Nazis had been bussed out, using riot-shields for the first time ever on the UK mainland, slugged it out with demonstrators in an event now known as the Battle of Lewisham.

This is the territory where Karim's radical friend Jamila lives in Hanif Kureishi's *The Buddha of Suburbia* (1990), very different to the novel's main setting in Bromley:

> The area in which Jamila lived was closer to London than our suburb, and far poorer. It was full of neo-fascist groups, thugs who had their own pubs and clubs and shops. On Saturday they'd be out in the High Street selling their newspapers and pamphlets. They also operated outside the schools and colleges and football grounds, like Millwall and Crystal Palace. At night they roamed the streets, beating Asians, and shoving shit and burning rags through their letter-boxes. Frequently the mean, white, hating faces had public meetings and the Union Jacks were paraded through the streets, protected by the police.[111]

The Lewisham riots form part of the back story to 'lad lit' supremo Tony Parsons's novel *Stories We Could Tell* (2006), which takes place during the events of one day and night in August 1977. Not *any* night, but the pivotal cultural and social turning point marked by the death of Elvis Presley: 'It was the end of a summer day in 1977 and there was something in the air'. We see disillusioned music journalist Leon Peck destroying new singles by David Soul, the Commodores, Showaddywaddy and Brotherhood of Man. Just as mainstream pop culture itself is about to be shattered, so the Lewisham riots, which Peck had attended a week earlier, symbolize a new kind of politics, a new mood of confrontation, unease, violence:

> I was there, he thought, touching the bruise on his cheekbone where he had been clipped by the knee of a policeman on horseback. I saw it happen. While many of his peers were dreaming of seeing Aerosmith at Reading, Leon had been in the middle of the riot at Lewisham, crushed in with the protesters being forced back by the police and their horses, and he had felt as if the world was ending.[112]

Around a mile due south of Lewisham centre, Catford is best known, curiously, for its dog track (which closed in 2005) and for the giant plaster cat atop the Catford (shopping) Centre, and for its early and controversial adoption of Brutalist architecture. John Betjeman

himself could not save the famed Gothic Revival town hall from the
blocky concrete (though the Art Deco Broadway Theatre escaped).
Two ornate Edwardian theatres were also torn down to make way for
the Brutalist Eros House, as Ian Nairn explains:

> A monster sat down in Catford and just what the place needed.
> No offence meant: this southward extension of Lewisham High
> Street badly wanted stiffening. Now there is a punchy concrete
> focus ('you know, that funny new building') both close to
> and at a distance, from the desolate heights of the Downham
> Estate, where it stands straight up to the afternoon sun. Rough
> concrete is put through all its paces, front convex eaves on
> Sainsbury's to a staircase tower which is either afflicted with an
> astounding set of visual distortions or is actually leaning. Again,
> no offence meant. Unlike many other avant-garde buildings,
> particularly in the universities, this one is done from real
> conviction, not from a desire for self-advertisement. The gaunt
> honesty of those projecting concrete frames carrying boxed-out
> bow windows persists. It is not done at you, and it transforms
> the surroundings instead of despising them. This most craggy
> and uncompromising of London buildings turns out to be full
> of firm gentleness.[113]

Mr Gawber, in Theroux's *The Family Arsenal*, lives, unhappily,
in Catford:

> Volta Road, Catford, was in his eyes a corridor of cracked
> Edwardian aunts in old lace, shoulder to shoulder, shawled
> with tiles and beaked with sloping roofs; the upper gables
> like odd bonnets with peaks jutting over the oblongs of
> window lenses and the dim eyes blinded by criss-crossings
> of mullioned veils. With the long breasts of their bay-fronts
> forward and their knees against bruised, clawed steps, they
> knelt in perpetual genuflection, their flat, grey faces set at one
> another across the road, as if – gathering dust – they were
> dying in their prayers. They were tall enough to keep Volta
> Road in shadow for most of the day. In among these four-
> storey houses one's primness stood out in the senility, paler
> than all the rest, with a low hedge and clematis beside the

door and a garden gnome fishing in a dry bird-bath, Number Twelve, Gawber's.[114]

Gawber feels displaced by the area's slide into inner-city decay:

> Once, this road had the preserved well-tended look of the nearby roads of lesser houses, small-shouldered bungalows with freshly painted trim, owned by families for their cosy size and kept in repair. But the houses on Volta Road – with servants' bells in every room and names like *The Sycamores* – had fallen into the hands of speculators and building firms and enterprising landlords – who partitioned them with thin walls, sealing off serving-hatches and doors, building kitchens in back bedrooms, installing toilets in broom cupboards, bolting a sink or a cooker on a landing so that the stacked dishes were in full view of the street.[115]

He is not too happy about recent arrivals to Catford, either:

> The native families were dispersed, and Mr Gawber thought: I am a relic from that other age. Latterly, he had studied the new families. They were limpers and Negroes and Irishmen who wore bicycle clips; dog-faced boys in mangy fur coats and surly mothers with red babies and children with broken teeth and very old men who inched down the sidewalk tapping canes. All of them escapees who had arrived and would never go.[116]

2 'THE HOWLING DESERT'
Southeast London, II: From Camberwell to Peckham, Dulwich, Herne Hill and Forest Hill

In his landmark study of the global suburb, *Bourgeois Utopias* (1987), Robert Fishman argues for south London as the first recognizable London suburbia, even as the first in the world. London was surrounded by a string of suburbs, all in the open country about 'three to five miles from the core'; most of them were located, in fact, at 'Dulwich, Walworth, Camberwell, and Clapham'.[1] Much of the fiction set in south, especially southeast, London comes in two types: the nostalgic lament for a lost paradise (destroyed by suburbia), and the struggle to find any sense of home, community or even beauty in what Sherlock Holmes notoriously calls 'The howling desert of south London'.[2]

Camberwell

Camberwell, an area lying between 2 and 3.5 miles south of London Bridge, is at the centre of a wide swathe of rapidly built Victorian south London inner suburbs: to the east Peckham, New Cross, Lewisham and Greenwich, and to the west Brixton, Clapham and Battersea. Camberwell and Peckham were among the first industrial, mass working- and lower-middle-class suburbs, in Britain and in the world. These are the 'railway suburbs', the 'clerks' suburbs', built rapidly from the 1860s for an expanding population of city clerks, public administrators, shop-workers and semi-skilled workmen. Originally a Surrey village ('Ca'brewelle' is mentioned in the Domesday Book), Camberwell was known for its fields, abundant fruit trees and varied fauna. Daniel Defoe, in his *Tour through the*

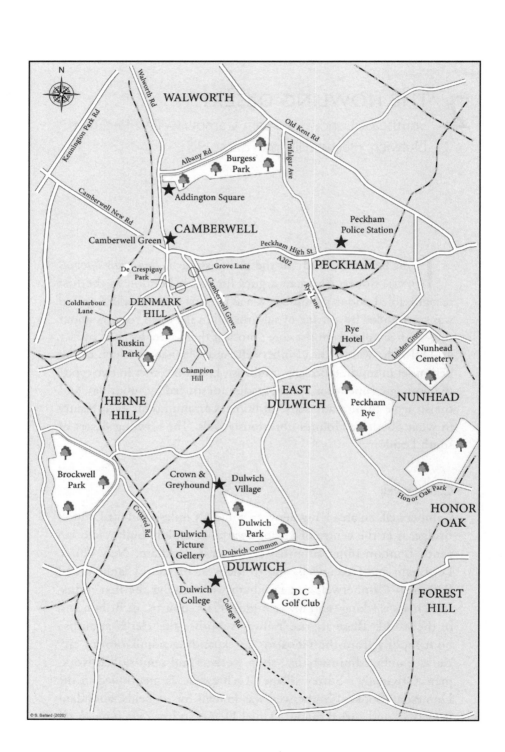

Whole Island of Great Britain (1724–7), noted, 'suppose you take your view from the little rising hills about Clapham, there you see the pleasant villages of Peckham and Camberwell, with some of the finest dwellings about London'. The famed Camberwell Beauty butterfly was first identified in 1748 and Camberwell enjoyed a brief late Georgian heyday (still in evidence in the grand villas and townhouses lining leafy Camberwell Grove and Grove Lane).

Camberwell-born Victorian poet Robert Browning had a liking for exploring the still-wild hills of south London from his home in Commercial Way down to Dulwich Woods in the 1820s. William Sharp explains in his 1890 *Life of Robert Browning*:

> In his early years Browning had always a great liking for walking in the dark. At Camberwell he was wont to carry this love to the point of losing many a night's rest. There was, in particular, a wood near Dulwich, whither he was wont to go. There he would walk swiftly and eagerly along the solitary and lightless byways, finding a potent stimulus to imaginative thought in the happy isolation thus enjoyed, with all the concurrent delight of natural things, the wind moving like a spirit through the tree-branches, the drifting of poignant fragrances, even in winter-tide, from herb and sappy bark, imperceptible almost by the alertest sense in the day's manifold detachments. At this time, too, he composed much in the open air . . . not only many portions of 'Paracelsus', but several scenes in 'Strafford', were enacted first in these midnight silences of the Dulwich woodland.[3]

William Allingham, a struggling Irish poet, kept a diary of his keen visits to noted literary figures in the mid-nineteenth century and recalls a meeting with Leigh Hunt, in 1847, while the latter reels off some entertaining opinions:

> 'Dickens – a pleasant fellow, very busy now, lives in an old house in Devonshire Terrace, Marylebone.
>   'Carlyle – I know him well.
>   'Browning – lives at Peckham, because no one else does! A born poet but loves contradictions. Shakespeare and Milton write plainly, the Sun and Moon write plainly, and why

can't Browning?' I suggested he was the Turner of poetry, to which Leigh Hunt replied, 'Now, you've said it! He's a pleasant fellow, has few readers, and will be glad to find you admire him.'[4]

Much Camberwell-set writing retains a sense of an original arcadia despoiled by mass industrial suburban growth. John Ruskin spent his childhood at 28 Herne Hill and in young adult life moved down the road towards Camberwell, to 163 Denmark Hill, in 1847. Ruskin vividly recalls an Edenic childhood on the pre-suburban London periphery. In his autobiographical *Praeterita* (1885–9) Ruskin recalls that, as a child in the 1820s, 'the little domain answered every purpose of paradise to me'.[5] Ruskin repeatedly returns to rhapsodic descriptions of the uninterrupted panorama seen from the house on the hill: 'It stood in command of seven acres of healthy ground . . . half of it in meadow sloping to the sunrise, the rest prudently and pleasantly divided into an upper and lower kitchen garden; a fruitful bit of orchard, and chance inlets and outlets of woodwalk.'[6]

> A slender rivulet, boasting little of its brightness, for there are no springs at Dulwich, yet fed purely enough by the rain and the morning dew, here trickled – there loitered – through the long grass beneath the hedges, and expanded itself, where it might, into moderately clear and deep pools, in which, under their veils of duck-weed, a fresh-water shell or two, sundry curious little skipping shrimps, any quantity of tadpoles in their time, and even sometimes a tittlebat, offered themselves to my boyhood's pleased, and not inaccurate, observation.[7]

For Ruskin, even Camberwell Green seemed like a demi-paradise, this particular Eden even having a hint of latent evil:

> There was one Elysian field for me in the neglected grass of Camberwell Green. There *was* a pond in the corner of it, of considerable size, and unknown depth – probably, even in summer, full three feet in the middle; the sable opacity of its waters adding to the mystery of danger . . . on its western edge grew a stately elm, from whose boughs, it was currently reported, and conscientiously believed, a wicked boy had fallen

into the pond on Sunday, and forthwith the soul of him into a deeper and darker pool.[8]

Felix Mendelssohn, temporarily living nearby at 168 Denmark Hill in the early 1940s, there composed one of the piano pieces in the fifth book of *Songs without Words*. This was originally called 'Camberwell Green' but was later renamed 'Spring Song'.

But trouble was looming on Denmark Hill. 'The view from the ridge on both sides was,' Ruskin remembers, 'before railroads came, entirely lovely; westward at evening, almost sublime.'[9] 'It's the railways – and rail passengers.' Ruskin's arcadia is eventually destroyed, not by gradual suburban encroachment from the distant, expanding city, but, dramatically, by the sudden coming of the enlarged Crystal Palace building (rebuilt and relocated from Hyde Park to Sydenham/Penge) in 1854. What annoyed Ruskin most were the hordes of working-class day-trippers and pleasure-seekers arriving via specially built train lines and two new stations.

A fascinating insight into early suburban life of the 1830s, as semi-rural Camberwell villadom began to attract more successful City types, can be seen in Charles Dickens's early collection *Sketches by Boz*. The tale 'Horatio Sparkins' concerns the Maldertons, newly affluent Camberwellians, who can afford a grand villa, Oak Lodge, on what seems a lot like either Camberwell Grove or the bottom of leafy Grove Lane. Dickens describes this social-climbing family:

> The family were ambitious of forming acquaintances and connexions in some sphere of society superior to that in which they themselves moved; and one of the necessary consequences of this desire, added to their utter ignorance of the world beyond their own small circle, was, that any one who could lay claim to an acquaintance with people of rank and title, had a sure passport to the table at Oak Lodge, Camberwell.[10]

Mr Malderton, of 'Lloyd's, the Exchange, India House, and the Bank', has made a 'few successful speculations', which have 'raised him from a situation of obscurity and comparative poverty, to a state of affluence'.[11] The Maldertons' primary task is to get their unpromising daughter married:

> Miss Teresa Malderton was a very little girl, rather fat, with
> vermilion cheeks, but good-humoured, and still disengaged,
> although, to do her justice, the misfortune arose from no lack
> of perseverance on her part. In vain had she flirted for ten years;
> in vain had Mr. and Mrs. Malderton assiduously kept up an
> extensive acquaintance among the young eligible bachelors
> of Camberwell, and even of Wandsworth and Brixton; to say
> nothing of those who 'dropped in' from town. Miss Malderton
> was as well known as the lion on the top of Northumberland
> House and had an equal chance of 'going off'.[12]

The problem is that in this raw, new suburban environment the
Maldertons have an uncertain status. Nobody knows who they are;
and they know nobody. Horatio Sparkins, at first meeting, seems very
promising material for Teresa Malderton; well-dressed, worldly, possibly aristocratic. Eventually, 'mysterious, philosophical, romantic,
metaphysical Sparkins' ('"Then", said everybody, "he must be *some-
body*"') is unmasked, revealed to be in fact a lowly draper's assistant, one
Mr Samuel Smith. It takes the Maldertons years to recover from this:

> Years have elapsed since the occurrence of this dreadful
> morning. The daisies have thrice bloomed on Camberwell-
> green; the sparrows have thrice repeated their vernal chirps in
> Camberwell-grove; but the Miss Maldertons are still unmated.
> Miss Teresa's case is more desperate than ever; but Flamwell
> is yet in the zenith of his reputation; and the family have the
> same predilection for aristocratic personages, with an increased
> aversion to anything *low*.[13]

Camberwell is also, at the end of the nineteenth century, one of
the key sites of that rapidly expanding tribe: the lower-middle-class
clerk. As a result of the increasing demand in finance, banking, admin-
istration and retail, and facilitated by cheap tram fairs (though many
clerks walked the 2–4 miles to work and back), whole sections of inner
suburban south London became populated by clerks and their families. One of the earliest, and best-known, literary examples is Jaggers's
legal clerk, Wemmick, in Dickens's *Great Expectations* (1861). After
work, Wemmick takes Pip 'down to Walworth'. Pip is unsure of the
area and isn't sure that he has arrived anywhere in particular: 'At first

with such discourse, and afterwards with conversation of a more general nature, did Mr Wemmick and I beguile the time and the road,
until he gave me to understand that we had arrived in the district of
Walworth.'[14] Wemmick's home is a literalized suburban fantasy:

Wemmick's house was a little wooden cottage in the midst of
plots of garden, and the top of it was cut out and painted like
battery mounted with guns.

'My own doing,' said Wemmick. 'Looks pretty; don't it?'

I highly commended it. I think it was the smallest house I
ever saw; with the queerest gothic windows (by far the greater
part of them sham), and a gothic door, almost too small to get
in at.

'That's a real flagstaff, you see,' said Wemmick, 'and on
Sundays I run up a real flag. Then look here. After I have
crossed this bridge, I hoist it up – so – and cut off the
communication.'

The bridge was a plank, and it crossed a chasm four feet
wide and two deep. But it was very pleasant to see the pride
with which he hoisted it up and made it fast; smiling as he did
so, with a relish and not merely mechanically.

'At nine o'clock every night, Greenwich time,' said
Wemmick, 'the gun fires. There he is, you see! And when you
hear him go, I think you'll say he's a Stinger.'

The piece of ordnance referred to was mounted in a separate fortress, constructed of lattice-work. It was protected from
the weather by an ingenious little tarpaulin contrivance in the
nature of an umbrella.

'Then, at the back,' said Wemmick, 'out of sight, so as not to
impede the idea of fortifications – for it's a principle with me,
if you have an idea, carry it out and keep it up – I don't know
whether that's your opinion –'

I said, decidedly.

'– At the back, there's a pig, and there are fowls and rabbits;
then I knock together my own little frame, you see, and grow
cucumbers; and you'll judge at supper what sort of salad I can
raise. So, sir,' said Wemmick, smiling again, but seriously too, as
he shook his head, 'if you can suppose the little place besieged,
it would hold out a devil of a time in point of provisions.'[15]

This sense of social displacement, desperate display, anxious role-play, snobbery and fakery recurs in a much later Victorian Camberwell-set novel, George Gissing's *In the Year of Jubilee* (1894). Lodging at 76 Burton Road in Brixton, Gissing, unfamiliar with south London, went on long walks around Brixton, Camberwell and Peckham, and was stunned by the crass features of modern popular culture springing up. These were the signs of emergent modern suburban culture that we will see in the Peachey–French home, 'a house in De Crespigny Park':

> unattached, double-fronted, with half-sunk basement, and a flight of steps to the stucco pillars at the entrance. De Crespigny Park, a thoroughfare connecting Grove Lane, Camberwell, with Denmark Hill, presents a double row of similar dwellings; its clean breadth, with foliage of trees and shrubs in front gardens, makes it pleasant to the eye that finds pleasure in suburban London. In point of respectability, it has claims only to be appreciated by the ambitious middle-class of Camberwell. Each house seems to remind its neighbour, with all the complacence expressible in buff brick, that in this locality lodgings are *not* to let.[16]

Here we meet Ada (lazy, magazine-reading, self-indulgent), Beatrice (restless, shallow, entrepreneurial-minded New Woman) and Fanny (manipulative, scheming). Over on Grove Lane, Nancy Lord (the novel's original title was 'Miss Lord of Camberwell') is uneasily caught between two worlds, being both a restless young woman, defying precedent by having sex before marriage and having a secret wedding, but also becoming, at the novel's close, a respectable suburbanite – and escaping from Grove Lane:

> Grove Lane is a long acclivity, which starts from Camberwell Green, and, after passing a few mean shops, becomes a road of suburban dwellings. The houses vary considerably in size and aspect, also in date – with the result of a certain picturesqueness, enhanced by the growth of fine trees on either side. Architectural grace can nowhere be discovered, but the contract-builder of to-day has not yet been permitted to work his will; age and irregularity, even though the edifices be but so

many illustrations of the ungainly, the insipid, and the frankly
hideous, have a pleasanter effect than that of new streets built
to one pattern by the mile. There are small cottages overgrown
with creepers, relics of Camberwell's rusticity; rows of tall and
of squat dwellings that lie behind grassy plots, railed from the
road; larger houses that stand in their own gardens, hidden by
walls. Narrow passages connect the Lane with its more formal
neighbour Camberwell Grove; on the other side are ways
leading toward Denmark Hill, quiet, leafy. From the top of the
Lane, where Champion Hill enjoys an aristocratic seclusion, is
obtainable a glimpse of open fields and of a wooded horizon
southward.

It is a neighbourhood in decay, a bit of London which does
not keep pace with the times. And Nancy hated it. She would
have preferred to live even in a poor and grimy street which
neighboured the main track of business and pleasure.[17]

All characters, but especially the women, are presented as rootless,
philistine, flashy and shallow. Beatrice even launches a subscription-
based 'fashion club', relying on the principle that 'out of every 500
women, you can reckon on 499 of them being fools'. The subsequent 'South London Fashionable Dress Supply Association' – a sort
of Christmas club for 'ignorant and pretentious women' too 'weak-
minded to save their own money'[18] (though, the reader needs to be
reminded, not 'technically fraud') – is a great commercial success.

Another flashy Camberwell figure is the narrator's wife's mysterious benefactor in the famed music hall song 'Wot Cher! Knocked 'em
in the Old Kent Road' (1891). 'Knocked 'em' refers to the neighbours'
shocked response to the couple's impressive new cart ('shay') provided
by 'rich uncle Tom' down in Camberwell.

Last week down our alley came a toff
Nice old geezer with a nasty cough.
Sees my missus, takes his topper off
In a very gentlemanly way!
'Ma'am' says he, 'I 'ave some news to tell,
Your rich uncle Tom of Camberwell,
Popp'd off recent, which it ain't a sell,
Leaving you 'is little donkey shay.'

Contrary to popular perception, many of Arthur Conan Doyle's Sherlock Holmes stories have a suburban, rather than city centre, setting; and the raw, still half-built south London suburbs in particular offer the requisite Holmesian touches: mud, fog, mystery, labyrinthine layout, inscrutable and displaced individuals. In the inaugural Holmes tale, *A Study in Scarlet* (1887), E. J. Drebber and Joseph Stangerson, the first murder victims in the series (Drebber is murdered in a house on Brixton Road), stay 'at the boarding-house of Madame Charpentier, in Torquay Terrace, Camberwell'. For Watson, the space between Baker Street and the murder scenes is uncharted territory. Visiting the policeman who had found one of the victims, Holmes and Watson travel to a grim spot between Camberwell and Kennington Park (where Holmes leaves Watson to get back to town):

> our cab had been threading its way through a long succession of dingy streets and dreary by-ways. In the dingiest and dreariest of them our driver suddenly came to a stand. 'That's Audley Court in there', he said, pointing to a narrow slit in the line of dead-coloured brick. 'You'll find me here when you come back.'
>
> Audley Court was not an attractive locality. The narrow passage led us into a quadrangle paved with flags and lined by sordid dwellings. We picked our way among groups of dirty children, and through lines of discoloured linen, until we came to Number 46, the door of which was decorated with a small slip of brass on which the name 'Rance' was engraved. On enquiry we found that the constable was in bed, and we were shown into a little front parlour to await his coming.[19]

In *The Sign of the Four* (1890), the lengthy second Sherlock Holmes story, Watson is soon disorientated by a tortuous journey south of the river to see mysterious clients, twins Thaddeus and Bartholomew Sholto. The first destination is to see Thaddeus, somewhere near Camberwell:

> At first I had some idea as to the direction in which we were driving; but soon, what with our pace, the fog, and my own limited knowledge of London, I lost my bearings, and knew nothing, save that we seemed to be going a very long way.

Sherlock Holmes was never at fault, however, and he muttered the names as the cab rattled through squares and in and out by tortuous by-streets. 'Rochester Row,' said he. 'Now Vincent Square. Now we come out on the Vauxhall Bridge Road. We are making for the Surrey side, apparently. Yes, I thought so. Now we are on the bridge. You can catch glimpses of the river.' We did indeed get a fleeting view of a stretch of the Thames with the lamps shining upon the broad, silent water; but our cab dashed on, and was soon involved in a labyrinth of streets upon the other side. 'Wandsworth Road,' said my companion. 'Priory Road. Lark Hall Lane. Stockwell Place. Robert Street. Cold Harbour Lane. Our quest does not appear to take us to very fashionable regions.'

We had, indeed, reached a questionable and forbidding neighbourhood. Long lines of dull brick houses were only relieved by the coarse glare and tawdry brilliancy of public-houses at the corner. Then came rows of two-storied villas, each with a fronting of miniature garden, and then again interminable lines of new staring brick buildings – the monster tentacles which the giant city was throwing out into the country. At last the cab drew up at the third house in a new terrace. None of the other houses were inhabited, and that at which we stopped was as dark as its neighbours, save for a single glimmer in the kitchen-window.[20]

Camberwell also appears at the start of the 'The Five Orange Pips' from *The Adventures of Sherlock Holmes* (1892), when we are informed that one of the numerous cases the detective had solved, in 1887, was the infamous 'Camberwell poisoning case': 'Holmes was able,' Watson tells us, 'by winding up the dead man's watch, to prove that it had been wound up two hours before, and that therefore the deceased had gone to bed within that time – a deduction which was of the greatest importance in clearing up the case.'[21]

A later Camberwellian clerk, the titular character in Shan Bullock's novel *Robert Thorne: The Story of a London Clerk* (1907), also experiences the contradictions of suburban life. Arriving from Devon and securing a much sought-after, and extremely tedious, clerking job at Somerset House (walking the 3 miles there and back every day), Thorne is very aware of being an insignificant member of that

anonymous mass of hard-working, lower-middle classes. He fears that
his testimony may not be valid – or interesting:

> I wish I could write a drama of official life . . . a magnificent
> drama indeed the writer of this record would write! Besides,
> supposing it written, who in this world would find interest in
> it? . . . Men hunched over desks in dreary rooms; telephones,
> revolving stamps, fire buckets; a pale-faced youth eating
> bread and cheese in a suburban bed-sitting-room; a foolish
> couple bending over a crib in a kitchen in Dulwich . . . what
> subjects, great heaven, for drama in this Twentieth Century!
> Why, all that is only life – a page from the awful Day-book of
> London town.[22]

Thorne is at first rather fond of the Kennington area around his
Camberwell New Road lodgings. On a Sunday walk we hear how he
goes on a walk 'through Myatt's fields, then a market garden, up into
Denmark Hill, where a cove named Ruskin lived (so Bertie said), and
down a lane into Dulwich'.[23] Thorne finds this pastoral all a great relief
from the tax office drudgery: 'trees and hedges were breaking into leaf.
Birds sang. Children sported. Lovers went whispering arm in arm.'
This is Thorne's 'first glimpse of kindly things in the London desert'.
Thorne gets married, has a baby and moves to a small flat in Dulwich:

> Our excursions with the perambulator out into the social
> world were of course few: generally, we had to find outdoor
> diversion nearer home. Marketing was still a weekly pleasure.
> On fine evenings we took the air on Peckham Rye. On
> Saturday afternoons we saw a cricket match, and later on a
> football match, in the playing fields at Honor Oak; sometimes
> adventured as far as Greenwich Park or had tea somewhere in
> Dulwich. Once or twice we took sandwiches and milk in the
> perambulator and spent most of a Sunday on One Tree Hill;
> and some of my holidays that year (for we found it impossible
> once more to visit father) were devoted to little excursions into
> the country.[24]

Thorne is curious as to exactly what kind of place he inhabits,
and who lives there, and he goes out exploring the 'various residential

zones of our neighbourhood'. Here they walk 'from the humble little roads of our own particular zone . . . into the brighter zone where the houses had brass knockers . . . thence into the genteel air of the red-brick villa region, some detached and screened from the vulgar gaze by privet hedges or high oak fences'.[25] This exploratory zeal comes in useful when Thorne and his new wife go house-hunting. 'Nell and I were sticklers about drains', we learn. Eventually they spot something they like: 'There was a house off Peckham Rye which we kept under observation for a long time.' It seems to have everything: 'Nice garden – fine open front – bay windows – quiet neighbourhood – tradesmen's entrance – servants' room – tiled hall – and dirt cheap at £42 a year'.[26] They take it and move in.

> Ours was a pleasant enough home, if humble – one of a row of six-roomed cottages in a quiet neighbourhood near Denmark Hill. In front was a privet hedge behind an oak fence, and a tiny flower bed under the parlour bay window; at the back, within brick walls, was a small garden having a grass plot, two beds with a subsoil of sardine tins and brickbats, a poplar at the bottom, and a lilac-tree near the scullery window. The hall door had its brass knocker and letter-box. The rooms were small but comfortable; downstairs a dining-room, drawing-room, kitchen and scullery, upstairs two bedrooms and a little back room containing a chair, a table, and a shelf of books which it pleased us to call the Study. You will see that, despite circumstances, we were finding our feet in the social world, making the best show we could. The brass knocker, the bay window, the dining and drawing rooms, establish the fact; whilst the Study gives evidence that already we had in view the great suburban ideal of being superior to the people next door.[27]

Augustus Carp, Esq. by Himself: Being the Autobiography of a Really Good Man is the fake memoir of another Camberwell clerk. Published anonymously in 1924 (the author later revealed as Sir Henry Bashford, a senior medical officer), and described by Anthony Burgess as 'one of the great comic novels of the twentieth century', this records the youthful adventures of the insufferably pompous and priggish Carp. Of his father, Carp says:

he was one of the most respected and trustworthy agents of
the Durham and West Hartlepool Fire and Burglary Insurance
Company, a sidesman of the Church of St James-the-Less in
Camberwell, and the tenant of Mon Repos, Angela Gardens.
This was one of some thirty-six admirably conceived houses of
a similar and richly ornamented architecture, the front door of
each being flanked and surmounted by diamond-shaped panes
of blue and vermilion glass; and though it was true that this
particular house had been named by the landlord in a foreign
tongue, it must not be assumed that this nomenclature in any
way met with my father's approval. On the contrary, he had
not only protested, but such was his distrust of French morality
that he had always insisted, both for himself and others, upon a
strictly English pronunciation.[28]

As the elder Carp comes down in the world – decamping from St
James-the-Less to 'St James-the-Lesser-Still, Peckham Rye', then 'St
James-the-Least-of-All, Kennington Oval' – Augustus grows up in
Camberwell. We see him at 'Hopkinson House School for the Sons
of Gentlemen', which was 'conveniently situated in Jasmine Grove on
the southern outskirts of Camberwell' and was 'daily attended by some
seventy or eighty of the sons of the Peckham and Camberwell gentry'.[29]
Carp soon acquires prim and uncomprehending self-righteousness.
Carp is terrified of the 'tobacconist and the publican . . . the cigarette
that will so inevitably lure him into loose and licentious company,
and the fermented liquor that will only too surely encase him in a
drunkard's coffin'.[30]

> I hastened to enrol myself as a member of the Peckham Branch
> of the Non-Smokers' League as well as of the Kennington
> Division of the Society for the Prohibition of the Strong Drink
> Traffic. Congenial in every way, I not only discovered in these
> an enormous sphere for the exercise of my influence, but the
> membership of both societies conferred the privilege of wearing
> a small badge or bone medallion.[31]

Vera Brittain, in *Testament of Youth* (1933), her memoir of the years
1900–1925, describes her terrifying and grim Denmark Hill lodgings
as a trainee nurse in 1915. Here, after relatively comfortable billeting

in Buxton, a posting to London meant she was now the 'quarter-possessor of a bare-boarded room divided into cubicles'. This was cold, dark, dirty and overcrowded, and Brittain recalls it all with a horrified fascination.

> Each morning at 7 a.m. we were due at the hospital, where we breakfasted, and went on duty at 7.30. Theoretically we travelled down by the workmen's trams which ran over Champion Hill from Dulwich, but in practice these trams were so full that we were seldom able to use them, and were obliged to walk, frequently in pouring rain and carrying suitcases containing clean aprons and a change of shoes and stockings, the mile and a half from the hostel to the hospital. As the trams were equally full in the evenings, the journey on foot had often to be repeated at the end of the day.[32]

Fred Bason, a working-class bookseller based in Walworth and Camberwell, kept a diary in the 1930s. One day in 1933 he was 'at a loss quite what to record':

My little shop is in New Church Road, Camberwell, S.E.5. It is ten minutes' walk from my home in Walworth. I get to the shop by passing through Albany Road over Wells Bridge Street which crosses over the Surrey Canal, which should have been filled in by Camberwell Council years ago. The canal is rarely used and it's smelly. All the dead dogs and cats are thrown in it.
   Once in 1920 I saw a youngish woman throw herself into it. She was a tall, fine woman of around thirty-seven. I couldn't swim – I've never been able to do so. So I shouted out loud and a public house owner at the corner of the canal bank came running up. He jumped in. She fought him and wanted to get drowned and nearly drowned him as well. I kept on yelling and a couple of men and women came running from the other side of the canal over the bridge to where they were. It is very deep in the extreme centre of the canal, but the sides are not more than four feet deep. One of the men got into the water at the side and the publican, who had knocked the woman out, got her to the man at the edge and between us we all got her on the bank. When the woman came round again she kept on crying

that she wanted to die, and it took the men all their time to stop her throwing herself in again.[33]

Post-Second World War Camberwell, like its neighbour Brixton, became a favoured destination for Caribbean migrants. The lives of second-generation Caribbean migrants, born and raised in the UK but excluded by racism, poverty, family breakdown and lack of opportunity, are addressed in a series of books by Alex Wheatle. His first novel, *Brixton Rock* (1999), follows fifteen-year-old Brenton Brown, living in a hostel near Camberwell Green, at the beginning of 1980:

> Brenton meandered along the vegetable and fruit-filled streets and decided to trot home. On Coldharbour Lane he observed the lively atmosphere of the packed Soferno-B shack, filled with black youths listening out for the latest releases as the bass-line boxed the shop windows.
>
> What he didn't notice was two black guys standing on the other side of the road, opposite the record shop. They had just come out of the barbershop there, although neither of them appeared to be trimmed. They were the brethren of Terry Flynn; Flynn himself was inside, receiving a briefing from the ghetto news.
>
> Brenton walked past the bustling unemployment exchange, unaware that youths had summoned Terry Flynn and were shadowing him. Carrying his trainers in a plastic bag, Brenton turned left off Coldharbour Lane, looking up at the white-painted tower blocks of Barrington Road . . .
>
> Terry Flynn and his spars continued to stalk their prey as Brenton strolled behind the back of another tower block. Here the avenging trio saw their chance. Brandishing a flick knife, Terry Flynn and his cohorts hurtled towards their unsuspecting target.[34]

Close by, yet a world away from Brenton Brown's turf, Jenny Eclair's *Camberwell Beauty* (2000), part of the 'mummy-lit' sub-genre that has evolved over the last couple of decades, offers a comedic panorama of various lives on one Camberwell street, recognizably a fictional amalgam of upmarket Camberwell Grove and Grove Lane:

Welcome to south London, to one of the nicest streets in one
of the country's vilest boroughs: Lark Grove, SE5. A determined
middle-class oasis of skips and bay trees, where Volvos sniff each
other's bumpers, and men called Giles live with women called
Samantha. This is a satellite-dish-free zone of tall houses with
big front doors, standing shoulder to shoulder, five floors apiece.
Come inside, shut the door and smell the coffee. You could
almost be in Kensington . . .

This is a colourful area, full of girls with dyed purple fringes
and savage dogs on strings, where junkies fall down and the
drunks trip over them and nobody raises a pierced eyebrow.
Here, there is vomit on the pavements, syringes in the gutter
and graffiti all over . . . Here live the mad, the bad, the arty and
the ordinary. You can get a very nice house in these parts for a
fraction of what it would cost somewhere else. The architecture
is chipped but good, and there are blue plaques littered about
where famous music hall comics once lived, drank, ran out of
jokes and committed suicide.[35]

Monty Python's Terry Jones bought a large three-storey house in
Grove Park, Camberwell, in 1969, and fellow Python Michael Palin
described his regular visits in his diaries:

It's another splendid morning and I go down to Camberwell
on the bus. It's good to be able to pace one's life, so that if I
want to take an extra 30 minutes to get to Terry's by bus I can.
The walk at the other end is a slog, but on a day like this it's all
justified by the feeling of busy, buzzing London life all around.
Faces in the sunshine . . .

Terry suggests a beer for lunch and we have a couple of
pints at a rather unpleasantly refurbished Young's pub beside
Peckham Common. Sitting next to us are a very old middle-
aged couple, a little tipsy. They have two Pekinese dogs which
they treat with affected bantering politeness. The woman licked
pieces of chocolate before giving them to the dog and the man
accused Terry of coming from Wrexham.[36]

The status of Camberwell as an index of suburban respectability –
of class, social standing – returns in historical novelist Sarah Waters's

79

novel *The Paying Guests* (2014). Here the position of the suburban home figuring as the centre of social and national concerns – of class, gender and power – is examined and given a contemporary sensibility by including issues of desire and sexual identity. The setting is a grand villa on Camberwell's Champion Hill, which now, in 1922, partly because of the annihilation of the entire male household in the First World War, must be made over into a boarding house. Frances Wray and her widowed mother take in paying boarders, Lilian and Leonard Barber, who are clearly of a lower, 'clerkly' class. Frances, looking out the window, anxiously awaits the arrival of the Barbers:

> She stood at a window in the largest of the rooms – the room which, until recently, had been her mother's bedroom, but was now to be the Barbers' sitting-room – and stared out at the street. The afternoon was bright but powdery. Flurries of wind sent up puffs of dust from the pavement and the road. The grand houses opposite had a Sunday blankness to them – but then, they had that every day of the week. Around the corner there was a large hotel and motor-cars and taxi-cabs occasionally came this way to and from it; sometimes people strolled up here as if to take the air. But Champion Hill, on the whole, kept itself to itself. The gardens were large, the trees leafy. You would never know, she thought, that grubby Camberwell was just down there. You'd never guess that a mile or two further north lay London, life, glamour, all that . . . A tradesman's van was approaching the house. This couldn't be them, could it? She'd expected a carrier's cart, or even for the couple to arrive on foot – but, yes, the van was pulling up at the kerb, with a terrific creak of its brake . . . Feeling trapped and on display in the frame of the window, she lifted her hand, and smiled.[37]

Conventional roles and norms are reversed. Where Frances is forced to cook, wash, clean and dust endlessly, laboriously maintaining all the paraphernalia of the still Victorian home, Lilian tends to sleep in and doesn't do much apart from dress up and decorate her rooms. Frances is dull, timid and cash-strapped; Lilian fashionable, well-dressed and with money to spend.

Where Waters revisits the early 1920s, Emily Bullock's novel *The Longest Fight* (2015) looks back at Camberwell in the early 1950s. This is a very different Camberwell, a claustrophobic and brutal post-war world of extreme poverty, violence and child abuse, of boxing, dingy pubs and petty gangsters, among the ruined streets near the Peckham Canal. Living in a grubby alley, near Addington Square, this is the tatty, raw, still severely bomb-damaged Camberwell of factories, canals and dereliction. Here is boxing trainer and wannabe promoter Jack Munday out with his new protégé Frank:

> It was warmer outside than in the house; a buttery daylight covered the pavements and buildings. They headed up Lomond Grove past Mrs Bell's, smell of mangy cat and flyblown bread; the hardware shop on the corner, sticky tar and chalky carbolic. Jack could find his way around by his nose alone. Bombs had stomped out the northeast corner of Addington Square, the top end of Medlar Street, and most of Hillingdon Street was flattened. But when Jack turned down Cowan Street flashes of light from broken glass and weathered rubble made it seem as though the old Watkins Bible Factory had risen again; hot ink and a dampened paper smell hung in the dusty air. *Wot no bibles* daubed with red paint on a heap of bleached bricks . . . Jack waited in a patch of sun that slithered across the bomb site between the factory rubble and the church. In the distance, wrecking balls hovered over Peckham like bluebottles. Jack could almost smell summer in the air, the Thames tide carrying it up from the coast: fish and chips in newspaper, sweet melting ice cream.[38]

Peckham

To the east of Camberwell, along the A202, Peckham was, like its neighbour, well into the mid-nineteenth century, a rural mix of market gardens, pasture land, some older grand houses, and numerous inns and watering points for cattle herders in transit from Kent to London. Following the Peckham opening of the Grand Surrey Canal in 1826, London's first regularly stopping tram service (by Thomas Trilling, in 1851) and railways (Peckham Rye, 1865, and Queens Road Peckham, 1866) provided the catalyst that rapidly transformed the Anglo-Saxon 'village by the hill' into populous, sprawling, speculatively built lower-middle-class suburbia. This pastoral hinterland was utterly transformed, with long streets of terraces and semis, with shops, stables, pubs and churches, with small factories and workshops, all built quickly in the 1860s and '70s. Rye Lane would go on to become an important shopping street (Jones & Higgins, south London's premier department store, opened there in 1867) and a centre for light industry (the Bussey firearms factory opened in 1870). Peckham's complex cultural footprint thus includes Blakean sublimity; middle-class conformity and respectability; lower-middle-class dour, hard-working clerkdom and shopkeeping; surviving Georgian and early Victorian villas as well as modern council estates; high urban crime and gang culture, and, since the arrival of the Overground, a nascent hipster zone of re-purposed car parks and Victorian factories.

Peckham has a particular resonance in the British popular imagination. These suburbs are often rendered in fiction, film and TV as insular and run-down, a scrappy landscape of brutal tower blocks, council estates or unremarkable Victorian terraces, populated by a shifting cast of dodgy market traders, wide boys, frustrated small shopkeepers, petty criminals, aspirational migrants and narrowly domesticated householders. Worse still, the area is often considered as not even constituting a place at all. This is poet Alan Brownjohn, meditating on the traffic-choked A202, linking Camberwell to Peckham:

Along its length it despoils, in turn, a sequence
Of echoless names: Camberwell, Peckham,
New Cross Gate; places having no recorded past
    Except in histories of the tram.[39]

This is south London as nowhere, a site that does not exist as it lacks the markers of broader cultural resonance or significance, which has no meaningful history, ignored or exempt from the cultural archive.

The sense of Peckham's otherworldly or sacred element is established with Peckham Rye's best-known appearance in literary history. Poet and artist William Blake had an ecstatic vision of angels on Peckham Rye sometime in the 1760s. 'As he grew older', Blake's first biographer, Alexander Gilchrist, tells us, 'the lad became fond of roving out into the country, a fondness in keeping with the romantic turn'. For the Soho-born Blake, open countryside in the late eighteenth century was just a mile or so south of the river. Gilchrist describes a 'country' walk route for Blake from the family home:

After Westminster Bridge . . . came St George's Fields, open
fields and scene of 'Wilkes and Liberty' riots in Blake's boyhood;
next, the pretty village of Newington Butts, undreaming its 19th
century bad eminence in the bills of cholera-mortality; and then,
unsophisticate green field and hedgerow opened on the child's
delighted eyes. A mile or two further through the 'large and
pleasant village' of Camberwell with its grove (or avenue) and
famed prospect, arose the sweet hill and vale and 'sylvan wilds' of
rural Dulwich, a 'village' even now retaining some semblance of
its former self. Beyond, stretched, to allure the young pedestrian
on, yet fairer amenities: southward, hilly Sydenham; eastward, in
the purple distance, Blackheath.[40]

Young Blake then reaches Peckham:

On Peckham Rye (by Dulwich Hill) it is, as he will in after
years relate, that while quite a child, of eight or ten perhaps, he
has his 'first vision'. Sauntering along, the boy looks up and sees
a tree filled with angels, bright angelic wings bespangling every
bough like stars.[41]

For this Peckham vision, according to Gilchrist, Blake narrowly avoids
a thrashing from his honest father, 'for telling a lie'. Yet he would also
have other visions in the south London hinterland, including of God
appearing at a window in Lambeth. Again, the theme here is of a
pastoral hinterland trashed by new industry. In plate 84 of *Jerusalem*
(1804–20), Blake writes:

Awake . . .
Highgates heights & Hampsteads, to Poplar Hackney & Bow:
To Islington & Paddington & the Brook of Albions River
We builded Jerusalem as a City & a Temple; from Lambeth
We began our Foundations; lovely Lambeth! O lovely Hills
Of Camberwell, we shall behold you no more in glory & pride
For Jerusalem lies in ruins & the Furnaces of Los are builded
   there[42]

Nunhead Cemetery, just to the east of Peckham Rye, was opened
in 1840, the sixth of the 'Magnificent Seven' cemeteries, designed to

accommodate the accumulating dead of teeming London. Charlotte Mew, influential proto-Modernist, lauded by Hardy and Woolf, set an astonishing and moving poem, 'In Nunhead Cemetery' (1916), here:

> It is the clay what makes the earth stick to his spade;
> He fills in holes like this year after year;
> The others have gone; they were tired, and half afraid
> But I would rather be standing here;
>
> There is nowhere else to go. I have seen this place
> From the windows of the train that's going past
> Against the sky.

Mew's brother, Henry, had been interred in Nunhead in 1901.

By the 1860s Peckham was a mix of working-class toilers, middle-class respectability and semi-rural obscurity (and with excellent rail links to Kent), which is partly why Charles Dickens chose the place to hide his mistress Ellen 'Nelly' Ternan. Dickens met the young actress in 1857 and, separating from his wife the next year, had plenty of time to pursue his secret affair. Desperate to keep all this quiet, and yet practical, he surreptitiously rented a house for her, Windsor Lodge, in Linden Grove, Nunhead, just to the east of Peckham Rye. Claire Tomalin in her 2012 biography of Dickens explains how he assumed the Nunhead/Peckham alias 'Charles Tringham', and how the couple had to 'discourage friendly and curious neighbours who might notice the comings and goings of Mr Turnham . . . and remark on his resemblance to Mr Charles Dickens'.[43] The secret liaison generated numerous rumours: that the couple had a child, who died in infancy; that Dickens really died, or at least was taken mortally ill, in Peckham, and was whisked away to die, officially, in respectable Gad's Hill Place, Higham.

Yet Dickens could see that the chaos of the industrializing city was fast approaching even pastoral Peckham. As Dickens records in his last completed novel, *Our Mutual Friend* (1864–5), this entire territory, from New Cross down to Nunhead, Brockley and Peckham, was, in the 1860s, undergoing profound changes:

> down in that district of the flat country tending to the Thames, where Kent and Surrey meet, and where the railways still

bestride the market-gardens that will soon die under them. The schools were newly built, and there were so many like them all over the country, that one might have thought the whole were but one restless edifice with the locomotive gift of Aladdin's palace. They were in a neighbourhood which looked like a toy neighbourhood taken in blocks out of a box by a child of particularly incoherent mind, and set up anyhow; here, one side of a new street; there, a large solitary public-house facing nowhere; here, another unfinished street already in ruins; there, a church; here, an immense new warehouse; there, a dilapidated old country villa; then, a medley of black ditch, sparkling cucumber-frame, rank field, richly cultivated kitchen-garden, brick viaduct, arch-spanned canal, and disorder of frowziness and fog.[44]

Throughout the nineteenth century, Peckham, especially around Peckham Rye, continued its development as a genteel, middle-class suburb. William Pett Ridge's 1898 comic novel *Mord Em'ly* provides a useful picture of the increasing polarity of urban Walworth and respectable Peckham suburb. The novel's titular heroine, Mord (or Maud), lives in a rowdy, overcrowded slum in the Walworth area near Elephant and Castle and runs with the all-girl teenage Gilliken Gang, fighting off their main rivals, the Bermondsey Gang. Here, living on the streets all day, she encounters a range of larger-than-life characters: urchins, coppers, shopkeepers, boxers, street toughs, all manner of criminals and chancers. This area was notorious for its violent gangs. Nearby Lambeth had the Hooligan Boys in the 1890s, and Clarence Rook's 1899 Elephant and Castle-set investigative novel *The Hooligan Nights* featured the criminal activities of the legendary Patrick Hooligan (not to mention 'Young Alf', 'Billy the Snide' and others). Mord is eventually arrested and incarcerated, after being identified by a malicious, over-eager constable. To keep her off the streets, Mord is sent into domestic service in middle-class suburban Peckham. This suburban house arrest is the antithesis of her previous Walworth life:

It seemed to Mord Em'ly that the people in the road [Lucella Road, Peckham] led lives that were ordered by some precise and stringent Act of Parliament. By half-past eight in the morning every man in every house had come out, had pulled the doors to, and had run off to catch the train to the City, an exodus which also used to take place (at an earlier hour) at Pandora Buildings [Mord's Walworth home]; but whereas there it signalled opportunity for free conversation, in Lucella Road it seemed that the women-folk remained indoors, and kept themselves in rigid seclusion.[45]

Any sign of individual identity is discouraged in Peckham: 'I think we shall decide to call you Laura if you stop with us', her employer explains, 'we always call our maids Laura. It's a family tradition.'[46] The silent, rigid, self-improving (one family member goes off to an evening 'lecture in Rye Lane on "Spiders and their Habits"'), early-to-bed, respectable suburb is, of course, a prison for feisty Mord. She fantasizes about 'obtaining a pocketful of pebbles . . . screaming loudly and breaking windows all the way'. She looks out of her Peckham attic window 'to see the glare of the sky away north, beyond the grey, melancholy mist, a glare that she knew was the reflection of the lighted streets of London . . . there was no sound except the occasional creak that restless houses in the suburbs give in the days of their youth'.[47] Mord does eventually escape – to Australia.

In the mid-1960s Ian Nairn, in his idiosyncratic *Nairn's London*, could still laud Peckham as the last outpost of a disappearing vibrant London working-class culture:

> now that the East End has been gutted by bombs and the wrong sort of building, Rye Lane is one of the few cockney streets left inside the county of London. Cockney life has gone outside instead – to Mitcham or Slough or Romford, where the pressure of kind people trying to live your life for you is not so strong. But Rye Lane must always have been one of the best. It is an old road, hence narrow and with a few bends in it, and unquenchable vitality has pulsed through it for ninety years. It is not only the Victorian detail that is full of life, but the jazz modern and the dayglo'd window displays. Everything fits except timidity, and a Rye Lane shopfront of 1933 matches a Rye Lane shopfront of 1963 better than either resemble their prototypes. In the same way the display on a coster's barrow, a supermarket and a jeweller's shop are all part of the same family.[48]

Peckham's position as a solidly working- and lower-middle-class suburb, the home of the dull and everyday, is at the heart of Muriel Spark's strange and discomfiting tale of a jilted bride and domestic diabolism, *The Ballad of Peckham Rye* (1960). At one point Spark clearly evokes the spirit of border balladry, retelling the events of the story as a kind of semi-mythic romance. Nobody is quite sure what happened:

> The affair is a legend referred to from time to time in the pubs when the conversation takes a matrimonial turn. Some say the bridegroom came back repentant and married the girl in the end. Some say, no, he married another girl, while the bride married the best man. It is wondered if the bride had been carrying on with the best man for some time past. It is sometimes told that the bride died of grief and the groom shot himself on the Rye.[49]

The novel tells the tale of a peculiar clash as an outsider, Dougal Douglas, arriving from nowhere (Scotland), casts a spell and spreads confusion as he undertakes his peculiar 'research' into life in very real Peckham. Even events that happen in the present, as the novel starts, have an unreality about them:

> Humphrey hit him. Trevor hit back. There was a fight. Two courting couples returning from the dusky scope of the Rye's broad lyrical acres stepped to the opposite pavement, leant on the railings by the swimming baths, and watched. Eventually the fighters, each having suffered equal damage to different features of the face, were parted by onlookers to save the intervention of the police.[50]

The novel is a detailed portrait of Peckham and we get a clear picture of the actual layout of the place. At the start (the story is told mostly in one long flashback) we see Humphrey returning to Peckham having walked out on his wedding some weeks earlier:

> He got back into the little Fiat and drove along the Grove and up to the Common where he parked outside the Rye Hotel . . . He walked across to the White Horse . . . Next he visited

the Morning Star and the Heaton Arms. He finished up at the Harbinger.[51]

These, apart from the Harbinger, were real pubs in Peckham. We then see Humphrey's earlier escape from Peckham, after running from the altar: 'Humphrey got to the door, into his Fiat, and drove off by himself to Folkestone . . . He drove past the Rye, down Rye Lane roundabout to Lewisham, past the Dutch House and on to Swanley, past Wrotham Hill and along the A20 to Ditton, where he stopped for a drink.'[52]

This is a very strange prelude – arriving at, and leaving, Peckham – as, when the novel finally gets going, we see that the characters in this suburb are very much trapped in the place. This is a pre-1960s, claustrophobic, white working-class respectable world of small engineering companies, factories and warehouses, of young school-leavers saving up to get married as soon as possible, of apprenticeships for the boys and factory work for the girls, of threadbare hops, dance halls and dingy pubs. As one factory-owner's wife laments, 'One of Richard's great mistakes . . . was insisting on our living in Peckham. Well the house is alright – but, I mean, the environment. There are simply no people in the place. Our friends always get lost finding their way here; they drive around for hours.'[53]

Douglas has a self-proclaimed 'human research' mission in Peckham, as part of which he successfully wheedles his way into paid positions at two small factories. He wants to focus on the people of Peckham: 'I shall have to do research into their inner lives. Research into the real Peckham. It will be necessary to discover the spiritual well-spring, the glorious history of the place.'[54] He later stresses, to a different gullible factory owner, the importance of 'observing the morals of Peckham', and provides a complex theory of the 'four types of morality observable in Peckham'.[55] He even undertakes formal research into Peckham's past:

> I copied it out of an old book in the library. My research. Mendelssohn wrote his 'Spring Song' in Ruskin Park. Ruskin lived on Denmark Hill. Mrs Fitzherbert lived in Camberwell Grove. Boadicea committed suicide on Peckham Rye probably where the bowling green is now, I should imagine . . . we have five cemeteries here around the Rye . . . did you know that Nunhead reservoir holds twenty million gallons of water?[56]

Finally, at the end of the novel, as Douglas heads back north over the river, there is one brief episode of Blakean splendour, centred again on Peckham Rye. As Humphrey, now finally married, drives past the Rye, he sees a possible glimpse of another world:

> It was a sunny day for November, and, as he drove swiftly past the Rye, he saw the children playing there and the women coming home from work with their shopping bags, the Rye for an instant looking like a cloud of green and gold, the people seeming to ride upon it, as you might say there was another world than this.[57]

Iris Murdoch, in *Under the Net* (1954), famously decided that 'There are some parts of London which are necessary and others which are contingent. Everywhere west of Earl's Court is contingent.' Murdoch isn't that keen on the south, either. Characters in the novel search for a film studio somewhere north of Peckham, 'situated in a suburb of south-east London', and this, we hear, is 'where contingency reaches the point of nausea'.[58] This uncertain place 'in and around the Old Kent Road' itself becomes mingled with the fantasy spaces created in the film studio. The suburb becomes an impregnable fortress, the 'field of Waterloo', a 'piece of ancient Rome', stuffed with lights, scenery and performing extras. A performance of 'Catiline inflaming the Roman plebs' turns into a real south London riot, with fighting, explosions and tangles with the police.[59] This phantasmagoric nowhere also has the sickening, nightmare quality of being impossible to leave:

> It was hours later, or so it seemed to my feet, and we were still walking along the Old Kent Road. It was some time now since my triumph at having escaped so cleverly had given place to dejection at finding that we had no money and that there was nothing for it but to keep on walking northward. There had been a moment when I thought of taking a taxi and making Dave pay at the other end, and the reflexion that Dave had already paid for one taxi for me that evening and might have no more ready cash would not have deterred me had I been able to find a taxi; but to those southern wastes the cruising taxi never comes and it was long since I had dismissed this as a hopeless vision.[60]

This place of parks and commons, small industry and bustling commerce, stolid working- and lower-middle-class 'clerkly' respectability, like so much of south London, declined and changed drastically in the post-war period. The widespread destruction and demolition, particularly in north Peckham, of acres of Victorian semis and villas (and the closing of the canal) and their replacement by small developments of terraces and maisonettes, tower blocks and sprawling, deck-access Brutalist housing, drastically reshaped the area. This sense of loss is evoked in Graham Swift's 1996 novel *Last Orders*. The Old Kent Road, of course, is the route Chaucer's pilgrims take in *The Canterbury Tales*, and *Last Orders* involves a contemporary pilgrimage as a bunch of assorted Bermondsey geezers escort the ashes of comrade Jack Dodds down the Old Kent Road and along the A2 to Margate, where Dodds's mortal remains are to be ceremonially thrown into the sea. The novel is also concerned with the older Peckham of the 1950s and '60s, of the characters' youth. Their route is clearly described: 'down past Albany Road and Trafalgar Avenue and the Rotherhithe turn . . . past the gas works, Ilderton Road, under the railway bridge'.[61] Yet the suburb depicted here is fast disappearing, epitomized by the long list of formerly landmark Old Kent Road pubs they pass – 'Green Man, Thomas à Becket, Lord Nelson' – in the process of taking last orders for ever.

Much of Peckham's working- and lower-class white residents migrated out this way in the 1970s and '80s, out to greener, and whiter, pastures in the outer suburbs. This is the exodus of the despised white working class also described by an aggrieved Michael Collins in his 2004 study *The Likes of Us* (echoing Millwall FC's belligerent chant 'No One Likes Us; We Don't Care'):

There had been little emigration from Southwark in the 1960s, beyond the few skilled workers who followed their jobs to new towns, or those uprooted to make way for the new estate who opted for a new council home on the outskirts of the Greater London area. In the 1980s, the younger generation of families who had been established locally since as far back as the 1890s and beyond broke the chain to form part of a mass exodus to the satellite suburbs of Greater London that spilled into Kent – Bexley, Eltham, Welling, Erith, Sidcup.[62]

Stephen Kelman's novel *Pigeon English* (2012), loosely based on the notorious murder of ten-year-old Damilola Taylor on the stairs of a Peckham block of flats, depicts a north Peckham of tower blocks, street gangs, drug dealers and casual murder. Kelman's key strategy here is to use, as an innocent narrator, an eleven-year-old Ghanaian immigrant, Harrison 'Harri' Opoku, who has recently moved with his mum and sister into a tower block off Peckham High Street:

> The buildings are all mighty around here. My tower is as high as the lighthouse at Jamestown. There are three towers all in a row: Luxembourg House, Stockholm House and Copenhagen House. I live in Copenhagen House. My flat is on floor 9 out of 14. It's not even hutious, I can look from the window now and my belly doesn't even turn over. I love going in the lift, it's brutal, especially when you're the only one in there.[63]

But also of course, at the same time Harri doesn't understand what he is seeing, or what this place really is, often unaware of the danger that surrounds him. Police helicopters, dingy alleyways, ranting winos and drug-users, even crime scenes, are not fearful to him. Harri's world is seen through a frame of childhood interests and manias and interpreted through scraps of popular culture. A boy is murdered, yet Harri responds to this through clichés gathered from *CSI* and other TV shows: 'Sellotape can do lots of different detective jobs. You can catch finger prints in it or hairs. You can use it to make traps . . . You can even catch the criminals themself if you have enough, like if you made it into a spiderweb.'[64]

Ben Judah, in his grim 2016 investigation into hidden migrant London, *This Is London*, visits Peckham police station, 'Frontline Peckham', and talks to a policeman coming off duty. Judah's policeman, a Nigerian who arrived in the capital in 1989, is shocked at the changing patterns of migration – from Africa, Asia, latterly Eastern Europe – he has seen:

> Last night we got a call, to one of the estates near the river, dem ones that look over the blocks into the lights of the Canary Wharf . . . just there over the river. Because there was a Pole sleeping in the bin chutes. He was begging me, 'Arrest me, arrest me,' trying to provoke me, going, 'Please arrest me for being drunk and disorderly' . . .

> The English are vanishing. London is no longer an English
> city at all . . . London is a patchwork of ghettos. Right
> here in Peckham, you have the Africans, over the river in
> Whitechapel we have the Bengalis, further east from there we
> have the Pakistanis, and west from here in Brixton we have
> the Jamaicans.[65]

Sandi Toksvig's memoir-travelogue *Between the Stops* (2019) ties
together various points of interest on the rambling Number 12 bus
route ('a red double-decker that meanders for just over seven and a
half miles from Dulwich library . . . to the BBC's Broadcasting House')
with incidents and reflections from Toksvig's life:[66]

> There used to be a tile works near here where bricks were
> made from the local clay. I like that Peckham clay made these
> great suburbs. I've been reading a book called *The Pickwicks
> of Peckham*, which is a 'compilation of the deeds, thoughts,
> adventures and aspirations of the members of the London
> Explorers' Club'. The bus passes Nigel Road on our left. It
> was here, at No. 24, Sage Cottage, that William Margrie, the
> skipper of the London Explorers' Club, made his home. He
> founded the club in September 1930, giving it the splendid and
> understated motto *Arise proud Peckham and lead the world!*
> . . . Margrie believed that he was a perfect example of a new
> evolutionary stage in human development, which he called
> Peckham Man. It never ceases to amaze me how many women
> struggle with self-belief while the majority of men have no
> trouble with it at all. He must have been insufferable.[67]

Dulwich

Dulwich (really meaning the very different East Dulwich and Dulwich
Village) is just south of Peckham and comprises part of that loop
of grander, and greener, mid- to late Victorian suburbs, partly built
around a chain of south London hills, that includes, eastwards, Forest
Hill, Catford, Eltham and Bexleyheath, and, to the west, Balham,
Streatham, Wandsworth Common and Wimbledon.

Dulwich Village has long been dominated by the wealthy Dulwich
Estate (and the private Dulwich College) and has successfully avoided

most forms of twentieth-century urban development (apart from the car – though London's last toll gate is here). 'Dulwich', Iain Sinclair reckons, 'is loud with all the silent trumpets of decency and hard-earned privilege'.[68] From the early nineteenth century, at least, it has played the role of urban village, a well-preserved sleepy pastoral retreat complete with grassy verges, cutesy finger-pointing signposts and lots of white-painted picket fences. Romantic poet, agitator, journalist and confidant of Shelley and Byron, Leigh Hunt, in the essay 'A Walk from Dulwich to Brockham', takes a trip out to the countryside at Dulwich in 1823:

> The stage took us to the Greyhound at Dulwich, where, though we had come from another village almost as far off from London on the northern side, we felt as if we had newly got into the country, and eat a hearty supper accordingly. This was a thing not usual with us; but then everybody eats 'in the country'; – there is 'the air'; and besides, we had eaten little dinner, and were merrier, and 'remote'. On looking out of our chamber window in the morning, we remarked that the situation of the inn was beautiful, even towards the road, the place is so rich with trees; and returning to the room in which we had supped, we found with pleasure that we had a window there, presenting us with a peep into rich meadows, where the haymakers were at work in their white shirts . . . We had not seen Dulwich for many years, and were surprised to find it still so full of trees. It continues, at least in the quarter through which we passed, to deserve the recommendation given it by Armstrong of 'Dulwich, yet unspoil'd by art'.[69]

The joke here is that by 1817 Dulwich did in fact boast John Soane's Picture Gallery. Hunt and companion, however, are becalmed by the rich country air and don't make it as far as the gallery: 'We know not whether it was the sultriness of the day, with occasional heavy clouds, but we thought the air of Dulwich too warm, and pronounced it a place of sleepy luxuriance.'[70]

Dulwich, by now self-consciously rustic and provocatively remote, proves to be the ideal retirement spot for Dickens's convivial bon viveur Samuel Pickwick Esq., in *The Pickwick Papers* (1836).

'The house I have taken,' said Mr Pickwick, 'is at Dulwich; it
has a large garden, and is situated in one of the most pleasant
spots near London. It has been fitted up with every attention to
substantial comfort; perhaps to a little elegance besides; but of
that you shall judge for yourselves. Sam accompanies me there.
I have engaged, on Perker's representation, a housekeeper – a
very old one – and such other servants as she thinks I shall
require. I propose to consecrate this little retreat, by having a
ceremony, in which I take a great interest, performed there.
I wish, if my friend Wardle entertains no objection, that his
daughter should be married from my new house, on the day
I take possession of it. The happiness of young people,' said
Mr Pickwick, a little moved, 'has ever been the chief pleasure of
my life. It will warm my heart to witness the happiness of those
friends who are dearest to me, beneath my own roof.'[71]

At the novel's close we see Pickwick in his twilight years:

He is somewhat infirm now, but he retains all his former
juvenility of spirit, and may still be frequently seen contemplating the pictures in the Dulwich Gallery, or enjoying
a walk about the pleasant neighbourhood on a fine day. He is
known by all the poor people about, who never fail to take their
hats off, as he passes, with great respect; the children idolise
him, and so indeed does the whole neighbourhood. Every year
he repairs to a large family merry-making at Mr Wardle's; on
this, as on all other occasions, he is invariably attended by the
faithful Sam, between whom and his master there exists a steady
and reciprocal attachment.[72]

In his 1898 study *South London*, Walter Besant recalls the village's
heyday earlier in the century:

Look at Dulwich – the peaceful and picturesque village of
Dulwich on this map of 1834. It lies among its trees, its gardens,
and its fields; the venerable college of Alleyn is the glory of
the village – nothing more beautiful than this almshouse, with
its hall and its picture gallery. Yet the people flocked out to
Dulwich less for the picture gallery than for the shady walks,

the fields, and a certain tavern – the Greyhound – which was beloved by everybody, and believed to contain a particular brew of beer, a particular kind of old Jamaica for punch, and a particular vintage of port not to be found anywhere else, even in a City company's cellars. There was, in fact, no more favourite place of resort for the better sort of citizens of London than Dulwich in the summer. For the poorer sort it was too far off, and cost too much in conveyance. The Dulwich stage ran two or three times a day; it was not too long a drive from the City; the young men rode – in those days the young men could all ride – even John Gilpin thought he could ride; they hired a horse as we now get into a cab. For those who lived in any suburb on the south, Dulwich was an easy walk. Not far from the college and the village – Mr Pickwick lived there in 1834 – were the Dulwich fields, as beautiful and interesting as those of Battersea were the contrary; there were, I think, five of them in succession. The little stream called the Effra rose somewhere in the neighbourhood, and ran about, winding through the fields in a deep channel, with rustic bridges across.[73]

G. A. Sala, in his 1859 satirical London investigation *Gaslight and Daylight*, mocks the ridiculous pretension of so many suburban house descriptions:

I recognise cottages, villas, and lodges, with the addition of 'hermitages', 'priories', 'groves', 'boxes', 'retreats', &c., on all suburban roads; – in Kensington, Hammersmith, and Turnham Green; in Kingsland, Hackney, and Dalston; in Highgate, Hampstead, and Hornsey; in Camberwell, Peckham, and Kennington; in Paddington, Kilburn, and Cricklewood; their roads, approaches, and environs, inclusive.[74]

Especially Dulwich:

What should the '*cottage ornée*' be like, I should wish to know (to jump from villas to cottages), but that delightful little box of a place at Dulwich, where a good friend of mine was wont (wont, alas!) to live. The strawberries in the garden; the private theatricals in the back parlour; the pleasant excursions on week days to the old College – (God bless old Thomas Alleyne and Sir Francis Bourgeois, I say! had the former done nothing worthier of benediction in his life than found the dear old place, or the latter not atoned for all the execrably bad modern pictures he painted in his life-time, by the exquisitely beautiful ancient ones he left us at his death); – the symposium in the garden on Sundays; the clear church-bells ringing through the soft summer air; the pianoforte in the boudoir, and Gluck's 'Che faro senza Euridice?' lightly, gently elicited from the silvery keys (by hands that are cold and powerless now), wreathing through the open window; the kind faces and cheerful laughter, the timid anxiety of the ladies concerning the last omnibus home at night, and the cheerful recklessness with which they subsequently abandoned that last omnibus to its fate, and conjectured impossibly fortuitous conveyances to town, conjectures ultimately resolving themselves into impromptu beds. How many a time have I had a shake-down on the billiard-table of the *cottage ornée*?[75]

Rupert Psmith (silent P, he says, 'as in pshrimp'), hero of P. G. Wodehouse's 1910 novel *Psmith in the City*, with a job waiting for him in the City at the 'New Asiatic Bank', roams sleepy Dulwich for somewhere to live. Wodehouse himself, as a *Puer Alleyniensis* or 'boy of Alleyn', an ex-Dulwich College schoolboy, knew the area very well. Psmith, we learn,

had settled on Dulwich as the spot to get lodgings, partly because, knowing nothing about London, he was under the impression that rooms anywhere inside the four-mile radius were very expensive, but principally because there was a school at Dulwich, and it would be a comfort being near a school. He might get a game of fives there sometimes, he thought, on a Saturday afternoon, and, in the summer, occasional cricket.[76]

Wodehouse describes the curious dissonance of optimistic place names and down-at-heel reality:

Wandering at a venture up the asphalt passage which leads from Dulwich station in the direction of the College, he came out into Acacia Road. There is something about Acacia Road which inevitably suggests furnished apartments. A child could tell at a glance that it was bristling with bed-sitting rooms.[77]

This is no arcadia, we learn:

It was a repulsive room. One of those characterless rooms which are only found in furnished apartments. To Mike, used to the comforts of his bedroom at home and the cheerful simplicity of a school dormitory, it seemed about the most dismal spot he had ever struck. A sort of Sargasso Sea among bedrooms.

He looked round in silence. Then he said: 'Yes.' There did not seem much else to say.

'It's a nice room,' said the pantomime dame. Which was a black lie. It was not a nice room. It never had been a nice room. And it did not seem at all probable that it ever would be a nice room. But it looked cheap.[78]

Improbably, Raymond Chandler, master of hard-boiled detective fiction, was another 'boy of Alleyn', whose time at Dulwich College even overlapped with Wodehouse's for one term, though they never actually met. Chandler, of course, then living in Upper Norwood, created famed private eye Philip Marlowe, who would later walk down the very different streets of Los Angeles. In the 1912 essay 'Houses to Let', Chandler criticized the self-satisfied bourgeoisie he encountered in Dulwich: 'the paramount bourgeois spirit . . . those clean smug bookcases which seem to cry aloud that they have as little as possible to do with literature or learning'.[79]

In the family saga *The Fortnight in September* (1931) by R. C. Sherriff (best known for the First World War play *Journey's End*), we see the Stevens family, living in 'Corunna Road', Dulwich, prepare to take their regular annual holiday. They are heading, as they have done for over twenty years, to the same boarding house, Seaview, down at Bognor. Mrs Stevens is extremely anxious about making the arduous journey, via East Dulwich and Clapham Station. Mrs Stevens inhabits a very enclosed world:

The Embankment – stretching out without break to right and left, divided the world for Mrs Stevens. On her side was

Dulwich and her home: long friendly roads, dotted here and there with the houses of people she knew. On her side, too, half a mile across the housetops, loomed the Crystal Palace, which sometimes in the autumn flashed golden squares of sunset over to them. Away beyond lay the open country and the trees . . .

On the far side of the Embankment lay the other half of Mrs Stevens' world: the half she scarcely knew. Herne Hill, Camberwell, and the lights of London that shone in overcast skies like sulphur candles in a dark, disused sick-room – that washed away, on fine nights, a little of the deep blue of the starlit heavens.

At the end of Corunna Road an asphalt footpath dived under the Embankment and emerged the other side, but Mrs Stevens seldom penetrated far into this other part of the world. She shopped in Dulwich, and had her friends there. Fine Saturday afternoons called them south, to the open fields and trees, out Bromley way.

Although she had lived at 22 Corunna Road for all her twenty married years, Mrs Stevens had little idea of what lay directly opposite the end of their garden – beyond the Embankment.[80]

Howard Jacobson's grotesque 1998 comedy *No More Mr Nice Guy* positions Dulwich as the ghastly un-asked-for suburban trap from which there is no escape. Frank Ritz, 'after so many shut-the-fuck-ups and get-the-fuck-outs', tries to flee Dulwich, travelling across London and west along the A40 towards Oxford, on a middle-age road trip towards his own past. He is, initially, elated: 'He's out. Free. Feeling fifteen, not fifty. Call me Kerouac.'[81] Life in Dulwich recedes:

He's over the river and on the Shepherd's Bush flyover, following the signs to Oxford . . . Where has he been for the last half-century? What has he been doing? Where has he been? His car's ten years old and it's got four thousand miles on the milometer. How many trips to Sainsbury's is that? Where's he been? He's been at home, turning down the volume of his life.[82]

In Dulwich, Frank has long been employed as a professional 'crap-watcher', that is, 'The best television critic in the country'. Frank likes to think of himself as a 'Rabelaisian man': he 'drank, he fornicated, he pigged out, he belched, he farted, he rose on the arched dolphin back of his dick'. Obnoxious and ageing, consumed with rancid self-hatred, Frank is convinced that Dulwich is not at all for him, and cannot figure out how he actually got there:

> But then he would have liked a penthouse or an apartment in
> a huddled mansion block to sink his Babylonian whirlpool in.
> Something with a Malibu terrace giving out on to the odours
> of the city, the fried food, the petrol fumes, the screams. Life.
> Life with a whiff of death in it. And what does he get instead?
> A whitewashed cottage on a village green in Dulwich. Dulwich!
> A garden. A wooden fence. Space. Death with a whiff of life
> in it.[83]

Frank's wife, Mel – angry, diet-faddish and bulimic, herself a not-able 'crap-producer' (of pornographic fiction) rather than producer – reminds him that this suburban existence is *exactly* what he wants: 'you may not think it . . . but you are living, in every particular, the life you want. That's why you stay.' Going along with Frank's taste for sexual debasement, on one sexual escapade, Mel drives her husband out to the countryside, 'blindfolded like "O", a mystery tour, down a lane, up a lane, off the beaten . . . deep into a forest, was it?' At the destination she orders him to strip, but to keep his socks on, and pose for photographs 'draped around a tree' or, nymph-like, 'arranged on the forest floor with everything akimbo'. Frank then hears the 'clop of a tennis ball' and suddenly, horrifically, realizes exactly where he is: 'Jesus Christ, Mel, this is Dulwich Park! We live here!'[84]

Dulwich doubles as 'Dulburb' in Will Self's 2000 novel *How the Dead Live*. Here, freshly deceased Londoners turn up in suburbs, called 'cystricts', which operate as 'quarantine, or clearing houses for the newly dead'. These areas, such as 'Dulston' in the north and 'Dulburb' in the south (clear echoes of their real-life counterparts), are located precisely in those forlorn real suburban places where the distinctions between life and death are already blurred:

> I'd been to Dulburb a few times . . . it was where the most
> comfortable dead liked to rest, in substantial semis, behind
> shaven privet hedges, in back of broad sidewalks, beside quiet

roads, the tarmac surfaces of which were so bluey-brown they seemed like infinitely slow moving, turbid waters.[85]

It gets worse:

> No, not Dulburb, at once illimitable and confined, like all the parts of London the dead inhabited. Not Dulburb, where every mile or so the houses pared away from a brief stretch of dual carriageway and you found the same mouldering parade of identical shops – the butcher, the baker, the greengrocer, the ironmonger – as you'd encountered a mile back. Not Dulburb, where the roundel of the tube station at Dulburb North was followed by the roundel at Dulburb Common and then, eventually, the roundel at Dulburb South.[86]

Herne Hill

Herne Hill is a mile or so to the west of Dulwich (Village), on the way to Brixton. John Ruskin thought it paradise:

> walking . . . through a mile of chestnut, lilac and apple trees, hanging over the wooden palings on each side – suddenly the trees stopped on the left, and out one came on the top of a field sloping down to the south into Dulwich valley – open field animate with cow and buttercup, and below, the beautiful meadows and high avenues of Dulwich, and beyond, all that crescent of the Norwood hills.[87]

Revisiting the bucolic site of his childhood home in 1880, Ruskin was stunned at the devastation caused by creeping suburbanization at Herne Hill:

> No existing terms of language known to me are enough to describe the forms of filth, and modes of ruin, that varied themselves along the course of Croxted Lane. The fields each side of it are now mostly dug up for building, or cut through into gaunt corners and nooks of blind ground by the wild crossings and concurrencies of three railroads. [The road] is bordered on each side by heaps of – Hades only knows

what! – mixed dust of every unclean thing that can crumble in drought, and mildew of every unclean thing that can rot or rust in damp; ashes and rags, beer-bottles and old shoes, battered pans, smashed crockery, shreds of nameless clothes, door-sweepings, floor-sweepings, kitchen garbage, back-garden sewage, old iron, rotten timber jagged with out-torn nails, cigar-ends, pipe-bowls, cinders, bones, and ordure, indescribable.[88]

In *Liquid City* (1999), Iain Sinclair undertakes a pilgrimage across south London to Herne Hill, walking all the way across town from Hackney to interview the nearly forgotten poet and academic Eric Mottram. Mottram had been part of the British Poetry Revival movement of the late 1960s and 1970s and an important pioneer of American literary studies in the UK (having also personally known individual Beats, particularly William Burroughs). He is interesting for Sinclair because of his links, and those of his fellow poets (J. H. Prynne, Barry MacSweeney, Allen Fisher, Brian Catling), with shamanism, broadly conceived. Shamanism became, in the late 1960s, a newly fashionable term that included the original features of the Asiatic/Siberian tribal holy man or doctor, a seer or spiritual guide, but with added elements of the poet, the underground leader, the (urban) guide to esoteric and hidden knowledge and forgotten practices, the charismatic rebel. Mottram had written the *Book of Herne*, a poetry collection containing shamanistic lore. In *Liquid City*, Sinclair suggests that Mottram is clearly *in the wrong place*: like J. G. Ballard camped out at Shepperton for fifty years, Mottram is in exile, a key cultural figure inexplicably detained on the suburban fringes. Sinclair is clearly uncomfortable en route to this southern hinterland, away from his usual psychogeographic turf. Tramping through Peckham, along these 'funeral streets with nothing to watch', Sinclair suggests that Mottram must be uncomfortable living out here ('Eric Mottram at Herne Hill, communing with the ghost of Ruskin'[89]), beyond the psychogeographic pale:

Eric, I remember, the last time I saw him, was talking about moving away. He doesn't want to spell it out. He won't say it. He says it: 'Alien noises'. Ghetto blasters. Pyramids of voodoo speakers. 'Brutal'. 'Extreme' . . . dustbin lids rolling down

Herne Hill; baseball bats clubbing gay activists in Brockwell Park; the rattle of commuter trains; gangsta-rage in Brixton. Reality, Eric discovers, is chewing up theory. Barriers of Gold Medal shockers won't defend the property against wired raiding parties.[90]

Forest Hill

Forest Hill lies southeast of Dulwich. The area was originally part of the ancient Great North Wood and is one the long chain of south-east London hills that sit around 6 miles southeast of London Bridge. It was rapidly suburbanized by the Victorians, attracted by the area's breezy hilltop location; a railway station (then known as Dartmouth Arms) arrived in 1839, and long streets of roomy villas were soon built for the middle classes. Some of these were in fact extremely grand, the grandest of all being that of tea merchant, amateur ethnologist and, later, museum founder Frederick Horniman. The quirky Horniman Museum, famed for some startling taxidermized animals, thrives.

Ella Hartley sticks up for the suburbs, and has a kind word for Forest Hill, in William Pett Ridge's 1909 Clapham-set comedy *Sixty-nine Birnam Road*. As the Boulogne boat-train meanders through the south London suburbs to Charing Cross, a Mrs Featherstone is provoked by the sight through the window: 'The suburbs, the poor mistaken suburbs! The long straight roads with houses on either side all precisely alike . . . When they say something is suburban this is what they mean.'[91] Ella will have none of it:

'You're wrong', she cried, rapidly. 'You're altogether wrong. People take their souls and their own bodies and their lives with them, and whether they reside in Berkeley Square or at Forest Hill, then can be themselves . . . There's as much intelligence in the suburbs as anywhere else in London; more. There's as much happiness in the suburbs as anywhere else in London; more. There's as much goodness and decency of behaviour in the suburbs as anywhere else in London; more.'[92]

Forest Hill is central to Jonathan Meades's nasty comedy *The Fowler Family Business* (2002). This concerns the drastic undoing of the life and family of grotesque Henry Fowler (the family business being funerals). Fowler – proving Ella Hartley wrong – embodies all the worst traits of the stereotypical suburban lower-middle-class man: loud, aggressive, tasteless, both sexually inhibited *and* perverse, snobbish, self-regarding and oblivious to others. Odious Fowler thinks of himself as very much part of his beloved patch of south London; he is pompously attached to the place where we see him grow up, with strong ties to place, family and tradition: 'he thought of himself severally, that is, as father, husband, bearer of the familial tradition, loving son, reliable undertaker, loyal subject to of his sovereign, member of Dulwich and Sydenham Golf Club'.[93]

More exactly, more absurdly, he 'thought of himself as a *south* Londoner, a *South-east* Londoner'. Fowler's London, as he looks out from Forest Hill, 'stretched across the hills from Honor Oak to South Norwood, bounded by Dulwich and Penge'. Absurdly, the suburb – in direct contradiction to all the known and observable historical data, the facts of 'centrifugence . . . chronology, sequence, cause, rail spread' – takes priority over the city. For Fowler, in fact, 'the Smoke is attached to South London'. Fowler, indeed, considers himself 'blessed': all this 'was his enchanted garden'.[94]

Of course, this cannot be allowed to prevail: Fowler is soon horribly expelled from this easy identification with place. There are numerous hints, early in the novel, that this corner of southeast London is no blessed land after all, but in fact an ill-fated site of random bad luck and gruesome violence. The Fowler family have a slack-jawed devotion to unfunny, diminutive, accident-prone 1960s TV clown Charlie Drake, 'who lived nearby in Lawrie Park Road'. 'Ooh he's going to come a cropper Mother!' predicts Fowler senior, glued to *The Charlie Drake Show*. There were, we learn, on the roads in Forest Hill in the 1960s, 'deaths galore' and 'random cullings' resulting from widespread speeding or drink-driving. This of course was a slice of luck for the Fowler family business:

'It's Nature's way. Nature always finds a way. War, disease, pogroms, the South Circular Road, a faulty earth. You make the place too safe and, well – it's not just the trade that's going to feel it. The world'll be full of old 'uns. Miserable old parties like yours truly . . . life was meant to be a banana skin. Look at the Bible, my lad.'[95]

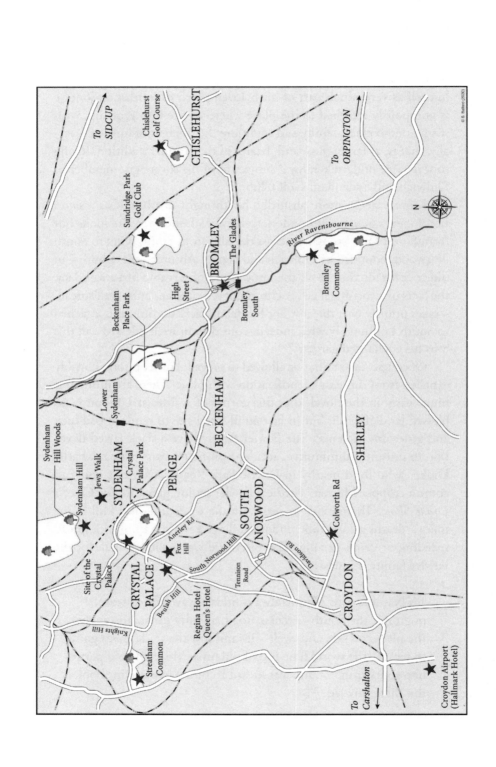

3 'A STRANGE FEELING IN THE AIR'

Outer Southeast London: From Sydenham to Penge,
Crystal Palace and the Norwoods, South Norwood,
Bromley, Chislehurst and Croydon

Sydenham, Penge and Upper Norwood, around 8 miles south-east of the City of London, form part of a hilly ridge that runs across this part of suburban London and hints at the limits of London itself. From vantage points in the north and centre of town, this appears to be London's final southern edge, clearly marked by the Eiffel Tower-like Crystal Palace TV transmitter. Indeed in a track by beloved early 1990s pop pranksters Carter USM, 'Midnight on the Murder Mile', concerning a night out in New Cross, the far-away transmitter tower's glowing red lights provide orientation and a glint of meaning. The heroine of Stella Gibbons's novel *Westwood* (1945) surveys from Highgate Hill bomb damage caused during the Second World War, and observes that on the 'outskirts of the city, out towards Edmonton and Tottenham in the north and Sydenham to the south, there was a strange feeling in the air'.[1] Sydenham is the southern limit.

Sydenham

Sydenham was a remote and rural district until natural mineral springs were discovered in the 1640s. Later, the Croydon Canal passed through Sydenham, and the London and Croydon Railway followed its route, opening up the area in the mid-1840s. The biggest event in Sydenham's history came with the re-siting of the vast iron and glass Crystal Palace Great Exhibition building from Hyde Park, in 1854. This, along with its remote, hilly and wooded setting, made it an ideal wealthy Victorian suburb, and numerous large family villas were built. Ian Nairn describes bosky, hard-to-find Sydenham Hill station in *Nairn's London* (1966):

This is the quintessence of true suburbia, the illusion of
rurality more effective here than the real thing would be.
From College Road there is no sign of platform or signals,
just a tiny entrance surrounded by trees . . . only the walls
and roof keep tigers from eating late passengers for the eight
fifty-seven.[2]

These green, remote and elevated qualities appealed to Eleanor
Marx (Karl's beloved youngest daughter), gifted and tireless early fem-
inist, socialist, activist and agitator. Eleanor Marx had been born and
brought up in squalid rooms in Dean Street, Soho, where two other
Marx children had earlier died. Partly through a £7,000 bequest from
Friedrich Engels, she moved, in 1895, with her caddish, faithless lover
Edward Aveling, to a spacious house at tree-lined, rural-feeling 7 Jews
Walk, Sydenham. From here she excitedly wrote a letter to her sister
Laura: 'the house we are about to buy . . . (Edward swears this is my
only reason for buying it) is in JEWS WALK, Sydenham'.[3] She also
wrote, before moving in: 'I am Jewishly proud of my house in Jews
Walk.'[4] Eleanor's move to Sydenham, to 'The Den', as she named the
house, was not to be a happy one. Aveling turned out to be devious,
untrustworthy and semi-criminal (he was 'short with the face and
eyes of a Lizard', according to a baffled George Bernard Shaw) and
soon departed The Den, taking Eleanor's money and anything that
could be sold. Depressed, betrayed and isolated, she confided to her
half-brother:

MY DEAREST FREDDY, – This morning I received a note: 'I am
coming back. Will be home early to-morrow.' (That means
to-day.) Then a telegram: 'Will be home again at half-past one.'
I began work at once in my room – and Edward appeared
surprised and highly offended that I did not throw myself into
his arms. So far he has made no attempt at excuse or apology.
I have therefore – after I had waited to see if he would begin –
said that we must talk over our business affairs, and that I could
not forget the treatment to which I had been subjected. To this
he did not reply. I said, moreover, that you would probably
come, and if you can come to-morrow or any other evening
this week I hope you will. It is only right that in the presence
of both of us he should come to an understanding. If, therefore,

you can come to-morrow, do so; if not, let me know when you can come . . .

    Ever, dear Freddy, yours,

TUSSY

The Den, Sydenham, Sept. 1, 1897[5]

The following year Marx discovered that Aveling had in fact secretly married an actress named Eva Frye. Marx writes again, increasingly desperate:

> MY DEAR FREDDY, – Come tonight if you can. It is a shame to worry you, but I am so lonely, and I am face to face with a most dreadful situation: Absolute ruin – everything, even to the last penny, or deepest shame before the whole world. It is frightful. It presents itself to me even worse than it is. And I need someone with whom I can take counsel. I know that the final decision and responsibility will rest with me – but a little counsel and friendly assistance will be of immeasurable value.
>
>   So, dear Freddy, come. I am broken-hearted. – Yours
>
> TUSSY
>
> The Den, Jews Walk, Sydenham, February 3, 1898[6]

On the afternoon of 31 March, Marx sent her maid round to the local chemist with a note. This requested 'prussic acid' (cyanide) for 'the dog'. By the time the maid had come back from returning the poison receipt book to the chemist, Eleanor Marx was near death. She was dead by the time the doctor arrived. Aveling has long been suspected of her murder: the note to the chemist had been signed with his initials – or had Eleanor forged them? A codicil to Marx's will, hurriedly written after she uncovered Aveling's secret marriage, was destroyed. Aveling disappeared with the Engels inheritance. Eleanor Marx had left Aveling one final note: 'My last word to you is the same as I have said during all these long, sad years – love'. Adding to the drama, Aveling himself died, of kidney disease, just six months later.

Lower Sydenham makes a bizarre appearance in Paul Theroux's grim political thriller *The Family Arsenal* (1976). Here, plodding, commuting Mr Gawber misses his usual station (Catford Bridge) on his way home and gets out just one stop later, at Lower Sydenham. This minor oversight induces profound uncanny disorientation – and grotesque consequences – for Gawber. He has no absolutely idea where he is:

> He walked down the platform with such uncertainty his shoes seemed too large for him. He was walking with another man's feet. The name on the station signboard was recognizable, but this particle of the familiar in so strange a place confounded him. The platform had no roof, and when the train drew out it was empty – the other passengers had quickly deserted it. And yet he enjoyed it and was surprised to notice how he lingered to savour the feeling and acquaint himself with the station. He said to himself with wondering pleasure, 'I've never been here before!'[7]

This unreal and uncertain territory that Gawber has stumbled into ('he almost laughed: he was delighted by this sense of being lost so near his home') is also where, in a gloomy pub, The Locomotive, he comes across both Hood, a disgraced former U.S. diplomat fresh from Hanoi and now loose in London, and despicable south London wide boy Weech. All three, in an unsettling scene laced with menace, drink at the bar. Afterwards, outside, in the long summer grass, on a footpath that leads back to Lower Sydenham station, Hood efficiently breaks Weech's neck. Weech's body is destined to be dumped at nearby Honor Oak Park, at 'that wooded mound he saw was called One-Tree Hill'.[8]

In 1986 novelist Kazuo Ishiguro was living in Sydenham, trying to write *The Remains of the Day*. Deciding to eliminate all distractions, Ishiguro stuck to a plan: to lock himself away and write all day, every day, for four weeks. This incarceration produced a certain delirium:

> On my first Sunday off I ventured outdoors, on to Sydenham High Street, and persistently giggled – so Lorna told me – at the fact that the street was built on a slope, so that people coming down it were stumbling over themselves, while those going up were panting and staggering effortfully. Lorna was concerned I had another three weeks of this to go, but I explained I was very well, and that the first week had been a success.[9]

Curiously, Sydenham's village-feeling remoteness also appealed to U.S. rock and folk critic Robert Shelton, who was trying to find somewhere quiet to finish his biography of Bob Dylan, *No Direction Home* (1986). According to Michael Gray, Shelton chose to leave the distraction of New York City to get the book written and so 'moved to a tiny cottage up an unmade road off Sydenham Hill in south-east London'.[10] This turned out to be an unwise move. Isolated, cramped, lonely, broke, increasingly cranky and over-guarded, Shelton took years to finish the book. Gray hints at a lyric from Dylan's 'Tangled Up in Blue' to paint the scene:

> So Shelton . . . landed up in a miserable, philistine part of London where there was no music in the cafes at night (there were no cafes at night), it could take ninety minutes to get in or out of the West End, and there was certainly no equivalent to the camaraderie and streetlife of Greenwich Village. In Sydenham he was just a middle-aged American, getting divorced from Carol, his third wife (there had been two short-lived marriages in his youth), who had hoped in vain that Bob might turn her into a country-music star.[11]

Penge

Just over a mile south of Sydenham, the nondescript Victorian suburb of Penge, another area boosted by the arrival of the Crystal Palace just up the hill, becomes, for Victorian social topographer, campaigner and novelist Walter Besant, a perfect example of benighted suburban sprawl. For him, in his 1899 survey and study *South London*, this place is the epitome of the destructive suburban sprawl that has destroyed an idyllic past:

> We have not only destroyed the former beauty of South London: we have forgotten it. Ask a resident of Penge – one of the many thousands of Penge – what this suburban town was like seventy years ago. Do you think he can tell you anything of Penge Common? Has he ever heard of any Penge Common? . . . Again, is there anyone in Penge who now remembers the hanging woods? They hung over a hillside, and were as beautiful as the hanging woods of Cliveden. But, like the Common, they are gone.[12]

Penge is the setting for famed barrister Horace Rumpole's first ever criminal case, as recorded in John Mortimer's *Rumpole and the Penge Bungalow Murders* (2004). The metropolitan suburbs are ideal territory for crime, and so for crime fiction. Supposedly writing his memoirs and recalling his first case in that far-off and mysterious time, the early 1950s, Penge provides the ideal analogue of a far-off and mysterious place: 'I had, for many years, been aware', Rumpole tells us, surprisingly, 'of Penge'.[13]

> I had . . . a clear memory of Penge, a small suburb beside the
> island of parkland surrounding the old Crystal Palace, now
> burned down, where I used to go on walks with my father . . .
> I even remembered the streets of bungalows which had sprung
> up in the 1930s to accommodate the growing population of
> the families of bank clerks, department store managers and
> commercial travellers who looked on Crystal Palace Park as
> their particular and privileged glimpse of the countryside.[14]

Former RAF bomber crew and companions Denis ('Jerry') Jerold and Charlie ('Tail-End') Weston are both murdered, shot, in their respective Penge bungalows, seemingly by Jerold's disaffected – and decidedly non-militaristic – son, Simon. Simon Jerold seems destined to hang for this, especially as the victims are (or so it seems) irreproachable war heroes, and his brief, one C. H. Wystan QC, is complacently convinced of the boy's guilt and lazily indifferent to his fate. Rumpole, young, idealistic and already awkward, is convinced that Simon Jerold is innocent, and is appalled at the indifference, ignorance and snobbery that could casually lead to his execution. Unusually, Rumpole travels down to obscure Penge to inspect the crime scene personally:

> It looked dusty and neglected, as though a feeling of guilt, the
> result of a violent death, still hung about it, and for which
> the room itself took some sort of blame . . . we had walked
> through the sifting rain to the row of identical bungalows in
> a dead-end street behind Penge Road. There was a police car
> parked outside number 3, the home of the Jerolds . . . So we
> stood in the room, which seemed small to have accommodated
> a party of half-drunk wartime heroes and a sudden tragedy. The
> bungalows were identical, so 'Tail-End' Charlie had precisely

the same accommodation as his pilot officer. Jerry's front door opened on to a small hall not much more than a small passage, with another door opening into the sitting room . . . it seemed a meagre place to come home to after the daring splendours of a victorious war.[15]

Crystal Palace and the Norwoods

Norwood (West, Upper and South) refers to the Great North Wood, the ancient oak forest that ran for almost 3 miles across a swathe of south London ridges and hills, from just to the north of Croydon almost up to Camberwell. Daniel Defoe noted in his *Tour through the Whole Island of Great Britain* that this area was 'more open and more woody than any other part so near London, especially about Norwood, the parishes of Camberwell, Dullege and Luseme'.[16] Most of the woodland was cleared at the end of the eighteenth century, Dulwich Wood being the only remaining wild fragment. The biggest change in the area came with the relocation, from Hyde Park, of Joseph Paxton's Crystal Palace exhibition building in 1854. This defined the area to the extent that it gradually became known as Crystal Palace.

Before the Crystal Palace building arrived, Norwood was considered fashionably remote, respectable, pastoral, with broad roadways and spacious villas, a spa and – because of the hills – no railways. This is the suburb that melancholic Mr Watkins Tottle dreams of in a tale first published in 1835 and included in Dickens's *Sketches by Boz*. In his room in town, Tottle dreams of the suburbs. He is 'wrapt in profound reveries', fantasies of marriage, of a family, of idealized suburban living. We learn that, with closed eyes, his 'fancy transformed his small parlour . . . into a neat house in the suburbs'.[17] When Tottle eventually travels down to Norwood, the suburb is transformed by Tottle's dream-like perceptivity and appears strangely unreal:

> The sun that rose on the next day but one, had never beheld a sprucer personage on the outside of the Norwood stage, than Mr. Watkins Tottle; and when the coach drew up before a cardboard-looking house with disguised chimneys, and a lawn like a large sheet of green letter-paper, he certainly had never lighted to his place of destination a gentleman who felt more uncomfortable.[18]

Here Tottle 'indulges in the most delicious reveries of future bliss' and grotesquely fantasizes some non-existent romantic interest from a certain Miss Lillerton. Tottle, of course, is horribly mistaken: he is not the intended recipient of Miss Lillerton's affections, but a mere messenger, a useful 'elderly gentleman'. A few weeks later, we learn, 'the body of a gentleman unknown, was found in the Regent's canal.'[19]

In Dickens's novel *David Copperfield* (1850–51), the young David is articled to lawyers Spenlow and Jorkins, and Mr Spenlow personally takes David down to Norwood in his 'handsome phaeton'. Copperfield's visit is envied by other clerks, as 'the house at Norwood was a sacred mystery'. Spenlow, like suburbanite Wemmick in *Great Expectations*, clearly keeps his city and suburban selves very much apart.

> There was a lovely garden to Mr Spenlow's house; and though that was not the best time of the year for seeing a garden, it was so beautifully kept, that I was quite enchanted. There was a charming lawn, there were clusters of trees, and there were perspective walks that I could just distinguish in the dark, arched over with trellis-work, on which shrubs and flowers grew in the growing season. 'Here Miss Spenlow walks by herself,' I thought. 'Dear me!'
>
> We went into the house, which was cheerfully lighted up, and into a hall where there were all sorts of hats, caps, greatcoats, plaids, gloves, whips, and walking-sticks. 'Where is Miss Dora?' said Mr. Spenlow to the servant. 'Dora!' I thought. 'What a beautiful name!'
>
> We turned into a room near at hand (I think it was the identical breakfast-room, made memorable by the brown East Indian sherry), and I heard a voice say, 'Mr. Copperfield, my daughter Dora, and my daughter Dora's confidential friend!' It was, no doubt, Mr Spenlow's voice, but I didn't know it, and I didn't care whose it was. All was over in a moment. I had fulfilled my destiny. I was a captive and a slave. I loved Dora Spenlow to distraction![20]

When the vast and revolutionary iron and glass building (the name 'Crystal Palace' was applied disparagingly in *Punch* magazine, referring to a tawdry attempt to build a 'palace of very crystal') was emptied at Hyde Park after the Great Exhibition of 1851 finished, it was dismantled, then transported largely by horse-drawn carts and rebuilt, considerably enlarged and reshaped, on a dramatic new site at the top of Sydenham Hill, between Sydenham and Upper Norwood, in 1854. Not everyone was pleased. Sage and critic John Ruskin, living in nearby Denmark Hill, was dismissive: 'Then the Crystal Palace came, for ever spoiling the view through all its compass'.[21] But it's not just the ruined field and lanes, the noise, the sudden arrival of day-tripping Cockney pleasure-seekers. In a pamphlet published in 1854, Ruskin can be seen struggling with the *meaning* of the Palace.

> I read the account in the *Times* newspaper of the opening of the Crystal Palace at Sydenham as I ascended the hill between Vevay and Chatel St. Denis . . . It is indeed impossible to limit, in imagination, the beneficent results which may follow from the undertaking thus happily begun. For the first time in the history of the world, a national museum is formed in which a whole nation is interested; formed on a scale which permits the exhibition of monuments of art in unbroken symmetry, and of the productions of nature in unthwarted growth, – formed under the auspices of science which can hardly err, and of wealth which can hardly be exhausted; and placed in the close neighbourhood of a metropolis overflowing with a population weary of labour, yet thirsting for knowledge, where contemplation may be consistent with rest, and instruction with enjoyment. It is impossible, I repeat, to estimate the influence of such an institution on the minds of the working-classes. How many hours once wasted may now be profitably dedicated to pursuits in which interest was first awakened by some accidental display in the Norwood palace.[22]

But later Ruskin reveals his true feelings. The iron and glass palace, gigantic, functional and temporary, is, for Ruskin, horribly emblematic of industrial modernity itself. He sees it as crude, mechanical, detached from tradition or relation to place, showy and empty, mass-produced. Tellingly, Ruskin uses a domestic analogy to disparage the palace: 'in the centre of the nineteenth century, we suppose ourselves to have invented a new style of architecture, when we have magnified a conservatory!'[23] Ruskin worries that the palace, ostensibly morally uplifting and informative – exhibition centre, technology showcase and concert space – is *really* a fun-place or fairground, offer-ing diverting spectacles such as sporting events, boating, music and dancing, eating and drinking, fireworks and fountains.

Fyodor Dostoevsky, in his 1864 novella *Notes from Underground*, also mocks the transparent utopianism of the Crystal Palace build-ing. In particular he seems to have in mind Nikolai Chernyshevsky's influential utopian novel *What Is to be Done?* of the previous year, wherein one character famously dreams of a beautiful building (the Crystal Palace having sparked much debate in Russia) crammed with beautiful people. Dostoevsky will have none of it:

> You believe in a palace of crystal that can never be destroyed –
> a palace at which one will not be able to put out one's tongue or
> make a long nose on the sly. And perhaps that is just why
> I am afraid of this edifice, that it is of crystal and can never be
> destroyed and that one cannot put one's tongue out at it even
> on the sly.[24]

The most severe criticism of the Crystal Palace, a disgusted percep-tion of the place as not at all uplifting or educational, or as a showcase for the triumphs of Empire and industrial civilization, but rather as a tawdry and mindless centre for proletarian mass entertainment, occurs in a telling episode in George Gissing's grim novel *The Nether World* (1889). The 'netherworld' here is the dreadful abyss of the Clerkenwell slums. In order to briefly escape from this hellish place, newlyweds Bob Hewett and Pennyloaf Candy plan to spend their wedding day having fun down at the palace. So, on trains from the city, 'Away they sped, over the roofs of South London, about them the universal glare of sunlight, the carriage dense with tobacco-smoke' on their way out to the 'palis':[25]

> Thus early in the day, the grounds were of course preferred to
> the interior of the glass house. Bob and Pennyloaf bent their
> steps to the fair. Here already was gathered much goodly
> company; above their heads hung a thick white wavering cloud
> of dust. Swing-boats and merry-go-rounds are from of old the
> chief features of these rural festivities; they soared and dipped
> and circled to the joyous music of organs which played the same
> tune automatically for any number of hours, whilst raucous

voices invited all and sundry to take their turn. Should this
delight pall, behold on every hand such sports as are dearest to
the Briton, those which call for strength of sinew and exactitude
of aim. The philosophic mind would have noted with interest
how ingeniously these games were made to appeal to the
patriotism of the throng. Did you choose to 'shy' sticks in the
contest for cocoa-nuts, behold your object was a wooden model
of the treacherous Afghan or the base African. If you took up
the mallet to smite upon a spring and make proof of how far
you could send a ball flying upwards, your blow descended
upon the head of some other recent foeman. Try your fist at the
indicator of muscularity, and with zeal you smote full in the
stomach of a guy made to represent a Russian. If you essayed the
pop-gun, the mark set you was on the flank of a wooden donkey,
so contrived that it would kick when hit in the true spot. What
a joy to observe the tendency of all these diversions! How
characteristic of a high-spirited people that nowhere could be
found any amusement appealing to the mere mind, or calculated
to effeminate by encouraging a love of beauty.[26]

It only gets worse as the day progresses. As night falls, the fireworks,
then serious drinking, then the fighting starts. The crowd now are
physically repulsive. For Gissing, this is pure *fin de siècle* degeneration;
the reverse of Chernyshevsky's beautiful vigorous youths:

Observe the middle-aged women; it would be small surprise
that their good looks had vanished, but whence comes it they
are animal, repulsive, absolutely vicious in ugliness? Mark the
men in their turn: four in every six have visages so deformed
by ill-health that they excite disgust; their hair is cut down to
within half an inch of the scalp; their legs are twisted out of
shape by evil conditions of life from birth upwards. Whenever
a youth and a girl come along arm-in-arm, how flagrantly
shows the man's coarseness! They are pretty, so many of these
girls, delicate of feature, graceful did but their slavery allow
them natural development; and the heart sinks as one sees them
side by side with the men who are to be their husbands . . . A
great review of the People. Since man came into being did the
world ever exhibit a sadder spectacle?[27]

The 1919 literary curiosity, the famously misspelled *The Young Visiters* by precocious nine-year-old Daisy Ashford, is partly set at the Crystal Palace. We can see how this novel was so popular at the time: a society novel, earnest, both knowing and innocent, unintentionally funny, apparently artless and seeming to offer an unknowing child's-eye view of the world, albeit heavily filtered through Ashford's compulsive reading. Many thought J. M. Barrie himself must have been the author. Here Mr Salteena travels to London to meet the Earl of Clincham, who will magically instruct the former in the arts of becoming more like a gentleman: 'I am quite alright as they say but I would like to be the real thing can it be done' (all spellings and punctuation as in the original). Salteena's friend Bernard advises him, 'Why don't you try the Crystal Pallace he asked several peaple Earls and even dukes have privite compartments there'. Next day, after 'a little whiskey to make him feel more at home' and a curry,

Mr Salteena found a tall policeman. Could you direct me to the Crystale Pallace if you please said Mr Salteena nervously.

Well said the geniul policeman my advice would be to take a cab sir.

Oh would it said Mr Salteena then I will do so.

He hailed a Hansome and got speedily in to the Crystal Palace he cried gaily and holding his bag on his knees he prepared to enjoy the sights of the Metropilis. It was a merry drive and all too soon the Palace heaved in view. Mr Salteena sprang out and paid the man and then he entered the wondrous edifice. His heart beat very fast as two huge men in gold braid flung open the doors. Inside was a lovely fountain in the middle and all round were little stalls where you could buy sweets and lemonade also scent handkerchiefs and many dainty articles. There were a lot of peaple but nobody very noteable.

At last after buying two bottles of scent and some rarther nice sweets which stuck to his teeth Mr Salteena beheld a wooden door on which was nailed a notice saying To the Private Compartments.

Ah ha said Mr Salteena to himself this is evidently my next move, and he gently pushed open the door straitening his top hat as he did so. Inside he found himself in a dimly lit passage with a thick and handsom carpet. Mr Salteena gazed round and

beheld in the gloom a very superier gentleman in full evening
dress who was reading a newspaper and warming his hands
on the hot water pipes. Mr Salteena advanced on tiptoe and
coughed gently as so far the gentleman had paid no attention.
However at the second cough he raised his eyes in a weary
fashion. do you want anything he asked in a most noble voice.

Mr Salteena got very flustered. Well I am seeking the Earl
of Clincham he began in a trembly voice are you by any chance
him he added most respectfully.

No not exacktly replied the other my name happens to be
Edward Procurio. I am half italian and I am the Groom of the
Chambers.[28]

Lawrence Durrell's first important novel, *The Black Book* (1938),
is partially set in the Queens Hotel, Crystal Palace (renamed here
the Regina Hotel), where the Durrell family lived briefly before their
celebrated decamp to Corfu. Here, Durrell describes a group of eccen-
trics and intellectual outcasts (including a certain Lawrence Lucifer),
holed up in the seedy hotel, all struggling to escape from the spiritual
sterility (and dreadful weather) of moribund pre-war England, trying
to evade a moth-eaten 'English Death':

This is the day I have chosen to begin this writing, because
today we are dead among the dead; and this is an *agon* for the
dead . . . It is today at breakfast . . . that I am dying again the
little death which broods forever in the Regina Hotel: along
the mouldering corridors, the geological strata of potted ferns,
the mouse-chawed wainscoting which the deathwatch ticks. Do
not ask me how. Do not ask me why, at this time, on a remote
Greek headland in a storm, I should choose, for my first real
book, a theatre which is not Mediterranean. It is part of us here,
in the four damp walls of a damp house, under an enormous
wind, under the sabres of rain . . . When I am in the Regina
I am dead again.[29]

The hypnotic, arch prose surveys the south London landscape, creating
a tone of apocalyptic 1930s doom and T. S. Eliot-like cultural exhaustion and Baudelarian decadence, with sparks of deranged Lawrentian
and Surrealist visioning:

From Peckham where the children sail their boats, where the lovers play with each other and go mad on the dark common after dark, away to the lairs of Lee Green, where you can smell Blackheath stalking upward into the darkness, leper-like, eaten by roads and villas. From the fag end of Anerley where the tram lines curve away above a wilderness of falling tombstones; Elmers End, a locality of white stumps in the snow; to the Crystal Palace stuck against the sky, dribbling softly, pricked with lamps. Lawrence knew this world. Look up suddenly into the night. O ponderous phalloi, you have impregnated the world, you are the hostage of these delicate girls whose virginities are hard as the iron rails of the beds on which they toss![30]

Fittingly, as the novel was being finished in 1936, the palace burned down, its glass and iron and lead all melting, falling and running downhill along the gutters of Anerley Road.

In 1969 Angela Carter also brilliantly used the run-down, decaying Victoriana of Crystal Palace as a setting for *The Magic Toyshop*, her exploration of childhood, adolescent sexuality and visionary transformation. The palace itself has vanished; yet stone foundations, embankments, sweeping staircases and the odd lion remain (as they do today), offering Carter an ideal ghostly and exhausted Victorian ambience. Fifteen-year-old Melanie, after the sudden death of her parents, goes to live with her uncle Philip and aunt Margaret, and Margaret's younger brothers, Francie and Finn, in grimy and windswept hill-top Crystal Palace. It is a long, long drive out to the mysterious new south London house from Victoria station: 'still farther', Finn says, until

they reached a wedge-shaped open space on a high hill with, in the centre, a focus, a whimsical public lavatory ornately trimmed with rococo Victorian wrought ironwork and, drooping over it, a weary sycamore tree with white patches on its trunk, like a skin disease. There were a number of shops, all brightly lighted now. A fruitshop, with artificial grass banked greenly in the windows and mounds of glowing oranges, trapped little winter suns; groping, mottled hands of bananas . . . A butcher's shop, where a blue-aproned, grizzle-headed man in a bloodstained straw boater reached between two swinging carcasses of lamb for sausages from a marble slab.[31]

Melanie's new home turns out to be at the back of a dark, cavernous and run-down toyshop, in a location where nothing is exactly either real or knowable. Melanie's first impression is that it is strange and stagey, and not London:

> 'We might as well not be in London at all . . . we might as well be somewhere else' . . . Melanie had been told that they had come to live in a great city but found herself again in a village, a grey one. The isolation of the Flower household on its South Suburban hill-top was complete. Melanie left the house, a basket on her arm and a list in her pocket like a French housewife, only to do the shopping . . . But where was London and the bustle and anonymity of a great city? She could see the lights of it from the upper windows but never got any nearer.[32]

The decaying Victorian house is claustrophobic and threadbare, harsh, cold and potentially violent, her semi-criminal cousins wild and unpredictable, and it represents the nasty present day; not the glory days of Victorian suburbia or Melanie's own well-appointed upper-middle-class past.

> It was a high and windy suburb. The square, its shabby focus, topped a steep hill and these streets ran sharply down; once stately and solid streets, fat with money and leisure, full of homes for a secure middle class with parlours in which its bustled daughters could play 'The Last Rose of Summer' and 'Believe me if all those Endearing Young Charms' politely on rosewood pianos antlered with candlesticks; and roast-beef coloured dining-rooms where the gentlemen mellowed over rich, after-dinner port . . . And, now, crumbling in decay, over-laden with a desolate burden of humanity, the houses had the look of queuing for a great knacker's yard.[33]

This version of the Crystal Palace suburb is, then, like a dying dream of the Victorian age itself (and of Melanie's previous secure and affluent childhood). Finn and Melanie even go for a walk to the now-derelict and uncanny site of the palace building itself, where Finn points out:

'All that there is left of the National Exposition of 1852, Melanie. They held it here, in a pleasant village outside London, and ran up to a hundred excursion trains a day out to it. They built this vast Gothic castle, a sort of Highland fortress, only gargantuan, and filled it with everything they could think of, to show off.'[34]

The abandoned Crystal Palace Park becomes the dark forest of legend – a secret Gothic place, gloomy, rank, chaotic and disordered:

The park lay in sodden neglect, sprawling over its rank acreage as if it had passed out. Trees had carelessly let go great branches or had toppled down entirely, throwing their roots up into the air. Bushes and shrubs, uncared for, burst bonds like fat women who had left off their corsets, and now many spilled out in mantraps of thorny undergrowth.[35]

This is where Melanie has her first kiss.

Crystal Palace Park, or rather, the bus terminus on the Parade, is also a mysterious location in Magnus Mills's absurdist *The Maintenance of Headway* (2009). Mills, himself a former bus driver, entertains with details of driving a bus and, crucially, complex theories of bus time-tabling and fleet management. The novel's title, we learn, is the key paradoxical 'guiding principle' in all public transport provision: the notion that it is highly desirable to establish a fixed gap between all individual buses on any given route. The novel concerns the complex and arduous struggle to adhere to this quasi-mystical principle in real road conditions for a group of drivers and dreaded inspectors on a south London bus route (seemingly an amalgam of the 12 and 343 bus routes). The route terminates at Crystal Palace Park. The maintenance of headway is not easy:

The fact is it's almost impossible to run a proper bus service in this city. The forces ranged against success are just too numerous . . . The streets are higgledy-piggledy and narrow; there are countless squares and circuses, zebra crossings and pelicans . . . All those shops, and all those pedestrians pouring into the road. Then there are the daily incidentals: street markets, burst water mains, leaking gas pipes, diesel spillages . . .[36]

This is a comically fatalistic world where all attempts to control and manage complex real-time systems (with absurd theories such as the 'Theory of Early Running', the 'Law of Cumulative Lateness', the 'Three Bears syndrome') come into conflict with messy and unscientific human individual initiatives, desires and common-sense perceptions, such as the tendency to speed up if late, to make humane unscheduled stops and so on. 'There's absolutely no excuse for being early' is the inspectors' repeated mantra. The drivers are trapped in the system: 'If we're late the people don't like it. If we're early the officials don't like it. And if we're on time we don't like it.' The Crystal Palace terminus, known here as the 'southern outpost', offers a temporary respite for the harassed drivers:

> The southern outpost was a remote and desolate place. In the previous century an enormous glasshouse had stood here, high on a hill, boldly reflecting the achievements of empire. Thousands of citizens had flocked to gaze upon it, but eventually it had collapsed under its own weight . . . Nowadays the site was used as somewhere for buses to turn around.[37]

The narrator looks out, wanting to escape the system. He tries to engage another driver in conversation:

> 'Nice view from up here, isn't it?' (The southern outpost afforded a marvellous vista across the garden suburbs south of the city, extending on clear days to the wooded shires beyond. To see it properly, though, you had to get out of your bus.)
>   'Can't say I've noticed', said Dean.[38]

South Norwood

Arthur Conan Doyle lived at 12 Tennison Road, South Norwood, between 1891 and 1894, the years when the early, and best, Sherlock Holmes stories were being written. Norwood appears in many of his famed detective's cases. In the early, long Holmes story *The Sign of the Four* (1890), Holmes and Watson try to solve the 'Mysterious Business at Upper Norwood', as the newspapers have it. This complex plot involves the Indian Rebellion of 1857, imperial adventures, secret pacts, murder, stolen money and treasure brought back to Britain by one Major John Sholto. After visiting the home of the major's son, Thaddeus Sholto, in Brixton, a suburban villa with a resplendent Hindu servant and rich oriental furnishings, the investigation moves further on, into the unknown, down to distant Lower Norwood to visit Thaddeus's twin, Bartholomew. Bartholomew lives at Pondicherry Lodge, a suburban villa bought by their father:

> It was nearly eleven o'clock when we reached this final stage of our night's adventures. We had left the damp fog of the great city behind us, and the night was fairly fine. A warm wind blew from the westward and heavy clouds moved slowly across the sky, with half a moon peeping occasionally through the rifts. It was clear enough to see for some distance, but Thaddeus Sholto took down one of the sidelamps from the carriage to give us a better light upon our way.[39]

This bleak outpost of a house is like a fortified station on the imperial margins: 'Pondicherry Lodge stood in its own grounds and was girt round with a very high stone wall topped with broken glass. A single narrow iron-clamped door formed the only means of entrance.'[40]

Bartholomew is found dead, with a note on a piece of torn paper: 'The sign of the four'. Holmes and Watson also then traverse a bewildering reverse route – from Norwood back to central London – when they set the 'ugly' tracker dog, Toby, to try and follow the trail of the stolen loot. Watson looks out the cab window and marvels at the sights of morning in south London:

> We had during this time been following the guidance of Toby down the half-rural villa-lined roads which lead to the metropolis. Now, however, we were beginning to come among continuous streets, where labourers and dockmen were already astir, and slatternly women were taking down shutters and brushing door-steps. At the square-topped corner public-houses business was just beginning, and rough-looking men were emerging, rubbing their sleeves across their beards after their morning wet. Strange dogs sauntered up and stared wonderingly at us as we passed, but our inimitable Toby looked neither to the right nor to the left, but trotted onwards with his nose to the ground and an occasional eager whine which spoke of a hot scent.

We had traversed Streatham, Brixton, Camberwell, and now found ourselves in Kennington Lane, having borne away through the side-streets to the east of the Oval. The men whom we pursued seemed to have taken a curiously zigzag road, with the idea probably of escaping observation.[41]

Norwood also features in a later Holmes tale, 'The Adventure of the Norwood Builder' (1903), where, it is reported, a 'most sensational crime has been committed'. The victim appears to be the Norwood builder himself, one Jonas Oldacre, murdered at home, his body burned. Holmes travels down to Norwood to investigate, as he retells it to Watson: 'This place, Deep Dene House, is a big modern villa of staring brick, standing back in its own grounds, with a laurel-clumped lawn in front of it. To the right and some distance back from the road was the timber yard which had been the scene of the fire.'[42]

The devious Oldacre is flushed out from a cunning secret sealed compartment he had built himself – 'a little, wizened man . . . like a rabbit out of its burrow' – by Holmes and others shouting 'Fire! Fire!' Oldacre appears, an 'odious face – crafty, vicious, malignant, with shifty, light-grey eyes and white lashes'.[43] Oldacre, deeply in debt, had faked his own murder, aiming to then pass his estate on to himself – as a fictitious double.

This potential for duplicity out in the suburbs is demonstrated in another Sherlock Holmes case set nearby, 'The Adventure of the Yellow Face' (1893), featuring a remote 'nice eighty-pound-a-year villa at Norbury'. Mr Grant Munro describes this idyllic location.

Our little place was very countrified, considering that it is so close to town. We had an inn and two houses a little above us, and a single cottage at the other side of the field which faces us, and except those there were no houses until you got halfway to the station.[44]

It is at this cottage window that Munro first sees a frightening 'livid, dead yellow' face. Again this case rests on fake identity – here a literal masking – and foregrounds another key theme of the entire detective series, the perceived threat to an idyllic-seeming suburban existence from imperial or exotic others returning to London. The suburbs provide difficult cases for Holmes to crack. In this instance, amazingly, even Holmes's famed method fails – he makes an erroneous deduction – and he admits: 'If it should ever strike you that I am getting a little over-confident in my powers . . . kindly whisper "Norbury" in my ear.' Other Holmes quests out to the south London suburbs from Baker Street include 'The Man with the Twisted Lip' (Lee), 'The Adventure of the Beryl Coronet' (Streatham), 'The Adventure of the Veiled Lodger' (Brixton), 'The Adventure of the Cardboard Box' (Croydon) and 'The Adventure of the Greek Interpreter' (Beckenham).

Conan Doyle also wrote in other genres. In the suburban romance *Beyond the City: The Idyll of a Suburb* (1893), he sets out an idealized version of suburban happiness: healthy, airy, close to nature, both communal and cosily familial. *Beyond the City* concerns three families who have, like Conan Doyle, moved out to the new suburbs, to the future:

> The cottage from the window of which the Misses Williams had looked out stands, and has stood for many a year, in that pleasant suburban district which lies between Norwood, Anerley, and Forest Hill. Long before there had been a thought of a township there, when the Metropolis was still quite a distant thing, old Mr Williams had inhabited 'The Brambles', as the little house was called, and had owned all the fields about it. Six or eight such cottages scattered over a rolling country-side were all the houses to be found there in the days when the century was young. From afar, when the breeze came from the north, the dull, low roar of the great city might be heard, like the breaking of the tide of life, while along the horizon might be seen the dim curtain of smoke, the grim spray which that tide threw up. Gradually, however, as the years passed, the City had thrown out a long brick-feeler here and there, curving, extending, and coalescing, until at last the little cottages had been gripped round by these red tentacles, and had been absorbed to make room for the modern villa. Field by field the estate of old Mr Williams had been sold to the speculative builder, and had borne rich crops of snug suburban dwellings, arranged in curving crescents and tree-lined avenues. The father had passed away before his cottage was entirely bricked round, but his two daughters, to whom the property had descended, lived to see the last vestige of country taken from them. For years they had clung to the one field which faced

their windows, and it was only after much argument and many heartburnings, that they had at last consented that it should share the fate of the others. A broad road was driven through their quiet domain, the quarter was re-named 'The Wilderness', and three square, staring, uncompromising villas began to sprout up on the other side. With sore hearts, the two shy little old maids watched their steady progress, and speculated as to what fashion of neighbours chance would bring into the little nook which had always been their own.[45]

A good sense of how these suburbs looked in the second half of the nineteenth century can be gleaned from some of the paintings of the Impressionist and Pointillist Camille Pissarro, who had fled to London from France, together with Édouard Manet and Alfred Sisley, during the Franco-Prussian War and the Paris Commune. Pissarro painted many scenes of the changing landscape:

> In 1870 I found myself in London with Monet, and we met Daubigny and Bonvin. Monet and myself were very enthusiastic over the London landscapes. Monet worked in the park, whilst I, living at Lower Norwood, at that time a charming suburb, studied the effects of fog, snow, and springtime. We worked from Nature, and later on Monet painted in London some superb studies of mist.[46]

Among the first Impressionist pictures to be exhibited in London was Pissarro's *Fox Hill, Upper Norwood* (1870), a snowy view that shows the developing road as still a winding, rural muddy lane.

Coincidentally, more than twenty years later the highly esteemed French Naturalist novelist Émile Zola, faced with fines and possible imprisonment for his famous *J'accuse* open letter to the French government in 1895, hurriedly left Paris and ended up at the Queens Hotel, Crystal Palace (where the Durrells were also to stay), and spent much of his time roaming Norwood, taking regular cycle trips, like Conan Doyle, and obsessively photographing the new suburban landscape. He seemed particularly entranced by that dashing sign of modernity and New Woman liberty: female cyclists.

Shena Mackay's novel *Dunedin* (1992) features a gloomy and down-at-heel south London as we follow depressed, damaged and lonely brother and sister Olive and William Mackenzie sharing a house in West Norwood: 'south east London really is the pits,' Olive thinks to herself, 'I don't think I can stand living here much longer.'[47] Olive and William are the grandchildren of minister Jack Mackenzie, a missionary to Dunedin, New Zealand, in the first decades of the twentieth century, whom we meet in the first and last sections of the novel. As the novel shifts forward to 1989, 'Dunedin' is now a dilapidated, decaying Victorian house and south London, specifically West Norwood, is very much an exhausted, post-imperial location, full of the dull detritus of the everyday: uninspiring corner shops, tatty pubs, packed buses grinding up and down the hills. William, however, still sees the area through its cultural past:

> Although 'The Case of the Norwood Builder' was not one of Sherlock Holmes' more spectacular adventures, William liked to think that it conferred a certain sinister distinction on his part of London. Less leafy, more urban now than then, and than when Camille Pissarro painted Norwood, Dulwich and Crystal Palace, the suburb is still full of blossom in the spring. Buses lumber in heavy traffic up the hill where carriage lamps once glittered in black rain and snow blurred the pale green streetlamps . . . Beyond Knight's Hill are secretive parks and half-hidden walks through what were once the gardens and woods of large houses; somewhere, lost, is Beulah Spa, a fashionable watering-place whose brilliance gushed briefly and trickled away.[48]

Bromley

Bromley, around 8 miles southeast of London Bridge, and 1 mile east of Lower Norwood, was originally a thriving market town, firmly placed in Kent. It is now a key suburban town, one of several dispersed commercial and retail hubs around London and the centre of the London Borough of Bromley. Bromley is intriguing as it features in much commentary and fiction as being paradoxically both boring and impenetrable, and so the ideal of a London suburb, but at the same time is also presented as being unique, being the key suburb, the suburb of all suburbs. Southeast London suburbs, Andy Medhurst argues, are not 'just *any* suburbs, but paradigmatic suburbs'. Medhurst notes 'sound historical fact' for Bromley's suburban typicality: its status as the world's original industrial suburb, with the development of the world's first commuter railway, and thus its establishment as a space of transition, instituting an integral polarity of work and domestic space, of spatial displacement from its own originary suburban centre.[49] Bromley is, as Simon Frith argues, where David Bowie was brought up, 'the quintessential suburban star'; it is also home of 'the quintessential suburban fans, the Bromley contingent' and, 'we might add, Hanif Kureishi's quintessential suburban novel, *The Buddha of Suburbia*.'[50]

H. G. Wells was born in Bromley in 1866 and loathed the place. 'This brain of mine came into existence', he recalls in *Experiment in Autobiography* (1934), 'and began to acquire reflexes and register impressions in a needy shabby home [47 High Street] in a little town called Bromley in Kent, which has since become a suburb of London.'[51] In this candid autobiography he describes how Bromley, with its 'morbid sprawl of population', spread and engulfed the area's rural beauty.

> The country round Bromley was being fast invaded by the spreading out of London; eruptions of new roads and bricks and mortar covered lush meadows and, when I was about fifteen or sixteen, that brown and babbling Ravensbourne between its overhanging trees was suddenly swallowed up by a new drainage system, but my father managed to see and make me see a hundred aspects of the old order of things, a wagtail, a tit's nest, a kingfisher, an indisputable trout under a bridge, sun-dew in a swampy place near Keston, the pollen of pine trees drifting like a mist, the eagle in the bracken root.[52]

In fact, Wells was not simply against the growth of London, nor straightforwardly anti-suburban. His visionary books of futurology *Anticipations* (1901) and *A Modern Utopia* (1905) even imagine a kind of ideal type of suburb, founded on Ebenezer Howard's 'Garden City' principles, at a clear distance from grubby Victorian London. These will not at all be like the 'over-ripened gardens and the no longer brilliant villas of Surbiton and Norwood, Tooting and Beckenham'. 'It will certainly be a curious and varied region, far less monotonous than our present English world . . . abundantly wooded, breaking continually into park and garden, and with everywhere a scattering of houses'.[53]

Wells's *When the Sleeper Wakes* (1899) tells of Graham, a Londoner (and precursor of Woody Allen's *Sleeper*) who falls into a deep, medically induced sleep and wakes up in 2100. South London is transformed: 'Nothing remained of it here but a waste of ruins, variegated and dense with thickets of the heterogeneous growths that had once adorned the gardens of the belt, interspersed among levelled brown patches of sown ground, and verdant stretches of winter greens.'[54]

Also, by this time, a group of enormous airport-style flying stages have been built: 'They formed three groups of two each and retained the names of ancient suburban hills or villages. They were named in order, Roehampton, Wimbledon Park, Streatham, Norwood, Blackheath and Shooters Hill.'[55] These structures, we learn, in a passage removed in the version revised in 1910 as *The Sleeper Awakes*, were surrounded by

> theatres, restaurants, newsrooms and places of pleasure and indulgence of various sorts that interwove with the prosperous shops below. This portion of London was in consequence commonly the gayest of all its districts, with something of the meretricious gaiety of a seaport or city of hotels . . . At various levels through the mass of chambers and passages beneath these, ran, in addition to the main moving ways of the city which laced and gathered here, a complex system of special passages and lifts and slides for the convenient interchange of people and luggage between stage and stage. And a distinctive feature of the architecture of this section was the ostentatious massiveness of the metal piers and girders that everywhere broke the vistas and spanned the halls and passages, crowding and twining up to meet the weight of the stages and weighty impact of the aeroplanes overhead.[56]

The loathing of speculative late Victorian suburban growth is most clear in Wells's political, and most autobiographical, novel *The New Machiavelli* (1911), written as the autobiography of radical Richard Remington. The 'beginning of true suburbanisation', Wells writes here, means an 'invading and growing disorder', where 'one walked past scaffold-poles into litter and fragments of broken brick and cinder mingled in every path'.[57] The 'Bromstead' (Bromley)-born narrator is stunned by the 'interminable extent of London's residential suburbs;

mile after mile one went, between houses, villas, rows of cottages, streets of shops . . . I have forgotten the detailed local characteristics – if there were any.'[58] He adds: 'All effect of locality or community had gone from these places . . . there was no general meeting place any more'.[59] Bromley/Bromstead is described in detail:

> First, then, you must think of Bromstead a hundred and fifty years ago, as a narrow irregular little street of thatched houses strung out on the London and Dover Road, a little mellow sample unit of a social order that had a kind of completeness, at its level, of its own. At that time its population numbered a little under two thousand people, mostly engaged in agricultural work or in trades serving agriculture. There was a blacksmith, a saddler, a chemist, a doctor, a barber, a linen-draper (who brewed his own beer); a veterinary surgeon, a hardware shop, and two capacious inns. Round and about it were a number of pleasant gentlemen's seats, whose owners went frequently to London town in their coaches along the very tolerable high-road.[60]

But then came the suburbs, that 'coming flood of mechanical power', which haphazardly threw up factories, brickfields, gasworks, railways, schools and endless streets of shoddy houses. The picture becomes one of horror, of

> digging and wheeling, of woods invaded by building, roads gashed open and littered with iron pipes amidst a fearful smell of gas, of men peeped at and seen toiling away deep down in excavations, of hedges broken down and replaced by planks, of wheelbarrows and builders' sheds, of rivulets overtaken and swallowed up by drain-pipes. Big trees, and especially elms, cleared of undergrowth and left standing amid such things, acquired a peculiar tattered dinginess rather in the quality of needy widow women who have seen happier days.[61]

For Remington, seeing the place as an adult, it is equally grim:

> The whole of Bromstead as I remember it, and as I saw it last – it is a year ago now – is a dull useless boiling-up of human

activities, an immense clustering of futilities. It is as unfinished as ever; the builders' roads still run out and end in mid-field in their old fashion; the various enterprises jumble in the same hopeless contradiction, if anything intensified. Pretentious villas jostle slums, and public-house and tin tabernacle glower at one another across the cat-haunted lot that intervenes. Roper's meadows are now quite frankly a slum; back doors and sculleries gape towards the railway, their yards are hung with tattered washing unashamed; and there seem to be more boards by the railway every time I pass, advertising pills and pickles, tonics and condiments, and suchlike solicitudes of a people with no natural health nor appetite left in them.[62]

In 1934 Wells refused an offer of the freedom of the town: 'Bromley has not been particularly gracious to me nor I to Bromley', he told the council committee, 'and I don't think I want to add the freedom of Bromley to the freedom of the City of London and the freedom of the City of Brussels – both of which I have.'[63]

The perceived weirdness of the outer suburbs is central to Richard Gordon's Bromley-set mock-anthropological survey *Good Neighbours* (1974). Gordon, best known for his 'Doctor' series of comic novels, presents the goings-on in 'BRI 2AX' as obscure and bizarre alien rituals that require careful interpretation. Chapters such as 'Totems and Taboos', 'Coming of Age in the Suburbs', 'Tribal Rites and Customs' and 'The Life Cycle of the Suburbanite' mimic ethnographic research as they seek to explain this strange place. Gordon, 'like Gauguin in Tahiti, like Stevenson in Samoa', is the outsider turned native, as he keenly scrutinizes the densely private neighbourhood for any meaningful signs: new people moving in, clothes lines, bins or make of car. In research mode he also attempts a rudimentary taxonomy of Bromley types, from keen gardener (*Digitus viridis*), to tennis player (*Pseudowimbledonia*).[64]

Also in the 1970s, 'Mersey Sound' poet Adrian Henri published 'Death in the Suburbs', a poem set in Orpington, around 3 miles southeast of Bromley, which offers outsiders a bemused view of south London suburbia. Henri offers an introduction to how he came to write it:

A couple of years ago I found myself unavoidably detained for a whole morning and part of an afternoon in a place called

Orpington. If you don't know Orpington if you think of
somewhere like Crosby, or Oxten or Wallasey and multiply it
by ten you get somewhere near Orpington. I had to spend a
whole morning there – it was early spring, it was very beautiful
– the gardens were flowering and I suddenly had this kind of
little nagging thought that I couldn't quite . . . and I wrote
lots of things in my little notebook and went away and then
a few months later I realised what the thought was which was
if the world was ever going to end it would start ending in
Orpington. So this begins with a little bit of my version of
Mother Shipton's Prophecy.[65]

Here Henri focuses on the normality of Orpington, a familiar everyday scene that soon tips into its opposite. So, at first glance, we get the
hypernormal everyday stuff, the bird-songy, bucolic ideal of 'pink-and-
white vistas / villas detached and undetached / islanded with flowering
cherry'. But then, 'the earth / moves / sudden / tiny snowstorms of
cherryblossom', a 'slow-growing crescendo', and everything shifts. The
familiar everyday objects of suburban domesticity – the photographs,
ready-meals, letters, teenage posters, stereo systems – are 'whirled helpless in a vortex'. The suburb is so familiar and placid, something bad
must happen: 'The end of the world will surely come / in Bromley
South or Orpington'.[66]

Bromley's utter normality, a normality that is in fact quite strange,
is central to that best-known Bromley novel (if not the best-known
London suburban novel), Hanif Kureishi's *The Buddha of Suburbia*.
Bromley here appears as a hellish trap that the unbelonging hero
Karim Amir (an 'Englishman born and bred, almost') must escape,
'over the river to London proper'.[67] The novel is clearly split into two
halves, 'In the Suburbs' and 'In the City', and in the first half Bromley
seems to be presented in traditionally negative terms. It is quiet and
dull, a place of boring routine and predictable, over-planned lives:
'Life for commuters was regulated to the minute.'[68] There is no surprise or spontaneity: 'there were no excuses to be made in the evenings:
no one went out, there was nowhere to go.'[69] There is little chance of
escape for Karim's unhappily married parents:

Divorce wasn't something that would occur to them. In the
suburbs people rarely dreamed of striking out for happiness.

It was all familiarity and endurance: security and safety were the reward of dullness . . . It would be years before I could get away to the city, London, where life was bottomless in its temptations.[70]

The stifling domesticity is policed by ever-present neighbourly surveillance. Anything hinting of difference is jumped upon as everyone must conform. 'In the suburbs there had been few things that seemed more petty than the fear everyone had of their neighbour's opinion. It was why my mother could never hang out the washing in the garden without combing her hair.'[71] Nearby Penge is 'full of neo-fascist groups' actively demonstrating on the streets, and mixed-race Karim is routinely taunted and racially abused: 'I was sick too of being affectionately called Shitface and Curryface, and of coming home covered in spit and snot and chalk and wood-shavings . . . Every day I considered myself lucky to get home from school without serious injury.'[72]

Worst of all for wannabe bohemian Karim, with his fixation on Bowie, Beatniks, Coltrane and Camus, is the philistine lack of serious and high culture. The 'English passion' here, Karim coolly assesses, is 'not for self-improvement or culture or wit . . . but for DIY', that is, for 'the painstaking accumulation of comfort'.[73] Actually, Karim realizes, there *is* one other cultural pursuit: 'They were fanatical shoppers in our suburbs. Shopping was to them what the rumba and singing is to Brazilians. Saturday afternoons, when the streets were solid with white faces, was a carnival of consumerism as goods were ripped from shelves.'[74]

Bromley is the place to go for anyone attempting to investigate the state of contemporary suburbia, or the nation. Roger Silverstone's influential 1997 collection of essays *Visions of Suburbia* opens with our editor emerging form Bromley South station and walking up Bromley High Street, desperately trying to make it all cohere. Silverstone notes chain stores, a 'ravaged shopping precinct', department stores, fast-food outlets, and churches, suburban villas, a 1959 pink Cadillac. An eccentric restaurant, Caligula ('live opera on Sunday and Monday'), stands in for the clutter and random eclecticism of the suburb:

a cornucopia of an eating house, whose frontage is decorated with pages torn from the magazine *Understanding Science* as well as the *Collected Works of Walter Scott* (including *The Bride of Lammermoor*), and made over to look like a *fin de siècle* prostitute's boudoir, stuffed to bursting with silks and satins, lampshades, feathers, pearls, toys, birdcages, bottles, dead clocks and china birds, the flotsam and jetsam of suburban fantasy, the whole misassembled as if in a car boot sale in Marrakesh.[75]

Chislehurst

Within a mile east of Bromley, London's outer southern suburbs are flatter, greener, more open. A sense of confusing featureless and spreading repetition – being both London and not London – appears in H. G. Wells's *Tono-Bungay* (1909), a novel of pseudoscientific quackery and magical elixirs, and highly critical of emergent suburban consumption and mass culture. George Pondevero, travelling into London by the South-Eastern Railway,

> marked beyond Chislehurst the ever-growing multitude of villas, and so came stage by stage through multiplying houses and diminishing interspaces of market garden and dingy grass to regions of interlacing railway lines, big factories, gasometers, and wide reeking swamps of dingy little homes, more of them and more and more. The number of these and their dinginess and poverty increased, and here rose a great public house and here a Board School and here a gaunt factory; and away to the east there loomed for a time a queer incongruous forest of masts and spars. The congestion of houses intensified and piled up presently into tenements; I marvelled more and more at this boundless world of dingy people.[76]

In Graham Swift's novel of suburban secrecy and detection, *The Light of Day* (2003), private eye George and his client Sarah (who later have an affair, though an unconventional one as she is jailed for the murder of her husband) meet up in Chislehurst. George is stunned that the single interesting fact he knows about Chislehurst appeals to Sarah's interest in French culture.

> 'Napoleon died there', I said, 'eighteen . . . seventy-something. He was the Napoleon who died in Chislehurst.'

Not just a detective, not just a pretty nose.

'I lived in Chislehurst – grew up there. It's how I know. It's the only reason I know.'

'George, *I* lived in Chislehurst – well, Petts Wood – when I was a girl'.

Sometimes fate comes and gives you a pat on the back.

'They lived where the golf course is now,' I said. 'Chislehurst Golf Course. Their house became the club house. My dad used to play there. They were the Emperor and Empress who lived on a golf course.'[77]

A mile east of Chislehurst, Sidcup features in Harold Pinter's *The Caretaker* (1959), as an (often-repeated) improbable source of validation and salvation for homeless Davies:

DAVIES: (*With great feeling*) If only the weather would break! Then I'd be able to get down to Sidcup!
ASTON: Sidcup?
DAVIES: The weather's so blasted bloody awful, how can I get down to Sidcup in these shoes?
ASTON: Why do you want to get down to Sidcup?
DAVIES: I got my papers there![78]

And repeated later:

DAVIES: I got plenty of references. All I got to do is to go down to Sidcup tomorrow. I got all the references I want down there.
MICK: Where's that?
DAVIES: Sidcup. He ain't only got my references down there, he got all my papers down there. I know that place like the back of my hand. I'm going down there anyway, see what I mean, I got to get down there or I'm done.
MICK: So we can always get hold of these references if we want them.
DAVIES: I'll be down there any day, I tell you. I was going to go down today, but I'm . . . I'm waiting for the weather to break.[79]

Further south at Orpington and St Mary Cray, Iain Sinclair, in *Downriver* (1991), discusses with Peter Riley, a book dealer and poet, a visit to the house of forgotten modernist poet Nicholas Moore – 'stuck out there in the wilderness, in outer suburbia'.[80]

> He thought it was an accident. A fairly pleasant place, when he first moved. His house was on the edge of the development, next to fields. But within a few years, of course, the whole area had been covered in suburbia. Nothing in sight except identical houses. He had really established a personal island, or islet, in the middle of a huge mud estuary.[81]

Sinclair decides to go on a pilgrimage, following the rivers Darent and Cray from the Thames, to locate and photograph Moore's house. Sinclair, of course, far from his usual patch, has a dismal time, with terrible pubs, shrieking lorries, blocked access, and even getting *lost*:

> Now the problems really begin. I am disoriented by a fury of traffic, screaming to get away, or cutting – with no signals – into one of many identical service roads. Unknowingly (fume-crazy), I drift north-east, losing all the river's wisdom: go back on myself towards Erith and the Thames. The first roundabout is a vortex of unconvincing promises: no offered destination holds the slightest attraction for me. Feebly, I aim for the highest ground and shuffle into one of Nicholas Moore's nightmares: unlittered streets, clean cars, safe margins of grass, lace curtains that twitch faintly as I pass, like the last flicker of breath in an oxygen tent . . .
>
> Moore's left-hand maisonette is a pebbledash and red-brick affair, oddly angled. I had visited it often in dreams – of which this was only the most recent version. But 'my' house was a mirror image. I pictured it on the other side of the street.[82]

Croydon

Croydon, 10 miles south of Charing Cross and about 3 miles beyond Crystal Palace, 'is the town, above all others', according to Jonathan Glancey, 'that would be a city'.[83] Occupying an important position on key routes between London and the south coast, Croydon was an important parish and market town for hundreds of years, a London Borough by 1886, a thriving industrial commercial centre in the nineteenth century, and in the 1960s and '70s notoriously welcomed car-culture out-of-town modernity. Up went huge multi-storey car parks, urban dual carriageways, underpasses and roundabouts, shopping centres and precincts and concrete tower blocks – an era nicely captured in Martin Parr's collection *Boring Postcards* (1999). This was followed, in subsequent decades, by glass and steel towers, corporate skyscrapers and more shopping malls, new major transport hubs and a tram system, so that Croydon now has the feel of a semi-independent 'edge city'. It was designated in the London Mayor's 'London Plan 2016' as a 'town centre', one of a network of a dozen urban developments on the suburban fringe, ripe for 'commercial development and intensification'.

D. H. Lawrence's first job was at Croydon's Davidson Road Elementary School (a state school for children aged ten to fourteen), in north Croydon, from October 1908 to January 1912. Lawrence lodged for most of that time with a Mr and Mrs Jones in nearby Colworth Road. While here he published short stories, his first novel, *The White Peacock* (1911), and worked on an early draft of *Sons and Lovers*. Lawrence seems quite taken by Croydon, especially in contrast to his grimy and constricting colliery home town of Eastwood, near Nottingham. Croydon was busy and bright, modern and exciting, close to London and its cultural activities but also still semi-rural (a 'bit like Derbyshire', he reckons), and Lawrence was soon, like an H. G. Wells Edwardian hero 'going-places', exploring London, bicycling out to its hinterlands, to Dorking, Reigate, Wimbledon and Richmond. Lawrence's biographer Brenda Maddox sets the scene:

> Croydon . . . a temple of Edwardian self-satisfaction, with heavily ornamented new buildings and three hundred trains a day to London. In the distance, high on Sydenham Hill, the Crystal Palace gleamed like a vision of the future. Double-decker trams ploughed down the middle of the roads, with passengers hanging from the sides beneath signs advertising the products of imperial prosperity: Heinz 57 Varieties, Dewar's Whisky, Lipton's Tea, Beecham's Pills and Bird's Custard.[84]

In this letter of 1908 to Mabel Limb, a childhood friend from Eastwood, Lawrence describes his new life:

12 Colworth Rd, Addiscombe, Croydon
Thursday Evening

My Dear Mabel,

Here I am a stranger in a strange land. Croydon is a big, rambling place, not very interesting but clean and open. I have the best of digs with exceedingly nice people in a smart, quiet quarter. The schools are big, new and finely appointed, but teaching is wearisome here, there is so much red tape and so little discipline . . . I find that I can go to London by motor-bus for fourpence. I am not so far from the Crystal Palace: I can see it from the school playground . . . This place suits me but it makes me so heavy and sleepy.[85]

In another letter to old flame Louie Burrows, a few days later, Lawrence expands on his new job:

School – a great big new imposing red-brick handsome place, with a fair amount of open space – looking across in front over great stacks of timber, over two railways to Norwood, where the music-hall folk live in big houses among the trees, and to Sydenham, where the round blue curves of the Crystal Palace sweep out into view on fairly clear days.[86]

Lawrence's story 'Fly in the Ointment', written in 1910, is set in his Croydon period, and recounts how a small bunch of primroses, sent from back 'home' in the Midlands by Muriel, an old flame, destabilizes the schoolmaster-narrator, plunging him back into another world:

those mauve primroses had set my tone for the day: I was dreamy and reluctant; school and the sounds of the boys were unreal, unsubstantial; beyond these were the realities of my poor winter-trodden primroses, and the pale hazel catkins that Muriel had sent me. Altogether, the boys must have thought me a vacant fool; I regarded them as a punishment upon me.[87]

At his lodgings the narrator, later that night, confronts a burglar, another instance of intrusion from another world, from the present, and one familiar to Lawrence from the Davidson Road school. This school was the first time Lawrence had come across real poverty, with its abandoned or neglected children who were often dirty, hungry, ragged – and aggressive. In the story the intruder is a 'slum rat', 'thin', 'pinched looking', a kid who 'evidently came of a low breed', someone the narrator sees as non-human: 'I had no fellow feeling with him. He was something beyond me.'[88] 'He sat stubborn and would not answer. I thought of the gangs of youths who stood at the corner of the mean streets near the school, there all day long, month after month, fooling with the laundry girls and insulting passers-by.'[89]

Croydon is presented in the story as magical, enchanted – 'I rejoiced exceedingly when night came, with the evening star, and the sky flushed dark blue, purple over the golden pomegranates of the lamps'[90] – a theme continued in another story from the Croydon years, 'The Witch à la Mode'. In this story, Bernard Coutts, on returning to England, rather than going directly to see Constance, his dull fiancée, instead undertakes a dangerous detour to his old flame Winifred Braithwaite in Croydon. This subverted passion will be trouble: 'when Bernard Coutts alighted at East Croydon he knew he was tempting Providence.'[91] In this bizarre tale of sexual frustration and warped desire (at one stage Winifred's dress catches fire) the Croydon setting itself symbolically represents Coutts's anguished desire:

> One by one the arc lamps fluttered or leaped alight, the strand of copper overhead glistened against the dark sky that now was deepening to the colour of monkshood. The tram-car dipped as it ran, seeming to exult . . . Soon the car was running full-tilt from the shadow to the fume of yellow light at the terminus, where shop on shop and lamp beyond lamp heaped golden fire on the floor of the blue night. The car, like an eager dog, ran in home, sniffing with pleasure the fume of lights.[92]

On another journey, from Shirley back to Croydon, to Winifred's lodgings, the landscape is presented as a beautiful modernized version of pastoral.

> At last, on the high-up, naked down, they came upon those meaningless pavements that run through the grass, waiting for the houses to line them. The two were thrust up into the night, above the little flowering of the lamps in the valley. In front was the daze of light from London, rising midway to the zenith,

just fainter than the stars . . . Below, in a cleft in the night, the long, low garland of arc-lamps strung down the Brighton Road, where now and then the golden tram-cars flew low along the track, passing each other with a faint angry sound.[93]

Where Lawrence casts Croydon as presenting transformative modernity, lovable nostalgist John Betjeman offers us a suburb that obliterates the past. In 'Croydon' (1932), we learn of a house in old Croydon where 'Uncle Dick was born', where he would walk through the bucolic woodlands of Coulsdon, full of 'pear and apple' and 'bud and blossom', to get to Whitgift. This route, in the present of the poem, of course, has been wiped out by time and suburbanization.[94]

Betjeman is both snobbishly repelled and fascinated by the booming 1930s suburbs and new towns. In 'Love in a Valley' (1937) he borrows the title, metre and sensibility of Victorian poet George Meredith's poem 'Love in the Valley', but transplants it to stream-lined suburbia. 'Take me, Lieutenant, to that Surrey homestead!' the poem's jolly speaker announces, as the couple motor down, somewhere near Addiscombe, and we see the house, surrounded by pinewoods, rhododendrons, summer houses and tennis courts and the poet enraptured with domestic fittings, with the steel lanterns and enamelled doors, the cosy orange glow of a gas fire, the promise of the patter of children's feet.[95]

Croydon's modernity is neatly illustrated by its famed aerodrome, opened in 1920 and then expanded in the 1930s. It was pioneering in a number of ways: it was the first in Britain to offer international flights (to France), the first to have a dedicated terminal building, and the first to have an air traffic control tower. 'Pylon poet' Stephen Spender's 'The Landscape near an Aerodrome' describes the grace of an incoming plane, 'More beautiful and soft than any moth', gliding down over the city edges, packed with chimneys, 'squat buildings' and factories, 'the outposts / Of work'. Neatly reversing the standard poetic 'Nature is Good / Technology is Bad' polarity, in this case 'The plane is more beautiful and softer than any moth', as it silently 'Glides over suburbs'.[96]

Elizabeth Bowen's 1932 novel *To the North* was very much concerned with the modernity of 1930s London, with communications, cars, planes, travel and speed, and describes how the heroine Emmeline and her lover Markie set off from Croydon Airport to Le Bourget, near Paris: 'The roar intensified, there was an acceleration of movement about the aerodrome as though they were about to be shot out of a gun; blocks were pulled clear and they taxied forward at high speed, apparently to the coast.'[97]

As they take off, Markie, who is on his first flight, is not impressed, soon opening up a 'rather dull report'. Emmeline, on the other hand, is transfixed:

> But to Emmeline some quite new plan of life, forgotten
> between flight and flight, seemed once more to reveal itself;
> she sat gazing down with intensity at the lay-out of gardens.
> No noise, no glass, no upholstery boxed her up from the
> extraordinary: as they smoothly mounted and throbbed
> through the shining element she watched trees and fields in the
> blue June haze take on that immaterial loveliness, that foreign
> and clear intensity one expects of the sky.[98]

Croydon Aerodrome also features in two key 1930s detective novels, which seem to address both the excitement and terror of this new form of transport. Freeman Wills Crofts's 1934 thriller *The 12.30 from Croydon* is an early version of the 'inverted' detective story: we know the details of crime and criminal early on, and readerly interest is maintained in establishing why it was done and whether the perpetrator will ever be caught. Here, Charles Swinburne, in urgent need of money to save his business and to get married, plans to bump off his rich uncle Andrew Crowther. This will be achieved through administering poison on a flight from Croydon to Paris. At first the trip seems dull as the weary party, down from Yorkshire, take the special Croydon air-bus from Victoria station, through 'miles of wet streets' and along the 'drab and dingy buildings which edged them'.[99] But then we see the thrilling pre-flight preparations and take-off through the excited eyes of ten-year-old Rose Morley:

> Without feeling anything unusual she saw there was a little
> space, a few inches, below the great wheel! The space increased.
> It became a foot, a yard, several yards. They were flying!
>
> 'Oh!' gasped Rose, delighted and yet just the least little
> bit afraid.
>
> 'Now we're off', said Peter somewhat unnecessarily, but
> she scarcely heard him. She was too busy looking down on

Croydon. As far as she could see, they were not rising: the ground instead was sinking quickly down from them in some quite inexplicable way. Two or three hundred yards below them Croydon seemed a far prettier place than it had looked on the way from Town. There were hills and hollows and the roads wound about in curves, and there was any amount of green between the houses. From the bus she had only seen streets and shops.[100]

At Paris, old Crowther is found dead in his seat.

Written a year later, in 1935, Agatha Christie's *Death in the Clouds* also features an in-air murder, this time on the Paris-to-Croydon leg. The victim is found dead (wasp sting? poison dart?) before arrival at Croydon. Luckily, Hercule Poirot is on the same flight. Air rage is also previewed here, as passengers are prevented from leaving the plane. "'Nonsense!' cried Lady Horbury angrily. "Don't you know who I am? . . . But it's absurd, absolutely absurd . . . I shall report you to the company. It's outrageous that we should be shut up here with a dead body.'"[101]

The once-popular R. F. Delderfield, probably best known for *To Serve Them All My Days* and the multi-volume *God Is an Englishman* saga of the early 1970s, lived as a child in Addiscombe, a mile or so east of Croydon. This area became the background for his two-novel sequence *The Dreaming Suburb* and *The Avenue Goes to War* (both 1958). 'The Avenue', Delderfield tells us, 'is not any particular Avenue, and might exist in any suburb of Greater London',[102] adding, 'I like to think of this book as a modest attempt to photograph the mood of the suburbs in the period between the break up of the old world and the perambulator days of an entirely new civilisation'[103] – that is, between 1919 and 1947. The novel sequence starts in 1947 (before going back to spring 1919) with the older Avenue being largely destroyed and brutally reshaped by post-war redevelopment:

In the Spring of 1947 the bull-dozers moved down the cart-track beside Number Seventeen and . . . ravaged the Avenue and despoiled its memories . . . Soon the Avenue itself was swallowed up in a tangle of new roads, new crescents, new avenues, each lined with semi-detached houses, quite unlike the terraced houses of the original curve.[104]

Manor Park Avenue in Addiscombe marks London's limit, at least for now:

> The Avenue ran in a scimitar curve from Shirley Rise, off the Lower Road leading to London, to the eastern entrance of the Recreation Ground . . . and was thus the southernmost rim of the most southerly suburb . . . Behind it lay the older, more sedate section of the suburb, a dozen or so roads built in the eighteen-sixties, and named after generals and incidents of the Indian Mutiny.[105]

Yet we know that this is not final: the Avenue is bulldozed. Suburban boundaries are always changing and evolving.

Anne Billson's 1993 short story 'Sunshine' enquires whether Croydon is actually part of London or not. Here a group of twelve women live in a 'tiny terraced house in Croydon' as part of a quasi-cult led by charismatic Charlie, dressed all in white, who orders his disciples to go up to London and carry out surrealist-type pranks on the Tube: busking, performance, confronting litterers, purposely misdirecting tourists . . . and pushing people under trains. Croydon turns out to be the ideal location for harbouring detached derangement:

> Croydon was good, he explained, because Croydon wasn't just a town, it was a state of mind. It was a part of London, and at the same time it wasn't London at all. London was a dangerous place. Stay in London too long, Charlie always said, and you would find yourself sucked back into the pit. But you could stand in Croydon, on the edge, and peer in without falling in.[106]

Just west of Croydon, Carshalton features in Henry Williamson's *The Dark Lantern* (1951), presented as the paradisiacal village of Cross Aulton in the 1890s:

> The village of Cross Aulton in Surrey was twelve miles from Hyde Park Corner as the coach drove; but ten by way of the London, Epsom, and Dorking Railway. The parish comprised nearly three thousand acres, of which four hundred were meadow land, twenty-four were water – being the river and its many tributary spring and rillets breaking out of the chalky

subsoil – and the remainder occupied by railways, public roads, and market gardens. And of these four square miles of arable, lying under the chalk downs, most of the fields were used for the cultivation of herbs, for seasoning and medicinal purposes. It was the variety of the colours and scents of these two thousand odd acres of herbs surrounding the village of old red brick, and bright water running everywhere from the springs – in the gutters, down the shady lanes, along ditches in the woods, through the pond divided by the road – which had given Cross Aulton the reputation among City men of being the jolliest village south of the River. Its numerous brooks held many trout, pink-fleshed and quick-growing from the ample insect and shell food in the glassy waters; a pack of foxhounds was kennelled in the village; there were the beagles, for running after hares across furrows in winter – 'Nothing like it for the liver, old chap'; and above all, there was an express service of twenty-five minutes by train to the City.[107]

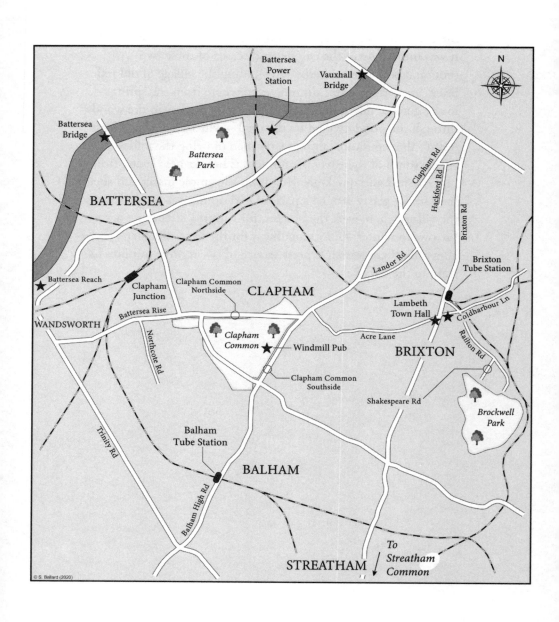

4 'SO VERY GREY AND MEAN'

Southwest London: From Brixton to Clapham, Battersea, Wandsworth, Balham, Tooting and Streatham

The suburbs of southwest London feel very different from the suburbs just to their east, at Camberwell, Peckham and New Cross. Especially when approached from key river bridges (Vauxhall, Chelsea, Battersea, Wandsworth) the place feels on a somewhat larger scale, airier, broader, more planned, compared to the denser clutter a mile or so east. The main routes in – the Brixton, Clapham, South and Lambeth roads – are broader and multi-laned, statelier, less industrial, lined with grander multi-storey Victorian villas and flats. As we will see, Clapham itself in the eighteenth century counts as the ground zero of the original house-and-garden, pastoral and picturesque upper-middle-class suburb. Even today Clapham, Battersea and Wandsworth, gentrified early, are grander, posher suburbs than their southeast London equivalents.

Brixton

Brixton is first recorded in writing as 'Brixistane', in 1067, and was mostly undeveloped until the opening of Vauxhall Bridge, a mile and a half to the north, in 1816, with Brixton, Stockwell and Kennington all rapidly becoming suburban villages. A scattering of large villas were built, set back along the grand main roads spreading south from the new Thames bridges; the arrival of railways in the 1860s later saw the construction of narrower side streets and terraces of much smaller houses. Grand shops, shopping arcades and indoor markets arrived in the 1880s (Electric Avenue, off the High Street, boasting Britain's first

ever electric street lighting), along with theatres, music halls and cinemas, so that by 1900 Brixton was quite a destination in itself. By the
end of the nineteenth century, however, the area on its uppers, many
of the larger villas had been converted into lodging houses, attracting
a considerable contingent of theatre folk, including Dan Leno and the
slapstick impresario Fred Karno. After severe bombing and depopu-
lation, post-war Brixton, with its cheap and shoddy housing (and the
use of the Clapham South air-raid shelter as a hostel), became popular
with new arrivals from the Caribbean.

Vincent van Gogh lodged in Brixton, at 87 Hackford Road, in
1873–4, while working for an art dealer in Covent Garden. Van Gogh
really took to his lodgings, staying with a widow and her daughter,
Ursula and Eugenie Loyer. He wrote in a letter home on 2 July 1873:

> The neighbourhood where I live is very pretty, and so peaceful
> and convivial that one almost forgets one is in London.
>
> In front of every house is a small garden with flowers or
> a couple of trees, and many houses are built very tastefully in
> a sort of Gothic style.
>
> Still, I have to walk for more than half an hour to reach the
> countryside.
>
> We have a piano in the drawing room, and there are also
> three Germans living here who really love music, which is
> most agreeable.[1]

Young Van Gogh enjoyed the convivial atmosphere, the lengthy
walking commute into town over Vauxhall Bridge, and the strenuous
walks (anticipating his later obsessive Provençal hikes) to nearby open
countryside:

> I haven't yet been to the Crystal Palace and the Tower, nor to
> Tussaud's; I'm not at all in a hurry to go and see everything. For
> the time being I have enough with the museums, parks, &c.,
> which attract me more.
>
> I had a nice day last Monday. The first Monday in Aug. is a
> holiday here. I went with one of the Germans to Dulwich, an
> hour and a half outside L., to see the museum there, and after-
> wards we walked to a village about an hour further on. The
> countryside here is so beautiful; many people who have their

business in L. live in some village or other outside L. and come to the city every day by train. Perhaps I'll soon be doing that as well, if I can find a cheap room somewhere. But I find moving so terrible that I'll stay here as long as possible.[2]

Another reason for Van Gogh's happiness at Hackford Road is, some suspect, an affair he had with one of the two Loyer women (nobody is sure which). He left the Brixton house very suddenly, his mother writing cryptically: 'since the summer he has been abnormal. The secrets of the Loyers did him no good.' Later, in 1914, Van Gogh's sister-in-law Jo revealed: 'Vincent felt great sympathy for the mother, fell in love with the daughter, Ursula' (though the daughter was actually named Eugenie).[3]

The gloomy, impenetrable Brixton villas set well back along the shaded and monumental Brixton Road prove to be an ideal location for Sherlock Holmes's first murder investigation, his first outing, in Conan Doyle's 1887 novella *A Study in Scarlet*. Holmes, settling in to his newly found Baker Street HQ, receives a note: 'My dear Mr Sherlock Holmes, there has been a bad business during the night at 3 Lauriston Gardens, off the Brixton Road'.[4] Holmes is not at all sure that he wants to leave the apartments to go down to Brixton: 'I'm not sure about whether I shall go', he dithers, 'I am the most incurably lazy devil'.[5] This sluggishness sets the tone for Conan Doyle's treatment of Brixton, which is presented as dull and heavy and muddy, bleached of any animating colour. 'It was a foggy, cloudy morning' as they set out, Watson records, 'and a dun-coloured veil hung over the house-tops, looking like the reflection of the mud-coloured streets beneath'.[6] The mire presents a direct challenge to Holmes's forensic skills:

> Number 3, Lauriston Gardens wore an ill-omened and
> minatory look. It was one of four which stood back some
> little way from the street, two being occupied and two empty.
> The latter looked out with three tiers of vacant melancholy
> windows, which were blank and dreary, save that here and there
> a 'To Let' card had developed like a cataract upon the bleared
> panes. A small garden sprinkled over with a scattered eruption
> of sickly plants separated each of these houses from the street,
> and was traversed by a narrow pathway, yellowish in colour,

and consisting apparently of a mixture of clay and of gravel. The whole place was very sloppy from the rain which had fallen through the night.[7]

As part of the strange inertia that Brixton provokes, contrary to Watson's expectations, Holmes does not rush in to the crime scene; rather, 'with an air of nonchalance which . . . seemed to me to border upon affectation, he lounged up and down the pavement, and gazed vacantly at the ground, the sky, the opposite houses and the line of railings'.[8] Once inside the villa, the entropic stillness and inertia is complete. The corpse, out here in London's modern suburb, is a horrific throwback to prehistoric times:

> My attention was centred upon the single, grim, motionless figure which lay stretched upon the boards, with vacant sightless eyes staring up at the discoloured ceiling . . . On his rigid face there stood an expression of horror, and as it seemed to me, of hatred, such as I have never seen upon human features. This malignant and terrible contortion, combined with the low forehead, blunt nose, and prognathous jaw, gave the dead man a singularly simious and ape-like appearance, which was increased by his writhing, unnatural posture.[9]

Conan Doyle chooses Brixton, for its anonymity and raffish mystery, in other Sherlock Holmes stories: in 'The Adventure of the Blue Carbuncle', the goose, in which an ingenious thief hides the titular jewel, is bred by entirely innocent Mrs Oakshott of 117 Brixton Road; south Brixton is the home of 'The Veiled Lodger', horribly disfigured (from her circus days) and suicidal; and 'The Disappearance of Lady Frances Carfax' sees Lady Frances, swindled of her money, brought to 36 Poultney Square, Brixton, chloroformed and very nearly disposed of by being buried alive in a coffin.

Brixton's attraction, in the 1880s and '90s, as digs for the expanding army of music-hall and theatre troupers provides the background for two key Brixton-set novels. It is central to Balham-born and Clapham-dwelling Angela Carter's last novel, *Wise Children* (1991), concerned with doubling and mirroring, disavowal – and being on the wrong side of the river:

Q. Why is London like Budapest?

A. Because it is two cities divided by a river.

Good morning! Let me introduce myself. My name is Dora Chance. Welcome to the wrong side of the tracks.

Put it another way. If you're from the States, think of Manhattan. Then think of Brooklyn. See what I mean? Or, for a Parisian, it might be a question of *rive gauche, rive droite*. With London, it's the North and South divide. Me and Nora, that's my sister, we've always lived on the left-hand side, the side the tourist rarely sees, the *bastard* side of Old Father Thames.[10]

On the one side, fame, riches and showbiz, located across the river in the glamorous West End; on the other side, the tawdry reality of the no-longer-famous, bright lights dimmed and eking out a shadowy afterlife at 49 Bard Road (Brixton's Shakespeare Road):

You can see for miles, out of this window. You can see right across the river. There's Westminster Abbey, see? Flying the St George's cross, today. St Paul's, the single breast. Big Ben, winking its golden eye. Not much else familiar, these days. This is about the time that comes in every century when they reach out for all that they can grab of dear old London and pull it down. Then they build it up again, like London Bridge in the nursery rhyme, goodbye, hello, but it's never the same.[11]

Sarah Waters's Victorian-set novel *Tipping the Velvet* (1998) also sets down-at-heel Brixton against West End glamour. Here we see innocent Nan, a newcomer fresh in from Whitstable, Kent, making that familiar journey from central London down to new lodgings in south London:

Once we had left the West End and crossed the river, the streets grew greyer and quite dull. The houses and the people here were smart, but rather uniform, as if all crafted by the same unimaginative hand: there was none of that strange glamour, that lovely queer variety of Leicester Square. Soon, too, the streets ceased even to be smart, and became a little shabby; each corner that we passed, each public house, each row of shops and houses, seemed dingier than the one before . . . I kept my face pressed to the window, wondering when we should ever leave behind these dreary districts and reach Greasepaint Avenue, our home.

At last, when we had turned into a street of tall, flat-roofed houses, each with a line of blistered railings before it and a set of sooty blinds and curtains at its windows, Mr Bliss broke off his talk to peer outside and say that we were almost there. I had to look away from his kind and smiling face, then, to hide my disappointment. I knew that my first, excited vision of Brixton – that row of golden make-up sticks, our house with the carmine-coloured roof – was a foolish one; but this street looked so very grey and mean.[12]

The landlady proudly displays on the walls numerous signed portraits of famous theatre folk: 'I marvelled to think that they had all stayed here, in Ginevra Road, with comely Mrs Dendy as their host.'[13]

Paul Vaughan recalls a 1930s Brixton childhood in his memoir *Something in Linoleum* (1994), before the family move out to modern New Malden:

Brixton, sw2. A clattering, grimy district, but in its time it too had been a semi-rural refuge for the better off, seeking escape from the crowds and the dirt of the city. True, Brixton in the twenties and thirties still retained a few signs of Edwardian desirability. Certain roads were favoured by members of the respectable middle class, and for some reason – it was said they found the rents lower – quite a few theatrical families who helped to elevate the tone of the place: the Lotingas, the Lupinos and the Liveseys, Naughton and Gold (later of the Crazy Gang), the O'Gorman Brothers . . . The overdressed daughters of one of the O'Gormans, called oddly Maureen and Noreen, went to my first school, arriving each day in frilly dresses and patent leather pumps, dressed alike as though they were twins.[14]

The genteel Brixton of the 1950s is the fitting home of an ageing, alienated, melancholy commuting clerk in V. S. Naipaul's early novel *Mr Stone and The Knights Companion* (1963). Here, lonely bachelor Mr Stone seems to be dangerously losing any sense of substantive reality, anchored only by obsessive habits and ongoing battles with next door's annoying cat. During a transport strike, along with a small army of fellow commuters, Stone walks home from the West End, down 'long streets of dark brick and stucco peeling like the barks of the pollarded plane trees'.[15]

> He had now reached Brixton, with its large, glass-fronted shops, its modernistic police station and antique food stalls, its crowds of black and white. Here the walkers were not noticeable. There were long but manageable queues at the bus stops. Several buses arrived; many people got off. He jumped a queue, found himself within the warding-off arm of a conductor on a 109 bus, and rode home. He was grateful for the ride. He was beginning to feel fatigued and his breath was failing . . . Taller and taller he grew, firmer and firmer he walked, past the petty gardens of petty houses where people sought to accommodate themselves to life, past the blank, perceptive faces of cats, past the 'To Let' and 'For Sale' signs.[16]

In *City of Spades*, Colin MacInnes's 1957 novel of London, and south London in particular, in the process of being transformed by immigration and youth culture, recently arrived Nigerian Johnny Fortune ventures out, 'south side of the Thames in Brixton', to meet Ghanaian Billy Whispers, who lives in 'a solitary house among ruins'. 'This Brixton house stood all by itself among ruins of what I suppose was wartime damages, much like one tooth left sticking in an old man's jaw.'[17] Scruffy and cheap, Brixton here is already attracting migrants to its rundown terraced houses and flats. Whisper's tall rambling house is subdivided and packed. Billy Whispers, again a sign of the future, deals marijuana (Fortune sees it being grown in a greenhouse):

> 'But tell me,' I said, 'if it's not enquiring. You didn't grow all that hemp you have from outside in your greenhouse?'
>   'No, no. Is an experiment I'm making, to grow it myself from seed.'
>   'Otherwise you buy it?'
>   He nodded.
>   'You can get that stuff easy here?'

'It can be got . . . most things can be got in London when
you know your way around.'

He gave the weed a final tender lick and roll, and handed
it to me by the thin inhaling end.[18]

Fortune is stunned when the weed kicks in: 'Smack! Up in my head I
got a very powerful kick from that hot weed which I'd been smoking.
A kick like you get from superior Congo stuff, that takes your brain
and wraps it up and throws it all away.'[19]

Brixton loses its seedy suburban sedateness in the 1950s and '60s
and becomes something else altogether, on its way to becoming the
inner city. In her 1977 essay 'D'you Mean South?' Angela Carter melo-
dramatically recalls 1950s Brixton: 'Nights were made hideous by the
rhythmic jangle of the swung bicycle chains of Teddy Boys who often
stabbed one another on late buses.'[20]

Patrick Keiller's celebrated 1994 film *London* follows a psychogeographic tour of the capital by Robinson, a mysterious peripatetic
flâneur-philosopher, who displays a keen interest in Brixton's indoor
markets, much like Walter Benjamin with the Paris Arcades, seeing
them as exemplary spaces of modernity:

> In his enthusiasms for crowds and public places, Robinson
> is a modernist . . . whenever he is occupied with his literary
> researches, he takes a bus to Brixton Market, where he works
> in a café in one of the arcades. He is trying to establish a
> connection between the Russian Formalists of the revolutionary
> period, with their interest in Sterne and *Tristram Shandy* and
> the poet Guillaume Apollinaire, who visited Brixton in 1901.
> He loves the modernity of Brixton, Electric Avenue, the bon
> marché, the railways crossing over Atlantic Road. He told
> me about the passengers of the ss *Empire Windrush*, the first
> post-war immigrants recruited from Jamaica who were housed
> in the deep shelters under Clapham Common when they
> first arrived.[21]

In the film, set during the febrile atmosphere of the 1992 General
Election, Robinson also riffs on the fact that about-to-be prime minister John Major, the much-mocked epitome of grey suburbanism and
traditionalism (recall his stealing of Orwell's vision of Englishness as a

matter of warm beer, long shadows and cycling spinsters), grew up in Brixton in the 1950s, after his father's garden ornament business went bust. In fact, as Sinclair points out in *Lights Out for the Territory*, this isn't quite the full picture: Major 'has in fact a far more exotic provenance: an inner city hustler with an Angela Carter background'. 'Being nothing in himself . . . he symbolises nonentity.'[22]

By the 1970s, with the national economic crisis and a decade of disinvestment, neglect, unemployment and racial tensions, Brixton gained a reputation as tough inner city. In Kureishi's *Buddha of Suburbia*, our Bromley suburban hero, Karim, with his uncle Ted, on their way to see Tottenham play, is stunned at what he sees out of the train window in the inner suburbs:

> The train took Ted and me and our sandwiches up through
> the suburbs and into London . . . Before crossing the river
> we passed over the slums of Herne Hill and Brixton, places
> so compelling and unlike anything I was used to seeing that
> I jumped up, jammed down the window and gazed out at the
> rows of disintegrating Victorian houses. The gardens were full
> of rusting junk and sodden overcoats; lines of washing criss-
> crossed over the debris. Ted explained to me, 'That's where the
> niggers live. Them blacks.'[23]

Black experience in the Brixton of the 1970s and '80s is explored in a series of gritty popular novels by Alex Wheatle. Wheatle lived in a hostel in Brixton as a teenager (described in 1999's *Brixton Rock*) and later got caught up the 1981 riots (featuring in 2001's *East of Acre Lane*). *Brixton Rock*, set in 1980, describes the life of parentless fifteen-year-old Brenton Brown, living in a children's home in Camberwell and hanging out mostly in Brixton. Here we see him travelling on the 36 bus from Camberwell to Lambeth Town Hall, Brixton, for the 'sound-system event of the year':

> One beret-topped guy apparently couldn't wait for the music to
> start. For in the rear of the upper deck, taking up most of the
> room on the double seat, he had his fingers on the control of
> an enormous Brixton suitcase – which was more like a London
> trunk. He was playing a tape of all the latest reggae releases
> from Jamaica, massaging the appetite of the roots heads.

A fearful conductor emerged from the stairwell, wearing a cap and his ticket machine strapped to his chest. He stole a glance at the DJ's luggage, then eyed the vociferous passengers before slipping back down the stairs.

The conductor was a picture of relief as the throng of black youngsters vacated the bus at Brixton Town Hall. A mass of people grouped near the entrance, blocking the path of pedestrians and watching a big white rental van park awkwardly near a zebra crossing.[24]

In *East of Acre Lane* we see Lincoln, known as Biscuit, trying to negotiate his way around a grimly isolating and frequently violent landscape with little chance of escape. He lives at home with his large family on a sprawling, constricting estate:

> The council estate that housed Biscuit's family and countless others, stretched between two bus stops along Brixton Road, and was three blocks deep. Biscuit made his way to his home slab and climbed four flights of concrete stairs, eyeing the graffiti that seemed to have been written when the block was built. The sight of the dark brown brickwork brought a powerful relief that not even the filthy syringes that were breeding in dark corners could repel. He winced as he observed the panoramic view of the tower block where Nunchaks had threatened his life. The sky was a malevolent grey, and to the east, beyond Kennington, he saw the hint of a threatening sunrise creeping over the tower blocks of Elephant and Castle.[25]

With very few other options, Biscuit is dragged into a petty drug-dealing scam and casual work. We see how the riot sparks and explodes out of a combination of anger and frustration, boredom and desperation, and institutionalized police racism and intimidation:

> On hearing the almost deafening sound of what seemed like a thousand sirens, the main body of rioters had retreated to the junction of Mayall Road and Railton Road. Coffin Head and others ran into an off-licence and helped themselves to bottles of all shapes and sizes. The man behind the counter stood still, utterly dumb-struck. Sceptic was gathering bricks from the

crumbling walls of an abandoned terrace . . . Onlookers peered out of upstairs windows, following the same sight path as Brenton, and a few of them took photos. Shop-owners thought it best to close business early . . .

Brenton saw the police reinforcements make their beach-head at the junction of Coldharbour Lane and Atlantic Road. He had never seen so many police vehicles in his life, and judging by the sirens there were more to come. He sensed the unease of the crowd as the police formed themselves into a line and started advancing. 'MURDER!' screamed a youth. A second later, a barrage of missiles darkened the afternoon sun. The sound of bottles smashing on the ground and masonry colliding against vehicles filled the atmosphere. Coffin Head had noticed that Molotov cocktails were being prepared by some residents. Yardman Irie, dressed in green army garb, threw a lump of wood into the police lines. 'ARMAGEDDON!' he screamed.[26]

While Brixton is in flames in the early 1980s it also provides a setting for another, very different fiction that records a certain kind of British slackerdom. Cheap rents and an extensive squatting scene, numerous music venues, bars and pubs, the enlivening presence of Caribbean and other migrant culture, the edge provided by poverty and crime, mean that Brixton also attracted those looking for a bohemian subculture. Cult writer Martin Millar's *Lux the Poet* (1988) takes place against the background of the 1981 riot, but the hero of this novel is a very different (teenage) character from Wheatle's: 'At seventeen, Lux the poet is a natural optimist, undeterred by life's misfortunes.'[27] Lux is an insufferable, cloying poet, recently ejected from his squat and wandering aimlessly around Brixton, quite oblivious to what is going on around him.

The misfortunes that Lux is not too worried about include having nowhere to live and no Giros coming from the social security, but he figures it will work out all right in the end.

He strides through the riot, not too worried about it, on his way to Pearl's house. 'Hello', he says, passing by someone he knows who is busy throwing rocks at the police across the street.

He gets a nod in return.

Lux is friendly to most people, and polite.[28]

Like a character misplaced from a different genre, adrift in the wrong place, Lux wanders obliviously right through the middle of the Brixton riots, the disturbances 'rumbling away from the early afternoon, heating up as the evening comes'.[29]

> Lux, hair set in a spectacular red and yellow forest fire around his head, skin looking very young and smooth, finds that he has reached an impassable roadblock. On his side of the road are masses of rioters. Separated by some burning cars are hordes of police. The rioters throw stones and petrol bombs. The police throw them back and beat on their riot shields with their truncheons, trying to unnerve the rioters prior to making an advance.
> Lux looks on, wondering what it is all about.
> 'What's it all about?' he asks the nearest person. The nearest person looks at him like he is crazy.[30]

Geoff Dyer's Brixton-set novel *The Colour of Memory* (1989) provides a snapshot of a now vanished time: the aimless and aleatory lives of a set of 1980s twenty-something slackers, intellectuals and misfits, trying to create a particular kind of bohemia (beatnik, modernist, jazzy) while subsisting on the dole, part-time work and housing benefit. These friends are all signing on, mostly squatting or have managed to blag a council flat, many of them quasi-artists dabbling in creative work, usually stoned or drunk, falling in love, analysing their friendships and relationships, listening to Coltrane – and writing novels. Brixton here provides a combination of inner-city/inner-suburban edge and danger, with its background threat of violence and poverty, and a continual supply of pubs, clubs, music, parties and high-rise roof-top hangouts.

> Something was happening. You could tell something was happening by the way everybody was asking everybody else what was happening. Railton Road was cordoned off. Police were everywhere. I was back in the DIY shop, wishing I measured things more accurately . . . Ten minutes later all the stock from outside was bundled in and the shutters were yanked down.[31]

Living a marginal life as would-be artists on the dole in the 1980s also generates a fear of the inauthentic, a sense among these middle-class dropouts that they are fakes, slumming it, the whole thing just a temporary performance. The narrator and his friends look for the real, for urban edge, but also have a sense that their own presence is destroying this very element:

> Later that evening . . . we walked down to the Atlantic. A lot of police were still around, walking the streets in twos and threes or waiting in buses parked some distance off in case anything happened . . . The Atlantic was right at the focus of all this activity. It used to be a dingy boozer; then it got to be very popular as people were drawn by the slight uneasiness and the fact that there was live jazz and the bar stayed open until midnight. After eleven it tended to fill up with people from the Albert, the pub across the road that was always packed with trendies complaining about how trendy and packed it was . . .
>
> People began leaving the pub and we started walking home. Steranko turned right at the top of Cold Harbour Lane and Carlton dashed for a bus, waving to me as it pulled away. There was hardly anyone around. A few cars went past. It occurred to me that the whole idea of street life in this country came into existence at exactly the moment when, it was claimed, the streets became unsafe to walk in.[32]

This Brixton novel is also haunted by loss. The narrator aims to fix these Brixton memories, to capture and preserve small moments, tiny episodes of significance, before they vanish:

> Standing there, waiting for the lights to change, I felt a strong sense of converging definition. It was one of those moments which, even as experienced, is obscurely touched by the significance with which it will be invested by the future, by memory: this is how I was, this is how we were; this is how we spent our time, wasting whole afternoons and not caring because it was winter and there were so many afternoons still ahead.[33]

In Patrick Neate's *The London Pigeon Wars* (2003), partially set in (and above) Brixton and Clapham, we see the lives of another group, this time 'thirtysomethings', aged 27 to 34, for whom 'degrees of wealth, power and happiness significantly diverge for the first time'.[34] Unlike Dyer's dole-bohos, this generation is in work (fashion designer, IT guy, minor actor and so on), have 'projects' and are busy and driven, if disappointed with how their 'careers' have turned out. We see them gathering:

> This party? It was full of successful London people. They were not all rich or powerful or happy but at least they took the starring roles in the imagined movies of their own lives. They were good at London and knew how to chew on the city like cows on the cud, pick it clean like jackals, gorge on its waste like pigeons.[35]

At the same time, we see the human ('peepnik') activity from a pigeon perspective, and the two worlds later come into contact. Like the humans, the pigeons are territorial and have conflicts between central and suburban. The 'wars' of the title refer to battles between different pigeon flocks (with the murder of one individual called Brixton23, 'above the Brixton tarmac'), as one group, the 'Surbs', are on their way back from a raid on central London's 'Pigeon Front', over Sainsbury's just off Acre Lane.

> Gunnersbury was at the apex of our formation as we
> passed Brixton station and began, with the confidence of
> proximate Surb territory, to climb high over Acre Lane. I had
> Gunnersbury's left flank and Sutton9, a crude hulk of a pigeon
> and typical suburban heartlander, had the right. The rest of
> our party was made up of the usual suspects: radical, young
> hotheads (all fly-by-night realists and high-pitched calls) and
> older extremists who'd spent their whole lives waiting for a
> cause like this to follow . . . Brixton23 was right at the back;
> our tailguard.[36]

Painter and poet Allen Fisher titled his 1985 poetry sequence *Brixton Fractals*. In the last of its poems, 'Birdland', Brixton is a place of fragments that will not cohere: 'Beneath helicopters / Brixton abandoned / challenges the closure of meaning / so far removed, nothing will have taken place but the place'.[37] The only place where Brixton presents any kind of knowable unity is in the poem's introduction:

'Brixton is that part of southwest London extending south/north geo-histographically from its prison and windmill down through the high road to the police station on one axis, and from the employment exchange in Coldharbour through the market to the Sunlight Laundry Factory east/west on another.'[38]

Fractals, meaning a seemingly irregular or fragmented pattern, but one that yet adheres to some kind of underlying regularity or consistent set of rules, here proves a useful metaphor. For Fisher, it is one way to make sense of Brixton, the chaos, the randomness, the abrupt discontinuities, the noise and clatter, all worked on and transformed by the power of perception. Fractals, he tells us, 'provides a technique of memory and perception analysis. It can be used to sharpen out-of-focus photographs; to make maps of the radio sky; to generate images from human memory'.[39]

> Endless destruction
> makes Brixton
> Call it the coexistence of prohibitions and
> their transgression
> Call it carnival and spell out jouissance and horror,
> a nexus of life and description, the child's
> game and dream plus discourse and spectacle.[40]

The chaos and anonymity of Brixton also features in Shena Mackay's south London-set *Dunedin*, as we see unbalanced and delusional Olive Mackenzie steal a baby from a carriage at Brixton station.

> He was in her arms . . . She heard a scream behind her as she was swallowed in the surge of people shoving towards the escalator. The heat and bad temper of the time of day were in her favour. Nobody reacted to the mother's scream; everybody was too concerned with fighting up the escalator and getting to the bus stops. The baby, who had been shocked into silence, opened his mouth to yell as they reached the street, but his voice was drowned by the traffic and a preacher shouting at people to repent, and the vendors of Hard Left tracts.
> Olive, who had often cursed it, now blessed the fact that nobody bothered to queue for buses any more. She saw one coming and shoved through the crowd, thrusting herself and

the baby onto the platform and up the stairs. She sat down beside a youth with a personal stereo.[41]

A short story from 2011 by sometime-Brixton resident Tibor Fischer, 'Crushed Mexican Spiders', presents a similar picture of inner-city clamour and aggravation, with a strange twist, on London's imposing anonymity:

> Ahead of her, struggling up the stairs strugglingly was a mother and pushchair, laden with bags and a screaming kid. Homebound workers salmoned passed without offering a hand, blinkered by visions of supper or respite.
>
> The comatose staff of London Underground didn't think of helping the mother. She wouldn't be helping either. Ten years ago when she had moved to London, she would have. Imperceptibly but perceptibly the city toxified you. Parking across strangers' driveways, not saying thank you when a door was held open for you, murder. Somehow it got you.
>
> London informed you that you got nothing for a lifetime of decency; not a free glass of water. Not that behaving badly necessarily got you anywhere, but it was generally easier and more fun; and finally any career criminal from Albania or genocidist from Rwanda passing through London got the same medical treatment as you and better housing rights.
>
> You didn't want to become the sort of person who didn't help an entoiled mother, but you became one. No one had helped her when she had needed it. And now her help muscles had withered away. Single mothers were especially annoying because of their dishonesty . . .
>
> Outside, on the pavement, a Portuguese junkie was kneeling, while a buxom exorcist wielding a bible intoned with two back-up entreaters and sprinkled him with holy water.
>
> Sidestepping the adjuration she threaded her way through the clumps of beggars, drug-dealers, thugs and seething commuters that made up Brixton.[42]

Tom McCarthy's Brixton-set novel *Remainder* (2005) concerns an unnamed narrator who has a catastrophic accident – something half-remembered, something 'falling from the sky' – and receives £8.5

million in compensation. The narrator, possibly brain-damaged, or dreaming, or dead, then becomes obsessed with the precise details of everyday passing events and routines, with action and gesture. Obsessively walking backwards and forwards from his flat to a phone box ('the nearest one was just around the corner, on Coldharbour Lane'), ensuring that he follows the exact same route, footstep for footstep, he becomes dizzied by his own inauthenticity:

> Two men who'd walked out of a café next to the tyre shop were looking at me. I realized that I was jerking back and forth like a paused video image on low quality machines. It must have looked strange. I felt self-conscious, embarrassed. I . . . remained standing on the pavement for a few more seconds while I pretended to weigh up several options and then come to an informed decision. I even brought my finger into it, the index finger of my right hand. It was a performance for the two men watching me, to make my movements come across as authentic.[43]

The narrator is stunned by the fact that he is always watching himself perform everyday routines:

> I'd always been inauthentic. Even before the accident, if I'd been walking down the street just like De Niro, smoking a cigarette like him, and even if it had lit first try, I'd still be thinking: *Here I am, walking down the street, smoking a cigarette like someone in a film.* See? Second-hand. The people in films aren't thinking that. They're just doing their thing, real, not thinking anything.[44]

But now, this sense of the inauthentic becomes bound up with an obsession with the minutiae of past life, small insignificant events that are always forgotten, and how these are half-captured and replayed in the memory. He experiences a moment of profound déjà vu at a Brixton party. A minor crack in the bathroom wall conjures up a half-remembered house, a scene, on an ordinary day – with a staircase, a cat, a roof, someone frying onion. He copies the crack onto an old piece of wallpaper and takes it home. A strange plan takes shape, while walking across Brixton. He will, with his money, pay a team to reconstruct, to actually build, that house as a real house, with all attendant details, as he has remembered it.

> I walked down to the main Brixton intersection, where the giant box junction spreads across the tarmac from the town hall to the Ritzy cinema. It must have been midnight or so. Brixton was alive and kicking. There were red and yellow sports cars gridlocked on Coldharbour Lane, black guys in baseball caps touting for cab firms, younger black guys in big puffy jackets pushing cannabis and crack, black girls with curled and flattened hair and big round hips wrapped up in stretchy dresses shouting into mobiles, white girls queuing outside the Dogstar, chewing gum and smoking at the same time. They all came and went – people, lights, colours, noise – on the periphery of my attention. I walked slowly, with the strip of wallpaper, thinking of the room, the flat, the world I'd just remembered.
>
> I was going to recreate it: build it up again and live inside it. I'd work it out from the crack I'd just transcribed.[45]

In Roma Tearne's *Brixton Beach* (2009), Sri Lankan Tamil Stanley Fonseka escapes increasing disorder and threat of civil war in that country, and moves to London, settling in Brixton, followed later by his Singhalese wife Sita and their daughter Alice. Where Sri Lanka, still Ceylon, is presented as lushly and dreamily tropical, vibrant, abundant and colourful, south London comes as a shock. Sita, at first, refuses to leave the house, or even get out of bed much. Then, 'without any warning, she went out'. She buys an *A to Z* and, 'armed with an umbrella against the threatening rain',[46] heads for the markets:

> She enjoyed wandering through the rubbish-strewn streets listening to the voices of the stallholders, smelling the frying onions and beef burgers, while picking up a bargain. No one knew her, no one even noticed her, but in a strange and complicated way, in spite of the dull soot-ridden rain and the lack of sun, the place reminded her of home. She could not explain this. London itself had no significance for her except as a constant contrast to her home. She walked with her sight turned inward.[47]

Alice grows up and gets married, and is haunted by childhood memories of her grandparents' paradisiacal beach house, up the coast from Colombo, especially now that the country is being torn apart by a civil war:

> In their new home in Brixton, after a honeymoon of a week
> of cloudy weather in the Lake District, a sudden memory of
> the Sea House broke over Alice like a squall of monsoon rain.
> It caught her unawares and took her breath away, floating in
> the September sky like a kite released from its string. Because
> of this when they returned, she gave their home in Brixton a
> name. She called it Brixton Beach.
> 'What?' asked Tim, confused.
> He watched her fixing up the sign she had painted. She
> seemed uncharacteristically determined. He remembered his
> mother's warning.
> 'Are you mad?' he asked. 'What will the neighbours think?'[48]

Clapham

About a mile west of Brixton, and under 2 miles south of the river across from Chelsea, Clapham was a hamlet named in the Domesday Book. By the seventeenth century it had already become an attractive proposition for the wealthier merchant class wanting easy commutes to the increasingly filthy and teeming city. Importantly, historian Robert Fishman considers the place as one of the world's first suburbs: 'as early as the 1790s Clapham had become a true suburb'.[49] For London historian Donald Olsen, it is the 'most famous of all the Georgian suburbs'.[50]

Samuel Pepys went down to Clapham, visiting on 25 July 1663, and was impressed with the houses, gardens and air of cosy domesticity:

> After some debate, Creed and I resolved to go to Clapham, to
> Mr Gauden's . . . When I came to Mr Gauden's one first thing
> was to show me his house, which is almost built . . . I find it
> very regular and finely contrived, and the gardens and offices
> about it as convenient and as full of good variety as ever I saw
> in my life. It is true he hath been censured for laying out so
> much money; but he tells me he built it for his brother, who

is since dead (the Bishop), who, when he should come to
be Bishop of Winchester, which he was promised (to which
bishopric at present there is no house), he did intend to dwell
here . . . By and by to dinner, and in comes Mr Creed; I saluted
Mr Gauden's lady, and the young ladies, he having many pretty
children, and his sister, the Bishop's widow; who was, it seems,
Sir W. Russel's daughter, the Treasurer of the Navy . . . [whom]
I find to be very well-bred, and a woman of excellent discourse
. . . Towards the evening we bade them Adieu![51]

In fact, Pepys liked Clapham so much he chose it as his retirement spot.
This period's other famed diarist, Deptford's John Evelyn, visits him
in his new home on 23 September 1700: 'I went to visit Mr Pepys, at
Clapham, where he has a very noble and wonderfully well-furnished
house, especially with Indian and Chinese curiosities: the offices and
gardens well accommodated for pleasure and retirement.'[52]

In 1792 the wealthy banker and philanthropist Edward Thornton
bought a large manor house, Battersea Rise House, on the northwest
corner of Clapham Common, on what is now the A3, and lived there
with his cousin William Wilberforce. Two of Thornton's brothers had
already bought large villas nearby, on the Common. The vast landscaped gardens at Battersea Rise House were large enough to build
two more huge houses, with Wilberforce moving into one when he
got married in 1797. This was the nucleus of the so-called 'Clapham
Sect' (nicknamed the 'Clapham Saints'), a neighbourhood network
of wealthy, powerful and highly influential and industrious Anglican
Evangelicals who agitated for Christian social and moral regeneration, most famously working successfully for the abolition of slavery
and the slave trade. Key members, associates and descendants of the
group reads like a Who's Who of Victorian British cultural grandees (Macaulay, Trevelyan, Wilberforce, Tennyson, Darwin, Leslie
Stephen) and on down, in the early twentieth century, to various of
the Bloomsbury Group: Strachey, Fry, Woolf and Forster. Clapham
itself is central here, as many of the public-spirited Saints' ideals were
also key to the creation of a particular kind of suburban ideal: close to
the city (with transport links, in this case the opening of Westminster
Bridge in 1750), set in bucolic landscapes, and at the same time offering a sheltered domestic zone where the nuclear family, children
especially, could thrive in quiet, spacious, quasi-pastoral conditions.

Large detached villas in landscaped 'Picturesque' settings were the ideal. In 1844 James Stephens describes the famed oval library at the Thornton place, with its astonishing mix of different worlds, of Cabinet meetings with domestic life:

> The chamber . . . became the scene of enjoyments . . . For there, at the close of each succeeding day, drew together a group of playful children, and with them a knot of legislators, rehearsing, in sport or earnestly, some approaching debate; or travellers from distant lands; or circumnavigators of the worlds of literature and science; or the Pastor of the neighbouring church . . . the lord of this well-peopled enclosure rejoiced over it with a contagious joy.[53]

For Marianne Thornton, Edward's daughter (and E. M. Forster's great-aunt), the huge, rambling house, with library and garden free to roam, became part of that common theme of middle-class suburban writing, the enchanted childhood: 'To the day of my death,' she writes, 'I shall think nothing so lovely as the trees and the lawn at Battersea Rise.'[54]

Clapham was considered an ideal location for boarding schools: far from the city's dangers – and far from meddling observers. Percy Bysshe Shelley's two sisters were trapped at the brutal Fenning's boarding school on Clapham Common. When he visited in January 1811, he was appalled to discover that one sister, as punishment for some trivial offence, was forced to wear a spiked iron collar all day, as she later recounted:

> His ire was greatly excited at a black mark hung round one of our throats, as a penalty for some small misdemeanour. He expressed great disapprobation, more of the system than that one of his sisters should be so punished. Another time he found me, I think, in an iron collar, which certainly was a dreadful interment of torture in my opinion.[55]

In 1829 the painter and antiquarian John Thomas Smith went down to Clapham to visit a Mr Esdaile, an amateur art collector who just happened to have 'a Virgin and Child, attributed to Albert Durer . . . [and] works of Rubens, Ruysdael, Salvator Rosa, &c.' on display in his home near the Common:

On arriving at Mr Esdaile's gate, Mr Smedley remarked that this was one of the few commons near London which had not been enclosed. The house has one of those plain fronts which indicated little, but ascending the steps, I was struck with a similar sensation to those of the previous season, when I first entered this hospitable mansion . . . the visiter [*sic*], immediately he enters the hall, is presented with too much at once, for he knows not which to admire first, the choice display of pictures which decorate the hall, or the equally artful and delightful manner in which the park-like grounds so luxuriantly burst upon his sight.[56]

Railways and industry arrived in nearby Battersea during the mid-nineteenth century and the grander, single-family mansions and villas with huge gardens, all built in the late eighteenth century and the early nineteenth, were demolished and replaced with smaller semis and terraces. E. M. Forster, researching his biography of Marianne Thornton, his great-aunt, visited the site of Battersea Rise after it had been demolished in 1907, the area redeveloped for a new middle-class influx:

I have identified the area with difficulty. It is completely covered with very small two-storied houses . . . Not one tree survives. Clapham Common survives, but so messed about, so full of roads and railings, and notices and huts and facilities and infelicities, that Marianne and her mama would not recognise it.[57]

Nobody visiting Battersea Rise today would consider these to be 'small houses'.

The new middle- and lower-middle-class suburbia, built around the turn of the twentieth century, is brilliantly captured by William Pett Ridge in *Outside the Radius: Stories of a London Suburb* (1899). The stories here all revolve around Claphamites' uncertain social status in the shifting and evolving landscape of the then-new mass suburb. The narrator is a keen surveyor of the street, watching closely for signs of class status, change, deviation, habit and routine. 'The Crescent', between the 'Common' and the 'Old Town', it is stressed at the start, is actually a *real* place and seems grander than other streets:

The Crescent looks like a shortcut to somewhere; but it is not a shortcut, and people who are deluded by this come from the Common, which gapes long and wide and open near to us, an oasis in a desert for villas, and take The Crescent, meaning to reach the Old Town, but find themselves brought out into the Common again in great confusion. The Crescent has been built for something like twelve years, and is thus an historic road compared with other streets near, which are one day blank spaces, next day a row of thirty-five-pound villas; the day after inhabited by joyful young married people, taking the brightest views of everything.

'The best of it is,' say the new inhabitants, artfully, 'that they don't dare build opposite.'

But they do build opposite, and two rows of houses are up, with lanky, shivering, unrobed trees on either side; baby Virginia creepers beginning to crawl up the walls, and titles over every front door, before you have realized the fact that building has commenced.[58]

The narrator, keen to make it clear that the Crescent is still a cut above other streets, and that each has a unique character and is solidly middle class, gives us a detailed inventory of the houses and their interiors, opening up the secrets of the suburban villa:

Every house has its front lawn, which is not perhaps so much a lawn as a rather large sod of turf; green iron railings with head ornaments (which ornaments young Mohawks from the Old Town and the riverside loot on dark evenings, and take home, I assume, to decorate their rooms as other men bring home the skins of big game); a tessellated pavement leading from the gate to the front door, a suggestion of a porch. Lace curtains drape the ground-floor windows in summer, but fly away when in October the signal is given by Number Nine, otherwise The Limes, leaving for a day a blank space, filled later by dark curtains which take duty for the winter. In the windows occur here and there attempts in the direction of individuality, and of these I give a complete inventory:

Bamboo stands with ferns in giant egg-shells.

Webster's Dictionary.

A stuffed cockatoo.
St Paul's Cathedral in white wax.
Bust of the late Mr Spurgeon.
Photograph of Her Majesty.
The Three Graces under a glass shade.
Upstairs, glistening brass lines bisect the windows horizontally, and backs of lounging mirrors fill the lower space between curtains.[59]

The narrator is our guide to this dimly understood new habitat and describes everyday routines for us. This is commuter territory:

At about eight-twenty every week-day morning The Crescent dispatches its grown-up male inhabitants in search of gold. The adventurers set out, each with a small brown bag, and, excepting on rainy mornings, are silk-hatted, because there are many ways of getting on in the City, but none apparently in which a silk hat is not indispensable. Some of these pioneers leave home with a good-tempered wave of the hand to a wife who is at the window urging a baby to make gestures of adieu with its small plump hands; others pull the door after them as far as they can and usually attempt to open the gate the incorrect way (than which nothing aggravates so much the crossness of a man). They hurry across the Common to the station muttering as men will who have been prevented by time's progress from finishing a debate with the opposition. I like to see the cheerful kind.[60]

We catch an unhappier glimpse of Clapham commuters in Oscar Wilde's *De Profundis* (1895), a 'letter' he wrote in prison exploring the events that led to his incarceration:

On November 13th, 1895, I was brought down here from London. From two o'clock till half past two on that day I had to stand on the centre platform of Clapham Junction in convict dress, and handcuffed, for the world to look at . . . Of all possible objects I was the most grotesque. When people saw me they laughed. Each train as it came in swelled the audience. Nothing could exceed their amusement. That was, of course, before they knew who I was. As soon as they had been informed, they laughed still more. For half an hour I stood there in the grey November rain surrounded by a jeering mob.[61]

Clapham, in H. G. Wells's *Love and Mr Lewisham* (1900), stands in for the vast, anonymous hinterland of London. The novel's hero moves to London, hearing that Ethel Henderson, his first love, has moved to the area somewhere ('Clapham – that's almost in London, isn't it?') and wanders the Clapham streets hoping to catch a glimpse of her. Eventually he finds her and, in a chapter titled 'Love in the Streets', the couple walk home every night from work in South Kensington (at Imperial College) to Clapham:

Every week night through November and December, save once, when he had to go into the far East to buy himself an overcoat, he was waiting to walk with her home. A curious, inconclusive affair, that walk, to which he came nightly full of vague longings, and which ended invariably under an odd shadow of disappointment. It began outside Lagune's most punctually at five, and ended – mysteriously – at the corner of a side road in Clapham, a road of little yellow houses with sunk basements and tawdry decorations of stone. Up that road she vanished night after night, into a grey mist and the shadow beyond a feeble yellow gas-lamp, and he would watch her vanish, and then sigh and turn back towards his lodgings.[62]

Modernist poet, thinker, journalist, soldier and all-round character (coiner of the terms 'Cubist' and 'Surrealism', and implicated in the 1911 theft of the *Mona Lisa*) Guillaume Apollinaire journeyed in 1904 from Paris to London, more exactly to Landor Road in north Clapham. He was desperately trying to track down one Annie Playden, with whom he had fallen in love when both lived in Germany. The Playden family were not amused by the agitated caller. Neither was Annie; she explained that she had made plans to emigrate to America. Apollinaire later wrote about this, in the poem 'The Emigrant from Landor Road' ('My ship will sail tomorrow for America / And I will never return').[63] Apollinaire was fascinated by the fog, anonymity, menace, huge distances and romance of the *fin de siècle* metropolis. His first major collection, *Alcools*, contains the poem 'The Song of the Poorly-loved', which recalls his visit to Clapham to see Annie:

> One misty London evening
> Some hoodlum who resembled
> My love came up to me
> And shot me such a glance
> I lowered my eyes in shame.
>
> I followed this punk who was
> Whistling his hands in his pockets
> Between houses that appeared like
> The Red Sea's parted waters
> I was Pharaoh he the Hebrews.[64]

For Psmith, in P. G. Wodehouse's *Psmith in the City*, Clapham is in the worrying condition of quite possibly *not existing*. In Chapter Fifteen, 'Stirring Times on the Common', we see Psmith eager 'to ascertain that such a place as Clapham Common really exists'. Junior bankers, Psmith and Mike, have a colleague, Waller, who turns out to be a radical socialist and invites the pair down to a protest on Clapham Common ('Evidently listening to the speakers was one of Clapham's fashionable Sunday amusements'). But first they have to find the place, as Psmith explains:

> One has heard of it, of course, but has its existence ever been proved? I think not. Having accomplished that, we must then try to find out how to get to it. I should say at a venture that it would necessitate a sea-voyage. On the other hand, Comrade Waller, who is a native of the spot, seems to find no difficulty in rolling to the office every morning. Therefore – you follow me, Jackson? – it must be in England. In that case, we will take a taximeter cab, and go out into the unknown, hand in hand, trusting to luck.[65]

A brawl breaks out, the pair are chased by angry locals, and they run for it, escaping by jumping onto a tram. Psmith is appalled by this:

'Wounded leaving the field after the Battle of Clapham Common. How are your injuries, Comrade Jackson?'

'My back's hurting like blazes,' said Mike. 'And my ear's all sore where that chap got me. Anything the matter with you?'

'Physically,' said Psmith, 'no. Spiritually much. Do you realize, Comrade Jackson, the thing that has happened? I am riding in a tram. I, Psmith, have paid a penny for a ticket on a tram. If this should get about the clubs! I tell you, Comrade Jackson, no such crisis has ever occurred before in the course of my career.'

'You can always get off, you know,' said Mike.[66]

In the 1930s and '40s, Clapham becomes associated with a certain inner-suburban seediness and squalor. In James Curtis's hard-boiled, tough-talking 1938 thriller *They Drive by Night*, Shorty Mathews, newly released from Pentonville, is falsely wanted for murder. Meanwhile, Hoover, the real murderer, a psychopathic misogynist serial killer (who fancies himself the 'Lone Wolf, the Napoleon of crime, the Undetectable, the mastermind'), bases himself in unnoticed Clapham, commuting up to the West End only to seek out more victims. Clapham is suitably shabby and anonymous for Hoover. This is a place 'where like Harun ar Rashid, he condescended to walk among the multitude, in the midst of poor people of Battersea and Clapham'.[67] We spot him before a trip: 'A man was sitting in a cheap multiple tea-shop near Clapham Junction. He had drunk his coffee and was now nervously pulling a matchbox to pieces with nicotine-stained fingers. His lips slavered as he talked to himself.'[68] He moves off along Clapham High Street:

For a while he stood, with his eyes pressed against the windows of a big store, watching assistants putting underwear on a figure. One of them noticed him and nudged the other. He moved off. Near the station there was, he knew, a shop that sold cheap American sex magazines.

A knot of girls got off a bus at the corner, so he stood watching them. His pupils dilated as he stared at the seams that ran up the back of their stockings. He clutched hard the coins in his pocket, trying to make out, without looking, which were silver and which were copper. Yes, he had enough.[69]

Clapham is also a key outpost of 'Greeneland', those seedy, squalid zones in many of Graham Greene's fictions, populated by exhausted and morally conflicted characters searching for meaning in a Godless universe. Greene himself lived at 14 North Side, Clapham, just off the Common, and a visit here, 'Excursion in Greeneland', is well described by writer and famed Soho habitué and memoirist Julian Maclaren-Ross:

> One day in 1956 I was walking home with a friend who lived off Clapham Common when pointing to a gutted ruin with a façade of blackened brick he said: 'That used to be a Queen Anne house before the blitz. Beautiful place I believe. It belonged to Graham Greene.'
>
> 'I know,' I said. 'I lunched there once. In 1938,' and my friend was suitably impressed.
>
> It was noon and summer when I arrived at that house eighteen years before, aged twenty-six and carrying a copy of *Brighton Rock* wrapped in a *Daily Express* containing James Agate's review of the novel . . . I had not found the house easily since there are three tube-stations and three sides to the Common, Clapham Common North, Clapham Common South, and Clapham Common West, and I am incapable of telling which is which without the help of a compass. I did not carry a compass. I had moreover mislaid Graham Greene's letter which gave precise instructions for getting to his house.[70]

Maclaren-Ross goes on:

> The drawing-room stood open at the top of the stairs: it was small, as was the house itself. Perhaps it was the kind called a Bijou house, I wouldn't know. Someone like Denton Welch would have been able to describe the interior and enumerate the articles of period furniture which I'm told it contained, but this bit is quite beyond me. The armchair I sat down in seemed like any other armchair, though rather low, and I saw immediately in a bookcase nearby the works of Joseph Conrad, which didn't come as a surprise.[71]

The drawn blinds, the use of a dumb-waiter, the odd food, the silence of Mrs Greene, make this an uncanny experience. At the end of lunch, another odd scene:

> when we rose from the table Greene said to me apologetically: 'It's an awful nuisance, but They are asking to see you I'm afraid. I wonder if you'd mind.'
>
> 'Why of course not,' I said mystified. 'I'd like to see Them very much.'
>
> 'I'm sorry but we'll get no peace otherwise,' he said, leading the way up another, darker flight of stairs. I could hear a strange twittering sound coming from behind the door in front of which he halted.
>
> 'By the way,' I asked slightly nervous. 'What are They?' imagining giant parrots or pet vultures brought from Africa, or even elderly female relatives, not quite certifiable but confined nevertheless to their rooms.
>
> 'They are in here,' Greene said, opening the door for me to precede him, and I found myself facing a large railed cot raised off the floor to about the level of my chest. From behind the bars of this cage two small, extremely pretty blonde girls peered out at me unblinking. They were perhaps aged about four and five respectively.[72]

Greene and his visitor then venture out across the common for a jug of beer from the nearby Windmill pub, a custom also described in Greene's 1951 Clapham-set novel *The End of the Affair*. This atmospheric novel tells, in a complex narrative of multiple chronological shifts, starting during the pre-war summer of 1939, of the wartime affair between cynical, embittered novelist Maurice Bendrix and Sarah, wife of Henry Miles, a senior civil servant. Bendrix and the Mileses live on opposite sides of the Common. Rainy post-war Clapham is dark, threadbare and grubby, full of seedy or defeated characters. Clapham is the location of what Bendrix calls 'the heavy scene', which he itemizes as 'the daily newspaper, the daily meal, the traffic grinding towards Battersea, the gulls coming up from the Thames'.[73] Bendrix, living on the 'wrong side' of the common, heads for the pub (renamed 'The Pontefract Arms'), on a 'black wet January night on the Common, in 1946', when 'the avenues of the Common . . . ran with rain'. Awkwardly, he bumps into Henry:

> It was strange to see Henry out on such a night: he liked his comfort and after all – or so I thought – he had Sarah. To me comfort is like the wrong memory at the wrong place or time . . . There was too much comfort even in the bed sitting-room I had at the wrong – the south – side of the Common, in the relics of other people's furniture. I thought I would go for a walk through the rain and have a drink at the local . . .
>
> Directly I began to cross the Common I realized I had the wrong umbrella, for it sprang a leak and the rain ran down under my mackintosh collar, and then it was I saw Henry. I could so easily have avoided him; he had no umbrella and in the light of the lamp I could see his eyes were blinded with the rain. The black leafless trees gave no protection; they stood around like broken waterpipes and the rain dripped off his stiff dark hat and coat and ran in streams down his black civil servant's overcoat.[74]

Later in the novel Bendrix recounts a VI attack as he and Sarah are lying in bed:

> It was the first night of what were later called the VIs in June 1944 . . . When the sirens went and the first robots came over, we assumed that a few planes had broken through our night defence . . . at that moment, lying in the dark on my bed, we saw our first robot. It passed low across the Common and we took it for a plane on fire and its odd deep bumble for the sound of an engine out of control. A second came and then a third.[75]

In Greene's earlier novel *It's a Battlefield* (1934) we see the Metropolitan Police Assistant Commissioner being driven, with a senior civil servant, down to Brixton jail to see a convicted killer, Drover, sentenced to hang. The commissioner is prodded by the secretary to read the possible popular reaction should Drover, a communist activist, hang: 'If you can answer for – shall we say, the docks, for Paddington, for Notting Hill, and King's Cross, the suburbs, Balham, and Streatham.'[76] From the ministerial car window, this part of south London appears as the natural home of the downtrodden ordinary:

> Over Battersea Bridge the gulls came sweeping down to the level of the glass, and the lights from the Embankment crossed the grey flow, touched two barges piled with paper, rested on the mud, and the stranded boats and the walls of the mill . . . The fish-and-chip shops were opening, and all down the Battersea Bridge Road and past Clapham Junction, through a wilderness of trams and second-hand clothes shops and public lavatories and evening institutes, the Assistant Commissioner wondered, as he often wondered, at the beauty of the young tinted faces. Their owners handed over pennies for packets of fried chips, they stood in queues for the cheapest seats at the cinemas, and through the dust and dark and degradation they giggled and chattered like birds. They were poor, they were overworked, they had no future, but they knew the right tilt of a beret, the correct shade of lipstick.[77]

Gabriel's domineering father in Paul Bailey's *Gabriel's Lament* (1986), extremely proud of his Clapham villa, 'Blenheim', in the early 1960s, is not at all impressed by the arrival of new neighbours, the Campbells, from Trinidad via Coventry:

> 'As the Ace of Spades, God help us', spluttered my father, his inventive powers of description for once failing him. They were dark brown, the Campbells, to be absolutely precise, I said . . .
>
> 'But people who move into a house at dead of night, when decent citizens are in their beds, they're not to be trusted. It doesn't bode well, that sneaky sort of behaviour. I've signed a petition.'
>
> 'A petition? What kind of petition?'
>
> 'I can't remember the exact words . . . A fellow called Weekes wrote it, solicitor type, command of the language . . . The gist of it is that the residents hereabouts don't relish the prospect of them, those Campbells, living in the Avenue. Not at all, they don't. Most definitely not.'
>
> 'Why, Father?'
>
> 'Oaf, oaf, oaf – do I have to spell it out?'

'You do.'

'They lower the tone.'

'The tone, Father?'

'Yes, the tone, Father. They bring the neighbourhood down.'[78]

After his father dies, Gabriel hears that the Campbells had received worse treatment from other neighbours, the Robinsons at 'Tintagel', who had 'sorely tried their Christian patience – turds, human turds, Robinson turds, had been dropped through their letter box or dumped on their door-step, and Mr Robinson, who was a church warden, had phoned them for several weeks at three in the morning to let them know they were monkeys.'[79]

For Ian Nairn in 1966, Clapham, though neglected and shabby, contains the bare bones of an ideal 'London village'. Here he is standing in the Old Town:

> The blunt end, with a good pub in it, points at Clapham
> Common, just a few yards away, and the Common plays an
> enchanting game, dancing in with foliage from two directions
> without breaking up the space. This is the perfect recipe for a
> neighbourhood: shops, open space, houses, a natural centre,
> and even a Georgian church (Holy Trinity) just around the
> corner. Now nobody cares much: it is all dog-shit and
> bus-tickets. But it could easily be marvellous.[80]

The marvellousness merges with house price hyper-inflation, a credit boom, and an influx of workers in financial services to make the place a highly desirable location. As Clapham resident Angela Carter recalled:

> In 1960, I went for a job on a glossy magazine and said, with
> typical south London sullen defiance: 'Balham', when the
> editor asked me where I lived. She drummed her enamelled
> fingertips on her leather desk for a long time, then enquired,
> almost solicitous: 'Do you find that perfectly convenient?' It
> was terribly convenient for the Northern Line, but she did not
> mean that. Where I live now is only two stops nearer the West
> End on the Northern Line; but these days she would be more

likely to say: 'Clapham? Why, some friends of mine have just moved there.'

When the bourgeoisie got priced out of, first, Hampstead and Highgate – how long ago it seems! – and then from Camden Town and Islington, and the alternatives got priced (who'd have thought it?) out of Ladbroke Grove, there was nowhere else for *all*, repeat all, the poor sods to go, was there?[81]

Mr Phillips, in John Lanchester's 2000 novel of the same name, is an archetypally anxious middle-aged Clapham suburbanite: disappointed, quizzical and confused, timid, a (secretly) unemployed accountant, who sets off from Clapham every morning and just pretends to go to work as usual:

The houses in the Crescent are low-squatting semi-detached Edwardian villas – a word which always gives Mr Phillips a mental glimpse of people in togas on the set of *Up Pompeii*. They look more cramped then they are, with decent space at the back and sometimes an attic too, as well as three upstairs bedrooms. If houses were faces the street would be a row of well-fed Tories, golfers, Gilbert and Sullivan enthusiasts.[82]

Clapham is used as exemplary representative of a very different urban condition in Lanchester's state-of-the-nation novel *Capital* (2012). People here – a rich banker and his family, their Spanish nanny, a Polish builder, an elderly survivor of the original white working class and her Banksy-type son, an over-qualified Zimbabwean traffic warden, an under-used Senegalese Premiership footballer, an Asian family who run the corner shop – do not meet. They only have the street in common and the fact that they all receive a menacing postcard: 'We Want What You Have'. Everyone is affected by the property bubble. 'For most of its history', we learn, 'the street was lived in by more or less the kind of people it was built for: the aspiring the not-too-well-off'. But then, as house prices rise and rise, the street becomes a 'casino', a casino where 'you were guaranteed to be a winner':[83]

This happened at first slowly, gradually, as average prices crept up through the lower hundred thousands, and then, as people from the financial industry discovered the area and house prices in general began to rise sharply, and people began to be paid huge bonuses . . . then, suddenly, prices began to go up so quickly that it was as if they had a will of their own. There was a sentence that rang down the decades, a very English sentence: 'Did you hear what they got for the house down the road?'[84]

We don't see much of Clapham here – the houses are now investment instruments. Yet, in good Marxist fashion, as the houses become commodities rather than homes, they become weirdly animated, alive:

> Once the parents had gone off to work and the children off to school you saw fewer people in the street in the daytime, except builders; but the houses had things brought to them every day. Vans from Berry Brothers and Rudd brought wine; there were two or three vans for dog walkers . . . cleaners, plumbers, yoga teachers, and all day long, all of them going up to the houses like supplicants and then being swallowed up by them. There was laundry, there was dry-cleaning, there were FedEx and UPS, there were dog beds, printer ribbon, garden chairs, vintage film posters, same-day DVD purchases, eBay coups, eBay whims and impulse buys.[85]

Roger Yount, the banker, only actually gets to see Clapham towards the end of the novel, after being fired – this is September 2008. Now, with time on his hands, this is the first time Roger has had a look around in the daytime. 'Weekends were all about Euro bankers with their sweaters over their shoulders,' he thinks, 'the yummy mummies on their phones, the British military fitness crowd shouting at their idiotic punters.' Weekdays were different:

> The Common demographic was different in the middle of the day, middle of the week. It was more underclassy. Four homeless men were sitting on a park bench drinking Tennent's Super, while a woman, looking just as rough as they did, harangued them about some injustice . . . Three truanting teenagers were practising skateboarding on the pavement and into the road . . . a few yards away, a scowling skinhead, in his late thirties, so old enough to know better, was letting his pit bull shit on the path, and visibly daring anyone to say something to him about it.[86]

House price inflation, a looming credit crunch, the banker invasion of Clapham and estate agents' imaginative rezoning of London districts are central to *Clapham Lights* by Tom Canty (2013). Here estate agent Craig Tennant is trying to persuade a couple that the house they are viewing is really in desirable Clapham and not in nearby Balham, and definitely not Streatham:

'What's this called?' Jane asks, gazing at the parkland on either side of the road.

'Um, this is Balham Common.'

'It said Tooting Bec Common on the sign back there,' Paul says.

'Yes, it's um, both. Balham Common and Tooting Bec Common are the same place, on either side of the road. Clapham Common is just at the other end of the road. Really close.'[87]

Things get worse once they are all at the house, and the couple are increasingly suspicious.

'What road is that?'

'That's Balham High Road.' Craig coughs and adjusts his belt.

Jane rubs her bump as Paul gets to his feet and gazes out of the window to the street. A group of young boys are kicking a football at a snarling pit bull terrier tethered to a gatepost. He takes his phone out of his pocket.

'They don't live around here,' Craig says, looking over Paul's shoulder.

'How do you know?' Paul says concentrating on his phone. 'I've just put this address into Google maps and it comes up as Streatham *not* Balham.' He glares at Craig.

'Err . . . well . . . the address is Streatham, but the house is in Balham.' Craig backs towards the corner of the room.

'So it's in Balham *and* Streatham?' Jane says.[88]

Novelist Julie Myerson, in *Home: The Story of Everyone Who Ever Lived in Our House* (2004), attempts to situate her own story within that of her unremarkable Clapham family home.

This summer, we've lived at 34 Lillieshall Road for exactly fifteen years. It's a narrow, three-storey, slightly subsiding, dirty red-brick, mid-Victorian Clapham terrace with a mature, spreading hydrangea in front of the bay window and a glossy scented jasmine that climbs up past the front door to the first-floor window . . . I loved 34 Lillieshall Road from the start but I was never someone who thought she'd stay anywhere long. And then one day it dawned on me that I have lived here ten years and might actually be here another ten. Might even grow old here.[89]

Casually stripping part of a wall reveals surprising depths.

It felt strangely moving and intimate, scraping the layers off – history unpeeling itself. There was a smell of dissolving paper, of oldness – the hiss of the steamer in the silence, the sight of naked walls. Even patches of mauveish, higgledy Victorian brick in some places where the plaster fell away in large, crumbling, worrying chunks . . . And the layers of paper curled and rolled off and dropped to the floor – and, quite perfectly preserved, half a dozen different patterns were revealed; imitation wood grain (the sixties?), brown zigzags (the fifties?) – then a bold Art Deco style in cobalt and scarlet (the twenties?) . . . Each layer – imperfectly glued, faded, merged – revealed another.[90]

'Each faded layer of wallpaper', Myerson notes, 'seemed to hint at a whole crowd of lost people, faces, souls.'[91] Myerson's research eventually unearths sixty-odd former residents, many families and groups, going back to the 1870s and earlier.

Battersea

To its west and north, down into Battersea Rise, Clapham merges into Battersea. 'For centuries', suburban historian Nick Barratt writes, Battersea 'had been little more than a village next to the Thames, connected to the north bank since 1771 by a rickety wooden bridge'.[92] Then, transformed by suburbanization and then the railway (at Clapham Junction, in 1863), Battersea became increasingly industrial and populous. The area soon gained a grim reputation. The area to the north, along the river, then known as Battersea Fields, attracted a mixed bunch of those considered to be lowering the tone – gamblers, revellers, gypsies, fairground folk, even a duel featuring the Duke of Wellington – and was transformed in the late 1840s into a Royal Park.

Victorian poet and educator Matthew Arnold spent an unpleasant few days inspecting schools in the area in 1852. He explained to his wife: 'This certainly has been one of the most uncomfortable weeks I ever spent. Battersea is so far off, the roads so execrable and the rain so incessant . . . There is not a yard of flagging, I believe, in all Battersea.'[93]

Battersea-born novelist Pamela Hansford Johnson, in her memoir *Important to Me* (1974), recalls her first impressions of the area's grubby reality and her family's snobbish need to keep themselves, their side, separate from the 'Other Battersea':

> St Mark's Church stands almost at the peak of the Other Battersea Rise. We called it that because we lived on the opposite one. The Rise sweeps down from Clapham Common (our side) down to the junction of St John's and Northcote Roads, and up again to Wandsworth Common, to the west. We lived in a large brick terrace house bought by my grandfather some time in the eighties, when it looked out on fields where sheep might safely graze. But by the time I was born, the railway had come, and the houses had been built up right over hills between it and us. Not pretty, I suppose.[94]

Johnson's first novel, *This Bed Thy Centre* (1935), is set around Clapham Common and Battersea and is an attempt, she says in the introduction, 'to tell the truth about a group of people in a London suburb, whose lives were arbitrarily linked'.[95] The opening chapter, 'Locality', tracks the rising sun, gradually illuming, 'over the Common and through the pond', over each character who will figure in the novel.[96] The novel, with a shocking frankness for 1935, observes a cast of young and old working-class characters in cycles of sexual frustration and ignorance, thwarted romance, disappointment, religious mania, grinding work, illness, suicide and just carrying on. Yet, even in the 1930s, there are signs that older working-class Battersea is doomed:

> As the neighbourhood fell with the falling year, so it mounted with the springtime.

'We don't know ourselves', said Parsons, eyeing, from his barrow, a new and ostentatious fruitshop that had opened on the corner of the street.

'No competition in the cat's meat trade', Ma Ditch called, waving a bunch of lights at him. 'They don't put up super pussy butcher's, thank God.'

'We're going to 'ave a new town 'all', said Mrs Parsons, 'all designed modern by a famous architect.'

'They'll make us the capital of England, soon', Parsons observed. 'What about 'Aig Crescent, now they've broadened it? Looks like Regent Street . . .'

'Even the people seem different some'ow'. Ma Ditch sniffed contemptuously. 'Young tart in a fur coat was down 'ere yesterday with 'er dog. "O what a lovely liver", says she, all posh. "Little Bobbykins, thank the lady nicely." Makes me sick.'[97]

Penelope Fitzgerald's *Offshore* (1979) describes a motley barge community berthed at Battersea Reach in the early 1960s. Battersea is shown here as still isolated and eccentric, in an almost Victorian murky and muddy riverscape. A passing pleasure steamer points it all out for the onboard tourists: 'Battersea Reach, ladies and gentlemen. On your right, the artistic colony. Folk live on those boats like they do on the Seine, it's the artist's life they're leading there.'[98] Well, not really, though life is fun for six-year-old Tilda and her older sister Martha, living on the *Grace*: no school, no adult authorities, very few rules; but no pocket money:

Like the rest of London's river children, they knew that the mud was a source of wealth, but they were too shrewd to go into competition with the locals from Partisan Street for coins, medals and lugworms. The lugworms, in any case, Willis had told them, were better on Limehouse Reach. Round about *Grace* herself, the great river deposited little but mounds of plastic containers.

Every expedition meant crossing the Bridge, because the current on Battersea Reach, between the two bridges, sets towards the Surrey side. The responsibility for these outings, which might or might not be successful, had worn between Martha's eyebrows a faint frown . . .

Below the old Church at Battersea the retreating flood had left exposed a wide shelf of mud and gravel. At intervals the dark driftwood lay piled. Near the draw dock some longshore-men had heaped it up and set light to it, to clear the area. Now the thick blue smoke gave out a villainous smell, the gross spirit of salt and fire. Tilda loved that smell, and stretched her nostrils wide.[99]

In his memoir *An Immaculate Mistake* (1990), Paul Bailey recalls a tough working-class Battersea childhood – his dad a road sweeper, his mum a domestic servant – just before the war:

Our new home was almost identical to our old one, now demolished, at the opposite end of the same street. We lived upstairs in the two-storeyed house, in four poky rooms, connected by a landing. The view from the front-room window was of other identical houses – some clean, some not so, as my mother was quick to notice – and beyond them the tall chimneys of the gasworks and the candle factory. From the back bedroom, I saw railway lines, along which goods trains rumbled at night, and an embankment where dandelions bloomed each spring.[100]

Bookish, imaginative (nicknamed 'The Professor', obviously), developing a taste for drama and classical music, slowly realizing he may be 'a pansy', Bailey recalls the contradictions, confusions, frustrations and humour of working-class Battersea. It is defined by deference, caution, bizarre rules and ancient wisdom codified into odd sayings ('there's boys, and then there's boys'), and an obsession with demonstrating cleanliness achieved in such grimy conditions (the 'immaculate' of the title). Young Bailey must not stand out in any way:

I did not, could not, reveal that I was what they call a pansy. They would not have believed me anyway. I came from working stock, and my ancestors had toiled long and hard to make a humble living. It was common knowledge that pansies were the sons of the idle rich, who had nothing better to do than to be waited on, hand and foot . . . You wouldn't find a pansy in our part of London. Across the river, yes, in Kensington – where it was pointed out to me, the Central School was situated – but not here in Battersea.

I was a Battersea pansy, wary of displaying his true colours in the sunlight. I belonged, as did so many others of the same peculiar genus, in the shade.[101]

John Walsh, in *The Falling Angels* (1999), his memoir of growing up on Battersea Rise in the later 1950s and the '60s, points out how E. M. Forster would be appalled if he could see what had become of the place where his great-aunt, Marianne Thornton, had lived in that grand villa:

> The Battersea end of Clapham Common was a dump, a service area for Clapham Junction: the busiest, nosiest and dirtiest railway junction in the country. It was a stridently working-class and immigrant neighbourhood then; a tough, coarse-grained part of inner suburbia. The skinhead phenomenon of the late sixties started around the Junction, where gangs of forty or fifty bald adolescents with braces and Doc Marten boots would congregate, before marauding across the Common in search of homosexuals, hippies and (later on) Asian youths to bash up.[102]

The Walshes, though originally Irish immigrants, didn't fit in, being the *wrong kind* of Irish immigrants. They were middle class and aspirational (GP father, private school and music lessons for the kids), not the hard-drinking, raucous, labouring Irish of fable, and so were out of place between the various types of local population: indigenous white cockneys, black and Asian immigrants, the Polish and Irish working classes:

> It would have been pleasant to grow up in a town, or to feel oneself becoming part of a town; but we weren't a town. We weren't a village. We were barely a district. We were just an artery, a migratory conduit, just as England had mutated into 'Airstrip One' in Orwell's *Nineteen Eighty-Four*. Huge, coughing trucks, immense Italian juggernauts, transporters carrying cages of new and reconstituted cars from Dagenham and Cowley to London dealers came wheezing and crashing up the Rise each night . . . making my whole bed shake.[103]

Walsh complains that this was *his* 1960s London: 'not all London was swinging. Battersea certainly wasn't, despite *Up the Junction*.'[104] Nell Dunn's sketches of grimly hedonistic Battersea working-class life on the cusp of affluence, first published in 1963, caused an uproar when a BBC TV version, directed by Ken Loach, was shown in *The Wednesday Play* slot in 1965. A film version, directed by Peter Collinson, followed in 1968 and a tie-in edition of the book was promoted with the tagline 'Innocence in Battersea lasts as long as the flower remains unsooted by the power station'. Here the narrator, Lily (like Dunn herself) comes across from Chelsea to Clapham Junction, drinking and hanging out with Sylvie and Rube and working in the local sweet factory. This is a narrowly confined, cockney landscape of small and dirty factories and factory work, noisy pubs, overcrowded terraces, meagre street markets, ancient poverty and much casual violence and petty criminality. Dunn offers to show us this place, we, the reader looking over the narrator's shoulder:

> We are at a party in a block of LCC flats: plates of ham sandwiches, crates of brown ale and Babycham, the radiogram in the lounge, pop-song oblivion with the volume knob turned to full . . .
>
> Rube, face deadpan, dances the Madison, brown velvet skirt, red patent sling-backs.
>
> The record finishes. She whispers in my ear, 'Isn't he a darlin'? I don't half fancy a snog tonight.' Her black hair hangs long and thick. 'He's a couchty-mouch. After going steady for six months you get a bit fed up, snoggin' with the same bloke every night. And I've noticed when we're out Terry'll start staring at some other bird. He'll say to me, "You all right, love?" And then his eyes will wander off and get affixiated on some silly cow. "What are you lookin' at then?" I says. "Am I so borin'?"'
>
> The thick-set fellow comes over and holds out a hand to Rube. 'You Romeo' she says, following him onto the floor, a faint smell of hair-oil and a brown suit.
>
> Out on the concrete balcony dusky Fulham stretches away.[105]

But this is also now a place, though still restrictive, beginning to be transformed by consumerism and the sexual revolution. What is new here is a breezy sexual frankness. The young women are assertive, confident and sexually adventurous. They work, go shopping, go out drinking and dancing, go out with who they like:

> We were crushed in the toilets. All round girls smeared on pan-stick.
>
> 'I can't go with him, he's too short.'
>
> 'All the grey glitter I put on me hair come off on his cheek and I hadn't the heart to tell him.'
>
> 'I wouldn't mind goin' with a married man 'cept I couldn't abear him goin' home and gettin' into bed with his wife.'
>
> 'Me hair all right?'
>
> 'Yeah, lend us yer lacquer.'
>
> 'Now don't get pissin' off and leavin' me.' Rube pulled at her mauve skirt so it clung to her haunches and stopped short of her round knees.
>
> Outside revving bikes were splitting the night.
>
> 'Where we going?'
>
> 'Let's go swimmin' up the Common.'
>
> 'We aint got no swim-suits with us.'
>
> 'We'll swim down one end and you down the other. It's dark, ain't it?'[106]

Battersea's reputation as a tough, working-class suburb is foregrounded in Michael de Larrabeiti's children's books featuring the Borribles, first published in 1976. The Borribles live, secretly, in Battersea Park and are a combination of sprites or mischievous elves, thieving opportunist Victorian street urchins and street gangs. They are skinny, feral, with 'sharp faces', burning eyes and quick wits, live outside the law, move in the dark and shadows, their telltale pointy elf ears hidden by woolly hats or ratty long hair. Borribles, in fact, are a mutation, an adaptation of abandoned or neglected human children, those who run away or have been labelled 'unmanageable'. These kids disappear, everyone thinking they must have been put into care, when in fact they they've been 'borribled'. These are, of course, Battersea's very own proletarian rivals to Wimbledon's cute, helpful, civic-minded Wombles; here renamed 'Rumbles'. As the series opens, in *The Borribles*, we see a 'Rumble', way off course, trapped in Battersea Park:

Timbucktoo shook himself free of the two Borribles and, though his hands were bound, he got to his feet and glared haughtily down his snout, his red eyes blazing.

'Why I'm fwom Wumbledon of course, you dirty little tykes. You'd better welease me before you get into sewious twouble.'

'I knew it', said Knocker turning to Lightfinger with excitement. 'A Rumble from Rumbledon. Ain't it strange as how they can't pronounce their *r*s?'

'So that's a Rumble', said Lightfinger with interest. 'I've often wondered what they looked like – bloody ugly' . . .

'You wevolting little stweet-awabs', the Rumble had lost his temper, 'how dare you tweat me in this fashion?'

''Cos you're on our manor, that's how, you twat', said Knocker angrily.[107]

In this first novel of the trilogy, a group of Borribles set off on an accurately plotted journey, undetected, across southwest London, down backstreets, across canals, through parks and waste land to attack the tiresome Rumbles on their own turf at Wimbledon.

Lanchester's anti-hero in *Mr Phillips* drops into Battersea Park on his aimless, time-filling perambulations around southwest and central London. Faced with the overwhelming chaos and randomness of the universe, typified here by the busy Battersea Park commotion of cyclists and skaters, parading peacocks, earnest joggers and shrieking boaters, Mr Phillips resorts to a double-entry bookkeeping system, his favourite method of establishing control: 'Now, walking in Battersea Park, Mr Phillips feels the long-suppressed need to draw up a tranquilising double-entry. The thing to imagine was that the park suddenly ceased to function as a going concern, and all its assets and liabilities were frozen in the moment of disposal.'[108] He also sits on a park bench, sneakily ogling some young women playing tennis:

Mr Phillips concentrates his attention on the girls while pretending to pay attention to the other two pairs – in other words, he holds his head pointing in one direction while secretly keeping his eyes on the middle. One girl's dress rides up when she serves, to show a glimpse of leg all the way up to her bum. Her legs and arms are the colour of Weetabix. She's blonde and has a pony tail which flaps around her head and shoulders as she moves. Mr Phillips wonders if they change ends after two games and if so whether he has the nerve to stay around long enough to get a better look at the darker girl.

'It's Wimbledon that brings them out', says a man beside Mr Phillips.[109]

The man turns out to be a creepy pornographer ('magazine publishing, Top Shelf'), trawling the park for 'basic research'.

In Kate Pullinger's 1989 novel *When the Monster Dies*, mostly set in Vauxhall, Australian couple Irene and Karl are working, as electrician and designer respectively, on a refurbishment of the defunct Battersea Power Station. The couple turn out to be unlikely anarchist cultural terrorists and decide to blow up the building as a protest against the mighty industrial landmark being turned into a tacky theme park (as was one of the plans at the time). On the night of the blast, Karl phones a warning through to the building and they drag their friends out to Vauxhall Bridge to watch:

> When they were halfway across the bridge Karl suddenly shouted 'Stop!' and turned towards the river. Battersea Power Station stood bulky and solid on the horizon, its chimneys like Stonehenge on Salisbury Plain. They pause and waited. Mary held her breath. And then in silence, the northeast corner of the building began to crumble. As though in slow motion, one chimney fell like a great pine. Clouds of dust billowed and then flames shot up as the interior began to burn. The sound came too late, booming and echoing down the river, like the roar of a great wounded beast. Mary began to cry and Finn put his arm round her. Bits of the building continued to fall.[110]

Wandsworth

Wandsworth, just to the southwest of Battersea and directly west of Clapham, takes its name from the Wandle, another of London's lost rivers (and mentioned in Izaak Walton's 1653 *The Compleat Angler* for its stunning variety of fish). The river powered numerous mills, and the area soon became industrialized (textiles, hats, metalworks, milling and brewing) and the river, of course, heavily polluted. In the nineteenth century, as with neighbouring Clapham, the attraction of open pasture and farmland, along with a picturesque common, attracted wealthier villa-building residents. 'Traffic-choked and unattractive', decides Ed Glinert in his *Literary London*, 'Wandsworth has no great literary tradition'.[111]

One unlikely Wandsworth resident was French Enlightenment polymath and genius Voltaire, best known for the satire *Candide*. In May 1726, fearing a lengthy prison sentence for defaming a powerful aristocrat, Voltaire offered to go into exile instead of to the Bastille. Despite his fame Voltaire had very few connections in England: 'I was without a penny, sick to death of a violent ague, a stranger, alone, helpless, in the midst of a city, wherein I was known to nobody.'[112] Luckily, he was then invited to stay at the house of a well-connected and wealthy City silk and wool merchant, Everard Fawkener, with a fine house on the High Street of the village-like Wandsworth. Voltaire wrote home: 'Another London citizen [Fawkener] that I had seen but once in Paris carried me to his own country house, wherein I lead an obscure and charming life . . . without going to London, and quite given over to the pleasures of indolence and friendship.'[113]

Graham Swift's debut novel, *The Sweet Shop Owner* (1980), is set in Sydenham and Wandsworth. The novel chronicles unchanging suburban domestic, personal and commercial routines, from the late 1930s up to Willy Chapman's death, the day of the novel's action, in 1974: 'How monotonously, how anonymously those years passed.'[114] The suburb is familiar and strange at the same time. Chapman notices how, while there is 'nothing new', 'everything was eternally new'.[115] He describes it all to his absent estranged daughter:

You can see it all from here, Dorry. The world ahead of you. Down there on the right, the stretch of High Street where it flanks the common. Traffic lights beyond. Then the railway bridge: green sign with a white arrow pointing to the station. Domed roof of the Town Hall, gabled roof of Gibbs' department store. There are the shops, straight ahead, on Common Road, where she used to get all her things; Mason's the butcher's, Cullen's, Henderson's. Beyond them – you could have seen the clock tower once, over the rooftops – the school where my parents toiled to send me. And, far-distant, half-left, poking up from the shoulder of the hill, the grey, ill-proportioned spire of St Stephen's.[116]

Chapman, ill with angina, wanders dazed across the hot suburb on the last day of his life – also his last day as a sweet shop owner as he closes up the shop – the past as vivid as the present, stunned by the passing of time and the frame of everyday routines built to give it meaning:

> The pain in his chest gave little evil prods. He moved to the door, twisted round the plastic sign to 'Closed', released the latch and slipped across the two bolts at the top and bottom.
>   There. It was done.
>   He sat on his stool. No need to hurry. Half-past five. They would be coming home now, in their hordes; work over, pleasure in store. Down at the station the trains would unload from Cannon Street and London Bridge; hot and crumpled commuters, sweaty and fidgety from the stifling carriages, but freed, at last. Across the road the Prince William would open its cool saloons to receive them. The landlord would be blessing the sunshine. Thirsty weather: good for trade. And along the High Street the shops which kept the normal hours would be closing. Business done: life begins.[117]

Balham

Balham, a half-mile south of Clapham on the A24, part of the ancient Roman Stane Street linking London to Chichester, was originally the small village of Belgeham. Like Clapham a place of desirable picturesque landscaped villas in the eighteenth century, Balham gradually filled with richer bankers and merchants, then the middle and working classes slowly arrived, and the open commons and fields were filled with terraces and semis.

Edward Thomas, probably best known as a war poet and for the frequently anthologized 'Adlestrop' ('Yes, I remember Adlestrop') and above all for his nature writing, was actually a suburbanite, born in Battersea and living in his youth on Shelgate Road, Clapham. *The Happy-go-lucky Morgans* (1913) is an autobiographical novel that tells linked stories of 'Abercorran House', the idyllic country house that pre-dates suburban Abercorran Street in Balham. 'My story', it opens, 'is of Balham and of a family dwelling in Balham who were more Welsh than Balhamitish'.[118] The story starts as the narrator recalls the older house, now gone, but once set in a fondly remembered deep countryside, the rolling rural landscape becoming regularized suburbia: 'Abercorran Street is straight, flat, symmetrically lined on both sides by four-bedroomed houses in pairs, and it runs at right angles out of Harrington Road into another road which the pair of four-bedroomed houses visible at the corner proclaim to be exactly like it.'[119]

The narrator conjures his idyllic pre-suburban Balham childhood centred on the family and their servants, the rambling, thrilling house with its library, huge kitchen and the room

> without a name which was full of fishing-rods, walking-sticks, guns, traps, the cross-bow, boxes of skins, birds' eggs, papers . . . its four-and-twenty elms that stood about the one oak in the long grass and buttercups and docks, like a pleasant company slowly and unwillingly preparing to leave that three-acre field which was the garden of Abercorran House and called by us The Wilderness – a name now immortalised, because the christener of streets has given it to the one beyond Abercorran Street.[120]

The countryside is now covered over and unrecognizable:

> Today the jackdaws at least, if they ever fly that way, can probably not distinguish Abercorran Street and Wilderness Street from ordinary streets. For the trees are every one of them gone, and with them the jackdaws. The lilies and carp are no longer in the pond, and there is no pond. I can understand people cutting down trees – it is a trade and brings profit – but not draining a pond in such a garden as the Wilderness and taking all its carp home to fry in the same fat as bloaters, all for the sake of building a house that might just as well have been anywhere or nowhere at all. I think No. 23 Wilderness Street probably has the honour and misfortune to stand in the pond's place, but they call it Lyndhurst.[121]

The last servant to leave the old house, now in temporary stasis before demolition and suburbia arrives, the trusty and wise Ann, while recalling 'those days', reassures that the Balham of the present is also a great place:

> It would be blasphemous to suppose that God ever made
> any but the best of worlds – not a better, but a different one,
> suitable for different people than we are now, you understand,
> not better, for that is impossible, say I, who have lived in
> Abercorran – town, house, and street – these sixty years – there
> is not a better world.[122]

In Ian McEwan's 2001 novel *Atonement*, Briony Tallis walks from
St Thomas' Hospital down to Balham to seek absolution from her
estranged sister Cecilia. Uncertain whether to continue or not, she
walks back, 'retracing her steps, in the direction of Clapham High
Street'.[123] She decides to go on. The following marks her perception
of Balham:

> She left the café, and as she walked along the Common she felt
> the distance widen between her and another self, no less real,
> who was walking back towards the hospital. Perhaps the Briony
> who was walking in the direction of Balham was the imagined
> or ghostly persona. This unreal feeling was heightened when,
> after half an hour, she reached another High Street, more or less
> the same as the one she had left behind. That was all London
> beyond its centre, an agglomeration of dull little towns. She
> made a resolution to never live in any of them.[124]

Later we realize that none of this actually happened, that Briony
did not walk to Balham to seek forgiveness from her sister, and that
Cecilia was probably killed in the Balham tube disaster of October
1940 when, during the Blitz, a huge bomb hit the station, killing 64
people sheltering there.

The comedy sketch 'Balham, Gateway to the South', originally
written for a radio show in 1949 by Frank Muir and Denis Norden,
narrated by Peter Sellers, but best known from its appearance on
his 1958 LP *The Best of Sellers*, satirizes the breezy and bombastic U.S.
travelogue commentaries of the day (Balham becoming 'Bal-Ham'),
and presents the suburb as an eccentric mix of quaint odd customs
and peculiar locals:

> Bal-ham! Gateway to the South! We enter Balham through the
> verdant grasslands of Battersea Park, and at once we are aware

that here is a land of happy, contented people who go about their daily tasks in truly democratic spirit.

This is busy High Street, focal point of the town's activities. Note the quaint old stores, whose frontages are covered with hand-painted inscriptions, every one a rare example of native Balham art. Let us read some of them as our camera travels past [all done in silly voices].

'Cooking apples! Choice eaters!'
'A Song to Remember at the Tantamount Cinema!'
'A suit to remember at Montague Moss!'
'Cremations conducted with decorum and taste.'
'Frying tonight. Bring your own paper.'
'Rally Thursday, Berkeley Square. Viscountess Lewisham and Mrs Gerald Legge. Up the ruling classes!'

We now enter old Balham. Time has passed by this remote corner. So shall we.

Tooting

Half a mile further south along the A24, Balham blends into Tooting Bec and then Tooting. Tooting, undeveloped and open, and not too far from London, became a popular location for those institutions and buildings increasingly expelled from London: asylums (the Surrey County Pauper Lunatic Asylum), two 'fever hospitals', and workhouses. Tooting's Infant Pauper Asylum became the centre of a notorious scandal in 1849, when 148 children died of cholera within two weeks at the overcrowded, gimcrack institution. Charles Dickens was outraged by this, as he mentions in an investigative essay, 'A Walk in a Workhouse' (1850).

And this conveys no special imputation on the workhouse of the parish of St. So-and-So, where, on the contrary, I saw many things to commend. It was very agreeable, recollecting that most infamous and atrocious enormity committed at Tooting – an enormity which, a hundred years hence, will still be vividly remembered in the byways of English life, and which has done more to engender a gloomy discontent and suspicion among many thousands of the people than all the Chartist leaders could have done in all their lives.[125]

Thomas Hardy, known for creating the fictional territory of Wessex, spent much time living in London suburbia, and some of that, from 1878 to 1881, in Trinity Road, Tooting. Hardy was fairly well known at the time, having already published *Far from the Madding Crowd* and having completed *The Return of the Native*. The curious work 'The Early Life of Thomas Hardy' (seemingly a biographic work by Hardy's second wife but actually ghosted by Hardy himself from diaries and memos) notes that he had 'decided that the practical side of his vocation of novelist demanded that he should have his head-quarters in or near London'.[126] Mark Ford, in his study of Hardy's unlikely London years, *Thomas Hardy: Half a Londoner*, sets the scene:

> It was close to Wandsworth Common railway station, with its regular service into Victoria – as well as, more ominously, the Surrey County Pauper Lunatic Asylum (founded in 1840). The suburban streets of the area were still somewhat raw, having been laid out in the previous two decades, as London's suburban railway network expanded . . . Tooting must have seemed, like Surbiton, a suitable compromise between the urban and the rural.[127]

Thirty years later, Tooting features in the poem 'Beyond the Last Lamp (Near Tooting Common)', describing miserable lovers (Hardy was very miserable in his marriage for years).

> While rain, with eve in partnership,
> Descended darkly, drip, drip, drip,
> Beyond the last lone lamp I passed
> Walking slowly, whispering sadly,
> Two linked loiterers, wan, downcast:
> Some heavy thought constrained each face,
> And blinded them to time and place.[128]

Critic J. Hillis Miller, in an essay on Hardy, argues for the importance of Tooting as a real place. 'The function of the circumstantial subtitle of "Beyond the Last Lamp"', Miller argues,

> is, among other things, to invite the reader to try out for it out for herself or himself. It is as though the subtitle were saying:

'Tooting Common exists. It is a real place to be found on any map of the region. Go there on a rainy night and see for yourself. If you find the right lane and go beyond the last lamp you will find the sad lovers still pacing back and forth there. Or at any rate you will do so if you have read this poem.' And who could say that this would not be the case? Go and see for yourself.[129]

Kit Wright, in an echo of W. B. Yeats's desire for a remembered quiet spot in the famed 'The Lake Isle of Innisfree', eulogizes Tooting in a 2000 poem, 'A Love Song of Tooting'. Tooting is a place of contentment and contemplation, of allotments in which to spend tranquil summers. In this place, 'The blackbird's *obbligato* / fulfils its liquid line'.[130]

'Crickleden', approximating the area of Tooting, is the location of the Pentecostal church and rectory of St Mary's in A. N. Wilson's comic novel *My Name Is Legion* (2004).

London goes to sleep early, and in bad weather – it had been bad weather for months – Londoners keep indoors . . . Where the suburban sprawls of south London began, the air of absolute desertion outside was complete, though tower blocks and, in streets lined with trees, upstairs windows still burned their electric bulbs. Five miles south, and west, of the Queen and Buckingham Palace and Westminster lay the unplanned ugliness and sprawl of Crickleden. Go past the deserted clock tower at the end of the High Road, walk as if you are going to Crickleden Junction and you will come to a huge Calvary, the white, tortured figure of the crucified Christ disturbingly realistic in the neon street-lit glare; and beside it, a noticeboard which reads SHRINE OF OUR LADY OF CRICKLEDEN. And behind it, looming up into the rain and the blackened sky, is the huge barn-like church.[131]

Streatham

Directly east of Tooting and around a mile south of Brixton on the A223, Streatham developed primarily because of its place on the key route through to Croydon and on down to the south coast. Like

Clapham and Balham, Streatham attracted rich City merchants with a taste for rural living, who, aided by a regular coach service along the new turnpikes, built a string of huge villas and mansions there.

One of these proto-suburban grandees was brewer and Southwark MP Ralph Thrale, who purchased 89 acres and built a mansion, Streatham Park, in grounds overlooking Streatham Common. Later, his son, Henry Thrale, and his wife Hester, invited down key artistic and literary figures of the day, including Edmund Burke, Joshua Reynolds, Frances ('Fanny') Burney and, most frequently of all, Samuel Johnson. Twelve portraits of the Thrales' most esteemed guests painted by Reynolds were hung in the dining room: Burney called them the 'Streatham Worthies'.

Johnson seems to have been attracted by the house itself, its excellent table, the prestigious company, the walks across the park and through the Surrey countryside. As he wrote to Hester Thrale in March 1779, from Lichfield: 'You do not think it much makes me forget Streatham. However it is good to wander a little, lest one should dream that all the world was Streatham, of which one may venture to say, none but itself can be its parallel.'[132]

His dogged companion and biographer James Boswell argued that the Streatham years were beneficial:

Nothing could be more fortunate for Johnson than this connection. He had at Mr Thrale's all the comforts and even luxuries of life; his melancholy was diverted, and his irregular habits lessened by association with an agreeable and well-ordered family. He was treated with the utmost respect, and even affection. The vivacity of Mrs Thrale's literary talk roused him to cheerfulness and exertion, even when they were alone. But this was not often the case; for he found here a constant succession of what gave him the highest enjoyment, the society of the learned, the witty, and the eminent in every way, who were assembled in numerous companies, called forth his wonderful powers, and gratified him with admiration, to which no man could be insensible.[133]

Novelist Frances Burney was very excited to receive a coveted invitation down to Streatham to visit the Thrales, in August 1778:

London, August. – I have now to write an account of the most consequential day I have spent since my birth: namely, my Streatham visit.

Our journey to Streatham was the least pleasant part of the day, for the roads were dreadfully dusty, and I was really in the fidgets from thinking what my reception might be, and from fearing they would expect a less awkward and backward kind of person than I was sure they would find.

Mr Thrale's house is white, and very pleasantly situated, in a fine paddock. Mrs Thrale was strolling about, and came to us as we got out of the chaise.

'Ah,' cried she, 'I hear Dr Burney's voice! and you have brought your daughter? – well, now you are good!'

She then received me, taking both my hands, and with mixed politeness and cordiality welcoming me to Streatham. She led me into the house, and addressed herself almost wholly for a few minutes to my father, as if to give me an assurance she did not mean to regard me as a show, or to distress or frighten me by drawing me out. Afterwards she took me up stairs, and shewed me the house, and said she had very much wished to see me at Streatham, and should always think herself much obliged to Dr Burney for his goodness in bringing me, which she looked upon as a very great favour.[134]

Later she meets Dr Johnson himself:

'No,' answered Mrs Thrale, 'he will sit by you, which I am sure will give him great pleasure.'

Soon after we were seated, this great man entered. I have so true a veneration for him, that the very sight of him inspires me with delight and reverence, notwithstanding the cruel infirmities to which he is subject; for he has almost perpetual convulsive movements, either of his hands, lips, feet, or knees, and sometimes of all together.

Mrs Thrale introduced me to him, and he took his place. We had a noble dinner, and a most elegant dessert. Dr Johnson, in the middle of dinner, asked Mrs Thrale what was in some little pies that were near him.

'Mutton,' answered she, 'so I don't ask you to eat any, because I know you despise it.'

'No, madam, no,' cried he, 'I despise nothing that is good of its sort; but I am too proud now to eat of it. Sitting by Miss Burney makes me very proud to-day!'

'Miss Burney,' said Mrs Thrale, laughing, 'you must take great care of your heart if Dr Johnson attacks it; for I assure you he is not often successless.'

'What's that you say, madam?' cried he; 'are you making mischief between the young lady and me already?'

A little while after he drank Miss Thrale's health and mine, and then added: ''Tis a terrible thing that we cannot wish young ladies well, without wishing them to become old women!'

'But some people,' said Mr Seward, 'are old and young at the same time, for they wear so well that they never look old.'

'No, sir, no,' cried the Doctor, laughing; 'that never yet was; you might as well say they are at the same time tall and short. I remember an epitaph to that purpose, which is in –

(I have quite forgot what, – and also the name it was made upon, but the rest I recollect exactly:)

'– lies buried here;
So early wise, so lasting fair,
That none, unless her years you told,
Thought her a child, or thought her old.'[135]

Streatham Spa, the water first discovered in 1659, attracted many visitors; the mineral water itself was also sold in town, at St Paul's and other sites: recommended dose, 3 cups. George Bell in his 1926 Greater London travelogue *Where London Sleeps* visits Streatham Spa (in its later, Georgian-built form) and is amazed at the modernity of the operation, overseen by the Ministry of Health.

That morning I had Streatham Spa to myself, and all its memories. No human being was in sight. That did not look as if much business was doing, in these days when we have lost the faith of our forefathers; but there was a bell, and a ring brought the attendant Hebe. Yes, the water was still on sale, and I had my glass of it freshly drawn by the maid of the well, finding it mildly warm, bright and by no means unpleasant to the taste

. . . To reach the well you strike away left from the highway
on which the trams and buses journey just before sighting the
police station, go down Sunnyhill Road and up over the rise,
to descend again to the Valley Road. These directions may be
necessary, for there is no announcement made, and were you
to ask that common source of all information, a policeman, for
Streatham Spa he might stare, wondering: never had he seen it
on his beat. It is the last of London's suburban spas to be kept
open for the public service (did they know it?) when, one after
another, all the others have closed down.[136]

Carolyn Steedman, in her autobiographical study *Landscape for
a Good Woman* (1987), recalls a working-class Streatham post-war
childhood of straitened circumstances and semi-poverty:

Upstairs, a long time ago, she had cried, standing on the bare
floorboards in the front bedroom just after we moved to this
house in Streatham Hill in 1951, my baby sister in her carry-cot.
We both watched the dumpy retreating figure of the health
visitor through the curtainless windows. The woman had said:
'This house isn't fit for a baby'. And then she stopped crying,
my mother, got by, the phrase that picks up after all difficulty
(it says: it's like this; it shouldn't be like this; it's unfair; I'll
manage): 'Hard lines, eh, Kay?'[137]

Steedman is particularly sharp on her aspirational mother's frustration and anger at never having enough money, at being forced to
save and make do, especially as the new consumerism and affluence
is glimpsed in and around 1950s south London. Steedman finds out
that Streatham in fact has a literary pedigree, one that applies to her
own experience:

When I was about seventeen I learned that V. S. Naipaul had
written *A House for Mr Biswas* in Streatham Hill, a few streets
away from where we lived . . . But for my mother, as for Mr
Biswas, the house was valuable in itself because of what it
represented of the social world; a place of safety, wealth and
position, a closed door, a final resting place. It was a real dream
that dictated the patterns of our days.[138]

Kingsley Amis, born in Norbury (just south of Streatham), often expresses his revulsion at the south London suburbs. Of Norbury, in a BBC interview, he remarks:

> My roots? Well, there aren't any, because Norbury is a non-place. It was originally just a railway station put up in the nineteenth century when they were extending its lines to the coast. So it is not really a place, it's an expression on a map really. I should say I came from Norbury station.[139]

Amis's late novel *Stanley and the Women* (1984) describes a trip through south London in his sporty Apfelsine car, towards a hospital somewhere near Shooter's Hill, and notes the crucial difference between a place and an area:

> It was raining busily away when I started on my disagreeable journey. I took the Apfelsine through the middle – straight down the hill, along past the office, across Blackfriars Bridge, to the Elephant and into the Old Kent Road . . . South of the river I was on home ground, or not far off. By the time I got to New Cross I had come to within five miles of where I had been born and brought up.
>
> For all I knew, this part and that part had been different then, built at different times with different ideas, anyhow not interchangeable. That was no longer so, if it ever had been, unless perhaps you happened to have an eye for churches. Not that I cared, of course – I had left South London for good as soon as I had the chance. And yet in a sense what I saw from the Apfelsine was the same as ever, was cramped, thrown up on the cheap and never finished off, needing a lick of paint, half empty and everywhere soiled, in fact very like my old part as noticed when travelling to and from an uncle's funeral a few weeks back. Half the parts south of the river were never proper places at all, just collections of assorted buildings filling up gaps and named after railway stations and bus garages. Most people I knew seemed to come from a place – Cliff Wainwright and I got out of an area.[140]

5 'UNCONGENIAL NEIGHBOURS'

Outer Southwest London: From Wimbledon to
Putney, Mortlake, Richmond, Twickenham, Teddington,
Kingston, Shepperton, Surbiton, New Malden and
Worcester Park

The outer southwest suburbs, from Kew to Kingston, notably along the Thames, are presented in much early London writing as stylized and picturesque pastoral delights. Home to Alexander Pope, Robert Walpole and James Thomson, among others, the place provided, close to London, an unspoilt river, woodland, meadows, vast parks, rolling hills – and a refuge, a neoclassical idealized arcadia. Thomson in particular eulogized the area, as his 'vale of bliss', with its 'dales, woods, lawns' and 'softly-swelling hills'. A Victorian commemorative plaque to Thomson (who unfortunately seems to have been taken ill and died after being out on his beloved river a little too much), put up at Pembroke Lodge in Richmond Park, states:

Ye who from London's smoke and turmoil fly,
To seek a purer air and brighter sky,
Think of the Bard who dwelt in yonder dell
Who sang so sweetly what he loved so well.

The craze for castellated riverside 'Gothic' villas, underground mosaiced grots and sickly nymphs is nicely satirized by Thomas Love Peacock, whose nouveau riche Ebenezer Mac Crotchet builds a 'Crotchet Castle' in the novel of that name (1831). Jerome K. Jerome also gently mocks the false 'Heritage' Englishness of the mazy river, the hazy history, the endless pubs and beds all supposedly frequented by 'Good Queen Bess', as if going slowly upriver is somehow tantamount to travelling back in time, to mythic English history at Runnymede, Windsor and so on. J. G Ballard, further upstream in his Shepperton

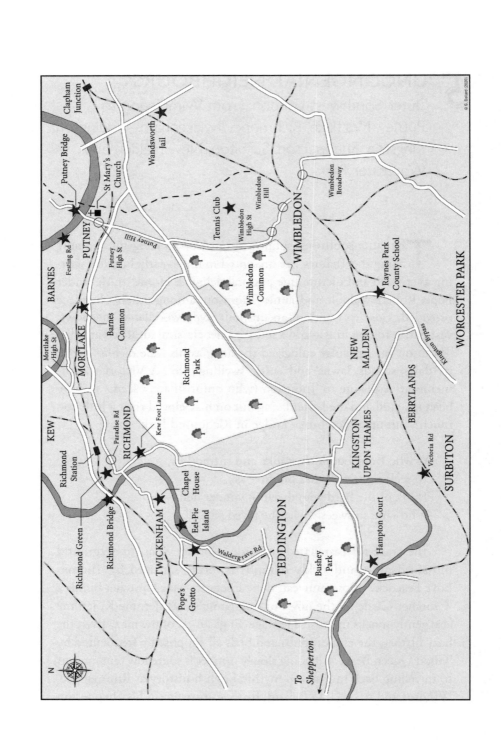

semi, also of course revels in the fantasy versions of England on show, his one composed of dull TV-drenched afternoons, local shops, motorway infrastructure, airports, retail parks – and the film studios where 'real' versions of his remembered Shanghai childhood, of *Empire of the Sun* (1984), are painstakingly recreated.

Wimbledon

Wimbledon, around 8 miles southwest of central London, starts as a village straggling around St Mary's church (there has been a church on the site since the eleventh century). The High Street was developed from the original medieval village through the eighteenth century, and then the railway, arriving, early for south London, in 1838, and being built down the steep hill, inaugurated much later nineteenth-century suburban growth. This split of older 'village' and newer 'town' remains locally significant. After a landmark victory over Earl Spencer's attempt to table a private parliamentary bill to have the whole of Wimbledon Common enclosed, parcelled up and sold, this remains the largest expanse of heathland in Greater London. Wimbledon remains, as Ed Glinert warns in his *Literary London*, 'Expensive, snooty and culturally moribund' and not known for anything much outside the annual tennis tournament.[1]

In 1803 a fifteen-year-old Arthur Schopenhauer, later notorious as the profoundly pessimistic philosopher of Will, accompanied his parents on a long tour of Europe. While the parents visited the Lake District, young Arthur was temporarily enrolled at a typically austere and abusive private boarding school, the Wimbledon School for Young Noblemen and Gentlemen. Schopenhauer was properly miserable in Wimbledon, and would always think of it as an incarceration. His biographer David Cartwright notes that:

> Despite the advantages Arthur enjoyed as a special boarder, the strained and uninspiring atmosphere of Wimbledon School must have been particularly difficult. He was disposed to being boisterous, independent, and curious, and he had a propensity for entering into quarrels, both intellectual and physical. It is difficult to imagine that his character would have suffered transformations into that of a quiet, demure, and obedient student. It is likely, therefore, that he suffered the rod on more

than one occasion and [his mother's] account of the disciplinary practices at Wimbledon School were derived from Arthur's personal experiences. If a student failed to learn a lesson or misbehaved at play, the punishment was to memorize a page of Latin or Greek. If the student failed this, he was sent to Lancaster's office, where he received seven or eight stout blows with the cane. This was done, [his mother] observed, 'with no regard as to whether the boy was six or sixteen, and in a most disgraceful manner'.[2]

The Wimbledon experience seems to have influenced Schopenhauer's notorious atheism, especially his life-long contempt for established religion, church-led education and Christian superstition. As he states in *Parerga and Paralipomena* (1851),

There is no nation which it is so painful to see methodically stupefied by the most degrading blind faith than the English who surpass the others in intelligence. The root of the evil is that there is no ministry of public instruction and hence that this has hitherto remained entirely in the hands of the parsons. These have taken good care that two-thirds of the nation shall not be able to read and write; in fact, from time to time, they have even have the audacity with the most ludicrous presumption to yelp at the natural sciences. It is, therefore, a human duty to smuggle into England, through every conceivable channel, light, liberal-mindedness, and science, so that those best-fed of all priests may have their business brought to an end.[3]

In Michael Frayn's 1967 Fleet Street-set comic novel *Towards the End of the Morning*, John Dyson and his wife Jannie, with two children, definitely decide that they do not 'want to live in the suburbs, in an ugly house with uncongenial suburban neighbours miles from town'.[4] They decide, then, to try and find a less expensive Georgian or Regency house in an ideal ungentrified location, not exactly in the centre of London but not too far out either. Forever on the edge of their vision, the harder they look, the more this kind of place vanishes. They land, at last, somewhere that sounds like Wimbledon:

Little by little they made concessions to themselves, swinging from each last concession to reach the next. They decided that they were prepared to settle for an Early Victorian house, provided it was central. Then they agreed that they were prepared to go a little way out, provided they could find an Early Victorian house. Like Tarzan swinging himself from branch to branch through the jungle, Dyson and his wife swung themselves farther and farther out from the centre of London, and farther and farther on through the nineteenth century, until they arrived at the year 1887, and number 43 Spadina Road, s.w.23. Here the descending curve of demand at last met the unyielding base-line of supply. Looked at in one way, what they had acquired was an ugly suburban house with uncongenial neighbours, miles from town, which had cost all the money they could raise by mortgage, plus all the savings and borrowings they had intended to use for modernization and repair. But they didn't look at it in that way. And in any case, the uncongenial neighbours would soon be driven out by the great influx of congenial architects, journalists, civil servants, and university lecturers who would come flooding in to follow the Dysons' example.[5]

We know this will not end well. And, of course, 'the middle classes did not come to Spadina Rd, s.w.23.' In addition, where liberal, right-thinking Dyson prides himself on being 'entirely in favour of both the working classes and West Indians', in reality his new neighbours do not make his life any easier: 'the particular West Indians and working classes living next door to him seemed to be very hard to get to know'.[6] In a novel very much concerned with the effects of entropy, the inevitable tendency of the universe to become disordered and chaotic, the Dyson house is on the front line:

God had his eye on the house, there was no doubt about it. Slowly but surely he was gathering it to his bosom. He was coming in through the walls as rain, up from the ground as rising damp, down through the chimney as birds, and moving in mysterious ways throughout the fabric as dry rot, green mould, mice, and earwigs. Dyson won brief tactical advantages with Polyfilla and emulsion paint, only to find that God had accomplished some vast strategic infiltration behind his back. The sad truth, Dyson realized, was that it was an unfair fight.[7]

Nigel Williams has set a sequence of comic novels, and a set of short stories, in Wimbledon. *The Wimbledon Poisoner* (1990), the first of the 'Wimbledon Trilogy', concerns one Henry Farr, who decides to murder his wife for no good reason than 'simply that he could think of no other way of prolonging her absence from him indefinitely'. Williams's Wimbledon here is a landscape familiar from endless clichés: curtain-twitching, sexually repressed, obsessive, fussy, eccentric and banal. It is full of stock characters, racist, sexist, unimaginative, frustrated, and usually seen from a soured, aggrieved white, male middle-class viewpoint. Farr is a suburban everyman, awkward, disappointed, repressed, clumsy, permanently irritated, misanthropic, 'English' in a very old-fashioned way, pointlessly writing a 'Complete History of Wimbledon'. The joke here is that timid Farr could plan and execute murder – in Wimbledon, of all places. Wimbledon is both dull and weird:

> The lights were on in all the houses up Maple Drive. At number 23 the Indian was seated, motionless, in his bay window. On the top floor of 32, Mrs Mackintosh stared nervously out at the dark street. Mrs Mackintosh had Alzheimer's disease. 'Has my husband gone out now?' the expression on her face seemed to say. 'Or is he due back at any moment?' . . . At 49 all the curtains were drawn and at 51 Mrs Archer had left the front door open, perhaps in the hope that Mr Archer would return.[8]

Henry's task is to closely observe locals and their habitat:

> He turned right into Caldecott Road, left into Howard's Avenue, right on to Mainwaring Road and up the wide thoroughfare that led to Wimbledon Hill. In all these streets, thick with lime trees, estate agents' boards and large, clean cars, there were no people to be seen at all. Henry knew all the houses – the double-fronted mansion with the Mercedes in the driveway, the row of early Victorian workmen's cottages, fastidiously repaired, the occasional bungalow or mock Gothic affair with turrets – he knew what each was worth,

and he followed their fortunes, decay, repair, sale, in the way a countryman might watch the seasons.[9]

Occasionally, more serious undercurrents are noted in Williams. In the story 'Keep Wimbledon White', new Asian arrivals, the Maliks, have racist graffiti sprayed on their house:

> After two weeks his house looked like a parcel that had been readdressed to the point of illegibility. Whoever was leading the campaign had scrawled on almost every available square of brickwork. On the garage roof they had written WE DON'T WANT PAKKY BARSTIDS HERE and on the path aerosolled the legend OUR KIDS WANT TO SPEKE ENGLISH, to which Hanif [Malik] responded, 'the man has a point! There are clearly too many wogs here. You can't even speak your own language anymore!'[10]

It turns out that Hanif Malik himself is the culprit, stirring up sympathy, burning down his own house to collect the insurance, then moving on to do the same in another unsuspecting suburb: 'He winked and placed his finger to his nose. "Keep Wimbledon White! I say," he chuckled, "and turn Virginia Water brown. I've got three acres and a swimming pool. Come down and bring that delightful family with you."'[11]

Louis de Bernières' 1999 play for radio *Sunday Morning at the Centre of the World* is inspired by Dylan Thomas's *Under Milk Wood*, and partly recalls the author's time spent living above a shop in Earlsfield (adjacent to Wimbledon: between the tennis club and Wandsworth prison). The play attempts to excavate the forgotten pasts and the numerous voices overlapping in this unremarkable suburb, as de Bernières explains in his introduction to the published script:

> One can discern the history of a community by following the succession of names on the stones; in Earlsfield cemetery there are the great tombs of Victorian bourgeois, and war graves of Australians who died of wounds upon returning from Gallipoli. One can place the arrival of Poles and West Indians. One can tell when young women stopped dying in childbed, one can tell when it was that young men started to die in motorcycle

crashes, and again when it was that they started to die of drugs. There was another graveyard nearby containing the bones of Huguenots, the people from whom I am descended. I am wedded to the idea that the dead are as much a part of the community as the living, something that perhaps Dylan Thomas also felt. If I were dead, but still aware, I would be frustrated at not being able to address the living, and so I let the dead of Earlsfield speak.

This piece is my farewell embrace to the polymorphous people of Earlsfield.[12]

In Jane Gardam's 1996 story 'The Latter Days of Mr Jones', old Jones is a relic of a different, pre-war age, living on in the Wimbledon house where he was born, prone to spending days sitting on the common and being teased by schoolkids ('now, children wore jeans and hunkish white sand-shoes at all seasons, or they were in track suits and he could not tell if they were boys or girls . . . they were all fat and always eating').[13] Jones is an innocent, an eccentric misfit, with little grasp of contemporary mores. His contact with the kids gets him into terrible trouble: 'He was the mildest of men and seemed unware of anything the children did to him. He said little and drew back beneath his beetle brows, and stared across the Common at things the children had never seen and would never see.'[14]

Though odd Mr Jones doesn't change, Wimbledon does: derelict, then squatted, and then gentrified:

The people in the houses were very different too. There were no servants living in, except for nannies who had apartments on top floors and cars to take the children to school. Husbands were not much in evidence except when out jogging early and late – in their ski-suits. They were called 'partners'. The women Mr Jones thought looked rather like rats. Anxious rats with frightening jobs in the city – or in several cities – and in what seemed to Mr Jones their late middle age they appeared in couture maternity clothes that emphasised their condition so grossly that he had to look away . . . His neighbours told him they could get him more than two million for his house, but he didn't seem to understand.[15]

Neat and predictable Wimbledon, yet punctuated with crime and passion, appears in Graham Swift's *The Light of Day* (2003). Here, semi-disgraced ex-cop George Webb runs a detective agency from an office over Wimbledon Broadway, and the novel obsessively details his restless investigations around sw19, this 'safe-as-houses land where nothing is meant to disturb the peace'.[16] Except, in this case, adultery, violent jealousy, imprisonment and murder:

> The sun feels warm through the windscreen, but the street's full of people hunched in coats, chins buried in scarves. I drive along the Broadway, past the station, towards the Hill. From Wimbledon's lower end (my end) to the snooty village on the hill. Past Worple Road. Then at Woodside I turn right, and then left into St Mary's Road, and I'm into the leafy, looked-after, quiet zone of houses set back from the street, of lawns and drives and hedges and burglar alarms. Rooftops backed by trees . . .
>
> A zone, as you climb the hill, of verges and double garages and wrought iron and speed bumps and private nursery schools. But don't knock it. If you make your living how I do, then make it where they'll pay your fees, and where – with all they've got – they can still (you'd be surprised) do the strangest things.
>
> And don't knock it anyway. This home-and-garden land, this never-never land where nothing much is ever meant to happen. These Wimbledons and Chislehursts. What else is civilization for?[17]

Putney

North of Wimbledon, and stretching up to the loop in the Thames as it rounds Fulham, Putney has an Anglo-Saxon-derived name and appears in the Domesday Book. Famed for its delicious salmon (until the nineteenth century) and its ferry, from the sixteenth century Putney became a popular location for courtiers and wealthier merchants, eager for a riverside location close to town. In H. G. Wells's novel *Tono-Bungay* (1909), George Ponderevo, as he travels the entire length of the tidal Thames, muses on the unique character of this southwest Thameside suburban London (especially as Bromley, Wells's home town, is, on the contrary, considered 'a boundless world of dingy people').[18]

To run down the Thames so is to run one's hand over the pages
in the book of England from end to end. One begins in Craven
Reach and it is as if one were in the heart of old England.
Behind us are Kew and Hampton Court with their memories
of Kings and Cardinals, and one runs at first between Fulham's
episcopal garden parties and Hurlingham's playground for the
sport instinct of our race. The whole effect is English. There
is space, there are old trees, and all the best qualities of the
homeland in that upper reach. Putney, too, looks Anglican
on a dwindling scale.[19]

Putney achieved fame during the Civil War when Cromwell chose
it as a temporary headquarters for his army, a period that also led to the
Putney Debates in the parish church, involving wide-ranging political discussions, including the case for universal suffrage. Victorian
historian Edward Walford describes the scene:

Old deceased historians and local authorities, we may here
state, differ widely in their accounts of the manner in which
Cromwell passed his time while domiciled at Putney. Thus,
while the former represent him as being entirely engrossed with
State affairs – holding conferences, and issuing mandates all
tending to the future overthrow of royalty; the latter, on the
other hand, would lead us to believe that his one thought was
the beautifying of the place, and that his chief occupation
was the planting of mulberry-trees all over Putney.[20]

Probably the first modern historian, and a key Enlightenment
figure castigated for his barbed anti-Church views, Edward Gibbon
was born in Putney in 1737. In his autobiography (again, one of the
first in the genre) he is surprisingly hard-nosed concerning the early
deaths of his six siblings.

I was born at Putney in Surrey, the twenty-seventh of April
. . . in the year one thousand seven hundred and thirty-seven,
within a twelve-month after my father's marriage with Judith
Porten, his first wife. From my birth I have enjoyed the right
of primogeniture; but I was succeeded by five brothers and
one sister, all of whom were snatched away in their infancy.

They died so young and I was myself so young at the time of
their deaths, that I could not then feel, nor can I now estimate
their loss, the importance of which could only have been
ascertained by future contingencies. The shares of fortune to
which younger children are reduced by our English laws would
have been sufficient, however, to oppress my inheritance; and
the compensation of their friendship must have depended on
the uncertain event of character and conduct, on the affinity
or opposition of our reciprocal sentiments. My five brothers,
whose names may be found in the Parish register of Putney,
I shall not pretend to lament; but from my childhood to the
present hour I have deeply and sincerely regretted my sister,
whose life was somewhat prolonged, and whom I remember
to have seen an amiable infant.[21]

Young Gibbon is soon packed off to a local school:

In my ninth year (January, 1746), in a lucid interval of
comparative health, my father adopted the convenient and
customary mode of English education; and I was sent to
Kingston-upon-Thames, to a school of about seventy boys,
which was kept by Dr Woodson and his assistants. Every
time I have since passed over Putney Common I have always
noticed the spot where my mother, as we drove along in the
coach, admonished me that I was now going into the World,
and must learn to think and act for myself. The expression may
appear ludicrous; yet there is not, in the course of life, a more
remarkable change than the removal of a child from the luxury
and freedom of a wealthy house to the frugal diet and strict
subordination of a school; from the tenderness of parents and
the obsequiousness of servants, to the rude familiarity of his
equals, the insolent tyranny of his seniors, and the rod, perhaps,
of a cruel and capricious pedagogue.[22]

Algernon Swinburne, the notorious Decadent poet and friend of
numerous Pre-Raphaelites, was removed to Putney in 1879, then aged
42, in an attempt to break his addiction to both excessive drinking
and certain peculiar sexual habits. He lived on there in semi-obscurity,
writing little, slowly becoming that curious anomaly, a figure keenly

identified with one literary period living on well into another. A 1914 essay by the Victorian-Edwardian humorist Max Beerbohm recalls a curious visit made in 1899 to the poet's house, The Pines, now 11 Putney Hill. Beerbohm is slightly amazed that this key figure of the 1870s continues to live on in a contemporary suburban villa. He is met by Swinburne's companion Theodore Watts-Dunton:

> On the day appointed 'I came as one whose feet half linger'. It is but a few steps from the railway-station in Putney High Street to No. 2. The Pines. I had expected a greater distance to the sanctuary – a walk in which to compose my mind and prepare myself for initiation. I laid my hand irresolutely against the gate of the bleak trim front-garden, I withdrew my hand, I went away. Out here were all the aspects of common modern life. In there was Swinburne. A butcher-boy went by, whistling. He was not going to see Swinburne. He could afford to whistle. I pursued my dilatory course up the slope of Putney, but at length it occurred to me that unpunctuality would after all be an imperfect expression of reverence, and I retraced my footsteps.
>
> No. 2 – prosaic inscription! But as that front-door closed behind me I had the instant sense of having slipped away from the harsh light of the ordinary and contemporary into the dimness of an odd, august past. Here, in this dark hall, the past was the present. Here loomed vivid and vital on the walls those women of Rossetti whom I had known but as shades. Familiar to me in small reproductions by photogravure, here they themselves were, life-sized, 'with curled-up lips and amorous hair' done in the original warm crayon, all of them intently looking down on me while I took off my overcoat – all wondering who was this intruder from posterity. That they hung in the hall, evidently no more than an overflow, was an earnest of packed plenitude within. The room I was ushered into was a back-room, a dining-room, looking on to a good garden. It was, in form and 'fixtures', an inalienably Mid-Victorian room, and held its stolid own in the riot of Rossettis. Its proportions, its window-sash bisecting the view of garden, its folding-doors (through which I heard the voice of Watts-Dunton booming mysteriously in the front room), its mantel-piece, its

gas-brackets, all proclaimed that nothing ever would seduce them from their allegiance to Martin Tupper . . .

While I stood talking to Watts-Dunton – talking as loudly as he, for he was very deaf – I enjoyed the thrill of suspense in watching the door through which would appear – Swinburne. I asked after Mr. Swinburne's health. Watts-Dunton said it was very good: 'He always goes out for his long walk in the morning – wonderfully active. Active in mind, too. But I'm afraid you won't be able to get into touch with him. He's almost stone-deaf, poor fellow – almost stone-deaf now.' He changed the subject, and I felt I must be careful not to seem interested in Swinburne exclusively. I spoke of 'Aylwin.' The parlour maid brought in the hot dishes. The great moment was at hand.

Nor was I disappointed. Swinburne's entry was for me a great moment. Here, suddenly visible in the flesh, was the legendary being and divine singer. Here he was, shutting the door behind him as might anybody else, and advancing – a strange small figure in grey, having an air at once noble and roguish, proud and skittish.[23]

'I did not know it at the time, but Putney was a good address to grow up in,' historian Tony Judt writes in *The Memory Chalet* (2010), his memoir of growing up above a hairdresser's (where his parents worked) on the busy and exciting Putney High Street:

Even the High Street was still rooted in a self-contained past. There were already, of course, 'chain stores': Woolworths, Marks & Spencer, The British Home Stores, etc. But these were small outlets and far outnumbered by locally owned shops selling haberdashery, tobacco, books, groceries, shoes, ladies' wear, toiletries and everything else. Even the 'multiples' were somehow local: Sainsburys, a small store with just one double-window, still had sawdust on its floor. You were served by polite, slightly haughty assistants in starched blue-and-white aprons, resembling nothing so much as the proud employees in the photograph on the back wall showing the little shop on the day it opened many decades before. The 'Home and Colonial' grocers further down the High Street carefully distinguished between its overseas and home-grown supplies: 'New Zealand lamb', 'English beef' and so on.

But the High Street was my mother's territory. *I* shopped in Lacy Road, which boasted an off-licence whence I was dispatched for cider and wine; a small tailors' establishment; and two 'sweet shops'. One of these was generic and modern, at least by '50s standards, offering fruit gums, packaged chocolate, and Wrigley's chewing gum. But the other – darker, danker, dirtier and otherwise depressing – was far more intriguing. It was run (and, I assume, owned) by a shrivelled, mean-spirited old crone who would resentfully weigh out from an array of large glass bottles a quarter-pound of gobstoppers or liquorice while grumbling at the impatience and sartorial insufficiency of her customers: 'I've been serving grubby little boys like you since the old Queen's jubilee, so don't try to fool me!' By the old Queen, of course, she meant Victoria, whose jubilee had been celebrated in Putney in June 1887.[24]

The magical 1970s children's TV cartoon favourite *Mr Benn* was set in Putney. Mr Benn, a bowler-hatted suburban everyman, leaves 52 Festive Road and walks along a very typical London suburban street to a fancy-dress shop, where, once an outfit is chosen and tried on, he leaves the changing room by a *second* door and is transplanted into another dimension: Outer Space, Wild West, Merrie England. 'I set it in my street in Putney, London', creator and animator David McKee explains, 'but changed "Festing Road" to "Festive Road", because "Festing" sounded too much like "festering".'[25]

Barnes, Mortlake and Kew

Just upstream of Putney to the west, the riverside suburbs of Barnes, Mortlake and Kew are strung along double U-shaped bends in the Thames, before the river turns south, down to Richmond. Mortlake is best known as home of Elizabethan astrologer, astronomer, magician, mathematician, philosopher and scientist John Dee. The occult and the 'scientific' were at this point inseparable, and as Peter Ackroyd notes: 'in London it is impossible to distinguish magic from other versions of intellectual and mechanical aptitude. Dr Dee, the great Elizabeth[an] magus of Mortlake, for example, was an engineer and a geographer as well as an alchemist.'[26] Dee was a favourite of Elizabeth I, as adviser and guide, and also had connections with key members of court: Francis Walsingham, Philip Sidney and Robert Cecil. This explains the choice of Mortlake as the location of his home, as his biographer Charlotte Fell Smith explains:

> Its nearness to London and to the favourite places of Elizabeth's residence – Greenwich, Hampton Court, Sion House, Isleworth and Nonsuch – was at first considered a great advantage, and the journey to and from London was almost invariably made by water. The Queen desired her astrologer to be near at hand.[27]

The house also housed one of Europe's largest libraries:

> He took up his abode with his mother, in a house belonging to her at Mortlake, on the river Thames. It was an old rambling place, standing west of the church between it and the river. Dee added to it by degrees, purchasing small tenements adjoining, so that at length it comprised laboratories for his experiments, libraries and rooms for a busy hive of workers and servants . . . Nothing of the old premises now remains, unless it be an ancient gateway leading from the garden towards the river.[28]

Dee's reputation for occult mysticism and possible secret influence on those in power appeals to contemporary psychogeographers, and, sure enough, Iain Sinclair, in *Liquid City*, describes a walk down to Mortlake, to John Dee House, next to St Mary's church, with fellow occultist Alan Moore (territory also covered in Sinclair's 1994 novel *Radon Daughters*):

> Come this far and London loses its gravitational pull, the drag of dirty words, the textual palimpsest. Between Mortlake and Richmond, reversing the ride Queen Elizabeth made when she wished to consult Dee, is a green path. Leading to follies and fountains. Metaphors of benevolence and continuity. Gardens and palaces. Privileged places we could visit but not occupy. Temporary visas for Arcadia. Permission to log the post at Teddington that marks the limits of the tidal Thames.[29]

Richmond

A small village known as 'Shene' for centuries, Richmond really took off in the early sixteenth century, when Henry VII rebuilt the manor house as a royal palace and called it 'Richmond' after his Yorkshire holdings. With the royal presence Richmond expanded and prospered, the riverside location and gentle hills proving popular attractions for those wanting to escape London's squalor. By the eighteenth century many impressive grand houses and villas had been built, the green had been developed as an ideal village green, the park (Britain's largest) laid out and a pretty bridge built. Richmond, with its leafy, hilly, riverside setting, became for many writers the ideal picturesque London suburb.

Scottish poet James Thomson (famed for *The Seasons* and the words to 'Rule, Britannia') was delighted with Richmond:

> O vale of bliss! O softly-swelling hills!
> On which the Power of Cultivation lies,
> And joys to see the wonders of his toil.
> Heavens! what a goodly prospect spreads around,
> Of hills, and dales, and woods, and lawns, and spires,
> And glittering towns, and gilded streams, till all
> The stretching landscape into smoke decays![30]

Thomson also described the view from his house on Kew Foot Lane, just off Richmond Hill:

> Which way, Amanda, shall we bend our course?
> The choice perplexes. Wherefore should we choose?
> All is the same with thee. Say, shall we wind
> Along the streams? or walk the smiling mead?
> Or court the forest glades? or wander wild
> Among the waving harvests? or ascend,
> While radiant Summer opens all its pride,
> Thy hill, delightful Shene? Here let us sweep
> The boundless landscape; now the raptur'd eye,
> Exulting swift, to huge Augusta send,
> Now to the sister-hills: that skirt her plain,
> To lofty Harrow now, and now to where
> Majestic Windsor lifts its princely brow.[31]

Richmond was a favourite holiday location for Charles Dickens and family, though of course, this being Dickens, these tended to be quite energetic affairs. He recounts in a letter to Daniel Maclise:

Beard is hearty, new and thicker ropes have been put up at the tree, the little birds have flown, their very nests have disappeared, the roads about are jewelled after dusk by glow-worms, the leaves are all out and the flowers too, swimming feats from Petersham to Richmond Bridge have been achieved before breakfast, I myself have risen at 6 and plunged head foremost into the water to the astonishment and admiration of all beholders.[32]

In Dickens's *Great Expectations* (1861), Pip escorts Stella from Cheapside down to Richmond, where she has been sent by Miss Havisham. On the journey they talk 'principally about the way by which we were travelling, and about what parts of London lay on this side of it, and what on that':[33]

We came to Richmond all too soon, and our destination there, was a house by the Green; a staid old house, where hoops and powder and patches, embroidered coats, rolled stockings, ruffles and swords, had had their court days many a time. Some ancient trees before the house were still cut into fashions as formal and unnatural as the hoops and wigs and stiff skirts; but their own allotted places in the great procession of the dead were not far off, and they would soon drop into them and go the silent way of the rest.

A bell with an old voice – which I dare say in its time had often said to the house, Here is the green farthingale, Here is the diamond-hilted sword, Here are the shoes with red heels and the blue solitaire – sounded gravely in the moonlight, and two cherry-coloured maids came fluttering out to meet Estella. The doorway soon absorbed her boxes, and she gave me her hand and a smile, and said good night, and was absorbed like-wise. And still I stood looking at the house, thinking how happy I should be if I lived there with her, and knowing that I never was happy with her, but always miserable.[34]

Radical reformer and journalist William Cobbett dissents from the predominantly positive views of Richmond. In *Rural Rides* (1830), his survey of the dire conditions of farm workers in southern England in the 1820s, he describes a journey, on Wednesday, 25 September 1822, out from Kensington. 'My object', he explains, 'was, not to see inns and turnpike roads, but to see the *country*; to see the farmers at *home*, and to see the labourers *in the fields*.'[35]

> We went through the turnpike-gate at Kensington, and immediately turned down the lane to our left, proceeded on to Fulham, crossed Putney-bridge into Surrey, went over Barnes Common, and then, going on the upper side of Richmond, got again into *Middlesex*, by crossing Richmond-bridge. All Middlesex is *ugly*, notwithstanding the millions upon millions which it is continually sucking up from the rest of the kingdom; and, though the Thames and its meadows now-and-then are seen from the road, the country is not less ugly from Richmond to Chertsey-bridge, through Twickenham, Hampton, Sunbury and Shepperton, than it is elsewhere. The soil is a gravel at bottom with a black loam at top near the Thames; further back it is a sort of spewy gravel; and the buildings consist generally of tax-eaters' showy, tea-garden-like boxes, and of shabby dwellings of labouring people who, in this part of the country, look to be about half *Saint Giles's*: dirty, and have every appearance of drinking gin.[36]

Mr Jennings in Sheridan Le Fanu's famed Gothic tale of malicious haunting, 'Green Tea' (1869), lives in semi-seclusion, way out of town, in a dark, 'quiet house at Richmond'.[37] Jennings takes the omnibus home from the City to Richmond, fortified by said strong green tea. One night, he sees two reddish lights winking in the murk:

> There was very little light in the 'bus. It was nearly dark. I leaned forward to aid my endeavour to discover what these little circles really were. They shifted their position a little as I did so. I began now too perceive an outline of something black, and I soon saw with tolerable distinctness the outline of a small black monkey, pushing its face forward in mimicry to meet mine; those were its eyes, and I now dimly saw its teeth grinning at me.[38]

The implacable monkey follows him home through the dark, deserted Richmond streets, keeping very close, almost brushing against Jennings:

> I came up here to this drawing-room. I just sat here. The
> monkey then got upon a small table that then stood *there*. It
> looked dazed and languid. An irrepressible uneasiness as to
> its movements kept my eyes always upon it. Its eyes were half
> closed, but I could see them glow. It looked steadily at me. In
> all situations, at all hours, it is awake and looking at me. That
> never changes.[39]

Henry James in 'The Suburbs of London' (1877) argues that cities like Paris and London have some of their finest landscapes and build-ings in the suburbs: 'There is nothing more charming in Europe than the great terrace at Saint Germain; there are few things so picturesque as Richmond bridge and the view thence along either bank of the Thames.'[40] He continues:

> by the time you reach Richmond, which is only nine miles
> from London, this suburban prettiness touches its maximum.
> Higher in its course the Thames is extremely pretty; but nothing
> can well be so charming as what you see of it from Richmond
> bridge and just above. The bridge itself is a very happy piece of
> picturesqueness. Sketches and photographs have, I believe, made
> it more or less classical. The banks are lined compactly with
> villas embowered in walled gardens, which lie on the slope of
> Richmond hill, whose crest, as seen from below, is formed by the
> long, bosky mass of Richmond park . . . I will therefore content
> myself with observing that, to take a walk in Richmond park and
> afterward repair to the Star and Garter inn to satisfy the appetite
> you have honestly stimulated, is as complete an entertainment as
> you are likely to find. It is rounded off by your appreciation of
> the famous view of the Thames from the window of the Inn –
> the view which Turner has painted and poets have versified.[41]

The hero of H. G. Wells's *The Time Machine* (1895) lives on such a hill in Richmond. As he sits on his machine, cycling out through the decades and then the centuries, it is Richmond and its environs that he sees dissolving around him:

The landscape was misty and vague. I was still on the hill-side
upon which this house now stands, and the shoulder rose above
me grey and dim. I saw trees growing and changing like puffs
of vapour, now brown, now green; they grew, spread, shivered,
and passed away. I saw huge buildings rise up faint and fair,
and pass like dreams. The whole surface of the earth seemed
changed – melting and flowing under my eyes. The little hands
upon the dials that registered my speed raced round faster and
faster . . . I saw great and splendid architecture rising about
me, more massive than any buildings of our own time and yet,
as it seemed, built of glimmer and mist. I saw a richer green
flow up the hill-side, and remain there without any wintry
intermission.[42]

Later, having met the disappointingly fey future inhabits of Richmond,
the decadent Eloi, lounging around in their crumbling Great Hall,
the Time Traveller pops outside. The gentle hills around Richmond,
seen at twilight, the same yet slightly different, provide a frisson of
the year 802,701:

The calm of evening was upon the world as I emerged from
the great hall and the scene was lit by the warm glow of the
setting sun. At first things were very confusing. Everything was
so entirely different from the world I had known – even the
flowers. The big building I had left was situated on the slope of
a broad river valley, but the Thames had shifted perhaps a mile
from its present position. I resolved to mount to the summit of
a crest, perhaps a mile and a half away, from which I could get
a wider view of this our planet in the year Eight Hundred and
Two Thousand, Seven Hundred and One AD . . .
    Looking round with a sudden thought, from a terrace on
which I rested for a while, I realized that there were no small
houses to be seen. Apparently the single house, and possibly
even the household, had vanished. Here and there among
the greenery were palace-like buildings, but the house and the
cottage, which form such characteristic features of our own
English landscape, had disappeared.
    'Communism', said I to myself.[43]

In Wells's 1897 novel *The War of the Worlds*, the Martians first arrive, in giant cylinders from the sky, on Horsell Common, just outside Woking in Surrey, around 22 miles southwest of London. (This, coincidentally, is just 15 miles from Dorking, the site of George Chesney's influential invasion novella *The Battle of Dorking* (1871), the work that inaugurated a mini literary tradition of fearful alien invasion – in this case German.) Wells clearly takes great delight in trashing first Woking then a series of pretty southwest riverside suburbs up to central London, describing smashed houses and churches, horrified panicking locals and endless lines of refugees: 'London in danger of suffocation! The Kingston and Richmond defences forced! Fearful massacres in the Thames Valley!'[44] The destruction starts on a Friday and the narrator escapes from Woking, just ahead of the stumbling advancing Martian tripods, as they exterminate everything beneath with their formidable Heat-Ray. He gets into the river around Weybridge and Shepperton, and witnesses a rare victory for the, mostly ineffective, earthling military.

> The shell burst clean in the face of the Thing. The hood bulged, flashed, was whirled off in a dozen tattered fragments of red flesh and glittering metal.
>
> 'Hit!' shouted I, with something between a scream and a cheer.
>
> I heard answering shouts from the people in the water about me. I could have leapt out of the water with that momentary exultation.
>
> The decapitated colossus reeled like a drunken giant; but it did not fall over. It recovered its balance by a miracle, and, no longer heeding its steps, and with the camera that fired the Heat-Ray now rigidly upheld, it reeled swiftly upon Shepperton. The living intelligence, the Martian within the hood, was slain and splashed to the four winds of heaven, and the Thing was now but a mere intricate device of metal whirling to destruction. It drove along in a straight line, incapable of guidance. It struck the tower of Shepperton Church, smashing it down as the impact of a battering-ram might have done, swerved aside, blundered on, and collapsed with a tremendous impact into the river out of sight.[45]

The narrator's brother, we hear, is at this time in central London, and we see him slowly absorbing the unfolding terror coming up from the southwest suburbs. On the Sunday morning he is at Waterloo, eager for news:

> One or two trains came in in from Richmond, Putney and Kingston, containing people who had gone out for a day's boating and found the locks closed and a feeling of panic in the air. A man in a blue-and-white blazer addressed my brother, full of strange tidings.
>
> 'There's hosts of people driving into Kingston in traps and carts and things, with boxes of valuables and all that', he said. 'They come from Molesey and Weybridge and Walton, and they say there's been guns heard at Chertsey, heavy firing, and that mounted soldiers have told them to get off at once because the Martians are coming.'[46]

Meanwhile the narrator is moving slowly, gradually closer to central London: through Sunbury ('dead bodies lying in contorted attitudes'[47]); Hampton Court, Bushey Park, Twickenham ('uninjured by either Heat-Ray or Black Smoke'[48]); crossing over Richmond Bridge ('up the hill Richmond town was burning briskly'[49]); to Kew ('the upper-works of a Martian fighting-machine loomed in sight over the house-tops'[50]); Sheen and Mortlake (holed up in a house unfortunately smashed by a fifth Martian cylinder that landed on it and stood 'amid the smashed and gravel-heaped shrubbery'[51]). Then to Putney ('the bridge was almost lost in a tangle of this [red] weed, and at Richmond, too, the Thames water poured in a broad and shallow stream across the meadows of Hampton and Twickenham'[52]). Further on he meets 'The Man on Putney Hill', an artilleryman who rails against the effete mass of suburbanites so easily wiped out, who are proving to be just easy food for Martians, and suggests forming a resistance movement that would live in the drains and sewers of London:

> All these – the sort of people that lived in these houses, and all those damn little clerks that used to live down that way – they'd be no good. They haven't any spirit in them – no proud dreams and no proud lusts; and a man who hasn't one or the other – Lord! What is he but funk and precautions? They just used

to skedaddle off to work – I've seen hundreds of 'em, bit of
breakfast in hand, running wild and shining to catch their little
season-ticket train . . . Well, the Martians will just be a godsend
to these. Nice roomy cages, fattening food, careful breeding,
no worry.[53]

Finally, the narrator crosses Putney Bridge, through Fulham and on
to 'Dead London'.

In his shockingly frank *Journal of a Disappointed Man* (1919),
W.N.P. Barbellion (a protective *nom de plume*) describes events on a
Sunday in March 1914:

In the afternoon, took a 'bus to Richmond. No room outside,
so had to go inside – curse – and sit opposite a row – curse
again – of fat, ugly, elderly women, all off to visit their married
daughters, the usual Sunday jaunt. At Hammersmith got on the
outside, and at Turnham Green was caught in a hail storm. Very
cold all of a sudden, so got off and took shelter in the doorway
of a shop, which was of course closed, the day being Sunday . . .
  The next 'bus took me to Richmond. Two young girls sat in
front, and kept looking back to know if I was 'game'. I looked
through them. Walked in the park just conscious of the singing of Larks and the chatter of Jays . . . To shelter from the rain
sat under an oak where four youths joined me and said, 'Worse
luck', and 'Not half', and smoked cigarettes. They gossiped and
giggled like girls, put their arms around each other's necks. At
the dinner last night, they said, they had Duck and Tomato
Soup and Beeswax ('Beesely, you know, the chap that goes
about with Smith a lot') wore a fancy waistcoat with a dinner
jacket. When I got up to move on, they became convulsed with
laughter. I scowled.
  Had tea in the Pagoda tea-rooms, dry toast and brown bread
and butter. Two young men opposite me were quietly playing
the fool . . . On rising to go, one of the two hilarious youths
removed my cap and playfully placed it on top of the bowler
which his friend was wearing.
  'My cap, I think', I said sharply, and the young man
apologised with a splutter. I glared like a kill-joy of sixty.[54]

Virginia and Leonard Woolf moved out of central London to Richmond in 1914 (living on The Green before moving to Hogarth House in March 1915) and stayed until 1924. Here, Virginia Woolf slowly recovered from a severe mental breakdown, and the Woolfs entertained many literary visitors, including Dora Carrington, E. M. Forster and T. S. Eliot. They also set up the Hogarth Press in the basement, publishing work by Woolf, Katherine Mansfield and T. S. Eliot, and the works of Sigmund Freud (James Joyce's *Ulysses*, however, was turned down). Woolf records walks in the parks and along the river; this one on the day of the Armistice, 1918:

> Monday 11 November 1918.
> Twenty-five minutes ago the guns went off, announcing peace. A siren hooted on the river. They are hooting still. A few people ran to look out of the windows. The rooks wheeled around, & were for a moment, the symbolic look of creatures performing some ceremony, partly of thanksgiving, partly of valediction over the grave. A very cloudy still day, the smoke still toppling over heavily towards the east; & that too wearing for a moment a look of something floating, waving, drooping . . . So far neither bells nor flags, but the wailing of sirens and intermittent guns.[55]

Woolf later describes a 'peace day' procession through Richmond, on 20 July 1919:

> After sitting through the procession and the peace bells unmoved, I began after dinner to feel that if something was going on, perhaps one had better be in it . . . The doors of the public house at the corner were open and the room crowded; couples waltzing; songs being shouted, waveringly, as if one must be drunk to sing. A troop of little boys with lanterns were parading the green, beating sticks. Not many shops went to the expense of electric light. A woman of the upper classes was supported dead drunk between two men partially drunk.
> We followed a moderate stream flowing up the Hill. Illuminations were almost extinct half way up, but we kept on till we reached the terrace. And then we did see something – not much indeed, for the damp had deadened the chemicals.

Red and green and yellow and blue balls rose slowly in the air, burst, flowered into an oval of light, which dropped into minuter grains and expired. There were hazes of light at different points. Rising over the Thames, among trees, these rockets were beautiful; the light on the faces of the crowd was strange; yet of course there was grey mist muffling everything and taking the blaze off the fire. It was a melancholy thing to see the incurable soldiers lying in bed at the Star and Garter with their backs to us, smoking cigarettes and waiting for the noise to be over.[56]

One day, T. S. Eliot comes to Sunday lunch. He reads aloud from a strange new long poem:

Eliot dined last Sunday & read his poem. He sang it & chanted it, rhymed it. It has great beauty & force of phrase: symmetry; & intensity. What connects it together, I'm not so sure. But he read till he had to rush . . . & discussion was thus curtailed. One was left, however, with some strong emotion. 'The Waste Land', it is called; & Mary Hutch, who has heard it more quietly, interprets it to be Tom's autobiography – a melancholy one.[57]

In 'The Fire Sermon', the third section of Eliot's *The Waste Land* (1922), one of the poem's mythical 'Thames Daughters' speaks of the modern age:

Trams and dusty trees.
Highbury bore me. Richmond and Kew
Undid me. By Richmond I raised my knees
Supine on the floor of a narrow canoe.[58]

In 1923 the Woolfs decided to move back into London: 'I'm heartless about poor old Hogarth [House], where for nine years we have been so secure.'[59] The Woolfs' suburban sojourn is also taken up in Michael Cunningham's 1998 novel *The Hours*. Here, Richmond is a cage, one that 'continues its decent, peaceful dream of itself', complete with hostile servants, enforced routines of walks, meals and early bedtimes, and restrictions on work. London, on the other hand, promises the freedom of walking, exhilaration and, maybe, madness. At one point Woolf nearly escapes:

> Virginia descends the stairs to the rail station. The Richmond station is at once a portal and a destination. It is columned, canopied, full of a faint burnt smell, slightly desolate even when crowded (as it is now), lined with yellow wooden benches that do not encourage lingering. She checks the clock, sees that a train has just pulled away and the next will not leave for almost twenty-five minutes. She stiffens. She had imagined (foolish!) stepping straight onto a train or, at most, waiting five or ten minutes. She stands impatiently before the clock, then walks a few slow paces down the platform. If she does this, if she gets on the train that leaves in, what, twenty-three minutes, and goes to London, and walks in London, and catches the last train back . . . Leonard will be insane with worry . . . She is better, she is safer, if she rests in Richmond; if she does not speak too much, write too much, feel too much; if she does not travel impetuously to London and walk through its streets.[60]

This suburban phobia is further developed in the 2002 film version of the novel, scripted by David Hare:

> I choose not the suffocating anaesthetic of the suburbs, but the violent jolt of the capital, that is my choice. The meanest patient, yes even the very lowest, is allowed some say in the matter of her own prescription. Thereby she defines her humanity. I wish, for your sake, Leonard, I could be happy in this quietness . . . But if it is a choice between Richmond and death, I choose death.[61]

J. R. Ackerley's 1968 memoir, *My Father and Myself*, records two traumatic family secrets: Ackerley's active homosexuality, and his father's bizarre double life. On the surface this is a dull and respectable upper middle-class Edwardian Richmond family:

> He left Blenheim House, our third Richmond residence, at eight o'clock every morning for breakfast at his office. Any nosy Parker keeping a watch upon our house would have seen the

front door opened punctually at that hour by the butler, and
my father descend the steps in his grey Edward VII hat, his light
fawn or heavy overcoat, his umbrella on his arm, a cigar in his
mouth, drawing on his wash-leather gloves. He would halt for
a moment in the front rose garden to exchange a word or two
with Scott the gardener (if that bibulous old man had arrived)
about the roses, the racing, or the weather, he would make some
little joke (perhaps about the Epsom Salts he had just taken
and would he reach his office or even the station in time?), old
Scott would dissolve into wheezy laughter, the butler would
stand with the gate ready open, my father would pass through
and walk down Richmond Hill to the station. Punctually at
six-thirty p.m. he would return for dinner, often bringing with
him a present for my mother, flowers or some delicacy for
the table.[62]

Later, after his father's death, Ackerley opens a letter to be opened
'only in the case of my death':

Now for the 'secret orchard' part of my story. For many years
I had a mistress and she presented me with twin girls ten years
ago and another girl eight years ago. The children are alive and
are very sweet things and very dear to me. They know me only
as Uncle Bodger, but I want them to have the proceeds of my
Life Insurance.[63]

Ackerley's father had a secret family, living just down the road, 'in a
house near Barnes Common'. His fastidious commutes incorporated
regular visits to his other family, in a house that 'lay on the main route
between Richmond and his Bow Street office'.[64]

Twickenham and Teddington

Twickenham is a mile upstream from Richmond (the river here running loosely south–north) and around 10 miles southwest of central
London. Twickenham, originally sited slightly upriver, opposite Eel
Pie Island, seems to be an ancient place, with some pottery fragments
unearthed dating to 3000 BC and evidence of Roman building. In the
early sixteenth century, with both Richmond and Hampton Court

as royal palaces, Twickenham became a popular place for grander courtiers to build riverside homes. In 1595 Francis Bacon, pioneering scientist and statesman, was given a mansion, Twickenham Park, by Elizabeth I.

Bacon's house was taken over by Lucy Harrington, Countess of Bedford, who formed there a prestigious salon visited by Ben Jonson, George Chapman and John Donne. Donne wrote 'Twicknam Garden' with Twickenham Park in mind:

Blasted with sighs, and surrounded with tears,
Hither I come to seek the spring,
And at mine eyes, and at mine ears,
Receive such balms as else cure every thing.[65]

By the eighteenth century Twickenham had become one of London's most fashionable suburbs. The great poet and satirist Alexander Pope moved here in 1719, partly because, as a Catholic, he was unwelcome in London society, and partly because his suspicious, cutting and ironic temperament enjoyed a distance from the fashionable centre. He eventually became known as the 'Wasp of Twickenham', especially after his long poem *The Dunciad* (1728) viciously attacked famed society and literary figures as being marvels of profound stupidity:

At last, the Gods and Fate have fix'd me on the borders of . . .
Twickenham. It is here I have pass'd an entire year of my life,
without any fix'd abode in London, or more than casting a
transitory glance (for a day or two at most in a month) on the
pomps of the Town.[66]

Over the years Pope had a formidable Palladian-style house built (partly designed by James Gibbs), and designed and laid out an impressive and highly original landscaped informal garden, the first of its kind. Pope was striving for a fashionable Picturesque effect, the house and garden artfully composed in a 'naturalistic' (that is, highly artificial) manner designed to delight the spectator. Even nature was roped in to add effects: 'Our river glitters beneath an unclouded sun, at the same times that its banks retain the verdure of showers: our gardens are offering their first nosegays; our trees, like new acquaintance brought happily together, are stretching their arms to meet each other.'[67]

In addition, Pope had constructed a magnificent and fashionable 'faery' grotto, full of statuary, inscriptions, sparkling stones, glinting mirrors, light effects and a framed view of the river, with even a small brook babbling through it all. In a letter from 1725 Pope describes this marvel:

> Let the young ladies be assured I make nothing new in my gardens without wishing to see the print of their fairy steps in every part of 'em. I have put the last hand to my works of this kind, in happily finishing the subterraneous way and grotto: I found there a spring of the clearest water, which falls in a perpetual rill, that ecchoes thro' the cavern day and night. From the river Thames, you see thro' my arch up a walk of the wilderness, to a kind of open Temple, wholly compos'd of shells in the rustic manner; and from that distance under the temple you look down thro' a sloping arcade of trees, and see the sails on the river passing suddenly and vanishing, as through a perspective glass. When you shut the doors of this grotto, it becomes on the instant, from a luminous room, a *Camera obscura*; on the walls of which all the objects of the river, hills, woods and boats, are forming a moving picture in their visible radiations; and when you have a mind to light it up, it affords you a very different scene; it is finished with shells interspersed with pieces of looking-glass in angular forms, and in the cieling [*sic*] is a star of the same material, at which when a lamp . . . is hung in the middle, a thousand pointed rays glitter and are reflected over the place.[68]

The house became a major visitor attraction, easily seen from the river and painted many times. One of Pope's many esteemed visitors was Voltaire, then living in exile in Wandsworth. A visit in 1724 is described by Oliver Goldsmith:

> M. Voltaire has often told his friends, that he never observed in himself such a succession of opposite passions as he experienced upon his first interview with Mr Pope. When he first entered the room and perceived our poor melancholy English poet,

naturally deformed, and wasted as he was with sickness and study, he could not help regarding him with the utmost compassion. But when Pope began to speak, and to reason upon moral obligations, and dress the most delicate sentiments in the most charming diction, Voltaire's pity began to be changed into admiration, and at last even into envy. It is not uncommon with him to assert, that no man ever pleased him so much in serious conversation.[69]

Another memorable anecdote (though there is no definitive source for this; some have connected it to Thomas 'Elegy Written in a Country Churchyard' Gray) concerns Voltaire when staying for a while with Pope at Twickenham. After Pope complained about feeling unwell, his concerned mother asked him why his health was so poor. Replied Voltaire, 'Oh those damned Jesuits, when I was a boy, buggered me to such a degree that I shall never get over it as long as I live.'[70]

Less than a mile down the road from Pope, in 1747, the antiquarian and writer Horace Walpole MP, son of former prime minister Robert Walpole, acquired from a Mrs Chevenix ('the noted toy-woman') the lease on a house known locally as Chopped Straw Hall which also came with some acres of land. Walpole soon demolished the house and, changing its name, declared: 'I am going to build a little Gothic castle at Strawberry Hill.' Over the next few decades the house was slowly transformed into a fantasy suburban Gothic castle. Medieval in conception – based on Gothic cathedrals, tombs, antiquarian prints of ruins – Strawberry Hill eventually acquired battlements, winding corridors, complicated ceilings, draperies, carvings and gilding, and even a spooky tower.[71] The design pre-dated and informed the vogue for Gothic Revival architecture that later spread through the country. Walpole wrote:

To the Hon. H. S. Conway.
Twickenham, June 8, 1747.
You perceive by my date that I am got into a new camp, and have left my tub at Windsor. It is a little plaything-house that I got out of Mrs. Chenevix's shop, and is the prettiest bauble you ever saw. It is set in enamelled meadows, with filigree hedges:

A small Euphrates through the piece is roll'd,
And little finches wave their wings in gold.

Two delightful roads, that you would call dusty, supply me continually with coaches and chaises; barges as solemn as barons
of the exchequer move under my window; Richmond Hill and
Ham Walks bound my prospect; but, thank God! The Thames
is between me and the Duchess of Queensberry. Dowagers
as plenty as flounders inhabit all around, and Pope's ghost
is just now skimming under my window by a most poetical
moonlight.[72]

He later proudly writes of developments at Strawberry Hill:

To Sir Horace Mann.
   Strawberry Hill, June 12, 1753.
   . . . The enclosed enchanted little landscape, then, is
Strawberry Hill; and I will try to explain so much of it to you
as will help to let you know whereabouts we are when we are
talking to you . . . Directly before it is an open grove, through
which you see a field, which is bounded by a serpentine wood
of all kind of trees, and flowering shrubs, and flowers. The lawn
before the house is situated on the top of a small hill, from
whence to the left you see the town and church of Twickenham
encircling a turn of the river that looks exactly like a seaport
in miniature. The opposite shore is a most delicious meadow,
bounded by Richmond Hill, which loses itself in the noble
woods of the park to the end of the prospect on the right,
where is another turn of the river, and the suburbs of Kingston
as luckily placed as Twickenham is on the left: and a natural terrace on the brow of my hill, with meadows of my own down
to the river, commands both extremities. Is not this a tolerable
prospect? You must figure that all this is perpetually enlivened
by a navigation of boats and barges, and by a road below my
terrace, with coaches, post-chaises, waggons, and horsemen
constantly in motion, and the fields speckled with cows, horses,
and sheep.
   Now you shall walk into the house. The bow-window below
leads into a little parlour hung with a stone-colour Gothic

paper and Jackson's Venetian prints, which I could never endure while they pretended, infamous as they are, to be after Titian, &c., but when I gave them this air of barbarous bas-reliefs, they succeeded to a miracle: it is impossible at first sight not to conclude that they contain the history of Attila or Tottila, done about the very æra. From hence, under two gloomy arches, you come to the hall and staircase, which it is impossible to describe to you, as it is the most particular and chief beauty of the castle. Imagine the walls covered with (I call it paper, but it is really paper painted in perspective to represent) Gothic fretwork: the lightest Gothic balustrade to the staircase, adorned with antelopes (our supporters) bearing shields; lean windows fattened with rich saints in painted glass, and a vestibule open with three arches on the landing-place, and niches full of trophies of old coats of mail, Indian shields made of rhinoceros's hides, broadswords, quivers, longbows, arrows, and spears – all *supposed* to be taken by Sir Terry Robsart in the holy wars.[73]

Experiencing a nightmare at the Castle (involving a grotesque hand in medieval armour) sparked Walpole's writing of what is now considered the first ever Gothic novel, *The Castle of Otranto* (1764).

Two hundred years later, Gavin Ewart wrote 'Strawberry Hill', as part of his *Londoners* series of poems. He is bemused to note that the place 'purchased for fun in 1747' and made into a gothic fantasy with 'suits of armour, monks and chivalry / With Dutch stained glass and golden antelopes', is now used as a 'Catholic Training College'.[74]

This stretch of the river that runs from Twickenham up to Hampton Court is the setting for Thomas Love Peacock's wide-ranging 1831 satire of Romantic and Gothic excess, *Crotchet Castle*. Ebenezer Mac Crotchet, set on 'enriching himself at the expense of the rest of mankind, by all then recognised modes of accumulation on the windy side of the law',[75] makes a fortune in the City and decides to build a weekend villa on the river:

In one of those beautiful vallies, through which the Thames (not yet polluted by the tide, the scouring of cities, or even the minor defilement of the sandy streams of Surrey,) rolls a clear flood through flowery meadows, under the shade of old beech woods, and the smooth mossy greensward of the chalk hills

(which pour into it their tributary rivulets, as pure and pellucid
as the fountains of Bandusium, or the wells of Scamander, by
which the wives and daughters of the Trojans washed their
splendid garments in the days of peace, before the coming of
the Greeks); in one of those beautiful vallies [*sic*], on a bold
round-surfaced lawn, spotted with juniper, that opened itself
in the bosom of an old wood, which rose with a steep, but not
precipitous ascent, from the river to the summit of the hill,
stood the castellated villa of a retired citizen.[76]

Nouveau riche Crotchet, who has now dropped the 'Mac', is not at all
traditionally aristocratic (and is hiding his Scottish-Jewish ancestry),
not really a country squire, but, with an 'inborn love of disputation',
decides to open up Crotchet Castle:

Being very hospitable in his establishment and liberal in
his invitations, a numerous detachment from the advanced
guard of the 'march of intellect', often marched down to
Crotchet Castle.

When the fashionable season filled London with exhibitors
of all descriptions, lecturers and else, Mr Crotchet was in his
glory; for, in addition to the perennial literati of the metropolis,
he had the advantage of the visits of a number of hardy annuals,
chiefly from the north, who, as the interval of their metropolitan flowering allowed, occasionally accompanied their London
brethren in excursions to Crotchet Castle.[77]

In 1851 Alfred Tennyson, by this time Poet Laureate, moved to
Chapel House (now 15 Montpelier Row), Twickenham, in order to
escape from oppressive London society. He was determined to deflect
unwanted fans visiting: 'so you have found me out,' he greeted
one unscheduled visitor, Francis Palgrave, compiler of *The Golden
Treasury*.[78] One admirer who did get through was young Irish poet
William Allingham:

Coventry Patmore . . . let me know that I might call on the
great Poet, then not married and living in Twickenham.

Saturday, June 28, was the appointed day, and in the warm
afternoon I walked from Twickenham Railway Station to

Montpelier Row, quite away from the village. It proved to be a single row of about a dozen moderate-sized houses that seemed dropped by accident among quiet fields and large trees . . .

I was admitted, shown upstairs into a room with books lying about, and soon in came a tall, broad-shouldered swarthy man, slightly stooping, with loose dark hair and beard. He wore spectacles, and was obviously very near-sighted. Hollow cheeks and the dark pallor of his skin gave him an unhealthy appearance. He was a strange and almost spectral figure. The Great Man peered close at me, and then shook hands cordially, yet with a profound quietude of manner. He was then about forty-one, but looked much older, from his bulk, his short-sight, stooping shoulders, and lose careless dress. He looked tired and said he had been asleep and was suffering from hay-fever.[79]

Later, the poet Coventry Patmore arrived and the gents went upstairs to smoke cigars:

Over our port we talked of grave matters. T. said his belief rested on two things, a 'Chief Intelligence and Immortality'. – 'I could not eat my dinner without a belief in immortality. If I didn't believe in that, I'd go down immediately and jump off Richmond Bridge.' Then to me, rather shortly, 'Why do you laugh?' I murmured that there was something ludicrous in the image of his jumping off Richmond Bridge. 'Well', he rejoined, 'in such a case I'd as soon make a comic end as a tragic' . . .
We walked to Richmond railway station, I feeling that a longing of my life had been fulfilled, and as if I had been familiar for years with this great and simple man.[80]

Others who made the trip down to Twickenham included Julia Margaret Cameron, Thomas and Jane Carlyle, John Everett Millais and William Makepeace Thackeray. The Who's Pete Townshend moved into the same house in 1985.

Thom Gunn's 1971 poem 'Last Days at Teddington' touchingly evokes the summer suburban ideal of the intermingling of outdoor and indoor, as 'the windows wide through day and night' allow sights, sound and smells to circulate; now the 'garden like a room', now the house 'in bloom'.[81]

Book-dealing occult diviner Todd Sileen, in Iain Sinclair's novel *Radon Daughters* (1994), is on a mad quest for psychogeographic resonances and cultural harmonics in the area, and having walked a long way down from Whitechapel, is exhausted, delirious and overexposed to unfamiliar elements, such as sunlight and fresh air:

> We saunter broad terraces, significant fakes, boathouses, barbecued chicken on the breeze, skiffs riding the swell. But there is a squalor mortgaging the Palladian, lice in the periwig. The notion of the Thameside village as a retreat. Horatian exiles for poets, Catholics, the mistresses of princelings. Caves and shrines. A steady drift from the corrupted centre . . .
>
> Now the pressure really bites; to cover (honour/activate) *all* the points of interest, the deposits of aboriginal virtue (Marble Hill, the fountains and statues of York house, Pope's gardens and Grotto, Strawberry Hill, the birthplace of Gerald Kersh in Teddington) without diverting us from the narrative quest, the miles that must be knocked off before the sun sets.[82]

Twickenham's Eel Pie Island – a curious mid-river 500-metre-long islet (or eyot), and once famous for a raffish Hotel that helped launch the 1960s British blues revival, then rock, including the Rolling Stones, The Who and Pink Floyd – features in Ben Aaranovitch's fantasy novel *Rivers of London* (2011). This novel concerns PC Peter Grant, of a little-known London Metropolitan Police department dealing with supernatural crimes. PC Grant, accompanying DCI Nightingale, is called to attend to a disturbance on a boat near Eel Pie Island. Grant knows the place: 'a collection of boatyards and houses on a river islet barely 500 metres long. The Rolling Stones had once played a gig there.'[83] On the way back into town they piece together what has happened:

> We returned to the Jag and the fickle embrace of its 1960s heating system. As we returned through Richmond town centre, the right way round the one-way system this time, I asked Nightingale whether Nathaniel the troll had been helpful.
>
> 'He confirmed what we suspected,' he said. That the boys in the boat had been followers of Father Thames, had come downstream to raid the shrine at Eel Pie Island and been

caught by followers of Mother Thames. They were doubt-
less well tanked up, and probably did set their own fire while
trying to make their escape. Downstream, the Thames was the
sovereign domain of Mother Thames, upstream, it belonged to
Father Thames. The dividing line was at Teddington Lock, two
kilometres upstream from Eel Pie Island.

'So you think Father Thames is making a grab for turf?' I
asked. It made these 'gods' sound like drug dealers. Traffic was
noticeably heavier heading back – London was waking up.

'It's hardly surprising that the spirits of a locality would
exhibit territoriality,' said Nightingale.[84]

Kingston

Kingston upon Thames, half a mile (upriver) from Teddington and
around 12 miles southwest of central London, has long been a key
position as a river crossing; its wooden bridge was the only one above
London Bridge until 1750. Jerome K. Jerome's narrator 'J.' wittily sets
the scene in *Three Men in a Boat* (1889), as this is where the chaotic
boat trip upriver to Oxford begins:

I mused on Kingston, or 'Kyningestun', as it was once
called in the days when Saxon 'kinges' were crowned there.
Great Cæsar crossed the river there, and the Roman legions
camped upon its sloping uplands. Cæsar, like, in later years,
Elizabeth, seems to have stopped everywhere: only he was
more respectable than good Queen Bess; he didn't put up at
the public-houses.[85]

Investigative journalist George Augustus Sala, author of the saucy
London guide *Twice Round the Clock*, describes a daring escape from
a grim boarding school, a Mr Bogryne's establishment at 'Bolting
House, Ealing', in his autobiography *Gaslight and Daylight* (1859). He
is aiming for Portsmouth and a ship:

I caught a glimpse of myself in the polished plate-glass window
of a baker's shop and found myself to be a very black grimy
boy. Vagabondism had already set its mark upon me . . . I
plodded down the Wandsworth road; blushing very much as

> I passed people in clean shirts and well-brushed clothes, and
> pretty servant-maids, dressed out in ribbons like Maypoles,
> laughing and chattering in the gardens and at the doors of
> suburban villas.[86]

He staggers on:

> By some circuitous route which took me, I think, over
> Wandsworth Common and through Roehampton and Putney,
> I got that evening to Kingston-upon-Thames. The sun was
> setting, as I leaned over the bridge. I was tired and hungry . . .
> Was it to be barn, or hay-rick, or outhouse – or simply field,
> with the grass for a pillow, and the sky for a counterpane?[87]

He meets a beggar, who takes him to a nearby 'union', or workhouse, and explains how it works: 'You have to work your bed out.
Here, Kingston way, you wheels barrows; at Guildford you pumps; at
Richmond you breaks stones; at Wandsworth they makes you grind
corn in a hand-mill till your fingers a'most drops off at yer wrists.'[88]

Kingston, then, is where J., George and Harris, plus Montmorency
the dog, set off upriver in *Three Men and a Boat*:

> The quaint back streets of Kingston, where they came down
> to the water's edge, looked quite picturesque in the flashing
> sunlight, the glinting river with its drifting barges, the wooded
> towpath, the trim-kept villas on the other side, Harris, in a
> red and orange blazer, grunting away at the sculls, the distant
> glimpses of the grey old palace of the Tudors, all made a sunny
> picture, so bright but calm, so full of life, and yet so peaceful,
> that, early in the day though it was, I felt myself being dreamily
> lulled off into a musing fit.[89]

The narrator dwells on some typical travelogue-style topics
of cosy national history and heritage but soon digresses (just like
their meandering trip) and we hear a new kind of voice, breezy and
comically irreverent:

> She was nuts on public-houses, was England's Virgin Queen.
> There's scarcely a pub of any attractions within ten miles

of London that she does not seem to have looked in at, or stopped at, or slept at, some time or other. I wonder, now, supposing Harris, say, turned over a new leaf, and became a great and good man, and got to be Prime Minister, and died, if they would put signs up over the public-houses that he had patronized: 'Harris had a glass of bitter in this house'; 'Harris had two of Scotch cold here in the summer of '88'; 'Harris was chucked from here in December, 1886'.

No, there would be too many of them! It would be the houses that he had *never* entered that would become famous. 'Only house in south London that Harris never had a drink in!' The people would flock to it to see what could have been the matter with it.[90]

Soames Forsyte, in Galsworthy's *The Man of Property* (1906), the first part of the endless series 'The Forsyte Saga', intends to build a new house out of London. Galsworthy was born in a huge house with an estate at Kingston, and this became part of the model for Forsyte House in the novels:

Within twelve miles of Hyde Park Corner, the value of the land certain to go up, would always fetch more than he gave for it, so that a house, if built in really good style, was a first-class investment.

The notion of being the one member of his family with a country house weighed but little with him; for to a true Forsyte, sentiment, even the sentiment of social position, was a luxury only to be indulged in after his appetite for more material pleasure had been satisfied.

To get Irene outside London, away from opportunities of going about and seeing people, away from her friends and those who put ideas into her head! That was the thing! . . .

It would be everything to get Irene out of town. The house would please her, she would enjoy messing about with the decoration, she was very artistic![91]

Eventually the house is finished (complete with purple leather curtains) and is inspected:

The carriage put them down at the door, and they entered.

The hall was cool, and so still that it was like passing into a tomb; a shudder ran down James's spine. He quickly lifted the heavy leather curtains between the columns into the inner court.

He could not restrain an exclamation of approval.

The decoration was really in excellent taste. The dull ruby tiles that extended from the foot of the walls to the verge of a circular clump of tall iris plants, surrounding in turn a sunken basin of white marble filled with water, were obviously of the best quality. He admired extremely the purple leather curtains drawn along one entire side, framing a huge white-tiled stove. The central partitions of the skylight had been slid back and the warm air from outside penetrated into the very heart of the house.

He stood, his hands behind him, his head bent back on his high, narrow shoulders, spying the tracery on the columns and the pattern of the frieze which ran round the ivory-coloured walls under the gallery. Evidently, no pains had been spared. It was quite the house of a gentleman.[92]

In D. H. Lawrence's *The Rainbow* (1915), Ursula Brangwen, trapped and frustrated at home in Derbyshire, gets an invite from a school: 'came an intimation from Kingston-on-Thames. She was to appear at the Education Office of that town on the following Thursday, for an interview'.[93] This is against her father's wishes, who wants her to get a local job, and Ursula dreams of escape to Kingston:

She passed shadowily through the day, unwilling to tell her news to her mother, waiting for her father. Suspense and fear were strong upon her. She dreaded going to Kingston. Her easy dreams disappeared from the grasp of reality.

And yet, as the afternoon wore away, the sweetness of the dream returned again. Kingston-on-Thames – there was such sound of dignity to her. The shadow of history and the glamour of stately progress enveloped her. The palaces would be old and darkened, the place of kings obscured. Yet it was a place of kings for her – Richard and Henry and Wolsey and Queen Elizabeth. She divined great lawns with noble trees, and terraces whose steps the water washed softly, where the swans sometimes came to earth. Still she must see the stately, gorgeous barge of the Queen float down, the crimson carpet put upon the landing stairs, the gentlemen in their purple-velvet cloaks, bare-headed, standing in the sunshine grouped on either side waiting.

'Sweet Thames, run softly till I end my song.'[94]

The children's writer Jacqueline Wilson (with 35 million books sold in the UK alone) lived as a child in Kingston, and the place makes many appearances in her work, as 'Kingstown'. Opal Plumstead, in the novel of that name, lives with her parents and sisters at Primrose Villa, Kingstown, just before the First World War:

> I lived in a house called Primrose Villas. It was a pretty name, but our home was small and stark, one of ninety-eight built in bright red brick in an ugly terrace. We didn't have any primroses in our garden – just a dusty privet hedge, a square of grass, and some puny rose bushes at the front. We had no garden at all at the back, just a bleak yard with a washing line and an outdoor WC. The word 'villa' implies a large spacious house, but ours was the opposite. It had a meagre front parlour, a living room and kitchen downstairs, and two bedrooms and a box room upstairs.[95]

Only when neighbouring naughty kids, Stella and Eliza, turn up do things change.

Shepperton

Although a full 6 miles southwest from Kingston, still on the Thames, Shepperton demands inclusion here for one reason: J. G. Ballard. For Ballard, lowly Shepperton's mix of transport infrastructure, waterworks and golf clubs, the small streets of unassuming semis, all on the urban periphery (16 miles from the centre), made it the ideal mid-century modern suburb. It was, he notes, 'the everywhere of suburbia, the paradigm of nowhere'.[96] Ballard moved into his notoriously nondescript (and famously never-cleaned) Shepperton semi in 1960. 'I think I chose Shepperton because of its film studios,' he suggests in his autobiographical *Miracles of Life* (2008), 'which gave it a slightly raffish air.'[97] His wife was not so impressed: 'Mary assumed that we would stay there for no more than sixth months, but three years later, after the success of *The Drowned World*, there still seemed little hope of moving, which I think depressed her.'[98] Ballard lived there to the end of his life, in 2009, and found it enchanting. In his semi-autobiographical novel *The Kindness of Women* (1991), the narrator describes a walk with his children and dogs:

> I set off with Henry and Alice down the sun-filled street. Polly the retriever had decided to join us. He trotted beside Alice . . . The modest houses in Charlton Road sat in their quiet suburban gardens, but seeing them through the dog's and the children's eyes transformed the rosebushes and rockeries, the freshly painted front doors and forgotten roller skates. They became more vivid, as if aware that Polly and the children would soon forget them, and were urging themselves more brightly into existence. Our own house was as modest as the others – my salary . . . barely matched the small mortgage – but Miriam, Henry, and Alice turned it into an endless funfair of noise and cheer. Behind other doors in Charlton Road were other Miriams. Young wives and their children strolled the streets of Shepperton and played in their gardens like agents of an exuberant foreign power.[99]

Shepperton's mix of banal, edge-of-London suburbia (undistinguished semis, afternoon TV, boredom and perversity) along with modern infrastructure (motorways and service stations, film studios, reservoirs, airports, shopping malls and giant sheds) were like a dream of the future. Shepperton, which 'had begun to colonise the whole country',[100] was also the setting for Ballard's novels *Crash* (1973) and *The Unlimited Dream Company* (1979).

The strange, transformative power of the suburb's latent unconscious is at the centre of *The Unlimited Dream Company*. Here, a pilot, suggestively named Blake, crashes his Cessna into the Thames at Shepperton, and the 'quiet suburban town' undergoes, under Blake's messianic influence, a bizarre transfiguration. The unlikely suburb becomes tropicalized:

> The air was bright with flowers and children. Without realizing it, Shepperton had become a festival town. As I strode past the

open-air swimming pool I could see that the entire population
was out in the streets. A noisy holiday spirit rose from
thousands of voices. Sunflowers and garish tropical plants with
fleshly fruits had sprung up in the well-tended gardens like
vulgar but happy invaders of an over-formal resort. Creepers
hung from the neon sills above the shop-fronts, trailed lazy
blooms among the discount offers and bargain slogans.
Extraordinary birds crowded the sky. Macaws and scarlet ibis
watched from the roof of the multi-storey car-park, and a
trio of flamingos inspected the cars outside the automobile
showroom, eager for these burnished vehicles to join the
vivid day.[101]

As the 'pagan God' of the suburbs, Blake transforms Shepperton into a
perverse 1970s sexual paradise, with typically suburban features finding
new uses:

I set off for the centre of Shepperton. The great arms of the
banyan tree had seized the pavement outside the post office and
filling-station as if trying to pull the whole of Shepperton into
the sky. I strode down the empty street, and touched the first
of the lamp standards, anointing it with my semen. A fire vine
circled the worn concrete and rose to the lamp above my head
where it flowered into a trumpet of blossom.[102]

Ballard was still exploring the area in his last novel, *Kingdom Come*
(2006), in which Richard Pearson is out looking for the semi-mythical
motorway town of Brooklands:

Already I was lost. I had entered what the AA map represented
as an area of ancient Thames Valley towns – Chertsey,
Weybridge, Walton – but no towns were visible around me,
and there were few signs of permanent human settlement. I was
moving through a terrain of inter-urban sprawl, a geography
of sensory deprivation, a zone of dual carriageways and petrol
stations, business parks and signposts to Heathrow, disused
farmland filled with butane tanks, warehouses clad in exotic
metal sheeting . . . Nothing now made sense except in terms
of a transient airport culture. Warning displays alerted each

other, and the entire landscape was coded for danger. CCTV cameras crouched over warehouse gates, and filter-left signs pulsed tirelessly, pointing to the sanctuaries of high-security science parks.[103]

Surbiton

Back towards London, Surbiton is just over a mile south of Kingston. There is something intrinsically comic about Surbiton (perhaps because it sounds fictional, like '*suburb*iton'). Surbiton was created in the 1850s as a new town distinguished from neighbouring Kingston, largely because the latter didn't want a railway running through it, and quickly became a desirable suburb, sometimes called 'Queen of the London Suburbs' (a title also claimed by Ealing). Surbiton's sense of self-satisfied superiority and reputation as the essence of middle-class, smug English suburban dullness appears in numerous works of fiction (and TV sitcoms).

In the 1870s the area was at the outer limit of London's suburban spread and was the home, surprisingly enough, of Victorian England's foremost nature writer, Richard Jefferies. Jefferies gleefully presented London as a vast, stinking toxic swamp in his future-set dystopian fantasy *After London* (1885), but actually quite enjoyed the town-meets-countryside boundary of Surbiton, as he explains in his highly wrought 'spiritual autobiography', *The Story of My Heart* (1883):

> From my home near London I made a pilgrimage almost daily to an aspen by a brook. It was a mile and a quarter along the road, far enough for me to walk off the concentration of mind necessary for work. The idea of the pilgrimage was to get away from the endless and nameless circumstances of everyday existence, which by degrees build a wall about the mind so that it travels in a constantly narrowing circle. This tether of the faculties tends to make them accept present knowledge, and present things, as all that can be attained to. This is all – there is nothing more – is the iterated preaching of house-life. Remain; be content; go round and round in one barren path, a little money, a little food and sleep, some ancient fables, old age and death.[104]

Jefferies's account of his walks, and the abundance and variety of wildlife he routinely came across, were collected as *Nature Near London* (1883):

It is usually supposed to be necessary to go far into the country to find wild birds and animals in sufficient numbers to be pleasantly studied. Such was certainly my own impression till circumstances led me, for the convenience of access to London, to reside for a while about twelve miles from town. There my preconceived views on the subject were quite overthrown by the presence of as much bird-life as I had been accustomed to in distant fields and woods.

First, as the spring began, came crowds of chiffchaffs and willow-wrens, filling the furze with ceaseless flutterings. Presently a nightingale sang in a hawthorn bush only just on the other side of the road. One morning, on looking out of window, there was a hen pheasant in the furze almost underneath. Rabbits often came out into the spaces of sward between the bushes.

The furze itself became a broad surface of gold, beautiful to look down upon, with islands of tenderest birch green interspersed, and willows in which the sedge-reedling chattered. They used to say in the country that cuckoos were getting scarce, but here the notes of the cuckoo echoed all day long, and the birds often flew over the house. Doves cooed, blackbirds whistled, thrushes sang, jays called, wood-pigeons uttered the old familiar notes in the little copse hard by. Even a heron went over now and then, and in the evening from the window I could hear partridges calling each other to roost.

Along the roads and lanes the quantity and variety of life in the hedges was really astonishing. Magpies, jays, woodpeckers – both green and pied – kestrels hovering overhead, sparrow-hawks darting over gateways, hares by the clover, weasels on the mounds, stoats at the edge of the corn. I missed but two birds, the corncrake and the grasshopper lark, and found these another season. Two squirrels one day ran along the palings and up into a guelder-rose tree in the garden. As for the finches and sparrows their number was past calculation.[105]

Surbiton as a byword for the everyday features in Keble Howard's *The Smiths of Surbiton: A Comedy without a Plot* (1906). This is the first of a series of novels dealing with the mostly mundane, domestic – yet always cheerful – lives of a lower-middle-class suburban couple. Here, Ralph and Enid Smith, just married, buy a house in Surbiton. Ralph works as a clerk in an insurance office, doing nicely on £350 a year:

> Altogether, then, the young couple had felt fully justified in renting, on a five years' lease, that desirable residence known as The Pleasance. The name of the house, idyllic though it might be, formed only one of the numerous attractions. There was the little garden in the front, for example, and there was the rather larger garden in the back. There was the pretty little drawing-room, with the little French windows opening on to the tiny balcony. There were the airy kitchen, the five bedrooms, and the dainty little bath-room. Finally there was the admirable situation 'two minutes from river and seven from station'. The house, by the way, boasted a number, but the Smiths had decided to dispense with it. Their note-paper bore the simple address, The Pleasance, Eton Road, Surbiton.[106]

The Smiths do well and move to a more pretentious residence in Surbiton:

> known to the tradespeople, the postal authorities, and the world in general as Valley View . . . It contained three reception and seven bedrooms, to say nothing of the lounge-hall and the electric-light fittings. The garden, tastefully laid out, was large enough for lawn-tennis and croquet. There were apple trees and plum trees, a greenhouse, strawberry-beds, and vegetables in abundance.
>
> In short, Valley View was just the house to which a man who has worked steadily and industriously for nearly forty years, who has married happily and brought up a family, whose employers have grown to look upon him as a staunch, good friend, whose eldest son is playing his part in the development of the Colonies, and whose eldest daughter is about to take her place as a younger of local society, may fairly consider himself entitled wherein to pass the gentle, closing years of his life.[107]

E. M. Forster finds hints of the eternal, the poetic and the ecstatic in the unlikely confines of a Surbiton alley in his 1911 fable 'The Celestial Omnibus':

> The boy who resided at Agathox Lodge, 28, Buckingham Park Road, Surbiton, had often been puzzled by the old sign-post that stood almost opposite. He asked his mother about it, and she replied that it was a joke, and not a very nice one, which had been made many years back by some naughty young men, and that the police ought to remove it. For there were two strange things about this sign-post: firstly, it pointed up a blank alley, and, secondly, it had painted on it in faded characters, the words, 'To Heaven'.[108]

The boy looks up and down his street:

> At the present moment the whole road looked rather pretty, for the sun had just set in splendour, and the inequalities of rent were drowned in a saffron afterglow. Small birds twittered, and the breadwinners' train shrieked musically down through the cutting – that wonderful cutting which has drawn to itself the whole beauty out of Surbiton, and clad itself, like any Alpine valley, with the glory of the fir and the silver birch and the primrose. It was this cutting that had first stirred desires within the boy – desires for something just a little different, he knew not what, desires that would return whenever things were sunlit, as they were this evening.[109]

Running up the blind alley, between the walls of two villas, he spots a sign: 'Sunrise and Sunset Omnibuses', return tickets available from the driver. The boy gets in the coach (the driver turns out to be Sir Thomas Browne) and they set off through some fog and head for somewhere that should have been 'Richmond Hill', and then up through the air and onto a shimmering rainbow:

> The boy looked below, past the flames of the rainbow that licked against their wheels. The gulf also had cleared, and in its depths there flowed an everlasting river. One sunbeam entered and struck a green pool, and as they passed over he saw three

maidens rise to the surface of the pool, singing, and playing with something that glistened like a ring.[110]

The boy returns, much to his parents' annoyance, transformed: full of imagination, profound joy and a deep knowledge of Keats and Shelley. Pompous snob, local bigwig Mr Bons, is outraged at the boy's outrageous lies and pretensions to culture, and demands to go out on the next trip. Things don't go well:

> From the *Kingston Gazette, Surbiton Times*, and *Raynes Park Observer*.
> The body of Mr Septimus Bons has been found in a shockingly mutilated condition in the vicinity of the Bermondsey gas-works. The deceased's pockets contained a sovereign-purse, a silver cigar-case, a bijou pronouncing dictionary, and a couple of omnibus tickets. The unfortunate gentleman had apparently been hurled from a considerable height. Foul play is suspected, and a thorough investigation is pending by the authorities.[111]

In the 1970s, thanks to the BBC sitcom *The Good Life* (1975–8), Surbiton becomes the epitome of boring and complacent English suburbanism. Yet of course, the supposedly ordinary contain within them the seeds of weirdness (Tom and Barbara and Margo and Jerry were *very* weird). This strangeness is captured in Bernice Rubens's 1987 novel *Our Father*, where God Almighty himself makes several unscheduled appearances in Surbiton. Explorer Veronica Smiles has just met aristocrat Edward Boniface on the train back from Victoria Station to Surbiton after returning from a trip to a desert:

> The train stopped at Berrylands. Surbiton was next. Normally at this stop, on her way home from expeditions, she had grown excited, longing to be home, to acknowledge singly every familiar object in her rooms, to consolidate herself in that base that she would normally leave again. At this stop she would rise and assemble her luggage and make her way down the aisle to the exact exit door that, on her arrival, would align her with the platform bridge that would lead her to the taxi-rank. But this time she made no move, stiffening herself as if to will the train not to move forward. All of a sudden she didn't want to reach

her stop and to have to say goodbye to this man, the first in her life to whom she had actually volunteered conversation.[112]

A week later in Surbiton she has a surprise encounter:

> Her car refused to start, so she ran all the way, collected the first loaf that came out of the oven and sprinted out of the shop. The streets were deserted. It would be an hour before the first trains left for the city. She savoured her aloneness as she savoured it in the desert, that appetite of hers that had first lured her to the solitary wastes of the world. So she was slightly irritated to see a figure approach her from the opposite direction. As she ran toward home, nibbling on the crust of the hot bread, she saw that he was God. She pulled up sharply as she reached Him.
> 'What are you doing in Surbiton?' she asked crossly.
> 'I am everywhere,' He said.
> Everywhere, she thought, as long as there's not a soul around to witness it. 'Then I'll see you in the market on Thursday,' she said. 'Twelve o'clock under the tower.' Let Him get out of that one.[113]

Comedian Julian Clary lived in Surbiton as a child and describes some early impressions in his autobiography *A Young Man's Passage* (2005):

> I had an Action Man (the first of many), while my sisters had Sindy dolls. They had boxes full of outfits with matching shoes and accessories, and my Action Man had a choice between camouflage all-in-ones or black slacks with matching polo neck. It was a ridiculous situation and I did the only thing I could. Very soon my Action Man was Surbiton's first cross-dressing experiment. (I blame the wallpaper.) Stretch fabrics looked particularly fetching on his well-toned torso and rippling limbs.[114]

In John Burnside's memoir *Waking Up in Toytown* (2010), the author recounts his efforts to escape alcoholism, dead-end jobs, drift and a potential mental breakdown by looking for a solidly normal life:

That was what I wanted, more than anything. A normal life. Sober. Drug-free. Dreamless. In gainful employment. A householder. A taxpayer. A name on the electoral roll. A regular, everyday sort of guy. The next-door neighbour whose name you can never remember, the one who keeps himself to himself but is basically OK. I wanted, in short, to be comfortably numb . . .

So I went to the suburbs.

I went to the suburbs because I wished to live deliberately, to front only the essential facts of life, and see if I could not learn what they had to teach, and not when I came to die, discover that I had not lived. I wanted the order that other people seemed to have, the non-apophenic order of a normal life.[115]

And where does Burnside go for his 'normal life'? To 'Surbiton, or somewhere like it'. Yet Burnside actually ends up in Guildford; for this is, after all, an imaginary Surbiton, an idealized location: 'my Surbiton was a Surbiton of the mind, a dreamscape that I was constructing around a *soi-disant* outsiders' confusion of the normal and the banal':[116]

Surbiton. Shorthand for a place that almost existed, a simplified world of autumn leaves and buses and a house in a side street where a man could live clean and true – and alone, of course, with his books and music and not even a Siamese cat for company.[117]

New Malden and Worcester Park

New Malden, 2 miles east of Surbiton, was originally developed as a suburb in the 1860s, but really only took off with the great suburban expansion in the interwar years. Paul Vaughan describes this in his memoir *Something in Linoleum* (1994). The Vaughans were part of a new exodus in the 1930s, out to the raw, modern peripheral suburbs:

This was where the postal district numbers came to an end. We weren't in London, we were in Surrey, and it mattered. My mother was captivated by the newness of it all, the 'villagey' High Street, with a neat little railway station, trees growing out of the pavement and hardly a Cockney accent to be heard. There was a tea shop with tables outside, fixed into the pavement in the form of concrete mushrooms. There wasn't much traffic, and, instead of noisy double-decker omnibuses labouring along the city roads, there was a single-decker 'country' bus that chugged through New Malden on its way to the county town (county town!) of Kingston-upon-Thames.[118]

This was all made possible by the car and the new bypasses: 'the most important thing about the situation of our new house', proudly named 'Wayside', 'was that it stood on the Kingston Bypass.' At first the Vaughans are thrilled by the startling modernity of the new roads and traffic zooming past their brand-new semi, 'as along its modern dual carriageway bowled the compact little motors, mostly black or navy blue, Morris Tens and Ford Eights or V-Eights, with running boards and starting handles, sometimes dickey seats and windscreens you could open, adventuring to the coast for the day'.[119] But there was another side to this:

> 'Wayside' . . . the name implied a soft-edged, sentimental view of the house's location, and of the murderous traffic that roared past, rising to its peak on hot summer weekends. Acre Lane [Brixton] this was not. Here the needs of the people and the needs of the motor car collided head-on. Most weeks in the *Wimbledon Borough News* or *Surrey Comet* you could read a headline reporting fresh casualties in the war that smouldered on our doorstep. DEATH-TRAP ON BYPASS – People Afraid to Send Children to School . . . TWO KILLED ON BYPASS – Motor Cyclists in Triple Crash . . . BYPASS TRAGEDY – Poor Lighting Criticized. From the landing window or the 'lounge' of 'Wayside' there was a clear view of the South Lane junction where some of the most spectacular accidents would regularly occur – the screaming of brakes, a sharp bang, a reverberating skitter of metal fragments, followed by even more sinister noises: the moans of the victims, the screams of women bystanders.[120]

There was also another surprising aspect to suburban modernity in New Malden. Vaughan attends a newish school, Raynes Park County, whose inspirational headmaster, John Garrett, had known

W. H. Auden while at Oxford. Garrett gets Auden to compose the
school motto – 'To each his need, from each his power' (adapted from
Marx) – and even to write the school song:

> My life was shaped by two quite different phenomena of the
> 1930s: the rapid redistribution of the population that went
> with the creation of the London suburbs; and the literary and
> artistic movement of the times. In Raynes Park, SW20, The Man
> on the Clapham Omnibus came face to face with the Auden
> Generation.[121]

Auden visited the school and the area, and seems, Vaughan reckons,
to have had New Malden in mind when writing certain anti-suburban
lines in his work, such as these from his play *The Ascent of F6* (1936),
written with Christopher Isherwood and featuring Mr and Mrs A.
(Average?), an archetypal timid suburban couple:

> The eight o'clock train, the customary place,
> Holding the paper in front of your face,
> The public stairs, the glass swing-door,
> The peg for your hat, the linoleum floor . . .
> Then the journey home again
> In the hot suburban train
> To the tawdry new estate.[122]

In H. G. Wells's 1909 'New Woman' novel *Ann Veronica*, the
heroine is trapped in suburban domestic respectability in dreary
Morningside Park, clearly modelled on Worcester Park:

> Morningside Park was a suburb that had not altogether, as
> people say, come off. It consisted, like pre-Roman Gaul,
> of three parts. There was first the Avenue, which ran in a
> consciously elegant curve from the railway station into an
> undeveloped wilderness of agriculture, with big, yellow brick
> villas on either side, and then there was the pavement, the little
> clump of shops about the post-office, and under the railway
> arch was a congestion of workmen's dwellings. The road from
> Surbiton and Epsom ran under the arch, and, like a bright
> fungoid growth in the ditch, there was now appearing a sort

of fourth estate of little red-and-white rough-cast villas, with meretricious gables and very brassy window-blinds.[123]

'Ye gods!' she exclaims, looking around the place, '*what* a place! Stuffy isn't the word for it.'[124] Ann is discontented with her 'beautiful, safe and sheltering home', her Victorian, controlling and patronizing father, and the tedium of the suburb, and longs to escape to London. She forms an escape plan with the help of the one nearby family with 'artistic quality', the Widgetts:

> All this was exciting and entertaining. Her aunt returned before her packing was done, and Ann Veronica lunched with an uneasy sense of bag and hold-all packed up-stairs and inadequately hidden from chance intruders by the valance of the bed. She went down, flushed and light-hearted, to the Widgetts' after lunch to make some final arrangements, and then, as soon as her aunt had retired to lie down for her usual digestive hour, took the risk of the servants having the enterprise to report her proceedings and carried her bag and hold-all to the garden gate, whence Teddy, in a state of ecstatic service, bore them to the railway station. Then she went up-stairs again, dressed herself carefully for town, put on her most businesslike-looking hat, and with a wave of emotion she found it hard to control, walked down to catch the 3.17 up-train.[125]

Would-be discerning architect (actually supply teacher) Albert Angelo, in B. S. Johnson's 1964 novel of the same name, has it in for Worcester Park:

> Albert's full contempt was reserved for Worcester Park: St. Helier was bad but unpretentious, but Worcester Park was both very bad and pretentious at the same time. Street upon street of semi-detached mock-timbered gables, Norman arches on the porches, Gothic windows in the halls, bakelite door furniture throughout, intensely unimaginative front garden layouts, identical wrought iron gates, twee lanterns to light the porches. William Morris was responsible for having started the movement which led to all this, Albert thought, but surely he could not have approved of Worcester Park?[126]

6 'REAL STABILITY'

West London: From Hammersmith to Chiswick, Brentford, Hounslow, Southall, Ealing, Shepherd's Bush and White City

This part of the west London suburbs is, in the literary imaginary, largely characterized by roads and transit, and by experiments in modernity. Chiswick's Bedford Park becomes the first Arts and Crafts garden suburb, providing the very latest in up-to-date metropolitan living: the 'new traditionalism' of a revived Queen Anne suburban house in a carefully landscaped setting. Key road, rail and canal routes to the west became, in the interwar years, London's first real trunk road for cars (the Great West Road, then, later, Western Avenue, the Hammersmith Flyover and the Westway): the age of the car arrived in London. The streamlined modernity of the west London suburb was also evident in the rapid construction of numerous Art Deco factories, film studios, warehouses and workshops, along with long lines of 'Runroamin' semis stretching out for miles either side of the raw tarmac. This was modernity, some of it even illuminated to provide the spectacle of the neon-lit 'Golden Mile'.

This was all obsessively written about by a long list of fascinated 1930s writers – Stephen Spender, George Orwell, Evelyn Waugh, Aldous Huxley, Elizabeth Bowen – all mesmerized by this startling, streamlined, futuristic landscape, dedicated to speed and popular consumption, producing cars, records and domestic and electrical appliances. And all of them mostly appalled. In the 1970s there came extensive demolition and urban regeneration, then even a brief hint of the futuristic urban motorway. Finally, we also have here the appearance of transformed high streets and neighbourhoods, as mass migration from the Indian subcontinent irrevocably changed and enriched these suburbs for ever.

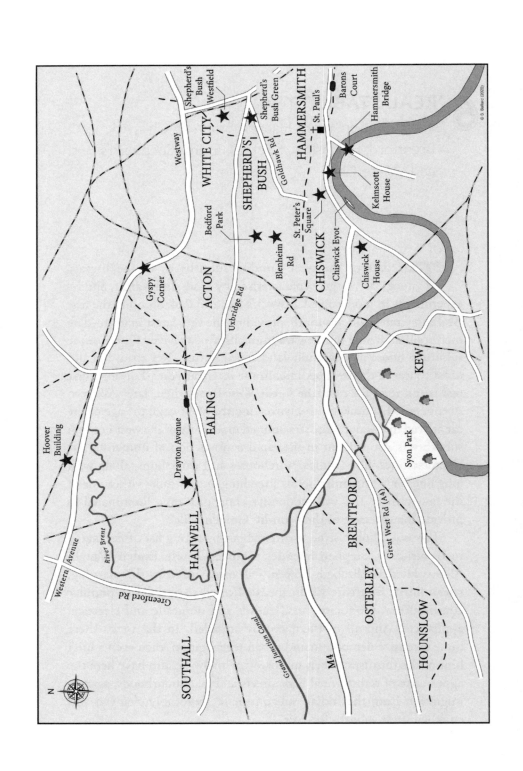

© S. Ballou (2002)

Hammersmith

Hammersmith, 4.5 miles southwest of Charing Cross, just west of Kensington, is strung along the north bank of the Thames opposite Barnes and Putney, and beneath the elevated A4, the key route out to Heathrow and the west. Well served by access to key routes (including, in 1827, London's first suspension bridge), Hammersmith quickly industrialized in the nineteenth century, bringing depots, factories, engineering works, a huge food-processing industry, a famed plant nursery, and much working- and lower-middle-class housing.

On leaving Cambridge in 1632, John Milton went to live with his parents, who had retired down to Hammersmith from Bread Street in the City, partly to escape the plague. Milton left an account of his studies in these years:

> At my father's country place, whither he had retired to spend
> his declining years, I devoted myself entirely to the study of
> Greek and Latin writers, completely at leisure, not, however,
> without sometimes exchanging the country for the city,
> either to purchase books or to become acquainted with some
> discovery in mathematics or music, in which I then took the
> keenest pleasure.[1]

Daniel Defoe, in his extensive *Tour through the Whole Island of Great Britain* (1724–7), is already impressed with Hammersmith and can see its future potential:

> In the village of Hammersmith, which was formerly a long
> scattering place, full of gardeners' grounds, with here and there
> an old house of some bulk: I say, in this village we see now not
> only a wood of great houses and palaces, but a noble square
> built as it were in the middle of several handsome streets, as if
> the village seem'd enclin'd to grow up into a city. Here we are
> told they design to obtain the grant of a market, tho' it be so
> near to London, and some talk also of building a fine stone
> bridge over the Thames; but these things are yet but in embryo,
> tho' it is not unlikely but that they may be both accomplished
> in time, and also Hammersmith and Chiswick joining thus,
> would in time be a city indeed.[2]

Moll Flanders moves to Hammersmith in Defoe's (anonymously published) 1722 picaresque novel, to accommodation provided by Moll's latest, married, admirer:

> He met me at Reading in his own chariot, and taking me into that, left the servants and the child in the hired coach, and so he brought me to my new lodgings at Hammersmith; with which I had an abundance of reasons to be very well pleased, for they were very handsome rooms, and I was very well accommodated.[3]

Here Moll aims for some kind of respectability:

> And now I was indeed in the height of what I might call my prosperity, and I wanted nothing but to be a wife, which, however, could not be in this case, there was no room for it; and therefore on all occasions I study'd to save what I could ... against a time of scarcity, knowing well enough that such things as these do not always continue; that men that keep mistresses often change them, grow weary of them, or jealous of them, or something or other happens to make them withdraw their bounty; and sometimes the ladies that are thus well used are not careful by a prudent conduct to preserve the esteem of their persons, or the nice article of their fidelity, and then they are justly cast off with contempt.
>
> But I was secur'd in this point, for as I had no inclination to change, so I had no manner or acquaintance in the whole house, and so no temptation to look any farther. I kept no company but in the family where I lodg'd, and with the clergyman's lady at next door; so that when he was absent I visited no body, nor did he ever find me out of my chamber or parlour whenever he came down; if I went anywhere to take the air, it was always with him.[4]

Pip also finds pleasant lodging with Herbert Pocket's family at Hammersmith, it being a desirable area for respectable clerks, when he first comes to stay in London in Dickens's *Great Expectations* (1861):

This collation disposed of at a moderate price (considering the grease, which was not charged for), we went back to Barnard's Inn and got my little portmanteau, and then took coach for Hammersmith. We arrived there at two or three o'clock in the afternoon, and had very little way to walk to Mr Pocket's house. Lifting the latch of a gate, we passed direct into a little garden overlooking the river, where Mr Pocket's children were playing about. And unless I deceive myself on a point where my interests or prepossessions are certainly not concerned, I saw that Mr and Mrs Pocket's children were not growing up or being brought up, but were tumbling up.

Mrs Pocket was sitting on a garden chair under a tree, reading, with her legs upon another garden chair; and Mrs Pocket's two nurse-maids were looking about them while the children played. 'Mamma,' said Herbert, 'this is young Mr Pip.' Upon which Mrs Pocket received me with an appearance of amiable dignity.

'Master Alick and Miss Jane,' cried one of the nurses to two of the children, 'if you go a bouncing up against them bushes you'll fall over into the river and be drownded, and what'll your pa say then?'[5]

Pip starts to get involved in some traditional Hammersmith pastimes:

In the evening there was rowing on the river. As Drummle and Startop had each a boat, I resolved to set up mine, and to cut them both out. I was pretty good at most exercises in which country boys are adepts, but as I was conscious of wanting elegance of style for the Thames – not to say for other waters – I at once engaged to place myself under the tuition of the winner of a prize-wherry who plied at our stairs, and to whom I was introduced by my new allies. This practical authority confused me very much by saying I had the arm of a blacksmith. If he could have known how nearly the compliment lost him his pupil, I doubt if he would have paid it.[6]

William Morris moved into Kelmscott House, on Upper Mall, Hammersmith, in 1879 and would travel between this and the *other* Kelmscott House, in Oxfordshire, some 125 meandering miles upstream. This journey is recapitulated in Morris's utopian novel *News from Nowhere* (1890), concerning one William Guest, whom we first see returning home to grubby Hammersmith one evening by 'underground railway', 'that vapour-bath of hurried and discontented humanity', where he is 'stewed discontentedly'. He walks to his house, 'which stood on the banks of the Thames, a little way above an ugly suspension bridge'.[7] The place seems a little different:

> There was a young moon halfway up the sky, and as the home-farer caught sight of it, tangled in the branches of a tall old elm, he could scarce bring to his mind the shabby London suburb where he was, and he felt as if he were in a pleasant country place . . . He came right down to the river-side, and lingered a little, looking over the low wall to note the moonlit river, near upon high water, go swirling and glittering up to Chiswick Eyot; as for the ugly bridge below, he did not notice or think of it.[8]

The next day, after a restless night's sleep, Guest awakes to find Hammersmith very different indeed. It is suddenly summer, and the Thames is oddly clear and sparkling; well-dressed, robust, hearty types are out swimming and catching salmon. The filthy factories, the smoking chimneys, the lead-works, all gone, the 'ugly' iron suspension bridge replaced by a carved, medieval-style stone one with houses and workshops on it. The date it was built? 2003.

> The date shut my mouth as if a key had been turned in a padlock fixed to my lips; for I saw that something inexplicable had happened . . . So I tried to look unconcerned, and to glance in a matter-of-course way at the banks of the river, though this is what I saw up to the bridge and a little way beyond; say as far as the site of the soap-works. Both shores had a line of very pretty houses, low and not large, standing back a little way from the river; they were mostly built of red brick and roofed with tiles, and looked, above all, comfortable, and as if they were, so to say, alive and sympathetic with the life of the dwellers in them. There was a continuous garden in front of them, going down to the water's edge, in which the flowers were now blooming luxuriantly, and sending delicious waves of summer

scent over the eddying stream. Behind the houses, I could see great trees rising, mostly planes, and looking down the water there were reaches towards Putney almost as if they were a lake with a forest shore.[9]

Taking its cue from Morris's Thameside Hammersmith arcadia, A. P. Herbert's popular romantic novel *The Water Gipsies* (1930) focuses on the life of a family of bargees and the romantic entanglement of its principal character, Jane Bell. The novel begins near Hammersmith Bridge, with Jane and her sister on a sailing barge. Industry certainly isn't absent from the river around Hammersmith:

> The tide was rising again, and one of the first tugs came through Hammersmith Bridge . . . A man called a greeting from the tug to a watchman at the boat-houses . . . The tug went lazily past them, with a lazy chunk-chunk of the engine and a lazy swish at the bows, till at last the red eye narrowed too and was gone . . . The mud, the reeds, had disappeared, and the water was lapping against the wall. There were two red eyes passing now, and all down the river the tugs were hooting to warn the wharves at which they were to call. The busy hour of the river was beginning.[10]

Richard Marsh's cultish *fin de siècle* horror tale *The Beetle* (1897) opens with starving, unemployed clerk Robert Holt tramping through southwest London, looking for a place to stay for the night, walking out from Fulham in the dismal rain:

> I had come to Hammersmith as a last resource. It had seemed to me that I had tried to find some occupation which would enable me to keep body and soul together in every other part of London, and that now only Hammersmith was left. And, at Hammersmith, even the workhouse would have none of me!
> Retreating from the inhospitable portal of the casual ward, I had taken the first turning to the left, – and, at that moment, had been glad to take it. In the darkness and the rain, the locality which I was entering appeared unfinished. I seemed to be leaving civilisation behind me. The path was unpaved; the road rough and uneven, as if it had never been properly made.

Houses were few and far between. Those which I did encounter, seemed, in the imperfect light, amid the general desolation, to be cottages which were crumbling to decay.[11]

Eventually Marsh comes to an odd-looking house:

It was not a large one. It was one of those so-called villas which are springing up in multitudes all round London, and which are let at rentals of from twenty-five to forty pounds a year. It was detached. So far as I could see, in the imperfect light, there was not another building within twenty or thirty yards of either side of it.[12]

Here, paralysed with fear, he makes terrifying acquaintance with The Beetle.

On a sudden I felt something on my boot, and, with a sense of shrinking, horror, nausea, rendering me momentarily more helpless, I realised that the creature was beginning to ascend my legs, to climb my body. Even then what it was I could not tell, – it mounted me, apparently, with as much ease as if I had been horizontal instead of perpendicular. It was as though it were some gigantic spider, – a spider of the nightmares; a monstrous conception of some dreadful vision. It pressed lightly against my clothing with what might, for the entire world, have been spider's legs. There was an amazing host of them, – I felt the pressure of each separate one. They embraced me softly, stickily, as if the creature glued and unglued them, each time it moved.[13]

In 1929, writer and poet Robert Graves, his wife Nancy, the American poet Laura Riding, who was then Graves's lover, and the Irish poet Geoffrey Phibbs set up a bohemian ménage in a house in St Peter's Square, Hammersmith. As one might guess, things didn't go at all well, though there is some confusion as to what actually happened on one notorious evening. Novelist Naomi Mitchison claimed, many years later, to have been there and to remember:

I was at the party when Laura Riding jumped out of the window. It was a party of big names in the Arts and I was escaping from one of the top portrait painters. I would have liked to be seen forever young and lovely, but if it meant going to bed with him – no. Then there was a wild row going on and Laura Riding jumped out of the window and Robert Graves jumped after her, but sensibly ran downstairs so that it was an easy jump. I disliked Laura so much that I would have preferred her to have been bashed to bits, but not at a party.[14]

Graves and Riding, after recovering from serious injury, escaped to Mallorca.

In James Curtis's hard-boiled 1936 thriller *The Gilt Kid*, the kid is being led out of town, west somewhere, on a job, by fellow burglar Scaley. The kid, though calm, has a very bad feeling about it all, particularly the destination:

Hammersmith Road. The bus travelled on, a mechanical thing driven by a mechanical man. When the bell rang once, the driver stopped the vehicle; when it rang twice, he started it again. When the lights were against him, he stopped; when they were with him he went on. There was no need to think. He just did his job. When he had finished the day's work, when he had punched the time clock, he would have become a man again. Until then he was just another unit in the industrial system.
Hammersmith Broadway.
Life, movement and vitality once more. Above and beyond all a smell of fried fish and chips. One of London's focal centres.
Scaley heaved himself, not without reluctance, out of his seat.
'Get off here, mate,' he said.
The kid followed him down the steps. He was feeling exalted. The first job he had done since he came out of prison. Well, he had never been caught on the job yet. Been chased off out of the gaff times without number, but never been caught there. He hoped his luck was going to be good.[15]

Hammersmith-born experimental novelist B. S. Johnson set his 1973 novel *Christie Malry's Own Double-entry* in the area. Malry, living 'near Hammersmith Bridge, in the stump of Mall Road left after the flyover and associated highway improvements', proves to be an unusual kind of trainee accountant.[16] He gleefully adopts the double-entry bookkeeping system he is learning to reuse as a reliable form of moral redistribution: every single time he is offended, annoyed, frustrated or angered, he will note the event on a detailed spreadsheet and then seek a restitutive and fitting revenge. This starts out small (vandalism, pranks) but soon escalates, expanding to include Molotov cocktails and a mass cyanide poisoning at the Barn Elms reservoirs, just across the river from Hammersmith.

> The lorry was already loaded with drums of the chemical . . .
> He loosened the caps with a chain wrench, and removed them
> with heavy-duty rubber gloves on. Starting the lorry by bridging
> across the ignition switch took a little more time than opening
> the door, but was equally as simple and does not bear further
> elucidation here. Then he opened the gates, drove out, closed
> the gates, drove on across Hammersmith Bridge and turned
> fourth left into Merthyr Terrace, no martyr. No one was of
> course on duty at this time of night to see him cut the u-bolt of
> the padlock with one brachyureate nip of a pair of bolt-cutters,
> open the gates and drive in.
>   Christie did not waste time looking. A short track led up
> the bank of the reservoirs, and at the nearest point he reversed
> the lorry to the edge and actuated the tip-up mechanism the
> lorry (of course) had. As the drums began to rumble through
> the open tailgate, Christie jumped out and watched them. In
> the low sunlight he saw the crystalline white powder pour out,
> begin to dissolve and make its way into the planet's water.[17]

The next day, mostly in west London, 'a total of just over twenty thousand people died of cyanide poisoning'.[18]

Hammersmith is also happily recalled in Johnson's 1963 novel *Albert Angelo*, as wannabe architect Angelo revisits his childhood home:

> The sun on St Paul's Hammersmith lifts me. Its proportions are
> miraculous, miraculous. Who did it [. . .] Gough, yes, Gough
> and Roumieu, and someone else. Forget the other. My first real
> isometric drawing was of St Paul's. My first real. Miraculous.
> And my parents (whatever that may mean) were married there,

at St Paul's. The flyover, Hammersmith flyover, too, pleases me. It sets off the church, is a fine piece of architecture itself. Graceful, curving away as though on tiptoe. But the sun emphasises which is the better.

Under, along, down towards the river. Towards the house of my parents.[19]

Hammersmith proves to be equally strange in Irvine Welsh's *Trainspotting* (1993). Here we see Renton returning to London, looking for the old gang:

Ah walk doon Hammersmith Broadway, London seeming strange and alien, after only a three-month absence, as familiar places do when you've been away. It's as if everything is a copy of what you knew before, similar, yet somehow lacking in its usual qualities, a bit like the way things are in a dream. They say you have to live in a place to know it, but you have to come fresh tae it tae really see it . . .

Everything in the street seems soft focus. It's probably lack of sleep and lack of drugs.[20]

Chiswick

A mile west of Hammersmith, further along the Great West Road, Chiswick still had market gardens and orchards until the later nineteenth century. Much of the area was not built up until the interwar years; one reason for this was the domination of the area by the Dukes of Devonshire, who had become owners of the spectacular Chiswick House. This was a huge and hugely influential Palladian suburban villa, built by Lord Burlington and finished in 1729, with extensive gardens that influenced the English landscape movement. The duke offered patronage to Pope, Swift, Gay and Handel, and over the centuries Chiswick House itself was visited by Voltaire, Rousseau, George Washington, Thomas Jefferson, William Ewart Gladstone, Queen Victoria – and The Beatles, in 1966, for the 'Paperback Writer' video.

William Makepeace Thackeray went to school in Chiswick, and his novel *Vanity Fair* (1848) opens with a section titled 'Chiswick Mall', setting the scene as Amelia Sedley and Becky Sharp are about to leave 'Miss Pinkerton's academy for young ladies'. Becky chucks her leaving present, Dr Johnson's *Dictionary*, out of the carriage window:

> While the present century was in its teens, and on one sunshiny morning in June, there drove up to the great iron gate of Miss Pinkerton's academy for young ladies, on Chiswick Mall, a large family coach, with two fat horses in blazing harness, driven by a fat coachman in a three-cornered hat and wig, at the rate of four miles an hour. A black servant, who reposed on the box beside the fat coachman, uncurled his bandy legs as soon as the equipage drew up opposite Miss Pinkerton's shining brass plate, and as he pulled the bell, at least a score of young heads were seen peering out of the narrow windows of the stately old brick house. Nay, the acute observer might have recognised the little red nose of good-natured Miss Jemima Pinkerton herself, rising over some geranium pots in the window of that lady's own drawing-room.
>
> 'It is Mrs Sedley's coach, sister,' said Miss Jemima. 'Sambo, the black servant, has just rung the bell; and the coachman has a new red waistcoat.'
>
> 'Have you completed all the necessary preparations incident to Miss Sedley's departure, Miss Jemima?' asked Miss Pinkerton herself, that majestic lady – the Semiramis of Hammersmith, the friend of Dr Johnson, the correspondent of Mrs Chapone herself.[21]

Alain-Fournier's 1913 novel of lost love, *Le Grand Meaulnes*, describes how teenager Augustin stumbles across an enchanting, dreamlike, three-day-long fete in a grand country house. Here, Augustin falls in love, but is rejected. Oddly, later, he realizes that he cannot locate where this house was. The novel's title is sometimes translated as 'The Lost Domain', and this sense of youthful obsession, an inability to return to a first love, fading glamour (and the frenzied party at the centre of it all) is supposed to have influenced F. Scott Fitzgerald's *The Great Gatsby*. Intriguingly, Alain-Fournier worked as a translator at the Sanderson's wallpaper factory, Chiswick, in the summer of 1905 and based the novel's fictional party on the elaborate annual summer fete at the factory's well-resourced social club.

Iain Sinclair records how Patrick Keiller, in the latter's journals, comments on the curious sense of unreality experienced by many displaced European intellectuals roaming the capital's suburbs.

> Dostoevsky, Rimbaud and Verlaine . . . Strindberg, Alain-Fournier – they were all in London at one time or another – (and Gustave Doré, and Van Gogh) – and all have left some sort of record of their impressions, which are naturally strange, only half-recognisable, like a dream of a place one knows. I particularly like Alain-Fournier's appreciation of the suburban villas of Chiswick and Kew, and of the atmosphere of London summer Sunday afternoons at the beginning of the century, and his saying that of all towns, he would prefer London to be unhappy in.[22]

London's influential first 'garden suburb' was built at Bedford Park, just north of the District line at Turnham Green. This was begun in 1876 by a speculative builder, Jonathan Carr, who aimed to create a superior, spacious and organically planned suburb with large, variegated, Queen Anne-style houses (some designed by Edward William Godwin, part of the Aesthetic Movement), landscaped, planted with trees and set back from the road, and seeking to promote a discrete community feel with church, shops and even a club. In 1887 Bedford Park became home for the Yeats family, at 3 Blenheim Road. Jack Yeats, an unsuccessful portrait painter, was attracted to the bohemian raffishness of the area, as R. F. Foster, the biographer of his son W. B. Yeats, explains:

> A milieu where respectable bohemianism met popular aestheticism suited both JBY and his eldest son. The population of Bedford Park included artists, journalists, academics, poets, playwrights, a celebrated pet anarchist (Sergius Stepniak) and an oddly high proportion of retired military men, attracted by the low house prices. Bargain-basement aestheticism existed within convenient range of William Morris's enterprises at Hammersmith . . . The Yeatses were quickly a Bedford Park fixture.[23]

While at Bedford Park, Yeats met Maude Gonne and Oscar Wilde and wrote 'An Old Song Re-sung' (later renamed 'Down by the Salley

Gardens'), 'The Wanderings of Oisin' and perennial favourite 'The
Lake Isle of Innisfree'. His sister, Lily Yeats, later recalled:

> In Bedford Park one evening, Helen Acosta & Lolly painting
> and I sat there sewing – Willy bursting in having just written,
> or not even written down but just having brought forth
> 'Innisfree', he repeated it with all the fire of creation and his
> youth – he was I suppose about 24. I felt a thrill all through me
> and saw Sligo beauty, heard lake water lapping, when Helen
> broke in asking for a paint brush . . . None of us knew what a
> great moment it was. Not that 'Innisfree' is one of his greatest,
> but it is beautiful & perhaps the best known.[24]

Influential German architectural historian Hermann Muthesius,
author of the landmark study *The English House* (1908), was very
impressed with Bedford Park:

> There was at the time virtually no development that could
> compare in artistic charm with Bedford Park, least of all had
> the small house found anything like so satisfactory and artistic
> and economic solution as here. And herein lies the immense
> importance of Bedford Park in the history of the English house.
> It signifies neither more nor less than the starting point of the
> smaller modern house, which immediately spread from there
> over the whole country.[25]

Bedford Park's lush, decadent aestheticism also appears at the
opening of G. K. Chesterton's 'metaphysical thriller' *The Man Who
Was Thursday* (1908), but renamed 'Saffron Park':

> The suburb of Saffron Park lay on the sunset side of London,
> as red and ragged as a cloud of sunset. It was built of a bright
> brick throughout; its skyline was fantastic, and even its ground
> plan was wild. It had been the outburst of a speculative builder,
> faintly tinged with art, who called its architecture sometimes
> Elizabethan and sometimes Queen Anne, apparently under
> the impression that the two sovereigns were identical. It was
> described with some justice as an artist's colony, though it
> never in any definable way produced any art. But although its

pretensions to be an intellectual centre were a little vague, its pretensions to be a pleasant place were quite indisputable. The stranger who looked for the first time at the quaint red houses could only think how very oddly shaped the people must be who could fit into them. Nor when he met the people was he disappointed in this respect. The place was not only pleasant, but perfect, if once he could regard it not as a deception but rather as a dream.[26]

This decadent dreaminess of Saffron Park/Bedford Park – all mauves and Chinese lanterns and lurid sunsets – is particularly in evidence on the evening that Gregory Syme, an undercover policeman posing as an anarchist (codename 'Thursday'), attends a party.

> More especially this attractive unreality fell upon it about nightfall, when the extravagant roofs were dark against the afterglow and the whole insane village seemed as separate as a drifting cloud. This again was more strongly true of the many nights of local festivity, when the little gardens were often illuminated, and the big Chinese lanterns glowed in the dwarfish trees like some fierce and monstrous fruit.[27]

The Seeds of Pleasure (1932), the second part of Patrick Hamilton's trilogy of seedy, infernal London, 'Twenty Thousand Streets under the Sky', sees domestic skivvy Jane 'Jenny' Taylor, with 'two old fossils' to look after, out drinking, for the first time in her life, in Hammersmith. She and her friend Violet have been picked up by a couple of cads, Andy and Rex. All very drunk, they tumble into Andy's car and head towards Chiswick; Jenny is so thrilled she starts talking as if in the movies:

> And then the car had started, and she felt the wind on her face. Gee, this was fun! And to think she'd never been in a car before! Gee, this was just what she was wanting to clear her head.
>   They were back in the Broadway in less than a minute, and flying along King Street in the direction of Chiswick.
>   'Where are we going?' cried Jenny, against the speed and wind. But no one answered her. The young man was yodel-ling, and Rex and Violet were cuddling each other with raucous

laughter behind; and Andy, now wrapped in the authoritative taciturnity of the driver, did not see fit to answer.

Gosh – he was getting up a pace! . . . Ravenscourt Park . . . Stamford Brook . . . She knew the route well enough – she had come that way earlier in the evening by tram . . . She supposed it was safe – going at this pace. There were very few vehicles on the road, but he was overtaking them all. She supposed it seemed risky to her because she had never been in a car before . . .

Here they were! – scouring along the Chiswick High Road itself! Chiswick! As they whizzed past the Green she looked over towards the home of the two old fossils. And to think of them sleeping peacefully in bed, and she out here. It must be pretty well midnight. Gee, what a life!

And now they had passed Gunnersbury, and had turned up to the right, and were ripping up the wide, smooth, deserted spaces of the Great West Road . . . Gee! – it was like a racing track – no wonder he put on speed. It was like being in an aeroplane.[28]

But this is no movie. They hit something: 'With a grating noise and a thud, a man and his bicycle were hurled helplessly against the side of the car, and left behind in the darkness.'[29]

In Mavis Cheek's novel *Pause between Acts* (1988), abandoned Joan Battran goes to see her estranged husband's new girlfriend, and compares suburban Chiswick, unfavourably, to urban Notting Hill:

She lived, of course, in Notting Hill. All thrusting and thriving and cosmopolitan, with a hundred names to every front door and rooms without net curtains full of pot plants and esoteric posters. I had lived here once – so had Jack, though in a better part of the same area. It was the life we both eschewed when we got married and bought the house in Chiswick less than a year ago. Chiswick had milkmen who whistled and came regularly each morning – real stability. Notting Hill sold its milk in cartons and nobody knew your name. The area felt quite alien to me now as I stomped through the slush to her hallowed portals.[30]

Todd Sileen, the one-legged book-dealing occultist in Iain Sinclair's 1994 novel *Radon Daughters*, is on a meandering journey down from Whitechapel to Mortlake for research related to John Dee, the Elizabethan magus, when, around Chiswick, he at last 'crosses the water'. He finds that he doesn't fit in:

> We can't have it all. Chiswick Eyot at low tide, a tufty islet in a bath of mustard. Sacrifices have to be made. The houses of William Morris and Hogarth the Painter, the obelisk (*Imitatio Ruris*) in the grounds of Lord Burlington's villa.
>
> Sileen rattles his coins, gesturing to the parade of waterside pubs. We'd never get through the door. Blue plaque territory, gourmands in distressed corduroy. Yellow and red Labour party endorsements in the windows of wisteria-enveloped Georgian mansions.[31]

Brentford

Further downriver, opposite Kew, Brentford ('Ford over the River Brent'), first appears to history as 'Breguntford' in 705. Once the (probable) county town of Middlesex, its importance stemmed from its key position on river, canal and key routes to the west. Brentford industrialized in the nineteenth century, with major gasworks, factories and docks, supplemented by key industries developing along Western Avenue in the interwar years.

Brentford is where Mrs Boffin heads in search of an 'eligible orphan' in Dickens's *Our Mutual Friend* (1864–5), the said child in the care of his grandmother, Mrs Betty Higden:

> The abode of Mrs Betty Higden was not easy to find, lying in such complicated back settlements of muddy Brentford that they left their equipage at the sign of the Three Magpies, and went in search of it on foot. After many inquiries and defeats, there was pointed out to them in a lane, a very small cottage residence, with a board across the open doorway, hooked on to which board by the armpits was a young gentleman of tender years, angling for mud with a headless wooden horse and line. In this young sportsman, distinguished by crisply curling auburn head and a bluff countenance, the Secretary descried the orphan.

It unfortunately happened as they quickened their pace, that the orphan, lost to considerations of personal safety in the ardour of the moment, overbalanced himself and toppled into the street. Being an orphan of a chubby conformation, he then took to rolling, and had rolled into the gutter before they could come up.[32]

The new bypasses and dual carriageways of suburban west London, the A4 Great West Road from Chiswick to Brentford (John Betjeman's 'Great Worst Road') and, to the north, Western Avenue (later Westway), were built in the 1920s and '30s and appeared as startlingly streamlined and modern. Lined with miles of new 'Dunroamin' semis and smart, white Art Deco factories and warehouses of the new, Americanized, industries (Gillette, Firestone, Hoover, Curry's), they seemed to be the future and were best viewed from a speeding car on broad, empty roads. These gleaming new industrial units were often floodlit, so providing a glamorous backdrop (nicknamed the 'Golden Mile') for the speeding motorist. This is what J. B. Priestley could see in his chauffeur-driven jaunts along Western Avenue, recorded in his 1934 state-of-the-nation travelogue, *English Journey*:

> Along Western Avenue the traveller will see, a few miles only from the heart of the Empire's capital, a gleaming palace in dazzling white and red, with soaring white towers, the walls are almost of glass, set like a glittering gem in the midst of green lawns and gay flower-beds. With its flat roof and general design, it might almost be the palace of some Oriental potentate.[33]

Flying over the same suburban west London are a couple of Bright Young Things in Evelyn Waugh's satire *Vile Bodies* (1930). The sight is too much for Nina:

> Nina looked down and saw inclined at an odd angle a horizon of straggling red suburb: arterial roads dotted with little cars; factories, some of them working, others empty and decaying; a disused canal; some distant hills sown with bungalows; wireless masts and overhead power cables; men and women were indiscernible except as tiny spots; they were marrying and shopping and making money and having children. The scene

lurched and tilted again as the aeroplane struck a current
of air.
     'I think I'm going to be sick,' said Nina.[34]

Louis MacNeice's long poem *Autumn Journal* (1938), an account
of the author's life in the final year of peace, combining global events
with rhythms of everyday life soon to be shattered, also includes a
phatasmagoric rainy night-time car journey from London to Oxford
along Western Avenue:

> The next day I drove by night
>   Among red and amber and green, spears and candles,
> Corkscrews and slivers of reflected light
>   In the mirror of the rainy asphalt
> Along the North Circular and Great West roads
>   Running the gauntlet of impoverished fancy
> Where housewives bolster up their jerry-built abodes
>   With *amour propre* and the habit of Hire Purchase.
> The wheels whished in the wet, the flashy strings
>   Of neon lights unravelled, the windscreen-wiper
> Kept at its job like a tiger in a cage or a cricket that sings
>   All night through for nothing.
> Factory, a site for a factory, rubbish dumps,
>   Bungalows in lathe and plaster, in brick, in concrete,
> And shining semi-circles of petrol pumps
>   Like intransigent gangs of idols.[35]

Just to the northwest, Hayes, near where George Orwell grew up, is
the setting for a rare poem by him from 1934, 'On a Ruined Farm near
the His Master's Voice Gramophone Factory'. This describes a beloved,
but now alien, landscape being grubbed up by 'factory-towers':

> I can neither
> Dwell in that world, nor turn again
> To scythe and spade, but only loiter
> Among the trees the smoke has slain.[36]

This strange new techno-futuristic landscape of suburban west
London motorways *is* the future in Aldous Huxley's dystopian *Brave*

New World (1931). Here, as we fly west 'over the six kilometre zone of parkland that separated Central London from its first ring of satellite suburbs', we see the zones of state-sanctioned compulsory fun:[37]

> The green was maggoty with foreshortened life. Forests of Centrifugal Bumble-puppy towers gleamed between the trees. Near Shepherd's Bush two thousand Beta-Minus mixed doubles were playing Riemann-surface tennis. A double row of Escalator Fives Courts lined the main road from Notting Hill to Willesden. In the Ealing stadium a Delta gymnastic display and community sing was in progress . . .
>
> The buildings of the Hounslow Feely Studio covered seven and a half hectares. Near them a black and khaki army of labourers was busy revitrifying the surface of the Great West Road. One of the huge travelling crucibles was being tapped as they flew over. The molten stone poured out in a stream of dazzling incandescence across the road; the asbestos rollers came and went; at the tail of an insulating watering cart the steam rose in white clouds.
>
> At Brentford the Television Corporation's factory was like a small town.[38]

This is the landscape described in Elizabeth Bowen's novel *To the North* (1932):

> The roads were empty: Oxford, where they hoped to breakfast, was still asleep, so they rushed the Chilterns and breakfasted at High Wycombe . . . They swerved north a little at Uxbridge and spun into London by the great empty by-pass of Western Avenue. Small new shops stood distracted among the buttercups; in the distance aerial glassy white factories were beginning to go up among forlorn may trees, branch lines and rusty girders: here and there one was starting to build Jerusalem.[39]

Gabriel Harvey, in Paul Bailey's *Gabriel's Lament* (1986), has, after many years of bedsits and shared flats around London, finally ended up living near the river in Chiswick:

> I live by the Thames these days at Chiswick . . . I can see the river at all hours, in all its moods. Even on the darkest night,

it is a glittering presence. On just such a night, a week ago, the
water looked thick and still as I walked slowly home from the
Steam Packet. I was almost at my door when I noticed what
appeared to be a body floating on the calm surface. Had the
richest of my wealthy neighbours, I wondered, succumbed to
despair as the result of a setback on the stock exchange? Was the
merchant banker a sudden pauper?

Fanciful questions, morbid imaginings – the corpse was
a log.[40]

Robert Rankin's comic fantasy – or, as Rankin prefers, 'far-fetched
fiction' – series the 'Brentford Trilogy' (concluding in 2019 after eleven
novels) chronicles the low-life antics of ill-assorted pub, bookie and
allotment dwellers in a semi-squalid Brentford landscape of dodgy
pubs, cafés and heavy traffic. Yet the twist here is that the key characters, Jim Pooley and John Vincent Omally, are also locked into a kind
of epic battle with a character who seems to be a homeless tramp, but
is also, really, the reincarnation of Pope Alexander IV, the 'Antipope'
of the first book's title. Boring Brentford is actually the battlefield of
clashing cosmic forces. As Soap Distant, the 'founder and sole member
of the Brentford and West London Hollow Earth Society', points out:

How many times have I propended my theories regarding
the lands beneath and their interterrestrial occupants, and
how many times have I offered irrefutable proof as to their
existence . . . Beneath the surface of the globe . . . is the vast
and beautiful land of Agharta, and in that sunken realm at the
very centre of the planet, Shamballah, capital city of Earth.
Here in unimaginable splendour dwells Rigdenjyepo, King of
the World, whose emissaries, the subterranean monks of black
habit, weave their ways through the endless network of ink-dark
corridors which link the capital cities of the ancient world.[41]

Soap's house, 15 Sprite Street, from which 'strange noises had been
heard in the nights coming as from the bowels of the earth',[42] seems
to offer access to this world beneath:

The wall dividing the front room from the back parlour had
been removed along with all the floorboards and joists on the

ground floor. The section of flooring on which the three now stood was nothing more than the head of a staircase which led down and down into an enormous cavern of great depth which had been excavated obviously with elaborate care and over a long period of time. A ladder led up to the bedroom, the staircase having been long ago removed.

Omally stared down into the blackness of the mighty pit which yawned below him. 'Where does it go to?' he asked.

'Down,' said Soap. 'Always down but also around and about.'[43]

Hounslow

Hounslow, around a mile southwest of Brentford along the London Road, almost at Heathrow, again derives its identity from straddling the main routes out of London. William Cobbett in *Rural Rides* (1830) is appalled by the place:

A much more ugly country than that between Egham and Kensington would with great difficulty be found in England. Flat as a pancake, and, until you come to Hammersmith, the soil is a nasty stony dirt upon a bed of gravel. Hounslow-heath, which is only a little worse than the general run, is a sample of all that is bad in soil and villainous in look.[44]

At this time the heath would have been vast and remote, and, with the main Bath Road, later the A4, running across it, ideal highwayman territory, as Walter Bell describes in his suburban travelogue *Where London Sleeps* (1926):

You might have known the roads by the gallows fruit that ripened along their sides. Gibbets at intervals marked the way, the guiding signposts. A horseman with no other aids to direction would travel surely by riding from one to the other. By the short rope, or may be in iron chains, the relics of malefactors who had worked along these roads dangled from the beam, intended as solemn warnings for a better course of life, which precious few in that age heeded. Not unseldom a wind blew over the heath, sharpening at times to a gale, and then these grisly phantoms would take unto themselves movement, though denied life, swaying to the creaking of the chains in a dreadful death dance.[45]

These main thoroughfares (the Great West Road, Staines Road, the Chertsey Road, the M4), promising escape to the west, remain intrinsic parts of any west London psychic geography. Gautam Malkani's 2006 Hounslow-set novel, *Londonstani*, features car- and speed-loving 'rudeboys, then we be Indian niggas, then rajamuffins, then raggastanis, Britasians, fuckin Indobrits. These days we try an use our own word for homeboy an so we just call ourselves desis.'[46] Here Jas is getting a lift in tough, cool Hardjit's 'pimped-up Beemer':

> The world going by outside the window tells me that in the olden times, before the airport, Hounslow must've been one a them batty towns where people ponced around on cycles stead a drivin cars. Why else we got such narrow roads? Some a them were so narrow that the trees on each side had got their branches castrated to stop them fightin in the middle. In't no leaves on em either, even in the summer. Talk bout a shitty deal for the trees. Castrated an no pubes. Standin there like giant, upright versions a the dried-up sticks a dog-shit that lay at their feet. If I was a cycleriding, tree-huggin, skint hippy I might've given a shit bout the trees an all the posters pinned to them for some Bollywood film that'd been released two weeks ago, the new Punjabi MC single that came out a month ago or ads for a bhangra gig in Hammersmith that happened a year ago. But I in't, so stead I hope the skint people who work for the local council would just finish the fuckin job and chop em all down. Make way for more billboards, more fuckin road. Only proper-sized roads round here were the Great West Road an London Road, both a them runnin along either side a this part of Hounslow like garden fences to an airport at the back where the garden shed should be (they called it Heathrow cos it's bang in the middle a Hounslow Heath or someshit). Lucky for us there weren't no other cars cruisin down all these side roads squashed between the garden fences. There were hardly any parked cars along the pavements either, partly cos the staff car parks at Heathrow were full but mostly cos all a the houses

round here had got their front gardens concreted over an turned into driveways. Big wheelie rubbish bins an recycling boxes where the plants, flower beds an garden paths used to be. No sign a the other stuff I drew on houses when my playschool teacher moved me up from crayons to colouring-in pencils. None a them smokin chimneys an those lollipop-like trees were missin too.[47]

Southall

Southall is north of Hounslow, between the M4 and the M40, around 8 miles west of Hyde Park. Spurred by the arrival of the Grand Junction Canal at the end of the late eighteenth century and then the railway some forty years later (Brunel's Great Western Railway had a depot here), industrial production really took off in the nineteenth century, with Southall becoming home to the largest margarine factory in the world as well as the renowned AEC bus factory, making the famed Routemasters. Asians from the Punjab began arriving in the early 1950s, initially attracted by available factory work (and, jokingly, the proximity to the airport); over the decades Southall became known as 'Little India'. By the 1970s the area was racially tense, with an anti-National Front protest turning violent in 1979 and a major riot involving skinheads and local Asians in the summer of 1981.

The riot is referenced in John King's 2008 novel *Skinhead*, where we see skinhead Ray, on 4 July 1981,

> going over to Southall to see the 4-Skins, Last Resort and Business play at the Hamborough Tavern . . . Southall is a chance for the boys in West London to see these bands, and it's a ten-minute train ride from Slough, there's five of them making the trip, and coming out of the station they're the only white faces, there's more Indians here than in Slough, and it's a fair old hike to the pub so they jump on a bus to the Broadway . . . a police car shoots past, sirens blaring, and Ray and the others see a big gang of locals looking over at them and one of them's carrying a long stick, Nick reckons it's a sword, and Ray can see a knife, and it's dawned on him that skinheads are supposed to hate immigrants and maybe these Indians believe what they read in the papers, perhaps they don't know what

Oi and street punk is all about, and he's heard plenty of people moaning about how the wogs and the jungle bunnies are taking over, but none of the skins he knows are interested in party politics, and anyway, his uncle was one of the original skins and all he ever listens to is reggae.[48]

Yet Ray soon enough gets stuck in and the fighting is clearly seen in racist terms:

Somehow Ray stays on his feet, fights back, most of them are his size or smaller, even the older ones, and he smacks two more in the face, and it's like he's in Calcutta or Bombay, in one of those films on the telly where the savages are after the white man and they're going to chop him up if they can just get him on the ground, and he keeps thinking about the knife, doesn't want to die, but he's angry he's being attacked for being white, on the streets of his own country . . . and Ray isn't going to give up, he's English and proud.[49]

In Tim Lott's 1996 memoir *The Scent of Dried Roses*, Lott is driving west towards Southall, where he grew up, away from Notting Hill, the place he has escaped to. His mother has just committed suicide, and lines from her terrible final note are stuck in his head:

This will be so bad for everybody but I hate Southall, I can see only decay, I feel alone.

I am driving towards Southall, to try to reimagine the place I grew up in, that I left twenty years ago. The place that Jean could no longer stand to live in. I turned the phrase from her note over and over in my mind.

I arrive through Greenford, the first stop off the Western Avenue on the way to Southall. I drive past the anonymous shops. There is an ugly 1950s church, Our Lady of the Visitation, just before Cardinal Wiseman High School. My school, Greenford County Grammar, would play them at football. To the right, the Golf Links estate, white high-rise blocks, where I would go to visit friends from my school who were not lucky enough to be owner-occupiers, Ds and Es rather than C2s. Here, the skinheads would gather to brood and swagger, but racial attacks were largely unheard of, or perhaps simply unreported, at least until Gurdip Singh Chaggar was murdered outside the Dominion Cinema in 1976. After that there were the National Front march in 1979, when Blair Peach died at the hands of the Special Patrol Group, and then the Southall Riots in 1981.[50]

Lott wants to make it clear that he left Southall, and his mother became increasingly unhappy there, not because of the area's transformation from a white working-class area to a largely Asian one, but because 'Southall was a dump, because it was nowhere, like most of subtopian England.'[51] He drives on:

> Into Southall proper . . . The signs read Curried Halal Meats, the Queens Style Carpet Centre, the Shahi Nan Kebab, Fine Fabric: Specialists in Sarees and Dhuptas, the White Hart Pub – now Shadows Night Club, Karaoke Most Evenings, West London's Fun Club. Past the White Hart and the town hall, boarded up and crumbling: These Premises Controlled by Security Officers. There are mock Doric columns, bathetic, supporting the roof to the entrance. Beyond and to the right, the plaster melted wedding cake of Southall Mosque. To the left, Mohammed Jewellers. Diagonally opposite, the astonishing folly of what was once the Southall Palace Cinema, its two giant Golden Dragons still intact and looking down at the street scene. Now it had been broken up into small market units selling cloth, gewgaws and pencils.[52]

In Nirpal Dhaliwal's 2006 novel *Tourism*, Bhupinder 'Puppy' Johal, a Sikh from Southall, also thinks the place is a total dump and can't wait to leave and head for London proper:

> We smoked our cigarettes looking at Allenby Road, the front line separating Southall from Great Britain. This street is where the Punjabi tribe starts in force, leading downhill into the brown-skinned, petit bourgeois suburbia of Lady Margaret Road, which itself leads to the bustle, often mayhem, of the Uxbridge Road, Southall's high street. Cross over the road, go down the other side of the hill, and you come to Ruislip

Road, Greenford's main street. The faces are whiter there, the pavements aren't full of people hawking Bollywood soundtracks while their asylum claims are processed.[53]

His loathing for Sikh Southall centres on his mother:

Behold!, the Asian family: unit of tradition, moral strength and business acumen. Behold!, my mother: matriarch and fulcrum, proud bearer of sons, stately in her new sari, her one eyebrow draped across her forehead like a trophy pelt, her moustache downy like an adolescent boy's.

It was a lousy type of revenge. For her disappointments, we suffered a mother who looked like an animal. Walking with her through streets, down supermarket aisles, we felt ashamed, revolted, and guilty for feeling so. And there was the weight: a stone gained when each of us came of age not meeting her expectations. She was five feet tall, weighed as much as a man and sported a beard.[54]

For Johal, growing up in Southall in the 1970s was a nightmare:

At school every Asian was habitually called a Paki, but I was given special treatment. My joodha – or 'top-knot' or 'bobble-head' as they called it – made me the focus of relentless abuse. I'd be pushed around the playground, slapped and taunted; they'd descend on me like harpies, trying to knock it off my head. I'd walk, sobbing, to the nurse's office, holding the hankie my mother had wrapped it in, as they tugged at my hair which now fell over my face and shoulders. I was ten years old. My last two years at primary school were impossible. Before then, no one had noticed me. I had no friends, apart from Asaf, and he wasn't a friend, just another 'stani' who'd been ostracised from the herd . . . The other Asian kids ignored my suffering; they were glad I was taking the heat and not them. The blacks were only too happy to join in; in fact, black boys were among my worst tormentors.[55]

Ealing

Famed for its film studios (the oldest in the world in continuous use, starting in 1902), Ealing had an envious reputation in the late nineteenth century as a middle-class utopia, and by the turn of the century had gained the nickname 'Queen of the Suburbs'. This describes both what it retained – being still relatively rural and villagey, with good train links to town, varied and well-built housing stock – and also what it managed to avoid: polluting industry and the working classes.

The unnamed sixteen-year-old beatnik narrator of Terry Taylor's *Baron's Court, All Change* (1961) loathes being stuck in unhip Ealing/Acton, especially as things are starting to happen just a little further east in Notting Hill:

> It was an early summer's evening and the streets looked inviting but there wasn't a soul about. No kids even – and it was a shame. They were clean houses, not good ones; all painted well enough and some were even bright – but they were all the same – every one of them. Even the people were, somehow. They belonged to the place like a tribe. If the natives saw anything their eyes weren't accustomed to – say, for instance, a Spade with his native costume on – they'd all stop and stare and think he'd come from Outer Space. Yet, only a very few miles away, when you're free from this thing they call Suburbia (a good name for it, don't you think?) that same Spade could walk down the street with his pyjamas on and nobody would take any notice.
>
> Down Drayton Avenue again I walked, taking giant steps to get me a train all the quicker; whistling loudly an improvised ten choruses of *Gone With the Wind*, until some old girl, her arms busy carrying some brawling brat, reached near me, so I had to let the imaginary piano take over, as the cries of this starving suburban bastard put me right off.[56]

The novel's title alludes to the boundary tube station where suburb gives way to city:

> The place where I lived comes under an area they call Greater London, which is such a ridiculous name I shan't make any

comment on it. So to get to the London which isn't so great but a bloody sight better, you have to board a tube train which goes on a twenty minute journey above ground till you come to a station called Baron's Court. Just as you leave Baron's Court station the train goes underground, and this never failed to give me a little thrill. At that point, when the train first goes into the tunnel, you are leaving Greater London, where the natives starve themselves to buy a new car to show off to their neighbours with, and enter the manor of the real Londoners. The ones the whole world have heard about and respect, and when you cross this border the people seem to change from puppets into human beings.[57]

George Orwell does not specify the exact location of 'Ellesmere Road, West Bletchley', home of disgruntled insurance agent and archetypal suburban man George 'Tubby' Bowling, in his pessimistic pre-war novel *Coming Up for Air* (1939). But we can guess: Ealing or maybe Hayes, further west. Robert Collis points out that there were five Ellesmere Roads in 1940; 'three in west London and one in Ealing, very like the one where the Bowlings live'.[58] Orwell is convinced we know the *type* anyway:

You know how these streets fester all over the inner-outer suburbs. Always the same. Long, long rows of little semi-detached houses – the numbers in Ellesmere Road run to 212 and ours is 191 – as much alike as council houses and generally uglier. The stucco front, the creosoted gate, the privet hedge, the green front door. The Laurels, the Myrtles, the Hawthorns, Mon Abri, Mon Repos, Belle Vue.[59]

Bowling's mood does not lighten when he leaves the house.

I had the street pretty much to myself. The men had bunked to catch the 8.21 and the women were fiddling with the gas-stoves. When you've time to look about you, and when you happen to be in the right mood, it's a thing that makes you laugh inside to walk down these streets in the inner-outer suburbs and to think of the lives that go on there. Because, after all, what *is* a road like Ellesmere Road? Just a prison with the cells all in a row. A line of semi-detached torture chambers where the poor little five-to-ten-pound-a-weekers quake and shiver, every one of them with the boss twisting his tail and his wife riding him like the nightmare and the kids sucking his blood like leeches.[60]

Much later we see Bowling return to London after a depressing pilgrimage to revisit a rural childhood idyll at 'Lower Binfield'.

And presently I struck into outer London and followed the Uxbridge Road as far as Southall. Miles and miles of ugly houses, with people living dull decent lives inside them. And beyond it London stretching on and on, streets, squares, back-alleys, tenements, blocks of flats, pubs, fried-fish shops, picture-houses, on and on for twenty miles, and all the eight million people with their little private lives which they don't want to have altered. The bombs aren't made that could smash it out of existence. And the chaos of it! The privateness of all those lives! John Smith cutting out the football coupons, Bill Williams swapping stories in the barber's. Mrs Jones coming home with the supper beer. Eight million of them! Surely, they'll manage somehow, bombs or no bombs, to keep on with the life that they've been used to?[61]

Shepherd's Bush and White City

Moving back in towards central London, squeezed in between the Uxbridge Road, the Westway and the West Cross Route, Shepherd's Bush (the name seeming to have originated from its use as a stopping place built for shepherds en route to London), around 5 miles west of Charing Cross, was largely undeveloped until the construction of the ornate buildings built for the 1908 Franco-British Exhibition and the Olympic Games. This site's twenty-odd stucco and marble palaces gave the north of the area its name: White City. Shepherd's Bush can boast TV sitcoms' *second* best-known address (after Tony Hancock's 23 Railway Cuttings, East Cheam): 24 Oil Drum Lane, site of *Steptoe and Son*'s rag and bone yard and dingy house. The former exhibition buildings were slowly dismantled, and the area was slowly reclaimed by housing estates and, in 1985, the BBC offices, but it remained semi-derelict until well into the 1990s. Regeneration arrived in the form of London's largest shopping mall, Westfield, opened in 2008.

Office clerk Edward Darnell, in Arthur Machen's 1904 story 'A Fragment of Life', lives a dull, routine-filled life in Shepherd's Bush; this place *seeming* to be an unremarkable Edwardian suburb:

> All day long a fierce and heavy heat had brooded over the City, and as Darnell neared home he saw the mist lying on all the damp lowlands, wreathed in coils about Bedford Park to the south, and mounting to the West, so that the tower of Acton Church loomed out of a grey lake. The grass in the squares and on the lawns which he overlooked as the 'bus lumbered wearily along was burnt to the colour of dust. Shepherd's Bush Green was a wretched desert, trampled brown, bordered with monotonous poplars, whose leaves hung motionless in air that was still, hot smoke. The foot passengers struggled wearily along the pavements, and the reek of the summer's end mingled with the breath of the brickfields made Darnell gasp, as if he were inhaling the poison of some foul sick-room.[62]

But, then, because this is Arthur Machen, gradually the mundane lifts and dissolves to reveal a very different Shepherd's Bush. Darnell, as he recounts to his wife over breakfast, has sensed other realities:

> 'Oh, I recollect now. That was the night I thought I heard the nightingale (people say there are nightingales in Bedford Park), and the sky was such a wonderful deep blue.'
>
> He remembered how he had walked from Uxbridge Road Station, where the green 'bus stopped, and in spite of the fuming kilns under Acton, a delicate odour of the woods and summer fields was mysteriously in the air, and he had fancied that he smelt the red wild roses, drooping from the hedge. As he came to his gate he saw his wife standing in the doorway, with a light in her hand, and he threw his arms violently about her as she welcomed him, and whispered something in her ear, kissing her scented hair. He had felt quite abashed a moment afterwards, and he was afraid that he had frightened her by his nonsense; she seemed trembling and confused. And then she had told him how they had weighed the coal.[63]

Parnell then decides that he would like to take a walking tour for his holiday; only this would be, perversely, 'a tour of London and its environs'. He sets off from Edna Road, Shepherd's Bush, and in an increasingly heightened visionary state perceives the presence of wonder and joy, even hints of past lives and epochs, beyond the veil of the customary and ordinary:

> 'I remembered one night I had gone farther. It was somewhere in the far west, where there are orchards and gardens, and great broad lawns that slope down to trees by the river. A great red moon rose that night through mists of sunset, and thin, filmy clouds, and I wandered by a road that passed through the orchards, till I came to a little hill, with the moon showing above it glowing like a great rose. Then I saw figures pass between me and the moon, one by one, in a long line, each bent double, with great packs upon their shoulders. One of them was singing, and then in the middle of the song I heard a horrible shrill laugh, in the thin cracked voice of a very old woman, and they disappeared into the shadow of the trees. I suppose they were people going to work, or coming from work in the gardens; but how like it was to a nightmare!
>
> 'I can't tell you about Hampton; I should never finish talking. I was there one evening, not long before they closed the gates, and there were very few people about. But the grey-red, silent, echoing courts, and the flowers falling into dreamland as the night came on, and the dark yews and shadowy-looking statues, and the far, still stretches of water beneath the avenues; and all melting into a blue mist, all being hidden from one's eyes, slowly, surely, as if veils were dropped, one by one, on a great ceremony! Oh! my dear, what could it mean? Far away, across the river, I heard a soft bell ring three times, and three times, and again three times, and I turned away, and my eyes were full of tears.'[64]

Between 1962 and 1970 the elevated Westway was built, a small part of what was once planned to be London's extensive modern urban motorway network, the so-called 'Motorway Box'. The tangled and multi-level elevated motorway interchange to the north of White City, at the junction with the West Cross Route, is the location for J. G. Ballard's 'autogeddon' Robinson Crusoe update, *Concrete Island* (1974).

> Soon after three o'clock on the afternoon of April 22nd 1973, a 35-year-old architect named Robert Maitland was driving down the high-speed exit lane of the Westway interchange in central London. Six hundred yards from the junction with the newly built spur of the M4 motorway, when the Jaguar had already passed the 70 m.p.h. speed limit, a blow-out collapsed the front nearside tyre. The exploding air reflected from the concrete parapet seemed to detonate inside Robert Maitland's skull. During the few seconds before his crash he clutched at the whiplashing spokes of the steering wheel, dazed by the impact of the chromium window pillar against his head. The car veered from side to side across the empty traffic lanes, jerking his hands like a puppet's. The shredding tyre laid a black diagonal stroke across the white marker lines that followed the long curve of the motorway embankment. Out of control, the car burst through the palisade of pinewood trestles that formed a temporary barrier along the edge of the road. Leaving the hard shoulder, the car plunged down the grass slope of the embankment. Thirty yards ahead, it came to a halt against the rusting chassis of an overturned taxi. Barely injured by this violent tangent that had grazed his life, Robert Maitland lay across his steering wheel, his jacket and trousers studded with windshield fragments like a suit of lights.[65]

Maitland is now effectively marooned in a deep patch of wasteland in the middle of the city:

> Shielding his eyes from the sunlight, Maitland saw that he had crashed into a small traffic island, some two hundred yards long and triangular in shape, that lay in the waste ground between three converging motorway routes. The apex of the island pointed towards the west and the declining sun, whose warm light lay over the distant television studios at White City. The base was formed by the southbound overpass that swept past seventy feet above the ground. Supported on massive concrete pillars, its six lanes of traffic were sealed from view

by the corrugated metal splash-guards installed to protect the
vehicles below.

Behind Maitland was the northern wall of the island, the
thirty-feet-high embankment of the westbound motorway from
which he had crashed. Facing him, and forming the southern
boundary, was the steep embankment of the three-lane feeder
road which looped in a north-westerly circuit below the overpass
and joined the motorway at the apex of the island. Although
no more than a hundred yards away, this freshly grassed slope
seemed hidden behind the overheated light of the island, by
the wild grass, abandoned cars and builder's equipment. Traffic
moved along the westbound lanes of the feeder road, but the
metal crash barriers screened the island from the drivers.[66]

Edward Platt explores a blighted and decaying Westway and
Western Avenue in his history of the area, *Leadville* (2000), fascinated
by the bizarre landscape of motorways lined with miles of beleaguered
semis, at the time threatened with redevelopment. 'The houses I had
seen beside the road began to preoccupy me', he records, 'I wanted
to know if Orwell had chosen the right place to look for England's
future.'[67] He starts knocking on doors around Gypsy Corner, in
North Acton:

The worst of times are the summer afternoons, when the flood
of traffic on Western Avenue thickens and congeals into a
fetid stew of metal which clogs the road and gums up the air.
Sometimes, Trevor Dodd wants to rush out and smash the cars
with a hammer. 'Everyone's beeping, everyone's bad-tempered,
it's hot, it's hard to breathe, it's stinking with all the exhausts
. . . it's just a wind-up'. He rests his hands on the window ledge
overlooking Western Avenue and then runs a finger along the
glass; it comes away smeared with dirt. 'Look how filthy the
window gets', he adds, disdainfully . . .

'It's dirty, it's dusty in the summer, and if it's raining, the
whole place goes brown – it's like this misty cloud all over the
road. Walk up to the shops and you get covered in dirty spray;
stand out there by the traffic lights and you get blown around
– the lorries come screaming through the junction at seventy
miles an hour, and you actually get moved off your feet.'[68]

In Sam Selvon's *Moses Ascending* (1975), Trinidadian Moses Aloeta, twenty years after we saw his and the other Caribbean 'boys' in Bayswater and Notting Hill in *The Lonely Londoner*s, has moved up – and out – to Shepherd's Bush. He is ascending, now becoming a landlord, buying a dilapidated house he sees advertised from his oldest friend in London, Tolroy: 'Highly desirable mansion in exclusive part of Shepherd's Bush. Vacant possession. Owner migrating to Jamaica.'[69]

> Galahad didn't know one arse about houses; it's true some of these terraces in London look like they might capsize any minute, but united we stand, divided we fall, and knowing Tolroy as I do, it stand to reason that he would not of bought no end-of-terrace house, but one plunk in the middle what would have support on both sides.
>
> True enough it turned out when I went to see it and get some more details from Tolroy, such as it had a five-year lease, two of which was gone, and it was due for LCC demolition. It sounded like the sort of thing I could afford.[70]

Moses's ascension is nicely literal:

> To cut a long story short, I clinch the deal with Tolroy. In this world you must not *heng* your hat too high. I would naturally of preferred a mansion in Belgravia or a penthouse in Mayfair, without too many black people around, but I had the feeling that if I didn't make the move now, I would be doomed to the basement brigade for the rest of my life.
>
> Having lived below the surface of the world all my life I ensconced myself in the highest flat in the house: if it had an attic I might of even gone higher still. It had a tall London plane what growing outside, and one of the branches stretch near the window. I would of prefer if it was a mango tree, or a calabash, to remind me of home, but you can't have everything. Also, being at the top of all them stairs was a deterrent to idlers and hustlers calling too frequently.[71]

Yet, for Moses, Ben Judah's Grenadian migrant in 2016, as recorded in *This Is London*, the area is nowhere to aspire to at all:

287

London was like someone had turned off the lights. Everything in White City was grey; the clouds, the concrete, the motorway, the estates.

'You didn't even need to tell me, I knew . . . That growing up here was rank. When I arrived at twelve years old, that smacked me right in the fucking face. I knew dat White City estate was way more corrupt . . . way more dangerous, more full of dis-illusion than anywhere in fucking Grenada . . . I swear within six months of being here I had lost 75 per cent of my morals. And I was ready to jack kids . . . and send anyone to sleep with dis fist.'[72]

Judah explains how it works:

Moses hugged the block. That's what everyone does when you got no dad and your mum is working night shifts scrubbing the toilets in BBC Television Centre – the other place they call White City. So, you get tight with the boys on the block. First it's only football. Then it's everyone jumping on their bikes to beef some estate that dared beat up some bruva for his fiver. You gotta keep up the respect. Otherwise those fuckers will be here spliffing on your lawn.[73]

Tim Lott's *White City Blue* (1999) is familiar Nick Hornbyesque lad-lit territory. Thirty-something Frankie Blue has lived in White City, with inadequates Tony, Colin and Nodge, all his life. He now needs to dump them, to try and move on, and in, with Veronica:

So now it's just another Tuesday night on the Goldhawk Road. I'm on my fifth bottle of Staropramen, trying to get well and truly binnered, but my mind feels absolutely unfogged. It's not a matter of wanting. I *need* to be drunk. Tonight I've got to tell them that I'm leaving them, that it's over, that it hasn't worked out, that I'm selling them down the river.

Diamond Tony, Nodge, and Colin are all with me, inside the Bush Ranger, watching the Rangers game on the satellite screen. A hundred other faces are upturned also, mostly male. They have scorched faces from Spanish tans, greased French crops, white lager-foam moustaches, MA 1 nylon jackets. Stone-washed jeans, white Reeboks, gold earrings, fake Ralphs from the Bush Market. It's all sports casual, surf-wear and over-designed running shoes, Nike Air Maxes up against the Reebok DMX 2000 series. The whole place has an odour of Fosters Ice and Lynx Aftershave. I like it. It smells like home.[74]

Semi-derelict White City is the setting for Nicholas Royle's psychological thriller *The Director's Cut* (2000). Here, among the abandoned buildings of the old Exhibition halls, Angelo feels he may have found what he's long being looking for: the 'Museum of Lost Cinema Spaces':

Across Rockwood Place from the Walkabout was the Shepherd's Bush Empire, which had screened its last movie in 1953. As Angelo made his way around the Green, checking out the former location of the Galaxy in the appallingly grim shopping centre on the south side of the Green, he reflected on the evidence that Shepherd's Bush had once been one of London's busiest neighbourhoods for cinema-going. Other picture houses – the Bioscope and the King's Hall Picture Palace – had operated on the north side of the Green. Angelo reached the Green's apex. Across six lanes of traffic was a huge white building. It was unknown to Angelo – his notebooks drew a blank – so not a former cinema, but a powerful building nonetheless and Angelo crossed the road to get a better look. The front door appeared to be padlocked and signs indicated that the premises were guarded by a security firm. Fly-posters for gigs, CDs, even books, were plastered over the filthy windows. Angelo wondered if there had been a mistake, if the hard-working compilers of Hammersmith and Fulham's list of cinemas past and present had somehow missed one, a big one. Moving to the edge of Holland Park roundabout, Angelo was able to see how the building extended beyond its fancy entrance: a long white shed with a largely ruined glass roof stretched back fully two hundred yards, then turned a ninety-degree corner and another shed ran west before turning another right angle to head north again. On their metal stilts, the long narrow sheds marched across a blasted, post-industrial landscape as far as the Central Line tube depot. Angelo felt something shift slowly within him.[75]

In Hanif Kureishi's *Gabriel's Gift* (2001), Hannah, a Polish au pair, is taking fifteen-year-old Gabriel (or is he taking her?) on a bus through west London from Shepherd's Bush, to meet his father:

> Hannah rarely went further than the local shops and market. As Gabriel led her to the bus stop and saw how alarmed she was by the swirling indifferent crowd and its numerous languages, he talked to her continuously. Still she insisted on taking his hand; not, he realized, to lead him, but for fear of getting lost herself.
>
> Seeing the various neighbourhoods from her point of view – for a while it seemed advantageous to pretend to himself that he was in Calcutta – he noticed that the bus, onto which they had had to clamber at the traffic lights as the driver appeared to see no other reason for slowing down, was driven by a monosyllabic lunatic who only stopped when shouted at by passengers, most of whom were listening to music on headphones. Other 'customers' chatted loudly on their mobiles and almost everyone else gibbered and swore to themselves. Then the bus – because of road works, he was told – didn't take its usual route but seemed to veer around West London almost at random, with the frantic passengers shouting instructions each time they saw a sign saying DIVERSION.
>
> She was solid, Hannah, and, back on the street, moved only slowly, with a kind of shuffle, whereas everyone else was engulfed by the stream; a moment's hesitation could engender a homicide. Gabriel tried to stand between her and this eventuality.[76]

7 'FINE THINGS TO BE SEEN'

Northwest London: From Kensal Green to Neasden,
Willesden, Kilburn, West Hampstead, Dollis Hill,
Wembley, Harrow, Ruislip and the Outer Northwest

Bounded and traversed by transport arteries (the A40 Westway,
the North Circular, major rail routes to the west and the
northwest), dotted with railway infrastructure, warehousing, big-box
sheds, distribution and data centres and retail parks, and miles of late
Victorian terraces and post-war estates, Neasden has long been presented as the epitome of sprawling, dull – even frightening – inner
suburbia. For many years *Private Eye* magazine ran a series of Neasden-
related absurdities: Neasden FC, for instance, playing in the 'North
Circular Relegation League', with their devoted fans – both of them.
Willie Rushton, comically, decides that he was glad he finally 'breezed
in' to 'Neasd-en'. Too close to London to count as John Betjeman's cosy
and nostalgic Metroland, this inner suburb/inner city is the scrappy
post-industrial zone you must pass through to get out to Metroland,
this particular dream zone not really starting until at least Harrow.

Yet, more recent fiction by Zadie Smith, Guy Gunaratne, Courttia
Newland, Robert McLiam Wilson, Edna O'Brien and others, while
seeing the violence, threat and seeming chaos of the place (often with
a sense of 'elsewhere in our blood', as Gunaratne has it), also reveal the
struggles to make it legible and meaningful, to make it a home. This writing revels in the creative energy and complexity of individuals, peoples,
histories, languages, classes and cultures all living in the same place.

Kensal Green

Kensal Green is dominated and defined by the huge cemetery to
the south of Harrow Road. Established in 1832, this was the first of

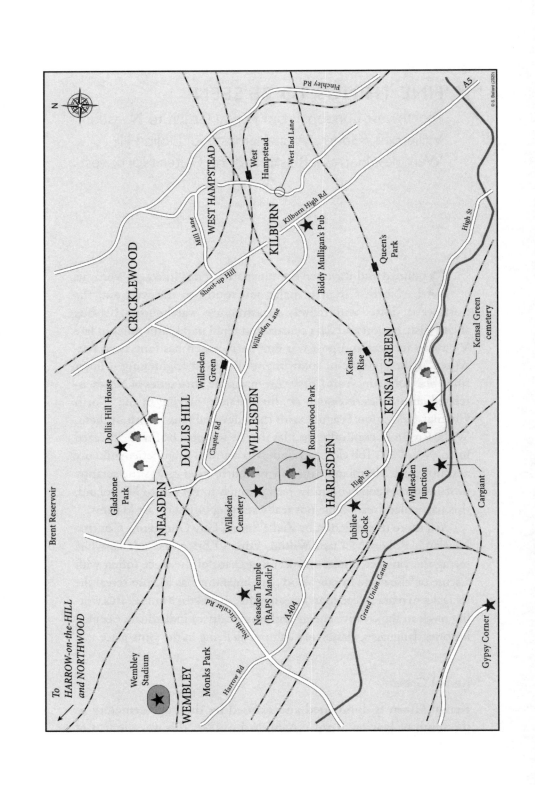

the so-called 'Magnificent Seven' ring of cemeteries constructed in the inner London suburbs to cope with the overflow from the city's bursting churchyards. With an interesting literary guest list, including Thackeray, Trollope and Wilkie Collins, the cemetery is mentioned in G. K. Chesterton's popular ballad 'The Rolling English Road': 'For there is good news yet to hear and fine things to be seen / Before we go to Paradise by way of Kensal Green.'[1]

In 1994 Iain Sinclair attended a memorial service at the cemetery for noirish British crime writer Robert Cook, whose best-known work appeared under the name Derek Raymond:

> I went with Marc Atkins to the memorial service in Kensal Green. Step through the gates and the ground is immediately familiar. You recognise these places as old friends when you meet them for the first time. It was a pleasant morning; we had half an hour to put on and wandered through the labyrinthine paths . . . Pyramids and stone mansions whose original pomposity had been weathered by long indifference into something more democratic; a sanctuary for wild nature, a trysting place for work-experience vampires. Irrelevant memory doses. Boasts and titles and meaningless dates.[2]

For the Soho literati attending the funeral, these are London's outer limits, strange and unfamiliar:

> Many of the folk from Kensal Green would never make it back to London proper. This was as close as they'd ever come to the countryside. The whiff of the Grand Union Canal had them reaching for the smelling salts. Some looked as if their powers of invention had been entirely used up in getting to the right venue on the right day. Others were so skeletal and waxy, it wasn't worth arranging a ride home. They only had to be matched with the right sepulchre, lifted onto an empty plinth.[3]

Patrick Keiller, the film-maker behind celebrated psychogeographic film *London* (1994), has a curious feeling cycling past Kensal Green Cemetery in summer 2008. Oddly, the cemetery wall has collapsed, 'so that passers-by could see in from the street for the first time since the wall was built in 1832 . . . to keep out the body snatchers'.[4] The collapsed wall also curiously chimes with the recent tottering of the global financial system and the oddness of *cycling* to this area's other notable landmark, the used car dealership Cargiant:

> Apart from the collapsed state of the cemetery wall, and the memory of the previous journey, the ride did not lead to any significant discovery, but it took place in a curious atmosphere of expectation, exacerbated by the weather, which recalled that described in the opening paragraphs of 'The Fall of the House of Usher', in which it was clear that the 'worst' of the collapse of the financial sector was still to come, an apprehension confirmed by the failure of Lehman Brothers two weeks later, and subsequent events, all of which felt at the time as if they might constitute a historic *moment*. Any sense of justification that accompanied this long-predicted turn of events was tempered for me by fear of financial shipwreck, following a misunderstanding with my employer, and especially since I was riding to what advertisements describe as Europe's largest car supermarket, in Harlesden, where I had identified a possible replacement for my car.[5]

Keiller then recalls a visit to the same area 28 years ago, one that was responsible for starting his film-making career:

> I had cycled along the same route once before on a Sunday afternoon in December 1980 when I had set out to look for a place that I had seen from a passing train a few days earlier. It was a north-facing hillside of allotments behind the corner of two streets of suburban houses, beyond the railway bridge above the North Circular Road . . . The view had seemed to me a curiously Northern-looking landscape to find in outer London, and I had thought it might be a subject for a photograph, which it was; but it led me to another more compelling spatial subject for a first film, so that this earlier bicycle journey had been, for me, a significant, even life-changing, event.[6]

A funeral service at Kensal Green is described in Courttia Newland's 1997 novel of west London estate life, *The Scholar: A West Side Story*, when Ron Bradley is buried after being beaten to death in police custody:

Ron's funeral was held in Kensal Green Cemetery in West London. The plot was adjacent to two older graves which held Teresa and Marcus Bradley, Ron and Bernice's mother and father. Teresa and Marcus had wanted to be buried in Dominica, their homeland, but they'd never been able to afford to return home; Ron's life assurance just about covered the cost of this third burial.

The grave was surrounded by friends and family – at least forty people Sean guessed, all sweltering in the mid-August sun. Although the boy had never seen a funeral before, he felt his uncle had received a beautiful send-off into the next world. The priest talked of the 'gentle giant' who'd befriended so many before his death; but neatly skirted around the blood clot found in Dr Phillip's autopsy. He also avoided mentioning three broken ribs, which police claimed were from Ron's earlier fight, although witnesses said his original assailants hadn't managed to land any blows: they were all too drunk.[7]

Neasden and Willesden

A mile further north, Willesden was, as the *London Encyclopaedia* tells, until the nineteenth century 'a rural area of exceptional charm, with small hamlets such as Neasden and Harlesden, a few large houses, farms and the village of Willesden itself'.[8] Transformed by railways (especially the Metropolitan Line in 1879), canals, factories and work-shops, the area rapidly industrialized in the later nineteenth century. By the post-war period the area was mostly working class, scruffy and decrepit, as local industries moved out, and proved attractive to newer Irish and Caribbean immigrants, and to Hindu migrants – creating a community that resulted in the building of the vast Neasden Temple, at the time the largest outside India. The area around Willesden Green is now gentrifying.

The area's pre-industrial reputation as pastoral idyll was matched by its being favoured by highwaymen and various outlaws on account of the many turnpikes approaching London. This can be clearly seen in William Harrison Ainsworth's best-selling Victorian potboiler *Jack Sheppard, A Romance* (1839). This 'Newgate novel' – that is, focused on and thought to glamorize the lives of criminals – recounts the adventures of the real-life thief Sheppard (also the prototype for John

Gay's Macheath in *The Beggar's Opera* of 1728), a much admired and mythologized rogue – famed, above all, for his incredible *four* daring escapes from prison, including twice from the notorious Newgate. Ainsworth relates how the abandoned Sheppard is raised as an apprentice by his stepfather, Owen Wood, living out at 'Dollis Hill, a beautiful spot near Willesden'.[9] Later, Sheppard ventures out to Willesden, through Kensal Green, on a job:

> he allowed his gaze to range over the vast and beautiful prospect
> spread out beneath him, which is now hidden from the
> traveller's view by the high walls of the General Cemetery, and
> can, consequently, only be commanded from the interior of that
> attractive place of burial, – and which, before it was intersected
> by canals and railroads, and portioned out into hippodromes,
> was exquisite indeed . . . he opened a gate, and struck into
> one of the most beautiful green lanes imaginable; which, after
> various windings, conducted him into a more frequented road,
> and eventually brought him to the place he sought. Glancing
> at the finger-post over the cage, which has been described as
> situated at the outskirts of the village, and seeing no direction
> to Dollis Hill, he made fresh inquiries . . .
> 'There is Dollis Hill,' said the man, pointing to a
> well-wooded eminence about a mile distant.[10]

This stretch of north London is presented as an enchanted landscape:

> Passing the old refectory, and still older church, with its reverend
> screen of trees, and slowly ascending a hill side, from whence he
> obtained enchanting peeps of the spire and college of Harrow,
> he reached the cluster of well-built houses which constitute the
> village of Neasdon [*sic*]. From this spot a road, more resembling
> the drive through a park than a public thoroughfare, led
> him gradually to the brow of Dollis Hill. It was a serene and
> charming evening, and twilight was gently stealing over the face
> of the country. Bordered by fine timber, the road occasionally
> offered glimpses of a lovely valley, until a wider opening gave a
> full view of a delightful and varied prospect. On the left lay the
> heights of Hampstead, studded with villas, while farther off a
> hazy cloud marked the position of the metropolis.[11]

Willie Rushton's recording of his comedy music hall-type ditty 'Neasden' was released by *Private Eye* in 1972, an example of the *Eye*'s relentless targeting of Neasden as the epicentre of dull, banal suburbia, with its numerous references to Neasden FC and the hallowed 'Neasden University'. Rushton points out all the exotic spots he has been to – Orpington, Tufnell Park and East Cheam, to name a few – and how none can match Neasden.[12]

The vast tangle of railway sidings and track infrastructure at Willesden Junction intrigued Leon Kossoff, who painted and sketched the scene endlessly. In *London Overground* (2015), following the 'Ginger Line', Iain Sinclair tries to locate the exact spot, on a bridge over the sprawling Willesden Junction railway yards, from which Kossoff produced his 1962 charcoal drawings:

> My view from the railway bridge was of resistant bushes, huge yellow hoists, reddish stones, rusty poles and blue-grey mesh fences. If I wanted anything close to the letterbox intensity of Kossoff's Willesden vision, I had to adapt an extreme telephoto mode, so that the overhead gantries are foreshortened, bleeding into a sequence of bridges, while horizontal diamond patterns of metalwork are countered by the curves of the track.
>
> NO ACCESS TO EUROTERMINAL.
>
> I poke about, trying to orientate myself, and hoping to identify the builder who rented Kossoff a draughty space in which to work. Hippie dope transfers have been plastered to the official sign, confirming its Euro credentials. DINAFEM. ORIGINAL AMNESIA. MOST AWARDED SATIVA FROM HOLLAND. HIGH LIFE CUP WINNER. Elective amnesia of the deadlands. Railside sheds have been made ready for cargoes from everywhere.[13]

Zadie Smith has made Willesden (and Harlesden) her own, presenting a contemporary multicultural and multi-class zone of confused identities and conflicting stories, with shifting polarities of escape and entrapment, aspiration and despair. Born and raised here, Smith knows this place well and guides us through dense, chaotic inner-suburban neighbourhoods. In the exuberant *White Teeth* (2000), Clara begs her new husband to take her away, away from an oppressive Jehovah's Witness mother, and 'as far away from Lambeth as a man of his means could manage – Morocco, Belgium, Italy'.[14] They make it as far as Willesden Green. Clara peers hopefully through the windscreen as they drive north:

> What kind of a place was this? That was the thing, you see, you couldn't be sure. Travelling in the front passenger seat of the removal van, she'd seen the high road and it had been ugly and poor and familiar (though there were no Kingdom Halls or Episcopalian churches), but then at the turn of a corner suddenly roads had exploded in greenery, beautiful oaks, the houses got taller, wider and more detached, she could see parks, she could see libraries. And then abruptly the trees would be gone, reverting back into bus-stops as if by the strike of some midnight bell; a signal which the houses too obeyed, transforming themselves into smaller, stairless dwellings that sat splay opposite derelict shopping arcades, those peculiar lines of establishments that include, without exception,
>> one defunct sandwich bar still advertising breakfast
>> one locksmith uninterested in marketing frills (KEYS CUT HERE)
>> and one permanently shut unisex hair salon, the proud bearer of some unspeakable pun (*Upper Cuts* or *Fringe Benefits* or *Hair Today, Gone Tomorrow*).
>> It was a lottery driving like that, looking out, not knowing whether one was about to settle down for life amongst the trees or amidst the shit. Then finally the car had slowed down in front of a house, a nice house somewhere midway between the trees and the shit.[15]

Willesden in the novel is at the real centre of shifting and simmering tensions of race, gender, class and identity:

> And the 52 bus goes two ways. From the Willesden kaleidoscope, one can catch it west like the children; through Kensal Rise, to Portobello, to Knightsbridge, and watch the many colours shade off into the bright white lights of town; or you can get it east, as Samad did; Willesden, Dollis Hill, Harlesden, and watch with dread (if you are fearful like Samad, if all you have learnt from the city is to cross the road at the sight of dark-skinned men) as white fades to yellow

fades to brown, and then Harlesden Clock comes into view, standing like Queen Victoria's statue in Kingston – a tall stone surrounded by black.[16]

In Smith's ambitious multi-voiced novel *NW* (2012), the areas of Willesden, Harlesden and Kilburn are presented as fragmentary and chaotic, with only temporary brief glimpses of the city swimming into view via the fleeting consciousness of characters:

> Pauline turns the page with violence. The window logs Kilburn's skyline. Ungentrified, ungentrifiable. Boom and bust never come here. Here busting is permanent. Empty State Empire, empty Odeon, graffiti-streaked sidings rising and falling like a rickety roller coaster. Higgledy-piggledy rooftops and chimneys, some high, some low, packed tightly, shaken fags in a box. Behind the opposite window, retreating Willesden. Number 37. In the 1880s or thereabouts the whole thing went up at once – houses, churches, schools, cemeteries – an optimistic vision of Metroland. Little terraces, faux-Tudor piles. All the mod cons! Indoor toilet, hot water. Well-appointed country living for those tired of the city. Fast-forward. Disappointed city living for those tired of their countries.[17]

By the novel's end, after a pointless random murder, Willesden has become nightmarishly claustrophobic, a place of sluggish progress-without-movement. Ambitious barrister Keisha (necessarily reinvented as Natalie) Blake, distressed, her life seeming to unravel, walks the area to make the chaotic townscape cohere, trying to tie memory, observation, sensation together. She aims to walks north, uphill, following the route outlined in the chapter headings: 'Willesden Lane to Kilburn High Road', 'Shoot Up Hill to Fortune Green', 'Hampstead to Archway', 'Hampstead Heath'.

> She turned left. Walked to the end of her road and the end of the next. Walked quickly away from Queen's Park. She passed into where Willesden meets Kilburn. Went by Leah's place, then Caldwell. In the old flat the kitchen window was open. A duvet cover – decorated with the logo of a football club – had been hung over the balcony to dry. Without looking where she

was going, she began climbing the hill that begins in Willesden and ends in Highgate. She was making a queer keening noise, like a fox. As she crossed the road a 98 bus swung by her steeply – it looked like it might capsize – and at first it seemed to be somehow the source of the strange red and blue light colouring the white stripes of the zebra crossing. Now she saw the police car parked in its shadow, roof lights turning silently . . . Can't I walk down there? asked Natalie. Incident, said the officer. He looked down at her. A big T-shirt, leggings and a pair of filthy red slippers, like a junkie. He looked at his watch. It's eight now. This road will be blocked for another hour or so. She tried to reach up on her toes to see round him. All she could see were more policemen and a white canvas tent off to the left, on the pavement opposite the bus stop. What kind of incident? He didn't answer. She was no one. She didn't merit answering. A kid on a BMX racer said, Someone got juked, innit.[18]

Christopher Boone, who is on the autistic spectrum, gets off at Willesden Station, after an overwhelming train and tube journey from Swindon to find his estranged mother's flat in Mark Haddon's *The Curious Incident of the Dog in the Night-time* (2013):

So I got to 451c Chapter Road, London NW2 5NG and it took me 27 minutes and there was no one in when I pressed the button that said Flat C and the only interesting thing that happened on the way was 8 men dressed up in Viking costumes with helmets with horns on and they were shouting, but they weren't real Vikings because the Vikings lived nearly 2,000 years ago, and also I had to go for another wee and I went in the alley down the side of a garage called Burdett Motors which was closed and I didn't like doing that but I didn't want to wee myself again . . .

So I sat down on the ground behind the dustbins in the little garden what was in front of 451c Chapter Road, London NW2 5NG and it was under a big bush. And a lady came into the garden and she was carrying a little box with a metal grille on one end and a handle on the top like you use to take a cat to the vet, but I couldn't see if there was a cat in it, and she had shoes with high heels and she didn't see me . . .

And then it was 11:32 p.m. and . . . a voice said, 'I don't care whether you thought it was funny or not,' and it was a lady's voice.

And another voice said, 'Judy look, I'm sorry, OK,' and it was a man's voice.

And the other voice, which was the lady's voice, said, 'Well, perhaps you should have thought about that before you made me look like a complete idiot.'

And the lady's voice was Mother's voice.[19]

Diana Evans's novel *26a* (2005) sees twins Georgia and Bessi Hunter, born to Nigerian parents, growing up at 26a Waifer Avenue, Neasden, up on the North Circular. In this minutely observed world the twins inhabit a room in the loft and rarely venture out further than nearby Gladstone Park, watching the rest of the world, even London events like Charles and Diana's wedding, on TV:

Neasden was like the high heel at the bottom of Italy. It was what the city stepped on to be sexy. London needed its Neasdens to make the Piccadilly lights, the dazzling Strand, the pigeons at Trafalgar Square and the Queen waving from her Buckingham balcony seem exciting, all that way away, over acres of rail track and miles and miles of traffic. The children of the city suburbs watched it all on TV. It was only very occasionally that the Hunters ventured past Kilburn because most of the things that they needed could be bought from Brent Cross, which had all the shops . . .

Neasden was easier. A little hilly place next to a river and a motorway with nodding trees and one stubby row of shops. One bank, one library, one optician, one chemist, one chip shop, one Chinese takeaway, pub, hairdresser, off-licence, cash 'n' carry, greengrocer and two newsagents, a full stop at each end of Neasden Lane. There was also a chocolate-smelling chocolate-biscuit factory said by the older locals to have driven people to madness. School-children were given unforgettable guided tours through it, the chocolate warm, melting, over freshly baked biscuits on conveyor belts.[20]

Ben Judah's hard-hitting book of street-level reportage *This Is London* (2016) visits Neasden and observes the area's downward transformation from Betjeman's prime suburbia – gnome-infested, neat, private and regimented, nearly all white and lower-middle-class – to becoming a gentrification-proof global slum.

> The mellow Georgian mansions and little cottage-pie lanes in Shepherd's Bush have suddenly gone. Harlesden's endless ladder of cramped, pompous Edwardian terraces, dotted with defunct gin palaces, has given way to bogus Tudor drives. And this is where gentrification ends, too. The English currency of status in this city is Victorian brick – and these niggling suburban semis are far from what the wealthy English dream for in London . . .
>
> There is trouble in Metroland. Betjeman's people have gone. The men who went on about Spitfires are mostly dead. Their sons were the ones who hated the suburbs; boys who grew their hair long, resentfully strummed guitars, and only came back for those cold awkward teas and finally to clear out the family house.
>
> The English don't want to live in this borough anymore. Betjeman would never recognize Brent. The white British population is around 18 per cent. South Asians make up 33 per cent. The black population, roughly 19 per cent. Between 2001 and 2011 the white British population of Brent tumbled: losing almost 30 per cent.[21]

The fictional 1970s Stones Estate, Neasden, is the setting for Guy Gunaratne's saga *In Our Mad and Furious City* (2018). One of the multiple narrators is called Selvon – a clear nod to the pioneer of London migrant fiction, Trinidad-born Sam Selvon, author of *The Lonely Londoners* (1956).

> See the four blocks rising behind the shop roofs, red shells and pointed arches pitched at the sky. I pick my pace up as I run through the market. Proper orphaned corner, this. Full of absent people stuck between bus stops and bookies. See them shuffling bodies. Lining up at cash machines and dole queues. Man only come around these Ends for a barber's, canned food or like batteries, ennet. Nuttan more. Pure minor commerce.

Any real money lands in spastic corners, in some bingo joint down near Wimpy sides or suttan. Don't make no sense to me. Every time I run past this place I feel like raggo, blessed I never grew up in Estate proper.

South Block is the nearest block to my road so I head through the market and toward the gate. Smell hits me hard as I turn into the stalls. See carrots and lemons and cabbages in boxes, piles of coloured fruit stacked in blue crates. Shopkeepers putting out their plastic pap. Mobile phone parts and baby clothes. Kitchenware hung on coat hangers. Run past it all, dodging the stools and the old dears. Maintain my breathing-tho, keep a compact chest.

South Block entrance goes over my head now. Stones Estate is four grey towers around me. The square space in the centre. See the walls. The graffiti is all over the brick walls, like scabby tagging reading short names in code. No-one around me, just my body in motion. Adidas and vest. See the broken windows and overflowing garbage. I run past the skips, littered with needles and suttan nasty, suttan foul. It reeks of piss and harsh filth washed up under darkness. Bunn that . . .

This Stones Estate got madness in it, everyone knows it. It don't touch me-tho. But every time I run here I think about my mates living up in these council flats with all this haggard muck.[22]

Kilburn

Just east of Willesden, Kilburn was established around an abbey in the twelfth century and developed along the Roman Watling Street (now the A5, Edgware Road and Kilburn High Road) and a river (the Westbourne, now another of London's lost rivers). Once famed for its natural springs, Kilburn really started to develop when the Metropolitan Railway arrived in the 1860s. It became a noted centre of Irish immigration from the early 1950s, colloquially known as 'County Kilburn', packed with pubs, clubs and dance halls owned and frequented by members of the Irish diaspora. The 1974 bombing of the famed Biddy Mulligan's pub on Kilburn High Road was the only example of loyalist terrorism on the British mainland.

Waguih Ghali's 1964 novel *Beer in the Snooker Club* follows Font and Ram, anglophile upper-class Egyptians, finding some freedom from Nasser's Egypt in late 1950s London:

> It was sunny and we walked; Edna between Font and myself,
> holding our arms. Up Park Lane to Marble Arch and on to
> Kilburn through Edgware Road. I had become a bit 'loud'
> lately, a sort of cocksureness which I loathed to see in others
> and yet was aware of in myself. I suppose if a young man feels
> he is loved by a rich and beautiful woman, it isn't unnatural
> for him to be a bit arrogant, but my arrogance was not natural
> . . . In Kilburn, Edna told us, a lot of Irish people lived. All
> I thought of when she said Irish was 'Black and Tan' which led
> me to think of boot polish.[23]

Ripley Bogle, in Robert McLiam Wilson's 1989 comic novel of that name, is a homeless Irish litterateur, stumbling around London, clearly echoing Leopold Bloom's Dublin adventures in Joyce's *Ulysses* (1922). Bogle visits a typical Kilburn boozer, already semi-delirious yet keen to experience real – that is, fake – 'Irishness': 'A Kilburn pub! S'blood, I'm back home already! A little piece of Ireland.'[24]

> A dark low-ceilinged chamber; wall mirrors reflect other
> fictional chambers, conjuring wide spaces bereft of glamour
> and generally confounding the eye. The cluttered butterthick
> air is filled with long troughs of tobacco smoke which curls and
> spirals around the groups of drinking men like some ghostly
> foliage sprouting from the mangled, match-thin stubs of rolled
> paper clamped between their wicked yellow fingers. There
> is a constant clamour – the sottish riot of Irishmen arguing,
> bawling, singing and shouting in rational, national disharmony.
> The odour of the place is a verminous, cloying blend of
> stingsweet whisky fumes, stale spilt beer and rotting carpets.
> It is heady and warming – a homely fragrance. Confusion is
> nourished; stomachs bubble and babble burgeons.[25]

The evening becomes increasingly phantasmagoric, and nasty. The appearance of a toilet bowl in the middle of a room, and a 'tiny, horrible, red hand' emerging from it, naturally, creates a riot:

Pandemonium breaks loose. The Drinkers, men and women,
scream in terror. They bolt wildly for the door. Many bodies
are trampled in the wild rush to escape that horror. Several
crazed old hags slit their own throats with broken beer glasses.
The tumult is dreadful, hellish, obscene. Death shepherds
his little flocks as heads are crushed, split and trampled by
maddened feet.[26]

In Chris Petit's noirish novel *The Hard Shoulder* (2001), hard
man Pat O'Grady returns, after a ten-year prison stretch, to an 1980s
Kilburn undergoing rapid change, the Irish moving out and being
replaced by newer migrants. The street itself seems banally familiar,
while O'Grady himself feels insubstantial, ghostly.

He took the stairs down to the street. He was still unfamiliar
with the process of everything and whatever he did felt
like it was at the wrong speed, even handing in his ticket
to the unmanned booth. Outside, the two railway bridges,
cutting the road at an angle just above the station entrance
and booming whenever a train passed over, were his first
familiar landmark. To his left Shoot Up Hill ran up towards
Cricklewood. To think he had once aspired to Cricklewood.
O'Grady turned right.
     The Kilburn High Road had been a ditch when he left,
and still was from what he could see. He wondered if Moran's,
where he'd had his first job, was still there. It was, the same.
The rest of the shops looked as fifth-rate as ever and the street
had not lost its air of having long since given up. Traffic was
clogging up in both directions. A white van parked half on
the pavement blocked the way, its orange tail lights winking
in unison. O'Grady had not seen indicators doing that before.
Apart from that, everything looked the same. It was a shock
to find so little changed. From what he had read there was
supposed to be a boom on.[27]

Kilburn High Road is where Edna O'Brien's short story 'Shovel
Kings' starts. The narrator makes contact with Rafferty, a labourer, the
'shovel king' of the title:

About six months after our first meeting I came upon Rafferty unexpectedly, and we greeted each other like old friends. I was on the Kilburn High Road outside a second-hand furniture shop, where he was seated on a leather armchair, smiling at passers-by, like a potentate. He was totally at ease out in the open, big white lazy clouds sailing by in the sky above us, surrounded by chairs, tables, chests of drawers, fire irons, fenders, crockery, and sundry bric-a-brac.

Offering me a seat, he said that the owner believed his presence perked up an interest in business, because once, when he had been singing 'I'll Take You Home Again, Kathleen', passers-by had stopped to listen and, as he put it, had browsed. Nearby, a woman haggled over the price of a buckled sieve, and a young mother was in vain trying to get her son off the rocking horse to which he was affixed. The white paint was scraped in several places, and the golden mane a smudged brown, but to the boy his steed was noble.

Rafferty rolled a cigarette, folded his tobacco pouch, and, impelled by some inner recollection, began to tell me the story of coming to London forty years earlier, a young lad of fifteen arriving in Camden Town with his father.[28]

West Hampstead

Adjacent to Kilburn, and just to the east, the area started as a collection of large villas on West End Lane: 'West Hampstead' was chosen for the name of the new Metropolitan Line station built in 1879. The Finchley Road is the suitably out-of-the-way place for Walter to stroll, after roaming Hampstead Heath, on a hot summer night in Wilkie Collins's novel *The Woman in White* (1859):

> I determined to stroll home in the purer air, by the most roundabout way I could take; to follow the white winding paths across the lonely heath; and to approach London through its most open suburb by striking into the Finchley-road, and so getting back, in the cool of the new morning, by the western side of the Regent's Park.[29]

This, at the junction of Frognal and West End Lanes and the Finchley Road, is where the strange meeting occurs:

> I had now arrived at that particular point of my walk where four roads met – the road to Hampstead, along which I had returned; the road to Finchley; the road to West End; and the road back to London. I had mechanically turned in this latter direction, and was strolling along the lonely high-road – idly wondering, I remember, what the Cumberland young ladies would look like – when, in one moment, every drop of blood in my body was brought to a stop by the touch of a hand laid lightly and suddenly on my shoulder from behind me.
>
> I turned on the instant, with my fingers tightening round the handle of my stick.
>
> There, in the middle of the broad, bright high-road – there, as if it had that moment sprung out of the earth or dropped from the heaven – stood the figure of a solitary Woman, dressed from head to foot in white garments; her face bent in grave inquiry on mine, her hand pointing to the dark cloud over London, as I faced her.
>
> I was far too seriously startled by the suddenness with which this extraordinary apparition stood before me, in the dead of night and in that lonely place, to ask what she wanted. The strange woman spoke first. 'Is that the road to London?' she said.[30]

In Barbara Vine's *King Solomon's Carpet* (1991), Jarvis Stringer (busy compiling a 'complete history of The London Underground') inherits a huge semi-derelict Victorian pile, once an eccentric school, in West Hampstead, where he lets out rooms to a wide cast of misfit Londoners:

> The building was a red-brick Victorian house in that West Hampstead street which runs parallel with the Metropolitan and Jubilee Lines of the London Underground. This large house, neo-Gothic in all respects but for its Italianate belvedere, stood about a third of the way between West Hampstead station and Finchley Road station, at which point the lines enter portals and dive underground. Its grounds were small

for so large a house, no more than two shrubberies dividing it from its neighbours, and at the rear a stretch of lawn with trees ran down to a fence. Through the palings of this fence the trains could be seen rolling past, northwards to Amersham and Harrow and Stanmore, southwards to inner London. They could be heard too, a constant if sporadic singing rattle. Silence came only in the deep watches of the night.

These lines had been there for many years when Ernest Jarvis bought the house in the twenties, the Metropolitan Railway having been extended from Swiss Cottage to West Hampstead in 1879. Ernest was well off, having his share of the Jarvis family money, and there was no reason why he should not have made his school in some more attractive part of NW6, up in the neighbourhood of Fortune Green for instance. Even his daughter did not know why he had chosen a house overlooking the railways or for that matter why he wanted to keep a school at all.[31]

Francine Snaith, the office temp in Rachel Cusk's *The Temporary* (1995), likes to believe she lives in West Hampstead, and *not* Kilburn:

Francine's flat was irrefutably placed at the western end of Mill Lane, and much as she might try to clothe the fact in whimsically stated preferences to longer walks in leafier branches of transportation, the tube at Kilburn was undeniably her most expeditious point of contact with the outside world. On the rare occasions – really only once or twice, in fact, and more toward the beginnings of things – on which Ralph had come to stay, she had directed him to the longer route, believing that her lair was better approached from the more seductive angle of West Hampstead. He had taken matters into his own hands, of course, by consulting a map.[32]

Dollis Hill

Just north of Willesden, Dollis Hill, one of the highest points in this area, was relatively undeveloped until after the First World War. In 1900 Mark Twain briefly moved into Dollis Hill House, built in 1823, and visited by Gladstone, Joseph Chamberlain and others, and was amazed at its still rural feel:

The rolling sea of green grass still stretches away on every hand, splotches with shadows of spreading oaks in whose black coolness flocks of sheep lie peacefully dreaming. Dreaming of what? That they are in London, the metropolis of the world, Post-office District, N.W.? Indeed no. They are not aware of it. I am aware of it, but that is all. It is not possible to realize it. For there is no suggestion of city here; it is country, pure & simple, & as still & reposeful as is the bottom of the sea.[33]

Where Twain found the place enchanting – 'Dollis Hill comes nearer to being a paradise than any other home I ever occupied'[34] – in Ian McEwan's 1990 novel *The Innocent* it becomes an emblem of suburban backwardness and dullness. The innocent here is gauche, awkward Leonard Marnham, contracted to work for a secret Anglo-American surveillance team in mid-1950s Berlin. The seedy, dangerous glamour of Cold War Berlin is compared throughout to Dollis Hill, where Marnham worked at the Post Office Research Station, where the world's first programmable computer, Colossus 1, was built during the war and used to crack German intelligence codes. 'Leonard still lived at home with his parents in Tottenham, and commuted each day to Dollis Hill,' we learn.[35] The dullness of this, his old life, is compared to thrilling, dangerous Cold War Berlin, especially as he has found sex: 'He had chased Maria away. She was the best thing to have happened to him since . . . His mind ran over various childhood treats, birthdays, holidays, Christmases, university entrance, his transfer to Dollis Hill. Nothing remotely as good had ever happened to him.'[36]

Wembley

Wembley lies along the Harrow Road a mile or so west of Neasden, across the North Circular Road. Although first mentioned in 825 as the village of Wemba Lea, Wembley really took off in the 1920s and '30s, with train and tram links to central London, the development of modern light engineering (GEC laboratories) and, famously, the 1924–5 British Empire Exhibition. The exhibition's aim, just as the Empire itself was seriously ailing, was to celebrate imperial glories by shrinking them and bringing them all to one place. Huge new reinforced concrete pavilions (one for each colony) and exhibition palaces were built on a vast 21-acre site. In a 1924 essay, 'Thunder at Wembley',

Virginia Woolf sniffily satirizes the exhibition's pompous straining for imperial grandeur:

> But at Wembley nothing is changed and nobody is drunk.
> They say, indeed, that there is a restaurant where each diner is
> forced to spend a guinea upon his dinner. What vistas of cold
> ham that statement calls forth! What pyramids of rolls! What
> gallons of tea and coffee! For it is unthinkable that there should
> be champagne, plovers' eggs, or peaches at Wembley. And for
> six and eightpence two people can buy as much ham and bread
> as they need. Six and eightpence is not a large sum; but neither
> is it a small sum. It is a moderate sum, a mediocre sum. It is the
> prevailing sum at Wembley.[37]

The exhibition's grandiose ambition to rule and order nature comes feebly unstuck as a distant storm approaches:

> Is it the wind, or is it the British Empire Exhibition? It is both
> . . . For either the sky has misread her directions, or some
> appalling catastrophe is impending. The sky is livid, lurid,
> sulphurine. It is in violent commotion. It is whirling water-
> spouts of clouds into the air; of dust in the Exhibition. Dust
> swirls down the avenues, hisses and hurries like erected cobras
> round corners. Pagodas are dissolving in dust. Ferro-concrete
> is fallible. Colonies are perishing and dispersing in spray of
> inconceivable beauty and terror which some malignant power
> illuminates. Ash and violet are the colours of its decay.[38]

Someone else who wasn't too impressed by the Wembley Empire Exhibition is Bertie Wooster in P. G. Wodehouse's 1924 story 'The Rummy Affair of Old Biffy'. Here Biffy – Charles Edward Biffen – as 'vague and woollen-headed a blighter as ever bit a sandwich', is dragged off to the 'good old exhibish',[39] with Bertie in tow, by a prospective father-in-law, Sir Roderick Glossop:

> Well, you know, I have never been much of a lad for exhibitions.
> The citizenry in the mass always rather puts me off, and after
> I have been shuffling along with the multitude for a quarter
> of an hour or so I feel as if I were walking on hot bricks.

About this particular binge, too, there seemed to me a lack of what you might call human interest. I mean to say, millions of people, no doubt, are so constituted that they scream with joy and excitement at the spectacle of a stuffed porcupine-fish or a glass jar of seeds from Western Australia – but not Bertram . . . By the time we had tottered out of the Gold Coast village and were working towards the Palace of Machinery, everything pointed to my shortly executing a quiet sneak in the direction of that rather jolly Planters' Bar in the West Indian section.[40]

The West Indian-themed bar is much more Wooster's idea of ethnographic exploration:

I have never been in the West Indies, but I am in a position to state that in certain of the fundamentals of life they are streets ahead of our European civilisation . . . A planter, apparently, does not consider he has had a drink unless it contains at least seven ingredients , and I'm not saying, mind you, that he isn't right. The man behind the bar told us the things were called Green Swizzles; and, if ever I marry and have a son, Green Swizzle Wooster is the name that will go down in the register, in memory of the day his father's life was saved at Wembley.[41]

Queenie, in the prologue of Andrea Levy's novel of multicultural 1940s London, *Small Island* (2004), recalls a childhood visit to the same exhibition:

The year we went to the Empire Exhibition, the Great War was not long over but nearly forgotten. Even Father agreed that the Empire Exhibition sounded like it was worth a look. The King had described it as 'the whole Empire in little'. Mother thought that meant it was a miniature, like a toy railway or model village. Until someone told her that they'd seen the real life-size Stephenson's Rocket on display. 'It must be as big as the whole world,' I said, which made everybody laugh . . .
    Hundreds and hundreds of people were tramping in through the gates of the exhibition, past the gardens and the lakes. Or milling about, chatting. Little kids being dragged to walk faster. Women pointing, old men wanting a seat. 'Over here! No, over

here . . . Over here's better.' The Empire in little. The palace of engineering, the palace of industry, and building after building that housed every country we British owned. Some of them were grand like castles, some had funny pointed roofs and one, I was sure, had half an onion on the top. Practically the whole world there to be looked at.[42]

Gordon Maxwell, in his 1925 tour of obscure London outskirts, *The Fringe of London*, finds that a neglected part of Wembley, Monks Park (now Tokyngton Park, just south of the stadium), was still classed as a rural district by the Post Office, despite being only 4 miles from Marble Arch: 'Monks Park I found (after some difficulty, for a mile away in industrial Willesden it seemed quite unknown) to be a small community of houses amidst the fields on the road to Harrow.'[43] He goes further and is amazed at what he finds:

Low-lying meadows (a hundred miles from London these would be called meads) through which the little river Brent winds its tortuous way. Oak, elm, willow and mountain ash grow by the banks, and close to the water's edge great patches of purple loosestrife and many another wild flower give a pleasing splash of colour . . . I wandered through these meads and explored the banks of the river for a couple of miles. Never in its whole course, I should think, does the Brent wind so much as through these fields; it is always meeting itself, coming round the corner in a most unexpected, but very delightful, way. The old half-ruined and disused sluice-gates which we came upon rather add to the picturesqueness of the little swift-flowing stream.[44]

In Martin Amis's state-of-the-nation novel *Lionel Asbo* (2012), the East London Asbo clan attends a wedding in Wembley, far from their home manor of Dalston:

Suddenly the train unsheathed itself from the black tunnel and soared out into the light of the May noon. And the weather – the air – was so fresh and bright, so swift and busy. Dawn said, 'Look, Des.' She meant Metroland. The orderly villas, the innocent back gardens, all aflutter in the swerving wind.

'I once came this way at night,' she said. 'And you look and you think. Every light out there stands for something. A hope. An ambition.'[45]

Kamila Shamsie's *Home Fire* (2017) centres on British Muslims living in Wembley. Here privileged Eamonn (son of a Pakistan-born British Home Secretary) walks from leafy Little Venice up to grimy Wembley, along the Regent's Canal towpath:

A kayak glided high above the stationary traffic of the North Circular, two ducks paddling in its wake. Eamonn stopped along the canal path, looked over the edge of the railing. Cars backed up as far as he could see. All the years he'd been down there in the traffic he'd taken this aqueduct for just another bridge, nothing to tell you that canal boats and waterfowl were being carried above your head. Always these other Londons in London. He typed 'canal above North Circular' into his phone, followed a link that led to another link, and was soon watching news footage of a bomb planted on this bridge by the IRA in 1939.[46]

Dimly recalled bits of dreary Wembley afternoons, visiting relatives, come back to him:

He left the canal path near high-rises embodying the word 'regeneration', and was soon on Ealing Road, walking past Gurkha Superstore, Gama Halal Meat, a Hindu temple intricately carved of limestone, cheerful stalls and restaurants. He couldn't point to anything in particular he recognised, yet he had complete certainty that he had looked out of a car window onto this street many times in his childhood . . .

On the High Road now, with its pound stores and pawn shops, glancing up every so often at the bone-white rainbow of Wembley Stadium for its reassuring familiarity – and then north toward Preston Road, where everything turned residential, suburban. Any one of these semi-detached houses could be the home in which he'd spent all those Eid afternoons, sitting pressed against his mother in an alliance that she tried to push him out of, knowing that he would rather be out in the garden playing cricket with the boy cousins whose invitations for him to join them were located confusingly at the border of the merely polite and the genuine.[47]

Harrow

The Metropolitan Line's expansion northwest out of Baker Street, by the 1880s to Neasden, Wembley and Harrow-on-the-Hill, and then eventually, over the next few decades, further out to Buckinghamshire and Hertfordshire, is memorable for its creation of so-called 'Metroland' (later, Metroland). The Metropolitan Railway had been permitted to buy up land and develop or oversee building projects along the line, and in 1915 the marketing department dreamed up the vision of 'Metroland', a cosy suburban pastoral comprising modern Tudorbethan semis, golf courses, country walks and a villagey feel with easy access to the countryside, all twenty minutes or so from town. The enterprise was a complete success and the company built houses, streets and even entire estates either side of the line from Wembley out to Chesham. Harrow or Wembley are considered the start of true Metroland.

'Metroland' became a buzz word, inspiring popular songs (such as one by George R. Sims: 'I know a land where the wild flowers grow / Near, near at hand if by train you go / Metroland, Metroland'), and even dance crazes. In Evelyn Waugh's first novel, *Decline and Fall* (1928), the Honourable Margot Beste-Chetwynde takes Viscount Metroland as her second husband, becoming Lady Metroland. The post-war spirit of Metroland, a place by the 1950s safely embalmed in distant nostalgia, was evoked in John Betjeman's 1954 collection *A Few Late Chrysanthemums*. This includes poems such as 'Middlesex' ('Gaily into Ruislip Gardens / Runs the red electric train, / With a thousand Ta's and Pardon's / Daintily alights Elaine');[48] 'Harrow-on-the-Hill' ('When melancholy Autumn comes to Wembley / And electric trains are lighted after tea');[49] and 'The Metropolitan Railway', where passengers travel from Harrow to Preston Road, observing the 'last green fields and misty sky', to Neasden: 'They felt so sure on their electric trip / That Youth and Progress were in partnership.'[50]

Betjeman also travels the line early in his 1973 BBC television film *Metro-Land*, an intensely nostalgic and somewhat cloying journey with the whimsical poet from Baker Street right out to Verney

Junction, Buckinghamshire. The early stops, around Neasden, are not considered up to much, and are snootily described as being typical 1930s suburbia, as Betjeman intones in the documentary:

> Out of the chimney-pots into the openness,
> Till we come to the suburb that's thought to be commonplace,
> Home of the gnome and the average citizen.
> Sketchley and Unigate, Dolcis and Walpamur.[51]

Deeper, still-rural Metroland stations are more like it, sleepy and attractive, 'down Hertfordshire way', at Chorleywood village:

> And wood smoke mingled with the sulphur fumes,
> And people now could catch the early train
> To London and be home just after tea.

Writer and naturalist Richard Mabey moved to a raw, unfinished sector of Metroland in the 1930s, and loved the frontier feel of the place, nothing like the marketed suburban dream. This was scrubby fields, scrappy woods and orchards, streams and rough tracks:

> I began drifting towards the Met's heartland as soon as I
> could ride a bike, aged about eleven, I guess . . . The Met Line
> and I were both arrowing in, from different directions, on
> the Chiltern Heartlands, a region too abstract to make any
> topographical sense to me at that age, but which held me in a
> powerful spell. There was a point on a hilltop where I would
> always pause on my cycle ride to school, and gaze in something
> close to rapture at the scene that unfolded southwards, the
> rising hills, the ancient beech groves, the ashwood where the
> first chiffchaff always sang . . . 'It was an unsettling feeling,'
> I wrote later, 'numinous, indefinable, a sense of something
> just beyond reach. At times it turned into an actual physical
> sensation that made the back of my legs tighten, as if I were
> peering down from a great height.'[52]

Julian Barnes uses his childhood at Northwood, further out along the Metropolitan Line from Harrow, as the setting for his novel *Metroland* (1990). Pretentious Francophile teenager Christopher feels that this is no place for a budding Paris *flâneur*: 'for a start, you usually needed a *quai*, or at the very least, a *boulevard*'.[53]

> '*Ou habites-tu?*' they would ask year after year, drilling us for French orals; and always I would smirkingly reply,
> '*J'habite Metroland!*'
> It sounded better than Eastwick, stranger than Middlesex; more like a concept in the mind than a place where you shopped. And so, of course, it was. As the Metropolitan Railway had pushed westward in the 1880s, a thin corridor of land was opened up with no geographical or ideological unity: you lived there because it was an area easy to get out of. The name Metroland – adopted during the First World War both by estate agents and the railway itself – gave the string of rural suburbs a spurious integrity.[54]

Aged thirty, though, Chris is back in Metroland, finding the place in fact rather practical, comfy and very handy for the countryside:

> On Sunday mornings I slip out of the house early. I turn left, past sensible detached houses: Ravenshoe, with its scatter of horse-chestnut flowers on the pavement; Vue de Provence, with its green shutters; East Coker, with a smirk-provoking carport. They have their names carved in Gothic letters on slices of wood which are screwed to trees.
> I pick my way across the golf course, watching an early drive catch the dew on its first bounce and pull up quickly, glistening. I like it here; I like the misty, different perspective.[55]

R. C. Sherriff's 1936 novel *Greengates* sees the retired Baldwins out for a walk along a favourite path near the fictional 'Welden', which lies out 'beyond Hendon'. Emerging from the woods they are shocked at the changes that have happened since their last visit: 'now there was little to be seen but rows of small new houses with an occasional sports ground in the distance'.[56] The old village has been absorbed by Metroland:

> The desolate charm of it – the wild, fragrant peace – had gone for ever; through the soft gorse field stretched broad, hideous

gashes of naked yellow clay, and clustering along them, like evil fungus to a fallen tree, were hideous new houses – stacks of bricks – pyramids of sewage pipes – piles of white timber – mud-stained lorries and sheets of hunched tarpaulin – a nightmare of perverted progress.[57]

The Baldwins are aghast; but then, seeing an open show house, take a quick tour and are seduced by the efficient, sleek modernity of the new houses under construction, especially the bright, clean, fitted bathroom, with the novelty of running hot water: 'It was impossible to be calm and blasé in the face of that final, glistening wonder.'[58] They decide to move from grubby Edgware to this new frontier, and they thrive:

> If you have not been to Welden Valley in the past ten years a visit will surprise you. A vast iron-grey by-pass road sweeps round upon its northern side, missing the old village by a hairsbreadth. 'To Welden ½-mile' brings you to a railway station, far different from the one that Tom and Edith Baldwin knew in the days when 'Greengates' was being built.
>
> You can no longer hear a solitary porter yawn through the stillness, for the sleepy little station has been attacked and captured by Metroland: colonised and civilised into producing six train loads of lively city people each day. The elms no longer creak their joints above the narrow, twisting lane that led to the village: the lane has grown into a broad, curving, concrete avenue upon which Woolworth's, Sainsbury's and Lyons have built their mansions and settled down.[59]

Just east of Harrow, Kenton is the place that historian Paul Barker lauds as the ideal suburb:

> Kenton is a vivid example of the kind of place I want to celebrate. Built mainly in the 1920s and 1930s, this is a suburb that few people, other than those who live there, have ever heard of. It lies, like a gentle enigma, at the meeting point of the north-west London boroughs of Harrow and Brent.[60]

Barker reels off the positives to be found at unremarkable Mayfield Avenue, Kenton. It is affordable, with good schools, doctors, connecting roads and plentiful public transport. Above all, it consists largely of 'that classic suburban creation, the semi-detached house':[61]

> In the early twenty-first century, Mayfield Avenue's spec-development semis are around the bottom of their fashionability cycle. There is nothing smart about them. But they are amazingly adaptable containers, I'd argue, as is Kenton itself. That is one test of the Good House or Good Neighbourhood they pass with flying colours. You can pour into these houses what you want.[62]

Ruislip

Past Harrow, one branch of the Metropolitan Line goes to Ruislip, 3 miles west. In Leslie Thomas's romp *Tropic of Ruislip* (1974), fictional 'Plummers Park' is an executive housing estate, the 'home of Flat-Roof Man',[63] 'thirty miles from Central London, in the latitude of Ruislip, in the country but not of it':[64]

> The estate was the strangest crop ever to grow on that old Hertfordshire farming land. When it was built some trees were permitted to remain like unhappy captives spared because they are old. They remained in clusters, sometimes embedded in garden walls as selling points for house-buyers desiring fresh air, twigs, greenness and autumn acorns for their children. It was rumoured that the builders had a mechanical squirrel which ran up trees to delight, deceive and decide prospective purchasers.
>
> The streets had, with commercial coyness, retained the sometimes embarrassing names of the various pastures and fields that now lay beneath concrete, crazy paving and statutory roses. Cowacre, Upmeadow, Risingfield, Sheep-Dip, The Sluice, and Bucket Way. Some of the new people said they found it embarrassing to give their address as Sows Hole Lane – provided for a policeman it always provoked suspicion – but others liked the rustic sounds.[65]

The flat-roofed, middle-class middle managers do not have it all their own way. Right next to this estate looms 'a monster council-housing development, built to rehouse families from slum London':[66]

Beneath the station burrowed a pedestrian tunnel nervously joining Plummers Park to the council estate. To venture through it was to leave one country for another: on one side fuchsias, and on the other sheets of newspaper drifting in the street winds. The path through the tunnel was their only direct link. Vehicles had to drive south or north and take the roads joining through neutral territory. Trouble was rare between the tenants of one side of the railway and the residents of the other (except for one violent morning in the launderette where some council clothes and some private garments became somehow mixed in a washing machine). Otherwise the people were not well enough acquainted to fight. They were merely strangers.[67]

Outer Northwest

Psychogeographer and walker Nick Papadimitriou stakes a claim on a huge portion of suburban and extra-suburban north and northwest London, the area corresponding very roughly to the old Middlesex county boundaries, stretching from Stanmore and Edgware in the south, up to St Albans, the Chilterns and Hertford to the north, and over to the River Lea in the east. Papadimitriou calls this forgotten area of no-longer existing Middlesex 'Scarp', after the Chiltern escarpment. In *Scarp* (2012) Papadimitriou calls this area a 'vast yet seemingly invisible presence [hovering] over the northern suburbs of London', a place 'seldom commented upon by either topographers or psychogeographers, and [that] seemingly possesses no cultural currency'.[68] Papadimitriou sets out to record, walk and write about this neglected landscape:

> Voices other than the merely historic surfaced on my walks: the groaning of South London villains entombed in motorway bridges; women long dead glimpsed with the inner eye when I stared through windows into warm-lit rooms passed on freezing afternoons; garish tales told by beings that confounded accepted notions of time; the outrage of mossy elementals lingering in relic woodlands.[69]

Scarp sees the author walking, thinking, responding, brooding on the huge task of making the landscape cohere, to mean something:

Finally I hit Uxbridge Road, which runs in parallel with
Scarp all the way from Stanmore in the east to Northwood, a
synthetic suburb established in the wake of the extension of the
Metropolitan Railway to Rickmansworth in the 1860s.

I wanted to tell you about these towns – Pinner, Hatch End,
Northwood Hills, Northwood – granting you a glimpse of
their inscape, but, truth be told, I can't be bothered. Yes, they
are easily subjected to abuse, their names cited in that droll,
pubby English way that refuses to recognise that everywhere is
somewhere . . . And yes, it is my duty to elevate them to expression, perhaps composing a complex cubist poetry that codifies
their crystalline facets, their fault-lines and their unconscious
impulses, but today is not the day.

As I wander west along Uxbridge Road it all looks too big to
even begin to take on.[70]

Paula Hawkins's best-selling thriller *The Girl on the Train* (2015)
concerns a commute from a fictional Buckinghamshire town, Ashbury
(possibly Aylesbury), to Euston, passing through endless northwest
London suburbia: 'The train crawls along; it judders past warehouses
and water towers, bridges and sheds, past modest Victorian houses,
their backs turned squarely to the track.'[71] This is banal, everyday suburbia, of course, the kind one passes en route to a dull day at work;
though, of course, it isn't at all, as the train starts

to pick up pace as suburbia melts into grimy north London,
terraced houses replaced by tagged bridges and empty buildings
with broken windows. The closer we get to Euston the more
anxious I feel; pressure builds, how will today be? There's a
filthy low-slung concrete building on the right-hand side of the
track about 500 metres before we get into Euston. On its side,
someone has painted: LIFE IS NOT A PARAGRAPH.[72]

8 'ASPIRING IN THE AIR'

North London: From Camden Town to Primrose Hill, Kentish Town, Holloway, Crouch End, Stoke Newington, Islington and Highbury

The area of north London covered here is a vast territory that contains many different versions of London suburbia. It includes the first industrialized dirty suburb, as Camden is brutally cut up by the railways. It becomes, as it is so close to working districts of Clerkenwell, and the City itself, the first part of urban London proper to become mass working- and middle-class suburbia. The place is full of Victorian clerks, like Bob Cratchit, and Holloway's Charles Pooter, daily walking to work in the City and back. It also, in the late 1950s, around Gloucester Crescent in Camden, and in Canonbury, Highbury and Angel, becomes the first place to see the 'knock-through' pioneering gentrifiers, returning from the outer suburbs and the provinces to restore decaying Georgian terraces and tidy knackered squares. Then of course, emerging from Barnsbury, New Labour territory in the 1990s, the frightening first glimpse of what geographers Tim Butler and Loretta Lees term 'super-gentrification'; as the global super-wealthy arrive and price out even the barristers and media folk. Overall, this version of a gentrified Islington seems to dominate the popular perception of a distinct 'North London' identity: as left-liberal, intellectual, family-oriented, comfortably middle class. Yet also, further out, we get other classic London suburban identities, especially the exclusive hilltop cutesiness of pastel-hued Primrose Hill, and the distinctly 'weird' (in a literary sense) enclave of Stoke Newington, with its historical echoes of Defoe, Poe, Machen and Alexander Baron.

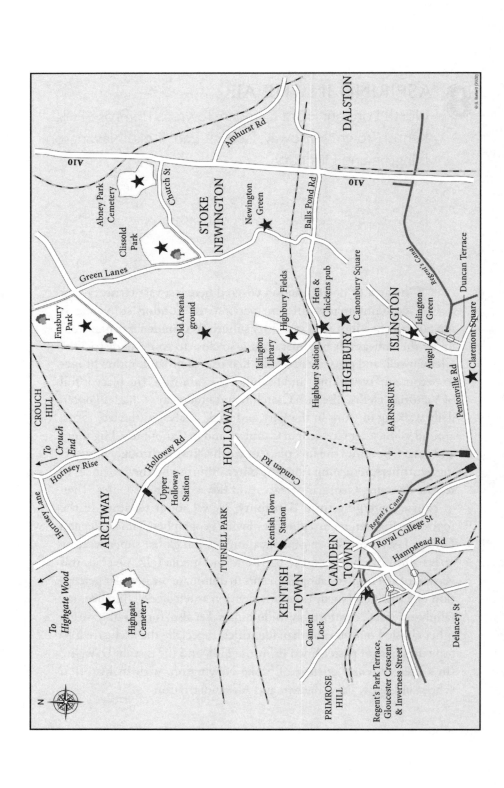

© S. Ballard (2020)

Camden Town

Developed comparatively late, in the 1780s and '90s, and still extensively rural into the nineteenth century, Camden Town was dramatically
changed by, first, the arrival of the Regent's Canal from 1816 and,
then, more seriously, by the coming of the railways after 1830. This
rapid modernization, driven by a desire to connect the new termini
at Euston, St Pancras and King's Cross, to the north, along with some
tricky engineering problems, deep excavations, long cuttings and tunnels, all executed by a vast army of navvies, was unusual in that the
disruption actually decreased the population for a while, as so much
of the place was simply torn down and brutally rearranged. Samuel
Palmer, writing in 1870, opened his description of Camden Town as
being 'a very considerable district, but of quite modern existence.
Indeed the first building erected in it was in 1750.'[1] It then belonged
to the parish of St Pancras:

> The alterations in this parish in the last fifty years are
> incalculable . . . At this time, when omnibuses and railways
> were unknown, St Pancras was the limit of the London
> tradesman's ambition. To pass a day in the fields of Camden
> and Kentish Town, or perhaps to venture as far as the hill of
> Highgate, was the boundary of his wishes; and after such an
> excursion he returned to his daily avocations with more zest
> than the excursionist of the present day, who in the same time
> is whirled away some fifty miles into the country.[2]

During these industrializing upheavals the young Dickens lived
in Camden Town, unhappily, at the time when his father was on his
way to debtors' prison. The Cratchits live here in 1843's *A Christmas
Carol* (where Scrooge dispatches the Prize Turkey) and, in *Sketches by
Boz* (1836), Camden forms part of the natural habitat of a universal
London type, the 'shabby genteel', the near-destitute individual living
in a 'damp back parlour in a new row of houses at Camden-town, half
street, half brickfield, somewhere near the canal', poor and ragged yet
eager to maintain some kind of respectable appearance.[3]

Permanently indebted Mr Micawber, in *David Copperfield* (1850),
also lives unhappily in Camden Town:

Our conversation, afterwards, took a more worldly turn; Mr
Micawber telling us that he found Camden Town inconvenient,
and that the first thing he contemplated doing, when the
advertisement should have been the cause of something
satisfactory turning up, was to move. He mentioned a terrace
at the western end of Oxford Street, fronting Hyde Park, on
which he had always had his eye.[4]

Dombey and Son (1848) provides a famous description of the extension of the London and Birmingham Railway, London's first mainline,
from its original terminus at Camden down to Euston in the mid-
1830s. This was a formidable engineering task due to the depth of the
cutting needed, the presence of canals that had to be crossed, and the
sticky, wet clay that had to be excavated (many of the Irish labourers
slipping, falling and drowning in the filthy mud):

The first shock of a great earthquake had, just at that period,
rent the whole neighbourhood to its centre. Traces of its course
were visible on every side. Houses were knocked down; streets
broken through and stopped; deep pits and trenches dug in the
ground; enormous heaps of earth and clay thrown up; buildings
that were undermined and shaking, propped by great beams of
wood. Here, a chaos of carts, overthrown and jumbled together,
lay topsy-turvy at the bottom of a steep unnatural hill; there,
confused treasures of iron soaked and rusted in something
that had accidentally become a pond. Everywhere were bridges
that led nowhere; thoroughfares that were wholly impassable;
Babel towers of chimneys, wanting half their height; temporary
wooden houses and enclosures, in the most unlikely situations;
carcases of ragged tenements, and fragments of unfinished
walls and arches, and piles of scaffolding, and wildernesses of
bricks, and giant forms of cranes, and tripods straddling above
nothing. There were a hundred thousand shapes and substances
of incompleteness, wildly mingled out of their places, upside
down, burrowing in the earth, aspiring in the air, mouldering
in the water, and unintelligible as any dream. Hot springs and
fiery eruptions, the usual attendants upon earthquakes, lent
their contributions of confusion to the scene. Boiling water
hissed and heaved within dilapidated walls; whence, also, the

glare and roar of flames came issuing forth; and mounds of ashes blocked up rights of way, and wholly changed the law and custom of the neighbourhood.

In short, the yet unfinished and unopened Railroad was in progress; and, from the very core of all this dire disorder, trailed smoothly away, upon its mighty course of civilisation and improvement.

But as yet, the neighbourhood was shy to own the Railroad. One or two bold speculators had projected streets; and one had built a little, but had stopped among the mud and ashes to consider farther of it. A brand-new Tavern, redolent of fresh mortar and size, and fronting nothing at all, had taken for its sign The Railway Arms; but that might be rash enterprise – and then it hoped to sell drink to the workmen. So, the Excavators' House of Call had sprung up from a beer shop; and the old-established Ham and Beef Shop had become the Railway Eating House, with a roast leg of pork daily, through interested motives of a similar immediate and popular description. Lodging-house keepers were favourable in like manner; and for the like reasons were not to be trusted. The general belief was very slow. There were frowzy fields, and cowhouses, and dunghills, and dustheaps, and ditches, and gardens, and summer-houses, and carpet-beating grounds, at the very door of the Railway. Little tumuli of oyster shells in the oyster season, and of lobster shells in the lobster season, and of broken crockery and faded cabbage leaves in all seasons, encroached upon its high places. Posts, and rails, and old cautions to trespassers, and backs of mean houses, and patches of wretched vegetation, stared it out of countenance. Nothing was the better for it, or thought of being so. If the miserable waste ground lying near it could have laughed, it would have laughed it to scorn, like many of the miserable neighbours.[5]

David Thomson's 1983 memoir of living in Regent's Park Terrace, *In Camden Town*, as well as noting its early promise as a site for early gentrification, conjures the place's grim industrial past.

Early in the morning of Friday, 2 October 1874, a train of six large barges pulled by a steamer tug worked its slow way through Camden Lock and got up speed on the straight between the Zoo and Prince Albert Road. The first barge, *Tilbury*, carried sugar, nuts, straw-boards, coffee, some barrels of petroleum and about five tons of gunpowder . . . *Limehouse* came next; *Susan* behind it had a little gunpowder on board. As *Tilbury* was passing under Macclesfield Bridge, which links Avenue Road with the north gate of Regent's Park, it blew up.[6]

The result was like a mini-earthquake, with the bridge destroyed, mounds of rubble thrown up, gas mains set alight, and, later, numerous dead bodies dredged up from the bottom of the canal.

By the late nineteenth century, Camden Town had acquired a grim reputation, a place for casual domestic violence and fetid corruption, nicely utilized in the Camden Town Group painter Walter Sickert's sickly interiors, including his notorious series of works *The Camden Town Murder*, inspired by the death of a prostitute, Emily Dimmock, in 1907. Sickert observed in a 1934 lecture:

It is said that we are a great literary nation but we really don't care about literature, we like films, and we like a good murder. If there is not a murder about every day they put one in. They have put in every murder which has occurred during the past ten years again, even the Camden Town murder. Not that I am against that because I once painted a whole series about the Camden Town murder; and after all murder is as good a subject as any other.[7]

Compton Mackenzie's novel *Sinister Street* (1913) captures the unease sensed by its protagonist, Michael, as he travels north through Camden:

when the cab had crossed the junction of the Euston Road with the Tottenham Court Road, unknown London with all its sly and labyrinthine romance lured his fancy onward. Maple's and Shoolbred's, those outposts of shopping civilisation, were left behind, and the Hampstead Road with a hint of roguery began. He was not sure what exactly made the Hampstead Road so disquieting . . . The road itself was merely grim, but it had a nightmare capacity for suggesting that deviation by a foot from the thoroughfare itself would lead to obscure calamities. Those bright yellow omnibuses in which he had never travelled, how he remembered them from the days of Jack the Ripper.[8]

Further along, up the Hampstead Road, it only gets worse.

Here was the Britannia, a terminus which had stuck in his mind for years as situate in some grey limbo of farthest London. Here it was, a tawdry and not very large public-house exactly like a hundred others. Now the cab was bearing round to the right, and presently upon an iron railway bridge Michael read in giant letters the direction Kentish Town behind a huge leprous hand pointing to the left. The hansom clattered through the murk beneath, past the dim people huddled upon the pavement, past a wheel-barrow and the obscene skeletons and outlines of humanity chalked upon the arches of sweating brick. Here was Kentish Town. It lay to the left of this bridge that was the colour of stale blood.[9]

Paul Verlaine and seventeen-year-old rebel poet Arthur Rimbaud arrived in London in 1872, escaping various spouses, families and debts. They seemed to enjoy the squalor and noise, much of London's raw modernity making its way into Rimbaud's poetry. They lived for a few months in 1873 at 8 Royal College Street, Camden, where their always fractious relationship exploded. The catalyst, as Graham Robb explains it (quoting Rimbaud), was Verlaine's returning from shopping with a fish and some oil:

By the end of June, the weak disciple was buckling under the strain. The last straw was as trivial as last straws usually are. On Thursday, 3 July, it was Verlaine's turn to do the shopping. He went out and came back with a fish and a bottle of oil.

'I was approaching the house when I saw Rimbaud observing me through the open window. For no good reason, he started to snigger. I climbed the stairs anyway and went in. "Have you any idea how ridiculous you look with your bottle of oil in one hand and your fish in the other?" said Rimbaud.'

A fish hit Rimbaud in the face and Verlaine headed for the stairs . . . and set off without packing his bags.[10]

In George Gissing's tale of literary scrabbling and hackery *New Grub Street* (1891), the hard-pressed Yule family live in Camden. We see Marian Yule, the daughter of literary hack Alfred Yule, and his unpaid research-drudge trudging home from the British Library:

> In Tottenham Court Road she waited for an omnibus that
> would take her to the remoter part of Camden Town; obtaining
> a corner seat, she drew as far back as possible, and paid no
> attention to her fellow passengers. At a point in Camden Road
> she at length alighted, and after ten minutes' walk reached
> her destination in a quiet by-way called St Paul's Crescent,
> consisting of small, decent houses. That at which she paused
> had an exterior promising comfort within; the windows were
> clean and neatly curtained, and the polishable appurtenances
> of the door gleamed to perfection.[11]

Terrifyingly, Alfred Yule, professional reader, comes to realize that he is losing his sight:

> He came out again by Camden Town Station. The coffee-stall
> had disappeared; the traffic of the great highway was growing
> uproarious. Among all the strugglers for existence who rushed
> this way and that, Alfred Yule felt himself a man chosen for
> fate's heaviest infliction.[12]

Dylan Thomas lived for a while at 54 Delancey Street in 1951, as he explained to American poet John Brinnin: 'Your letter just forwarded from Laugharne to our new London house of horror on bus and nightlorry route and opposite railway bridge and shunting station. No herons here.'[13]

Camden is strange and disorientating to Margaret in David Storey's 1960 novel *Flight into Camden*, as she escapes to London from Yorkshire to live with a married schoolteacher. She is not impressed: 'The street down to the tube station was piled high with mounds of rubbish from a market. It smelt strongly of fruit and vegetables. Howarth liked the sight and the smell. The stalls were being dismantled, but were still alight with glaring yellow gas lamps.'[14] But things improve:

In the afternoon he said he had some sort of surprise for me. He took me out of the house, and instead of walking down Inverness Street he took me in the opposite direction, walking between two rows of not unpleasant, heavily-painted houses. Within a few minutes a frieze of branches showed beyond the houses, then a broad stretch of grass and bare trees. He laughed at my surprise.

'But I'd never have thought,' I said, looking back at the roofs and chimneys, 'I'd never have guessed that this was here. It's like the sea . . . in the middle of all these buildings.'

'It's only Regent's Park.'[15]

David Thomson arrived in Camden in 1955, slightly ahead of the first wave of gentrifiers. Over the following decades, things slowly changed, as he recalled in 1980:

> September 28th, Sunday
>
> Yesterday, Saturday afternoon, we passed many people of a kind we never used to see in Camden Town before, people connected with the markets – buyers and sellers from the newest one by the Bucks Head and from Dingwalls Lock – the new name for Camden Lock. They were mostly young and there was a carefree feeling about them – some sitting and standing outside the Elephants Head, which was called the Boxers when we first came. They are very unlike the Inverness Street market people, some of whom are also very young, and unlike any groups one sees on weekdays – crowds enjoying themselves here at weekends, as strangers to us, and to most local people, like tourists . . . the very fact that they were enjoying themselves openly in the street is something new too. For, some years ago, no Camden Town pub, and least of all a working-class one like the Boxer, would have tables outside on the pavement.[16]

This is the same territory and people, the pioneering gentrifiers, identified in the sketches called 'Life and Times in NW1' that Alan Bennett wrote for his BBC TV series *On the Margin* (1966). Bennett invents typical gentrifying couples, such as Joanna and Simon Stringalong and Nigel and Jane Knocker-Threw. The following year Mark Boxer (penname Marc) reworked these into a cartoon strip under the same name for *The Listener*. Eccentric upper-middle-class, liberal, media types the Stringalongs, roughing it in gritty Georgian Camden Town, are faced with all manner of new middle-class dilemmas. A typical tagline runs:

> SIMON: Have you seen this scheme to route the Stansted extension slap through NW1?
> JOANNA: What a marvellous opportunity for a really valid protest movement. Moira can do a TV programme; we can have a party; and the Touch-Paceys can design a protest button.[17]

Bennett himself had moved into 23 Gloucester Crescent in 1969, when Camden was still shabby and neglected:

> I first saw the house in 1968. Jonathan Miller lives in the same street and Rachel, his wife, saw the 'For Sale' sign go up. It belonged to an American woman who kept parrots and there were perches in the downstairs room and also in its small garden. Slightly older than the other houses in the crescent, like many of them it had been a lodging house, so every room had its own gas meter and some had washbasins. I did most of the decorating myself, picking out the blurred and whitewashed frieze in the drawing room with a nail file, a job that these days would be done by steam cleaning, though then I was helped by some of the actors in my first play, *Forty Years On*, which was running in the West End.[18]

The Gloucester Crescent house became well known through its appearance in the 2015 film *The Lady in the Van*, written by Bennett and adapted from a memoir of the same name. This concerns a homeless woman who takes up residence in a Bedford van in Bennett's driveway for fifteen years, from the early 1970s on. Bennett describes the area in the immediately preceding years:

> It must have been . . . some time in the late Sixties, that the van first appeared in Gloucester Crescent. In those days the street was still a bit of a mixture. Its large semi-detached villas had originally been built to house the Victorian middle class, then it had gone down in the world, and though it had never

entirely decayed, many of the villas degenerated into rooming-houses and so were among the earliest candidates for what is now called 'gentrification', but which was then called 'knocking through'. Young professional couples, many of them in journalism or television, bought up the houses, converted them and (an invariable feature of such conversions) knocked the basement rooms together to form a large kitchen-dining-room. In the mid-Sixties I wrote a BBC TV series, *Life in NW1*, based on one such family, the Stringalongs, whom Mark Boxer then took over to people a cartoon strip in the *Listener*, and who kept cropping up in his drawings for the rest of his life. What made the social set-up funny was the disparity between the style in which the new arrivals found themselves able to live and their progressive opinions: guilt, put simply, which today's gentrifiers are said famously not to feel (or 'not to have a problem about'). We did have a problem, though I'm not sure we were any better for it. There was a gap between our social position and our social obligations. It was in this gap that Miss Shepherd (in her van) was able to live.[19]

Gloucester Crescent in fact produced a rich harvest of literary types, among them George and Diana Melly, Alice Thomas Ellis, Beryl Bainbridge, David Gentleman, V. S. Pritchett, Angus Wilson and A. J. Ayer.

Nina Stibbe, in her collection of letters published as *Love, Nina* (2013), describes arriving at 55 Gloucester Crescent from her native working-class Leicester, for a job as a live-in nanny: 'It's fantastic here, the house, the street, London. You can hear the zoo animals waking up in the morning.'[20] Her employer turns out to be Mary-Kay Wilmers, the bohemian and unworldly editor of the *London Review of Books*, and so various colourful Camden literary types casually cross the threshold: John Lahr, Jonathan Miller, Claire Tomalin – and, of course, Alan Bennett himself:

Of course he's *the* Alan Bennett. You'd know him if you saw him. He used to be in *Coronation Street*. He's got a small nose and Yorkshire accent.

He's very nice. He says, 'Don't be daft' etc. He's getting quite famous now (probably more so than Jonathan Miller

actually) but he's not bothered about it. He's very interested
in history, but he's rubbish on nature (like MK) although
he is very outdoorsy and does like it (nature) for walks etc.
(unlike MK) . . .

Once, late at night, when I was on my own, I thought
I could hear someone creeping around in the house (burglar or
worse). I got myself so scared I rang AB and asked him to come
over. He came over straight away (his mac over his pyjamas)
holding his brolly. He had a good look around. There was no
one. I was so embarrassed I almost wished there was. I said,
'I feel such an idiot.' And he said, 'Don't be daft.'[21]

A sense of the other Camden, as somehow blighted and darkly
unsettling, continues in the denouement of John le Carré's 1974 spy
thriller *Tinker Tailor Soldier Spy*. This takes place at a safehouse on
the Regent's Canal:

Lock Gardens, which presumably drew its name from the
Camden and Hampstead Road Locks nearby, was a terrace
of four flat-fronted nineteenth-century houses built at the
centre of a crescent, each with three floors and a basement and
a strip of walled back garden running down to the Regent's
Canal . . . the neighbourhood possessed no social identity and
demanded none.[22]

The house is placed under surveillance:

On the canal towpath, meanwhile, Guillam had resumed his
vigil of the house. The footpath is closed to the public one hour
before dark: after that it can be anything from a trysting place
for lovers to a haven for down and outs; both, for different
reasons, are attracted by the darkness of the bridges. That cold
night Guillam saw neither. Occasionally an empty train raced
past, leaving a still greater emptiness behind. His nerves were
so taut, his expectations so varied, that for a moment he saw
the whole architecture of that night in apocalyptic terms: the
signals on the railway bridge turned to gallows; the Victorian
warehouses to gigantic prisons, their windows barred and
arched against the misty sky. Closer at hand, the ripple of rats

and the stink of still water. Then the drawing-room lights went out; the house stood in darkness except for the chinks of yellow to either side of Millie's basement window. From the scullery a pin of light winked at him down the unkempt garden.[23]

Deborah Moggach's novel *Close to Home* (1979) depicts a Camden street during the long heatwave summer of 1976. 'Brinsley Street', here, is a typically grubby, traffic-choked Camden main road: 'it was a noisy road, a through route, part of a complicated traffic system that led towards King's Cross and the City. Day and night lorries rumbled past.'[24] Yet beyond the street, Moggach reveals the existence of another world: 'Brinsley Street was all fumes and noise; passers-by could scarcely guess at the sweet green release that lay behind the houses, the shade and silence and dappled patches of grass, the flowers and sleeping rats.'[25]

The residents, sharing over honeysuckled walls their rural secret, behaved differently here from the way they did in the street. In the street they had to shout to be heard, their eyes flickered always to their children, they had to press against the railings for the passers-by. Here, in the gardens, their own countryside, they felt private and sufficient unto themselves.[26]

Primrose Hill

To the northwest of Camden Town, just above Regent's Park, this former forest was cleared in the sixteenth century, which was when real primroses first appeared, and had long been a popular site for duelling, the odd murder, political demonstrations and a booming Second World War anti-aircraft battery. Latterly best-known for celebrity-spotting and picnics with stunning views. William Blake, keen on walking and thinking on Primrose Hill, set the place, in the epic visionary poem *Jerusalem*, as one of the future sites of the New Jerusalem that would be built in London:

The fields from Islington to Marylebone,
To Primrose Hill and Saint John's Wood,
Were builded over with pillars of gold,
And there Jerusalem's pillars stood.

Her little ones ran on the fields,
The Lamb of God among them seen,
And fair Jerusalem, His Bride,
Among the little meadows green.

Pancras and Kentish Town repose
Among her golden pillars high,
Among her golden arches which
Shine upon the starry sky.[27]

Claire Clairmont, living with her stepsister Mary Shelley and
her husband Percy Shelley in 1814, would frequently walk the hill
and especially the pond, where the poet seemed inordinately fond of
making and sailing paper boats. In fact, according to his close friend
and biographer Thomas Jefferson Hogg, Shelley would launch entire
flotillas of these boats until they absorbed water and slowly sank.

Sunday Oct 2nd. We all go to a Pond past Primrose Hill &
make Paper Boats & sail them . . .
    Wednesday Oct 5th. Go with Mary and Shelley to Primrose
Hill Pond and sail fire Boats – Return to Dinner.[28]

Two decades later, Charles Lamb's extensive London walks also
took him to Primrose Hill. In 'Detached Thoughts on Books and
Reading', from *The Last Essays of Elia* (1833), he records:

I do not remember a more whimsical surprise than having
been once detected – by a familiar damsel – reclined at my
ease upon the grass, on Primrose Hill (her Cythera), reading –
Pamela. There was nothing in the book to make a man seriously
ashamed at the exposure; but as she seated herself down by
me, and seemed determined to read in company, I could have
wished it had been – any other book. We read on very sociably
for a few pages; and, not finding the author much to her taste,
she got up, and – went away. Gentle casuist, I leave it to thee
to conjecture whether the blush (for there was one between us)
was the property of the nymph or the swain in this dilemma.
From me you shall never get the secret.[29]

A walk to pretty Primrose Hill was also considered just the thing for a talk between the notoriously estranged Victorian father and son in Edmund Gosse's 1907 memoir of that name:

> It was a very long time since we had spent a day out of London, and I said, on being coaxed back to calmness, that I wanted 'to go into the country'. Like the dying Falstaff, I babbled of green fields. My father, after a little reflection, proposed to take me to Primrose Hill. I had never heard of the place, and names have always appealed directly to my imagination. I was in the highest degree delighted, and could hardly restrain my impatience. As soon as possible we set forth westward, my hand in my Father's, with the liveliest anticipations. I expected to see a mountain absolutely carpeted with primroses, a terrestrial galaxy like that which covered the hill that led up to Montgomery Castle in Donne's poem. But at length, as we walked from the Chalk Farm direction, a miserable acclivity stole into view surrounded, even in those days, on most sides by houses, with its grass worn to the buff by millions of boots, and resembling what I meant by 'the country' about as much as Poplar resembles Paradise. We sat down on a bench at its inglorious summit, whereupon I burst into tears, and in a heart-rending whisper sobbed, 'Oh! Papa, let us go home!'[30]

In H. G. Wells's *The War of the Worlds* (1895) the narrator struggles northwards through devastated and 'dead London' (see Chapter Five), until he reaches Primrose Hill, where the Martians, after rampaging across London from Woking, have finally come to grief:

> Great mounds had been heaped about the crest of the hill, making a huge redoubt of it – it was the final and largest place the Martians had made – and from behind these heaps there rose a thin smoke against the sky . . .
>
> In another moment I had scrambled up the earthen rampart and stood upon its crest, and the interior of the redoubt was below me. A mighty space it was, with gigantic machines here and there within it, huge mounds of material and strange shelter-places. And scattered about it, some in their overturned war-machines, some in the now rigid handling-machines, and

a dozen of them stark and silent and laid in a row, were the
Martians – *dead*![31]

He scrambles to get closer.

> I stood staring into the pit, and my heart lightened gloriously,
> even as the rising sun struck the world to fire about me with
> his rays. The pit was still in darkness; the mighty engines,
> so great and wonderful in their power and complexity, so
> unearthly in their tortuous forms, rose weird and vague and
> strange out of the shadows towards the light. A multitude of
> dogs, I could hear, fought over the bodies that lay darkly in the
> depth of the pit, far below me . . . At the sound of a cawing
> overhead I looked up at the huge fighting-machine that would
> fight no more for ever, at the tattered red shreds of flesh that
> dripped down upon the overturned seats on the summit of
> Primrose Hill.[32]

Jean Rhys's Anna Morgan spends a typically unhappy summer
afternoon on Primrose Hill in *Voyage in the Dark* (1934):

> Sometimes it was hot that summer. The day we went to
> Savernake it was really hot. I had been sitting out on Primrose
> Hill. There were swarms of children there. Just behind my chair
> a big boy and a little one were playing with a rope. The little
> one was being tied up elaborately, so that he couldn't move his
> arms or legs. When the big one gave him a push he fell flat.
> He lay on the ground, still laughing for a second. Then his
> face changed and he started to cry. The big boy kicked him –
> not hard. He yelled louder. 'Nah then,' the big one said. He
> got ready to kick again. But then he saw I was watching. He
> grinned and undid the rope. The little boy stopped crying and
> got up. They both put out their tongues at me and ran off. The
> little one's legs were short and dimpled. When he ran he could
> hardly keep up. However he didn't forget to turn round and put
> his tongue out again as far as he could.
>   There was no sun, but the air was used-up and dead, dirty-
> warm, as if thousands of other people had breathed it before you.
> A woman passed, throwing a ball for a dog called Caesar . . .

'See-zah, See-zah!'
After a bit I went home and had a cold bath.[33]

Primrose Hill was an ideal location to set huge anti-aircraft gun placements in the Second World War. Louis MacNeice observes the preparations in 1938, recorded in *Autumn Journal*:

And I hear dull blows on wood outside my window;
They are cutting down the trees on Primrose Hill.
The wood is white like the roast flesh of chicken,
Each tree falling like a closing fan;
No more looking at the view from seats beneath the branches,
Everything is going to plan;
They want the crest of this hill for anti-aircraft[34]

Six years later the poet Sebastian Barnack, in Aldous Huxley's 1944 novel *Time Must Have a Stop*, actually hears the guns in action:

The guns on Primrose Hill were banging away with a kind
of frenzy; and though the desert was far away, though the
nightmare under those swooping planes was long past,
Sebastian felt some of the old quivering tensions – as if he
were a violin with knotted strings in the process of being
tuned up, excruciatingly sharp and sharper, towards the final
snapping point.[35]

A fantasy version of Primrose Hill, all nannies and butlers and jolly good manners, is also the setting for Dodie Smith's 1956 children's novel *The Hundred and One Dalmatians*. The fantasy is temporarily broken by the dark Cruella de Vil:

It was a beautiful September evening, windless, very peaceful.
The park and the old, cream-painted houses facing it basked
in the golden light of sunset. There were many sounds but no
noises. The cries of playing children and the whir of London's
traffic seemed quieter than usual, as if softened by the evening's
gentleness. Birds were singing their last song of the day and
further along the Circle, at the house where a great composer
lived, someone was playing the piano.[36]

The peace doesn't last long:

> At that moment, the peace was shattered by an extremely
> strident motor horn. A large car was coming towards them. It
> drew up at a big house just ahead of them, and a tall woman
> came out on to the front-door steps. She was wearing a tight-
> fitting emerald satin dress, several ropes of rubies, and an
> absolutely simple white mink cloak, which reached to the heels
> of her ruby-red shoes. She had dark skin, black eyes with a tinge
> of red in them, and a very pointed nose. Her hair was parted
> severely down the middle and one half of it was black and the
> other white – rather unusual.
> 'Why, that's Cruella de Vil,' said Mrs Dearly. 'We were at
> school together. She was expelled for drinking ink.'
> 'Isn't she a bit showy?' said Mr Dearly.[37]

Sylvia Plath, after Ted Hughes's desertion, and with two small
children, moved into a flat at 23 Fitzroy Road, attracted by the idea
of a previous occupant: W. B. Yeats. That winter, 1962–3, turned out
to be the coldest of the century and London was frozen for months.

> In London the day after Christmas (Boxing Day) – it began
> to snow: my first snow in England. For five years I had been
> tactfully asking, 'Do you ever have snow at all?' as I steeled myself
> to the six months of wet, tepid gray that make up an English
> winter. 'Ooo I do remember snow,' was the usual reply, 'when
> I were a lad.' Whereupon I would enthusiastically recall the huge
> falls of crisp and spectacular white I snowballed, tunneled in and
> sledded on in the States when *I* was young. Now I felt the same
> sweet chill of anticipation at my London window, watching the
> pieces of darkness incandesce as they drove through the glow of
> the street-light. Since my flat (once the home of W. B. Yeats and
> so marked on a round, blue plaque) has no central heating, my
> chill was not metaphorical but very real.
> The next day the snow lay about – white, picturesque,
> untouched, and it went on snowing. The next day the snow still
> lay about – untouched. There seemed to be a lot more of it. Bits
> plopped in over my boot tops as I crossed the unplowed street.
> The main road had not been plowed either. Random buses

and cabs crawled along in deep white tracks. Here and there men with newspapers, brooms and rags attempted to discover their cars.[38]

The Beatles' 1967 song 'The Fool on the Hill', written by Paul McCartney, is rumoured to be based on an experience McCartney had on Primrose Hill early one morning out walking his dog, Martha. Unreliable witness Alistair Taylor insists he was there.

We turned to go, when suddenly there was a man standing behind us. He was a middle-aged man, very respectfully dressed in a belted raincoat. There's nothing odd in that you might think, but he had come up behind us over the bare top of the hill in total silence. We were sure the man had not been there seconds earlier . . . he appeared miraculously. We exchanged greetings . . . and then walked away . . . when we looked around he'd vanished! There was no sign of the man. He had just disappeared from the top of the hills as if he'd been carried off into the air . . .
Paul is shaken; has to sit down for a minute. 'What the hell do you make of that? That's weird! He was there, wasn't he?'[39]

In Kingsley Amis's 1990 novel *The Folks That Live on the Hill*, Primrose Hill, where Amis lived in his sozzled, declining years, becomes 'Shepherd's Hill', where boozy retiree Henry Caldecote tries to makes sense of the modern world:

The bright May sunshine in the street suffered from what Bunty had half-supposed to be a rock concert in the nearer middle distance but now turned out to be merely the output of some sort of radio playing to no visible audience from the scaffolding on the house opposite. Further along, a burglar alarm pealed steadily and somewhere else what was perhaps another form of alarm sounded a continuous fluctuating whistle like an automaton pronouncing sorry-sorry-sorry-sorry without end. Somewhere else again a loud male voice blurted unformed syllables. And this was supposed to be a quiet suburb, handy for the centre, but still quiet.[40]

There is another side to Primrose Hill. Paul Charles's *Last Boat to Camden Town* (1998) sees Detective Inspector Christy Kennedy trying to solve the mystery of why one Edmund Berry has ended up dead in the Regent's Canal:

> The morning was sharp – he could see his breath before him, but at least it was dry. Kennedy never tired of the beauty of Primrose Hill, particularly on such early morning walks. The sky was a powerful blue and the green and brown colours of the hill combined to create his personal living picture-postcard. He felt very privileged to live where he did . . . His normal route to the office took him past Cumberland Basin. This morning, there were no signs whatever that twenty-four hours earlier, a man had lost (or maybe taken) his life there.[41]

Helen Falconer's first novel, *Primrose Hill* (1999), also presents a very different picture, of gritty inner-city estates, wasted lives and boredom. We see Si stretched out on the hill one summer night:

> I started to watch the stars, swimming into view light years above us. That summer, that's what I'd really been getting into about the hill, being able to see through a billion billion miles of open space, all the way up to the stars. It wasn't like being in London at all – not down in London where you couldn't see shit but up here, closer to the sky, like we'd been living in a manhole and climbed up and pushed off the cover. You could imagine you were right out of it, maybe on a mountain top somewhere, real air and a sky you could see. Down in the hot sweaty concrete valleys hunted the short-haired packs, with their knives and their YSL jeans, but up here we old pony-tailed long-hairs were well out of it. Even the 'Pah! Pah!' drunk was a harmless old fucker.[42]

As soon as he descends, trouble starts. Si calls his mum from a phone box:

> Listening to her talk, in the orange light of a street lamp I fingered the cards stuck all over the inside of the box – like, French maid into correction, busty blonde, 40, 20, 40, gives

golden showers (what? for fuck's sake) – and then this kid I'd
never seen before in my life jumps up out of the dark into
the orange light, leaping up against the glass like an animal in
the zoo, and starts hammering on it: 'Oi, *you*, I seen that, you
perve!' I nearly jumped out of my fucking skin.[43]

Kentish Town

A mile up the road from Camden, by the seventeenth century Kentish
Town had gained a reputation as an attractive rural location. Close
to town, but still wooded, spacious and elevated, bounded by the
sparkling River Fleet, the area was well known for its clean air and
health-giving pure water. Antiquarian William Stukeley describes how
he finds the place in 1759:

> After 9 years assiduous inquiry I found a most agreeable rural
> retreat at Kentish-town, 2 miles and ½ distant, extremely
> convenient for keeping my horses, and for my own amusement,
> the hither end of the village, between the castle inn and the
> chapel, an half-hour's walk over sweet fields. 'Tis absolutely
> and clearly out of the influence of the London smoak, a dry
> gravelly soil, and air remarkably wholsom . . . The house is new
> built for the most part; pretty, little, and elegant . . . I inclosed
> two acres of medow out of the great pasture, added to my
> garden, reduced it to a circular form, made a retired place like
> a hermitage.[44]

Mary Shelley returned to London a year after her husband drowned
off the Italian coast and in 1824 was sharing a Kentish Town lodging
with Jane Williams (previously part of the Shelley clan). The Shelleys,
with Claire Clairmont (Mary's stepsister and Byron's mistress), had
lived in the area before, one step ahead of bailiffs and landlords. On
28 July 1824 Mary wrote, unhappily, from Kentish Town to Edward
Trelawny, who had identified Percy Shelley's drowned body and had
accompanied Byron to fight for Greek independence:

> Here then we are, Jane and I, in Kentish Town . . . We live near
> each other now, and, seeing each other almost daily, for ever
> dwell on one subject . . . The country about here is really pretty;

lawny uplands, wooded parks, green lanes, and gentle
hills form agreeable and varying combinations. If we had
orange sunsets, cloudless noons, fireflies, large halls, etc. etc.,
I should not find the scenery amiss, and yet I can attach myself
to nothing here; neither among the people, though some are
good and clever, nor to the places, though they be pretty. Jane
is my chosen companion and only friend. I am under a cloud,
and cannot form near acquaintances among that class whose
manners and modes of life are agreeable to me and I think
myself fortunate in having one or two pleasing acquaintances
among literary peoples, whose society I enjoy without dreaming
of friendship.[45]

Dramatically, Shelley mentions seeing Byron's funeral cortège pass by
on the street outside:

You will not wonder that the late loss of Lord Byron makes
me cling with greater zeal to those dear friends who remain to
me. He could hardly be called a friend, but, connected with
him in a thousand ways, admiring his talents, and (with all his
faults) feeling affection for him, it went to my heart when, the
other day, the hearse that contained his lifeless form – a form
of beauty which in life I often delighted to behold – passed my
windows going up Highgate Hill on his last journey to the last
seat of his ancestors.[46]

Like all the other Victorian inner suburbs, Kentish Town's unspoilt
villagedom could not last, snubbed out by the arrival of trams and
trains, small industry, and a population and building explosion. The
sanitary reformer James Hole, in the 1860s, comments on Kentish
Town's rapid demise.

The inhabitant whose memory can carry him back thirty
years recalls pictures of rural beauty, suburban mansions and
farmsteads, green fields, waving trees and clear streams where
fish could live – where now can be seen only streets, factories
and workshops, and a river or brook black as the ink which now
runs from our pen describing it.[47]

John Betjeman's 1945 poem 'Parliament Hill Fields' recounts a nostalgic tram-ride down from Highgate, his childhood home, through north London, very precisely citing an extensive list of remembered place names, local features, destinations, well-known shops, churches and adverts: 'Bon Marché', 'Charrington's', 'Dale and Co', he remembers as they 'rocked past Zwanziger the baker's, and the terrace blackish brown / And the curious Anglo-Norman parish church of Kentish Town'.[48]

In 1974 Jonathan Raban, in *Soft City*, sees Kentish Town as the next stage, after Camden and Islington, for the outward spread of gentrification:

> Some London suburbs are traditional class ghettoes; ownership of a house in say, Golders Green or Cockfosters, merely reflects the income bracket and status within the middle class of the purchaser. But there is a great deal of soft territory where people buy houses to announce something distinct about themselves . . . As I write, it is becoming a very clear signal of personal identity to buy a house in Kentish Town, a recently resurrected dark quarter of the city, to which those who are discriminatory, left of centre, but scornful of the swarm of Islington camp-followers, are currently flocking. The NW5 postal district is moving into the pantheon of style, where it joins NI, NWI, NW3, SW6, W8 and others. A year or two ago it had all the characteristics of an area awaiting rediscovery: heavy dilapidation, absentee landlords, houses let off in single rooms, a high proportion of immigrants and students, and relatively low property prices. As these things go, it was a junk quarter, a natural piece of raw material for the stylistic entrepreneurs. Its very unlikeliness was part of its charm. Kentish Town is a mess of hilly streets around a tube station, sliced into segments by noisy through-roads. Most of the houses are survivals of the most notorious period of Victorian speculative jerry-building. They were erected in short terraces of what were accurately described by their builders as 'fourth-rate residences' . . . Kentish Town is one such slum; but time, and the pressure on metropolitan living space, have rendered its cramped terraces quaint . . . it now has 'possibilities'.[49]

Kentish Town neatly demonstrates his theory of the 'soft city', the idea that cities are imaginary and symbolic as much as they are concretely 'real':

> It has become an idea, the most precious of all commodities in this curious system. Three years ago I lived just above Kentish Town, and it was merely a place to be crossed in order to arrive at somewhere more interesting. Now it has an exact identity; it communicates thrift, intelligence, foresight, a refusal to be taken in by the showy charms of more obvious quarters. Thus transformed, it can now be used as a badge of affiliation to a caste, a symbol not of status but of taste and identity.[50]

Buchi Emecheta's first novel, *In the Ditch* (1972), is set in Kentish Town and describes the life of Nigerian single mother Adah, whose 'problems were many: how to study, keep her job and look after the kids'. Adah and the kids live in a block of council flats, 'Pussy Mansions':

> The stairs leading to the top flats were of grey stone, so steep were they that it took Adah and her kids weeks to get used to them. They were always smelly with a thick lavatorial stink. Most of the rubbish chutes along the steps and balconies were always overflowing and always open, their contents adding to the stink. The walls along the steep steps were of those shiny, impersonal bricks still seen in old tube stations, but even more like those Adah had seen in films of prisons. The windows were small and so were the doors. Most of the flats were in dark sympathy with the dark atmosphere. Ah yes, the Mansions were a unique place, a separate place individualised for 'problem families'. Problem families with real problems were placed in a problem place. So even if one lived in the Mansions and had no problems the set-up would create problems
> – in plenty.[51]

Holloway

Holloway means the Holloway Road. First appearing in records in the fifteenth century (a 'holloway' is a sunken, tree-screened lane), this

then became a turnpike and eventually a main route north, the Great
North Road. By the early nineteenth century the road was lined with
large villas and cottages for prosperous merchants and bankers, and
then, as it rapidly built up from the 1860s, became a very popular
location for the expanding army of lower-middle-class clerks toiling
in the City.

Such a clerk in Dickens's *Our Mutual Friend* (1865) is Reginald
'Rumty' Wilfer, a poor 'clerk in the drug-house of Chicksey, Veneering,
and Stobbles':

> R. Wilfer locked up his desk one evening, and, putting his
> bunch of keys in his pocket much as if it were his peg-top,
> made for home. His home was in the Holloway region north of
> London, and then divided from it by fields and trees. Between
> Battle Bridge and that part of the Holloway district in which
> he dwelt, was a tract of suburban Sahara, where tiles and bricks
> were burnt, bones were boiled, carpets were beat, rubbish was
> shot, dogs were fought, and dust was heaped by contractors.
> Skirting the border of this desert, by the way he took, when the
> light of its kiln-fires made lurid smears on the fog, R. Wilfer
> sighed and shook his head.
>
> 'Ah me!' said he, 'what might have been is not what is!'
>
> With which commentary on human life, indicating an
> experience of it not exclusively his own, he made the best of
> his way to the end of his journey.
>
> Mrs Wilfer was, of course, a tall woman and an angu-
> lar. Her lord being cherubic, she was necessarily majestic,
> according to the principle which matrimonially unites
> contrasts. She was much given to tying up her head in a
> pocket-handkerchief, knotted under the chin. This head-
> gear, in conjunction with a pair of gloves worn within doors,
> she seemed to consider as at once a kind of armour against
> misfortune (invariably assuming it when in low spirits or dif-
> ficulties), and as a species of full dress. It was therefore with
> some sinking of the spirit that her husband beheld her thus
> heroically attired, putting down her candle in the little hall,
> and coming down the doorsteps through the little front court
> to open the gate for him.[52]

The plot here revolves around the wealth generated by businessman John Harmon's so-called 'dust heaps', mini-mountains of junk, ashes and urban detritus, also located in north London, on the way out to the Wilfers', a mile or so 'over Maiden-Lane [York Way] way – out Holloway direction'.[53] Noddy Boffin, the inheritor of Harmon's huge wealth, becomes known as the 'Golden Dustman'.

Upper Holloway is also the location of the best-known suburban clerk in all of London-set suburban fiction: Mr Charles Pooter in George and Weedon Grossmith's *The Diary of a Nobody* (1892). Here we see him as he is just proudly moving into his new Holloway home.

> My dear wife Carrie and I have just been a week in our new house, 'The Laurels', Brickfield Terrace, Holloway – a nice six-roomed residence, not counting basement, with a front breakfast-parlour. We have a little front garden; and there is a flight of ten steps up to the front door, which, by-the-by, we keep locked with the chain up . . . We have a nice little back garden which runs down to the railway. We were rather afraid of the noise of the trains at first, but the landlord said we should not notice them after a bit, and took £2 off the rent. He was certainly right; and beyond the cracking of the garden wall at the bottom, we have suffered no inconvenience.[54]

Busy and content at first with various tradesmen, repairmen, delivery boys, visitors and neighbours, Pooter's grasp on suburban lower-middle-class reality soon heads into trouble, hinted at here already as the garden walls crumble. Lowly butchers and ironmongers prove unreliable or unreasonable, delivery boys and clerks always cheeky, visitors (Mr Cummings and Mr Gowing) soon exasperate. The house itself seems to rebel – a dodgy foot-scraper attacks visitors, doorbells fail, nothing will grow in the scrubby garden, things break or fail, or get lost:

> April 11. – Mustard-and-cress and radishes not come up yet. To-day was a day of annoyances. I missed the quarter-to-nine 'bus to the City, through having words with the grocer's boy, who for the second time had the impertinence to bring his basket to the hall-door, and had left the marks of his dirty boots on the fresh-cleaned door-steps.[55]

346

Although Pooter insists on his homeliness – 'What's the good of a home if you are never in it?' he argues – the novel is really an account of Pooter's incompetence and discomfort, how he doesn't fit into the comfy and ordered suburban world that he yearns for. Note his terrible attempts at home improvement:

April 25. – In consequence of Brickwell telling me his wife was working wonders with the new Pinkford's enamel paint, I determined to try it. I bought two tins of red on my way home. I hastened through tea, went into the garden and painted some flower-pots. I called out Carrie, who said: 'You've always got some new-fangled craze'; but she was obliged to admit that the flower-pots looked remarkably well. Went upstairs into the servant's bedroom and painted her washstand, towel-horse, and chest of drawers. To my mind it was an extraordinary improvement, but as an example of the ignorance of lower classes in matters of taste, our servant, Sarah, on seeing them, evinced no sign of pleasure, but merely said 'she thought they looked very well as they was before'.

April 26. – Got some more red enamel paint (red, to my mind, being the best colour) and painted the coal-scuttle, and the backs of our *Shakspeare* [*sic*], the binding of which had almost worn out.

April 27. – Painted the bath red, and was delighted with the result. Sorry to say Carrie was not, in fact we had a few words about it.[56]

A few days later, while in the bath, Pooter is momentarily terrified to find that the bath-water has turned blood-red.

As Holloway declines in the post-war era it becomes amenable to recent migrants. In Colin MacInnes's novel of new Commonwealth migrants, *City of Spades* (1957), Nigerian Johnny Fortune and his countryman Hamilton are looking for 'a taxi among the endless streets that led in the direction of his Holloway home'.[57] The pair need to be careful where they get out as taxi-drivers 'make their report on passengers they carry to the Law':

We walked from the taxi stop round several blocks, Hamilton glancing sometimes back along the streets behind, then dived in the basement of a silent house. Hamilton opened, and turned on the lights with a great smile. 'Welcome to my place,' he said, 'which is also to be from now on your home.'[58]

Fortune is surprised to be impressed:

It certainly was a most delightful residence: with carpets and divans, and shaded lamps and a big radiogram and comfort. He turned on the sound which gave out first Lena Horne. 'She! One of my favourites,' I told him.
    'Then listen to her, man, while I go change my shirt.'
    Up on his walls, Hamilton had stuck many photographs: like Billy Daniels, and Dr Nkrumah, and Joe Louis in his prime, and Sugar Ray; and also Hamilton's acquaintances, all sharply dressed and grinning – rocking high with charge, I'd say, when these snaps of them were taken.[59]

Playwright and provocateur Joe Orton lived in Noel Road, Angel, in the 1960s and has two key links to the Holloway Road. The first is the ornate Art Nouveau Islington Central Library on Holloway Road, where Orton and his lover, Kenneth Halliwell, spent an inordinate amount of time stealing books, artistically defacing either the blurbs or covers, then returning them to shelves. Additions included: 'READ THIS BEHIND CLOSED DOORS! And have a good s*** while you are reading!' The first volume of the collected plays by the Welsh dramatist Emlyn Williams now included such previously unknown works as *Knickers Must Fall*, *Olivia Prude*, *Up the Front* and *Up the Back*. The cover of a romance, *Queen's Favourite*, was altered with the addition of two semi-naked men wrestling. The *Collins Guide to Roses* was given a startling monkey peering out from a flower. Orton later recalled that he 'used to stand in the corners after I'd smuggled the doctored books back into the library and then watch people read them. It was very fun, very interesting.' The Islington libraries department, and the law, took this prank very seriously: after a lengthy investigation the two were discovered, arrested and jailed for six months.[60]
    Orton also kept a diary for a few years and, in riposte to Pooter, subtitled it 'Diary of a Somebody'. Pooter would not recognize *this* Holloway, especially the public toilets just down from Pooter's villa,

under the bridge on Holloway Road, a favoured location for Orton's cottaging:

4 March 1967

Spent this morning ringing up P. Willes, Peggy, Michael White and Oscar . . .

I took the Piccadilly line to Holloway Road and popped into a little pissoir – just four pissers. It was dark because someone had taken the bulb away. There were three figures pissing . . . Another man entered and the man next to the labourer moved away, not out of the place altogether, but back against the wall. The new man had a pee and left the place and, before the man against the wall could return to his place, I nipped in sharpish and stood next to the labourer. I put my hand down and felt his cock, he immediately started to play with mine. The young-ish man with fair hair, standing back against the wall, went into the vacant place. I unbuttoned the top of my jeans and unloos-ened my belt in order to allow the labourer free rein with my balls. The man next to me began to feel my bum. At this point a fifth man entered. Nobody moved. It was dark. Just a little light spilled into the place from the street, not enough to see immediately. The man next to me moved back to allow the fifth man to piss. But the fifth man very quickly flashed his cock and the man next to me returned to my side, lifting up my coat and shoving his hand down the back of my trousers. The fifth man kept puffing on a cigarette and, by the glowing end, watching. A sixth man came into the pissoir. As it was so dark nobody bothered to move . . . The little pissoir under the bridge had become the scene of a frenzied homosexual saturnalia. No more than two feet away the citizens of Holloway moved about their ordinary business. I came, squirting into the bearded man's mouth, and quickly pulled up my jeans. As I was about to leave, I heard the bearded man hissing quietly, 'I suck people off! Who wants his cock sucked?' When I left, the labourer was just shoving his cock into the man's mouth to keep him quiet. I caught the bus home.[61]

Orton and Halliwell had just returned from an expensive trip to Libya. 'It sounds as though eightpence and a bus down the

Holloway Road was more interesting than £200 and a plane to Tripoli',[62] Halliwell comments when he hears of Orton's escapades. After bludgeoning Orton's skull with a hammer a few months later, and before committing suicide, Halliwell left a note in Orton's diary:

> If you read his diary all will be explained.
> K.H.
> P.S. Especially the latter part.

The last week of Orton's diary was missing.

In J. M. O'Neill's novel of Irish labourers in London, *Duffy Is Dead* (1987), the titular Irish builder drops dead outside a bank on the Holloway Road. Landlord Robert Calnan (O'Neill had himself been landlord of the Duke of Wellington on nearby Balls Pond Road) has the task of sorting everything out and travels extensively around a gritty, still Irish, working-class north London:

> There was an undertaker's in Upper Street, managed by the Clincher Casey, for lower end of the market embarkations, and he caught a bus at the Archway. He passed the bank that would be for ever Duffy's memorial and watched the greasy passage of the Holloway Road to Highbury Corner. Holloway was cheap, Upper Street down-at-heel.
>
> Canonbury Chapels of Rest was closed for lunch but he found the Clincher in the next-door pub, saloon bar, impeccably behind his *Daily Telegraph*, half of bitter, cheese and wheaten bread. The Clincher was a Corkman, of refined enunciation and a whole range of funeral postures and grimaces that endeared him to Calnan. If you took the job on, Calnan thought, you worked at it.
>
> Calnan bought him a pale sherry and said: 'A fellow called Duffy is dead at the Whittington. Died on the road. They took him in.'[63]

Calnan loves to walk ('it was no effort on such caisson legs') and heads back, 'hardly more than a short step from Islington to the Trade Winds' at Dalston, passing Islington Green.[64]

The statue of Myddleton, an Islington patriarch of long, long ago, stood on the last triangular scrap of village green with ageing seats and trees yellowed in the late fall, the stumps of countless amputations scattered on their trunks like warts. The breeze was rising again and in a split second of traffic silence a dry rustle wafted down to him. At the public lavatory a drunk, or maybe a deranged old man, shouted something incoherent and was ignored by a zombie stream of urban forbearance. Behind him and the grass patch had been Collins' Music Hall: Calnan had drunk there and watched its last resurgence and sudden decline from entertainment to the sadness of tit, clit and smut. It was an office columbarium now, glass and glaze, part of the great featureless architecture of a strange new world.[65]

A fire in 1958 destroyed all but the facade of Collins' Music Hall; it currently houses a branch of Waterstones.

Rob Fleming runs a neglected record shop just off the Holloway Road in Nick Hornby's tale of 1990s lad inadequacy, *High Fidelity* (1995):

The shop smells of stale smoke, damp, and plastic dustcovers, and it's narrow and dingy and dirty and overcrowded, partly because that's what I wanted – this is what record shops should look like, and only Phil Collins fans bother with those that look as clean and wholesome as a suburban Habitat – and partly because I can't get it together to clean or redecorate it.

There are browser racks on each side, and a couple more in the window, and CDs and cassettes on the walls in glass cases, and that's more or less the size of it; it's just about big enough, provided we don't get any customers, so most days it's just about big enough. The stockroom at the back is bigger than the shop part in the front, but we have no stock, really, just a few piles of second-hand records that nobody can be bothered to price up, so the stockroom is mostly for messing about in. I'm sick of the sight of the place, to be honest.[66]

In Hornby's 2001 *How To Be Good*, David Carr makes a sort-of living with a newspaper column, 'The Angriest Man in Holloway', fulminating on a narrow range of personal grievances: old people, young people, middle-aged people, new things, old things and so on. These are, as his estranged wife sadly notes, 'tiny outlets for his enormous torrent of rage'.[67] She notes that Carr is

> rabidly conservative in everything but politics. There are people like that now, I've noticed, people who seem angry enough to call for the return of the death penalty or the repatriation of Afro-Caribbeans, but who won't, because, like just about everybody else in our particular postal district, they're liberals, so their anger has to come out through different holes. You can read them in the columns and the letters pages of our liberal newspapers every day, being angry about films they don't like or comedians they don't think are funny or women who wear headscarves.[68]

Carr then undergoes a bizarre transformation, becomes, seemingly, a completely different kind of extremist, discovering rabid altruism and setting out on an unbending quest to challenge the too-easy liberal moral imperatives of those 'who live in this income bracket and his postal district'.[69] He becomes savagely, excessively, 'good': giving away family wealth and possessions, including the kids' computers, helping total strangers, and personally housing the homeless in Holloway.

Archway Road, a steep hill at the northern end of the Holloway Road, offers panoramic views over London. Alan Ruthven, the central figure of Charlotte Riddell's 1861 novel *City and Suburb*, has his first, thrilling glimpse of London from here: 'Alan Ruthven passed under Highgate Archway on his way to London . . . behind him – white, straight and dusty, lay the Great North Road he had traversed – before him was the goal he desired to reach'.[70] He stops to take it all in:

> Truly London was stretching out no eager arms to welcome the stranger; wherefore Alan Ruthven sate him down on the turf under the shadow of those trees in which this very spring rooks are building their nests, to gaze at his leisure on the view present to him of the Monarch of Cities.
>
> Churches and houses, lines and lines of streets, a sea of roofs stretching away as far as the eye could reach; Pentonville, and Holloway, and Islington, to the left; Kentish Town, Primrose Hill, the Regent's Park, and the great tract appropriated to

fashion to the right; Tufnell Park, and Camden New Town, and Agar Town straight before, with the city, the heart of the gigantic body he beheld, lying far below. It was enough to stir the calmest spirit, to see that dream-London, of every country imagination, thus unveiled to view.[71]

Archway is also the setting for St George's comprehensive school in Zoë Heller's 2003 psychological thriller *Notes on a Scandal*:

The other thing that became known in those early weeks was that Sheba was experiencing 'class control issues'. This was not entirely unexpected. Because Highgate is part of its catchment area, people often assume that St George's is one of those safe, soft comprehensives, full of posh children toting their cellos to orchestra practice. But posh parents don't surrender their offspring to St George's. The cello-players get sent to St Botolph's Girls or King Henry's Boys, or to private schools in other parts of London. St George's is the holding pen for Archway's pubescent proles – the children of the council estates who must fidget and scrap here for a minimum of five years until they can embrace their fates as plumbers and shop assistants . . . The school represents – how to put it? – a very *volatile* environment.[72]

On 25 March 2005, on a walk right across London, Bill Drummond, formerly of million-quid-burning pop-pranksters The KLF, gets to Archway:

We move on down into Upper Holloway, edge around Tufnell Park, into Holloway proper and past the prison down into Kentish Town. This is all proper urban multicultural stuff, proper London. Graffiti, bendy buses, marauding gangs of school kids, Asian-owned mini-markets with a few hundredweight of fresh fruit and vegetables all polished and stacked up in boxes outside the shopfront, bill-boards for mobile-phone network providers, discarded B&H cartons and empty Sunny Delight bottles roaming free. This is the way inner cities should be.[73]

Crouch End

Just to the east of Holloway Road, Hornsey Lane leads up to Crouch End (its name deriving from *crux*, or cross, referring to the centre of a medieval street pattern). Though seemingly a fairly benign, prosperous, late Victorian middle-class suburb with a thriving high street, Crouch End does have a hint of weirdness.

Crouch End is London's outer limit in George Gissing's novel of hellish, industrial working-class Clerkenwell, *The Nether World* (1889). Here, one character commutes down to Clerkenwell from a small cottage in Crouch End.

> Look at a map of greater London, a map on which the town proper shows as a dark, irregularly rounded patch against the whiteness of suburban districts, and just on the northern limit of the vast network of streets you will distinguish the name of Crouch End. Another decade, and the dark patch will have spread greatly farther; for the present, Crouch End is still able to remind one that it was in the country a very short time ago. The streets have a smell of newness, of dampness; the bricks retain their complexion, the stucco has not rotted more than one expects in a year or two; poverty tries to hide itself with venetian blinds, until the time when an advanced guard of houses shall justify the existence of the slum.
>
> Characteristic of the locality is a certain row of one-storey cottages – villas, the advertiser calls them – built of white brick, each with one bay-window on the ground floor, a window pretentiously fashioned and desiring to be taken for stone, though obviously made of bad plaster. Before each house is a garden, measuring six feet by three, entered by a little iron gate, which grinds as you push it, and at no time would latch. The front door also grinds on the sill; it can only be opened by force, and quivers in a way that shows how unsubstantially it is made. As you set foot in the pinched passage, the sound of your tread proves the whole fabric a thing of lath and sand. The ceilings, the walls, confess themselves neither water-tight nor air-tight. Whatever you touch is at once found to be sham.[74]

Arthur Machen, cult/occult writer and lover of secret worlds, writing in 1920 finds himself on Hornsey Road as part of his attempt to locate the actual site of the mysterious, possibly mythic, 'Tottenham Hale' (see Chapter Ten). He starts out at King's Cross.

Here I took the 'bus for Hornsey Rise, and turned up the Caledonian Road, bordering on the mysterious region of Barnsbury, where you retreat when you wish to look upon the faces of your friends no more. The Caledonian Road amounts to a long hill and I am sure it must pass near Harmony Jail where Wegg read to Mr Boffin. The land has been built over since the day of Boffin, but built in a grey mood in grey bricks. I think I may call the general effect grimy: I am sure it is sad.

But the bright square by the Caledonian Road was but a momentary gleam, and we were passing over the canal – black, sluggish waters with drifts and puffs of steam rising from them, looking much as if they had issued from the infernal lake of the underworld. More grey wall, the crushing gloom of Pentonville prison, and so out into the Holloway Road and Seven Sisters Road into Hornsey Road.

And these are the regions into which you should bring the average man who thinks he knows London . . . take him to Hornsey Road and he will discover that his London is but a tiny Island in the midst of an unknown, unnavigated sea . . .

For it is not only the main ways, the more or less broad thoroughfares, that are beyond his ken; from these to right and left strike off the long roads to worlds undreamed of, perhaps climbing hills crowned with tossing trees, perhaps descending into dark, grey valleys, crawling sluggish through weary plains of houses, still leading beyond and beyond as if this huge London could have no ending. So it is on this Hornsey Road, a monotonous, tired way, with little to mark its weary length, save in one place where what was once a garden has run wild into green leaf and the willows are showing their catkins, and a pear tree displays creamy buds – against a dead factory wall.[75]

Ian Cunningham, in his *Reader's Guide to Writers' London* (2001), notes this area's connection to horror and fantasy writing. Crouch End became 'known as a haunt of horror writers – Clive Barker,

Peter Straub and Kim Newman are all former residents', and then became something of a favoured setting for so-called miserabilists including M. John Harrison, Michael Marshall Smith and Nicholas Royle.[76] Horror writer Stephen King, planning to meet fellow writer Peter Straub, gets lost in Crouch End, and turns this experience into a H. P. Lovecraft-style short story called, of course, 'Crouch End'. Doris Freeman, an American tourist, experiences a weird and horrifying Other Crouch End, seemingly leaking from another dimension altogether: investigating PCs Vetter and Farnham know that many similar unexplained cases exist on file at Crouch End police station:

> 'Highgate's mostly all right, that's what I think – it's just as thick as you'd want between us and the Dimensions in Muswell Hill and Highgate. But now you take Archway and Finsbury Park. *They* border on Crouch End, too. I've got friends in both places, and they know of my interest in certain things that don't seem to be any way rational. Certain crazy stories which have been told, we'll say, by people with nothing to gain by making up crazy stories.'
>
> 'Did it occur to you to wonder, Farnham, why the woman would have told us the things she did if they weren't true?'
>
> 'Well . . .'
>
> Vetter struck a match and looked at Farnham over it. 'Pretty young woman, twenty-six, two kiddies back at her hotel, husband's a young lawyer doing well in Milwaukee or someplace. What's she to gain by coming in and spouting about the sort of things you only used to see in Hammer films?'[77]

The narrator of Will Self's 'The North London Book of the Dead' (1991) spots his mother while walking on Crouch Hill:

> I was walking down Crouch Hill towards Crouch End on a drizzly, bleak, Tuesday afternoon. It was about three o'clock. I'd taken the afternoon off work and decided to go and see a friend. When, coming up the other side of the road I saw Mother. She was wearing a sort of bluish, tweedish long jacket and black slacks and carrying a Barnes & Noble book bag.[78]

This is no ordinary Tuesday-afternoon awkward encounter:

The impression I had of Mother in that very first glance was so sharp and so clear, her presence so tangible, that I did not for a moment doubt the testimony of my senses. I looked at Mother and felt a trinity of emotions: affection and embarrassment mingled with a sort of acute embarrassment. It was this peculiarly familiar wash of feeling that must have altogether swamped the terror and bewilderment that anyone would expect to experience at the sight of their dead mother walking up Crouch Hill.[79]

He digs deeper:

'Mother,' I said, 'what are you doing in Crouch End? You never come to Crouch End except to take the cat to the vet, you don't even like Crouch End.'

'Well, I live here now.' Mother was unperturbed. 'It's OK, it's a drag not being able to get the tube, but the buses are fairly regular. There's quite a few good shops in the parade and someone's just opened up a real deli. Want some halva?' Mother opened her fist under my face. Crushed into it was some sticky halva, half-eaten but still in its gold foil wrapping. She grinned again.

'But Mother, what are you doing in Crouch End? You're dead.'[80]

In Anthony Horowitz's *Killer Camera* (1999), a Crouch End car boot sale is the perfect location for a teenager to pick up a malevolent bargain:

There was a patch of empty land there; not a car park, not a building site, just a square of rubble and dust that nobody seemed to know what to do with. And then one summer the car-boot sales had arrived like flies at a picnic and since then there'd been one every week. Not that there was anything very much to buy. Cracked glasses and hideous plates, mouldy paperback books by writers you'd never heard of, electric kettles and bits of hi-fi that looked forty years out of date . . .

Matthew sighed. There were times when he hated living in London and this was one of them. It was only after his own birthday, his fourteenth, that his parents had finally agreed to

let him go out on his own. And it was only then that he realised he didn't really have anywhere to go. Crummy Crouch End
with its even crummier car-boot sale. Was this any place for a
smart, good-looking teenager on a summer afternoon?[81]

Amnesiac Christine Lucas, in S. J. Watson's 2011 best-seller *Before
I Go to Sleep*, wakes up every day *Groundhog Day*-style, with no
recollection at all of the past 25 years or so, and has to learn it all again:

I follow him down. He shows me a living room – a brown sofa
and matching chairs, a flat screen bolted to the wall which he
tells me is a television . . . None of it is familiar. I feel nothing
at all, not even when I see a framed photograph of the two of
us on a sideboard. 'There's a garden out the back,' he says and
I look through the glass door that leads off to the kitchen. It
is just beginning to get light, the night sky starting to turn an
inky blue, and I can make out the silhouette of a large tree, and
a shed sitting at the far end of the small garden, but little else.
I realize I don't even know what part of the world we are in.
  'Where are we?' I say.
  He stands behind me. I can see us both, reflected in the glass.
Me. My husband. Middle-aged.
  'North London,' he replies. 'Crouch End.'
  I step back. Panic begins to rise. 'Jesus,' I say. 'I don't even
know where I bloody live . . .'[82]

Stoke Newington

Moving southeast across Green Lanes and Harringay, skirting Finsbury
Park, Stoke Newington (meaning 'new town in the wood') first comes
to notice in Saxon times, being built along a key Roman route north
(now the A10). Many handsome Greek Revival villas were built here
in the early nineteenth century, but development was quite sparse for
the rest of the century. In the volume of *The Buildings of England* that
covers the outer areas of London, Nikolaus Pevsner could still argue
in 1953 that 'Stoke Newington is not entirely London yet. There lin-
gers round the timber spire of the old church something of a village
atmosphere.'[83] This is still true, and 'Stokey' manages to maintain, if
you squint, a vaguely bosky, villagey feel.

In the seventeenth century Stoke Newington became attractive to religious Dissenters, who were then not permitted to live in the city proper. The most prominent of these was Daniel Defoe, pamphleteer, journalist, government agent, spy, failed businessman and, later, that new-fangled thing, a novelist. Defoe moved to Stoke Newington in 1709 (also having been to school down the road at the Newington Green Nonconformist Academy), the place seeming a safe bet for someone who had already been jailed at Newgate and placed in the pillory. From 1718 Defoe began writing in Stoke Newington, among other ventures, a series of novels, including *Robinson Crusoe*, *Captain Jack* and *Moll Flanders*, and the quasi-factual 'eyewitness' account *A Journal of the Plague Year*. Between 1724 and 1726 Defoe published descriptions of thirteen tours that he completed around Britain, much of the information gleaned from his spying days. He doesn't, however, say much about where he lives, writing: '*Newington*, *Tottenham*, *Edmonton*, and *Endfield*, stand all in a Line N. from the city. The increase of buildings is so great in them all, that they seem, to a Traveller, to be one continued Street; especially Tottenham and Edmonton, and in them all, the new buildings so far exceed the old, especially in the value of them, and figure of inhabitants, that the fashion of the towns are quite altered.'[84]

A later volume of 1801, with a confusingly similar title, is little more informative, concentrating on Defoe's fellow Dissenter and resident of Stoke Newington, the hymn writer Isaac Watts: 'Stoke Newington, or Canonicorum; the church belonging to the Dean of St Paul's. In the manor-house of this village the pious Dr Watts resided thirty years, under the hospitable roof of Sir Thomas Abney.'[85]

Patrick Keiller's psychogeographic film *London* has a sequence set in Stoke Newington. Keiller's *flâneur* in the film is named after Defoe's best-known fictional character. In the sequence after Ridley Road, Robinson discovers Defoe's house in Stoke Newington, where he wrote *Robinson Crusoe*, and London is revealed to him as a place of 'shipwreck and a vision of Protestant isolation'.[86]

As a boy Edgar Allan Poe was a pupil at Manor House School, Newington Church Street, from 1817 to 1820. The school is evoked (even retaining the headmaster's real name, the Rev. John Bransby) in Poe's unsettling doppelgänger tale 'William Wilson' (1839). Here Wilson recalls his boarding school days in a large, rambling, Elizabethan house, in a misty-looking village of England . . . In truth, it was a dream-like and spirit-soothing place, that venerable old town. At this moment, in fancy, I feel the refreshing chilliness of its deeply-shadowed avenues, inhale the fragrance of its thousand shrubberies, and thrill anew with undefinable delight, at the deep hollow note of the church-bell, breaking, each hour, with sullen and sudden roar, upon the stillness of the dusky atmosphere in which the fretted Gothic steeple lay imbedded and asleep.[87]

Continuing the weird theme, Arthur Machen's short story 'N' (1938) concerns alternate realities existing in Stoke Newington. Here, Arnold hears stories and rumours of an unlikely paradise that exists, somehow, in the 'wild no man's land of the north', up in Stoke Newington. Arnold hears, for instance, of a Reverend Thomas, who had received a strange request from an even stranger parishioner, one Glanville, living in an unprepossessing Stoke Newington semi. 'I want to show you the view', Glanville offers to Thomas. Thomas is doubtful, not expecting much, as 'the streets of our London suburbs do not often offer a spectacle to engage the amateur of landscape and the picturesque', but looks anyway: 'I looked through the window, and saw exactly that which I had expected to see: a row or terrace of neatly designed residences, separated from the highway by a parterre or miniature park, adorned with trees and shrubs.' But then Granville exhorts:

'Look again.'
     I did so. For a moment, my heart stood still, and I gasped for breath. Before me, in place of the familiar structures, there was disclosed a panorama of unearthly, of astounding beauty. In deep dells, bowered by overhanging trees, there bloomed flowers such as only dreams can show; such deep purples that yet seemed to glow like precious stones with a hidden but ever-present radiance, roses whose hues outshone any that are to be seen in our gardens, tall lilies alive with light and blossoms that were as beaten gold . . . I might almost say that my soul was ravished by the spectacle displayed before me. I was possessed by a degree of rapture and delight such as I had never experienced.[88]

Arnold feels he must to go to Stoke Newington and see for himself, and of course is deeply disappointed, merely seeing 'everywhere there were blocks of flats in wicked red brick, as if Mrs Todgers had given Mr Pecksniff her notion of an up-to-date gaol', or as if 'Mr H. G. Wells's bad dreams had come true.'[89] Then Arnold hears a story from some old men in a pub, that the park opposite had once housed a 'lunatic asylum', and that one of the patients there was always babbling about the amazing view from the windows: 'And then, it seems, he began to talk the most outrageous nonsense about golden and silver and purple flowers, and the bubbling well, and the walk that went under the trees right into the wood, and the fairy house on the hill; and I don't know what.'[90]

There is unusual excitement in placid Stoke Newington in William Pett Ridge's suburban comedy *Nine to Six-thirty* (1910), as a distant fire is spotted and restless, trapped Barbara Harrison leaves the house and gleefully rushes off to investigate further:

Five minutes later she was out fully dressed, but plainly dressed, in Medburn Road. A few children to whom news had come tardily were running along, screaming to each other to hurry; she followed them at a good pace, with shoulders slightly bent, towards Church Street, thence into High Street, where folk standing up on tram-cars, information exchanged between conductors, and the general movement of folk to Stoke Newington Road, indicated the direction to be taken; even those in black, whose clear objective was Abney Park Cemetery, wavered and seemed inclined to re-trace steps. Going southward, she had the light in her eyes of one who has escaped from close supervision, something of the backward glance of one who fears pursuit. Everybody was speculating in regard to the exact whereabouts of the fire; fathers wearing silk hats reserved for the day, assured small boys who were making a brave endeavour to keep step that they must be close upon it now; mothers began to declare their inability to go further, saying recklessly, 'Well, it'll have to burn, that's all!' Fast-trotting ponies conveying large publicans and publicans' enormous wives were checked, and drawn to the side of the pavement to allow a scarlet fire engine to race past; the sight of this gave encouragement, and pedestrians took up the chase with new energy. At the Dalston

Lane corner, drivers of omnibuses bearing the word Clapton, but going to London Bridge, shouted cheerily, 'This way to the fi-yer; the fi-yer this way; a penny fare, the fare one penny, any more want to go to blazes?'[91]

The fire turns out to be down towards Bethnal Green Road. But not all is wasted, as Barbara arranges a date with a young man in Clissold Park, or so she thinks:

> Had Clissold Park been mentioned, or was it perhaps Finsbury Park? She was flurried at the time; it seemed possible error instead of truth remained in her memory. If she had only shown less impetuosity in interrupting him and in hastening away, the name could have been repeated and doubt dispelled. Barbara had some idea of leaving at once and hurrying up by a Green Lanes tram-car; reflection told her that Finsbury Park was of even greater extent than Clissold, and to search for him there would be like trying to discover one particular leaf. Perhaps it was better not to make any endeavour. Certainly this course would cancel the great difficulty foreseen all through the week; the moment when gloves were taken off and hands exposed. It was natural men should have a preference for soft white hands, that rested – what was the simile she had come across in a book? – like a snowflake in a firm warm grasp. Barbara walked towards the Church Street entrance, and looked up at the ambitious younger building that pretended to be a cathedral.
> 'Yours late too?' asked a short girl, with corkscrew curls, familiarly . . . 'If mine isn't here in five minutes from now, I shall be off.'[92]

Happy-go-lucky part-time gambler and idler Harry 'Harryboy' Boas, in Alexander Baron's 1963 novel *The Lowlife*, lives in Ingrams Terrace (real-life Foulden Road) just off Stoke Newington High Street. Living in a single room in a shared house, in a 'Victorian-Edwardian suburb swallowed up by London, broad streets, little villas, and big tradesmen's houses', Harryboy spends long days reading serious novels, napping, and, in the evening, losing quite a lot of money at Harringay dog track:

Ingrams Terrace – this is where I roomed – is part of a street that joins Stoke Newington High Street next to Amhurst Road, not far north of Dalston Junction. It was probably named after the Victorian spec builder who ran it up; mostly two-storied houses, with basements, some bigger like old-fashioned vicarages; and at the end houses with passages at the sides from street to back garden. Big rooms, high ceilings with moulding on them; small areas in front that used to have hedges or fancy iron railings but since the war have wooden fences or nothing at all; neglected gardens at the back trampled and heaped with rubbish. When I was a boy, these houses were occupied by superior working class families, who kept them in beautiful condition. Every year, when the fresh gravel and tar was laid on the road (and I can still smell the tar) the houses were bright with fresh paint. Now most of them are tenements.[93]

But this is no perceived deterioration or longing for the good old days:

The street is still clean. All the people are in work. Their cars jam the kerbs on both sides. All is quiet and decent. Negroes have come to live, more every month. And Cypriots. The Negroes are of marvellous respectability. Every Sunday morning they all go to the Baptist Chapel in the High Street. You should see the men, in beautiful pearl grey suits and old fashioned trilbies with curled brims, the big women full of dignity, and the little girls in white muslin and bonnets. It slays me. They are the Victorian residents of this street, come back a century later, with black skins.[94]

The top flat at 359 Amhurst Road, Stoke Newington, turned out to be the hideout of Britain's answer to the Baader-Meinhof terror group: the Angry Brigade. During 1970 and 1971 the 'Angries' had bombed various Tory MPs' homes, government sites, corporate HQS, and once the Biba boutique in Kensington High Street, as explained in their 'Communiqué #8':

All the sales girls in the flash boutiques are made to dress the same and have the same make-up, representing the 1940s. In fashion as in everything else capitalism can only go backwards – they've nowhere to go – they're dead. Life is so boring there is nothing to do except spend all our wages on the latest skirt or shirt.[95]

Ostensibly searching for stolen cheque books, the police raided the flat in August 1971:

> It was just after four o'clock by the time the police officers involved had gathered at Stoke Newington police station to prepare for the raid. Eight of them were to go in, including a woman police officer to deal with Anna Mendelson, and a uniformed dog-handler with an Alsatian. At just on 4:15 Sergeant Gilham led the way through the front door of number 359 and up the narrow stairs to the second floor. Inside John Barker was still asleep. Hilary Creek was in the same room, reading . . .
>
> Sergeant Gilham tapped on the glass pane in the door. Creek and Greenfield both got up and went into the hall to open the door. Greenfield thought it was the children from next door, but as soon as the catch was undone he knew his mistake. Gilham pushed in, waving his warrant . . . 'We're police officers and I have a warrant to search this flat', said Gilham.[96]

The police found ammunition, guns, 33 sticks of gelignite and det-onators, and a small duplicating machine that had been used for the Brigade's arty Situationist-inspired 'Communiqués'. In addition, a child's printing set was found, used to contact the press. The Angries appear in various guises in plays – Howard Brenton's *Magnificence* (1973) and James Graham's *The Angry Brigade* (2014) – and in novels: Doris Lessing's *The Good Terrorist* (1985), Jake Arnott's *Johnny Come Home* (2006) and Hari Kunzru's *My Revolutions* (2007).

This concentration of the occult and the anarchic is catnip for psychogeographers, of course, and Iain Sinclair turns up in Stoke Newington on one of his exhaustive and exhausting tramps in *Lights Out for the Territory* (1999). He is, as ever, on the trail of outsiders, in this case Defoe, Poe, Machen and Alexander Baron:

> Stoke Newington Road stretches onwards like the rubber neck of a chicken. We drift past exotic minimarts, deleted cinemas, tributary nameplates with literary associations. The Hasidic

foothills have always been disputed land: Jews escaping from
Whitechapel sweatshops, early West Indian immigrants (as
depicted in Alexander Baron's novel, *The Lowlife*). Baron,
troubled after the war, wandered the borough like a fetch:
watching, listening, hungry for the clues that would allow
him to reorientate himself . . . Stoke Newington is the perfect
location in which to stay lost: limboland, London's Interzone.
Large shabby properties that ask no questions. Internal exile
with a phoney rent-book. Stoke Newington is the place where
terrorists behave like unpublished poets, and poets cultivate
a justified paranoia. Drinking clubs, spielers, anarchist pubs:
they cluster around the nick with the worst reputation in
north London. A permanent, on-going, death in custody
protest.[97]

In Stoke Newington's Abney Park Cemetery, Sinclair notes an occult
symbol in the chapel at its centre, 'in blue paint: the eye within the
triangle' and the word 'DOG', some 'Special Brew occultism'. Maybe
this is the centre, the key to his entire series of walks:

We had brought ourselves to the heart of it, the vandalised
chapel in the woods, and we were confronted by just the
reversal we deserved. DOG. The word twisted our expedition
back to its source. It established this site as the x, the given, the
point from which the true walk would begin . . . The triangle of
concentration. A sense of this and of all the other triangulations
of the city: Blake, Bunyan, Defoe, the dissenting monuments in
Bunhill Fields. Everything I believe in, everything London can
do to you, starts there. The theatre of obelisks and pyramids,
signs, symbols, prompts, whispers. The lovely lies that take you
out into the light.[98]

Barrington Jedidiah Walker, the Jamaican immigrant in
Bernardine Evaristo's *Mr Loverman* (2013), claims to have foreseen
Stoke Newington's future while hanging out in Clissold Park way
back in the 1960s:

I remember the exact moment when the Kingdom of
Barrington was conceived.

A summer evening after work, and me and Morris was breezing off having a lager and a smoke in Clissold Park, delaying the return to our respective farmhouses until the squealing sucklings had been put to bed . . .

At some point I found myself paying proper attention for the first time to the three slummified Victorian houses on the walk opposite our spot. Vandalized windows, wrecked roofs, gardens being reclaimed by the forests of Ye Olde England. I said to Morris, 'Look how huge they is, spar. Once upon a time they must-a been built for the rich, and, you mark my words, one day the rich shall recolonize them. I, Barrington Jedidiah Walker, hereby predict the gentrification of Stoke Newington.'

Or something like that. Even if I didn't speak those words out loud to Morris *exactly*, it was on my mind.[99]

Islington

Islington was an eleventh-century Anglo-Saxon Settlement called Giseldone, meaning 'Gisla's Hill'. By the seventeenth century the village, growing along the original High Street and around the New Road (now Pentonville Road) at the Angel, had become known, on account of its spas, gardens, dairy pasture, pubs, tea-gardens and fairs, as 'merry Islington'. After growing rapidly into the nineteenth century, with the Regent's Canal, railways, a huge boost in population and new entertainment centres (music halls, theatres, department stores), Islington faced serious decline in the twentieth century. War-damaged housing stock was replaced by new large estates, but then, starting in the late 1950s, Islington also pioneered a new form of urban development: gentrification. Georgian and early Victorian terraces came back into fashion.

Ned Ward, satirist, irascible pub landlord, keen urban explorer and acute watcher of all aspects of London life at the turn of the eighteenth century, describes, in his *A Walk to Islington*, a trip to one of the numerous spas in this 'New Tunbridge Wells'. Rather than health and tranquillity, Ward describes, in lascivious detail, bizarre extremes of drunkenness and debauchery. 'In holiday time', our narrator states, 'When Whores have a more than an ord'nary Itching / To visit the Fields, and so Ramble a Bitching', the narrator goes to the 'New-River-Head' at Sadler's Wells:

Then I, like my Neighbours, to sweeten my Life,
Took a walk in the Fields; but for want of a Wife,
Was forc'd to take up with a Lady of Pleasure,
Who I turn'd off at Will, and enjoy'd at my Leisure:
We saunter'd about near the *New-River-Head*,
Where we pratled and tatled, tho' what 'twas we said,
If you'd have me Discover, indeed I must fail-you,
Because 'twas on Business improper to tell-you.
I found be her Words I her heart could Command,
So quickly we setled the matter in hand.
We rambled about 'till we came to a Gate,
Where abundance of Rabble peep'd in at a Grate,
To gaze at the Ladies amid'st of their Revels,
As fine all as *Angels*, but wicked as *Devils*.[100]

Roy Porter, in *London: A Social History*, suggests that Islington was one of the first suburban villages to become urbanized:

The first City suburb to be truly built-up. On high ground commanding a 'magnificent panorama' over London, Islington had a well which was credited with health-giving properties . . . It was a 'pretty neat town, mostly built of brick, with a church and bells; it has a small lake, or rather pond in the midst, though at present much neglected', thought Goldsmith. But Islington became the butt of satire rather like Neasden today. George Colman mocked its citizens in *The Spleen; or, Islington Spa*, the tale of a tailor who retired to the 'country' and found it deadly dull:
Would not he Islington's fine air forego
Could he again be choak'd in Butcher-Row.[101]

In his *A Tour through the Whole Island of Great Britain*, in the early 1720s, Daniel Defoe is already impressed by Islington's extent:

Islington is a large and populous village, and from the great increase of buildings nearly joining to the metropolis. It is said to have been built by the Saxons and in the reign of William the Conqueror to have been called *Isendon* or *Isledon*. The parish is extensive, and includes in it, Upper and Lower Holloway,

three sides of Newington-green, and part of Kingsland. At the
end of the village is a medicinal spring, called the Spa, and near
it, a celebrated and well-known place of amusement, called
Sadler's Wells.[102]

Charles Lamb lived in Colebrook Cottage, on Duncan Terrace
near Islington Green, from 1823 to 1827. The editor of his letters,
Thomas Noon Talfourd, explains how Lamb spent his time there: 'His
mornings were chiefly occupied in long walks, sometimes extending
to ten or twelve miles, in which at this time he was accompanied by
a noble dog, the property of Mr Hood, to whose humours Lamb
became almost a slave.'[103]

Hood's dog, Dash, seemed a bit of a handful, as Peter Patmore
(father of poet Coventry) explained in a footnote:

> Lamb made himself a perfect slave to the dog, whose habits were
> of the most extravagantly errant nature; for, generally speaking,
> the creature was half a mile off from his companion either
> before or behind, scouring the fields and roads in all directions,
> scampering up or down 'all manner of streets' and leaving Lamb
> in a perfect fever of irritation and annoyance; for he was afraid
> of losing the dog when it was out of sight, and yet could not
> persuade himself to keep it *in* sight for a moment by curbing its
> roving spirit. Dash knew Lamb's weakness in these particulars as
> well as he did himself, and took a due dog-like advantage of it.[104]

Sadly, the dog had to go. Yet it all turned out well: 'under his second
master we learn from the same source [Patmore] that Dash "subsided
into the best bred and best behaved of his species".'[105]

In his series of reports, stories and vignettes *Sketches by Boz* (1836),
Dickens finds Islington to be the natural abode of that unremarkable,
habituated, near-invisible archetype, the lower-middle-class clerk. In
'The Streets – Morning', Dickens notes the early morning commuters
from 'Somers and Camden towns, Islington, and Pentonville' who are
'fast pouring into the city': these 'middle-aged men . . . plod steadily
along, apparently with no object in view but the counting-house'.[106]
In 'Thoughts about People' we note one who 'would walk to the office
every morning from the back settlements of Islington'. When his work
for the day is over he

retires to his usual dining-place . . . [and] orders a small plate of roast beef, with greens, and half-a-pint of porter . . . Exactly at five minutes before the hour is up, he produces a shilling, pays the reckoning, carefully deposits the change in his waistcoat-pocket (first deducting a penny for the waiter) and returns to the office, from which, if it is not a foreign post night, he again sallies forth, in about half an hour. He then walks home, at his usual pace, to his little back room at Islington, where he has his tea; perhaps solacing himself during the meal with the conversation of his landlady's little boy, whom he occasionally rewards with a penny, for solving problems in simple addition.[107]

Dickens also set his early, outlandish 'The Lamplighter's Story' (1841) in Canonbury Square, at the north end of Upper Street. Tom Grig, a street lamplighter, is having a tough time in his chosen profession, threatened, as all his fellows were, by the arrival of more efficient gas (rather than oil). The story features a mad scientist figure, hard at work in a local landmark, the seventeenth-century Canonbury Tower:

Tom's new beat, gentlemen, was – I can't exactly say where, for that he'd never tell; but I know it was in a quiet part of town, where there were some queer old houses. I have always had it in my head that it must have been somewhere near Canonbury Tower in Islington, but that's a matter of opinion. Wherever it was, he went upon it, with a bran-new ladder, a white hat, a brown holland jacket and trousers, a blue neck-kerchief, and a sprig of full-blown double wall-flower in his button-hole. Tom was always genteel in his appearance, and I have heard from the best judges, that if he had left his ladder at home that afternoon, you might have took him for a lord.

He was always merry, was Tom, and such a singer, that if there was any encouragement for native talent, he'd have been at the opera. He was on his ladder, lighting his first lamp, and singing to himself in a manner more easily to be conceived than described, when he hears the clock strike five, and suddenly sees an old gentleman with a telescope in his hand, throw up a window and look at him very hard . . .

Gentlemen, he was one of the strangest and most
mysterious-looking files that ever Tom clapped his eyes on. He
was dressed all slovenly and untidy, in a great gown of a kind
of bed-furniture pattern, with a cap of the same on his head;
and a long old flapped waistcoat; with no braces, no strings,
very few buttons – in short, with hardly any of those artificial
contrivances that hold society together. Tom knew by these
signs, and by his not being shaved, and by his not being over-
clean, and by a sort of wisdom not quite awake, in his face, that
he was a scientific old gentleman. He often told me that if he
could have conceived the possibility of the whole Royal Society
being boiled down into one man, he should have said the old
gentleman's body was that Body.

The old gentleman claps the telescope to his eye, looks all
round, sees nobody else in sight, stares at Tom again, and cries
out very loud:

'Hal-loa!'

'Halloa, Sir,' says Tom from the ladder; 'and halloa again, if
you come to that.'

'Here's an extraordinary fulfilment,' says the old gentleman,
'of a prediction of the planets.'

'Is there?' says Tom. 'I'm very glad to hear it.'

'Young man,' says the old gentleman, 'you don't know me.'

'Sir,' says Tom, 'I have not that honour; but I shall be happy
to drink your health, notwithstanding.'

'I read,' cries the old gentleman, without taking any notice of
this politeness on Tom's part – 'I read what's going to happen,
in the stars.'[108]

Canonbury Park is the location of the family home in Mary
Vivian (Molly) Hughes's affectionate memoir of middle-class childhood, *A London Child of the 1870s* (1934). Hughes sets out to describe
her early life as a girl with four older brothers and 'an ordinary, suburban, Victorian family, undistinguished ourselves and unacquainted
with distinguished people . . . My early memories run from 1870,
when we moved into a big house in Canonbury, until 1879, when my
happy childhood was abruptly ended. I hope to show that Victorian
children did not have such a dull time as is usually supposed.'[109] This
she achieves, as the memoir recounts, with the security of a large

middle-class home, stories of adventure and tremendous freedom, street games and pastimes, passion and interests, trips and excursions, and an extremely vivid street life:

> The main attraction for all of us was the window. Our house stood at the corner of two roads, and our window had a good view down most of the length of one of them – Grange Road, affording us plenty of information of the doings of our neighbours and any passers-by. Up and down there went, much oftener than to-day, the hawkers of various goods, each with an appropriate cry: 'Flowers all a-blowing and a-growing', 'Ornaments for your fire stove' (unbelievably hideous streamers of coloured paper), 'A pair of fine soles', bird-cages, iron-holders, brooms, brushes, and baskets. The long, wailing cry was a signal for us to crowd on to the ottoman, to watch. Seeing our faces, the hawker would stop, look up eagerly and hold up his goods. Several times we sent one round to the back-door with the encouraging words 'Mamma would like some.' Then we went to the top of the stairs to listen to the drama below.[110]

Among other adventures is a family holiday to Cornwall:

> The next crisis was the fetching of the cab. At 7 o'clock in the morning there was no certainty of getting one quickly, and we kept rushing to the window until some one shouted, 'Here it comes'. If you saw that cab to-day your anxiety would be as to whether it could possibly stay the course to Paddington. The few 'growlers' still to be seen in the London streets are royal coaches compared with those of the 'seventies. They were like omnibuses, with the same dingy blue velvet, only much dirtier, and, as they were used for taking people to hospitals, my father used to call them 'damned fever-boxes' . . . Luggage was piled on the top, and we were packed in among rugs, umbrellas and hand-bags. At last the cabby climbed up to his seat and whipped up the horse. It took an hour or more to jog along from Canonbury to Paddington, but we did reach the enchanted spot at last.[111]

Arthur Machen sets a nasty murder story, 'The Islington Mystery' (1927), in the area. The story is a sort of rewrite of the notorious 1912 Dr Crippen case, where the doctor, having murdered his wife and buried her in the cellar at their house in Tufnell Park, was then arrested on a transatlantic liner, having gone on the run with his mistress, who was, quite ineptly, disguised as a boy. Only, this time, as the narrator advises us, the decidedly mediocre and unjustifiably famous Crippen – a 'foolish little man',[112] is replaced by the resourceful and tormented Mr Boale, who we are told in fact 'justifiably' murders his wife, 'a tartar and a scold'[113] who is 'full of energy and the pest of the neighbourhood, and more than a pest to her husband'.[114]

> But as to the Islington Mystery – this is how it fell out. There
> is an odd street, not far from the region which was once called
> Spa Fields, not far from the Pentonville or Islington Fields,
> where Grimaldi the clown was once accused of inciting the
> mob to chase an overdriven ox. It goes up a steep hill, and the
> rare adventurer who pierces now and then into this unknown
> quarter of London is amazed and bewildered at the very outset,
> since there are no steep hills in the London of his knowledge,
> and the contours of the scene remind him of the cheap lodging-
> house area at the back of hilly seaside resorts. But if the site is
> strange, the buildings on it are far stranger. They were no doubt
> set up at the high tide of Sir Walter Scott Gothic, which has
> left such queer memorials behind it. The houses of Lloyd Street
> are in couples, and the architect, combining the two into one
> design, desired to create an illusion of a succession of churches,
> in the Perpendicular or Third Pointed manner, climbing up the
> hill. The detail is rich, there are finials to rejoice the heart, and
> gargoyles of fine fantasy, all carried out in the purest stucco.
> At the lowest house on the right-hand side lived Mr Harold
> Boale and his wife, and a brass plate on the Gothic door said,
> 'Taxidermist: Skeletons Articulated'.[115]

Newly married Evelyn Waugh moved into 17a Canonbury Square in 1928. The square, by then neglected and shabby, was also somewhat remote from Waugh's desired West End haunts and he is forced to provide detailed directions to any visitors willing to travel. He informs aesthete and writer Harold Acton how best to get to this 'cheap district':

> Do please come & see us as soon as ever you can. A 19 bus from the corner of Theobalds Road, opposite the L.C.C. school where I learned carpentry, will take you to us in about ten minutes. If you ask the conductor to tell you when you reach Compton Terrace, & then walk up Canonbury Lane you will find our dilapidated Regency Square . . . We have very little furniture at present but I am anxious to show you what we have & to have your advice about decorations.[116]

George Orwell moved into flat 27b in the same square in 1944. Canonbury's springtime resurgence, especially since the entire area, like London in general, was still shabby, pock-marked and in a bad state of repair from war damage, provides the background for the 1946 essay on the insuppressible wonders of spring, 'Thoughts on a Common Toad':

> At any rate, spring is here, even in London N1, and they can't stop you enjoying it. This is a satisfying reflection. How many a time have I stood watching the toads mating, or a pair of hares having a boxing match in the young corn, and thought of all the important persons who would stop me enjoying this if they could. But luckily they can't. So long as you are not actually ill, hungry, frightened or immured in a prison or a holiday camp, spring is still spring. The atom bombs are piling up in the factories, the police are prowling through the cities, the lies are streaming from the loudspeakers, but the earth is still going round the sun, and neither the dictators nor the bureaucrats, deeply as they disapprove of the process, are able to prevent it.[117]

Canonbury Square, bomb-damaged and decayed, is also the setting for Winston Smith's shabby flat, at 'Victory Mansions', in Orwell's *Nineteen Eighty-four* (1949):

> It was a bright cold day in April, and the clocks were striking thirteen. Winston Smith, his chin nuzzled into his breast in

an effort to escape the vile wind, slipped quickly through the glass doors of Victory Mansions, though not quickly enough to prevent a swirl of gritty dust from entering along with him.

The hallway smelt of boiled cabbage and old rag mats. At one end of it a coloured poster, too large for indoor display, had been tacked to the wall. It depicted simply an enormous face, more than a metre wide: the face of a man of about fortyfive, with a heavy black moustache and ruggedly handsome features.[118]

The wartime Canonbury streets provide a suitably bleak view:

Outside, even through the shut window-pane, the world looked cold. Down in the street little eddies of wind were whirling dust and torn paper into spirals, and though the sun was shining and the sky a harsh blue, there seemed to be no colour in anything, except the posters that were plastered everywhere. The black moustachio'd face gazed down from every commanding corner. There was one on the house-front immediately opposite. BIG BROTHER IS WATCHING YOU, the caption said, while the dark eyes looked deep into Winston's own. Down at street level another poster, torn at one corner, flapped fitfully in the wind, alternately covering and uncovering the single word INGSOC. In the far distance a helicopter skimmed down between the roofs, hovered for an instant like a bluebottle, and darted away again with a curving flight. It was the police patrol, snooping into people's windows. The patrols did not matter, however. Only the Thought Police mattered.[119]

In Margaret Drabble's *The Garrick Year* (1964), Emma is looking for a house:

When David and I got so aimlessly married, we had to find somewhere to live; we wanted to buy a house, to affirm, I suppose, in solid bricks and mortar the absurd nature of what we had done . . . So I trudged all over London, and I enjoyed it.[120]

These are the early stages in Islington's famed pioneering gentrification, as all things Georgian are fashionable again:

The house that I found was the right thing. As soon as I saw it, it fitted neatly into some ready-made notch: it was an ordinary nineteenth-century terrace house in Islington, and on either side of the front door stood a small stone lion. Inside it had been modernized by a young couple who had since made a lot of money and moved off into a more fashionable area. It was all right: nothing remarkable, except for the plaster ceilings and one good ornate fireplace. But the back garden was up to the standard of the lions. It was surrounded by a high brick wall, but from the upstairs rooms one could see it and all the gardens in the row, and the impression was of old brick and shoots of greenery and grass and daffodils. Our garden was all weeds, but the one next door on the right had been looked after to perfection by an old man who had lived in the house through all the permutations of the area, from its days of respectable solidarity, the days in which Dickens refers to 'shady Pentonville', through the shabby slip into dusty urban poverty and back once more into the classless rise of chi-chi that David and myself quite adequately represented. His garden was a perpetual delight: the grass was mown and even, flowers grew at every season in every corner and the walls were covered with every variety of climbing, blossoming plant.[121]

Jonathan Raban was a keen observer of gentrification's expanding frontier in the 1960s, as it 'went steadily eastwards: across Camden . . . into Islington, Lower Holloway and Barnsbury':[122]

Perhaps Orwell himself was the first of these people, when he moved to Islington in the 1940s (though Canonbury Square, where he took a house, has always remained expensively sedate and leafy despite the fluctuations of the neighbourhood around it) . . .

This burrowing out of new postal districts inside the city is like a dive into a new frontier. Like a frontier, it produces edgy and painful encounters with the indigenous population (the sitting tenants, some of whom are immigrants, some Cockneys), who are alternately harassed with eviction notices and raised rents, and romanticised, like Fenimore Cooper Indians, as 'real'

people. Like a frontier, it offers ennobling privations: few restaurants, poor recreation areas, no delicatessens or antiques
shops . . . Enervated Georgian architecture suddenly becomes
beautiful, after every architectural writer since their erection
has glossed over them with a yawn. (Pevsner, writing about
Islington in the *London* volume of the Penguin *Buildings of
England*, sounds antediluvian today; he is *bored* by the most
lovely and desirable squares in the whole city . . .).[123]

Irma Kurtz's essay 'Islington' (1997) also recalls the gentrification
emerging during this period:

> Islington was a north London slum in the early stages of
> gentrification in the 1960s, and my new boss, Robert Carrier,
> the celebrated gourmet and cook, owned a big house in one
> of its prettiest squares: Gibson Square – 'the Gibson girls',
> Don-Don used to call Bob's ménage. His own basement flat
> in Bob's house was bright and airy and not at all what the
> word 'basement' brings to mind . . . I remember the small
> office we shared, jerry-built shelves running the length of it,
> I think it was near the top of the house; I'm sure it faced the
> garden. Details of this period are hazy not because of drink or
> drugs; luxury is an opiate too, and five-star memories have the
> sameness of blood heat.[124]

Put-upon office drudge Malry, in B. S. Johnson's novel *Christie
Malry's Own Double-entry* (1973), lives in Hammersmith and has a
girlfriend (the 'Shrike') with Islington connections, which Johnson
tries to explain, sort of:

> The Shrike's Old Mum lived, as you already know, up in
> Islington. Islington is certainly up from Hammersmith, which
> is only some sixteen feet above sea level, whereas old Islington
> lies mainly on a ridge whose southernmost point is Claremont
> Square in Finsbury. The exact height of Claremont Square
> escapes me for a moment, though I could look it up. Yes, I will.
> [Deliberate space] It is just above the hundred foot contour
> line, say fifteen feet, making a height of a hundred and fifteen
> feet in all. Claremont Square must have been a fine point to

view the city and the river at one time, before it was built on. But of course, that is not relevant for our purposes, since the Shrike's Old Mum lived just on the eastern side of the ridge, down off Essex Road, at the flats in Britannia Row. And I am not going out with theodolite and mate to determine just where she lived in relation to the hundred foot contour line, or to work out how high her flat took her above it in relation to ground level; no, not for you: nor anyone.[125]

John Berger's story 'Islington', from *Here Is Where We Meet* (2005), also focuses on the area's early gentrification: 'The borough of Islington has, during the last twenty-five years, become fashionable. In the 1950s and 1960s, the name Islington, when pronounced in central London or in the northwestern suburbs, conjured up a remote and faintly suspect district.'[126] The narrator's college friend Hubert bought a house in the area forty years earlier: '"They've moved to Islington!" a friend told me at the time. And this news was like a late autumn afternoon when the daylight hours are becoming noticeably shorter. There was something of a foreclosure about it.'[127] Hubert shows him around the house in the present:

> We took the stairs slowly. He held himself very upright. On the first landing he stopped and said: 'This terrace was built in the 1840s and the houses were destined for clerks who worked in the City. Poor man's Georgian, as you can see. And it didn't work out. Within a generation they had all been turned into lodging houses, with one or a couple of tenants living on each floor. And so it remained for a hundred years. When we arrived, forty years ago, the houses on the other side of the street didn't even have electricity. Only gas and paraffin lamps . . . Before we bought this house it was a brothel, serving the lorry drivers who delivered goods to London from the north.'[128]

In Linda Grant's 2011 baby boomer saga *We Had It So Good*, Stephen and Andrea, without really trying or wanting to, somehow manage to acquire a nice flat in Canonbury in the early 1970s, and eventually end up owning the entire house. This was a casual decision: '"We *should* buy it," Andrea said. "Why?" "It's a good house. The area is coming up – it will be harder to buy it if we wait."'[129]

After the squat, commune, whatever you want to call it, we
found a bedsit a couple of blocks away from where we are
now, and then a few months later we got the flat in this house.
We moved to Islington in 1972, when it was a run-down,
working-class section, and we've been here ever since, with
everything coming up around us, and now you have to be as
rich as Croesus to buy here because it's an easy commute to
the City. We're probably the poorest middle-class people in the
neighbourhood and we can only afford it because we started
so long ago. Everyone else is in hedge funds or worked for
Lehman's and Goldman Sachs. People we thought were the
devil when we were their age.[130]

In the novel we see the area's slow gentrification over the years, until,
eventually, it becomes a middle-class utopia:

Christmas in Islington. Andrea lit candles and put them in the
windows, she decorated a tree with lights and baubles, they
ate food she would not have allowed into the house at other
times of the year and the children walked past the churches and
wondered what people were *doing* going in there . . .

On New Year's Eve there were parties all along the street,
you ran from one to another. When they first began, the young
adults came bringing their babies, then their children . . .

You dressed up, you drank champagne, some of the hosts
hired young people dressed in black to open the door and take
the coats and serve the wine and canapés. At the far end of
the garden a few of the men, and women shivering in evening
gowns, ventured down to the fish pond to smoke a joint. Fairy
lights hung from the black trees. A line of frost along the fence,
and their feet sliding on the wet grass around the pond with its
old carp.[131]

Highbury

To the east of the Holloway Road, running from Highbury Corner
up to scruffy Finsbury Park, Highbury has maintained, in parts, a
certain Georgian and mid-Victorian grandeur, with leafy avenues

and crescents, huge stucco villas and terraces and pretty parks. Its greatest claim to fame in the nineteenth century was Highbury Barn, a grand restaurant later equipped with a huge outdoor concert and dancing area, the Leviathan Platform. The original dining attraction is mentioned in Thackeray's *Vanity Fair* (1848):

> And as if all things conspired in favour of the gentle Rebecca, the very elements (although she was not inclined at first to acknowledge their action in her behalf) interposed to aid her. For on the evening appointed for the Vauxhall party, George Osborne having come to dinner, and the elders of the house having departed, according to invitation, to dine with Alderman Balls, at Highbury Barn, there came on such a thunder-storm as only happens on Vauxhall nights, and as obliged the young people, perforce, to remain at home. Mr Osborne did not seem in the least disappointed at this occurrence.[132]

In T. S. Eliot's *The Waste Land* (1922), Highbury is just the perfect place to provide a frisson of the bathetic suburban tawdry. In the third section, 'The Fire Sermon', one of the poem's mythical 'Thames Daughters' speaks. She is echoing the murder of Pia in Dante's *Purgatorio*: 'remember me, who am La Pia. / Siena bore me; the Maremma undid me'.[133] Only, this now being the modern Waste Land, Dante's tragic story is given a tawdry contemporary twist involving a girl's sexual experiences in the *suburbs*.

> Trams and dusty trees.
> Highbury bore me. Richmond and Kew
> Undid me. By Richmond I raised my knees
> Supine on the floor of a narrow canoe.[134]

John Betjeman's 1932 poem 'The Sandemanian Meeting-house in Highbury Quadrant' describes the various journeys taken to get to Highbury. (The Sandemanians were an obscure Protestant sect, with Michael Faraday their best-known adherent.) Dramatically, we see and hear the travelling faithful, in 'red trams and the brown', rattling down along the iron rails of Holloway Road, and in trains from 'From Canonbury, Dalston and Mildmay Park' heading for the 'black platform, gaslit and dark' of Highbury Station.[135]

In Stella Gibbons's 1939 novel *My American* we see future writer Amy Lee living precariously in a very detailed presentation of then-working-class Highbury:

> She got off the tram at the Holloway Arcade and set out on the walk along Holloway Road to Highbury Fields, where she lived. It was not far, and she walked along so quickly and lightly that she almost ran, the cold rain beating in her face. No one bumped into her – she saw to that – but it was tiring dodging people, and once a car nearly ran her down as she crossed a road. Everyone shouted at her, looking frightened and furious. Her head felt queerer and queerer, but she took no notice of that, and as usual, enjoyed the walk. She took in the golden windows of the shops, the cold winter smell of the celery piled outside a greengrocer's, the lovely face of Dolores Castello gazing out dreamily from a cinema hoarding. Amy loved walking in London . . .
>
> At the pub called The Hen and Chickens she crossed over, turned down Corsica Street and left the trams and buses and bright shops behind, went along Calabria Road, then through Baalbec Road into Highbury Place. Here the Fields faced her, their tall trees behind a railing shining silver with the wet.
>
> The Fields are an open space like a half-heart, and sur-rounded by Highbury Crescent and Highbury Place, two rows of tall, early nineteenth century houses of dark brown brick with elegant details in their fanlights, railings and balconies. There is plenty of life in the fields, for the National School boys play football there and babies are brought from the poorer streets to sun-bathe and enjoy the bit of green, but the houses have the spell of the past on them.
>
> Amy went down Highbury Walk, where there are two or three quiet little shops, and stopped at one with 'D. Beeding, Baker and Confectioner' over it. This was where she lived.[136]

For supply teacher and aspiring architect Albert Angelo, in B. S. Johnson's 1964 novel of that name, Highbury is not promising territory:

They send you the next day, on the Friday, the last day of
the first week, to Crane Grove Secondary, up past Highbury
Corner, off the Holloway Road. The five- and six-storey
schools in this part stand above the three-storey streets like
chaotic constellations. Dead cinemas and a musichall sadden
corners, abandoned. Only Arsenal Stadium, older-looking in
its outdated modernity than last century's houses, competes
in height with the dark red brick, stonedressed schools. Swart
sleek diesels shaped as functionally as otters pass and re-pass
solemnly between strips of houses at eaves-level pulling trains
of rust-stained wagons.

You spend all day teaching simple English to the third-year
classes, fourteen-year-olds who have very little interest in learning: they are waiting only to leave school. You try to arouse
their interest by pointing out how basic a knowledge of at least
English must be. One boy says he can read the racing and that
that's enough for him . . .

Even the lavatory-gothic of the Union Chapel in Compton
Terrace cannot make you smile on your way back home, nor
the glimpse of Barry's Holy Trinity in Cloudesley Square
encourage you by a reminder that a good architect's early
work may be poor.[137]

In his football memoir *Fever Pitch* (1992) we see young Nick
Hornby coming up to London from a 'small, detached house in the
Home Counties' to see Arsenal play at the Highbury ground, the place
forming a surrogate home for estranged father and son:

Saturday afternoons in north London gave us a context in
which we could be together. We could talk when we wanted,
the football gave us something to talk about (and anyway the
silences weren't oppressive), and the days had a structure, a
routine. The Arsenal pitch was to be our lawn (and, being an
English lawn, we would usually peer at it mournfully through
driving rain); the Gunners' Fish Bar on Blackstock Road our
kitchen; and the West Stand our home. It was a wonderful
set-up, and changed our lives just when they needed changing
most, but it was also exclusive: Dad and my sister never really
found anywhere to live at all.[138]

Oddly enough, as the original stadium has since been demolished, parts of the ground and pitch are, quite literally, now homes and gardens.

Neil Gaiman's *Neverwhere* (1996) describes 'London Below', a place that exists, largely unseen, beneath or alongside visible London, or 'London Above'. The worlds connect in tunnels, doors and Tube stations, especially abandoned ones:

> 'Who are we looking for again, then?' he asked, more-or-less innocently. 'The Angel Gabriel? Raphael? Michael?'
>
> They were passing a Tube map. The Marquis tapped Angel station with one long dark finger: Islington.
>
> Richard had passed through Angel station hundreds of times. It was in trendy Islington, a district filled with antique shops and places to eat. He knew very little about angels, but he was almost certain that Islington's Tube stop was named after a pub, or a landmark. He changed the subject. 'You know, when I tried to get on a tube train a couple of days ago, it wouldn't let me.'
>
> 'You just have to let them know who's boss, that's all,' said Hunter, softly, from behind him.
>
> Door chewed her lower lip. 'This train we're looking for will let us on,' she said. 'If we can find it.'[139]

The comics writer Alan Moore (probably best known for *From Hell* and *V for Vendetta*) produced a CD of eight spoken-word monologues, *The Highbury Working: A Beat Séance* (2000), with experimental music backing by Tim Perkins, based on a live performance at The Garage, Highbury, in November 1997, which aimed to conjure the deep psychogeographic spirit of Highbury and capture the essence of the place. Moore discusses local cultural landmarks and figures: the area's Roman origins, Arsenal FC, occultist Aleister Crowley, record producer Joe Meek (with a DIY recording studio in his Holloway Road flat), the coming of the Tube. Highbury eventually transforms into the Angel Highbury:

> And up above them all the Angel Highbury stands a thousand feet tall, with her pinions fanned from Hampstead to Stoke Newington. Her robe is stitched together from the tattered cover fronts of pulp science fiction magazines, erupting from

the Fantasy Book Centre in Holloway Road. Her hair is woven from the blazing priory, long curls of flame caught in the wind that writhes about her face, a beacon fire against the sharp November dark.[140]

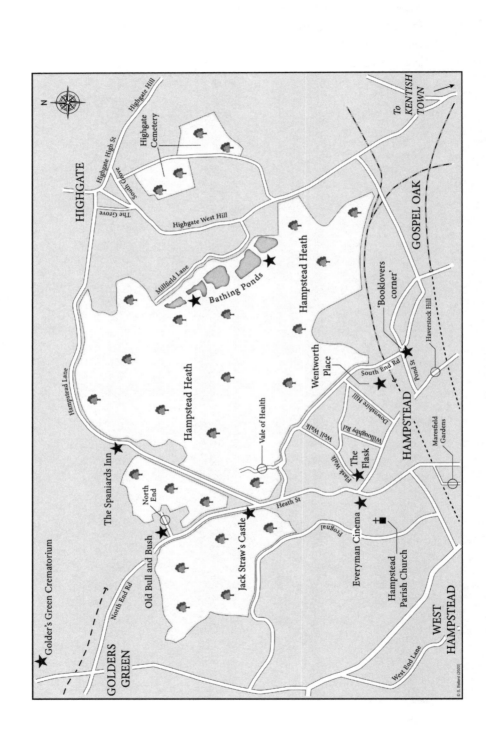

9 'SO NEAR HEAVEN'
Hampstead and Highgate

'What is Hampstead?'
'An artistic and thoughtful little suburb of London'[1]

'Hampstead is a bit of a joke, though many of its inhabitants are deadly serious about it,' reckons Ian Nairn.[2] Picturesque, cutesy, high up and hilly, packed with narrow winding streets and odd corners, well-preserved Georgian villas and a sprinkling of celebrities, with the vast spread of the Heath and Ponds and spectacular views over London, Hampstead is a special case. It seems to have become a self-consciously leafy, charming village already by the eighteenth century – and more or less stayed that way. Like Dulwich Village in the south, or bits of Kew, Richmond and Twickenham in the south-west, Hampstead seems to have evaded modernity, with industry, mass or public housing, redevelopment and infill, canals, roads and rail, and the building over of commons all successfully kept at bay by Hampstead's powerful, wealthy and active urban-village set.

Already in the 1860s William Howitt points out the area's unique status:

> The outskirts of London, in almost all directions, are rich
> in historical and biographical reminiscences. The Northern
> suburbs are amongst the most affluent in this respect. Before
> the aristocratic class acquired the tendency to spread itself over
> the flats of the West, the City itself and the hills which arose
> on its northern confines were the chosen abodes of its nobles

and wealthy merchants. Hampstead and Highgate bear even
to-day, amid all the changes of the last two centuries, the traces
of this former predilection of the affluent dwellers in and the
frequenters of the metropolis.[3]

The place, of course, has an impressive roster of literary and
literary-minded residents: various Romantic poets, Lord Alfred
Douglas, Robert Louis Stevenson, Edward Elgar, John Galsworthy,
Walter Besant, Charles de Gaulle, Enid Blyton, William Empson,
Gracie Fields, Harold Pinter, Marianne Faithfull and Judi Dench,
not forgetting Kate Moss, Boy George and Slash. Yet the 'Hampstead
novel' itself – those tales awash with upper-middle-class, over-educated
people suffering liberal anguish and committing adultery, supposedly
written by the likes of Margaret Drabble, Penelope Lively and Fay
Weldon – is, in fact, rather elusive. 'Hampstead novels' share a generic
tone and subject-matter rather than a specific setting.

Hampstead

Hampstead had already long been popular for its elevation, quiet
and clear air, and convenient distance from plagued London when,
around 1700, iron-rich mineral waters were discovered and the first
pump rooms built, in Well Walk. Fashionable London soon came up
the hill and tea-rooms, taverns, lodging houses, even a race-track and
a concert hall were provided. The influential Whig literary society
the Kit-Cat Club, including Walpole, Vanbrugh, Addison, Steele and
Congreve, began having their summer gathering at a tavern called the
Upper Flask, on Heath Street. From the 1820s Hampstead landowner
Sir Thomas Maryon Wilson was continually stymied in his attempts
to offload large tracts of Hampstead Heath to developers: eventually,
after pressure by well-connected preservationists such as J. S. Mill,
Thomas Hughes and Octavia Hill, the Metropolitan Commons Act
(1866) was passed to save common land throughout London.

Already, by 1724, Daniel Defoe, in his *A Tour through the Whole
Island of Great Britain*, is impressed:

Hampstead indeed is risen from a little country village,
to a city, not upon the credit only of the waters, tho' 'tis
apparent, its growing greatness began there: but company

increasing gradually, and the people liking both the place and the diversions together; it grew suddenly populous, and the concourse of people was incredible.[4]

Defoe considers it 'a most beautiful prospect indeed':

> On the top of the hill indeed, there is a very pleasant plain, called the Heath, which on the very summit, is a plain of about a mile every way; and in good weather 'tis pleasant airing upon it, and some of the streets are extended so far, as that they begin to build, even on the highest part of the hill. But it must be confest, 'tis so near heaven, that I dare not say it can be a proper situation, for any but a race of mountaineers, whose lungs have been used to a rarity'd air, nearer the second region, than any ground for 30 miles round it.
>
> It is true, this place may be said to be prepared for a summer dwelling, for in winter nothing that I know can recommend it: 'Tis true, a warm house, and good company, both which are to be had here, go a great way to make amends for storms, and severity of cold.
>
> Here is a most beautiful prospect indeed, for we see here Hanslop Steeple one way, which is within eight miles of Northampton, N.W. to Landown-Hill in Essex another way, east, at least 66 miles from one another; the pros-pect to London, and beyond it to Bansted Downs, south; Shooters-Hill, S.E. Red-Hill, S.W. and Windsor-Castle, W. is also uninterrupted: Indeed due north, we see no farther than to Barnet, which is not above six miles; but the rest is sufficient.[5]

Yet even then, Defoe notes there is a problem keeping out the riffraff further down the hill:

> Yet Hampstead is not much the less frequented for this, but as there is (especially at the Wells) a conflux of all sorts of company, even Hampstead itself has suffered in its good name; and you see sometimes more gallantry than modesty: So that the ladies who value their reputation, have of late more avoided the wells and walks at Hampstead, than they had formerly done.[6]

A little later, in the 1730s, Hampstead gained a curious notoriety after William Whiston, a renowned natural philospoher – a theologian and mathematician in the Newtonian mould – predicted a comet strike that would almost certainly destroy the world on 13 October 1736. Whiston was said to be quite clear about this, as he informed fourteen London tradesmen and five apprentices gathered near the Royal Exchange and appealing to the 'comet mania' of the time:

> Friends and fellow-citizens, all speculative science is at an end: the period of all things is at hand; on Friday next this world shall be no more. Put not your confidence in me, brethren, for to-morrow morning, five minutes after five, the truth will be evident; in that instant the comet shall appear, of which I have heretofore warned you. As ye have heard, believe. Go hence, and prepare your wives, your families, and friends, for the universal change.[7]

As Charles Mackay tells us in his 1841 best-seller *Memoirs of Extraordinary Popular Delusions*, thousands of Londoners headed out for the Hampstead heights for safety – and to watch the end of the world:

> No little consternation was created in London in 1736 by the prophecy of the famous Whiston, that the world would be destroyed in that year, on the 13th of October. Crowds of people went out on the appointed day to Islington, Hampstead, and the fields intervening, to see the destruction of London, which was to be the 'beginning of the end'.[8]

The genuine panic of the coming apocalypse was later ridiculed by Swift; outbreaks of religiosity with packed churches and national prayers, extravagant hand-outs to beggars, dramatic confessions of adultery, ships dumping inflammable cargoes into the Thames, even a run on the banks. Whitson's prediction of the comet was, in fact, accurate. However, when the promised ensuing biblical floods and flames failed to arrive, the chastised people of London and the Hampstead Heights 'headed for the taverns', where they returned to their 'usual state of indifference'; 'they drank, they whored, they swore, they lied, they cheated, they quarrelled, they murdered.'[9]

Evelina, in Frances ('Fanny') Burney's satirical 1778 novel of that name, spends an unpleasant, disagreeable evening at a fashionable Hampstead ball; a 'long projected and most disagreeable affair'. Evelina is harassed by prospective dance partners:

> For a few moments I very much rejoiced at being relieved from this troublesome man; but scarce had I time to congratulate myself, before I was accosted by another, who begged the favour of hopping a dance with me.
>
> I told him that I should not dance at all; but he thought proper to importune me, very freely, not to be so cruel; and I was obliged to assume no little haughtiness before I could satisfy him I was serious.
>
> After this, I was addressed much in the same manner, by several other young men; of whom the appearance and language were equally inelegant and low-bred; so that I soon found my situation was both disagreeable and improper, since, as I was quite alone, I fear I must seem rather to invite than to forbid the offers and notice I received; and yet, so great was my apprehension of this interpretation, that I am sure, my dear Sir, you would have laughed had you seen how proudly grave I appeared.[10]

Hampstead's reputation as a haven for literary types really takes off at the start of the nineteenth century, when renowned Scottish poet and dramatist Joanna Baillie moved to a large Hampstead house in 1802. She was visited there by Wordsworth, Byron and Keats, along with Sir Walter Scott and poets Anne Bannerman and Anna Laetitia Barbauld. A few years later, in 1816, so-called 'cockney poet' Leigh Hunt, after a spell in the Surrey County Gaol for defaming the Prince Regent ('a corpulent gentleman of fifty! . . . a violator of his word, a libertine over head and ears in debt and disgrace, a despiser of domestic ties, the companion of gamblers and demireps!'[11]), settled first in West End Lane and then the Vale of Health. He soon gathered a circle of Romantic types here, including William Hazlitt, Charles Lamb, Keats, and painters Joseph Severn and Benjamin Robert Haydon. But Shelley was the big draw. In December 1816, two visitors in particular were eagerly

waiting for Shelley to arrive from Marlow; these were Keats and Horace Smith. Keats had been hoping to make Smith's acquaintance for the past two months, but the witty parodist, full of a recent reading of Shelley's work, and anxious to see a poet with such a remarkable reputation, seemed hardly to notice the young man whose sonnet he had once picked out for praise. In any case, Shelley, once arrived and introduced, soon began to dominate the conversation, though he seems to have winced politely at some of Hunt's facetiousness. On a walk across Hampstead Heath in the fine weather, Smith deliberately sought out Shelley and the two tall men, striding out together, soon left Keats and the rest of the company behind.[12]

In March 1817, in a symbolic move from his old life as a medical student, Keats, with brother Tom, moved from damp, unhealthy lodgings in Cheapside up to 1 Well Walk, Hampstead:

On Saturday 1 March, in a spell of beautifully fine warm weather, Keats set out with a copy of *Poems* in his hand to give to Hunt. As he walked up Millfield Lane, Hampstead Heath, beside the Ponds he met on the wooded path Hunt himself. This seemed to both like an omen. Hunt invited Keats home to the Vale of Health to celebrate the publication. After dinner the weather was warm enough for them to take their wine in the garden, where the constellation of Orion, the Bull and the Pleiades shone brightly above them. In this starry and inspiring setting, the garden warm with early spring and the book of poems with its vernal promise between them, it seemed natural enough for the two poets to strike a poetic attitude. Shelley was no longer with them to turn the talk to more transcendental matters, and both may have felt the necessary luxury of being a little silly . . . At all events, Hunt felt moved to embody his admiration by picking and twining a chaplet of laurel and placing it on Keats's forehead: Keats, not to be outdone, wove together strands of ivy and put them on Hunt's head. To Hunt, the next move was obvious. They should each write a sonnet to mark the moment, with a fifteen minute time-limit.[13]

Keats would be somewhat mortified recalling this moment of levity as it could suggest that he wasn't taking his poetic calling seriously enough. He soon tired of Hampstead's literary set and Hunt's tiresome, possessive sponsorship:

> I went to Hunt's and Haydon's who live now neighbours.
> Shelley was there – I know nothing about any thing in this part
> of the world – every Body seems at Loggerheads. There's Hunt
> infatuated – there's Haydon's picture in status quo. There's Hunt
> walks up and down his painting room criticising every head most
> unmercifully – There's Horace Smith, tired of Hunt. 'The web of
> our Life is of mingled Yarn' . . . Yesterday Morning while I was
> at Brown's, in came Reynolds – he was pretty bobbish, we had
> a pleasant day – but he would walk home at night that cursed
> cold distance. Mrs Bentley's [the landlady's] children are making
> a horrid row . . . I am quite disgusted with literary Men and will
> never know another except Wordsworth – no not even Byron.[14]

After the death of his brother Tom at Well Walk in December
1818, Keats shared one of a pair of semi-detached houses, known as
Wentworth Place, on what was then John Street, on the southern edge
of the Heath. The next two years or so here were highly productive:
Charles Brown claims Keats wrote the perennial favourite 'Ode to a
Nightingale' in the Wentworth Place garden.

> In the spring of 1819 a nightingale had built her nest near my
> house. Keats felt a tranquil and continual joy in her song; and
> one morning he took his chair from the breakfast-table to the
> grass-plot under a plum-tree, where he sat for two or three
> hours. When he came into the house, I perceived he had some
> scraps of paper in his hand, and these he was quietly thrusting
> behind the books. On inquiry, I found those scraps, four or
> five in number, contained his poetic feeling on the song of our
> nightingale. The writing was not well legible; and it was difficult
> to arrange the stanzas on so many scraps. With his assistance
> I succeeded, and this was his 'Ode to a Nightingale', a poem
> which has been the delight of everyone.[15]

John Constable started visiting Hampstead in 1819 and also ended
up moving to Well Walk, to a house at number 3, in 1829. Up in
Hampstead, Constable could continue his obsessive cloud-watching

and 'systematic recording of skies and their related weather'.[16] He also liked the views: 'Our little drawing room commands a view un-equalled in Europe – from Westminster Abbey to Gravesend. The dome of St Paul's in the air, realizes Michael Angelo's idea on seeing that of the Pantheon – "I will build such a thing in the sky".'[17]

In Dickens's *Oliver Twist* (1838), Bill Sikes is on the run after killing Nancy and heads, naturally, for high ground to get out of London:

> He went through Islington; strode up the hill at Highgate
> on which stands the stone in honour of Whittington; turned
> down to Highgate Hill, unsteady of purpose, and uncertain
> where to go; struck off to the right again, almost as soon as he
> began to descend it; and taking the foot-path across the fields,
> skirted Caen Wood, and so came out on Hampstead Heath.
> Traversing the hollow by the Vale of Health, he mounted the
> opposite bank, and crossing the road which joins the villages of
> Hampstead and Highgate, made along the remaining portion
> of the heath to the fields at North End, in one of which he laid
> himself down under a hedge, and slept.
>
> Soon he was up again, and away, – not far into the country,
> but back towards London by the high-road – then back again
> – then over another part of the same ground as he had already
> traversed – then wandering up and down in fields, and lying on
> ditches' brinks to rest, and starting up to make for some other
> spot, and do the same, and ramble on again.[18]

In Wilkie Collins's 'Sensation' novel *Armadale* (1866), Hampstead Lane, the Vale of Health ('Fairweather Vale'), is the location for dodgy Dr Downward's creepy sanatorium, where Lydia Gwilt goes to try and murder Allan Armadale with poison gas capsules:

> Fairweather Vale proved to be a new neighbourhood, situated
> below the high ground of Hampstead, on the southern side.
> The day was overcast, and the place looked very dreary. We
> approached it by a new road running between trees, which
> might have once been the park-avenue of a country house.
> At the end we came upon a wilderness of open ground, with
> half-finished villas dotted about, and a hideous litter of boards,
> wheelbarrows, and building materials of all sorts scattered in

every direction. At one corner of this scene of desolation stood a great overgrown dismal house, plastered with drab-coloured stucco, and surrounded by a naked unfinished garden, without a shrub or a flower in it – frightful to behold. On the open iron gate that led into this enclosure was a new brass plate, with 'Sanatorium' inscribed on it in great black letters. The bell, when the cabman rang it, pealed through the empty house like a knell; and the pallid withered old manservant in black who answered the door looked as if he had stepped up out of his grave to perform that service. He let out on me a smell of damp plaster and new varnish; and he let in with me a chilling draft of the damp November air. I didn't notice it at the time – but writing of it now, I remember that I shivered as I crossed the threshold.[19]

Hampstead is wonderfully Gothic in Bram Stoker's *Dracula* (1897). This is where Lucy Westenra lures local kids out onto the dark, secluded Heath for vampiric purposes, as the novel describes in a breathless 'newspaper' account.

> The Westminster Gazette, 25 September
>
> A HAMPSTEAD MYSTERY
>
> The neighbourhood of Hampstead is just at present exercised with a series of events which seem to run on lines parallel to those of what was known to the writers of headlines as 'The Kensington Horror', or 'The Stabbing Woman', or the 'The Woman in Black'. During the past two or three days several cases have occurred of young children straying from home or neglecting to return from their playing on the Heath. In all these cases the children were too young to give any properly intelligible account of themselves, but the consensus of their excuses is that they had been with a 'bloofer lady'. It has always been late in the evening when they have been missed, and on two occasions the children have not been found until early in the following morning.[20]

All the missing Cockney urchins, encountering this 'bloofer' (beautiful) lady, were found alive, but 'slightly torn or wounded in the throat . . . The wounds seem as might be made by a rat or a small dog'. Lucy, of course, is dead: Van Helsing proposes that he and Dr Seward dine at Jack Straw's Castle and then stake out the nearby churchyard where Lucy had been buried:

> As we went further, we met fewer and fewer people, till at last we were somewhat surprised when we met even the patrol of horse police going their usual suburban round. At last we reached the wall of the churchyard, which we climbed over. With some little difficulty – for it was very dark, and the whole place seemed so strange to us – we found the Westenra tomb. The Professor took the key, opened the creaky door, and standing back, politely, but quite unconsciously, motioned me to precede him . . . The tomb in the day-time, and when wreathed with fresh flowers, had looked grim and gruesome enough; but now, some days afterwards, when the flowers hung lank and dead, their whites turning to rust and their greens to browns; when the spider and the beetle had resumed their accustomed dominance; when the time-discoloured stone, and dust-encrusted mortar, and rusty, dank iron and tarnished brass, and clouded silver-plating gave back the feeble glimmer of a candle, the effect was more miserable and sordid than could have been imagined . . .
>
> 'What are you going to do?' I asked.
>
> 'To open the coffin. You shall yet be convinced.' Straightaway he began taking out the screws, and finally lifted off the lid, showing the casing of lead beneath. The sight was almost too much for me. It seemed to be as much an affront to the dead as it would have been to have stripped off her clothing in her sleep whilst living; I actually took hold of his hand to stop him . . . I had expected a rush of gas from the week-old corpse . . . taking the edge of the loose flange, he bent it back towards the foot of the coffin, and holding up the candle into the aperture, motioned to me to look.
>
> I drew near and looked. The coffin was empty.[21]

For the Grossmiths' Holloway-based Charles Pooter, a pleasant weekend stroll over the fields to a Hampstead inn, The Cow and Hedge (a thinly disguised version of the famous Old Bull and Bush, on

North End Road), turns into yet another social humiliation. Sunday licensing laws then only permitted entry to legitimate travellers who had come some distance; and not to passing locals:

> April 15, Sunday
>
> At three o'clock Cummings and Gowing called for a good long walk over Hampstead and Finchley, and brought with them a friend named Stillbrook. We walked and chatted together, except Stillbrook, who was always a few yards behind us staring at the ground and cutting at the grass with his stick.
>
> As it was getting on for five, we four held a consultation, and Gowing suggested that we should make for 'The Cow and Hedge' and get some tea. Stillbrook said: 'A brandy-and-soda was enough for him.' I reminded him that all public-houses were closed till six o'clock. Stillbrook said, 'That's all right – bona-fide travellers.'
>
> We arrived; and as I was trying to pass, the man in charge of the gate said; 'Where from?' I replied: 'Holloway.' He immediately put up his arm, and declined to let me pass. I turned back for a moment, when I saw Stillbrook, closely followed by Cummings and Gowing, make for the entrance. I watched them, and thought I would have a good laugh at their expense. I heard the porter say: 'Where from?' When, to my surprise, in fact disgust, Stillbrook replied: 'Blackheath,' and the three were immediately admitted.[22]

In Conan Doyle's 1904 Sherlock Holmes story 'The Adventure of Charles Augustus Milverton', the title character, 'the king of all the blackmailers', is also deemed to be 'the worst man in London'. Soon-to-be-wed debutante Lady Eva Brackwell is Milverton's latest target, about whom he has obtained some early letters – 'imprudent, Watson, nothing worse'. Holmes and Watson plan to burgle Milverton's Hampstead home (craftily wearing home-made black silk masks) to retrieve the documents:

> Holmes and I put on our dress-clothes, so that we might appear to be two theatre-goers homeward bound. In Oxford Street we picked up a hansom and drove to an address in Hampstead. Here we paid off our cab, and with our great-coats buttoned up,

for it was bitterly cold and the wind seemed to blow through us, we walked along the edge of the Heath.

'It's a business that needs delicate treatment,' said Holmes. 'These documents are contained in a safe in the fellow's study, and the study is the ante-room of his bed-chamber . . . This is the house, this big one in its own grounds. Through the gate – now to the right among the laurels. We might put on our masks here, I think. You see, there is not a glimmer of light in any of the windows, and everything is working splendidly.'

With our black silk face-coverings, which turned us into two of the most truculent figures in London, we stole up to the silent, gloomy house. A sort of tiled veranda extended along one side of it, lined by several windows and two doors . . .

The place was locked, but Holmes removed a circle of glass and turned the key from the inside. An instant afterwards he had closed the door behind us and we had become felons in the eyes of the law. The thick, warm air of the conservatory and rich, choking fragrance of exotic plants took us by the throat.[23]

In his autobiography, *A Little Learning* (1964), Evelyn Waugh recalls Edwardian Hampstead, when it still 'bore plain marks of the character given to it in the late eighteenth century; a pleasure garden':[24]

I was four years old when my father built his house in what was then the village of North End, Hampstead. He was, in fact, the first of its spoliators. When we settled there the tube reached no further than Hampstead. Golders Green was a grassy cross-road with a sign pointing to London, Finchley and Hendon; such a place a place as where 'the Woman in White' was encountered. All round us lay dairy farms, market gardens and a few handsome old houses of brick or stucco standing in twenty acres or more; not far off there survived woods where we picked bluebells, and some streams beside which we opened our picnic baskets. North End Road was a steep dusty lane with white posts and rails bordering its footways. North End, the reader may remember, was the place where Bill Sikes spent the first night of his flight after the murder of Nancy.[25]

This doesn't last long and the spot is rapidly suburbanized, the postcode even changing from Hampstead to dreary Golders Green:

> My father deplored the change, and, as far as was possible, ignored it, because Hampstead had historic associations, with Keats and Blake and Constable, while Golders Green meant, to him, merely a tube station. I, at that self-conscious age, minded more, for I knew, as he did not, that the district had somehow acquired a slightly comic connotation.[26]

D. H. Lawrence moved into a house on the Vale of Health in summer 1915, one of many Hampstead properties let to him by friends and admirers:

> 1 Byron Villas, Vale of Health, Hampstead
>
> My Dear Kot,
>   You take the tube to Hampstead station, from thence walk straight up the hill to the Heath, & continue straight on, past the pond, along the Spaniards Road, a little way, till you come to the public house called Jack Straw's Castle. Across the road from this the path drops down the Heath straight into the Vale of Health, & the road winding to the right leads you to Byron Villas. I hope you will like our flat – I think you will.[27]

While out for a walk on the Heath a few weeks later, Lawrence and Frieda see a German Zeppelin airship:

> Then we saw the Zeppelin above us, just ahead, amid a gleaming of clouds: high up like a bright golden finger, quite small, among a fragile incandescence of clouds. And underneath it were splashes of fire as the shells fired from the earth burst. Then there were flashes near the ground – and the shaking noise. It was like Milton – then there was a war in heaven. But it was not angels. It was that small golden Zeppelin, like an oval world, high up. It seemed as if the cosmic order were gone, as if there had come a new order, a new heavens above us: and as if the world in anger were trying to revoke it. Then the small long-ovate luminary, the new world in the heavens, disappeared again.

I cannot get over it, that the moon is not Queen of the sky by
night, and the stars the lesser lights. It seems the Zeppelin is in
the zenith of the night, golden like a moon, having taken control
of the sky; and the bursting shells are the lesser lights . . . So it is
the end – our world is gone, and we are like dust in the air.[28]

Lawrence's short story 'The Last Laugh' (1924) is set in Hampstead:

There was a little snow on the ground, and the church had just
struck midnight. Hampstead in the night of winter for once
was looking pretty, with clean white earth and lamps for moon,
and dark sky above the lamps.
   A confused little sound of voices, a gleam of hidden yellow
light. And then the garden door of a tall, dark Georgian house
suddenly opened, and three people confusedly emerged. A girl
in a dark-blue coat and fur turban, very erect: a fellow with a
little despatch case, slouching: a thin man with a red beard,
bareheaded, peering out of the gateway down the hill that
swung in a curve downwards towards London.
   'Look at it! A new world!' cried the man in the beard,
ironically, as he stood on the step and peered out.
   'No, Lorenzo! It's only white-wash!' cried the young man
in the overcoat.[29]

In 1918, the year after she was diagnosed with tuberculosis, and
while waiting for her divorce to come through, the poet and short-
story writer Katherine Mansfield lived with the publisher John
Middleton Murry at 17 East Heath Road, polishing the entries in her
journal a long way from her native New Zealand:

I am the little Colonial walking in the London garden
patch – allowed to look, perhaps, but not to linger. If I lie
on the grass, they positively shout at me: 'Look at her, lying
on *our* grass, pretending she lives here, pretending this is
her garden, and that tall back of a house, with windows
open and the coloured curtains lifting, is her house. She is
a stranger – an alien. She is nothing but a little girl sitting
on the Tinakori hills and dreaming: "I went to London and
married an Englishman and we lived in a tall grave house with

red geraniums and white daisies in the garden at the back."
Im-pudence!'[30]

George Orwell's *Keep the Aspidistra Flying* (1936), a disturbing study
of poverty, isolation and sexual frustration, and a portrait of the profound *ressentiment* of the struggling, starving artist in a money-obsessed
world, is set in a dank and depressing Hampstead. Gordon Comstock,
a perpetually skint poet, toils in Mr McKechnie's bookshop, where he is
aghast at the stuff he has to sell ('all that soggy, half-baked trash massed
together in one place'), disgusted by the garish advertising posters
opposite the shop, and generally dwells on his favourite subject: 'the
futility, the bloodiness, the deathliness of modern life'.[31] McKechnie's
shop is based on real-life Booklovers' Corner (the 'corner' being South
End Road and Pond Street), the shop where Orwell worked in the
mid-1930s. It is now a branch of Le Pain Quotidien:

> He gazed out through the glass door. A foul day, and the wind
> rising. The sky was leaden, the cobbles of the street were slimy.
> It was St Andrew's day, the thirtieth of November. McKechnie's
> stood on a corner, on a sort of shapeless square where four
> streets converged. To the left, just within sight from the door,
> stood a great elm-tree, leafless now, its multitudinous twigs
> making sepia-coloured lace against the sky. Opposite, next to
> the Prince of Wales, were tall hoardings covered with ads for
> patent foods and patent medicines exhorting you to rot your
> guts with this or that synthetic garbage. A gallery of monstrous
> doll-faces – pink vacuous faces, full of goofy optimism.
> QT Sauce, Tru-weet Breakfast Crisps ('Kiddies clamour
> for their Breakfast Crisps'), Kangaroo Burgundy, Vitamalt
> Chocolate, Bovex.[32]

Comstock lives in a dingy room at the run-down '31 Willowbed Road
N.W.', specializing in 'single gentlemen', and again based on Orwell's
real-life digs in Willoughby Road, Hampstead.

> Willowbed Road, N.W., was not definitely slummy, only dingy
> and depressing. There were real slums hardly five minutes' walk
> away. Tenement houses where families slept five in a bed, and,
> when one of them died, slept every night with the corpse until

it was buried; alley-ways where girls of fifteen were deflowered by boys of sixteen against leprous plaster walls. But Willowbed Road itself contrived to keep up a kind of mingy, lower-middle-class decency. There was even a dentist's brass plate on one of the houses. In quite two-thirds of them, amid the lace curtains of the parlour window, there was a green card with 'Apartments' on it in silver lettering, above the peeping foliage of an aspidistra.[33]

Keats Grove also gets a mention as Comstock is invited by critic Paul Doring to a certain 'Coleridge Grove' for a literary soiree:

Coleridge Grove was a damp, shadowy, secluded road, a blind alley and therefore void of traffic. Literary associations of the wrong kind (Coleridge was rumoured to have lived there for six weeks in the summer of 1821) hung heavy upon it. You could not look at its antique decaying houses, standing back from the road in dank gardens under heavy trees, without feeling an atmosphere of outmoded 'culture' envelop you. In some of those houses, undoubtedly, Browning Societies still flourished, and ladies in art serge sat at the feet of extinct poets talking about Swinburne and Walter Pater. In spring the gardens were sprinkled with purple and yellow crocuses, and later with harebells, springing up in little Wendy rings among the anæmic grass; and even the trees, it seemed to Gordon, played up to their environment and twisted themselves into whimsy Rackhamesque attitudes. It was queer that a prosperous hack critic like Paul Doring should live in such a place. For Doring was an astonishingly bad critic.[34]

Doring is not at home. This tips Comstock over the edge: 'The sods! The bloody sods! To have played a trick like that on him! To have invited him, and changed the day and not even bothered to tell him!'[35]

In the 1920s the Spenders are living at 10 Frognal, Hampstead, and a distant relative, Caroline, is employed to help out, especially with the children, Stephen and Christine:

They reached the house and the door was opened by Ella, who greeted them with a most friendly smile. (Caroline noted that it was an ugly house in the Hampstead style, as if built from the box of bricks of a nineteenth-century German child. It was surmounted by an abortive tower at one corner, to vary the regularity of the roof. There was a stone-tiled hall, long and high, out of which doors led to a dining-room containing massive furniture, and to Harold Spender's book-lined study, which had a roll-top desk. Upstairs was a drawing-room, painted grey, and furnished in a style reminiscent of Mrs Spender's *art nouveau* phase. Above this there was a floor which contained several bedrooms.)

Caroline was introduced to Christine, who was 'almost ill with apprehension and shyness', and to Stephen, 'who gave her the limpest of handshakes'. They went in to tea and Mrs Schuster destroyed whatever was left of Christine's self-control by saying: 'Of course you must pour out tea, dear Christine, and don't drop the cups, and, oh, be careful, you're spilling the milk', etc.[36]

In Patrick Hamilton's 1929 novel *The Midnight Bell*, which later became the first part of the trilogy *Twenty Thousand Streets Under the Sky* (1935), desperately infatuated barman Bob takes Jenny, a West End prostitute and for him a 'complete and golden girl', up to a wintry Hampstead Heath for a romantic stroll. On returning to town, the mood is shattered:

On the heights of Hampstead the lamps were already lit. A crescent moon was out. Dead leaves rustled beneath their feet. The sensuous fervours of his passion had fled, but the charm remained, and quiet Nature conspired tender scenery for their romance. They hardly spoke.

When they reached the road between Jack Straw's Castle and the Spaniards, however, the high atmosphere was different.

'Oo – ain't it jes' cold!' she said; and it was. Bitterly cold – and windy, and dark. He took her arm. It was too cold and windy and dark even for romance. They hurried along.

They descended the hill towards the station, and were back again with people and unchanged reality. He had burned his emotions out, and was glad to speak of other things.

In the lift at Hampstead Station the strong light glared upon her powdered but faultless skin. He saw that she was tired, and so was he. The noise of the train obliterated – or at least suspended – any feeling of any kind.

Where was she going tonight? To earn her living?
Unthinkable thoughts. The situation was really ghastly.[37]

Orcadian poet Edwin Muir and his wife, the translator Willa Muir,
spent a very happy time in Hampstead in the early 1930s: 'By good
luck we managed to rent a charming, dilapidated house in Hampstead
. . . Hampstead was filled with writing people and haunted by young
poets despairing over the poor and the world, but despairing together,
in a sad but comforting union.'[38] Muir tries to figure out the reasons
for their happiness:

There seems to have been no objective reason for our
happiness in Hampstead, and when I try to resuscitate it now
it seems to have been made up of a confusion of things, many
of them quite trifling. First of all, we had many more friends
than in the years when we had lived abroad . . . George Barker
and Dylan Thomas dropped in at all hours . . . [John] Holms
often came, bringing with him Peggy Guggenheim, who told
us curious stories of the American colony in Paris after the
first war . . .
    The house itself was a source of happiness. It was an old
dilapidated Strawberry Hill Gothic house, which vibrated
gently whenever the underground train passed beneath it. A
plumber and repairer had attended to it for an absent-minded
trust for forty years. Plumbing had developed during that time,
but he had not. The roof of our bedroom leaked, and for the
first few weeks we had to sleep with a large umbrella over our
heads, in case of rain . . . The garden at the back was filled
with small bones and oyster-shells. An elderly lady who had
had the house before us had spent her days in bed, living on
mutton chops and oysters, throwing the bones and the shells
through the open window. As I look back at our troubles with
the house, they seem part of the pleasure it gave us, though they
must have been exasperating at the time. The fact was that we
were in love with its sweet, battered, Mozartian grace, and for
that were prepared to forgive it anything.[39]

Sigmund Freud, fleeing Nazi-annexed Vienna in 1938 along with
his wife, Martha; his daughter Anna; housekeeper, Paula Fichtl; and

a personal doctor, Josephine Stross. They lived first at Primrose Hill and then at 20 Maresfield Gardens, Hampstead, where Freud's study opened on to a typical flowery suburban garden.[40] He had some impressive visitors, including the Woolfs. H. G. Wells was considering lobbying for an Act of Parliament to confer immediate British citizenship on Freud, who wrote in a letter to Wells:

> 20 Maresfield Gardens
> London N.W.3
> July 16, 1939
>
> Dear Mr Wells
> Your letter starts with the question how I am. My answer is I am not too well, but I am glad of the chance to see you and the Baroness [Moura von Budberg] again and happy to learn that you are intending a great satisfaction for me. Indeed, you cannot have known that since I first came over to England as a boy of eighteen years, it became an intense phantasy wish of mine to settle in this country and become an Englishman. Two of my half-brothers had done so fifteen years before.
> But an infantile phantasy needs a bit of examination before it can be admitted to reality.[41]

Also fleeing the Nazis from Vienna, along with many others, novelist and sociologist Elias Canetti and his wife Veza moved to Hampstead in February 1939. The next summer they watch the Battle of Britain unfold from the Heath:

> In those days of September 1940, you could watch the dogfights between the British and the German planes from up on the Heath . . . In the middle of the day, you could look up at the sky, and watch the tracks of the planes, like watching some sporting event. It was so thrilling that you only had eyes for each particular duel as it was in progress . . . It was a particularly beautiful autumn day, the sky was clear and deeply blue and against it we could see the zigzags of the planes marked in little puffs of white. I won't try to describe what I saw, but I want to try and regain the feeling that gripped me then. I was very excited – I already said that it was like some sporting occasion – but felt utterly innocent, as though it

weren't a matter of people's lives and deaths. The planes and the men in them were fused to single beings, a kind of aerial centaur, you could say.[42]

In his cruel and sensational posthumous memoir *Party in the Blitz* (2005), Canetti is tough on the English ('the worst of England is the desiccation, the life as a remote-controlled mummy'), especially Hampstead literary celebrities. This includes T. S. Eliot (an 'abysmal character') and his 'costive-minimal work (so many spittoons of failure)'; and Iris Murdoch, 'the bubbling Oxford stewpot. Everything I despise about English life is in her.'[43] He recalls the titular party during the Blitz, at art critic Roland Penrose's house, 'higher than most of those on Downshire Hill'. As Canetti neutrally observes, as he descends from the top floor, things are getting a little out of hand:

The dancers, the women especially, had something lascivious about them, and they relished their own movements, as well as those of their partners. The atmosphere was thick and warm, and no-one seemed to be concerned that we could hear bombs coming down, it was a fearless and very lively group. I had started out on the top floor, I could hardly believe my eyes, then I walked down to the second floor, and believed them still less. Each room seemed more fiery than the one I had been in before. In the lower rooms, people sought a little privacy for themselves, couples sat embracing, the music pushed through us hotly, from top to bottom, people were hugging and kissing, nothing seemed indecent, in the basement there were the most astounding goings-on. The door into the garden was ajar, men in firemen's helmets reached for buckets of sand, which they carried out very fast, with sweat on their faces. They heeded nothing they saw in the room, in their haste to protect the burning houses in the neighbourhood, they reached blindly for the sand-filled buckets. There must have been any number of them, the couples, not quite so many down here, continued to hold each other hard, no-one let go of his or her partner, it was as though the panting, sweating labourers had nothing whatever to do with them, they were two different species, each oblivious to the other.[44]

Aldous Huxley's novel *Time Must Have a Stop* (1944) features the precocious poet Sebastian Barnack, thinking of Keats and mentally composing poetry as he walks through Hampstead:

> All over the world, millions of men and women lying in pain;
> millions dying, at this very moment; millions more grieving
> over them, their faces distorted, like that poor old hag's,
> the tears running down their cheeks. And millions starving,
> millions frightened, and sick, and anxious . . .
> As he walked down Haverstock Hill, Sebastian felt himself
> overcome by a vast impersonal sadness. Nothing else seemed
> to exist now, or to matter, except death and agony.
> And then that phrase of Keats's came back to him –
> 'The giant agony of the world!' The giant agony. He racked
> his memory to find the other lines. 'None may usurp this
> height . . .' How did it go?

> None may usurp this height, returned that shade,
> But those to whom the miseries of the world
> Are misery, and will not let them rest . . .

> How exactly right that was! And perhaps Keats had thought
> of it one cold spring evening, walking down the hill from
> Hampstead, just as he himself was doing now. Walking down,
> and stopping sometimes to cough up a morsel of his lungs and
> think of his own death as well as other people's. Sebastian began
> again, whispering articulately to himself.[45]

In John Wyndham's *The Day of the Triffids* (1951) one of the few sighted survivors of an asteroid storm, Bill Masen, comes across blinded scavengers on the Hampstead borders:

> We stopped somewhere near Swiss Cottage, and piled out.
> There were perhaps twenty people in sight, prowling with
> apparent aimlessness along the gutters. At the sound of the
> engines every one of them had turned towards us with an
> incredulous expression on his face, and as if they were parts of
> a single mechanism they began to close hopefully towards us,
> calling out as they came. The drivers shouted to us to get clear.

They backed, turned, and rumbled off by the way we had come. The converging people stopped. One or two of them shouted after the lorries; most turned hopelessly and silently back to their wandering. There was one woman about fifty yards away; she broke into hysterics, and began to bang her head against a wall. I felt sick.[46]

Hampstead itself is quite uncanny; the same, but subtly altered:

I recalled that in former days when I had come up to Hampstead Heath it had often been by way of a bus terminus where a number of small shops and stores clustered. With the aid of the street plan I found the place again easily enough – not only found it, but discovered it to be marvellously intact. Save for three or four broken windows, the area looked simply as if it had been closed up for a weekend.

But there were differences. For one thing, no such silence had ever before hung over the locality, weekday or Sunday. And there were several bodies lying in the street. By this time one was becoming accustomed enough to that to pay them little attention.[47]

Christopher Isherwood rented a house in Hampstead for a few trying months in the summer of 1961. He wrote: 'there is much that is lovable here but thank God it is not my home. Never do I cease to give thanks I left it.'[48]

June 8th 1961

Walked on the Heath this afternoon and made japam [Hindu chanting of a sacred name] and sat under a birch tree looking out over London. Such an 'English' scene: fair touches of pale gold light amidst the buildings (Turner), a steeple rising above swelling oaks (Constable), and a bright cumulus cloud against a dark thundery sky (Samuel Palmer). Some rain fell as I was walking home and I sheltered under a tree and was talked to by a weird little Filipino, accompanied by a big Dutch student. The Filipino asked me my profession, nationality, name, etc. and had heard of my books. We sort of flirted with each other; he was incredibly provocative. He is to be found, he told me, at the King

William IV pub and an espresso bar called The Geisha. It was a very strange meeting, a sort of 'recognition'. I laughed wildly, as if with a familiar friend, and even found myself pretending to hit him when he made some joke about *Diane* [1956 film with Lana Turner]. Home feeling unreasoningly elated.[49]

After some careful stalking, psychopathic Frederick Clegg, in John Fowles's *The Collector* (1963), tracks his victim, Miranda Grey, to the Everyman Cinema in Hampstead. Outside, he has his specially modified van ready:

She came out alone, exactly two hours later, it had stopped raining more or less and it was almost dark, the sky overcast. I watched her go back the usual way up the hill. Then I drove off past her to a place I knew she must pass. It was where the road she lived in curved up away from another one. There was trees and bushes on one side, on the other a whopping big house in big grounds. I think it was empty. Higher up there were the other houses, all big. The first part of her walk was in bright-lit streets.

There was just this one place.

I had a special plastic bag sewn in my mac pocket, in which I put some of the chloroform and CTC and the pad so it was soaked and fresh. I kept the flap down, so the smell kept in, then in a second I could get it out when needed.

Two old women with umbrellas (it began to spot with rain again) appeared and came up the road toward me. It was just what I didn't want, I knew she was due, and I nearly gave up then and there. But I bent right down, they passed talking nineteen to the dozen, I don't think they even saw me or the van. There were cars parked everywhere in that district. A minute passed. I got out and opened the back. It was all planned. And then she was near. She'd come up and round without me seeing, only twenty yards away, walking quickly. If it had been a clear night I don't know what I'd have done. But there was this wind in the trees. Gusty. I could see that there was no one behind her. Then she was right beside me, coming up the pavement. Funny, singing to herself.

I said, excuse me, do you know anything about dogs?[50]

In Bernard Kops's 1966 novel *The Dissent of Dominick Shapiro*, our sixteen-year-old hero can't wait to get out of the place:

> Across the road was Hampstead Heath. Well, not exactly; it was really the Heath Extension. They lived in Golders Green no matter how much they tried to kid themselves that it was Hampstead.
>
> Long ago he personally had put paid to such pretence. 'I live at Golders Green. I'm sixteen so it's not my fault. But I'm going to escape as soon as possible.'[51]

Young Dominick, though, admits that the place does have its compensations:

> Dominick left the house and wandered on the Heath Extension. There was no way out. Not tonight. There was not a soul about and a lone dog was howling and there was the wind. No, tonight was not a night for escape. It was so cold and there was a wonderful fire burning in the grate. Real coal. And his mother would make him a mug of hot chocolate. And his father would feel guilty and be sorry and tomorrow would be marvellous because of that guilt. He would probably bung him ten extra shillings pocket money.
>
> No. Escape would come, but it was out of the question tonight. He would not leave the womb tonight but would wait another day or two to be born.[52]

Kingsley Amis lived in Hampstead, on Flask Walk, from 1976 to 1982. The Hampstead area features in *Jake's Thing* (1978), more precisely the mythical '47 Burgess Avenue, NW16', the location not specified other than being equidistant between Golders Green, East Finchley, Highgate and Hampstead: somewhere near, but not in, Hampstead Garden Suburb. This is classic late Amis territory: ramshackle suburbia, having seen better days, seedy and oddly out of date. Number 47 belonged to one of 'two longish brick terraces put up a hundred years before to house the workers at some vanished local industry and these days much in demand among recently married couples, pairs of homosexuals and older persons whose children had left or never existed. Jake had bought no. 47 in 1969; he couldn't have afforded to now.'[53]

The house stood out among its neighbours by not having had anything done to its outside: no stucco, no curious chimneys, no colourful shutters, no trailing ferns in wire baskets, front door and window-frames and drain-pipes not painted cinnabar or orpiment or minium or light mushroom, and garden neither turned into a tiny thicket nor altogether removed to accommodate a car. Having no car had made it comparatively easy for Jake to prevent that last option but some of the others had taken toll of his powers of resistance. He opened and then shut the gate, which was not of wrought iron or imitation bronze, walked up the eight yards of gravel path and let himself in.[54]

To Jake, travelling into town on the bus, everything looks semi-derelict and empty:

Although there was no shortage of his fellow human beings on the pavements and in and out of shops, other places and spaces were altogether free of them, so recurrently that his mind was crossed by thoughts of a selective public holiday or lightning semi-general strike. A railway bridge revealed two or three acres of empty tracks and sidings; large pieces of machinery and piles of bricks stood unattended on a rather small stretch of mud; no one was in sight among the strange apparatuses in what might have been a playground for young Martians; a house that had stayed half-demolished since about 1970 overlooked a straightforward bomb-site of World War II.[55]

Joseph Connolly's 1996 comic novel *This Is It* sees Eric Pizer living a double life in Hampstead, in a 'rather large Edwardian house, once fairly splendid, just off Haverstock Hill':[56]

It was a nice room, a comfortable room – the big ground-floor bay-windowed room that he had never been allowed into when a boy. In some ways, Eric's mother – he couldn't remember his father, and certainly it never did to bring him up – had been a very go-ahead, bookish, eccentric sort of woman: typically, Eric supposed, what people used to call *Hampstead*. God knows what Hampstead as an adjective meant nowadays – anything people wanted it to mean, but always derogatory (and always, for some dumb reason, with the aitch dropped if the Heath or the bloody funfair were under discussion). But in other ways, in other ways Eric's mother had been a pillar of middle-class rectitude. Each morning, she would walk him to The Hall preparatory school, and then strut back to the house, having bought a small cottage loaf in Rumbold's in Belsize Village, and some Cow & Gate Farmer's Wife Double Devon Cream at the dairy.[57]

Will Self's dystopian novel *The Book of Dave* (2006) is set in two Hampsteads: one in the present day and one some five hundred years or so in the future. Hampstead-based exemplary black-cab driver Dave Rudman, depressed and angry, separated from and denied access to his son, records his rants and grievances – against women, against mothers, about separated fathers' access rights, what's wrong with London – and has them etched on steel plates and buried in his Hampstead back garden. Some centuries into the future, after global flooding and other catastrophes, these plates are unearthed. They form, for the surviving inhabitants of the now globally warmed, inundated islet of 'Ham', one of the few elevated, habitable points of the submerged land of 'Ing', the sacred 'Book of Dave'. The colony is thoroughly 'Dave-ish' in character and language. They speak an amalgam of Cockney, cabby-speak, and the Knowledge:

> The sea mist had retreated offshore, where it hovered, a white-grey bank merging with the blue screen above. Wot if Eye woz up vair, Carl thought, up vair lyke ve Flyin I? He put himself in this lofty perspective and saw Ham, floating like a water beetle, thrusting out angled legs of grey stone deep into the placid waters of its ultramarine lagoon . . .
> The real island was quite as vivified as any toyist vision, the southeast-facing undulation of land audibly hummed. Bees, drugged by the heat, lay down in the flowers, ants reclined on beds of leaf mould, flying rats gave a liquid coo-burble – then stoppered up. To the south a few gulls soared above the denser greenery of the Ferbiddun Zön.
> The little kids who'd left the manor with Carl had run on ahead, up the slope towards the Layn, the avenue of trees that

formed the spine of Ham. These thick-trunked, stunted crinkle-leafs bordered the cultivated land with a dark, shimmering froth. Carl saw brown legs, tan T-shirts and mops of curly hair flashing among the trunks as the young Hamsters scattered into the woodland.[58]

The narrator of Helen Simpson's 2006 short story 'Constitutional', out for a precisely timed lunchtime circuit of the autumnal Heath, newly pregnant, having just returned from a funeral, feeling old and contemplating ageing, decay, death, memory and the mysterious cycle of life, has the notion of time very much on her mind:

> The thing about a circular walk is that you end up where you started – except, of course, that you don't. My usual round trip removes me neatly from the fetid staffroom lunch-hour, conveniently located as the school is on the very edge of the Heath . . .
>
> When the sun flares out like this, heatless and long-shadowed, the tree trunks go floodlit and even the puddles in the mud hold flashing blue snapshots of the sky. You walk past people who are so full of their lives and thoughts and talk about others, so absorbed in exchanging human information, that often their gaze stays abstractly on the path and their legs are moving mechanically. But their dogs frisk around, curvet-ting and cantering, arabesques of pink tongues airing in their broadly smiling jaws. They bound off after squirrels or seagulls, they bark, rowrowrow, into the sunshine, and there is no idea anywhere of what comes next.
>
> This walk is always the same but different, thanks to the light, the time of year, the temperature and so on. Its same-ness allows me to sink back into my thoughts as I swing along, while on the other hand I know and observe at some level that nothing is ever exactly the same as it was before.[59]

Ian McEwan's short story 'My Purple Scented Novel' (2016) actually addresses the Hampstead novel. It features criminal literary envy between former rising star Parker Sparrow, unhappily living in Brixton, then having to move out of London altogether, and celebrated 'Hampstead novelist' Jocelyn Tarbet. Tarbet is, of course, famous, successful, rich, well-connected, virtually a national treasure, and lives, naturally, 'in a large Victorian house in Hampstead, right near the heath'.

> So it was a holiday of the senses to pitch up at Jocelyn and Joliet's for a weekend. The vast library, the coffee tables supporting that month's hardbacks, the expanses of dark polished oak floor, paintings, rugs, a grand piano, violin music on a stand, the banked towels in my bedroom, its awesome shower, the grownup hush that lay around the house, the sense of order and shine that only a daily cleaning lady can bestow. There was a garden with an ancient willow, a mossy Yorkstone terrace, a wide lawn, and high walls. And, more than all this, the place was pervaded by a spirit of open-mindedness, curiosity, tolerance, and a taste for comedy. How could I stay away?[60]

Sparrow, of course, loathes the man and schemes to bring his smoothly unwarranted success to a ghastly end.

Highgate

Just over a mile or so northeast of Hampstead Village, across the Heath, Highgate, taking its name from a tollgate across a major route out of London, was early considered a healthful, refreshing spot, known for fairs, dancing and merriment. By the late seventeenth century Highgate had become a favoured site for vast aristocratic mansions, built to take advantage of the air and the views, and to escape noxious and crowded London. England's premier aristocrats had huge mansions built, such as Arundel House, Lauderdale House and Cromwell House (although the last did not get this name until 1833). More grand villas, including Fitzroy House, joined these in the next century, along with inns and guest-houses, Highgate becoming something of a retreat for all manner of wearied Londoners.

The antiquary John Aubrey, in his proto-biographical study *Brief Lives*, which remained scattered across four manuscripts from his death in 1697 until nearly two centuries later, describes the curious end of pioneering writer, scientist and philosopher (and Lord Chancellor) Francis Bacon. Bacon, sometimes considered the originator of scientific method and formal empiricism, just could not help 'trying an experiment' while out in Highgate in 1626:

as he was taking the aire in a coach with Dr Witherborne
(a Scotchman, Physitian to the King), towards High-gate,
snow lay on the ground, and it came into my lord's thoughts,
why flesh might not be preserved in snow, as in salt. They were
resolved they would try the experiment presently. They alighted
out of the coach, and went into a poore woman's howse at
the bottom of Highgate hill, and bought a hen, and made the
woman exenterate it, and then stuffed the bodie with snow,
and my lord did help to doe it himselfe. The snow so chilled
him, that he immediately fell so extremely ill, that he could not
returne to his lodgings (I suppose then at Graye's Inne), but
went to the earle of Arundell's house at High-gate, where they
putt him into a good bed warmed with a panne, but it was a
damp bed that had not been layn-in in about a yeare before,
which gave him such a cold that in 2 or 3 dayes, as I remember
. . . he dyed of suffocation.[61]

Highgate, with its key position on a major route out of London, was
well known for its inns and hostelries, a fact picked up in Byron's long
narrative poem of adolescent angst, *Childe Harold's Pilgrimage* (1812–18):

Some o'er thy Thamis row the ribbon'd fair,
Others along the safer turnpike fly;
Some Richmond-hill ascend, some scud to Ware,
And many to the steep of Highgate hie.
Ask ye, Bœotian shades! the reason why?
'Tis to the worship of the solemn Horn,
Grasp'd in the Holy hand of Mystery,
In whose dread name both men and maids are sworn,
And consecrate the oath with draught, and dance till morn.[62]

Coleridge lived at Highgate from 1818 until the end of his life in
1834, staying with the physician James Gillman, first in South Grove
and then, as the number of visitors increased, in a larger house at 3 The
Grove. This arrangement was an attempt to cure his acute opium
addiction, as Gillman's nephew recalls:

Coleridge, in order to allay the pain of a disease, had acquired
the habit of 'opium eating' in the form of taking large doses of

413

laudanum. The vice became one of which he could not break himself, and at the age of forty-three he at last perceived that his only hope of redemption lay in a voluntary submission of his enfeebled will to the control of others.[63]

After an interview with Dr Gillman he is invited to stay at the house. The Gillmans certainly make a fuss of their star patient, even building an early loft conversion:

> The Gillmans gave our poet a more luxurious refuge at Highgate than he had had with the kind Morgans at Hammersmith. They were then living at No. 3 in The Grove and had a portion of the roof raised in order to gain a room where he could place his great book-chests and work undisturbed. His windows overlooked – and overlook still – a beautiful view of the Nightingale Valley, with the green heights behind, the shady walks and half-hidden valleys of Hampstead. In the depth to the left lies the great metropolis – through the smoky cloud of which many a soaring tower is visible; while the sky spreads forth all the rich colours of the Western sun.[64]

Coleridge attracted a long line of impressive visitors up the hill, including Ralph Waldo Emerson, William Wordsworth, Arthur Hallam and, inevitably, Charles Lamb, who turned up every Sunday for lunch. Coleridge did in fact bump into Keats once, while both were living on the Highgate and Hampstead hills, on Millfield Lane, on the Highgate side of the Heath. Keats recognized Coleridge's companion and secretary, Joseph Henry Green, from his old medical days. We have brief accounts from both sides. Keats describes the meeting in a letter to his sister:

> April 15, 1819
> Last Sunday I took a Walk towards Highgate and in the lane that winds by the side of Lord Mansfield's park I met Mr Green our Demonstrator at Guy's [Hospital] in conversation with Coleridge – I joined them, after enquiring by a look whether it would be agreeable – I walked with him at his alderman-after-dinner pace for near two miles I suppose. In those two Miles he broached a thousand things – let me see if I can give you a list

– Nightingales, Poetry – on Poetical Sensation – Metaphysics –
Different genera and species of Dreams – Nightmare – a dream
accompanied by a sense of touch – single and double touch – A
dream related – First and second consciousness – the difference
explained between will and Volition – so say metaphysicians from
a want of smoking the second consciousness – Monsters – the
Kraken – Mermaids – Southey believes in them – Southey's belief
too much diluted – A Ghost story – Good morning – I heard his
voice as he came towards me – I heard it as he moved away – I
had heard it all the interval – if it may be called so. He was civil
enough to ask me to call on him at Highgate. Good Night![65]

For his part, Coleridge is convinced that he sensed, even then, that
Keats was doomed:

A loose, slack, not well-dressed youth met Mr. [Green] and
myself in a lane near Highgate. [Green] knew him, and spoke.
It was Keats. He was introduced to me, and stayed a minute or
so. After he had left us a little way, he came back and said: 'Let
me carry away the memory, Coleridge, of having pressed your
hand!' – 'There is death in that hand,' I said to [Green], when
Keats was gone; yet this was, I believe, before the consumption
showed itself distinctly.[66]

Coleridge's position on a hill overlooking London, attracting visitors for his expansive and hypnotic 'Table Talk', proved an irresistible
metaphor for his lofty metaphysics; he became known as the 'sage
of Highgate'. There is surely a hint of mockery in Thomas Carlyle's
description:

Coleridge sat on the brow of Highgate Hill, in those years,
looking down on London and its smoke-tumult, like a
sage escaped from the inanity of life's battle . . . A sublime
man; who, alone in those dark days, had saved his crown of
spiritual manhood; escaping from the black materialisms, and
revolutionary deluges . . . a king of men . . . [he] sat there as a
kind of *Magus*, girt in mystery and enigma; his Dodona oak-
grove (Mr Gillman's house at Highgate) whispering strange
things, uncertain whether oracles or jargon.[67]

It was rumoured that Coleridge still seemed to have found ways of getting his laudanum fix, some from a Mr Dunn, the local 'Chemist and Druggist' on the High Street. Coleridge writes to Dunn concerning his 'Sciatic Nerve'. This is driving him wild with pain, he explains,

> as if four and twenty Rats 'all in a row' from the right Hip to the Ancle Bone were gnawing away at me . . . I must therefore have recourse to an Anodyne – till I can see my friend, Mr Green . . . You will therefore greatly oblige me by sending by the Bearer a Scruple of the Acetate of Morphium, in the accompanying little Bottle, which I shall try, a grain at a time, giving six hours, till the Pain is sufficiently lulled to permit me to have some Sleep.
>
> I will do myself the pleasure of calling on you and winding up my little account, as soon as this damp-begotten Vagrant, Rheumatism by name (for want of a better) shall have taken to his Heels, like the fugitive Turnkey in Sir W. Scott's Rob Roy, and left the Prison Door open for,
> My dear Sir,
> Your obliged Friend
> S. T. Coleridge[68]

Highgate Cemetery was consecrated in 1839, quickly becoming the most desirable of the 'Magnificent Seven' suburban cemeteries built to contain London's growing army of the dead; its theatrical and Gothic design, ornate landscaping and great views soon brought in sightseers as well as the deceased. Elizabeth 'Lizzie' Siddal, Victorian artist and muse (model for Millais's *Ophelia*), died of a laudanum overdose in 1862 and her distraught husband, Dante Gabriel Rossetti, in a romantic gesture, placed the sole manuscript of his complete poems in her coffin. Less romantically, several years later he wished to get them back and arranged for the coffin to be dug up and opened, as the writer Hall Caine recalls:

> Rossetti had buried the only complete copy of his poems with his wife at Highgate, and for a time he had been able to put by the thought of them; but as one by one his friends, Mr Morris, Mr Swinburne, and others, attained to distinction as poets, he began to hanker after poetic reputation, and to reflect with pain

and regret upon the hidden fruits of his best effort. Rossetti
– in all love of his memory be it spoken – was after all a frail
mortal; of unstable character: of variable purpose: a creature of
impulse and whim, and with a plentiful lack of the backbone
of volition. With less affection he would not have buried his
book; with more strength of will he had not done so; or, having
done so, he had never wished to undo what he had done; or
having undone it, he would never have tormented himself with
the memory of it as of a deed of sacrilege. But Rossetti had
both affection enough to do it and weakness enough to have it
undone. After an infinity of self-communions he determined
to have the grave opened, and the book extracted. Endless
were the preparations necessary before such a work could be
begun. Mr Home Secretary Bruce had to be consulted. At
length preliminaries were complete, and one night, seven and
a half years after the burial, a fire was built by the side of the
grave, and then the coffin was raised and opened. The body is
described as perfect upon coming to light.

Whilst this painful work was being done the unhappy
author of it was sitting alone and anxious, and full of self-
reproaches at the house of the friend who had charge of it.
He was relieved and thankful when told that all was over. The
volume was not much the worse for the years it had lain in the
grave. Deficiencies were filled in from memory, the manuscript
was put in the press, and in 1870 the reclaimed work was issued
under the simple title of *Poems*.[69]

John Betjeman, born down the hill at lowly Gospel Oak, was
three when in 1909 his family moved up to West Hill in Highgate
proper, which suited him well, as he recalls in the verse autobiography
Summoned by Bells:

Safe, in a world of trains and buttered toast
Where things inanimate could feel and think,
Deeply I loved thee, 31 West Hill!
At that hill's foot did London then begin,
With yellow horse-drawn trams clopping past the planes
To grey-brick nonconformist Chetwynd Road
And on to Kentish Town and barking dogs

And costers' carts and crowded grocers' shops . . .
Here from my eyrie, as the sun went down,
I heard the old North London puff and shunt,
Glad that I did not live in Gospel Oak.[70]

Stella Gibbons's 1945 novel *Westwood* is set in wartime Highgate and Hampstead; or between them. Margaret Steggles, considered unattractive and unmarriageable by her family in Highgate, fortuitously gets involved with the arty Challis clan, over in Hampstead. Margaret is determined to get in with them:

> The villages of Highgate and Hampstead confront one another across a mile or so of small valleys and hills and copses, the whole expanse of some six hundred acres of open land raised upon two broad and swelling hills which look over the immense grey expanse of old London on their southern side and the ever-growing red and white expanse of new London on their northern. Each village upon its hill is marked by a church spire, and both are landmarks for miles. Both villages are romantic and charming, with narrow hilly stretches and little two-hundred-year-old houses, and here and there a great mansion of William and Mary's or James the First's reign, such as Fenton House in Hampstead and Cromwell House in Highgate; but their chief charm dwells in their cold air, which seems perpetually scented with April, and in the glimpses at the end of their steep alleys of some massive elm or oak, with beyond its branches that abrupt drop into the complex smoky pattern (formed by a thousand shades of grey in winter and of delicate cream and smoke-blue in summer) of London.[71]

This is wartime Hampstead, just the year after the Blitz, when 'the roar of guns and the horrifying whine of falling bombs, and the hot reek of explosives had stifled the sweet damp scents of autumn'.[72] Yet the war has let nature back in:

> On the outskirts of the city, out towards Edmonton and Tottenham in the north and Sydenham in the south, there was a strange feeling in the air, heavy and sombre and thrilling, as if History were working visibly, before one's eyes. And

the country was beginning to run back to London; back
into those grimy villages linked by featureless roads from
which it had never quite vanished, and which make up the
largest city in the world. Weeds grew in the City itself; a
hawk was seen hovering over the ruins of the Temple, and
foxes raided the chicken roosts in the gardens of houses near
Hampstead Heath.[73]

Hampstead itself has changed, been reborn:

> Hampstead was less picturesque than it looked from a distance.
> Like the rest of London, it needed painting; it had been
> bombed; its streets were disfigured by brick shelters and its
> walls by posters instructing the population how to deal with
> butterfly or incendiary bombs; most of its small shops which
> had sold antiques or home-made sweets or smart hats before
> the war were empty; and its narrow streets were crowded with
> foreigners, for the village and its lower districts of Belsize Park,
> St John's Wood and Swiss Cottage had been taken over by the
> refugees, and their populations almost doubled. But there was
> a heartening note among all the sad sallow faces and unfamiliar
> accents; there were many young mothers with ringing voices,
> each pushing a pram with one fat baby in it like an acorn in its
> cup; hailing each other cheerfully across the turbaned heads of
> the aliens and asking each other what luck they had had with
> the biscuits or the fish.[74]

Howard Baker, 'a decent but unremarkable man', gets a taste of
Heaven in the form of an extended daydream, starting at Highgate
Hill, in Michael Frayn's *Sweet Dreams* (1973):

> Howard Baker . . . is sitting in front of a green light waiting for
> a green light because he is thinking. He is wondering:
>   – whether he is adequately insured;
>   – whether it's Hornsey Lane he is about to enter on the other
> side of Highgate Hill, or whether he has confused Highgate
> Hill with Highgate West Hill once again;
>   – whether life might really be coming to an end, as
> ecologists say;

— whether he should kiss Rose, the wife of the man he is on his way to see, when she opens the door for him;

— whether, conceptually, it would be helpful to try regarding the house as an extension of the car, rather than the other way about, and experiment with an internal trim based upon black simulated leather, with built-in ashtrays;

— whether he will be invited to lunch with Rose and Phil, and if not, whether to get a sandwich in a pub, or go straight back to the office, send out for sandwiches, and catch up on plans for the Manchester Marina scheme . . .

— whether the girl standing on the other side of Highgate Hill (or Highgate West Hill) with the long dark hair blowing forwards over her shoulder will turn so that he can see her face . . .

And she does. She turns to look at *him* . . .

So that's one thing settled. The problem of lunch he doesn't resolve, nor whether to kiss Rose, nor the question of internal trim in public housing. But he does find out whether it's Hornsey Lane on the other side of Highgate Hill (or Highgate West Hill).

It's not. It's a ten-lane expressway, on a warm midsummer evening, with the sky clearing after a day of rain.

The expressway! Of course! How obvious everything is when once it's happened.[75]

In Tracey Chevalier's historical novel *Falling Angels* (2001), two Edwardian girls develop a friendship at Highgate Cemetery, meeting as their respective families select attractive future plots:

> I had an adventure at the cemetery today, with my new friend and a naughty boy. I've been to the cemetery many times before, but I've never been allowed out of Mama's sight. Today, though, Mama and Papa met the family that owns the grave next to ours, and while they were talking about the things grown-ups go on about, Maude and I went off with Simon, the boy who works at the cemetery. We ran up the Egyptian Avenue and all around the vaults circling the cedar of Lebanon. It is so delicious there, I almost fainted from excitement.
>
> Then Simon took us on a tour of the angels. He showed us a wonderful child-angel near the Terrace Catacombs. I had never

seen it before. It wore a little tunic and had short wings, and its head was turned away from us as if it were angry and had just stamped its foot. It is so lovely I almost wished I had chosen it for our grave. But it was not in the book of angels at the mason's yard. Anyway, I am sure Mama and Papa agree that the one I chose for our grave is the best.

Simon took us to other angels close by and then he said he wanted to show us a grave he and his father had just dug . . . So we went and looked down into it, and although it was frightening, I also got the strangest feeling that I wanted to lie down in that hole.[76]

Audrey Niffenegger's novel *Her Fearful Symmetry* (2009) uses the setting of Highgate Cemetery to tell a modern ghost story. Elspeth, a one-time guide at the cemetery and now interred there, has left her house, overlooking the cemetery, to her two American nieces. Robert, Elspeth's lover, is a tour guide at the cemetery, fascinated by the place as a 'theatre of mourning, a stage set of eternal repose':[77]

The drizzle turned to rain as Robert came to Elspeth's mausoleum. He put up his umbrella with a flourish and sat down on the steps with his back against the door. Robert leaned his head back and closed his eyes. Less than an hour ago he had walked right past this spot with his tour. He had been chatting to the groups about wakes and the extreme measures the Victorians had taken for fear of being buried alive. He wished that the Noblin tomb was not on one of the main paths; it was impossible to give a tour without passing Elspeth, and he felt callous leading groups of gawping tourists past the small structure with her surname carved into it . . .

Robert settled into himself. The stone step he sat on was cold, wet and shallow. His knees jutted up almost to shoulder height. 'Hello, love,' he said, but as always felt absurd speaking out loud to a mausoleum. Silently he continued: *Hello. I'm here. Where are you?* He pictured Elspeth sitting inside the mausoleum like a saint in her hermitage, looking out at him through the grate in the door with a little smile on her face. *Elspeth?*[78]

The twins arrive at the house they have inherited:

> Beyond the wall, Highgate Cemetery spread before them,
> vast and chaotic. Because they were on a hill, they might have
> seen quite far down into the cemetery, but the density of the
> trees prevented this; the branches were bare, but they formed
> a latticework that confused the eye. They could see the top of
> a large mausoleum, and a number of smaller graves. As they
> watched, a group of people strolled towards them along a path
> and then stopped, evidently discussing one of the graves. Then
> the group continued towards them and disappeared behind the
> wall. Hundreds of crows rose into the air as one. Even through
> the closed window they could hear the rush of wings. The
> sun abruptly came out again and the cemetery changed from
> deep shade and grey to dappled yellow and pale green. The
> gravestones turned white and seemed to be edged with silver;
> they hovered, tooth-like amid the ivy.[79]

In Ruth Rendell's *The Vault* (2011), Chief Inspector Wexford is no
longer a policeman, no longer living at Kingsmarkham. He has retired
to Hampstead, but is bored and lonely:

> He wasn't going to stay in on Thursday and wait for Tom's call,
> but he took his mobile out with him. He walked by way of
> the Heath to Kenwood, intending to make it to Highgate, but
> that would have meant finding some sort of transport to bring
> him back. It was too far to walk both ways. Highgate could be
> saved for another day. St Michael's Church, where Coleridge
> had a memorial tablet, could wait till next week and so could
> Highgate Hill, where Dick Whittington and his cat turned to
> look down on London and its gold-paved streets. 'I would bet
> you anything you like', Wexford said to no one in particular,
> 'that he gave milk to his cat.'[80]

10 'IN ALL PLACES HIGH AND LOW'

Outer North London: Following the North Circular Road from Hendon to Finchley, Barnet, Cockfosters, Enfield, Palmers Green, Ponders End, Tottenham and Edmonton

In much London suburban writing, outer north London is the city's furthest reach, the point, as Gerald Kersh has it, where London 'gives up the game'. For Elizabeth Bowen's Emmeline, driving at dreamlike breakneck speed through the night-time city in the 1930s, this is where the grip and 'heat' of London fade and fall away, on the icy 'way to the North'. This area marks the high-tide mark of London's humanity escaping a destroyed dystopian cityscape in works by both H. G. Wells and John Christopher. It tends to feature as a place to which people escape, hide, retreat or retire, or it is just where they run out of road. We read of London's peripheral and terminal activities; of motorways and bypasses and the Great North Road, aerodromes and schools, hangar-like 'out-town' stores, giant sheds and psychiatric hospitals. Yet, for Stevie Smith, writing at Palmers Green, this outward sense is precisely the suburb's best attribute: her outer north is bright, breezy, healthy and unpretentious, perfect for the tumult of families, children, commuting, for everyday life: it is somewhere to live.

Hendon

At the foot of the M1, 7 miles northwest of Charing Cross, Hendon is probably best known for its early associations with flying: home to an aircraft factory, a flying school (set up by Louis Blériot himself), which was the site of the London Aerodrome in 1911, then an RAF base, and is now the Royal Air Force Museum. This link to aviation feels right; Hendon has the feel, like much of outer north London, of being on the periphery of the city, an interzone between town and routes north.

423

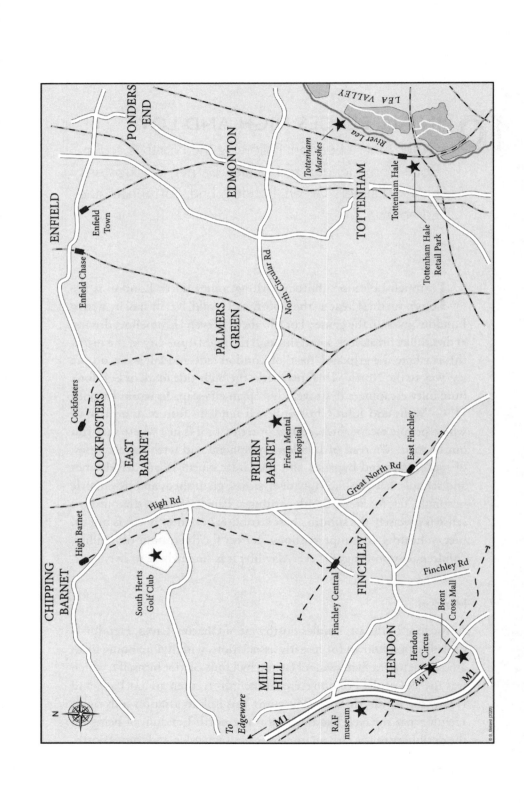

Thus, in Elizabeth Bowen's 1933 novel *To the North*, Emmeline is driving Mark 'Markie' Drinkwater at reckless speed in an open-top sports car through the 'warm lampy evening' of outer north London, heading out, escaping the pull of London, for the north. They 'swung up the winding curves of the Finchley Road, past Swiss Cottage station, past blind shop windows reflecting lamp-light and couples halting and sauntering in the cool restless night'.[1]

> Slackening speed for a moment [Emmeline] took the wide black Hendon Way; they bumped over tramlines; a long lit road running brighter with traffic crossed theirs. Left and right, homely windows were now beginning to darken, downstairs then up; large cars racing back to London shot ahead slipping vivid stretches of turf and kerb, sweeping fans of light over ceilings under which people lay half awake. A cold night smell came from the turf.[2]

They push further and further out toward the mythical north:

> The cold pole's first magnetism began to tighten upon them as street by street the heat and exasperation of London kept flaking away. The glow slipped from the sky and the North laid its first chilly fingers upon their temples, creeping down into his collar and stirring her hair at its roots. Petrol pumps red and yellow, veins of all speed and dangerous, leapt giant into their lights. As they steadily bore uphill to some funnel-point in the darkness – for though lamps dotted the kerb the road ran and deepened ahead into shades of pitch like a river – this icy rim to the known world began to possess his fancy, till he half expected its pale reflection ahead . . .
> Hendon Circus stood empty, asleep in lamplight: she crept so slowly over the cross-roads he thought she would surely turn. But she looked up round the façades of pretty suburban elegance and in at dark windows as though someone else had spoken, or someone up there might reply; this halt in her faculties made the car almost stop . . . Recollecting herself, she glanced at the clock on the dashboard, they gathered speed and went forward, uphill, then down. He saw 'The North' written low, like a first whisper, on a yellow AA plate with an arrow

pointing: they bore steadily north between spaced-out lamps, chilly trees, low rows of houses asleep, to their left a deep lake of darkness: the aerodrome.

'Hendon,' he said. 'I wish we were still flying.'[3]

Shorty Matthews finds himself in a similar spot in James Curtis's slang-rich, hard-boiled thriller *They Drive by Night* (1938). Shorty, freshly out of prison and already framed for a murder, has to get out of London quickly. He is on the edge of London heading north, in 'a little town that had risen from the status of a market town to a suburb'.[4]

He shook his head so that a dewdrop would fall off the end of his nose. It was far too cold for him to take his hands out of his pockets. As he walked he limped a little because his left shoe was beginning to give water. It had been a hell of a long walk so far even if he had taken a pennorth on a tram three times. The road forked and he stood undecided, looking at the signpost. One arm pointed to The North and the other to St Albans.

Well, there was one for you. Which was the best road to take? Oh hell, any road was all right just so long as it didn't go back to the Smoke. No, use your crust, kid. It was getting late and all and it was a hell of a cold night to do a skipper. Just outside this town on one of these roads there was a café where all the transport drivers pulled in. This was the joint to make for. Well, it was stone ginger that it was on the road north.[5]

Iain Sinclair, in *Lights Out for the Territory*, is naturally drawn to this peripheral territory of noirish semi-criminal London zones that feature in films from the 1930s and '40s:

Its boundaries were established by the distance a fugitive could run in attempting to avoid the consequences of a crime he had not committed. Arthur Woods' *They Drive by Night* (based on a novel by the excellent James Curtis) is a paradigm of the genre. Emlyn Williams, with his endemic head cold, and looking like an incomplete dissolve between Charlie Chaplin and Nigel Lawson, is the innocent on the lam – determined to prove that the countryside is never more than

a few badly-woven tussocks and a clapboard truckers' shack
in a perpetual thunderstorm.[6]

Sinclair, on a visit to film-maker Patrick Keiller, in the same work
discusses the latter's 1994 film *London* and a sequence at Brent Cross
shopping centre.

> Had he been a poet, *London*'s narrator confesses, Brent Cross
> would have been his inspiration. At last the camera moves,
> floats upwards on an escalator, gazing dreamily on plashing
> fountains, a Mogadon crowd numbed by the muzak of the
> spheres. The narrator speaks of noticing a 'small intense man'
> reading Walter Benjamin, for all the world like a card-carrying
> Cambridge poet. The instant of empathy is an illusion. The
> spectre vanishes into Willesden . . .
>   Beyond Brent Cross, Ikea, the bloated hangars of consumer-
> ism, London loses its grip. Keiller can wait, crouching in the
> stubble like an anchorite, for meaningful movement in the
> clouds.[7]

'Hendon,' Dina Rabinovitch informs us, 'unlike say, Jerusalem,
has not inspired great literary endeavour.'[8] But this has changed: 'No
more,' she adds. She is referring to Naomi Alderman's debut novel,
Disobedience (2006), set among Hendon's Jewish community:

> Hendon is a village. It exists within a city, certainly, one of the
> greatest in the world. It has links to this city, people travel to and
> fro between them. But it is a village. In Hendon, people know
> one another's business. In Hendon, a woman cannot walk from
> one end of the High Street to the other without encountering
> an acquaintance, perhaps stopping for a chat visiting the
> butcher, baker, grocer. In Hendon, only frozen vegetables and
> washing powder are bought in supermarkets; all other produce is
> purchased at small shops, in which the shopkeepers know their
> customers by name, remember their favourite items and put
> them by. Though there is a wider world, in Hendon all that is
> needed has been provided: Torah-true schools and kosher shops
> and synagogues and mikvahs and businesses that are closed on
> the Sabbath and matchmakers and burial societies.[9]

Ronit, revisiting Hendon after her father's death, finds a strange connection to the place:

> There are parks in Hendon. There are parks and trees, with wild grass growing and open-faced hills sweeping down to the Brent Cross Flyover and the A41. Once upon a time, long ago, there were farms here and farm people. Traces remain: stone-built houses and ancient roads with crooked names, though London has silted up this place that once was farmland. In the centre of the city, the land has quite forgotten that it was ever tilled and sown, though once it was. But Hendon, lacking age and wealth, remembers the seed and the soil.
>
> We who live in Hendon now like to imagine ourselves elsewhere. We carry our homeland on our backs, unpacking it where we find ourselves, never too thoroughly nor too well, for we will have to pack it up again one day. Hendon does not exist; it is only where we are, which is the least of all ways to describe us . . . It is not our place, and we are not its people, but we have found affection here. And, as King David told us, God is in all places, high and low, distant and near at hand. As surely as He is anywhere, God is in Hendon.[10]

Finchley

Finchley grew very slowly and, well into the nineteenth century, was largely a straggle of small villages. 'In some ways', historian Nick Barratt writes of Finchley, 'its claim to fame was more that it was an area to be driven through than visited. The Great North Road was a busy one.'[11] In Alexander Baron's *The Lowlife* (1963), gambler Harry 'Harryboy' Boas visits his sister:

> Debbie lives in Finchley, the smart part. Finchley, as few people know, is one of the millionaire quarters of London. There are roads in Finchley that make Kensington look poor. Houses at forty thousand, three-car garages (Rolls, Sonny's Jag and mummy's shopping Dauphine), driveways, grounds front and rear, and butlers. Not that Debbie married so high. A fifteen thousand pound house and a Spanish couple to look after it is all she's got, poor girl. All right, so she hasn't done so bad.[12]

In Buchi Emecheta's ground-breaking novel of Nigerian experience in 1960s London, *Second-class Citizen* (1974), Adah, new to England, and to London, gets a job in North Finchley Library:

> Spring had come very late that year, because it had been a long and bitter winter, and although it was June, the freshness in the air was like that of the first day of April.
>
> At Finchley Central, the train emerged from its underground tunnel into the open air like a snake from its hole. Adah let down the window and breathed in the cool, pure, watery air. It had rained the night before and there was wetness everywhere.
>
> She saw the back gardens of many, many houses, gardens with flowers of many varieties growing in profusion: lupins and peonies, delphiniums, sweet peas and columbines. The wonderful glow of alyssum on the verges of many garden paths gave a tidy edge to the carpet of green grass which seemed to cover the ground. The trees had burst into green, ceasing to look like the naked, dried-up, juiceless old women they had reminded Adah of when she first landed in England.[13]

Adah is amazed at the library's popularity:

> Only God knew what the people of North Finchley did with all the books they borrowed. The queue sometimes stretched so far that some people had to stand outside waiting, just to borrow books . . . In fact, working at the North Finchley Library was more of a 'Thank you, thank you' job than anything else. All in all, Adah was happy that she'd got a first-class job; she was happy that her colleagues at work liked her; she was happy that she was enjoying the work.[14]

In Tim Parks's first novel, *Tongues of Flame* (1985), it's Finchley in the late 1960s. Teenage Ricky's father, an Anglican priest, suddenly announces that he has been born again, 'baptized in the Spirit', and becomes evangelical. This brings a few changes:

> But everyone was talking about Satan. Rolandson was talking about him almost non-stop, and I remember he said at the Youth Fellowship on Saturday how Satan was present in the

words and music of certain progressive pop groups, called
Black Widow and Black Sabbath, who sang about witches and
black masses: so all members of the Youth Fellowship who
had bought records by these groups had to bring them into
the meetings over the next weeks and have them smashed to
smithereens in front of everybody.[15]

Ricky gets to see more of the people of Finchley than he would like:

The church started going out more into the community too,
buttonholing people on the High Road on Saturday morning,
taking their own tent in the Spring Carnival with three or four
services each evening, and sending out nightly parties to knock
at every front door in the neighbourhood and invite people to
our church.[16]

Barnet and Friern Barnet

Three miles further north from Finchley, Chipping Barnet, or High
Barnet (at 427 feet, one of the highest points in north London), lies
along what was once the medieval Great North Road, a key route out
of London to St Albans and the north of England. Once all forest
– *baernet* in Old English meant an area of land cleared by burning
– Barnet's position on this busy route, the importance of its annual
fair, its health-giving mineral springs, numerous inns and opportunities for recreation meant that it became a destination in its own right.
Samuel Pepys records a visit on 11 July 1664, as part of a trip to the
wells, searching, as ever, for a cure for his bladder stones.

But betimes up this morning, and, getting ready, we by coach
to Holborne, where, at nine o'clock, they set out, and I and
my man Will on horseback, by my wife, to Barnett; a very
pleasant day; and there dined with her company, which was
very good . . .
   Thence I and Will to see the Wells, half a mile off, and there
I drank three glasses, and went and walked and came back and
drunk two more; the woman would have had me drink three
more; but I could not, my belly being full, but this wrought
very well, and so we rode home, round by Kingsland, Hackney,

and Mile End till we were quite weary, and my water working at least 7 or 8 times upon the road, which pleased me well, and so home weary, and not being very well, I betimes to bed.

And there fell into a most mighty sweat in the night, about eleven o'clock, and there, knowing what money I have in the house and hearing a noyse, I begun to sweat worse and worse, till I melted almost to water. I rung, and could not in half an houre make either of the wenches hear me, and this made me fear the more, lest they might be gag'd; and then I begun to think that there was some design in a stone being flung at the window over our stayres this evening, by which the thiefes meant to try what looking there would be after them and know our company. These thoughts and fears I had, and do hence apprehend the fears of all rich men that are covetous and have much money by them. At last Jane rose, and then I understand it was only the dogg wants a lodging and so made a noyse. So to bed, but hardly slept, at last did, and so till morning.[17]

The Physic Well, temporarily reopened after being closed for a century, is visited by George Bell in the 1920s, in his eccentric 1926 travelogue *Where London Sleeps.* He descends gingerly into the unwelcoming pit:

The ladder head . . . stood not only out of the ground but out of the actual well. I descended its rungs, through an orifice too crabbed to pass prosperous men; and, as often before it had been to my advantage on antiquarian research, I am not of that figure. I passed into the twilight mystery of whatever might be below. The result was a complete surprise, as after but a few steps down I found a firm foothold. The world was left behind and above, and I was back two and a half centuries in time – the luck of it! – back in the days of King Charles II, when all this about me was fashioned; the days of the Court beauties, the scandal and the gossip, something of which I Imagine was centred around this place.[18]

It is in deserted Barnet that Oliver Twist, having tramped for nearly seven days towards London and covered more than 50 miles, first bumps into the Artful Dodger:

Early on the seventh morning after he had left his native place, Oliver limped slowly into the little town of Barnet. The window-shutters were closed; the street was empty; not a soul had awakened to the business of the day. The sun was rising in all his splendid beauty; but the light only served to show the boy his own lonesomeness and desolation, as he sat, with bleeding feet and covered with dust, upon a cold door-step.

By degrees, the shutters were opened; the window-blinds were drawn up; and people began passing to and fro. Some few stopped to gaze at Oliver for a moment or two, or turned round to stare at him as they hurried by; but none relieved him, or troubled themselves to inquire how he came there. He had no heart to beg. And there he sat.

He had been crouching on the step for some time: wondering at the great number of public houses (every other house in Barnet was a tavern, large or small): gazing listlessly at the coaches as they passed through: and thinking how strange it seemed that they could do, with ease, in a few hours, what it had taken him a whole week of courage and determination beyond his years to accomplish: when he was roused by observing that a boy, who had passed him carelessly some minutes before, had returned, and was now surveying him most earnestly from the opposite side of the way. He took little heed of this at first; but the boy remained in the same attitude of close observation so long, that Oliver raised his head, and returned his steady look. Upon this, the boy crossed over; and walking close up to Oliver, said, 'Hullo, my covey! What's the row?'

The boy who addressed this inquiry to the young wayfarer, was about his own age: but one of the queerest-looking boys that Oliver had ever seen. He was a snub-nosed, flat-browed, common-faced boy enough; and as dirty a juvenile as one would wish to see; but he had about him all the airs and manners of a man. He was short of his age: with rather bow-legs: and little, sharp, ugly eyes.[19]

In the second part of Thomas de Quincey's 'Sketches of Life and Manners' (1834), revised in 1853 as 'The Nation of London', we see the awe-struck teenaged author approaching London from the north:

Already at three stages' distance upon some of the greatest roads, the dim presentiment of some vast capital reaches you obscurely, and like a misgiving. This blind sympathy with a mighty but unseen object in your neighbourhood, continues to increase, you know not how. Arrived at the last station for changing horses, Barnet suppose, on one of the north roads, or Hounslow on the western, you no longer think (as in all other places) of naming the next stage; nobody says, on pulling up, 'Horses on to London' – that would sound ludicrous; one mighty idea broods over all minds, making it impossible to suppose any other destination. Launched upon this final stage, you soon begin to feel yourself entering the stream as it were of a Norwegian *maelstrom*; and the stream at length becomes a rush.[20]

Barnet, in H. G. Wells's *The War of the Worlds* (1895), is the scene of chaos and terror as refugees crowd northward to escape the advancing Martians:

So, designing to cross the Great North Road, they went on towards Barnet, my brother leading the pony to save it as much as possible . . . And as they advanced towards Barnet a tumultuous murmuring grew stronger.

They began to meet more people. For the most part these were staring before them, murmuring indistinct questions, jaded, haggard, unclear. One man in evening dress passed them on foot, his eyes on the ground. They heard his voice and, looking back at him, saw one hand clutched in his hair and the other beating invisible things. His paroxysm of rage over, he went on his way without once looking back.

As my brother's party went on towards the cross-roads to the south of Barnet, they saw a woman approaching the road across some fields on their left, carrying a child and with two other children, and then a man in dirty black, with a thick stick in one hand and a small portmanteau in the other, passed. Then round the corner of the lane, from between the villas that guarded it at its confluence with the highroad, came a little cart drawn by a sweating black pony and driven by a sallow youth in a bowler hat, grey with dust. There were three girls, East

End factory girls, and a couple of little children crowded in the cart . . .

For the main road was a boiling stream of people, a torrent of human beings rushing northward, one pressing on another. A great bank of dust, white and luminous in the blaze of the sun, made everything within twenty feet of the ground grey and indistinct and was perpetually renewed by the hurrying feet of a dense crowd of horses and of men and women on foot, and by the wheels of vehicles of every description.

'Way!' my brother heard voices crying. 'Make way!'

It was like riding into the smoke of a fire to approach the meeting point of the lane and road; the crowd roared like a fire, and the dust was hot and pungent. And, indeed, a little way up the road a villa was burning and sending rolling masses of black smoke across the road to add to the confusion . . .

So much as they could see of the road Londonward between the houses to the right was a tumultuous stream of dirty, hurrying people, pent in between the villas on either side; the black heads, the crowded forms, grew into distinctness as they rushed towards the corner, hurried past, and merged their individuality again in a receding multitude that was swallowed up at last in a cloud of dust.

'Go on! Go on!' cried the voices. 'Way! Way!'[21]

This apocalyptic scene is echoed in another science fictional post-apocalypse, John Christopher's *The Death of Grass* (1956). Here a deadly virus has wiped out global grain production, the world is on the verge of mass starvation, and the British government is about to commence nuking major cities to preserve resources. Some try to escape the capital:

The two cars drove north again, across the North Circular Road, and through North Finchley and Barnet. The steady reassuring voice on the radio continued to drone out regulations, and then was followed by the music of a cinema organ. The streets showed their usual traffic, with people shopping or simply walking about. There was no evidence of panic here in the outer suburbs. Trouble, if there were any, would have started in Central London.

They met the road-block just beyond Wrotham Park. Barriers had been set up in the road; there were khaki-clad figures on the other side. The two cars halted. John and Roger went over to the road-block. Already there were half a dozen motorists there, arguing with the officer in charge. Others, having abandoned the argument, were preparing to turn their cars and drive back.

'Ten bloody minutes!' Roger said. 'We can't have missed it by more; there would have been a much bigger pile-up.'

The officer was a pleasant, rather wide-eyed young fellow, clearly enjoying what he saw as an unusual kind of exercise.

'I'm very sorry,' he was saying, 'but we're simply carrying out orders. No travel out of London is permitted.'[22]

In Kinglsey Amis's 1971 novel *Girl, 20*, composer Roy Vandervane had 'moved some miles north of Hampstead . . . to a reputedly rather grand establishment on the fringes of the Hertfordshire country-side'.[23] Music critic Douglas Yandell has a tricky task to get there from central London:

I took an 11 bus along the Strand and got on to the North-Western Line . . . The train stopped at the end of the line, and I and not many other people got out. Following instructions, I telephoned from a box near the station entrance and gave some either female or effeminate person the news that I had arrived. I was told to start walking and to expect to be picked up by a car.[24]

The car arrives and they set off:

We turned off, climbed a long hill and emerged into an impressive thoroughfare with a wood and then a common on one side and infrequent large houses on the other . . . A pond, a real one this time, came into view on the common, and the car pulled off the road at one end of a considerable dwelling with plaster urns and large rhododendron bushes in front of it. I remembered Roy telling me that he had got the place for a song: yes, a song with mixed choir, double orchestra, brass band and organ.[25]

Just down Barnet Hill, Friern Barnet is the setting for Will Self's novel *Umbrella* (2012). Laingian psychologist Zack Busner is on his way to work at Friern Hospital, formerly Friern Mental Hospital, in 1970:

> the window is cracked open so that *Muswell Hill calypso* warms the cold Friern Barnet morning, staying with him, wreathing his head with rapidly condensing *pop breath. I'm an ape man, I'm an ape-ape man, oh I'm an ape man . . .* The lawns and verges are soft with dew, his arms and his legs are stiff . . . the Austin's steering wheel *plastic vertebrae bent double, kyphotic* . . . had pulled at his shoulders as he wrestled the car down from Highgate, then yanked it through East Finchley – knees jammed uncomfortably under the dashboard – then across the North Circular and past the blocks of flats screening the Memorial Hospital before turning right along Woodhouse Road . . . In his already heightened state he had looked upon the city as an inversion, seeing the parallelograms of dark woodland and dormant grass as man-made artefacts surrounded by growing brick, tarmac and concrete that *ripples away to the horizon along the furrows of suburban streets.*[26]

For Michael Hofmann, in his poem 'From A to B and Back Again' (1993), Barnet is one of 'the unconcerned suburbs' where, heading north on the Northern line, the train emerges from underground: 'There was Barnet, my glottal stop, trying hard / to live up to its name, colloquial and harmless and trite.'[27]

Cockfosters

Just east of Barnet, Cockfosters is perhaps known as the end, or the beginning, of the Piccadilly Line. In Helen Simpson's story 'Cockfosters' (2015), Julie has just got off a Piccadilly Line train at Green Park when she realizes that she has left her glasses on the train. With her friend Philippa, Julie resolves to go to all the way to the end of the line – Cockfosters – to reclaim them. The journey and destination provide neat metaphors of ageing and other kinds of final destinations: 'The next station is Cockfosters. This train will terminate there. Please ensure you take all your personal belongings with you.'[28]

COCKFOSTERS

As the train drew in to its destination, they were giggling and sticking their tongues out at each other like silly schoolgirls they had once been together.

Waiting on the platform were more than half a dozen cleaners with plastic bags and pincers poised to clear the carriages.

'They look efficient,' said Philippa, impressed.

'Very.'

'It obviously happens all the time, people forgetting stuff, leaving stuff behind.'

'*Un Chien Andalou!*', cried Julie. '*That* was the film I was telling you about!'

And she punched the air in triumph.

'Well done,' said Philippa.

By the time they had managed to recover the lost varifocals from the Supervisor's office, their spirits were high and still rising. Sunlight flooded the station concourse and stopped them in their tracks for a moment. They stood side by side, blinking, smiling.

'This train will terminate here,' came a station announcement. 'Cockfosters Station. This is the end of the line.'

'But not for us,' quipped Philippa, laughing, patting her friend's arm.[29]

Enfield

Further east, towards the A10 and the River Lea, the area was wooded and renowned for its rich pasture. The famed royal hunting grounds of Enfield Chase were enclosed by the twelfth century. Surprisingly, the area was also home to modern industry: the Royal Small Arms Factory opened in 1816, later producing such world-famous weapons as Lee–Enfield rifles and Bren light machine guns, and the Edison & Swan United Electric Light Company, progenitor of mass electronics manufacturing, opened up in nearby Ponders End in 1883.

Enfield's remoteness was ideal for schools. In the summer of 1803 the eight-year-old John Keats was sent to board at John Clarke's school in Enfield, an enlightened and progressive place, as Keats's biographer Robert Gittings tells us: 'small dormitories and family surroundings in a converted private house, a rural setting where the boys had their own garden plots, complete an almost idyllic picture'.[30] The school building was converted into Enfield station (later Enfield Town) in 1849 with the arrival of the Eastern Counties Railway; its brick facade, once attributed to Sir Christopher Wren, was dismantled in 1872 and acquired by the Victoria & Albert Museum, although it is now in storage.

> Keats's own contemporaries generally had his own prosperous middle-class background, but developed in widely varied ways, as musicians, artists, writers and lawyers. It was a school where character was appreciated as much as intellect, which accounts for the acceptance of Keats himself for, according to a contemporary, Edward Holmes, he was 'not in childhood attached to books'. His passion was, as several accounts confirm, for fighting, and, as Holmes goes on to say, 'He was a boy whom any one from his extraordinary vivacity & personal beauty might easily have fancied would become great – but rather in some military capacity than in literature'.[31]

In 1827 Charles and Mary Lamb consider a retreat from busy Islington to rural Enfield. On 9 August, Charles Lamb wrote to a friend: 'I write from Enfield, where we are seriously weighing the advantages of dulness over the over-excitement of too much company, but have not yet come to a conclusion.'[32] By mid-September they have moved, as he tells the poet Thomas Hood:

> Our new domicile is no manor house; but new, & externally not inviting, but furnish'd within with every convenience. Capital new locks to every door, capital grates in every room, with nothing to pay for incoming & the rent £10 less than the Islington one . . .
>
> It is not our intention to abandon Regent Street, & West End perambulations (monastic and terrible thought!), but occasion-ally to breathe the FRESHER AIR of the metropolis. We shall put up a bedroom or two (all we want) for occasional ex-rustication, where we shall visit, not be visited. Plays too, we'll see, – perhaps our own; Urbani Sylvani *and Sylvan Urbanuses* in turn. Courtiers for a spurt, then philosophers. Old, homely tell-truths and

learn-truths in the virtuous shades of Enfield, Liars again and mocking gibers in the coffee-houses & resorts of London. What can a mortal desire more for his bi-parted nature?

O, the curds & cream you shall eat with us here!

O, the turtle soup and lobster sallads we shall devour with you there!

O, the old books we shall peruse here!

O, the new nonsense we shall peruse over there!

O, Sir T. Browne, here!

O, Mr Hood and Mr Jerdan, there![33]

The novelist and travel writer Norman Lewis recalls an Edwardian childhood at Enfield Chase:

Forty Hill was once the northernmost place from which people might commute to London. It was on the borders of Enfield Chase, a landscape covered with ancient oaks, many of them hollow, cleared, in the far past, of human habitation by terrible kings, and designed for hunting stags. The land and its hamlets were owned and ruled by Colonel Sir Henry Ferryman Bowles, a sporadically benevolent tyrant who would not have been out of place in Tsarist Russia. Further sharers in this rural emptiness were the Meux brewery dynasty and Field Marshal French, commander of the British Expeditionary Force during the First World War. He retired here in advance of the great slaughter on the Somme, having publicly admitted that this was a war he did not understand, and that could only be won by trebling the number of cavalry engaged up to that date.[34]

Enfield's isolation here pulls the place back into the past:

Isolation in relatively empty country, crossed with byroads going nowhere in particular, had never quite released the village from the previous century. An early photograph of it could have been of Russia in about 1913, with small houses of all shapes scattered about a ragged little prairie remaining deep in mud or dust according to the season. Livings in Forty Hill, too, had always been scraped, and this, added to its cut-off location, made the place a sort of museum of outworn social attitudes that could only be remedied by more freedom of movement and more cash in pockets.[35]

Palmers Green

Just south of Enfield, Palmers Green had the distinction of being home to novelist and poet Stevie Smith for over sixty years. Smith, aged three, moved into a large late Victorian semi in Avondale Road with her parents and lived there for the rest of her life. The 1949 essay 'A London Suburb' sees Palmers Green in positive, life-affirming terms, 'wide open to the sky', and as a 'cheap place for families to live in and have children and gardens'. There, 'behind the fishnet curtains', lie not nasty secrets but life lived, 'family life – father's chair, uproar, dogs, babies and radio'. Smith's poems and novels paint a comic and breezy view of the messy and optimistic suburb.[36]

Smith could also be ambivalent about the joys of life in Palmers Green, as in her 1937 poem 'The Suburban Classes', voicing, with complex glee, some very common anti-suburban prejudices. Suburbanites are seen as stupid, lazy, far too numerous and, somehow, un-British: 'Menacing the greatness of our beloved England, they lie / Propagating their kind in an eight-roomed stye.'[37] The poem's ambivalent tone continues, speaking of 'a plan left to unfold'. This turns out to be a Swiftian 'Modest Proposal'-style scheme to eliminate all suburbanites by persuading them, using various means – 'it won't hurt' – to commit mass suicide.[38] The narrator of Smith's best-known novel, *Novel on Yellow Paper* (1936), also makes use of Palmers Green:

> My fiancé and I, did I say that my fiancé Freddy and I both live at Bottle Green? This is a healthy residential district to the north of London. None of your Hampsteads or Highgates or Golders Greens, but just straight north in a line with Enfield, which is where they make small arms and have a market place and a residential district even superior to Bottle Green.[39]

Where the somewhat detached narrator, Pompey, does not see herself as a typical product of the suburb ('I do not know it myself'), Freddy is supposedly the expert, for he 'certainly knows a whole lot about the people of Bottle Green, and he is a very keen observer is Freddy'.[40]

What *she* sees is lots of competitive snobbery and a squalid scramble for women to get married: 'The social round in England is very complicated, very intricate, but it is always the same in this way. Everybody is always trying to be the next step up.'[41]

> But now I must come back to the subject of Bottle Green. It is rather fascinating this subject. Yes it is rather fascinating this Bottle Green where I live, and where Freddy knows about the people. They have an idea you know, the unmarried girls have an idea, that if only they were married it would be all right, and the married women think, Well now I am married, so it *is* all right: Sometimes too of course it is all right, but sometimes they have to work very hard saying all the time: So now I am married, so now it is all right, so Miss So-and-So is not married, so that is not all right. So what.
>
> And the girls who are not married are often getting quite desperate oh yes they are becoming quite desperate, they are saying all the time, it is like the refrain in Three Sisters. It is the *leitmotiv* of all their lives. It is their Moscow. Marriage is to them: Oh if we could only go to Moscow. Oh if we could only get to Moscow.[42]

Ponders End

Ponders End is just east of Enfield, over towards the Lea Valley. You have to go through Ponders End in order to get to Gerald Kersh's fictional destination *Fowlers End* (1957), though you may not want to:

> This is how you find Fowlers End – by going northward, step by step, into the neighbourhoods that most strongly repel you. The compass of your revulsion may flicker for a moment at the end of the Tottenham Court Road . . . go ahead up Camden High Street towards the Camden Road, and so to Holloway, where the jail is; and past the allurements of this enclosed space, through the perpetual twilight of Seven Sisters Road, which takes you to Tottenham, where the only distraction is the Isolation Hospital for Infectious Diseases. Do not be led astray by this; go north to Edmonton and Ponders End. Who Ponder was and how he ended, the merciful God knows . . . Farther

yet, bearing north-east . . . there sprawls Fowlers Folly . . .
Some vestige of the ruin remains. Only a mile farther on . . .
is Fowlers End.

   Here the city gives up the game.
   This is it.[43]

We get a detailed description of the horrors of the place.

   Fowlers End is a special kind of tundra that supports nothing
   gracious in the way of flora and fauna. Plant a cabbage here
   in this soured, embittered, dyspeptic, ulcerated soil, and up
   comes a kind of bleached shillelagh with spikes on its knob.
   Plant a family, a respectable working-class family, and in two
   generations it will turn out wolves. Fowlers End is barren of
   everything but weeds. Even the dogs are throwbacks to their
   yellow-eyed predatory ancestors that slunk in the trail of the
   sub-men and ate filth. There is a High Street about a hundred
   yards long, and the most woebegone railway terminal on the
   face of the earth where, with a dismal and sinister smashing and
   groaning of shunting locomotives, all that is most unserviceable
   in the way of rolling stock comes in with coal and sulphur,
   scrap iron and splintery timber, and goes away with the stuff
   they make in the Fowlers End Factories . . .

   And what a High Street it was, in my time! Except for a
   few clumps of rusty television antennae, I don't think that
   the place will have changed that much unless some German
   bomb, well placed for once, happened to fall near-by – in
   which case, good riddance to it! It wouldn't have taken much
   more than a five-hundred-pounder to make rubble of the
   entire High Street, which, when I last measured it when I
   stepped out of the Pantheon to clear my lungs with a whiff of
   comparatively healthful carbon monoxide and sulphuric acid
   after a Children's Matinee, measured exactly eighty-five long
   paces from Godbolts Corner to the end of the tram line where
   Fowlers End begins.[44]

Tottenham and Edmonton

Moving back south, crossing the North Circular and passing down the Lea Valley, Tottenham, around 6.5 miles north of London Bridge, seems originally to have been Toteham, or 'Tota's hamlet', and developed along the old Roman Ermine Street (now the A10). By 1600 Tottenham was a thriving village, well known for its sparkling brooks and rivers and rural charm. An 1872 rail link from Enfield down to Liverpool Street stimulated development and by the 1890s the usual elements of the Victorian suburb were in place: music halls, theatres, pubs, light industry and streets of modest two-up, two-down semis and terraces. Tottenham suffered the usual post-war decline and neglect. It is probably best known today as the site of 1985's Broadwater Farm riot.

Tottenham's rural charms were set out in Izaak Walton's meditative *The Compleat Angler* (claimed to be the third most printed book in English, after the Bible and Bunyan's *Pilgrim's Progress*), which features a dialogue between wise veteran angler 'Piscator' and keen student and disciple 'Venator', on a rambling walk from 'Tottenham Hill' up to fish on the River Lea at Ware, Hertfordshire. Piscator explains:

> we are now almost at Tottenham, where I first met you, and where we are to part, I will lose no time, but give you a little direction how to make and order your lines, and to colour the hair of which you make your lines, for that is very needful to be known of an angler.[45]

The journey around Tottenham, through pleasant pastures and shady lanes, continues:

> Well, Scholar, having now taught you to paint your rod, and we having still a mile to Tottenham High-Cross, I will, as we walk towards it in the cool shade of this sweet honey-suckle hedge, mention to you some of the thoughts and joys that have possessed my soul since we two met together.[46]

At the end of the walk Venator is very grateful and has found a great place to sit and drink:

Pray let's now rest ourselves in this sweet shady arbour, which nature herself has woven with her own fine fingers; 'tis such a contexture of woodbines, sweetbriar, jasmine, and myrtle, and so interwoven, as will secure us both from the sun's violent heat, and from the approaching shower. And being sat down, I will requite a part of your courtesies with a bottle of sack, milk, oranges, and sugar, which, all put together, make a drink like nectar; indeed, too good for any but us Anglers.[47]

Daniel Defoe in his *A Tour through the Whole Island of Great Britain* notes suburban patterns emerging as early as 1725 (as has already been noted for Stoke Newington in Chapter Eight). He went on to add that in

especially *Tottenham* and *Edmonton*, the New Buildings so far exceed the Old, especially in the value of them, and figure of the inhabitants, that the fashion of the Towns are quite altered . . . [The buildings] generally belong to the middle sort of Mankind, grown Wealthy by Trade, and who still taste of London; some of them live both in the City, and in the Country at the same time: yet many of them are immensely Rich.[48]

Edmonton, just to the north, features in John Cowper's extremely popular ballad 'The Diverting History of John Gilpin' (1782), which describes the exploits of a City draper who sets out to be married at Edmonton, but is carried further off by his wayward horse:

Thus all through merry Islington
These gambols he did play,
Until he came unto the Wash
Of Edmonton so gay;

And there he threw the Wash about
On both sides of the way,
Just like unto a trundling mop,
Or a wild goose at play.
At Edmonton, his loving wife
From the balcony spied

Her tender husband, wondering much
To see how he did ride.

Stop, stop, John Gilpin! – Here's the house!
They all at once did cry;
The dinner waits, and we are tired;
Said Gilpin – So am I![49]

The infamous 1909 'Tottenham Outrage' involved a melodramatic
wages snatch by two Jewish-Latvian anarchists at the Schnurmann
rubber factory, and a resulting two-hour chase, involving dozens of
police and public, through Tottenham, across the River Lea and the
Tottenham Marshes, into Walthamstow and up to Epping Forest.
The pursuit involved, at various points, bicycles, a delivery cart, two
number 9 trams, a milk float, a horse and cart and a car. A policeman
and a young bystander died, as well as both robbers, who had fired
about four hundred rounds of ammunition. M. H. Baylis's novel *The
Tottenham Outrage* (2014) is based on this event, as a character, Rex,
discovers from a local history specialist, Dr Kovacs:

> 'So what evidence makes you conclude that people might be
> interested in a robbery that happened here in 1909?'
> 'It was the first hint of the Tottenham we live in now.
> Global, multicultural, connected. Latvian anarchists com-
> mitting crimes in London to fund acts of terror in Russia.
> Robbing a factory so dependent on a casual ever-shifting
> immigrant workforce that the bosses weren't even aware
> Helfeld and Lapidus had been on the payroll under false
> names. A rubber factory, I should add, that processed latex
> from our colonies in Singapore and India into bicycle-tyres
> for use on the cobbles of Tottenham.'[50]

Tottenham is visited in 1921 by Thomas Burke in his guide to
peripheral London, *The Outer Circle*:

> If you start from Holloway and pursue Seven Sisters Road to
> its end you will come to Tottenham. You may exclaim: 'Who
> on earth wants to come to Tottenham?' Well, quite a number
> of people live at Tottenham, and thousands of strangers go

regularly to Tottenham, not to see the parish church, or the
room where Queen Elizabeth slept, but to see the game of
football played at the ground of the Tottenham Hotspurs.

I first went to Tottenham one fine Saturday, when I had
nothing better to do. I had not meant to go to Tottenham.
A tramcar, labelled Waltham Cross, attracted me at Tottenham
Court Road by its bright colour and firm lines. I boarded it.
Until then my journey along Seven Sisters Road had ceased at
Finsbury Park. There seemed no just cause for going further.[51]

Burke is pleased that he made the trip:

There is a heartiness about it that comes refreshingly to the
visitor from Highgate, where heartiness is forbidden. Joy
persists. There are still songs to be sung. Here are still groups of
those who hear the chimes at midnight from All Hallows', and
play their pranks beneath the minatory chimneys that adjoin
the recreation ground. Here are still girls and gardens, and
moonrise, bold ribbons, shy silks and muslins; and the hearts
of the boys beat bravely. 'Back to her nest comes the swallows in
the Spring-time,' whispers Rodolphe in *La Bohème*; and if you
go to Tottenham at the time of the breaking of buds, you will
see in the faces of the factory boys and girls the recurrent throb
of beauty. While Highgate's motto reads: 'It *looks* so bad,' the
motto of Tottenham is: 'Who cares?'

They live well at Tottenham.[52]

Writer and occultist Arthur Machen is on a journey in search
of Tottenham Hale (see Chapter Eight). He recalls how this strange
obsession started:

I saw a queer little omnibus 'inside only', shoot around a corner
from nowhere in particular, pause a moment and shoot off, as
it declared, in the direction of Tottenham Hale . . . I had never
heard of such a place. I have made various inquiries again and
again, and I have not yet encountered anybody else who has
heard of it. And as I am a desirer of mysteries and unknown
things, I resolved that I would one day set forth and find
Tottenham Hale.[53]

After travelling up through north London by bus, Machen gets closer and closer, and it does not disappoint:

> And at first I was inclined to say: 'Where there is Tottenham Hale there is nothing.' It seems a void chaos of building, without limit, without meaning, without centre, lacking circumference. But by degrees its waste elements resolve themselves into some kind of a picture. I see coils of black smoke issuing sluggishly from tall factory chimneys; I see clouds of white steam rising from the yard of some works. There is no glimpse of open country, no prospect of high lands before me . . . There are roads in all directions which I cannot think lead to anything desirable, even if they lead anywhere at all, which I am inclined to doubt. There are sheds and workshops everywhere and fried fish seems the favourite delicacy and its stench contends with the reek of some nameless refuse crackling and reeking and smoking in a Gahanna fenced with corrugated iron. A grim place enough and if it reminds me of anything it is of the outskirts and back parts of an industrial town in Lancashire.[54]

In Ian McEwan's *The Innocent* (1990), Leonard Marnham returns to boring 1950s Tottenham for Christmas, back from thrilling sex and espionage work in West Berlin.

> And Tottenham, and all of London, was sunk in Sunday torpor. People were drowning in ordinariness. In his street the parallel walls of Victorian terraces were the end of all change. Nothing that mattered could ever happen here. There was no tension, no purpose. What interested the neighbours was the prospect of hiring or owning a television. The H-shaped aerials were sprouting on the rooftops. On Friday evenings his parents popped into the house two doors down to watch, and they were saving hard, having sensibly set their hearts against hire-purchase . . . The great struggle to keep Europe free was as remote as the canals of Mars. Down at his father's pub, none of the regulars had even heard of the Warsaw Pact, the ratification of which had caused such a stir in Berlin.[55]

Gretta Mulrooney's *Araby* (1998) follows Irish Londoner Rory Keenan returning to Ireland to see his dying mother, who had emigrated initially from Cork to Tottenham, and then back again, after selling 'their modest terraced house in Tottenham for an eighties-inflated profit beyond their dreams'.[56] That was ten years ago. He exchanges birthday and Christmas cards with his brother in Hong Kong, but otherwise knows nothing of his extended family:

> They had all emigrated to England and gone their various ways with negligible contact. My mother hardly ever spoke about her brothers and sisters, didn't even know where her youngest brother lived . . . Growing up in Tottenham I was surrounded by children who had close-knit families. My friends would come to school talking about the presents they received from aunts and uncles for their birthdays, family trips and holidays taken with cousins, celebratory family occasions. I would listen with envy and a sense of displacement, unable to reveal that I did have aunts, uncles and cousins, but I didn't see them because they had been adopted or gone missing or because there was no contact. It all seemed somehow shameful in comparison to my friends' wholesome networks . . . it added to my feeling of not quite belonging.[57]

For urban explorer Mark Mason, in *Walk the Lines* (2011), in which he traces the Tube lines by walking them above ground, Tottenham Hale is pretty much the end:

> The bridge continues over water. At first it's just the River Lee, whose houseboats lend a vaguely rustic feel but don't mark an end to the city. Soon, though, huge expanses of shimmering blue open up on either side – the reservoirs that separate Tottenham from Walthamstow . . . They really are the point at which London ends . . . In the distance, to the south, you can see Canary Wharf. But it *is* the distance. The towers there are part of London. This isn't.[58]

In the mid-2010s, Gary Budden and Kit Caless had an epiphany in a Tottenham branch of Subway:

The idea germinated in Tottenham Hale Retail Park . . . A walk through the park's rectangular brandscape of Aldi, Staples, Burger King, Poundland, Subway, Greggs and Argos is a walk through modern London.

It's a place where normal Londoners go about their day; passing through on their way to Tottenham Hale station or stopping off to get groceries for the evening. It's bland and functional. It is only used by people who know it is there. It feels out of date, yet part of the future. It is dull. And it is average. But it contains a wealth of stories just like any other part of the city.

It was here that the idea of *An Unreliable Guide to London* [their 2016 book] developed. Sitting in Subway we stuffed our mouths with meatball marinara and wondered why publishers weren't printing books set in the parts of London that we knew and interacted with on a daily basis. Why weren't writers writing about them? What novels had we read set in Hanwell, Cricklewood or Barking? These parts of the capital can feel like another world, another site that exists on the periphery of the imagined, lived in by millions.[59]

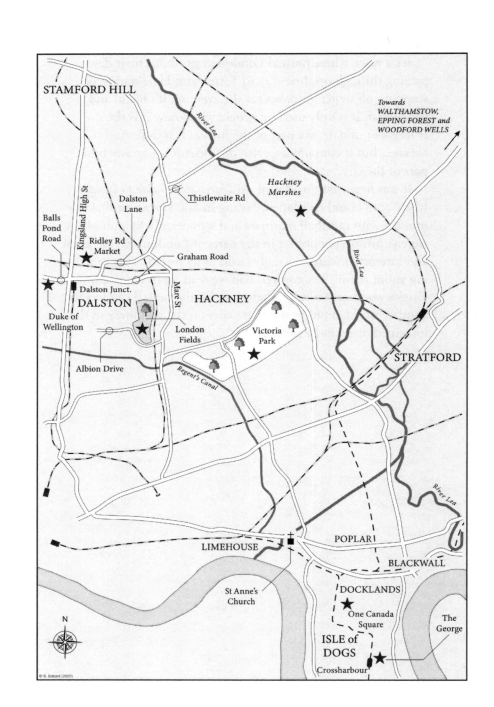

STAMFORD HILL

River Lea

Towards
WALTHAMSTOW,
EPPING FOREST and
WOODFORD WELLS

Hackney
Marshes

Dalston
Lane

Thistlewaite Rd

Balls
Pond
Road

Ridley Rd
Market

Kingsland High St

Graham Road

River Lea

Mare St

HACKNEY

Dalston Junct.

DALSTON

London
Fields

Victoria
Park

Duke of
Wellington

STRATFORD

Albion Drive

Regent's Canal

River Lea

POPLAR

LIMEHOUSE

BLACKWALL

DOCKLANDS

St Anne's
Church

One Canada
Square

The
George

ISLE of
DOGS

Crossharbour

N

© S. Ballard (2020)

11 'THE ODOUR OF OLD STONE'
East London: From Dalston to Hackney, Walthamstow, Stratford and the Isle of Dogs

London's eastward spread, beyond the City walls at Aldgate and Tower Hill, was quite piecemeal until the early eighteenth century. Until this point Hackney was a favoured rural spot, with streams, meadows, woodland and teeming market gardens, an ideal spot for the likes of Samuel Pepys to take an afternoon off. Increasing development, with docks, shipbuilding and industry along the Thames, and then the Regent's Canal and railways, soon changed all this, and Hackney was densely urban and industrial by the mid-nineteenth century. Destruction during the Blitz, de-industrialization, urban decay and 'white flight' in the 1950s in turn gave way to a radicalized Hackney from the later 1960s, as a form of counter-cultural gentrification arrived. Artists, radicals, anarchists, squatters, and then punks and crusties, moved into the rotting and freezing early Victorian terraces and villas – including, of course, that obsessive investigator of hidden, secret and obliterated London, Iain Sinclair. Since the 1990s Hackney has morphed yet again in ways that even Sinclair finds confusing: gentrifiers and hipsters on the one hand; and new groups of migrants (Kurdish, Turkish, Vietnamese) on the other.

Dalston

Dalston, straggled around the A10 about 3 miles north of London Bridge, is where fashionable Islington and Highbury come up against the far grubbier outer East End. A leafy Hackney Village for centuries, then a fashionable Victorian suburb, close to the City, Dalston declined in the 1960s and '70s, becoming attractive to hippies, squatters and newer immigrants – Turkish Cypriots, West African and from the Caribbean, following in the footsteps of earlier nineteenth-century Jewish refugees from Eastern Europe. Dalston is sort of in the East End (inspiring 'Walford' in the BBC's *EastEnders*), is ethnically and culturally diverse, and today rapidly gentrifying and newly accessible with the revival of the Overground line into this notoriously Tube-less sector, and with the Ridley Road market as a huge draw.

Roland Camberton's *Rain on the Pavements* (1951) is set in 1930s Dalston and Hackney and follows the life of one David Hirsch from age six to young adulthood. This is noisy, chaotic, pre-war Orthodox Jewish Dalston:

> Mrs Goldstein had a great deal to put up with on account of the vast, high wall of the corner house which backed so conveniently on to Brenton Street. It was known throughout Dalston, Hackney, Stoke Newington, Dibley and Clapton as positively the best wall on which to play wall-ey. It was so high and so broad, and it was windowless. The continual thump of balls against her kitchen and bedroom above drove Mrs Goldstein to distraction. She fought an energetic, though losing battle with the hordes of purposeful urchins who came, holding tennis balls, rubber balls, discarded golf balls, to shatter the quiet gloom of Brenton Street and play on her wall. By threats and appeals to parents, she was able to thin out the volley of local balls; but even so, on late summer evenings, lads whom no one knew, who jeered their menaces, found their way to peaceful Brenton Street and remorselessly pounded her wall with balls and, apparently, bricks.

The meeting beneath her wall of the Dibley Jewish Circle (Youth Section) would be a new source of annoyance.[1]

As Hirsch gets older he explores Dalston and its surroundings with his uncle, just three years his senior:

> David and Yunkel flung out their outposts to Hampstead and Purley and Wandsworth and Richmond, but failed to hold their enormous tracts of territory. They might carve their initials on a tree in Clapham Common, but on returning four months later, they scarcely even knew the right tram stop at which to get off.

On the other hand, exploration with Philip, if less ambitious, was more thorough. David and Philip set out to conquer only the boroughs immediately bordering Hackney, Dalston and Dibley – Stamford Hill, Stoke Newington, Clapton, Homerton, Cambridge Heath, and Bethnal Green on the one side; and Highbury, Islington, Hoxton, and Shoreditch on the other.

It was necessary to know every alley, every cul-de-sac, every arch, every passageway; every school, every hospital, every church, every synagogue; every police station, every post office, every labour exchange, every lavatory; every curious shop name, every kids' gang, every hiding place, every muttering old man . . . In fact, everything; and having got to know everything, they had to hold this information firmly, to keep abreast of change, to locate the new position of beggars, newsboys, hawkers, street shows, gypsies, political meetings.[2]

Ridley Road market is a favoured location:

> So Ridley it was. Yes. King Anthony was back, surrounded by a large crowd which listened seriously and even glumly to his analysis of Tudor and Hanoverian genealogy. The fire-swallowing man was there, furiously swallowing fire – ah to hell with the man! They decided to go. Let him go on swallowing fire! The manacled man writhed among his chains. There was a sharp snap which they thought at first might be his red and bursting neck, but which turned out to be the thick, massive chain again . . . The fishmongers, clothes dealers, cut-price confectioners, whelk-sellers, oyster-mongers, tattooists, blowers up of balloons, clairvoyants, comic-dealer, and discreet salesmen of toilet goods, murmured their comments, roared their cries; while bulging housewives, and others with pinched faces and five or six pale, snotty, whimpering children, protested and fingered and shoved. Amid the hoarse cries, the heaving crowd, and beneath the flickering, lurid lights of flares hissing from the tops of stalls, David and Philip wormed their way, holding hands for safety.[3]

The *Luftmensch* – literally 'airman', referring to an impractical dreamer and loafer – 'Harryboy' Boas in Alexander Baron's *The Lowlife* is in trouble. Evading gangsters on Stoke Newington High Street, he jumps on a southbound bus and heads to Dalston Junction:

> I sat on the rear bench of the bus and watched them through the back platform window. With an interest as unconcealed as my own the little man watched me through the windscreen of the Buick.
>
> We were coming into a more crowded part of the main road, where it becomes the Kingsland High Street. People thickened on the pavement, groups of boys and girls singing and yoo-hooing, people coming out of cinemas, the last stalls packing up in Ridley Road market and the last shoppers coming away, and the groups thickening into crowds as we neared the busiest crossroads in this part of London, Dalston Junction.
>
> For my purposes it didn't matter which way the traffic lights went at the Junction. In fact they were red. The bus pulled up as the pavement thickly crowded, and without any warning to my pursuers I swung by the handrail round from my seat, off the platform, slipping away into the crowd. Let them try to touch me in the middle of this mob. I didn't look back to see how they were coping with the problem of the crowds and of the traffic lights. I darted through the crowd and round the corner into Dalston Lane. The buses come down here almost in convoy. A few blocks up they separate, some following the curve of Dalston Lane and some going up Graham Road. Once again, either way suited me. I had chosen my ground.[4]

In the late 1960s, 99 Balls Pond Road, leading into Dalston Junction, was briefly the location for the Exploding Gallery, an influential squat-commune-collective that partly aimed to break down the barriers between art and everyday life. Poet Hugo Williams was there:

> It was the time of Kinetic Art and David [Medalla] was curator of Signals Gallery in Wigmore Street. Art was moving away from my protected world, but Hermine kept after it. Soon after we got married and moved into a house in Islington, Medalla instigated The Exploding Gallery Advance Drama, a commune in nearby Balls Pond Road. They would come

around for communal hot baths and snacks, there being no services at No.99. Hermine would go jumble-saling with them, or scrudging (looking for things in the street). It was now that our marriage took a crash course in hippie. Dance dramas were performed at the Roundhouse and Parliament Hill, where we later had annual birthday parties for our daughter, like a kind of ghost tribute to The Galaxy. In those days I was about half way between the thinking of The Galaxy and that of the other inhabitants of Balls Pond Road. Today I feel more sympathetic to what they were trying to do, which was personified for me by the form of Jill Drower, flitting magically through psychedelic happenings like a dryad of the night.[5]

In J. M. O'Neill's novel of 1980s Irish London, *Duffy Is Dead*, mentioned earlier, Robert Calnan runs the grotty Trade Winds pub at Dalston Junction. O'Neill himself was the landlord of the Irish pub The Duke of Wellington on Balls Pond Road throughout the 1970s (see Chapter Eight):

> The Trade Winds was alive; heat, smoke, a wavering shout of conversation enveloped him like a spouse as he pushed in the swing doors; his name was called out everywhere so that, in the style of some proletarian despot, he smiled at no one in particular, raised a hand in salutation as he moved.
>
> Morgan in full flow, covered the ring of the bar, smooth, effortless, on ice; his helpers, as smart as paint, Blondie and Sher, in flimsy skirts and tops, hard as nails, could giggle laughter, shout or spit, outswear a navvy. Calnan nodded; they smiled and winked, Morgan brought over a measure of brandy, a glass of beer.[6]

Calnan walks everywhere in this area where north London meets east:

> He walked the long stretch from Dalston to Shoreditch Church and stood looking at the roads fanning out to Hackney, Bethnal Green, Gardiner's Corner, the City, London Bridge, Clerkenwell. This was his London, always traces of elegance but like himself growing old. Shoreditch Church, at the gates of the City, was always reassuring in the stillness of early morning.[7]

Dalston Junction has attracted London's more unorthodox and interesting urban commentators. 'What is to be done about Dalston Junction?'[8] asks Patrick Wright in *A Journey Through Ruins*, detailing the place in 1991, just at the time when 'inner-city' London was at its post-war, post-Thatcher low point. Dalston seems chaotic, broken and traffic-choked, neglected and dangerous; 'I'm familiar with its vicious side,' Wright explains:

> I've seen the squalor and the main signs of grinding poverty . . .
> I've studied the psychotic antics of the man who spends a lot
> of his time on the traffic island at Lebon's Corner, reading the
> cracks in the asphalt and cleaning them out with a stick . . .
>
> Blight has its hideous aspect but, as I try to convince un-
> believing visitors, it can resemble a condition of grace. Dalston
> Lane is a jumble of residential, commercial and industrial
> activities, but zoning is not the only kind of development on
> which this street, if not its surrounding area, has missed out.
> In the Fifties it escaped the kind of standardization Ian Nairn
> described as subtopia ('Subtopia is the annihilation of the site,
> the steamrollering of all individuality of place to one uniform
> and mediocre pattern') . . .
>
> On Dalston Lane time itself seems to lie around in broken
> fragments: you can drop in on previous decades with no more
> effort than it takes to open a shop door. Pizzey's High Class
> Florist is still trading out of the Fifties, and the Star Bakery . . .
> offers immediate access to the decade before that. Until a year
> or so ago there was even a time-warped estate agency, advertis-
> ing houses at twenty-year-old prices. People would pause there
> and marvel at the opportunities they had missed.
>
> This has a human aspect, to be sure. The people of Dalston
> Lane have their own ways of being in the world. They walk
> about in a distinctly unsuburban manner and without neces-
> sarily following what planners would recognize as a proper 'line
> of pedestrian desire'. They saunter and dawdle and fail to wait
> for the green light before crossing the road. They hang about
> without apparent purpose. They do things remarkably slowly, if
> at all. They indulge in habits that are being extirpated from the
> national culture.[9]

Dalston is also, of course, catnip to Iain Sinclair, living just south-east of Dalston, towards London Fields. On their initial expedition from Hackney to Greenwich in *Lights Out for the Territory* (1997), Sinclair and Marc Atkins are

> closing on the junction, the crossroads, the epicentre of the notional Dalston Town . . .
>
> The quadrivium, or meeting place of four roads, is the spiritual centre of the area through which we are walking; it's where suicides and vampires would receive their toothpick through the heart. On the east/west axis, the hobbled spurt of Dalston Lane, labouring gamely under the burden of cultural significance imposed upon it by Patrick Wright in *A Journey Through Ruins*, goes head-to-head with Peter Sellers' comedic Balls Bond Road. And to the north, Ermine Street, lightly disguised as Kingsland High Street (Stoke Newington Road, Stoke Newington High Street), makes a bid for Stamford Hill, White Hart Lane and other inconsequential destinations. This cruciform reef of shops, stalls and small businesses, has died and returned to life more times than RL Stevenson's Master of Ballantrae. Not so much a failed shopping centre as a car boot sale in an open prison, tactfully invigilated by security guards in peaked caps.[10]

Lily Bloom is dead in Will Self's *How the Dead Live* (2000), yet finds herself in an afterlife retaining some dimly familiar London features: mainly the two key suburbs of the dead, 'Dulburb' (Dulwich) in the south, and 'Dulston' in the north.

> 'Like I say, girl – we're goin' to Dulston; it's a 'burb like any other, yeh-hey?'
>
> 'And where is Dulston?' The minicab has nosed on to Pentonville Road. 'I mean, we appear to be heading in the direction of Dalston.'
>
> 'Yairs, well. It's right alongside of it, y'know. It's like a skinny district, yeh? One minute yer on the Kingsland Road, the next turnin' into Dalston Lane. If yer not quick you can miss Dulston.'
>
> 'So, it's between Islington to the west and Dalston to the east?'

'Thass right.'

'And what's to the south?'

'Dalston again.'

'And the north?'

'Stoke Newington.'

'That doesn't make any sense. There isn't anything between these parts of London. Not unless Dulston is a made-up estate agents' kind of place.'

'Could be that. Could be y'don't know London quite as well as you think.'[11]

Dulston turns out to be a 'cystrict'; a kind of featureless London inter-zone where the dead turn up, but also somewhere the living pass through; and the living *don't notice*:

Dulston is even more characterless than other inner North East London suburbs I've known. The overwhelming impression the place gives is of colourlessness, an indifference towards municipal airs and graces.

Dulston is one of those districts you're always finding your-self lost in, rather than arriving at. It's the place you wind up in when you overshoot your destination or take the wrong turn. It's the 'burb as displacement activity . . . I realise that Dulston must be as big or as small as its beholders. It's a hidden pleat in the city's rolled-up sleeve; an invisible flare flapping in its trouser leg; a vent in the back of its jacket. Presumably, if the living stray into Dulston they see noth-ing of its true nature. For them it's merely a drive-by span of inattention, a glimpse of their own speeding car warped in a showroom window – before they find themselves traversing Hackney Marsh, or gawping at the Stamford Hill frummers, or heading into town. Dulston; you wouldn't know you were there at all – unless you were dead.[12]

Martin Amis's state-of-the-nation as dystopian grotesquery, *Lionel Asbo* (2012), takes place in the hellish, fictional 'London Borough of Diston' in east London: 'To evoke the London borough of Diston', Amis tells us, 'we turn to the poetry of Chaos: Each thing hostile / To every other thing: at every point / Hot fought cold, moist dry, soft hard, and the weightless / Resisted weight'.[13] Something malevolent is at work here:

> In Diston there were many thousands of pylons, and they all sizzled. The worst stretch of Cuttle Canal was as active as a geyser: it spat and splatted, blowing thick-lipped kisses to the hastening passers-by. Beyond Jupes Lanes sprawled Stung Meanchey (so christened by its inhabitants, who were Korean), a twelve-acre dump of house-high electronic waste, old computers, televisions, phones and fridges: lead, mercury, beryllium, aluminium. Diston hummed. Background radiation, background music for a half-life of fifty-five years.[14]

All this has had a curious impact on Diston's inhabitants. First, Desmond Pepperdine, at his school, Squeers Free, seems miraculously unscathed by this environment:

> On the face of it, Des was a prime candidate for persecution. He seldom bunked off, he never slept in class, he didn't assault the teachers or shoot up in the toilets – and he preferred the company of the gentler sex (the gentler sex, at Squeers Free, being quite rough enough). So in the normal course of things Des would have been savagely bullied, as all the other misfits (swats, wimps, four-eyes, sweating fatties) were savagely bullied – to the brink of suicide and beyond.[15]

For Desmond's uncle Lionel, it's a bit different:

> He was served his first Restraining Directive when he was three. Three years and two days: a national record (though disputed by other claimants). This was for smashing car wind-screens with paving stones; the authorities also noted his habit, when out shopping with his mother, of booting over display pyramids of bottles and tin cans; a childish interest in cruelty to animals was perhaps only to be expected, but Lionel went further, and one night made a serious attempt to torch a pet shop. Had he come along half a generation later, Lionel's first Restraining Directive would have been called a BASBO, or Baby ASBO . . . ASBO, which

(as all the kingdom now knew) stood for Anti-Social Behaviour Order.

What was the matter with him? Why did he *work* at being stupid? I mean (thought Des), if you spend about a third of your waking life in court, isn't it a bit bloody daft to change your name, by deed poll, on your eighteenth birthday, from Lionel Pepperdine to Lionel Asbo? All his uncle would say was that *Pepperdine's a crap name anyhow. And Asbo has a nice ring to it.*[16]

Hackney

Central Hackney, for our purposes east from Dalston, and bounded by Hackney Downs and Lower Clapton to the north and Victoria Park to the east, was famed, until the early nineteenth century, for its market gardens, pastures, clean air and healthy pursuits, a haven from the nearby filthy city. Then industry arrived, with timber yards and furniture-making mills along the Lea, then clothing sweatshops, crafts, brewing and manufacturing. Extensive interwar slum clearances meant that streets of Georgian and Victorian houses were swept away, replaced by London County Council flats. The post-war period saw the decline of manufacturing and industry and a fall in population, partly due to 'white flight' migration further out to Hertfordshire and Essex. The area has long been ethnically diverse, with Orthodox Jews arriving from the old East End (Stamford Hill, just to the north, having Europe's largest population of Hasidic Jews) and a large Turkish and Kurdish population: today, around 45 per cent of the population are BAME. Gentrification has now arrived in the shape of converted industrial units, a thriving foodie scene and rising property prices.

Hackney's pastoral charms were much appreciated by Samuel Pepys, who took many restorative trips here up from Seething Lane. Here he is on 25 April 1664:

> Thence, the young ladies going out to visit, I took my wife by coach out through the city, discoursing how to spend the afternoon – and conquered, with much ado, a desire of going to a play. But took her out at White-chapel and to Bednell-green; so to Hackny, where I have not been many a year, since a little child I boarded there. Thence to Kingsland by my nurse's house, Goody Lawrence, where my brother Tom and I was kept

when young. Then to Newington-green and saw the outside of Mrs Herberts house, where she lived, and my aunt Ellen with her; but Lord, how in every point I find myself to over-value things when a child. Thence to Islington, and so to St John's to the Red bull and there saw the latter part of a rude Prize fought – but with good pleasure enough. And thence back to Islington and at the Kings-head, where Pitts lived, we light and eat and drunk for remembrance of the old house sake. And so through Kingsland again and so to Bishopsgate, and so home with great pleasure – the country mighty pleasant; and we with great content home, and after supper to bed.[17]

The first volume of Henry Mayhew's epic *London Labour and the Labour Poor*, compiled in the 1840s, is a pioneering investigation into and analysis of London's myriad 'street-folk'. He notes that suburban Hackney was the centre for one of the oldest of the street trades: muffin- and crumpet-sellers:

> The sellers of muffins and crumpets are a mixed class, but I am told that more of them are the children of bakers, or worn-out bakers, than can be said of any other calling. The best sale is in the suburbs. 'As far as I know, sir,' said a muffin-seller, 'it's the best Hackney way, and Stoke Newington, and Dalston, and Balls Pond, and Islington; where the gents that's in banks – the steady coves of them – goes home to their teas, and the missuses has muffins to welcome them.'[18]

Walter Besant's social-reforming novel *All Sorts and Conditions of Men* (1882) sees two idealistic individuals (both, happily, with some money behind them) devise a plan to build, in the midst of the blighted East End, a 'Palace of Delight', a kind of cultural and educational centre for the area's working classes. The novel, incredibly enough, did in fact lead to the building of the 'People's Palace' on Mile End Road, which was later incorporated into Queen Mary College. The two philanthropists go for a walk from Stepney Green up to Victoria Park, Hackney:

> One Sunday afternoon when they were walking together – it was in one of the warm days of last September – in Victoria

Park, they had a conversation which led to really important things. There are one or two very pretty walks in that garden, and though the season was late, and the leaves mostly yellow, brown, crimson or golden, there were still flowers, and the ornamental water was bright, and the path crowded with people who looked happy, because the sun was shining; they had all dined plentifully with copious beer, and the girls had got on their best things, and the swains were gallant with a flower in the buttonhole and a cigar between the lips. There is, indeed, so little difference between the rich and the poor; can even Hyde Park in the season go beyond the flower and the cigar?[19]

The Gosse family were members of the local Hackney branch of a devout, fundamentalist protestant sect, the Plymouth Brethren, who expected Christ's return at any moment. Edmund Gosse produced, in *Father and Son* (1907), a notorious memoir of his scientist father's religious fanaticism and his own agonized religious doubts (although recently the accuracy of Gosse senior's inflexible severity has been questioned):

'The saints' was the habitual term by which were indicated the friends met on Sunday mornings for Holy Communion, and at many other times in the week for prayer and discussion of the Scriptures, in the small hired hall at Hackney, which my parents attended. I suppose that the solemn dedication of me to the Lord, which was repeated in public in my Mother's arms, being by no means a usual or familiar ceremony even among the Brethren, created a certain curiosity and fervour in the immediate services, or was imagined so to do by the fond, partial heart of my Mother. She, however, who had been so much isolated, now made the care of her child an excuse for retiring still further into silence. With those religious persons who met at the Room, as the modest chapel was called, she had little spiritual and no intellectual sympathy. She noted:
'I do not think it would increase my happiness to be in the midst of the saints at Hackney. I have made up my mind to give myself up to Baby for the winter, and to accept no invitations. To go when I can to the Sunday morning meetings and to see my own Mother.'

The monotony of her existence now became extreme . . . For over three years after their marriage, neither of my parents left London for a single day, not being able to afford to travel. They received scarcely any visitors, never ate a meal away from home, never spent an evening in social intercourse abroad. At night they discussed theology, read aloud to one another, or translated scientific brochures from French or German. It sounds a terrible life of pressure and deprivation, and that it was physically unwholesome there can be no shadow of a doubt.[20]

Playwright Bernard Kops, born in Jewish Stepney Green, recalls visiting his remarried father, in 1954, considering himself to have successfully moved out of the East End (Kops having likewise long escaped to bohemian Soho):

My father had married again, an old Russian woman with milk-white eyes. She was as blind as him, and could only speak Yiddish and Russian.

They lived in a house in Hackney. It was full of old Jewish people with hardly twenty words of English between them, yet they had all been in England for more than fifty years. They listened to Radio Moscow nearly all of the time, ate matzos and drank lemon tea continuously. Old Mr Adler was a very firm man of eighty, looking more like fifty, with his grey-blue eyes. He would completely ignore the criss-cross conversations about fried fish and family and pigeon-hole me in a conversation from across the other side of the room.

'I knew Gorki you know.' He sat silently for a while before continuing. 'He was no fool.' Then he smiled at me, and nodded his head and shrugged.

'What do you think of the terrible news?' my father would say. 'What do you think of the terrible weather,' an old crony would remark.

'What do you think of the wonderful progress in Russia?' 'St Petersburg! There was a city!'

None of them listened to the other. They all spoke all day, all lived in their own different worlds.

I was glad that my father had married again. For since my mother had died, he had been disappearing as a person, swallowing himself alive, but now he managed to walk five miles every day. He had started to collect silver paper for Guide Dogs for the Blind. It was about the only thing he could see in the street. I saw him once down Cambridge Heath Road stooping in the gutter. He spent several hours a week flattening it all out and rolling it into balls. He never took care crossing roads and was knocked over twice, but both times he stood up and walked on again.[21]

Hackney-born Harold Pinter evokes the place in a *New Yorker* interview from 1967:

I lived in a brick house on Thistlewaite Road, near Clapton Pond, which had a few ducks on it. It was a working-class area – some big, run-down Victorian houses, and a soap factory with a terrible smell, and a lot of railway yards. And shops. It had a lot of shops. But down the road a bit from the house there was a river, the Lea River, which is a tributary of the Thames, and if you go up the river two miles you find yourself in a marsh. And near a filthy canal as well. There is a terrible factory of some kind, with an enormous dirty chimney, that shoves things down to this canal.[22]

Evacuated during the Blitz, Pinter returns to Hackney just in time for the first Nazi VI flying bombs ('Doodlebugs') to arrive:

On the day I got back to London, in 1944, I saw the first flying bomb. I was in the street and I saw it come over . . . There were times when I would open our back door and find our garden in flames. Our house never burned, but we had to evacuate several times. Every time we evacuated, I took my cricket bat with me.[23]

Hackney, of course, belongs, really, to Iain Sinclair, prolific walker and psychogeographer, who moved into Albion Drive, in Haggerston, in 1969, almost at random. 'It's a habit I can't break,' he confesses in his study *Hackney, That Rose-Red Empire* (2009), 'the habit of Hackney; writing and walking, thirty years in one house. Thirty years of misreading the signs, making fictions.'[24]

Taking the right fork, into Albion Drive, brings me under the scratchy abundance of a fig tree that overhangs the pavement, heavy with sour-green grenades, polyps, empurpled fruit testicles. As twilight footsteps pad closer, ever closer, I suck the nectars, relishing pointless fecundity. In Hackney, we walk in a constant audition of sound, safe in the membrane of previous experience: the bad thing has not happened. Not yet, never. We are still here, still around; we must have made the right decision, crossed the road at the optimum time, avoided eye contact, jumped back from the kerb before the siren-screaming cop car rocketed over the humpbacked bridge. Motorcyclists slow significantly, sizing up our bags, checking on mobile-phone activity. Cycle bandits, out of nowhere, are at our shoulder. They nudge. Blade carving through straps. This is nothing, a toll on the privilege of living here; a community charge that sometimes, infrequently, steps over the mark: death. No longer a name on the electoral register, a statistic.

Preoccupied, contained in the dream of place, my harmless excursion, one walk fading into the footprint of the last, ruptures. With the breeze of the savage downward stroke, I swerve just enough to deflect the main force of the blow. Pain is nothing: a caressing slice into the skin of a balding cranium, no cerebellum-denting impact. It's a paper cut. Nothing, nothing at the time. A shock, when it happens on safe ground . . .

I have been stabbed in the head, that's all.[25]

The property 199 Grove Road, Hackney, is the home of the 'Skinhead Squad', an anarchist/nihilist/hooligan army dedicated to street violence, riot, yuppie-bashing, disorder and improbably frequent sexual encounters, in Stewart Home's comic pulp 'n' politics stomp *Red London* (1994). Here they urgently address the radical politics of . . . home decoration:

Fellatio [Jones] and Melody followed him through the automatic door that hisses as the bus pulled up. They crossed the street, took a short flight of steps at a fast run and split-seconds later, Melody found herself inside 199 Grove Road. At least a dozen layers of wallpaper were visible in the gloomy hallway. It looked as if some crazed convert to *nouveau realisme* had ripped the place apart in a romantic homage to the aesthetics of decay.

'Adolf began stripping the walls,' Fellatio explained, 'but once he realised that in places the wallpaper was the only thing between us and the outside world, he thought it best to leave well alone.'

'It's amazing how lazy people are,' Kramer put in, 'you can see that each successive occupier has simply lined the wallpaper up over whatever was already there. For almost a century nobody could be arsed to strip the walls when they redecorated.'

'This place is a dump!' Melody exclaimed as she seated herself at the kitchen table.

'I know,' Adolf admitted, 'it's one of the reasons why I'm determined to start a revolution. As soon as the Skinhead Squad takes control of East London, I'm gonna requisition myself a nice house with double glazing and central heating.'

'Listen to 'im complaining,' Fellatio bleated as he pointed one finger at his friend, ''es got the best bloody room in the 'ouse. That man is set up like Prince Zaleski – the only difference is we pass through a bomb-damaged terrace instead of a rotting mansion, as we make our way to the posh quarters occupied by our hero.'[26]

Peter Ackroyd's 1992 novel *English Music* sees 1920s Hackney through the eyes of nine-year-old Timothy Harcombe. He lives there with his father in Hackney Square. There is no Hackney Square, in fact, or wasn't, until 2014, when the developer Telford Homes announced 'the launch of Hackney Square, a sophisticated collection of 47 one, two and three-bedroom homes designed around an attractive landscaped courtyard . . . just a few minutes' walk from Mare Street and London Fields in the vibrant and cultural hub of Hackney'.[27] Ackroyd's square is a little different.

It was time for my father and me to return home, so he took my hand and we made our way back to Hackney Square. It was here that we lived in lodgings, on the ground floor of a house overlooking the ragged patch of grass and pebbles which comprised the 'garden' of the square itself. It was a quiet place, and set in such a maze of streets that it was almost undiscoverable except by those who actually inhabited it: it was part of a faded and dilapidated area, but on looking back I suspect that its very remoteness, its air of being withdrawn from the busy life of Kingsland Road or Brick Lane, made it appear more derelict than in fact it was. It seemed to be hiding from the world and, in its loneliness, had succumbed to internal decay. But my father loved it. He loved to inhale the odour of old stone and brick blackened by coal dust, although to me it resembled nothing so much as the smell of damp cardboard. He was fascinated by crumbling dissolution, whereas even at that age I detested it – detested perhaps, because it seemed to encroach upon my sense of my own self and even on occasion to supplant it.

'Let's get lost,' he said, on these journeys toward home. By which he meant that we would approach Hackney Square from a different direction to the usual one, and that we would make our way through what were to me less familiar streets and alleyways. 'Do you want to get lost, Tim?' There were occasions when we passed the burial grounds of Bunhill Fields and approached Hackney Square from the south through Old Nichol Street and Hand Alley; there were occasions when we would approach it from the north, by way of St Agnes Well and Bowling Green Walk; and often we would walk up Brick Lane before coming upon the church at Shoreditch.[28]

In Bernardine Evaristo's *Mr Loverman* (2013), Windrush-era immigrant Barrington Jedidiah Walker is off to meet Morris, his secret lover, at the Caribbean Canteen on Dalston Junction.

As I walk down Cazenove, I join the Friday lunchtime dance of the gentlemen of the Hasidim, silently wending and crisscrossing with the gentlemen of the Mohammedeen: the former dressed in the style of prewar Poland, with their black coats, bushy beards, and long ringlets hanging down from underneath their tall black hats, as they make their way to the synagogue; the latter attired in the style of twentieth-century Pakistan, with their white skullcaps, long cotton waistcoats, and *salwar kameezes*, as they also make their way to their house of spiritual sustenance, in this case the mosque.

Everybody minds their own business, which is good, because this here gentleman of the Caribbean, attired in the sharp-suited style of his early years, minds his own business too.

I can't remember when anything last kicked off, and when it does, it's because the youngbloods let their raging testosterones get the better of them.[29]

Walthamstow

About 3 miles northwest of Hackney, across the Hackney Marshes adjacent to the River Lea and its attendant reservoirs, Walthamstow is an ancient settlement, once enveloped by the vast Epping Forest that originally stretched out to the Essex coast, but then, of course, built over and industrialized in the later nineteenth century. Samuel Pepys, always on the lookout for a pretty rural spot, goes out to Walthamstow on 29 May 1661 with his neighbour Admiral William Penn (father of William Penn, founder of the Province of Pennsylvania):

> 29. *Kings birth day*. Rose earely; and having made myself fine and put six spoons and a porringer of Silver in my pocket to give away today, Sir W. Pen and I took Coach and (the weather and ways being foule) went to Waltamstowe . . . Back to dinner to Sir Wms; and then after a walk in the fine gardens, we went to Mrs Brown's, where Sir W. Pen and I were godfathers and Mrs Jordan and Shipman godmothers to her boy. And there, before and after the Christening, we were with the women, above in her chamber, but whether we carried ourselfs well or ill, I know not . . . All being done, we went to Mrs Shipman's, who is a great butter-woman; and I did see there the most of milke and cream, and the cleanest that ever I saw in my life. After we had filled our bellies with cream, we took our leaves and away. In our way we had great sport to try who should drive fastest, Sir W. Batten's coach or Sir W. Pen's chariot, they having four, and we two horses, and we beat them.[30]

Penn senior had his son schooled in the area, at Chigwell, and the pioneering biographer John Aubrey recorded in *Brief Lives* (1669–96) that it was at this school that Penn first had a mystical vision, which influenced his later conversion to Quakerism:

The first sense he had of God was when he was 11 yeares old at Chigwell, being retired in a chamber alone. He was so suddenly surprized with an inward comfort and (as he thought) an externall glory in the roome that he has many times sayde that from thence he had the scale of divinity and immortality, that there was a God and that the soule of man was capable of enjoying his divine communications. – His schoolmaster was not of his perswasion.[31]

William Morris was born in Walthamstow in 1834. When he was six his family moved to Woodford House, a grand mansion in 50 acres of woodland on the fringes of Epping Forest. In a letter Morris described Walthamstow as 'once a suburban village on the edge of Epping Forest, and once a pleasant place enough, but now terribly cocknified and choked up by the jerry-builder'.[32] In his 1890 socialist 'Utopian Romance' *News from Nowhere*, the narrator, William Guest, has newly awoken from a 160-year-long slumber. He finds himself in the mid-twenty-first century, one hundred years after the revolutionary socialist overthrow of industrial capitalism in 1952. He is trying to explain where exactly he comes from, and why he is so unfamiliar with the beautiful vision of London he encounters, now largely restored to its wild and wooded past:

'You see, I have been such a long time away from Europe that things seem strange to me now: but I was born and bred on the edge of Epping Forest; Walthamstow and Woodford, to wit.'

'A pretty place, too,' broke in Dick; 'a very jolly place, now that the trees have had time to grow again since the great clearing of the houses in 1955.'[33]

The Nowherians want to hear more about the past, thinking Guest is well read rather than two hundred years old. He finds that the 'strong sweet smell' of lavender

brought back to my mind my very early days in the kitchen-garden at Woodford . . . 'When I was a boy, and for long after, except for a piece about Queen Elizabeth's Lodge, and for the part around High Beech, the Forest was almost wholly made up of pollard hornbeams mixed with holly thickets. But when the Corporation of London took it over about twenty-five years ago, the topping and the lopping, which was part of the old commoners' rights, came to an end, and the trees were let to grow . . . I was very much shocked then to see how it was built-over and altered; and the other day we heard that the philistines were going to landscape-garden it. But what you were saying about the building being stopped and the trees growing is only too good news.'[34]

Stratford

Stratford (its Old English name literally meaning 'street-ford') developed from the realignment of the ancient Roman road from Aldgate, made possible by a bridge thrown across the River Lea in the early twelfth century. Its location by the Lea and its tributaries, which powered numerous mills, fostered the introduction of industrial concerns in timber, printing, distilling and porcelain, all of which were flourishing by 1800. Then, in the later nineteenth century, as polluting industry was pushed eastward out of the city and across the Lea, Stratford became a key industrial area dedicated to warehousing, engineering, chemicals and transport manufacture and infrastructure.

Foxe's Book of Martyrs, first published in 1563, memorializes accounts of Anglican martyrdom in a time of religious turmoil, including a well-known incident at Stratford:

> When these thirteen were condemned, and the day appointed they should suffer, which was the twenty-seventh day of June, anno 1556, they were carried from Newgate in London to Stratford-le-Bow (which was the place appointed for their martyrdom), and there divided into two parts, in two several chambers.
>
> Afterward the sheriff, who there attended upon them, came to the one part, and told them that the other had recanted, and their lives would be spared, willing and exhorting them to do the like, and not to cast away themselves; unto whom they answered, that their faith was not builded on man, but on Christ crucified . . .
>
> Now when he saw it booted not to persuade (for they were, God be praised, surely grounded on the Rock, Jesus Christ), he

then led them to the place where they should suffer: and being
all there together, most earnestly prayed unto God, and joyfully
went to the stake, and kissed it, and embraced it very heartily.

The eleven men were tied to three stakes, and the two
women loose in the midst without any stake; and so they were
all burnt in one fire, with such love to each other, and con-
stancy in our Saviour Christ, that it made all the lookers-on
to marvel.[35]

Daniel Defoe, in his early 1720s *Tour through the Whole Island of
Great Britain*, marvels at Stratford's growth:

Passing Bow-Bridge, where the County of Essex begins, the
first Observation I made was, That all the Villages which may
be called the Neighbourhood of the City of London on This, *as
well as on the Other sides thereof*, which I shall speak to in their
Order; I say, all those Villages are increased in Buildings to a
strange Degree, within the Compass of about 20 or 30 Years
past at the most.

The Village of Stratford, the first in this County from
London, is not only increased, but, I believe, more than doubled
in that time; every Vacancy filled up with new Houses, and Two
little Towns or Hamlets, as they may be called, on the Forest side
of the Town, entirely New, namely, Mary-land-Point, and the
Gravel-Pits, one facing the Road to Woodford, and Epping, and
the other facing the Road to Illford: And as for the hither-part,
it is almost joined to Bow, in spite of Rivers, Canals, Marshy-
Grounds, &c. Nor is this increase of Building the Case only, in
this and all the other Villages round London; but the increase of
the Value and Rent of the Houses formerly standing, has, in that
Compass of Years above-mentioned, advanced to a very great
Degree, and I may venture to say at least a fifth Part; some think
a third Part, above what they were before.[36]

Thomas Burke, in his 1921 exploration of out-of-the-way London,
The Outer Circle (1921), enjoys Stratford:

I like Stratford. It is joyously Cockney, while retaining the
external charms of a country market town. It has a theatre,

a music-hall, three time-worn inns, and the Broadway, which is a separate delight, amalgamating the charms of the others. The Parish Church, a mere infant as a London church – it was built in 1835 – was erected as a memorial to the Stratford martyrs who suffered on the green in the sixteenth century. High Street, Stratford-Langthorne, which begins at Bow Bridge and curls around Bow Church, is a straggling lane of tumbling cottages and over-hanging shops; very aromatic; for alongside Bow Creek are chemical, gas, oil, varnish, and pickle factories; and the Northern Outfall Sewer works its way here to the river at Barking Creek.[37]

In J. R. Ackerley's 1960 novel *We Think the World of You*, Frank, from leafy Barnes, is heading northeast across town to leafless Stratford: 'The long bus ride down the Mile End Road to Stratford seemed interminable . . . as the bus trundled along through the ugly, stricken landscape.'[38] At Stratford, Frank, for complex reasons, finds himself responsible for Evie, a neglected family dog:

In the alley-way, as soon as I had freed her, she had relieved herself of an evil-looking porridge of excrement. Then we happened in our ramblings upon an extensive bomb-site; half of what had once been a great block of council-flats had been demolished, providing what seemed to be the only open space, besides the Rec., in the neighbourhood. There, amidst the rubble and the rubbish, some stunted grass had managed to sprout, and picking my way through the debris to the centre, where the ground was clearer, I had seated myself upon a piece of fallen masonry and lighted a cigarette to calm my agitation.[39]

Stratford is no place, Frank feels, for a beautiful creature like Evie: 'An elegantly tailored dog . . . with a sharp watchful face framed in a delicate Elizabethan ruff. If Tom took her out every day round these mean streets, what use would that be to her? She ought to be bounding a daily ten miles over grass. She ought to be in the country.'[40]

Plaistow-born Joe Hawkins 'hated his parents with all the violence in his young body',[41] Richard Allen explains in *Skinhead* (1970), the first of a long series of skinhead/suedehead pulp novels, with lashings of ultraviolence, centred on East End white working-class grievance and subculture, reminiscing a world that never really existed:

> It was Saturday and West Ham were playing Chelsea at Stamford Bridge. He wished the match had been at Upton Park. A lot of his mates had stopped travelling across London to Chelsea's ground. Funny, he thought, how the balance of 'power' had shifted from East to West in a few years. He remembered when the Krays had been king-pins of violence in London and the East End had ruled the roost. Not now! Every section of the sprawling city had its claim to fame. South of the Thames the niggers rode cock-a-hoop in Brixton; the Irish held Shepherd's Bush with an iron fist; and the Jews predominated around Hampstead and Golders Green. The Cockney had lost control of his London. Even Soho had gone down the drain of provincial invasion. The pimps and touts there weren't old-established Londoner types. They came from Scouseland, Malta, Cyprus and Jamaica. Even the porno shops were having their difficulties with the parasitic influx of outside talent.
>
> Like most of his generation, Joe *knew* about these things. At one time, East Enders enjoyed a visit to Soho and mingling with the 'heavy boys' from Poplar and Plaistow and Barking. No longer. The word had circulated – stay away from Soho. Look for your heroes in Ilford, Forest Gate and Whitechapel. The old cockney thug was slowly being confined – to Bow, Mile End, Bethnal Green and their fringe areas. London was wide open now. To anyone with a gun, a cosh, an army of thugs.[42]

Urban trekker John Rogers, having moved to the Leytonstone area, feels that to fully understand the area he has to walk down through Leyton and Stratford to the Thames, as he describes in *This Other London* (2013): 'Looking south I traced a straight line through Stratford across Mill Meads to the point where the River Lea empties in the Thames at Leamouth. Between Leamouth and Barking Creek lies the ancient manor of Hamme.'[43] He continues:

> The excursion really starts as I enter Stratford. This stretch of the [Leyton] High Road is desperate, far enough off the beaten track to not have qualified for an Olympic makeover. If you

peer along the streets of run-down terraced houses you can see the Olympic Village glistening on Angel Lane like a glorious Gulag. It seems to have been modelled on a despot's palace.

I'd toyed with taking the trail along Leyton High Road into Angel Lane, following a route I've walked periodically over the last six years as the Olympic development evolved. But I'm keen not to lapse into a splenetic rant against land-grabs and property developers, frothing at the mouth about the breaking up of one of London's oldest housing co-ops at Clays Lane, the horror of the state-subsidized shopping mall through which visitors to the Olympic Stadium have to pass – the way to the 100-metres final being via Zara, handy for a cheap Third World T-shirt but hardly the Wembley Way.[44]

In Benjamin Zephaniah's 1999 novel *Face*, Martin and his schoolfriends escape briefly from Forest Gate (just east of Stratford) and head up to Wanstead Flats:

By the second week the sun had begun to shine, so Martin, Mark and Matthew started looking for action. On some days this meant going over to Wanstead Flats, grassland on the edges of Epping Forest where girls walked and where football was played. It was like a park with the attitude of a beach.

Martin loved the forest. He thought other areas of the East End were concrete jungles, with no space to breathe. The Flats were a quick escape to greenery. He knew the area well but he took much of its cultural diversity for granted. At school he learned how in the sixteenth century French Protestant refugees called Huguenots settled there, then Germans, Chinese, Vietnamese, Jews and Poles had settled too and the latest arrivals were Caribbeans, Africans, Asians and Bosnians.

Some things never change, though. Every bank holiday the funfair came to Wanstead Flats. All the girls would head there in their girl gangs with their best summer clothes on and the boy gangs would gather with their tough faces and their egos turned on full.[45]

Isle of Dogs

Once known as Stepney Marsh, the marshy Isle of Dogs peninsula (its etymology greatly contested; it's not an island and there never seems to have been any dogs) was partially drained in the Middle Ages, yet remained largely empty and forlorn until the huge docks arrived in the early nineteenth century. 'Docklands' was the name given in the 1980s to the regenerated eastern extent of the London docks (primarily Limehouse, the West and East India Docks, the Royal Docks and the Isle of Dogs), which was mostly derelict by the mid-1960s. This is the 8.5-mile extent of the 'Urban Development Area' set up by the London Docklands Development Corporation from 1981. For many commentators the rapid development of the Isle of Dogs peninsula – with generous tax incentives, public money and freedom from strict planning laws – has been the blueprint for much subsequent London regeneration. This has led to a rise in gated communities, 'public' corporate spaces that are actually private, increased surveillance, unaffordable prices and the marginalization and elimination of surviving working-class communities.

The antiquarian and diarist Ralph Thoresby recalls a curious sight on a summer boat trip downriver on 14 July 1714:

> Called upon by Mr. Boulter; coached it to the Tower; then took boat; coasted by St. Catherine's, Wapping, Shadwell, Radcliff, Limehouse, Poplar, and down to Blackwall, where we had a view of the turn of the river Thames; we called at the Isle of Dogs, to see the skeleton of a whale, forty-eight yards long, and thirty-five round.[46]

The southern part of the Isle of Dogs, inaccessible, marshy and windswept, quickly gained an unsavoury reputation. Samuel Pepys mentions the 'unlucky' Isle of Dogs in the 1660s, the very end of the peninsula along the river having a notorious gibbet where the rotting corpses of executed criminals (especially pirates), displayed in a rattling, hanging iron cage, were presented for all to see. Thomas Mozley, in his *Reminiscences* (1882), recalls travelling past when he was a boy:

> In 1820, and for many years after, the only inhabitants of the Isle of Dogs that I ever saw were three murderers hanging from

a gibbet. But all that part was quite out of London. In 1823, after being devoured by vermin at a wretched inn, the only one at Blackwall, I had to pick my way over planks, rough stones, and dirt, down a long shelving shore, to a boat in waiting to take passengers to the Edinburgh steamer.[47]

Dickens, in the 'Greenwich Fair' (1835) section of *Sketches by Boz*, notes how the aged sailors from the Seaman's Hospital would helpfully point out the sights across the Thames:

> The old pensioners, who, for the moderate charge of a penny, exhibit the mast-house, the Thames and shipping, the place where the men used to hang in chains, and other interesting sights, through a telescope, are asked questions about objects within the range of the glass, which it would puzzle a Solomon to answer.[48]

Henry Morley, writing in Dickens's journal *Household Words*, visits the London and Blackwall Railway station on the East India Dock, at the top of the Isle of Dogs, in 1852. This is the embarkation point for thousands of migrants heading out for the colonies, in this case, as he recounts in 'A Rainy Day on "The Euphrates"', poor and abandoned children bound for Australia and New Zealand:

> The 13th of January, 1852, was a decidedly wet day. *You*, reader, as a shadow, not affected by the weather; I, as a motionless, damp substance, under the porch of the Blackwall Railway station, looking up at the immense wet slate in the sky, and down at the few human sponges whom fate urged, for some motive or other, to a run across the puddles on the pier. The river before us had a languid, sickly look, as if it had just come from swallowing a sewer. As for the opposite shore, utterly flat, it seemed to be depressed entirely, on account of the uncomfortable aspect of the morning.
>
> It was our fancy to come down to Blackwall half-an-hour before the time appointed for embarkation on board the steamer which was to carry us alongside an emigrant ship, 'The Euphrates', ready to sail this afternoon, weather permitting.[49]

Walter Besant, in his guide *East London* (1899), muses on the origin of the area's name and its reputation:

> I have no suggestion to offer, except a vague suspicion that, as Pepys thought, there was a tradition of bad luck attaching in some form to the place, which was named accordingly. If a man on the downward path is said to be going to the dogs, a place considered as unlucky might very well have been called the Isle of Dogs. Now a level marsh without any inhabitants and adorned by gibbets and dangling dead bodies would certainly not be considered a lucky place.[50]

Despite commenting that 'needless to say there is not a single book-shop in the Isle of Dogs', Besant, is, in fact, mostly impressed with the place:

> Yet a walk around the Isle of Dogs is full of interest. To begin with, the streets are wide and clean; the houses are small, built for working-men; these are no houses of the better sort at all; the children swarm, and are healthy, well fed and rosy; the shops are chiefly those of provisions and cheap clothing. All round the shore there runs an unbroken succession of factories. These factories support the thousands of working-men who form the population of the Isle of Dogs. All kinds of things are made, stored, received and distributed in the factories of this industrial island . . . There are no slums, I believe, on the Isle of Dogs. I have never seen any Hooligans, Larrikins, or any of that tribe – perhaps because they were all engaged in work, the harder the better. You will not see any drunken men, as a rule, nor any beggars, nor any signs of misery. We may conclude that the Isle of Dogs contains an industrious and prosperous population . . . It is a place where one might deliberately choose to be born, because, apart from the general well-being of the people and the healthfulness of the air, there is a spirit of enterprise imbibed by every boy who grows up in this admirable island.[51]

In a thrilling chase in the second Sherlock Holmes tale, *The Sign of the Four* (1890), Holmes and Watson, in a police launch, are chasing down the *Aurora*, with its rollicking cargo of peg-legged criminal Jonathan Small and a box of priceless jewels. The chase has been in progress all the way downriver from Westminster Pier.

> She was still, however, well in view, and the murky, uncertain twilight was settling into a clear, starlit night. Our boilers were strained to their utmost and the frail shell vibrated and creaked with the fierce energy which was driving us along. We had shot through the Pool, past the West India Docks, down the long Deptford Reach, and up again after rounding the Isle of Dogs. The dull blur in front of us resolved itself now clearly enough into the dainty *Aurora*. Jones turned our search-light upon her, so that we could plainly see the figures upon the deck. One man sat by the stern, with something black between his knees over which he stopped. Beside him lay a dark mass which looked like a Newfoundland dog . . . At Greenwich we were about three hundred paces behind them. At Blackwall we couldn't have been more than two hundred and fifty. I have coursed many creatures in many countries during my chequered career, but never did sport give me such a wild thrill as this mad, flying man-hunt down the Thames. Steadily we drew in upon them, yard by yard . . . We were not more than four boat's lengths behind them, both boats flying at a tremendous pace. It was a clear reach of the river, with Barking Level upon one side and melancholy Plumstead Marshes upon the other.[52]

Homesick Scottish poet John Davidson, in his 1895 poem 'In the Isle of Dogs', describes how an organ-grinder transforms the filthy, clamouring docks, by 'magic sound', into a Scots 'northern isle', a 'green isle like a beryl set / In a wine-coloured sea'.[53]

> From the pavements and the roofs
> In shimmering volumes wound
> The wrinkled heat;
> Distant hammers, wheels and hoofs,
> A turbulent pulse of sound,
> Southward obscurely beat,
> The only utterance of the afternoon,
> Till on a sudden in the silent street

An organ-man drew up and ground
The Old Hundredth tune.[54]

The river here, polluted, oily, exhausted, is, of course, an ideal setting for T. S. Eliot's modern epic of cultural and spiritual death, *The
Waste Land* (1922):

The river sweats
Oil and tar
The barges drift
With the turning tide
Red sails
Wide
To leeward, swing on the heavy spar.
The barges wash
Drifting logs
Down Greenwich reach
Past the Isle of Dogs.[55]

Thomas Burke's orientalist tales of the exotic, erotic and decadent, *Limehouse Nights* (1917), are set in London's first Chinatown,
just to the north of the Isle of Dog's peninsula. In the Poplar-set
story 'The Father of Yoto', Marigold Vassiloff, a 'glorious girl' (a teenage prostitute), 'lives under the tremendous glooms of the East and
West India Docks', at the top of the Isle of Dogs. Burke insists that
we *know* this place: 'You know, perhaps, the East India Dock, which
lies a little north of its big brother, the West India Dock: a place of
savagely masculine character, evoking the brassy mood. By daytime a
cold, nauseous light hangs about it; at night a devilish darkness settles
upon it.'[56]

But then there are things we don't know, here – of these exotic
creatures 'with the lust for life racing in their veins', from the East and
the East End – and Burke has to tell us:

It may offend your taste, and in that case you may reject it. Yet
I trust you will agree that any young thing, moving in that dank
daylight, that devilish darkness, is fully justified in taking her
moments of gaiety as and when she may . . . There are minds to
which the repulsive – such as Poplar High Street – is supremely

beautiful, and to whom anything frankly human is indelicate, if not ugly. You need, however, to be a futurist to discover ecstatic beauty in the torn wastes of tiles, the groupings of iron and stone, and the nightmare of chimney-stacks and gas-works. Barking Road, as it dips and rises with a sweep as lovely as a flying bird's, may be a thing to fire the trained imagination, and so may be the subtle tones of flame and shade in the byways, and the airy tracery of the Great Eastern Railway arches. But these crazy things touch only those who do not live among them: who comfortably wake and sleep and eat in Hampstead and Streatham.[57]

Jack Lindsay's 1953 novel *Rising Tide* shows us London's docklands (especially the Victoria and Albert, or Royal, docks) before it became Docklands. This is a novel of poverty, brutal working conditions, industrial dispute and politics. Here Jeff and Phyl are going to see the weatherboard shack near the docks in which Sam and Molly Ricks have been squatting since the end of the war:

They went down a side-street by the Seamen's Hospital, through the thin March sunlight. Children in the roadway were kicking an indiarubber ball with a hole in it, while a dog barked jealously behind a gate. The small girl with the plaits was there dancing a hopscotch game by herself, still singing. They turned into Custom House Fields, which stood deserted this afternoon; then they skirted the Connaught Approach of the Albert Dock, and moved into the open fields.

'I never knew all this was here,' said Phyl, halting with the air of someone finding a new room in a familiar house. She stared at the wide space of straggling grass and bush, with three hobbled horses on the left and a clump of shacks on a slightly raised level well ahead. 'It looks so odd – all this wasteland, and the docks only a few yards away' . . .

The path became narrow and she let him lead the way between the patches of tall grass and the scratchy bushes, the heaps of coiled rusting wire and the treacherous channels. Then in a few moments they climbed up on to the raised part, and she saw the gunpits . . . Fancy living in such a dump.[58]

V. S. Pritchett visits the (still just-working) docks in his 1962 travelogue *London Perceived*:

The docks break up this east London into grimy little Venices. How do you imagine the Isle of Dogs? It is a collection of high, black prison walls and streets without feature. There are rows of small houses, and then, over a dock wall, appears in huge white letters the startling single word *Philosopher*, or some other just as strange. You are looking at the name of a ship whose black bow overhangs the wall of the graving dock, dwarfing trains, buses, houses, everything. Between the new blocks of flats that have gone up since docklands was burned out during the Blitz rise the funnels and the masts; one is surprised to see ships, lightly domesticated, careless-looking, gay and trim, rising with the clean paint of the sea among London's dirty brick. There are havens on the Isle of Dogs, such as The Gun, one of the few remaining public houses with a terrace on the river, where on summer nights one looks at the river and its cold lights and listens to the clatter of the chains and conveyors of history; and where one waits for that peremptory, half-melancholy, half-majestic sound of a ship blowing as she silently glides out black in the night, almost through the pub yard, from the dock basin on her voyage. 'Nice boys. Very nice fellers they were. And spent a lot of money,' says the woman at the bar, looking towards the sound of the ship she cannot see. There will be no sing-song at the piano in the river room with that lot now. They have gone.[59]

In Alan Hollinghurst's *The Swimming-pool Library* (1988), we see rich, cultured Will, far from his usual luxurious West End locations, heading east along the District Line:

I looked out of the window at the widening suburbs, the housing estates, the distant gasometers, the mysterious empty tracts of fenced-in waste land, grass and gravelly pools and bursts of purple foxgloves. Modern warehouses abutted on the line, and often the train ran on a high embankment at the level of bedroom windows or above shallow terrace gardens with wooden huts, a swing or a blown-up paddling pool. Everywhere the impression was of desertion, as if on this spacious summer day just touched, high up, with tiny flecks of motionless cloud, the people had made off.[60]

The old Victoria and Albert docks at Silvertown, east of the Isle of Dogs, provoke a disorientating doubling:

I was amazed to think it was in the city where I lived, and consulted my *A–Z* surreptitiously so as not to set off with faked familiarity in the wrong direction. The culture shock was compounded as a single-decker bus approached showing the destination 'Victoria and Albert Docks'. Victoria and Albert *Docks*! To the people here the V and A was not, as it was in the slippered west, a vast terracotta-encrusted edifice, whose echoing interiors held ancient tapestries, miniatures of people copulating, dusty baroque sculpture and sequences of dead and spotlit rooms taken wholesale from the houses of the past. How different my childhood Sunday afternoons would have been if, instead of showing me the Raphael Cartoons (which had killed Raphael for me ever since), my father had sent me to the docks, to talks with stevedores and have them tell me, with much pumping and flexing, the stories of their tattoos.[61]

In Iain Sinclair's feverish incantation, and exorcism, of Thatcherite London, *Downriver* (1991), the nightmarish Isle of Dogs appears, in the midst of the area's rapid transformation, as 'The Isle of Doges (*Vat City plc*)': clearly a riposte to the London Docklands Development Corporation's slogan that the area would 'feel like Venice and work like New York'. For Sinclair it feels more like a tawdry theme park:

The avenues! Treeless, broad, focusing on nothing. Dramatic perspectives leading to no revelation: no statues of public men, no fountains, no slogans. Nothing. No beggars, no children, no queues for buses. This city of the future, this swampland Manhattan, this crystal synthesis of capital, is already posthumous: a memorial to its own lack of nerve. It shudders and lets slips its ghosts. It swallows the world's dross. Isle of Dogs, receiving station of everything that is lost and without value. A library of unregarded texts. Escaped pets.

Abortions. Amputated limbs. Hiding place of Idi Amin, Baby Doc Duvalier, Martin Bormann. There must be a showcase tower that contains nothing but the collected shoes of Imelda Marcos. There must be a pyramid filled with the severed heads of torturers, waiting for the quacks to steam them to reincarnation. Their red-veined eyes move, like the eyes in portraits: they watch us. There must be a gambling hell for all those who blaspheme against fate by calling themselves 'Lucky'; a sullen moustached Lord Lucan 'greets' a toothpick-chewing Luciano, who slips him a counterfeit nickel. There must even be a shrine where collectors of military fetishes can worship the single testicle of Adolf Hitler.[62]

Sinclair returns, five years later, in *Lights Out for the Territory*:

The Isle of Dogs. Anubis land, a reservation of jackals. Death's promontory. The whole glass raft is a mistake, glitter forms of anachronistic postmodernism (the swamp where that word crawled to die). Instant antiques. Skin grafts peeling before completion. The seductive sky/water cemetery of Thatcherism, cloud-reflecting sepulchre towers: an evil that delights the eye (the eye in the triangle). An astonishingly obvious solicitation of the pyramid, a corrupt thirst for eternity. (Climb the true tower of St Anne's Church, and stand among Hawksmoor's crumbling Portland stone lanterns, pyramids set above catacomb arches, designed to be seen *through*, to keep vision alive; the river, all points of the compass – even the futile bluntness of Canary Wharf's phallic topping.)

The planners have dabbled in geomancy, appeased the energy lines (while attempting to subvert them), and have achieved nothing beyond futile decoration. A city state built on self-regard.[63]

And again in 2002's trek around the M25, *London Orbital*:

Breakfast is a priority on these walks. Which is something of a problem in the desert between the neck of the Isle of Dogs at East India Dock Road and our access point to the Lee Navigation towpath at Bow Lock. The landscape is provisional.

Strategic planning runs up against sulking real estate, tacky old businesses that won't fade away, inconvenience stores, revenants from Thomas Burke's Chinatown. Marine provisioners have decayed into monosodium glutamate takeaways that leave you orange tongued, raging with thirst. Merchant marine outfitters peddle cheap camping-gear, unisex jeans, diving suits for non- swimmers . . .

East India Dock Road, with its evocative name, has a secondary identity as the A13, my favourite early morning drive. The A13 has got it all, New Jersey-going-on-Canvey Island: multiplex cinemas, retail parks, the Beckton Alp ski slope; fly-overs like fairground rides, three salmon-pink tower blocks on Castle Green, at the edge of Dagenham; the Ford water tower and the empty paddocks where ranks of motors used to sit wait-ing for their transporters. Beckton Alp ski slope; flyovers like fairground rides, three salmon-pink tower blocks on Castle Green, at the edge of Dagenham; the Ford water tower and the empty paddocks where ranks of motors used to sit wait-ing for their transporters. The A13 drains East London's wound, carrying you up into the sky; before throwing you back among boarded-up shops and squatted terraces. All urban life aspires to this condition; flux, pastiche. A conveyor belt of discontinued industries. A peripatetic museum, horizon to horizon, available to anyone; self-curated. The wild nature graveyard in Newham. Inflatable, corn-yellow potato chips wobbling in their mon-ster bucket outside McDonald's in Dagenham. River fret over Rainham Marshes.[64]

Detective Inspector Kate Miskin, in P. D. James's *Original Sin* (1994), takes the plunge and risks buying a flat in the new Docklands.

This flat, of course, wasn't what she had originally imagined. She had pictured herself in one of the great converted warehouses near Tower Bridge with high windows and huge rooms, the strong oak rafters and, surely, the lingering smell of spice. But even with a falling property market this had been beyond her means. And the flat, which after careful searching she had chosen, wasn't a poor second. She had taken the highest mortgage possible, believing that it was financially wise to buy the best she could afford. She had one large room, eighteen feet by twelve, and two smaller bedrooms, one with its shower en suite. The kitchen was large enough to eat in and well fitted. The south-west facing balcony, which ran the whole length of the sitting-room, was narrow but still wide enough to take a small table and chairs. She could eat out there in the summer . . .

And the flat had another great advantage. It was at the end of the building and with a double outlook and two balconies. From her bedroom she could see the wide gleaming panorama of Canary Wharf, the tower like an immense cellular pencil with its lead topped with light, the great white curve of the adjoining building, the still water of the old West India Dock and the overhead Docklands Light Railway with its trains like clockwork toys. This city of glass and concrete would become busier as new firms moved in. She would be able to look down on the multicoloured, ever-changing pageant of half a million scurrying men and women leading their working lives. The other balcony looked south-west over the river and the slower immemorial traffic of the Thames; barges, pleasure boats, the launches of the River Police and Port of London Authority, the cruise liners making their way upstream to birth at Tower Bridge.[65]

Geographer Anna Minton, writing in 2009 in her study of urban planning *Ground Control*, notes that the uncontrolled boosterism of Canary Wharf hasn't spread down to the rest of the Isle of Dogs:

Walking down towards the Isle of Dogs from Harbour Exchange Square, it seemed to me that South Quay had spread. But when I reached Crossharbour, which is the next stop on the Docklands Light Railway, a sharp dividing line between new Docklands and the old communities on the Isle of Dogs became clear. On one side of the road, by the station, are newly built office blocks and a host of construction sites, while on the other side is a dilapidated housing estate. In between is the George pub, which flies a flag of St George from its roof, and seems to mark a boundary point, set in the shadow of the skyscrapers, on the corner of one of Millwall's housing estates.

This pub could not be more different from the All Bar One of Reuters Plaza, and the contrast between the two sides of the road could not have been greater.

The George is a typical East End pub, which maintains the traditional division between the 'working men's bar' and the 'lounge'. I can guarantee that when I walked in on a Friday afternoon, no one from the offices opposite was drinking there. Carrying on down from the George into Millwall, I could see the towers looming. To my right was a low-rise 1960s' estate, badly in need of repair, with peeling paint flaking from the windows and doors. The people were entirely different, too. In place of the blackberried professionals in a hurry where a few mothers, some white, some Asian and veiled, pushing prams. A group of teenagers larked up the street.[66]

12 'THE OVERLOOKED CITY'

Outer East London: From Barking to Ilford, Romford, Dagenham, Rainham and Purfleet

The development of outer East London, the boroughs of Barking and Dagenham, Redbridge and Havering, followed a familiar pattern: from ancient Roman settlements (Gidea Park, Romford, was the original site of Durolitum, a sizable fort and staging post on the London to Colchester road); to thriving Saxon villages and communities situated near woods (Hainault Forest, Loughton Chase) and frequently centred around a church or big house (Barking Abbey, Havering Palace); then, inevitably, by the late nineteenth century, railways and industry. The huge Ford car plant opened on Dagenham Marshes in 1931, followed by chemicals, paints and munitions factories, a gigantic power station by the river, and all the other features of mid-century industrial landscapes: scrapyards, repair shops, dumps, workshops. The gigantic LLC-built Becontree Estate, the world's largest, was completed in 1934, bringing 100,000 people to the area. This landscape – of arterial roads, huge lorries, desolate factories, warehouses, logistics depots – is best evoked, in song, on Billy Bragg's joyous 'A13 Trunk Road to the Sea' (1985). Based on the famous R&B standard 'Route 66', which extols the joys of motoring from Chicago to LA, Bragg substitutes the A13 route from Wapping to Shoeburyness, Southend, the preferred route of East End or Essex boy racers speeding out to Canvey Island in the 1960s and '70s.

Barking

Around 10 miles east of Charing Cross and just outside the North Circular Road, which follows the River Roding as it curves down to

487

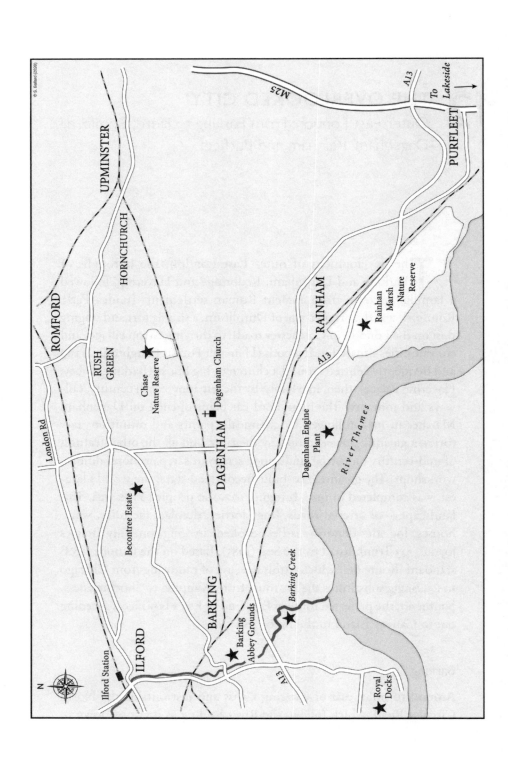

the Thames, Barking was one of the earliest Saxon settlements in Essex. It grew up next to the extensive Barking Abbey, which was the largest Benedictine nunnery in the country before the Reformation. Barking was dominated by fishing until the end of the nineteenth century (ships from here going out as far as Iceland), and then by freight yards, chemical processing and a huge gasworks at the adjacent Beckton. The Barking Riverside development is part of the vast Thames Gateway regeneration project, which aims to take post-industrial suburban London out into Essex and Kent.

Barking Abbey was founded in AD 666 (possibly incorporating tiles left over from the Roman period). It was one of the first Saxon Christian buildings and is mentioned by the Venerable Bede in his *Ecclesiastical History of the English People* (721), the first account of Christianity in Britain:

> In this monastery many signs and miracles were performed which have been written down by those who were acquainted with them as an edifying memorial for succeeding generations and copies are in the possession of many people . . . The plague which has been so often referred to and which was ravaging the country far and wide had also attacked that part of the monastery occupied by the men, and they were daily being carried away into the presence of the Lord. The mother of the congregation was anxiously concerned as to when the plague would strike that part of the monastery, separated from the men's community, in which dwelt the company of the handmaidens of the Lord. So when the sisters met together, she took to asking in what part of the monastery they would like their bodies to be buried and where they desired a cemetery to be made when they were snatched away from the world by the same catastrophe as the rest. Although she often inquired she received no definite answer from the sisters, but she and all of them received a most definite reply from the divine providence. On a certain night when the servants of Christ had finished their matin psalms, they went out of the oratory to the tombs of the brothers who had already died. While they were singing their accustomed praises to the Lord, suddenly a light appeared from heaven like a great sheet and came upon them all, striking such terror into them that they broke off the chant they were

singing in alarm. This resplendent light, in comparison with which the noonday sun seemed dark, soon afterwards rose from the place and moved to the south side of the monastery, that is, to the west of the oratory. There it remained for some time, covering that area until it was withdrawn from their sight into the heavenly heights. So no doubt remained in their minds that this light was not only intended to guide and receive the souls of Christ's handmaidens into heaven, but was also pointing out the spot where the bodies were to rest, awaiting the resurrection day.[1]

Daniel Defoe visits Barking early in his *Tour through the Whole Island of Great Britain* (1724–7): 'I went from Stratford to Barking, a large Market-Town, but chiefly inhabited by Fishermen, whose Smacks ride in the Thames, at the Mouth of their River, from whence their Fish is sent up to London to the Market at Billingsgate, by small boats.'[2] Defoe is very impressed by the Barking fleet's many uses:

One Thing I cannot omit in the mention of these Barking Fisher-Smacks, *viz.* That one of those Fishermen, a very substantial and experienced Man, convinced me, that all the Pretences to bringing Fish alive to London Market from the North Seas, and other remote Places on the coast of Great Britain, by the New-built Sloops called *Fish-Pools*, have not been able to do any thing, but what their Fishing-Smacks are able on the same Occasion to perform. These Fishing-Smacks are very useful Vessels to the Publick upon many Occasions; as particularly, in time of War they are used as Press-Smacks, running to all the Northern and Western Coasts to pick up Seamen to man the Navy, when any Expedition is at hand that requires a sudden equipment: At other Times, being excellent Sailors, they are Tenders to particular Men of War; and on an Expedition they have been made use of as *Machines*, for the blowing up Fortified Ports and Havens; as at Calais, St. Maloes, and other Places.[3]

Britain's worst maritime disaster in inland waters occurred in 1878 at Barking Creek, when the pleasure paddle steamer *Princess Alice*, with around nine hundred passengers returning to London Bridge after a day trip downstream to Sheerness, was sliced in two by a huge iron-hulled coal-carrier, the *Bywell Castle*. The *Princess Alice* sank in minutes and around 650 passengers died, many trapped below deck. All this happened within sight and earshot of both banks of the Thames, as many witnesses later testified. Adding to the horror, many struggling passengers were also poisoned by sewage and industrial effluent that had only just been released into the Thames from Barking Creek. News of the disaster appealed to the Victorian taste for sensation and sentiment. W. T. Vincent, then a reporter for the *Kentish Independent*, later told the story of the aftermath in his *Records of the Woolwich District* (1890), slightly misquoting Edward Young's poem 'Narcissa'.

> Ghastly Sights. – Soon policemen and watermen were seen by the feeble light bearing ghastly objects into the offices of the Steampacket Company, for a boat had just arrived with the first consignment of the dead, mostly little children whose light bodies and ample drapery had kept them afloat even while they were smothered in the festering Thames. I followed into the steamboat office, marvelling at the fate which had brought the earliest harvest of victims to the headquarters of the doomed ship, and, entering the board-room, the first of the martyrs was pointed out to me as one of the company's own servants, a man employed on the 'Princess Alice', and brought here thus soon to attest by his silent presence the ship's identity. The lifeless frames of men and women lay about, and out on the balcony, from which the directors had so often looked upon their fleet through the fragrant smoke of the evening cigar, there was a sight to wring out tears of blood from the eyes of any beholder. A row of little innocents, plump and pretty, well-dressed children, all dead and cold, some with life's ruddy tinge still in their cheeks and lips, the lips from which the merry prattle had gone for ever.
>
>> Lovely in death the beauteous ruins lay;
>> Far lovelier! Pity swells the tide of love.
>
> Callous as one may grow from frequent contact with terrors and afflictions, one could never be inured to this. It was a spectacle to move the most hardened official and dwell

for ever in his dreams. Then to think what was beyond out there in the river. It was madness![4]

Singer-songwriter Billy Bragg, the 'Bard of Barking', recalls growing up in the suburb and trying to invest it with a sense of wonder and place:

> Despite being a heavily industrialised east London suburb, Barking had its own adventures from history, some of which echoed the stories in my Ladybird books. The Anglo-Saxons founded an abbey on the banks of the river Roding c. AD666, which was raided by Vikings and burned to the ground during the time of Alfred the Great. When the Barking bypass was built in 1928, the council named the stretch that crossed the Roding Alfred's Way, presumably as a warning to any Viking raiders who might be contemplating a return trip.[5]

Bragg's song 'The Battle of Barking' (the title echoing an infamous dogfight over the town in 1939, when two Spitfires accidentally fought each other, resulting in the first RAF death of the Second World War) concerns the 2010 General Election scrap when Nick Griffin of the far-right British National Party, having come third with 17 per cent in 2005, was thought to have a chance in the Barking constituency up against the (New) Labour stalwart Margaret Hodge. Bragg compares the anti-racist struggle in Barking with older anti-racist and anti-totalitarian battles in Spain and Cable Street ('No pasáran').[6] These events are also the focus of Laura Fairrie's 2010 documentary *The Battle for Barking*.

This area – Dagenham, Romford and across the border into Essex – has a reputation for crime, both organized and low-level, that has resulted in the 'Essex Boys' tag as a criminal counterpart to the pejorative 'Essex girl' stereotype. This has inspired a string of pulpy, best-selling crime writers, such as Kimberley Chambers and, above all, the 'Queen of Crime', Martina Cole, who was brought up across the Essex border in Aveley, where the A13 meets the M25. Cole's work is set in outer east London and Essex, and in the fictional 'Grantley', which seems a lot like Grays, a riverside town beyond Rainham Marshes and across the M25, once under a thick blanket of cement dust from the factories that lined the Thames but more recently promoted to commuters as affordable housing built on the old chalk quarries, under the name Chafford Hundred.

> Melanie Harvey walked sedately along Bayler Street in Grantley.
> She had been born in the small Essex town, and she was now at college there. She felt this gave her an air of sophistication, being educated, and she was enjoying it, something her teachers would never have believed. But she loved the place, it was her home and it was where she wanted to work and raise her children. Especially since the new order had arrived. Grantley was growing, going up in the world and she wanted desperately to be a small part of it. Gradually the green belt was becoming flats and housing estates – private, of course. The older properties were being knocked down or renovated to make way for the commuters who liked being forty minutes from Fenchurch Street in a place that still felt countrified enough to justify bringing up children there; they would pay through the nose for a small three-bedroomed house.[7]

Ilford

Ilford is located a mile north of Barking, just beyond the North Circular Road. John Rogers, on one of his 'adventures in the overlooked city' in *This Other London* (2013), turns up for a look around:

> It is fair to say that Ilford has a poor self-image. It is ranked fourth in a national survey of 'Unhappiest places to live in Britain' . . . The High Street looks to be suffering from the effect of the Westfield mega mall opening a few miles down the Romford Road in Stratford . . . The Benetton store has been taken over by a pop-up fruit and veg shop. The elegant art deco department stores of the 1920s now house the Money Shop, Premier Work Support, Superdrug and Lidl.
> You sense a stoicism among the half-happy faces on the Broadway, though. When a V-2 rocket fell on the Ilford Hippodrome in 1945 the orchestra continued their performance of *Robinson Crusoe* drenched to the skin by a burst water tank above stage and covered in dust and rubble. The coat of arms for the old Borough of Ilford bears the slogan 'In Unity

Progress'. In his Potted History of the Borough Norman Gunby wrote, 'To anyone who may wonder or ask what history Ilford has, I would answer that there is history in every stone, in every particle of earth, and in every grain of sand'.[8]

Ben Judah's study of new kinds of immigrant life in the hidden spaces of the capital, *This Is London* (2016), includes a night-time drive out to Ilford:

Down terrace after terrace, hundreds of bay windows glow. These were once desirable suburban addresses: on Henley, Windsor and Hampton Road. But today these are where you find the immigrant share rooms. The ones they advertise on Polish websites, or in little cards stuck in grubby windows of the Pakistani newsagents. This is where England begins. And today the white British population of these dingy streets south of Ilford station is around 10 per cent.

The windows make me think. How these long net curtains, with their thickly sewn patterns of polyester flowers and roses, which glow yellow into the night-time, were once a sign someone had made it here in these hundreds, thousands of little houses, lined up one by one, with that little bay window, proudly out front. But not any more. The successful English hate these kind of curtains; they want either that bay window to glow out with cream, soft linen – or glint through wooden venetian blinds . . .

As I slow down I notice these terraces carry the sad names of the other, richer London – Richmond, Kingston or Eton Road. And they turn and turn, mutating between Pakistani homes and Eastern European tenements. But those net curtains, they are always the giveaways. These were left up when the landlords turned this pebbledash house into a tenement, as the English pulled out or died. You can always tell a slum house, where four Polish builders crash in bunk beds behind that chipped bay window, by those very same old and floral singed curtains.[9]

Romford

Around 4 miles east of Ilford, along the A12 Eastern Avenue, Romford is now the administrative centre of the London Borough of Havering and initially developed and grew due to its position on a key north–south route and its proximity to an important Roman garrison and to nearby Havering Palace. The railway arrived here early, in 1839, followed by significant suburban development in the early twentieth century with the building of a Garden Suburb at Gidea Park. More rapid suburban growth in the post-war period – the extensive Harold Hill estate was completed in 1958 – saw the population double. Home to a market since 1247, Romford is also a centre for shopping; Pevsner, in *London: East* (1952–65), notes: 'Visitors, by train or car, thus find themselves confined to the shopping streets, but this is Romford's raison d'etre. It has no less than five shopping centres, developed over the course of the c20.'[10]

Nature poet Edward Thomas reluctantly enlisted, in 1915, in the Artists Rifles, a Volunteer Reserve service of the army, and underwent military training at Hare Hall Camp, at Gidea Park, in 1916. He came to know the area well, with the Havering countryside appearing in his work. The 'Household Poems' of spring 1916 root his poetry in real places, using the names of villages, fields and streams.

> If I should ever by chance grow rich
> I'll buy Codham, Cockridden, and Childerditch,
> Roses, Pyrgo, and Lapwater,
> And let them all to my eldest daughter.
> The rent I shall ask of her will be only
> Each year's first violets, white and lonely . . .[11]

Humphry Repton moved to a small cottage at Gidea Park, Romford, in 1786. Short of money, Repton hit on the idea of combining his sketching ability, business acumen and some basic horticultural skills, and set himself up as a 'Landscape Gardener' (he seems to have coined the title). He produced pragmatic, workable designs, not like the forced Picturesque style dominant at the time, all fully costed and bound in handy so-called 'Red Books', which even offered for clients 'before' and 'after' views. He became wildly successful, and his best-selling *Observations on the Theory and Practice of Landscape*

Gardening, Including some Remarks on Grecian and Gothic Architectures was modestly dedicated to King George III.

TO

THE KING

HIS MAJESTY'S

MOST GRACIOUS PERMISSION

THIS WORK

IS HUMBLY INSCRIBED

HIS MAJESTY'S

MOST FAITHFUL, OBEDIENT

AND HUMBLE SUBJECT,

HUMPHRY REPTON

Hare Street, near Romford
Dec 31, 1803

Here is principle 9 from the book:

> Deception may be allowable in imitating the works of NATURE; thus artificial rivers, lakes and rock scenery, can only be great by deception . . . but in works of ART every trick ought to be avoided. Sham churches, sham ruins, sham bridge, and everything which appears what is is not, disgusts, when the trick is discovered.[12]

Dagenham

A couple of miles east of Barking along the A13, Dagenham is one of the oldest Saxon villages in Essex and retained a largely rural flavour until well into the twentieth century. Then, in 1921, the London County Council (LCC) started work on the vast Becontree housing estate, and Ford built its huge European factory there in 1931; other ancillary industries followed.

Defoe tells us about the famous Dagenham Breach, a marshy area caused by a break in the sea wall, initially from 1707 and again thereafter, that became something of a tourist spot:

We saw, passing from Barking to Dagenham, The famous
Breach, made by an Inundation of the Thames, which was so
great, as that it laid near 5000 Acres of Land under Water, but
which after near ten Years lying under Water, and being several
times blown up has been at last effectually stopped by the
application of Captain Perry; the Gentleman, who for several
Years had been employed, in the Czar of Muscovy's Works,
at Veronitza, on the River Don. This Breach appeared now
effectually made up, and they assured us, that the new Work,
where the Breach was, is by much esteemed the strongest of all
the Sea Walls in that Level.[13]

Famed prison reformer Elizabeth Fry founded the Association for
the Reformation of Female Prisoners in Newgate, in 1817 after visiting
that terrible place. Appalled by the almost medieval mistreatment of
women prisoners there, Fry agitated successfully, even appearing at a
parliamentary committee (the first woman to do so), for improved
conditions; food, bedding, clothes, and an end to using iron man-
acles and the practice of transportation to penal colonies. For summer
holidays the Fry family rented two small former fishing cottages at
Dagenham Breach, as daughter Katherine recorded:

It is difficult to convey the sort of enjoyment Dagenham
afforded us . . . there was fishing, boating, driving and riding
inland by day, and when night closed in over the wild marsh
scenery the cries of water birds, the rustling of the great beds of
reeds, the strange sounds from the shipping on the river gave
the place an indescribable charm.[14]

In Simon Blumenfeld's *Jew Boy* (1935), Alec and Olivia pass by
Dagenham on a day trip from Fenchurch Street to Southend:

Alec secured two seats in a non-smoker, and they sat happily
opposite each other. The train moved off grunting and
squeaking till it cleared the station. It stopped at two or three
more London stations, picking up passengers, who squeezed
miraculously into the compartments until the train was chock
full. Then it belched steadily towards the open country.

Alec glanced through his newspaper. There was nothing very interesting in it. He passed it to Olive, and looked out of the window . . .

Dagenham, the drabbest part of Essex, a scraggy county at best; it seemed to be full of rubbish dumps. And this was where they'd shot those poor families from the Bethnal Green slum clearance. Still, dreary as it might be, it was ten thousand times healthier than their old disease-ridden homes in the stinking Bethnal Green back streets. The authorities had neglected only one thing, they had omitted to move the factories and workshops to Dagenham as well. Extra rents, and fare money getting up to town, took a good slice from the men's wages, and it meant also getting up an hour earlier in the morning, and coming home an hour later in the evening. Dagenham fresh air wasn't much of a compensation for the loss of two hours a day, and the liveliness, and friendliness of the East End, especially when the money needed for food had to go in fares . . .

Laindon . . . stretches of mud . . . Benfleet. Change for Canvey Island . . . Tiny yachts sagging lazily on the water . . . Leigh . . . Southend at last. Southend![15]

The Becontree estate, just to the north of Dagenham, was part of the huge government-sponsored, LCC-built 'homes fit for heroes' project and was the largest council estate in the world at the time, as Nick Barratt explains:

By the time work was completed in 1938, some 27,000 homes had been built for 120,000 people. To achieve this, over 300 acres of farmland and scattered houses and cottages were compulsorily purchased, to be replaced by cottage-style houses set amid gardens, parks and green spaces. The whole site was designed in part with former slum dwellers in mind, but its attractive layout, and accommodation that included gas and electricity, inside toilets and fitted baths, made it appealing to the more well-to-do manual and blue-collar workers who were making their money in factories and the transport industry.[16]

The estate is the basis of an ethnographic study in Peter Willmott's *The Evolution of a Community* (1963). Willmott had worked with Michael

Young on the famous sociological work *Family and Kinship in East London* (1957), which studied close-knit, working-class Bethnal Green families leaving slummy Victorian terraces behind and relocating out to a post-war estate at Debden, near Chigwell. Willmott chose to go to Dagenham to address two major issues: 'One is the charge that the estate is "one class" – in other words, overwhelmingly working class; the other that it was a "dormitory".'[17]

> Throughout this book Dagenham has been compared with the 'traditional' working-class community. At the end one is impressed by how similar, not how different, they are. Local extended families, which hold such a central place in the older districts, have grown up in almost identical form on the estate, and so have local networks of neighbours – people living in the same street who help each other, mix together and are on easy-going terms. In people's attitudes to their fellows, their feelings about social status and class, their political loyalties, again, there are close parallels between the two districts. In part, Dagenham is the East End reborn.[18]

Willmott talks to one of the locals:

> It is a way of life, what is more, that satisfies most people. Many of them are not oppressed by the architectural monotony and dreariness which fill the visitor with gloomy amazement that people could live in such a place, let alone enjoy it. The inhabitants express affection for it. Mr Brooks, a toolmaker in an engineering factory, went to Dagenham when he was 16, and is now 38:
> 'I know Dagenham seems monotonous to people from outside,' he said, 'but when you've been living here for a while, the roads develop their own personalities – there are landmarks which you get to recognize in different turnings. Anyway, it's not the outside of the houses that matter, it's what's inside them. I've got a number of good friends here. Lots of the people round here know me. I get on extremely well with the shopkeepers in the district. My roots are here now and I am very happy indeed.'[19]

The 'Dagenham Dialogues' were a regular item in *Not Only . . . But Also*, a comedy series on BBC television that ran for three series from 1965 to 1970. Peter Cook and Dagenham-born Dudley Moore appeared as 'Pete' and 'Dud', two flatcap- and scarf-wearing working-class bar-room philosophers who discuss various topics: fine art, zoos, harassment by Hollywood icons ('bloody Jane Russell'), and thinking of the 'worst bloody thing that could happen to you'. Here they are at an art gallery:

> DUD: *(eating a sandwich)* Y'know, Pete. I reckon there's a lot of rubbish about in this gallery here.
> PETE: Not only rubbish, Dud, there's a lot of muck about. I've been looking all over the place for something good.
> DUD: I've been looking for that lovely green gypsy lady. You know, the one with . . .
> PETE: The one with the lovely shiny skin.
> DUD: Where is she? Nowhere.
> PETE: Nowhere.
>
> . . .
>
> DUD: But what I can't understand, frankly, Peter, is that there's not a Vernon Ward gallery in here.
> PETE: There's not a duck in the building, there's no Peter Scott, there's no Vernon Ward. Not a duck to be seen.
> DUD: Nothing. The marvellous thing about Vernon Ward is that of course he's been doing ducks all his life.
> PETE: Well, he's done more ducks than you've had hot breakfasts, Dud. If he's done anything he's done ducks.
> DUD: He's done ducks in all positions.
>
> . . .
>
> PETE: The thing what makes you know Vernon Ward a good painter is if you look at his ducks, you see the eyes follow you round the room.
> DUD: You noticed that?
>
> . . .
>
> PETE: . . . That's a sign of a good painting.[20]

Iain Nairn is on typical form in *Nairn's London* (1966), when describing St Peter and St Paul's church, Dagenham:

Marvellous nonsense, the work of a man who had Gothic fantasy in his blood. William Kent would have been proud of this one: William Mason obviously was, because he signed his name as architect all the way round the arch above the west door. A riot of curly details and a riot of materials too . . . Pure froth, without a care in the world; it is difficult to guess which Dagenham is the more alien to it: the original bleak village in the marshes, or the present chaotic spilling over of London's spare parts.[21]

Rainham and Purfleet

Dracula's English pad, Carfax Abbey, is located at Purfleet, 5 miles downstream from Dagenham. 'Tell me of London and of the house which you have procured for me', the Count, in Transylvania, asks his 'agent' Jonathan Harker. Harker notes that the Count, reclining on his sofa with his Bradshaw's railway guide and 'plans and deeds and figures of all sorts', is clearly obsessed with finding somewhere in exactly the right location (price not really a problem).[22] Harker tells the Count how he 'had come across so suitable a place':

> At Purfleet, on a by-road I came across just such a place as seemed to be required, and where was displayed a dilapidated notice that the place was for sale. It is surrounded by a high wall, of ancient structure, built of heavy stones, and has not been repaired for a large number of years. The closed gates are of heavy old oak and iron, all eaten with rust.
>
> The estate is called Carfax, no doubt a corruption of the old *Quatre Face*, as the house is four-sided, agreeing with the cardinal points of the compass. It contains in all some twenty acres, quite surrounded by the solid stone wall above mentioned. There are many trees on it, which made it in places gloomy, and there is a deep, dark-looking pond or small lake, evidently fed by some springs, as the water is clear and flows away in a fair-sized stream. The house is very large and of all periods back, I should say, to mediæval times, for one part is of stone immensely thick, with only a few windows high up and heavily barred with iron.[23]

Iain Sinclair is similarly on the prowl in *London Orbital* (2002), his account of a walk around the M25 and the outer limits of London, looking for any traces of Stoker's Dracula:

> The Gothic imagination invading – and undoing – imperial certainties of trade, law, class. *Dracula* announces the coming age of the estate agent. Nothing in the book works without the Count's ability to purchase, rent, secure property. Like the Moscow mafia buying into St George's Hill (proximity to Heathrow), Dracula chose Purfleet, alongside the Thames, so that he could ship out for Varna at a moment's notice. Being an immortal, the Count knew that he only had to hang on for a few years and he would have a bridge across the river, a motorway circuit around London: new grazing grounds. The future M25 was a magic circle, a circle in salt. The Vampire couldn't be excluded, he was already inside! Purfleet rather than Thurrock. The motorway was the perfect metaphor for the circulation of blood: Carfax Abbey to Harefield – with attendant asylums. Stoker predicted the M25, made its physical construction tautologous. The Count's fetid breath warmed Thatcher's neck as she cut the ribbon.[24]

REFERENCES

INTRODUCTION

1 St John Adcock, ed., *Wonderful London* (London, 1926), p. 26.
2 Jonathan Raban, *Soft City* (London, 1974).

1 'THE BASTARD SIDE' Southeast London, 1: From Deptford and New Cross to Greenwich, Woolwich, Blackheath, Brockley and Lewisham

1 Angela Carter, *Wise Children* (London, 1991), p. 1.
2 Walter Besant, 'South London, Part VIII: South London of To-day', *Pall Mall Gazette*, XVI (1898), repr. in Walter Besant, *South London* (London, 1899), p. 320.
3 Harry Williams, *South London* (London, 1949), p. 23.
4 Besant, *South London*, p. 309.
5 Jonathan Raban, 'My Own Private Metropolis', *Financial Times*, 9 August 2008.
6 Charles Higson, *Happy Now* (London, 1993), p. 5.
7 Anthony Burgess, *A Dead Man in Deptford* (London, 1993), pp. 4–5.
8 John Evelyn, *The Diary of John Evelyn*, ed. William Bray (London, 1901), vol. I, p. 273.
9 Ibid.
10 Ralph Thoresby, *The Diary of Ralph Thoresby*, ed. Joseph Hunter (London, 1830), vol. II, pp. 237–8.
11 Paul Theroux, *The Family Arsenal* (London, 1976), p. 16.
12 Ibid., p. 75.
13 Ibid., p. 131.
14 Ibid., p. 132.

15 Roy Porter, *London: A Social History* (London, 1994), p. xiv.
16 Ibid.
17 Ibid.
18 Alex James, *Bit of a Blur* (London, 2008), p. 34.
19 Ibid., p. 36.
20 Ibid., p. 38.
21 Blake Morrison, *South of the River* (London, 2008), p. 22.
22 Ibid., p. 55.
23 Ibid., p. 79.
24 Ibid., p. 82.
25 Kate Tempest, *The Bricks that Built the Houses* (London, 2016), p. 3.
26 Ibid., p. 4.
27 Ibid., p. 53.
28 Ibid., p. 167.
29 A. L. Kennedy, *Serious Sweet* (London, 2016), p. 19.
30 Ibid.
31 Ibid.
32 Ibid., p. 21.
33 Ibid., p. 513.
34 Samuel Pepys, *The Shorter Pepys*, ed. Robert Latham (Berkeley, CA, 1985), p. 379.
35 Ibid., p. 399.
36 Samuel Johnson, *The Major Works* (Oxford, 2008), p. 2.
37 James Boswell, *London Journal, 1762–1763* (London, 2010), p. 296.
38 Ibid., p. 297.
39 Joseph Jekyll, 'The Life of Ignatius Sancho', in *Letters of the Late Ignatius Sancho, An African*, ed. Joseph Jekyll (London, 1782), vol. I, p. vi.
40 Ibid., p. vii.
41 *Letters of the Late Ignatius Sancho, An African*, ed. Joseph Jekyll (London, 1782), vol. II, p. 172.
42 Thomas Pynchon, *Mason and Dixon* (London, 1997), p. 194.
43 Peter Ackroyd, *Hawksmoor* (London, 1993), p. 48.
44 Charles Dickens, *Sketches by Boz* [1836] (Harmondsworth, 1995), p. 135.
45 Ibid., p. 138.
46 Ibid., p. 139.

47 Ibid., p. 140.

48 William Makepeace Thackeray, *The Book of Snobs and Travels in London* (London, 1903), p. 217.

49 Hippolyte Taine, *Notes on England* [1872] (New York, 1885), pp. 7–8.

50 Henry James, 'London at Midsummer', *Lippincott's Magazine*, 20 (1877), pp. 603–11; repr. in Henry James, *English Hours* [1905] (New York, 2011), p. 96.

51 Ibid., p. 97.

52 Joseph Conrad, *The Secret Agent* [1907] (London, 2000), p. 7.

53 Ibid., p. 5.

54 Ibid., p. 59.

55 Ibid., p. 70.

56 Ibid.

57 Ibid., p. 152.

58 Nicholas Blake, *The Worm of Death* (London, 1961), p. 38.

59 Ibid., p. 101.

60 Iain Sinclair and Marc Atkins, *Liquid City* (London, 1999), p. 40.

61 Ibid., p. 41.

62 Iain Sinclair, *Lights Out for the Territory* (London, 1997), p. 43.

63 Ibid.

64 Stewart Home, *Come before Christ and Murder Love* (London, 1997), p. 69.

65 W. G. Sebald, *Austerlitz* (London, 2001), pp. 142–3.

66 Ali Smith, *There but for the* (London, 2011), p. 2.

67 Ibid., p. 3.

68 Ibid., p. 351.

69 Ibid., p. 356.

70 Bernadine Evaristo, *Lara* [1997] (London, 2009), p. 101.

71 Ibid., p. 119.

72 Sinclair, *Lights Out for the Territory*, p. 46.

73 Ibid., p. 47.

74 Stella Duffy, 'A Modest Woolwich Proposal', available at https://stelladuffy.blog, accessed 27 November 2019.

75 Stella Duffy, 'Notes to Support Funding Modestly Proposed to the Woolwich Tourist Board', in *33 East* (London, 2010); available at https://stelladuffy.blog, accessed 26 November 2019.

76 Charles Dickens, *A Tale of Two Cities* [1859] (London, 2003), p. 8.
77 Charles Dickens, *Our Mutual Friend* [1864–5] (London, 1997), p. 662.
78 Ibid., p. 665.
79 Ibid., p. 666.
80 James, *English Hours*, p. 102.
81 Julian Symons, *The Blackheath Poisonings* (London, 1992), p. 3.
82 Ibid., p. 157.
83 Ibid., p. 182.
84 Daniel Defoe, *A Tour through the Whole Island of Great Britain* [1724–7] (London, 1971), p. 115.
85 Italo Svevo, *This England Is So Different* (Leicester, 2003), p. 168.
86 Sinclair, *Lights Out for the Territory*, p. 347.
87 Ibid.
88 Ibid.
89 Paul Breen, *The Charlton Men* (London, 2014), p. 2.
90 Ibid., p. 1.
91 Ibid., p. 3.
92 Ibid., p. 4.
93 Edgar Wallace, 'The Treasure Hunt', *The Grand Magazine*, 46 (December 1924); repr. in Edgar Wallace, *The Mind of Mr J. G. Reeder* (London, 1925).
94 Ibid.
95 Edgar Wallace, 'The Man from the East', *The Grand Magazine*, 47 (1925); repr. as 'Sheer Melodrama' in *The Mind of Mr J. G. Reeder*.
96 Ibid.
97 Henry Williamson, *The Dark Lantern* [1951] (London 2011), p. 11.
98 Ibid.
99 Ibid., p. 22.
100 David Lodge, *Quite a Good Time to be Born* (London, 2015), p. 17.
101 Ibid., p. 18.
102 Walter de la Mare, 'The Riddle' [1903], in *The Riddle and Other Stories* (London, 1923), pp. 289–94.
103 Ibid.

104 E. Nesbit, *The Story of the Treasure Seekers* (London, 1899), p. 3.

105 E. Nesbit, *The Wouldbegoods* (London, 1901), p. 3.

106 Ibid.

107 Betty Miller, *Farewell Leicester Square* (London, 1941), pp. 52–3.

108 Tony Parker, *The People of Providence* (London, 1996), p. 21.

109 Ibid., p. 26.

110 Ibid., p. 34.

111 Hanif Kureishi, *The Buddha of Suburbia* (London, 1990), p. 56.

112 Tony Parsons, *Stories We Could Tell* (London, 2006), p. 4.

113 Ian Nairn, 'More Readers' Books of the Year', *The Guardian*, 31 December 2005.

114 Paul Theroux, *The Family Arsenal* (London, 1976), p. 35.

115 Ibid., p. 36.

116 Ibid., p. 37.

2 'THE HOWLING DESERT' *Southeast London, II: From Camberwell to Peckham, Dulwich, Herne Hill and Forest Hill*

1 Robert Fishman, *Bourgeois Utopias* (New York, 1999), p. 23.

2 Arthur Conan Doyle, *The Sign of Four* [1890], in *The Original Illustrated 'Strand' Sherlock Holmes* (London, 1989), p. 70.

3 William Sharp, *The Life of Robert Browning* (London, 1890), pp. 61–2.

4 William Allingham, *A Diary*, ed. Helen Allingham and D. Radford (London, 1907), p. 36.

5 John Ruskin, *Praeterita* [1886], in *The Library Edition of the Works of John Ruskin*, ed. E. T. Cook and Alexander Wedderburn (London, 1903–12), vol. xxxv, p. 36.

6 Ibid., p. 379.

7 John Ruskin, 'Fiction, Fair and Foul', in *On the Old Road* [1885], in *The Library Edition of the Works of John Ruskin*, vol. xxxiv, pp. 265–6.

8 Ruskin, *Praeterita*, p. 47.

9 Charles Dickens, *Sketches by Boz* [1836] (Harmondsworth, 1995), p. 409.

10 Ibid., p. 412.

11 Ibid.

12 Ibid., pp. 409–11.

13 Ibid., p. 426.

14 Charles Dickens, *Great Expectations* [1861] (Harmondsworth, 1980), p. 229.

15 Ibid.

16 George Gissing, *In the Year of Jubilee* [1894] (London, 1994), p. 5.

17 Ibid., p. 16.

18 Ibid., pp. 238–9.

19 Arthur Conan Doyle, *A Study in Scarlet* [1887], in *The Adventures of Sherlock Holmes* (London, 1996), p. 24.

20 Arthur Conan Doyle, *The Sign of Four* [1890], in *The Original Illustrated 'Strand' Sherlock Holmes*, p. 71.

21 Arthur Conan Doyle, 'The Five Orange Pips' [1891], in *The Original Illustrated 'Strand' Sherlock Holmes*, p. 175.

22 Shan F. Bullock, *Robert Thorne: The Story of a London Clerk* (London, 1907), pp. 216–17.

23 Ibid., pp. 19–20.

24 Ibid., p. 206.

25 Ibid., p. 207.

26 Ibid., p. 209.

27 Ibid., pp. 249–50.

28 H. H. Bashford, *Augustus Carp, Esq. by Himself: Being the Autobiography of a Really Good Man* [1924] (Harmondsworth, 1987), pp. 2–3.

29 Ibid., p. 24.

30 Ibid., p. 75.

31 Ibid.

32 Vera Brittain, *Testament of Youth* [1933] (London, 2019), p. 183.

33 Nicolas Bentley, ed., *Fred Bason's Diary* (London, 1957), p. 48.

34 Alex Wheatle, *Brixton Rock* [1999] (London, 2010), p. 39.

35 Jenny Eclair, *Camberwell Beauty* [2000] (London, 2012), pp. 1–2.

36 Michael Palin, *The Complete Diaries* (London, 2005), n.p.

37 Sarah Waters, *The Paying Guests* (London, 2015), p. 4.

38 Emily Bullock, *The Longest Fight* (Brighton, 2015), pp. 87–9.

39 Alan Brownjohn, 'Ode to the A202', repr. in *Collected Poems, 1952–2006* (London, 2014), p. 103.

40 Alexander Gilchrist, *The Life of William Blake* [1863] (Mineola, NY, 2017), p. 7.

41 Ibid., p. 8.

42 William Blake, *Jerusalem: The Emanation of the Giant Albion* [1804–20], in *The Complete Poetry and Prose of William Blake*, ed. David V. Erdman (Berkeley, CA, 2008), p. 243.

43 Claire Tomalin, *Charles Dickens* (London, 2012), p. 361.

44 Charles Dickens, *Our Mutual Friend* [1864–5] (London, 1997), p. 219.

45 William Pett Ridge, *Mord Em'ly* [1898] (London, 1992), p. 41.

46 Ibid., p. 45.

47 Ibid., p. 43.

48 Ian Nairn, *Nairn's London* [1966] (London, 2014), p. 198.

49 Muriel Spark, *The Ballad of Peckham Rye* [1960] (London, 1999), p. 14.

50 Ibid., p. 9.

51 Ibid., p. 7.

52 Ibid., pp. 8–9.

53 Ibid., p. 118.

54 Ibid., p. 17.

55 Ibid., p. 89.

56 Ibid., p. 74.

57 Ibid., p. 143.

58 Iris Murdoch, *Under the Net* (London, 1954), p. 164.

59 Ibid., p. 169.

60 Ibid., p. 173.

61 Graham Swift, *Last Orders* (London, 1996).

62 Michael Collins, *The Likes of Us* (London, 2004), p. 209.

63 Stephen Kelman, *Pigeon English* (London, 2012), p. 5.

64 Ibid., p. 87.

65 Ben Judah, *This is London: Life and Death in the World City* (London, 2016), p. 36.

66 Sandi Toksvig, *Between the Stops* (London, 2019), p. 1.

67 Ibid., pp. 61–2.

68 Iain Sinclair and Marc Atkins, *Liquid City* (London, 1999), p. 41.

69 Leigh Hunt, 'A Walk from Dulwich to Brockham', in *The Companion* (London, 1828), p. 319.

70 Ibid., pp. 319–20.

71 Charles Dickens, *The Posthumous Papers of the Pickwick Club*
    [1836] (London, 1838), pp. 345–6.

72 Ibid., p. 350.

73 Walter Besant, 'South London, Part VIII: South London of
    To-day', *Pall Mall Gazette*, XVI (1898), repr. in Walter Besant,
    South London (London, 1899), pp. 308–10.

74 G. A. Sala, *Gaslight and Daylight* (London, 1859), p. 227.

75 Ibid., p. 228.

76 P. G. Wodehouse, *Psmith in the City* [1910] (London, 2003),
    p. 26.

77 Ibid.

78 Ibid., p. 27.

79 Raymond Chandler, 'Houses to Let', *The Academy*,
    24 February 1912.

80 R. C. Sherriff, *The Fortnight in September* (London, 2008),
    p. 29.

81 Howard Jacobson, *No More Mr Nice Guy* (London, 2003),
    p. 12.

82 Ibid., p. 14.

83 Ibid., p. 7.

84 Ibid., p. 130.

85 Will Self, *How the Dead Live* (London, 2000), p. 277.

86 Ibid., p. 278.

87 Ruskin, *Praeterita*, p. 48.

88 Ruskin, 'Fiction, Fair and Foul', in *On the Old Road* [1885],
    in *The Library Edition of the Works of John Ruskin*, vol. XXXIV,
    p. 266.

89 Iain Sinclair, *Lights Out for the Territory* (London, 1997).

90 Sinclair and Atkins, *Liquid City*, p. 39.

91 William Pett Ridge, *Sixty-nine Birnam Road* (London, 1909),
    p. 16.

92 Ibid., pp. 16–17.

93 Jonathan Meades, *The Fowler Family Business* (London, 2002),
    p. 64.

94 Ibid., p. 63.

95 Ibid., p. 4.

3 'A STRANGE FEELING IN THE AIR' *Outer Southeast London: From Sydenham to Penge, Crystal Palace and the Norwoods, South Norwood, Bromley, Chislehurst and Croydon*

1 Stella Gibbons, *Westwood* [1946] (London, 2011), p. 2.
2 Ian Nairn, *Nairn's London* [1966] (London, 2014), p. 197.
3 Eleanor Marx, Letter to Laura Lafargue, 17 November 1895, available at www.marxists.org, accessed 5 July 2018.
4 Eleanor Marx, Letter to Laura Lafargue, 10 December 1895, available at www.marxists.org, accessed 5 July 2018.
5 Eleanor Marx, Letter to Freddy Demuth, 1 September 1897, available at www.marxists.org, accessed 5 July 2018.
6 Eleanor Marx, Letter to Freddy Demuth, 3 February 1898, available at www.marxists.org, accessed 5 July 2018.
7 Paul Theroux, *The Family Arsenal* (London 1976), p. 21.
8 Ibid., p. 23.
9 Kazuo Ishiguro, 'Kazuo Ishiguro: How I Wrote *The Remains of the Day* in Four Weeks', *The Guardian*, 6 December 2014.
10 Michael Gray, 'Writing Rock History in the Path of Dylan', *The Guardian*, 13 December 1995.
11 Ibid.
12 Walter Besant, 'South London, Part VIII: South London of To-day', *Pall Mall Gazette*, XVI (1898), repr. in Walter Besant, *South London* (London, 1899), pp. 312–13.
13 John Mortimer, *Rumpole and the Penge Bungalow Murders* (London, 2004), p. 13.
14 Ibid.
15 Ibid., pp. 62–3.
16 Daniel Defoe, *A Tour through the Whole Island of Great Britain* [1724–7] (London, 1971), p. 347.
17 Charles Dickens, *Sketches by Boz* [1836] (Harmondsworth, 1995), p. 495.
18 Ibid., p. 500.
19 Ibid., p. 535.
20 Charles Dickens, *David Copperfield* [1850–51] (London, 1992), pp. 330–31.
21 John Ruskin, *Praeterita* [1886], in *The Library Edition of the Works of John Ruskin*, ed. E. T. Cook and Alexander Wedderburn (London, 1903–12), vol. XXXV, p. 48.

22 John Ruskin, 'The Opening of the Crystal Palace considered in some of its relations to the prospects of art' [1854], in *The Library Edition of the Works of John Ruskin*, vol. XII, pp. 417–18.

23 Ibid., p. 419.

24 Fyodor Dostoyevsky, *Notes from Underground* [1864] (New York, 1992), p. 23.

25 George Gissing, *The Nether World* [1889] (London, 1983), p. 105.

26 Ibid., p. 106.

27 Ibid., p. 110.

28 Daisy Ashford, *The Young Visiters* [1919] (London, 1984), pp. 37–8.

29 Lawrence Durrell, *The Black Book* [1938] (London, 2012), pp. 20–23.

30 Ibid., p. 32.

31 Angela Carter, *The Magic Toyshop* (London, 1981), p. 43.

32 Ibid., p. 100.

33 Ibid., p. 110.

34 Ibid.

35 Ibid., p. 112.

36 Magnus Mills, *The Maintenance of Headway* (London, 2009), p. 18.

37 Ibid., p. 36.

38 Ibid.

39 Arthur Conan Doyle, *The Sign of Four* [1890], in *The Original Illustrated 'Strand' Sherlock Holmes* (London, 1989), p. 76.

40 Ibid.

41 Ibid., p. 87.

42 Arthur Conan Doyle, 'The Adventure of the Norwood Builder' [1903], in *The Original Illustrated 'Strand' Sherlock Holmes* (London, 1998), p. 576.

43 Ibid., p. 580.

44 Arthur Conan Doyle, 'The Adventure of the Yellow Face' [1893], in *The Original Illustrated 'Strand' Sherlock Holmes*, p. 323.

45 Arthur Conan Doyle, *Beyond the City* (London, 1892), pp. 10–11.

46 Camille Pissarro, Letter to Wynford Dewhurst, 1902, quoted

in Kate Flint, ed., *Impressionists in London: The Critical Reception* (London, 1984), p. 2.

47 Shena Mackay, *Dunedin* [1992] (London, 2016), p. 72.

48 Ibid., p. 78.

49 Andy Medhurst, 'Negotiating the Gnome Zone: Versions of Suburbia in British Popular Culture', in *Visions of Suburbia*, ed. Roger Silverstone (London, 1997), p. 243.

50 Simon Frith, 'The Suburban Sensibility in British Pop and Rock', in *Visions of Suburbia*, ed. Silverstone, p. 271.

51 H. G. Wells, *Experiment in Autobiography: Discoveries and Conclusions of a Very Ordinary Brain* (London, 1934).

52 Ibid.

53 H. G. Wells, *Anticipations* (London, 1902), p. 35.

54 H. G. Wells, *When the Sleeper Wakes* (London, 1899), chap. 16, 'The Aerophile'.

55 Ibid.

56 Ibid.

57 H. G. Wells, *The New Machiavelli* (London, 1911), chap. 2.

58 Ibid., chap. 3.

59 Ibid., chap. 2.

60 Ibid.

61 Ibid.

62 Ibid.

63 Cahal Milmo, 'War of the Words: How H. G. Wells Snubbed Bromley', *The Independent*, 29 December 2010.

64 Richard Gordon, *Good Neighbours: Four Seasons in Suburbia* [1976] (Looe, 2001), pp. 10–12.

65 Adrian Henri, comments on 'Death in the Suburbs', recorded in Liverpool, 5 October 1982, available at www.poetryarchive. org, accessed 5 December 2019.

66 Ibid.

67 Hanif Kureishi, *The Buddha of Suburbia* (London, 1990), p. 113.

68 Ibid., p. 65.

69 Ibid., p. 46.

70 Ibid., p. 8.

71 Ibid., p. 188.

72 Ibid., p. 63.

73 Ibid., p. 75.

74 Ibid., p. 65.

75 Silverstone, ed., *Visions of Suburbia*, p. 2.

76 H. G. Wells, *Tono-Bungay* [1909] (London, 1994), p. 73.

77 Graham Swift, *The Light of Day* (London, 2003), p. 76.

78 Harold Pinter, *The Caretaker* (London, 1963), p. 28.

79 Ibid., p. 60.

80 Iain Sinclair, *Downriver* (London, 1991), p. 310.

81 Ibid., p. 311.

82 Ibid., pp. 320–22.

83 Jonathan Glancey, 'What's so Funny about Croydon?', *The Independent*, 7 April 1996.

84 Brenda Maddox, *The Married Man: A Life of D. H. Lawrence* (London, 1994), p. 15.

85 James T. Boulton, ed., *The Letters of D. H. Lawrence*, vol. 1: *1901–1913* (Cambridge, 1979), p. 82.

86 Ibid., p. 83.

87 D. H. Lawrence, 'The Fly in the Ointment', *New Statesman*, 16 August 1913, pp. 595–7; repr. in D. H. Lawrence, *The Mortal Coil and Other Stories* (Harmondsworth, 1971), p. 60.

88 Ibid., p. 66.

89 Ibid., p. 65.

90 Ibid., p. 60.

91 D. H. Lawrence, 'The Witch à la Mode' [1911–13], in *The Mortal Coil*, p. 88.

92 Ibid., p. 89.

93 Ibid., p. 96.

94 John Betjeman, 'Croydon', in *Mount Zion* (London, 1932); repr. in John Betjeman, *Collected Poems* (London, 2006), p. 11.

95 John Betjeman, 'Love in a Valley', in *Continual Dew* (London, 1937); repr. in *Collected Poems*, p. 23.

96 Stephen Spender, 'The Landscape near an Aerodrome' [1933], in *New Collected Poems*, ed. Michael Brett (London, 2018).

97 Elizabeth Bowen, *To the North* [1933] (London, 1950), p. 183.

98 Ibid., p. 184.

99 Freeman Wills Crofts, *The 12.30 from Croydon* [1934] (London, 2016), chap. 1.

100 Ibid., n.p.

101 Agatha Christie, *Death in the Clouds* [1935] (London, 2008), p. 19.

102 R. F. Delderfield, *The Dreaming Suburb* [1958] (London, 2008), p. 2.
103 'Introduction', ibid., p. ix.
104 Ibid., pp. 1–2.
105 Ibid., p. 3.
106 Anne Billson, 'Sunshine', in *The Time Out Book of London Short Stories*, ed. Maria Lexton (London, 1993), p. 31.
107 Henry Williamson, *The Dark Lantern* [1951] (London 2011), p. 35.

4 'SO VERY GREY AND MEAN' Southwest London: From Brixton to Clapham, Battersea, Wandsworth, Balham, Tooting and Streatham

1 Vincent van Gogh, Letter to Willem Jacob van Stockum and Carolina Adolphina van Stockum-Haanebeek, 2 July 1873, available at http://vangoghletters.org, accessed 5 January 2017.
2 Vincent van Gogh, Letter to Willem Jacob van Stockum and Carolina Adolphina van Stockum-Haanebeek, 7 August 1873, available at http://vangoghletters.org, accessed 5 January 2017.
3 See Kate Kellaway, 'Does a House in Brixton Hold the Key to Vincent van Gogh?', *The Observer*, 27 April 2014.
4 Arthur Conan Doyle, *A Study in Scarlet* [1887], in *The Adventures of Sherlock Holmes* (London, 1996), p. 19.
5 Ibid.
6 Ibid.
7 Ibid., p. 20.
8 Ibid.
9 Ibid., p. 21.
10 Angela Carter, *Wise Children* (London, 1991), p. 1.
11 Ibid., p. 3.
12 Sarah Waters, *Tipping the Velvet* (London, 1999), p. 67.
13 Ibid., p. 69.
14 Paul Vaughan, *Something in Linoleum: A Thirties Education* (London, 1994), p. 7.
15 V. S. Naipaul, *Mr Stone and the Knights Companion* (London, 1963), p. 158.
16 Ibid., p. 159.
17 Colin MacInnes, *City of Spades* [1957], in *The Colin MacInnes Omnibus: His Three London Novels* (London, 1985), p. 26.

18 Ibid., p. 28.

19 Ibid., p. 29.

20 Angela Carter, 'D'you Mean South?', *New Society*, 28 July 1977, pp. 188–9; repr. in Angela Carter, *Shaking a Leg: Collected Journalism and Writings* [1997] (London, 2013), p. 311.

21 Transcript from Eva Ulrike Pirker, *Narrative Projections of a Black British History* (London, 2011), p. 64.

22 Iain Sinclair, *Lights Out for the Territory* (London, 1997), p. 298.

23 Hanif Kureishi, *The Buddha of Suburbia* (London, 1990), p. 43.

24 Alex Wheatle, *Brixton Rock* [1999] (London, 2010), p. 137.

25 Alex Wheatle, *East of Acre Lane* [2001] (London, 2006), p. 13.

26 Ibid., pp. 268–9.

27 Martin Millar, *Lux the Poet* (London, 1988; repr. Berkeley, CA, 2009), p. 4.

28 Ibid., p. 3.

29 Ibid., p. 5.

30 Ibid., p. 18.

31 Geoff Dyer, *The Colour of Memory* (London, 1989), p. 71.

32 Ibid., pp. 73–4.

33 Ibid., p. 86.

34 Patrick Neate, *The London Pigeon Wars* (London, 2003), p. 16.

35 Ibid., p. 18.

36 Ibid., p. 3.

37 Allen Fisher, 'Brixton Fractals' [1985], in *Gravity as a Consequence of Shape* (Cambridge, 2004), p. 82.

38 Fisher, Preface, ibid., p. xi.

39 Ibid.

40 Fisher, 'Brixton Fractals', ibid., p. 81.

41 Shena Mackay, *Dunedin* [1992] (London, 2016), p. 98.

42 Tibor Fischer, *Crushed Mexican Spiders* (London, 2011).

43 Tom McCarthy, *Remainder* [2005] (London, 2016), p. 15.

44 Ibid., p. 24.

45 Ibid., p. 64.

46 Roma Tearne, *Brixton Beach* (London, 2009), p. 63.

47 Ibid., p. 263.

48 Ibid., p. 324.

49 Robert Fishman, *Bourgeois Utopias* (London, 1989), p. 53.

50 Donald Olsen, *The Growth of the Victorian City* (Harmondsworth, 1979), p. 190.

51 Samuel Pepys, *The Diary of Samuel Pepys*, Saturday 25 July 1663, available at www.pepysdiary.com, accessed 7 December 2019.

52 John Evelyn, quoted in Edward Walford, *Old and New London* (London, 1878), vol. VI, p. 320, available at www.british-history.ac.uk, accessed 7 December 2019.

53 James Stephens, 'The Clapham Sect', *Edinburgh Review*, LXXX (July 1844), p. 132.

54 E. M. Forster, *Marianne Thornton, 1797–1887: A Domestic Biography* (London, 1956), p. 18.

55 John Addington Symonds, *Shelley* (London, 1878), p. 45.

56 John Thomas Smith, *A Book for a Rainy Day* (London, 1845), pp. 256–7.

57 Forster, *Marianne Thornton*, pp. 19–20.

58 William Pett Ridge, *Outside the Radius: Stories of a London Suburb* (London, 1889), pp. 3–4.

59 Ibid., p. 5.

60 Ibid., pp. 8–9.

61 Oscar Wilde, *De Profundis* [1905] (London, 1907), p. 83.

62 H. G. Wells, *Love and Mr Lewisham* [1900], available at www.gutenberg.org, accessed 10 April 2020.

63 Guillaume Apollinaire, 'L'émigrant de Landor Road' [1904], original available at www.poemhunter.com, accessed 1 July 2020.

64 Guillaume Apollinaire, 'La Chanson du Mal-Aimé', trans. Jack Hayes, available at http://alcools-jh.blogspot.com, accessed 8 December 2019.

65 P. G. Wodehouse, *Psmith in the City* [1910] (London, 2003), p. 101.

66 Ibid., p. 114.

67 James Curtis, *They Drive by Night* [1938] (London, 2008), p. 93.

68 Ibid., p. 94.

69 Ibid., p. 95.

70 Julian Maclaren Ross, 'Excursion in Greene Land', *London Magazine*, IV (December 1964), pp. 56–65; repr. in Henry J. Donaghy, ed., *Conversations with Graham Greene* (Jackson, MS, and London, 1992), p. 3.

71 Ibid., p. 4.

72 Ibid., pp. 8–9.
73 Graham Greene, *The End of the Affair* [1951] (London, 2011), p. 25.
74 Ibid., p. 8.
75 Ibid., p. 70.
76 Graham Greene, *It's a Battlefield* [1934] (London, 2002), pp. 13–14.
77 Ibid., p. 16.
78 Paul Bailey, *Gabriel's Lament* (London, 1986), pp. 178–9.
79 Ibid., p. 186.
80 Ian Nairn, *Nairn's London* [1966] (London, 2014), p. 191.
81 Carter, 'D'you Mean South?'
82 John Lanchester, *Mr Phillips* (London, 2000), p. 36.
83 John Lanchester, *Capital* (London, 2013), pp. 5–6.
84 Ibid., p. 5.
85 Ibid., p. 6.
86 Ibid., p. 475.
87 Tom Canty, *Clapham Lights* (ebook, 2013), n.p.
88 Ibid.
89 Julie Myerson, *Home: The Story of Everyone Who Ever Lived in Our House* (London, 2004), pp. 12–13.
90 Ibid., pp. 8–9.
91 Julie Myerson, 'How I Wrote the Biography of an Ordinary Terraced House', *The Guardian*, 21 June 2014.
92 Nick Barratt, *Greater London: The Story of the Suburbs* (London, 2012), p. 215.
93 Matthew Arnold, Letter to Frances Arnold, December 1852, quoted in Fred G. Walcott, 'Matthew Arnold, Her Majesty's Inspector of Schools', *Quarterly Review: A Journal of University Perspectives*, LX (1953), p. 243.
94 Pamela Hansford Johnson, *Important to Me* [1974] (London, 2012), p. 1.
95 Pamela Hansford Johnson, *This Bed Thy Centre* [1935] (London, 2012), p. 15.
96 Ibid.
97 Ibid., pp. 251–2.
98 Penelope Fitzgerald, *Offshore* [1979] (London, 2013), p. 10.
99 Ibid., pp. 76–7.
100 Paul Bailey, *An Immaculate Mistake: Scenes from Childhood and Beyond* (London, 1990), p. 16.

101 Ibid., pp. 92–3.
102 John Walsh, *The Falling Angels* (London, 1999), p. 52.
103 Ibid., p. 55.
104 Ibid., p. 58.
105 Nell Dunn, *Up the Junction* [1963] (London, 1968), pp. 30–31.
106 Ibid., pp. 10–11.
107 Michael de Larrabeiti, *The Borribles* [1976] (London, 2002), p. 5.
108 Lanchester, *Mr Phillips*, p. 60.
109 Ibid., p. 63.
110 Kate Pullinger, *When the Monster Dies* (London, 1989), p. 168.
111 Ed Glinert, *Literary London* [2000] (London, 2007), p. 387.
112 Voltaire, Letter to Nicolas-Claude Thieriot, quoted in Ian Davidson, *Voltaire: A Life* (London, 2012), p. 58.
113 Ibid., p. 63.
114 Graham Swift, *The Sweet Shop Owner* [1980] (London, 1997), p. 75.
115 Ibid., p. 117.
116 Ibid., p. 83.
117 Ibid., p. 213.
118 Edward Thomas, *The Happy-go-lucky Morgans* (London, 1913), p. 1.
119 Ibid.
120 Ibid., p. 3.
121 Ibid., p. 5.
122 Ibid., p. 299.
123 Ian McEwan, *Atonement* [2001] (London, 2007), p. 228.
124 Ibid., pp. 229–30.
125 Charles Dickens, 'A Walk in a Workhouse', *Household Words*, 25 May 1850, p. 204, available at www.victorianweb.org, accessed 9 December 2019.
126 Florence Emily Hardy, *The Life of Thomas Hardy* [1928–30] (London, 1962), p. 118; quoted in Mark Ford, *Thomas Hardy: Half a Londoner* (London, 2016), p. 187.
127 Ibid.
128 Thomas Hardy, 'Beyond the Last Lamp (Near Tooting Common)', *Harper's Monthly Magazine* (December 1911), p. 92; repr. in *The Collected Poems of Thomas Hardy* (London, 2002), p. 296.

129 J. Hillis Miller, 'Hardy', in *The J. Hillis Miller Reader* (Stanford, CA, 2005), p. 147.

130 Kit Wright, 'A Love Song of Tooting', in *Hoping It Might Be So: Poems, 1974–2000* (London, 2008), p. 11.

131 A. N. Wilson, *My Name Is Legion* (London, 2004), pp. 123–4.

132 Samuel Johnson, Letter to Hester Thrale, 29 May 1779, in *Letters to and from the Late Samuel Johnson, LL.D* (London, 1788), vol. II, p. 47.

133 James Boswell, *The Life of Samuel Johnson, LL.D* (London 1791), vol. I, p. 270.

134 Frances Burney, *The Diary and Letters of Madame D'Arblay* (London, 1842), vol. I, p. 62.

135 Ibid., pp. 63–4.

136 Walter George Bell, *Where London Sleeps: Historical Journeyings into the Suburbs* (London, 1926), pp. 171–2.

137 Carolyn Steedman, *Landscape for a Good Woman* (London, 1987), p. 2.

138 Ibid., p. 44.

139 'Kingsley Amis: The Memoirs', *Bookmark*, BBC2, 6 March 1991.

140 Kingsley Amis, *Stanley and the Women* [1984] (London, 2004), p. 130.

5 'UNCONGENIAL NEIGHBOURS' Outer Southwest London: From Wimbledon to Putney, Mortlake, Richmond, Twickenham, Teddington, Kingston, Shepperton, Surbiton, New Malden and Worcester Park

1 Ed Glinert, *Literary London* [2000] (London, 2007), p. 388.

2 David E. Cartwright, *Schopenhauer: A Biography* (Cambridge, MA, 2010), pp. 54–5.

3 Ibid., p. 58.

4 Michael Frayn, *Towards the End of the Morning* (London, 1967), p. 25.

5 Ibid., pp. 26–7.

6 Ibid., p. 27.

7 Ibid., p. 25.

8 Nigel Williams, *The Wimbledon Poisoner* [1990] (London, 2013), p. 12.

9 Ibid., p. 23.

10 Nigel Williams, *Scenes from a Poisoner's Life* (London, 1994), p. 55.

11 Ibid., p. 59.

12 Louis de Bernières, *Sunday Morning at the Centre of the World* (London, 2001), p. xiii.

13 Jane Gardham, *The People on Privilege Hill* (London, 1996), p. 46.

14 Ibid.

15 Ibid., pp. 48–9.

16 Graham Swift, *The Light of Day* (London, 2003), p. 19.

17 Ibid., p. 21.

18 H. G. Wells, *Tono-Bungay* [1909] (London, 1994), p. 73.

19 Ibid., p. 349.

20 Edward Walford, 'Putney', in *Old and New London* (London, 1878), vol. VI, pp. 489–503, available at www.british-history. ac.uk, accessed 10 December 2019.

21 Edward Gibbon, *The Autobiographies of Edward Gibbon*, ed. John Murray (London, 1887), p. 28.

22 Ibid., p. 43.

23 Max Beerbohm, 'No. 2. The Pines' [1914], in *And Even Now* (London, 1920), pp. 61–5.

24 Tony Judt, *The Memory Chalet* (London, 2010), pp. 53–4.

25 Ben Beaumont-Thomas, 'How We Made Cult Cartoon Mr Benn', interview with David McKee, *The Guardian*, 7 March 2017.

26 Peter Ackroyd, *London: The Biography* (London, 2000), p. 508.

27 Charlotte Fell Smith, *The Life of John Dee, 1527–1608* (London, 1909), p. 32.

28 Ibid., pp. 31–2.

29 Iain Sinclair and Marc Atkins, *Liquid City* (London, 1999), p. 85.

30 James Thomson, 'Summer', in *The Seasons* [1730], in *The Poetical Works of James Thomson* (London, 1887), lines 1434–43.

31 Ibid., lines 1401–13.

32 Charles Dickens, Letter to Daniel Maclise, 28 June 1839, in *The Selected Letters of Charles Dickens*, ed. Jenny Hartley (Oxford, 2012), p. 55.

33 Charles Dickens, *Great Expectations* [1861] (London, 2010), p. 256.

34 Ibid., p. 257.

35 William Cobbett, *Rural Rides* (London, 1830), p. 1.

36 Ibid., pp. 1–2.

37 Sheridan Le Fanu, 'Green Tea', *All the Year Round* (October–November 1869), repr. in Sheridan Le Fanu, *In a Glass Darkly* (London, 1872), p. 41.

38 Ibid., pp. 51–2.

39 Ibid., pp. 59–60.

40 Henry James, *The Suburbs of London* [1877], in *London Stories and Other Writings* (London, 1989), p. 221.

41 Ibid., pp. 232–3.

42 H. G. Wells, *The Time Machine* [1895], in *The Complete Short Stories of H. G. Wells* (London, 1987), p. 24.

43 Ibid., p. 33.

44 H. G. Wells, *The War of the Worlds* (New York and London, 1898), p. 130.

45 Ibid., pp. 100–101.

46 Ibid., pp. 120–21.

47 Ibid., p. 190.

48 Ibid.

49 Ibid., p. 191.

50 Ibid.

51 Ibid., p. 201.

52 Ibid., p. 239.

53 Ibid., p. 155.

54 W.N.P. Barbellion, *The Journal of a Disappointed Man* (London, 1919), pp. 112–13.

55 Virginia Woolf, *A Moment's Liberty: The Shorter Diary*, ed. Anne Olivier Bell [1977] (London, 1990), p. 61.

56 Ibid., p. 86

57 Ibid., p. 143.

58 T. S. Eliot, *The Waste Land* [1922] (London, 2010), lines 292–5.

59 Woolf, *A Moment's Liberty*, p. 170.

60 Michael Cunningham, *The Hours* (New York, 1998), pp. 168–9.

61 David Hare, *The Hours* (London, 2003).

62 J. R. Ackerley, *My Father and Myself* [1968] (Harmondsworth, 1971), p. 81.

63 Ibid., p. 136.

64 Ibid., p. 143.
65 John Donne, 'Twicknam Garden', in *Poems of John Donne*,
    ed. E. K. Chambers (London, 1896), p. 29.
66 Alexander Pope, *Letters* (London, 1737), vol. VII, p. 206.
67 Alexander Pope, *The Works of Alexander Pope Esq.* (London,
    1751), vol. VIII, p. 36.
68 Pope, *Letters*, vol. VII, pp. 171–2.
69 Oliver Goldsmith, *Memoirs of M. de Voltaire* [1761], quoted
    in Ian Davidson, *Voltaire: A Life* (London, 2012), p. 171.
70 Ibid.
71 Horace Walpole, *A Description of the Villa of Horace Walpole*
    (London, 1774), p. 1.
72 Horace Walpole, *The Correspondence of Horace Walpole with
    George Montagu* (London, 1837), vol. I, pp. 108–9.
73 Horace Walpole, *The Letters of Horace Walpole, Earl Orford*,
    ed. Peter Cunningham (London, 1861), vol. II, p. 338.
74 Gavin Ewart, *Londoners* (London, 1964), p. 34.
75 Thomas Love Peacock, *Crotchet Castle* (London, 1831), p. 3.
76 Ibid., pp. 1–3.
77 Ibid., p. 9.
78 John Batchelor, *Tennyson: To Strive, to Seek, to Find* (London,
    2014), p. 96.
79 William Allingham, *A Diary* (London, 1908), pp. 60–61.
80 Ibid., pp. 62–3.
81 Thom Gunn, 'Last Days at Teddington', in *Collected Poems*
    (London, 1994), p. 237.
82 Iain Sinclair, *Radon Daughters* (London, 1994), p. 149.
83 Ben Aaronovitch, *Rivers of London* (London, 2011), p. 96.
84 Ibid., pp. 105–6.
85 Jerome K. Jerome, *Three Men in a Boat* (London, 1889), p. 48.
86 G. A. Sala, *Gaslight and Daylight* (London, 1859), p. 349.
87 Ibid., p. 350.
88 Ibid., p. 353.
89 Jerome, *Three Men in a Boat*, p. 48.
90 Ibid.
91 John Galsworthy, *The Forsyte Saga*, vol. I: *The Man of Property*
    [1906] (London, 1978), p. 61.
92 Ibid., p. 226.
93 D. H. Lawrence, *The Rainbow* [1915] (London, 1979), p. 360.

94 Ibid., pp. 360–61.

95 Jacqueline Wilson, *Opal Plumstead* (London, 2014), p. 20.

96 J. G. Ballard, *The Unlimited Dream Company* [1981] (London, 1990), p. 35.

97 J. G. Ballard, *Miracles of Life* (London, 2008), p. 184.

98 Ibid.

99 J .G. Ballard, *The Kindness of Women* (London, 1992), p. 122.

100 Ibid., p. 81.

101 Ibid., p. 105.

102 Ibid., p. 127.

103 J. G. Ballard, *Kingdom Come* (London, 2006), p. 6.

104 Richard Jefferies, *The Story of My Heart* [1883] (London, 1901), p. 47.

105 Richard Jefferies, *Nature near London* (London, 1905), p. 1.

106 Keble Howard, *The Smiths of Surbiton: A Comedy without a Plot* (London, 1906), p. 8.

107 Ibid., p. 289.

108 E. M. Forster, 'The Celestial Omnibus' [1911], in *The Celestial Omnibus and Other Tales* (Mineola, NY, 2014), p. 29.

109 Ibid., p. 30.

110 Ibid., p. 36.

111 Ibid., p. 44.

112 Bernice Rubens, *Our Father* (London, 1987), p. 9.

113 Ibid.

114 Julian Clary, *A Young Man's Passage* (London, 2005), p. 22.

115 John Burnside, *Waking Up in Toytown* (London, 2010), p. 19.

116 Ibid., p. 28.

117 Ibid., p. 25.

118 Paul Vaughan, *Something in Linoleum: A Thirties Education* (London, 1994), p. 6.

119 Ibid., p. 58.

120 Ibid.

121 Ibid., p. 3.

122 W. H. Auden and Christopher Isherwood, *The Ascent of F6* [1936], in *Plays and Other Dramatic Writings, 1928–38*, ed. Edward Mendelson (Princeton, NJ, 1988), pp. 297–8.

123 H. G. Wells, *Ann Veronica* (London, 1909), p. 3.

124 Ibid.

125 Ibid., p. 99.
126 B. S. Johnson, *Albert Angelo* [1964] (London, 2003), p. 136.

6 'REAL STABILITY' West London: From Hammersmith to Chiswick, Brentford, Hounslow, Southall, Ealing, Shepherd's Bush and White City

  1 Barbara K. Lewalski, *The Life of John Milton* (New York, 2008), p. 54.
  2 Daniel Defoe, *A Tour through the Whole Island of Great Britain* [1724–7] (London, 1971), p. 347.
  3 Daniel Defoe, *Moll Flanders* [1722] (London, 1921), p. 99.
  4 Ibid., p. 100.
  5 Charles Dickens, *Great Expectations* [1861] (London, 1980), p. 209.
  6 Ibid., p. 218.
  7 William Morris, *News from Nowhere* [1890] (London, 1995), p. 4.
  8 Ibid., p. 5.
  9 Ibid., pp. 10–11.
 10 A. P. Herbert, *The Water Gipsies* (London 1930), p. 12.
 11 Richard Marsh, *The Beetle* [1897] (Ontario, 2004), p. 44.
 12 Ibid., p. 46.
 13 Ibid., p. 51.
 14 Naomi Mitchison, Letter, *London Review of Books*, xvi/7, 7 April 1994.
 15 James Curtis, *The Gilt Kid* [1936] (London, 2007), p. 125.
 16 B. S. Johnson, *Christie Malry's Own Double-entry* [1973] (London, 2001), p. 27.
 17 Ibid., p. 146.
 18 Ibid., p. 147.
 19 B. S. Johnson, *Albert Angelo* [1964] (London, 2003), pp. 20–21.
 20 Irvine Welsh, *Trainspotting* [1993] (London, 2011), p. 228.
 21 William Makepeace Thackeray, *Vanity Fair* [1848] (London, 1992), p. 3.
 22 Iain Sinclair, *Lights Out for the Territory* (London, 1997), p. 354.
 23 Roy Foster, *W. B. Yeats: A Life*, vol. I: *The Apprentice Mage, 1865–1914* (Oxford, 1998), p. 60.

24 Ibid., p. 79.
25 Hermann Muthesius, *Das englische Haus* (Berlin, 1908), p. 134.
26 G. K. Chesterton, *The Man Who Was Thursday* [1908] (London, 1986), p. 9.
27 Ibid., p. 10.
28 Patrick Hamilton, *Twenty Thousand Streets under the Sky* [1935] (London, 1998), p. 297.
29 Ibid.
30 Mavis Cheek, *Pause between Acts* [1988] (London, 1998), p. 5.
31 Ian Sinclair, *Radon Daughters* (London, 1994), p. 144.
32 Charles Dickens, *Our Mutual Friend* [1864–5] (London, 1997), p. 184.
33 Quoted in Michael Law, *The Experience of Suburban Modernity* (Manchester, 2014), p. 154.
34 Evelyn Waugh, *Vile Bodies* [1934] (London, 2000), p. 168.
35 Louis MacNeice, *Autumn Journal* (London, 1939), p. 45.
36 George Orwell, 'On a Ruined Farm near the His Master's Voice Gramophone Factory' [1934], in *Orwell's England* (London, 2001), p. 196.
37 Aldous Huxley, *Brave New World* [1932] (London, 1972), p. 58.
38 Ibid., pp. 58–9.
39 Elizabeth Bowen, *To the North* [1932] (London, 1950), p. 91.
40 Paul Bailey, *Gabriel's Lament* (London, 1986), p. 12.
41 Robert Rankin, *The Antipope* (London, 1981), p. 70.
42 Ibid., pp. 76–7.
43 Ibid., p. 78.
44 William Cobbett, *Rural Rides* (London, 1830), p. 61.
45 Walter George Bell, *Where London Sleeps: Historical Journeyings into the Suburbs* (London, 1926), pp. 202–3.
46 Gautam Malkani, *Londonstani* (London, 2006), p. 5.
47 Ibid., p. 17.
48 John King, *Skinheads* (London, 2008), pp. 130–31.
49 Ibid., p. 131.
50 Tim Lott, *The Scent of Dried Roses* [1996] (London, 2009), p. 25.
51 Ibid., p. 29.
52 Ibid., p. 28.
53 Nirpal Singh Dhaliwal, *Tourism* (London, 2006), pp. 40–41.
54 Ibid., p. 34.
55 Ibid., pp. 115–16.

56 Terry Taylor, *Baron's Court, All Change* [1961] (London, 2011), pp. 23–4.

57 Ibid., p. 59.

58 Robert Colls, *George Orwell: English Rebel* (Oxford, 2013), p. 267.

59 George Orwell, *Coming Up for Air* [1939] (London, 1948), p. 13.

60 Ibid., pp. 435–6.

61 Ibid., pp. 565–6.

62 Arthur Machen, 'A Fragment of Life', in *The House of Souls* (London, 1906), p. 35.

63 Ibid., p. 29.

64 Ibid., p. 55.

65 J. G. Ballard, *Concrete Island* [1974] (London, 2014), p. 7.

66 Ibid., pp. 11–12.

67 Edward Platt, *Leadville* (London, 2000), pp. 2–3.

68 Ibid., p. 9.

69 Sam Selvon, *Moses Ascending* [1975] (London, 2008), p. 1.

70 Ibid., p. 2.

71 Ibid., pp. 4–5.

72 Ben Judah, *This Is London: Life and Death in the World City* (London, 2016), pp. 117–18.

73 Ibid., p. 118.

74 Tim Lott, *White City Blue* [1997] (London, 2000), p. 23.

75 Nicholas Royle, *The Director's Cut* (London, 2001), p. 219.

76 Hanif Kureishi, *Gabriel's Gift* (London, 2001), p. 112.

7 'FINE THINGS TO BE SEEN' Northwest London: From Kensal Green to Neasden, Willesden, Kilburn, West Hampstead, Dollis Hill, Wembley, Harrow, Ruislip and the Outer Northwest

1 G. K. Chesterton, 'The Rolling English Road' [1913], in *The Flying Inn* (London, 1914), p. 252.

2 Iain Sinclair, *Lights Out for the Territory* (London, 1997), p. 340.

3 Ibid., p. 341.

4 Patrick Keiller, *The View from the Train* (London, 2013), p. 173.

5 Ibid.

6 Ibid., p. 174.

7 Courttia Newland, *The Scholar: A West Side Story* (London, 1997), p. 7.

8 Ben Weinreb and Christopher Hibbert, eds, *The London Encyclopaedia* (London, 1983), p. 991.

9 Harrison Ainsworth, *Jack Shepherd, A Romance* [1839] (London, 1898), p. 19.

10 Ibid., pp. 194–5.

11 Ibid., p. 196.

12 Willie Rushton, 'Neasden' (1972), full lyrics available at https://jon-doloresdelargo.blogspot.com, accessed 21 December 2019.

13 Iain Sinclair, *London Overground: A Day's Walk around the Ginger Line* (London, 2015), p. 181.

14 Zadie Smith, *White Teeth* (London, 2000), p. 46.

15 Ibid., p. 47.

16 Ibid., p. 164.

17 Zadie Smith, *NW* (London, 2012), p. 42.

18 Ibid., p. 263.

19 Mark Haddon, *The Curious Incident of the Dog in the Night-time* (London, 2003), pp. 232–3.

20 Diana Evans, *26a* (London, 2005), p. 9.

21 Ben Judah, *This Is London: Life and Death in the World City* (London, 2016), pp. 53–4.

22 Guy Gunaratne, *In Our Mad and Furious City* (London, 2018), pp. 9–10.

23 Waguih Ghali, *Beer in the Snooker Club* [1964] (London, 2010), p. 88.

24 Robert McLiam Wilson, *Ripley Bogle* (London, 1989), p. 155.

25 Ibid., p. 154.

26 Ibid., p. 174.

27 Chris Petit, *The Hard Shoulder* (London, 2001), p. 3.

28 Edna O'Brien, 'Shovel Kings', in *Saints and Sinners* (London, 2011), pp. 5–6.

29 Wilkie Collins, *The Woman in White* [1859] (Oxford, 1998), p. 19.

30 Ibid., pp. 19–20.

31 Barbara Vine, *King Solomon's Carpet* (London, 1991), pp. 15–16.

32 Rachel Cusk, *The Temporary* (London, 1995), p. 140.

33 Mark Twain, *Mark Twain, the Globetrotter* (ebook, 2017), n.p.

34 Ibid.

35 Ian McEwan, *The Innocent* [1990] (London, 2005), p. 3.

36 Ibid., p. 88.

37 Virginia Woolf, 'Thunder at Wembley', *Nation and Athenaeum*, 39 (June 1924), pp. 409–10; repr. in Virginia Woolf, *The Captain's Death Bed and Other Essays* (London, 1950), p. 169.

38 Ibid., p. 171.

39 P. G. Wodehouse, 'The Rummy Affair of Old Biffy', *Saturday Evening Post* (September 1924); repr. in P. G. Wodehouse, *Carry On, Jeeves* (London, 1925), pp. 132 and 147.

40 Ibid., p. 150.

41 Ibid., p. 151.

42 Andrea Levy, *Small Island* [2004] (London, 2014), p. 3.

43 Gordon S. Maxwell, *The Fringe of London* (London, 1925), p. 155.

44 Ibid., p. 156.

45 Martin Amis, *Lionel Asbo* (London, 2013), pp. 70–71.

46 Kamila Shamsie, *Home Fire* (London, 2017), n.p.

47 Ibid.

48 John Betjeman, *A Few Late Chrysanthemums* (London, 1954); repr. in John Betjeman, *Collected Poems* (London, 2006), p. 163.

49 Ibid., p. 148.

50 Ibid., p. 169.

51 John Betjeman, *Metro-land*, BBC 2, 26 February 1973; collected in *John Betjeman's England*, ed. Stephen Games (London, 2009), pp. 174–84.

52 Richard Mabey, *A Good Parcel of English Soil* (London, 2013), p. 62.

53 Julian Barnes, *Metroland* (London, 1980), p. 17.

54 Ibid., p. 34.

55 Ibid., p. 135.

56 R. C. Sherriff, *Greengates* [1936] (London, 2015), p. 101.

57 Ibid., p. 105.

58 Ibid., p. 114

59 Ibid., p. 311.

60 Paul Barker, *The Freedoms of Suburbia* (London, 2009), p. 15.

61 Ibid.

62 Ibid., p. 18.

63 Leslie Thomas, *Tropic of Ruislip* [1974] (London, 1997), p. 12.
64 Ibid., p. 11.
65 Ibid., pp. 11–12.
66 Ibid., p. 12.
67 Ibid., p. 13.
68 Nick Papadimitriou, *Scarp: In Search of London's Outer Limits* (London, 2012), pp. 1, 3.
69 Ibid., pp. 8–9.
70 Ibid., pp. 80–81.
71 Paula Hawkins, *The Girl on the Train* (London, 2015), p. 16.
72 Ibid., p. 22.

8 'ASPIRING IN THE AIR' North London: From Camden Town to Primrose Hill, Kentish Town, Holloway, Crouch End, Stoke Newington, Islington and Highbury

1 Samuel Palmer, *St Pancras* (London, 1870), p. 64.
2 Ibid., p. 17.
3 Charles Dickens, 'Shabby-genteel People', in *Sketches by Boz* [1836] (London, 1839), p. 143.
4 Charles Dickens, *David Copperfield* (London, 1850), p. 297.
5 Charles Dickens, *Dombey and Son* [1848] (London, 1921), pp. 62–3.
6 David Thomson, *In Camden Town* (London, 1983), p. 74.
7 Walter Sickert, Lecture at Thanet School of Art, 16 November 1934, quoted in Lisa Tickner, 'Walter Sickert: *The Camden Town Murder* and Tabloid Crime', in *Modern Life and Modern Subjects: British Art in the Early Twentieth Century* (New Haven, CT, 2000), pp. 11–47; available at www.tate.org.uk, accessed 28 December 2019.
8 Compton Mackenzie, *Sinister Street* (New York, 1914), vol. II, pp. 371–2.
9 Ibid., p. 372.
10 Graham Robb, *Rimbaud* (London, 2000), n.p.
11 George Gissing, *New Grub Street* [1891] (London, 1968), p. 115.
12 Ibid., p. 446.
13 John Brinnin, *Dylan Thomas in America* (Boston, MA, 1955), p. 131.
14 David Storey, *Flight into Camden* (London, 1960), p. 127.

15 Ibid., p. 134.

16 Thomson, *In Camden Town*, p. 88.

17 Quoted in Inigo Thomas, 'Mark Boxer and the LRB', LRB [*London Review of Books*] blog, 29 January 2015, available at www.lrb.co.uk, accessed 28 December 2019.

18 Alan Bennett, 'What I Did in 2014', *London Review of Books*, XXXVII/I (8 January 2015), pp. 37–9.

19 Alan Bennett, 'The Lady in the Van', *London Review of Books*, XI/20 (26 October 1989), pp. 3–10.

20 Nina Stibbe, *Love, Nina: Despatches from Family Life* (London, 2013), p. v.

21 Ibid., p. 18.

22 John le Carré, *Tinker Tailor Soldier Spy* (London, 1974), p. 317.

23 Ibid., p. 320.

24 Deborah Moggach, *Closer to Home* (London, 1979), p. 22.

25 Ibid.

26 Ibid., pp. 24–5.

27 William Blake, *Jerusalem: The Emanation of the Giant Albion* [1804–20], in *Poems of William Blake*, ed. W. B. Yeats (London, 1920), pp. 221–2.

28 Mary Kingston Stocking, ed., *The Journals of Claire Clairmont* (Cambridge, MA, 1968), p. 47.

29 Charles Lamb, 'Detached Thoughts on Books and Reading' [1833], in *The Complete Works in Prose and Verse of Charles Lamb: From the Original* (London, 1874), p. 148.

30 Edmund Gosse, *Father and Son* (London, 1907), p. 48.

31 H. G. Wells, *The War of the Worlds* (New York and London, 1898), pp. 277–8.

32 Ibid., pp. 279–80.

33 Jean Rhys, *Voyage in the Dark* [1934] (London, 1967), pp. 75–6.

34 Louis MacNeice, *Autumn Journal* [1939] (London, 2013), p. 113.

35 Aldous Huxley, *Time Must Have a Stop* (London, 1944), p. 270.

36 Dodie Smith, *The Hundred and One Dalmatians* [1956] (London, 1989), p. 8.

37 Ibid.

38 Sylvia Plath, 'Snow Blitz' [1963], in *Johnny Panic and the Bible of Dreams* (London, 1977), p. 125.

39 Keith Badman, *The Beatles: Off the Record* (ebook, 2009), n.p.

40 Kingsley Amis, *The Folks that Live on the Hill* [1990] (London, 2012), p. 5.

41 Paul Charles, *Last Boat to Camden Town* [1998] (London, 2016), p. 33.

42 Helen Falconer, *Primrose Hill* (London, 1999), p. 5.

43 Ibid., p. 7.

44 William Stukeley, *The Family Memoirs of the Rev. William Stukeley*, vol. iii, Publications of the Surtees Society 80 (London, 1887), p. 20.

45 Mrs Julian Marshall, *The Life and Letters of Mary Wollstonecraft Shelley* [1889] (New York, 1970), vol. ii, pp. 119–20.

46 Ibid., p. 119.

47 James Hole, *The Homes of the Working Classes, with Suggestions for their Improvement* (London, 1866), quoted in Roy Porter, *London: A Social History* (London, 1994), p. 259.

48 John Betjeman, 'Parliament Hill Fields', in *New Bats in Old Belfries* (London, 1945); repr. in John Betjeman, *Collected Poems* (London, 2006), p. 85.

49 Jonathan Raban, *Soft City* [1975] (London, 1981), pp. 108–9.

50 Ibid., p. 109.

51 Buchi Emecheta, *In the Ditch* [1972] (London, 1979), p. 21.

52 Charles Dickens, *Our Mutual Friend* [1864–5] (London, 1997), pp. 41–2.

53 Ibid., p. 58.

54 George and Weedon Grossmith, *The Diary of a Nobody* [1888] (London, 1998), p. 3.

55 Ibid., p. 9.

56 Ibid., pp. 19–20.

57 Colin MacInnes, *City of Spades* [1957], in *The London Novels* (London, 2005), p. 68.

58 Ibid., p. 69.

59 Ibid.

60 Natasha Frost, 'The Strange, Sad Story of Joe Orton, His Lover, and 72 Stolen Library Books', 9 August 2017, available

at www.atlasobscura.com, accessed 29 December 2019. See also www.joeorton.org.

61 Joe Orton, *The Orton Diaries*, ed. John Lahr (London, 1978), p. 233.

62 Ibid.

63 J. M. O'Neill, *Duffy Is Dead* (London, 1987), p. 31.

64 Ibid., p. 70.

65 Ibid.

66 Nick Hornby, *High Fidelity* [1995] (London, 2000), p. 39.

67 Nick Hornby, *How to be Good* (London, 2001), p. 36.

68 Ibid., pp. 35–6.

69 Ibid., p. 19.

70 Charlotte Riddell, *City and Suburb* (London, 1861), p. 1.

71 Ibid., p. 3.

72 Zoë Heller, *Notes on a Scandal* (London, 2003), p. 20.

73 Bill Drummond, 'Edge-lands', in *London: City of Disappearances*, ed. Iain Sinclair (London, 2006), p. 599.

74 George Gissing, *The Nether World* (London, 1889), pp. 251–2.

75 Arthur Machen, 'Tottenham Hale', in *Wonderful London*, ed. A. St John Adcock (London, 1926), p. 100.

76 Ian Cunningham, *A Reader's Guide to Writers' London* (London, 2001), p. 169.

77 Stephen King, 'Crouch End' [1980, revised 2003], in *Nightmares and Dreamscapes* (New York, 2017), p. 661.

78 Will Self, 'The North London Book of the Dead', in *The Quantity Theory of Insanity* [1991] (London, 2011), p. 6.

79 Ibid., pp. 6–7.

80 Ibid., p. 7.

81 Anthony Horowitz, 'Killer Camera' [1999], in *The Complete Horowitz Horror* (London, 2008), pp. 35–6.

82 S. J. Watson, *Before I Go to Sleep* (London, 2011), p. 22.

83 Nikolaus Pevsner, *London (except the Cities of London and Westminster)*, The Buildings of England (Harmondsworth, 1953), p. 427.

84 Daniel Defoe, *A Tour through the Whole Island of Great Britain* [1724–7] (Harmondsworth, 1971), pp. 337–8.

85 Clement Cruttwell, *A Tour through the Whole Island of Great Britain* (London, 1801), vol. v, p. 108.

86 Patrick Keiller, 'London in the Early 1990s', in *The View from the Train* (London, 2013), p. 90.

87 Edgar Allan Poe, 'William Wilson' [1839], in *The Complete Tales and Poems of Edgar Allan Poe* (London, 1982), p. 626.

88 Arthur Machen, 'N.', in *The Great God Pan and Other Horror Stories* (London, 2018), p. 311.

89 Ibid., p. 312.

90 Ibid., p. 314.

91 William Pett Ridge, *Nine to Six-thirty* (London, 1910), pp. 4–5.

92 Ibid., pp. 12–13.

93 Alexander Baron, *The Lowlife* [1963] (London, 2010), p. 12.

94 Ibid.

95 Pamela Cox and Annabel Hobley, *Shopgirls* (London, 2015), p. 226.

96 Gordon Carr, *The Angry Brigade: A History of Britain's First Urban Guerilla Group* [1975] (Oakland, CA, 2010), p. 103.

97 Iain Sinclair, *Lights Out for the Territory* [1997] (London, 2003), pp. 23–4.

98 Ibid., pp. 34–5.

99 Bernardine Evaristo, *Mr Loverman* (London, 2013), p. 115.

100 Ned Ward, *A Walk to Islington: With a Description of New Tunbridge-Wells, and Sadler's Musick-house* (London, 1699), p. 3.

101 Roy Porter, *London: A Social History* (London, 1994), p. 122.

102 Daniel Defoe, *A Tour through the Whole Island of Great Britain* [1724–7] (London, 1971), p. 321.

103 Charles Lamb, *The Letters of Charles Lamb, with a Sketch of his Life* (London, 1837), vol. 1, p. 192.

104 Ibid., p. 193.

105 Ibid., p. 194.

106 Charles Dickens, 'The Streets-morning', in *Sketches by Boz* [1836] (Harmondsworth, 1995), p. 72.

107 Charles Dickens, 'Characters, Chapter 1: Thoughts about People', ibid., p. 253.

108 Charles Dickens, 'The Lamplighter's Story', in *The Pic-nic Papers*, ed. Dickens (London, 1841), pp. 4–5.

109 M. V. Hughes, *A London Girl of the 1870s* [1934], in *A London Family, 1870–1900* (Oxford, 1946), pp. 2–3.

110 Ibid., pp. 5–6.

111 Ibid., p. 86.

112 Arthur Machen, 'The Islington Mystery', in *The Black Cap*, ed. Cynthia Asquith (London, 1927), p. 134.

113 Ibid., p. 138.

114 Ibid., p. 139.

115 Ibid., pp. 137–8.

116 Evelyn Waugh, Letter to Harold Acton, *c.* 22 September 1928, in *The Letters of Evelyn Waugh*, ed. Mark Amory (London, 1980), p. 37.

117 George Orwell, 'Some Thoughts on the Common Toad', *Tribune*, 12 April 1946; repr. in *The Collected Essays, Journalism and Letters of George Orwell*, vol. IV: *In Front of Your Nose, 1945–1950*, ed. Sonia Orwell and Ian Angus (London, 1968), p. 144.

118 George Orwell, *Nineteen Eighty-four* [1949] (London, 1989), p. 3.

119 Ibid., p. 4.

120 Margaret Drabble, *The Garrick Year* (London, 1964), p. 38.

121 Ibid., p. 39.

122 Jonathan Raban, *Soft City* [1975] (London, 1981), p. 84.

123 Ibid., pp. 85–6.

124 Irma Kurtz, 'Islington', in *Dear London: Notes from the Big City* (London, 1997), p. 91; repr. in Jerry White, ed., *London Stories* (London, 2014), p. 408.

125 B. S. Johnson, *Christie Malry's Own Double-entry* [1973] (London, 2001), p. 155.

126 John Berger, 'Islington', *Prospect*, 17 March 2005; repr. in John Berger, *Here Is Where We Meet* (London, 2005), p. 109.

127 Ibid., p. 110.

128 Ibid.

129 Linda Grant, *We Had It So Good* (London, 2011), p. 110.

130 Ibid., p. 74.

131 Ibid., p. 167.

132 William Makepeace Thackeray, *Vanity Fair* [1848] (London, 1868), p. 29.

133 Lawrence S. Rainey, ed., *The Annotated Waste Land with Eliot's Contemporary Prose* (New Haven, CT, 2006), p. 113.

134 T. S. Eliot, *The Waste Land* [1922] (London, 2010), lines 292–5.

135 John Betjeman, 'The Sandemanian Meeting-house in Highbury Quadrant', in *Mount Zion* (London, 1932), p. 32; repr. in John Betjeman, *Collected Poems* (London, 2006), p. 15.

136 Stella Gibbons, *My American* [1939] (London, 2011), pp. 10–11.

137 B. S. Johnson, *Albert Angelo* [1964] (London, 2003), pp. 46–7.

138 Nick Hornby, *Fever Pitch* [1992] (London, 1998), p. 18.

139 Neil Gaiman, *Neverwhere* [1996] (London, 2013), p. 138.

140 Alan Moore and Tim Perkins, *The Highbury Working, A Beat Séance*, RE-PCD03, 2000; transcribed text available at https://genius.com, accessed 1 January 2020.

9 'SO NEAR HEAVEN' *Hampstead and Highgate*

1 E. M. Forster, *A Passage to India* [1924] (Harmondsworth, 1979), p. 246.

2 Ian Nairn, *Nairn's London* [1966] (London, 2014), p. 216.

3 William Howitt, *The Northern Heights of London* (London, 1869), p. v.

4 Daniel Defoe, *A Tour through the Whole Island of Great Britain* [1724–7] (London, 1971), p. 339.

5 Ibid.

6 Ibid., p. 340.

7 'A True and Faithful Narrative of What Passed in London during the Great Consternation . . .' (London, *c.* 1730); repr. in *The Works of Jonathan Swift, Containing Additional Letters, Tracts and Poems*, vol. XIII: *Miscellanies in Prose* (Edinburgh, 1824), p. 273; this was originally published anonymously and has been attributed variously to John Gay (most probably), John Arbuthnot, Jonathan Swift and Alexander Pope.

8 Charles Mackay, *Memoirs of Extraordinary Popular Delusions and the Madness of Crowds* (London, 1841), vol. I, p. 223.

9 Jonathan Swift, 'Miscellanies in prose by Swift, Pope, Dr Arbuthnot', in *The Works of Jonathan Swift* (Edinburgh, 1824), vol. XIII, p. 287.

10 Frances Burney, *Evelina* [1778] (London, 1919), p. 232.

11 *The Examiner*, 22 March 1813.

12 Robert Gittings, *John Keats* (London, 1968), pp. 64–5.

13 Ibid., pp. 177–8.

14 John Keats, Letter to Benjamin Bailey, 8 October 1817, in *Selected Letters*, ed. Robert Gittings (Oxford, 2002), p. 26.

15 Charles Armitage Brown, *Life of John Keats*, ed. Dorothy Hyde Bodurtha and Willard Bissell Pope (Oxford, 1937), pp. 53–4.

16 Graham Reynolds, *Constable's England*, exh. cat., Metropolitan Museum of Art, New York (1983), p. 17.

17 John Constable, Letter to Bishop John Fisher, in Anthony Bailey, *John Constable: A Kingdom of His Own* (London, 2007), p. 176.

18 Charles Dickens, *Oliver Twist* [1838] (London, 1867), p. 226.

19 Wilkie Collins, *Armadale* [1866] (New York, 1874), p. 577.

20 Bram Stoker, *Dracula* [1897] (Oxford, 2011), p. 165.

21 Ibid., pp. 183–4.

22 George and Weedon Grossmith, *The Diary of a Nobody* [1890] (London, 2003), p. 42.

23 Arthur Conan Doyle, 'The Adventure of Charles Augustus Milverton', in *The Return of Sherlock Holmes* (London, 1904); repr. in Arthur Conan Doyle, *The Original Illustrated 'Strand' Sherlock Holmes* (London, 1998), pp. 649–50.

24 Evelyn Waugh, *A Little Learning: The First Volume of an Autobiography* (London, 1964), p. 41.

25 Ibid., p. 34.

26 Ibid., p. 35.

27 D. H. Lawrence, *The Letters of D. H. Lawrence*, vol. II: *June 1913–October 1916*, ed. George J. Zytaruk and James T. Boulton (Cambridge, 1981), pp. 389–90.

28 D. H. Lawrence, Letter to Lady Ottoline Morrell, 9 September 1915, in *The Selected Letters of D. H. Lawrence*, ed. James T. Boulton (Cambridge, 2000), p. 106.

29 D. H. Lawrence, 'The Last Laugh' [1924], in *The Woman Who Rode Away* (Cambridge, 2002), p. 122.

30 J. Middleton Murry, ed., *Journal of Katherine Mansfield* (London, 1962), p. 157.

31 George Orwell, *Keep the Aspidistra Flying* [1936] (London, 2000), pp. 3, 92.

32 Ibid., pp. 3–4.

33 Ibid., p. 23.

34 Ibid., p. 72.

35 Ibid., p. 74.

36 Stephen Spender, *World within World* (London, 1951), p. 26.

37 Patrick Hamilton, *Twenty Thousand Streets under the Sky* [1935] (London, 1987), pp. 114–15.

38 Edwin Muir, *An Autobiography* (London, 1955), p. 232.

39 Ibid., p. 327.

40 *Home movies from Freud Archives, 1939–Sigmund Freud*, U.S. Library of Congress, film/video, available at loc.gov, accessed 20 January 2020.

41 Ernst L. Freud, ed., *Letters of Sigmund Freud* (1960) (Mineola, NY, 1992), p. 459.

42 Elias Canetti, *Party in the Blitz* (London, 2005), p. 193.

43 Ibid., pp. 48, 247, 217.

44 Ibid., p. 200.

45 Aldous Huxley, *Time Must Have a Stop* (London, 1944), pp. 3–4.

46 John Wyndham, *The Day of the Triffids* [1951] (London, 1969), p. 135.

47 Ibid., p. 143.

48 Christopher Isherwood, *The Sixties: Diaries, 1960–1969* (New York, 2010), p. 62.

49 Ibid., p. 68.

50 John Fowles, *The Collector* [1963] (London, 2004), p. 27.

51 Bernard Kops, *The Dissent of Dominick Shapiro* (London, 1966), p. 9.

52 Ibid. p. 56.

53 Kingsley Amis, *Jake's Thing* (London, 1978), p. 14.

54 Ibid., p. 15.

55 Ibid., p. 33.

56 Joseph Connolly, *This Is It* (London, 1996), p. 7.

57 Ibid., p. 26.

58 Will Self, *The Book of Dave* (London, 2006), p. 1.

59 Helen Simpson, *Constitutional* (London, 2006), pp. 106–7.

60 Ian McEwan, 'My Purple Scented Novel', *New Yorker*, 28 March 2016, pp. 62–7.

61 John Aubrey, *Brief Lives* [1669–96], ed. Andrew Clark (Oxford, 1898), vol. I, pp. 75–6.

62 Lord Byron, *Childe Harold's Pilgrimage* (London, 1814), Canto I, stanza LXX, p. 46.

63 Alexander Gillman, *The Gillmans of Highgate* (London, 1895), p. 7.

64 Ibid., p. 9.

65 John Keats, Letter to Georgiana Keats, 15 April 1819, quoted in Sidney Colvin, *John Keats: His Life and Poetry, His Friends, Critics and After-fame* (London, 1917), p. 351.

66 Thomas Ashe, *The Table Talk and Omniana of S. T. Coleridge* (London, 1888), p. 180.

67 Thomas Carlyle, *The Life of John Sterling* (London, 1851), pp. 69–70.

68 Earl Leslie Griggs, ed., *Unpublished Letters of Samuel Taylor Coleridge* (London, 1932), pp. 330–31.

69 T. Hall Caine, *Recollections of Dante Gabriel Rossetti* (London, 1882), pp. 58–60.

70 John Betjeman, *Summoned by Bells* (London, 1960), p. 4.

71 Stella Gibbons, *Westwood* [1945] (London, 2011), p. 47.

72 Ibid., p. 48.

73 Ibid., p. 1.

74 Ibid., p. 50.

75 Michael Frayn, *Sweet Dreams* [1973] (London, 2015), p. 1.

76 Tracy Chevalier, *Falling Angels* (London, 2001), pp. 22–3.

77 Audrey Niffenegger, *Her Fearful Symmetry* (London, 2009), p. 65.

78 Ibid., pp. 32–3.

79 Ibid., p. 108.

80 Ruth Rendell, *The Vault* (London, 2011), p. 40.

10 'IN ALL PLACES HIGH AND LOW' *Outer North London: Following the North Circular Road from Hendon to Finchley, Barnet, Cockfosters, Enfield, Palmers Green, Ponders End and Tottenham*

1 Elizabeth Bowen, *To the North* [1932] (London, 1950), p. 316.

2 Ibid., p. 317.

3 Ibid., pp. 317–19.

4 James Curtis, *They Drive by Night* [1938] (London, 2008), p. 31.

5 Ibid., p. 32.

6 Iain Sinclair, *Lights Out for the Territory* [1997] (London, 2003), p. 307.

7 Ibid., p. 308.

8 Dina Rabinovitch, 'This Is Hendon', *The Guardian*, 4 March 2006.

9 Naomi Alderman, *Disobedience* (London, 2006), p. 123.

10 Ibid., pp. 216–17.

11 Nick Barratt, *Greater London: The Story of the Suburbs* (London, 2012), p. 221.

12 Alexander Baron, *The Lowlife* [1963] (London, 2010), p. 1.

13 Buchi Emecheta, *Second-class Citizen* [1974] (London, 1994), p. 43.

14 Ibid., p. 45.

15 Tim Parks, *Tongues of Flame* (London, 1985), p. 23.

16 Ibid.

17 Samuel Pepys, *The Shorter Pepys*, ed. Robert Latham (Berkeley, CA, 1985), pp. 403–4.

18 Walter George Bell, *Where London Sleeps: Historical Journeyings into the Suburbs* (London, 1926), p. 43.

19 Charles Dickens, *Oliver Twist* [1838] (London, 1846), pp. 39–41.

20 Thomas de Quincey, 'Sketches of Life and Manners', *Tait's Edinburgh Magazine*, n.s., 1 (1834), p. 84; revd as 'The Nation of London', in *Autobiographical Sketches* (Boston, MA, 1853).

21 H. G. Wells, *The War of the Worlds* [1898] (London, 2005), pp. 97–8.

22 John Christopher, *The Death of Grass* [1956] (London, 2009), p. 56.

23 Kingsley Amis, *Girl, 20* (London, 1971), p. 13.

24 Ibid., p. 17.

25 Ibid.

26 Will Self, *Umbrella* (London, 2012), pp. 1–2.

27 Michael Hofmann, 'From A to B and Back Again', in *The Honest Ulsterman*, 82 (1986), p. 16; repr. in Michael Hofmann, *Corona, Corona* (London, 1993) and Mark Ford, ed., *London: A History in Verse* (Cambridge, MA, 2012), p. 704.

28 Helen Simpson, *Cockfosters* (London, 2015), p. 9.

29 Ibid., pp. 10–11.

30 Robert Gittings, *John Keats* (London, 1968), p. 45.

31 Ibid.

32 Charles Lamb, Letter to Sir John Stoddart, 9 August 1827, in *The Letters of Charles Lamb*, ed. E. V. Lucas (London, 1935), vol. III, p. 114.

33 Charles Lamb, Letter to Thomas Hood, 18 September 1827, ibid., p. 132.
34 Norman Lewis, 'God Bless the Squire', in *The Happy Ant-heap* (London, 1998), p. 1.
35 Ibid., pp. 2–3.
36 Stevie Smith, 'A London Suburb', in *Flower of Cities: A Book of London* (London, 1949), p. 212; repr. in Stevie Smith, *Me Again: Uncollected Writings* (London, 1981), p. 104.
37 Stevie Smith, 'The Suburban Classes' [1937], in *Selected Poems*, ed. James MacGibbon (London, 2002), p. 27.
38 Ibid.
39 Stevie Smith, *Novel on Yellow Paper* [1936] (London, 2003), p. 145.
40 Ibid.
41 Ibid.
42 Ibid., pp. 146–7.
43 Gerald Kersh, *Fowlers End* [1957] (London, 1958), pp. 6–8.
44 Ibid., pp. 8–10.
45 Izaak Walton, *The Compleat Angler* [1653] (London, 1836), vol. II, p. 300.
46 Ibid., pp. 303–4.
47 Ibid., p. 309.
48 Daniel Defoe, *A Tour through the Whole Island of Great Britain* (London, 1725), vol. II, pp. 2–3.
49 William Cowper, 'The Diverting History of John Gilpin' [1782], in *The Works of William Cowper: His Life, Letters and Poems* (London, 1851), p. 606.
50 M. H. Baylis, *The Tottenham Outrage* (London, 2014).
51 Thomas Burke, *The Outer Circle: Rambles in Remote London* (London, 1921), p. 23.
52 Ibid., p. 27.
53 Arthur Machen, 'Tottenham Hale', in *Wonderful London*, ed. St John Adcock (London, 1938), vol. I, p. 104.
54 Ibid., p. 105.
55 Ian McEwan, *The Innocent; or, The Special Relationship* (London, 1990), p. 114.
56 Gretta Mulrooney, *Araby* (London, 1998), p. 4.
57 Ibid., pp. 56–7.
58 Mark Mason, *Walk the Lines: The London Underground, Overground* (London, 2011), p. 48.

59 Gary Budden and Kit Caless, eds, *An Unreliable Guide to London* (London, 2016), p. 12.

11 'THE ODOUR OF OLD STONE' *East London: From Dalston to Hackney, Walthamstow, Stratford and the Isle of Dogs*

1 Roland Camberton, *Rain on the Pavements* (London, 1951), pp. 36–7.
2 Ibid., pp. 64–5.
3 Ibid., p. 66.
4 Alexander Baron, *The Lowlife* [1963] (London, 2010), pp. 149–50.
5 Hugo Williams, 'A Cult of Inspired Amateurishness that Seized the 60s', *The Spectator*, 3 May 2014.
6 J. M. O'Neill, *Duffy Is Dead* (London, 1987), p. 11.
7 Ibid., p. 53.
8 Patrick Wright, *A Journey through Ruins: The Last Days of London* [1991] (Oxford, 2009), p. 11.
9 Ibid., pp. 13–14.
10 Iain Sinclair, *Lights Out for the Territory* (London, 1997), p. 15.
11 Will Self, *How the Dead Live* (London, 2000), pp. 163–4.
12 Ibid., pp. 175–6.
13 Martin Amis, *Lionel Asbo: State of England* (London, 2012), p. 19.
14 Ibid., p. 28.
15 Ibid., p. 20.
16 Ibid., p. 27.
17 Samuel Pepys, *The Diary of Samuel Pepys*, vol. v: *1664*, ed. Robert Latham and William G. Matthews (Berkeley, CA, 2000), pp. 132–3.
18 Henry Mayhew, *London Labour and the London Poor* (London, 1851), vol. I, p. 202.
19 Walter Besant, *All Sorts and Conditions of Men* [1882] (London, 1890), p. 112.
20 Edmund Gosse, *Father and Son* (London, 1907), pp. 9–11.
21 Bernard Kops, *The World Is a Wedding* (London, 1963), pp. 231–2.
22 Harold Pinter, *New Yorker* (25 February 1974), p. 34; quoted in Efraim Sicher, *Beyond Marginality: Anglo-Jewish Literature after the Holocaust* (Albany, NY, 1985), p. 94.

23 Ibid., p. 36; quoted in William Baker, *Harold Pinter* (London, 2008), p. 10.

24 Iain Sinclair, *Hackney, That Rose-red Empire* (London, 2009), p. 7.

25 Ibid., pp. 10–11.

26 Stewart Home, *Red London* (Edinburgh, 1994), pp. 20–22.

27 'Hackney Square, now Launched', available at www. telfordhomes.london, 25 September 2014, accessed 8 January 2020.

28 Peter Ackroyd, *English Music* (London, 1992), p. 13.

29 Bernardine Evaristo, *Mr Loverman* (London, 2013), pp. 112–13.

30 Samuel Pepys, *The Diary of Samuel Pepys*, vol. II: *1661*, ed. Robert Latham and William G. Matthews (Berkeley, CA, 2000), pp. 109–10.

31 John Aubrey, *Brief Lives* [1669–96], ed. Andrew Clark (Oxford, 1898), p. 132.

32 William Morris, Letter to Andreas Scheu, 5 September 1883, in *The Collected Letters of William Morris*, vol. II: *1885–1888*, ed. Norman Kelvin (Princeton, NJ, 1988), p. 227.

33 William Morris, *News from Nowhere* [1890] (Oxford, 2003), p. 15.

34 Ibid.

35 John Foxe, *Fox's Booke of Martyrs: The Acts and Monuments of the Church* [1563] (London, 1851), vol. III, pp. 737–8.

36 Daniel Defoe, *A Tour through the Whole Island of Great Britain* (Harmondsworth, 1971), pp. 47–8.

37 Thomas Burke, *The Outer Circle: Rambles in Remote London* (London, 1921), p. 194.

38 J. R. Ackerley, *We Think the World of You* (London, 1960), p. 18.

39 Ibid., p. 46.

40 Ibid., p. 47.

41 Richard Allen, *Skinhead* [1970] (London, 2015), p. 13.

42 Ibid., p. 15.

43 John Rogers, *This Other London: Adventures in the Overlooked City* (London, 2013), p. 29.

44 Ibid., p. 32.

45 Benjamin Zephaniah, *Face* (London, 1999), pp. 15–16.

46 Ralph Thoresby, *The Diary of Ralph Thoresby*, ed. Joseph Hunter (London, 1830), vol. II, p. 235.

47 Thomas Mozley, *Reminiscences, Chiefly of Towns, Villages and Schools* (London, 1885), vol. I, p. 364.

48 Charles Dickens, 'Greenwich Fair', *Evening Chronicle*, 16 April 1835; repr. in Charles Dickens, *Sketches by Boz* [1836] (London, 1837), vol. II, p. 287.

49 Henry Morley, 'A Rainy Day on "The Euphrates"', *Household Words*, IV/96 (24 January 1852).

50 Walter Besant, *East London* (New York, 1899), p. 92.

51 Ibid., pp. 93–5.

52 Arthur Conan Doyle, *The Sign of Four* [1890], in *The Original Illustrated 'Strand' Sherlock Holmes* (London, 1989), p. 99.

53 John Davidson, 'In the Isle of Dogs', in *The Last Ballad and Other Poems* (London, 1898), pp. 127–31; repr. in *London: A History in Verse*, ed. Mark Ford (Cambridge, MA, 2012), p. 457.

54 Ibid.

55 T. S. Eliot, *The Waste Land: A Facsimile and Transcript*, ed. Valerie Eliot [1971] (London, 2010), lines 266–76.

56 Thomas Burke, *Limehouse Nights* (New York, 1917), p. 41.

57 Ibid., pp. 42–3.

58 Jack Lindsay, *Rising Tide: A Novel of the British Way* (London, 1953), p. 10.

59 V. S. Pritchett, *London Perceived* (New York, 1962), p. 43.

60 Alan Hollinghurst, *The Swimming-pool Library* (London, 1988), p. 168.

61 Ibid., p. 169.

62 Iain Sinclair, *Downriver* [1991] (London, 2002), pp. 276–7.

63 Sinclair, *Lights Out for the Territory*, pp. 40–41.

64 Iain Sinclair, *London Orbital* (London, 2002), p. 39.

65 P. D. James, *Original Sin* (London, 1994), pp. 118–19.

66 Anna Minton, *Ground Control: Fear and Happiness in the Twenty-first-century City* (London, 2009), p. 7.

12 'THE OVERLOOKED CITY' Outer East London: From Barking to Ilford, Dagenham, Rainham and Purfleet

1 Bede, *The Ecclesiastical History of the English People*, ed. Judith McClure and Roger Collins (Oxford, 1999), pp. 184–5.

2 Daniel Defoe, *A Tour through the Whole Island of Great Britain* (Harmondsworth, 1971), p. 50.

3 Ibid., p. 6.
4 W. T. Vincent, *The Records of the Woolwich District* (London, 1890), vol. II, pp. 781–4.
5 Billy Bragg, 'Billy Bragg on Barking', *The Guardian*, 26 May 2018.
6 Billy Bragg, 'The Battle of Barking', *Fight Songs*, BB5112 (2011).
7 Martina Cole, *Broken* (London, 2005), p. 1.
8 John Rogers, *This Other London: Adventures in the Overlooked City* (London, 2013), p. 292.
9 Ben Judah, *This Is London: Life and Death in the World City* (London, 2016), pp. 358–60.
10 Nikolaus Pevsner and Bridget Cherry, *London: East*, vol. V: *Pevsner Architectural Guides: Buildings of England*, ed. Charles O'Brien (London, 2005), p. 198.
11 Edward Thomas, 'Household Poems, 1: Bronwen', available at www.theslowroom.com, accessed 3 January 2020.
12 Quoted in J. C. Loudon, *The Landscape Gardening and Landscape Architecture of the Late Humphrey Repton* (Edinburgh, 1840), p. 129.
13 Defoe, *Tour through the Whole Island of Great Britain*, p. 51.
14 Katherine Fry, available at www.e7-nowandthen.org, accessed 24 January 2020.
15 Simon Blumenfeld, *Jew Boy* (London, 1935), pp. 208–9.
16 Nick Barratt, *Greater London: The Story of the Suburbs* (London, 2012), p. 358.
17 Peter Willmott, *The Evolution of a Community: A Study of Dagenham after Forty Years* (London, 1963), pp. 13–14.
18 Ibid., p. 109.
19 Ibid., p. 110.
20 Peter Cook and Dudley Moore, 'At the Art Gallery', *Not Only . . . but Also*, BBC 2, 20 February 1965; repr. in Peter Cook and William Cook, *Tragically I was an Only Twin: The Comedy of Peter Cook* (London, 2003), pp. 116–17.
21 Iain Nairn, *Nairn's London* [1966] (London, 2014), pp. 188–9.
22 Bram Stoker, *Dracula* [1897] (Oxford, 2011), p. 24.
23 Ibid., p. 25.
24 Iain Sinclair, *London Orbital* (London, 2002), pp. 401–2.

A READER'S GUIDE

Aaronovitch, Ben, *Rivers of London* (London, 2011)

Ackerley, J. R., *My Father and Myself* [1968] (London, 1984)

—, *We Think the World of You* (London, 1960)

Ackroyd, Pete, *English Music* (London, 1992)

—, *London: The Biography* (London, 2000)

Adcock, St John, ed., *Wonderful London*, vol. 1 (London, 1926)

Ainger, Alfred, ed., *The Letters of Charles Lamb*, vol. 11 (London, 1897)

Alderman, Naomi, *Disobedience* (London, 2006)

Allen, Richard, *Skinhead* [1994], ebook (2015)

Allingham, William, *William Allingham: A Diary* (London, 1908)

Amis, Kingsley, *Girl, 20* (London, 1971)

—, *Jake's Thing* (London, 1979)

—, *Stanley and the Women* [1984] (London, 2004)

—, *The Folks that Live on the Hill* [1990] (London, 2012)

Amis, Martin, *Lionel Asbo* (London, 2013)

Arnold, Matthew, *Complete Poetical Works of Matthew Arnold*, ebook (2013)

Ashe, T., *The Table Talk and Onmniana of S. T. Coleridge* (London, 1888)

Ashford, Daisy, *The Young Visiters; or, Mr. Salteena's Plan* [1919] (London, 2008)

Atkins, Marc, and Iain Sinclair, *Liquid City* (London, 1999)

Aubrey, John, *Brief Lives* (Oxford, 1891)

Bailey, Paul, *An Immaculate Mistake: Scenes from Childhood and Beyond* (London, 1990)

—, *Gabriel's Lament* (London, 1986)

Baker, William, *Harold Pinter* (London, 2008)

Ballard, J. G., *Concrete Island* (London, 2014)

—, *The Kindness of Women* (London, 1991)

—, *Kingdom Come* (London, 2006)

—, *Miracles of Life: Shanghai to Shepperton: An Autobiography* (London, 2008)

—, *The Unlimited Dream Company* [1979] (London, 1992)

Barker, Paul, *The Freedoms of Suburbia* (London, 2009)

Barnes, Julian, *Metroland* (London, 1980)

Baron, Alexander, *The Lowlife* [1963] (London, 2010)

Barratt, Nick, *Greater London: The Story of the Suburbs* (London, 2012)

Bashford, Henry Howard, *Augustus Carp, Esq. by Himself: Being the Autobiography of a Really Good Man* [1924] (Harmondsworth, 1987)

Bason, Fred, *Diary* (London, 1957)

Batchelor, John, *Tennyson: To Strive, to Seek, to Find* (London, 2014)

Bell, Walter George, *Where London Sleeps* (London, 1926)

Bennett, Alan, 'Diary', *London Review of Books*, XXXVII/1 (January 2015), pp. 37–9

—, 'The Lady in the Van', *London Review of Books*, XI/20 (October 1989), pp. 3–10

Besant, Walter, *All Sorts and Conditions of Men* (London, 1913)

—, *East London* (London, 1901)

—, 'South London', *Pall Mall Gazette*, XVI (1898)

Betjeman, John, *Collected Poems* (London, 2006)

—, *Coming Home: An Anthology of Prose* (London, 1998)

—, *John Betjeman's Collected Poems* (London, 1972)

—, *Summoned by Bells* (London, 1960)

Blake, William, *Collected Poems* (London, 2005)

Blumenfeld, Simon, *Jew Boy* (London, 1935)

Boswell, James, and Gordon Turnbull, *London Journal, 1762–1763* (London, 2010)

Bowen, Elizabeth, *To the North* [1932] (London, 1999)

Breen, Paul, *The Charlton Men* (London, 2014)

Briggs, Julia, *A Woman of Passion: The Life of E. Nesbit, 1858–1924* (London, 1987)

Brinnin, John, *Dylan Thomas in America* (London, 1951)

Brownjohn, Alan, *Collected Poems, 1952–2006* (London, 2014)

Bullock, Emily, *The Longest Fight* (London, 2015)

Burke, Thomas, *Limehouse Nights* (London, 1926)

—, *The Outer Circle: Rambles in Remote London* (London, 1921)

Burnside, John, *Waking Up in Toytown* (London, 2010)

Byron, George Gordon Noel, sixth Baron Byron, *Childe Harold's Pilgrimage*, ed. H. F. Tozer (Oxford, 1885)

Caless, Kit, *An Unreliable Guide to London*, ebook (London, 2016)

Camberton, Roland, *Rain on the Pavements* (London, 1951)

Campbell, Ramsey, ed., *New Tales of the Cthulhu Mythos* (London, 1988)

Canty, Tom, *Clapham Lights*, ebook (Kidderminster, 2013)

Carlyle, Thomas, *The Life of John Sterling* (London, 1851)

Carr, Gordon, *The Angry Brigade: A History of Britain's First Urban Guerilla Group* (London, 2010)

Carter, Angela, *The Magic Toyshop* [1967] (London, 2006)

—, *Wise Children* (London, 1991)

—, and Jennifer S. Uglow, *Shaking a Leg: Collected Journalism and Writings* [1997] (London, 2013)

Cartwright, David E., *Schopenhauer: A Biography* (Cambridge, 2010)

Cheek, Mavis, *Pause Between Acts* [1988] (London, 1998)

Chesterton, G. K., *The Man Who Was Thursday* [1908] (Harmondsworth, 1986)

Chevalier, Tracy, *Falling Angels* (London, 2001)

Christie, Agatha, *Death in the Clouds* [1935] (London, 2001)

Christopher, John, *The Death of Grass* [1956] (London, 2009)

Clary, Julian, *A Young Man's Passage* (London, 2006)

Cobbett, William, *Rural Rides* [1830] (London, 1925)

—, *Rural Rides*, vol. 1 (London, 1966)

Cole, Martina, *Broken* (2005)

Collins, Michael, *The Likes of Us* (London, 2004)

Collins, Wilkie, *Armadale* (London, 1875)

—, *The Woman in White* [1859] (Oxford, 1998)

Collis, Robert, *George Orwell, English Rebel* (Oxford, 2013)

Conan Doyle, Arthur, *The Original Illustrated 'Strand' Sherlock Holmes* (London, 1989)

Connolly, Joseph, *This Is It* (London, 1996)

Coverley, Merlin, *South* (London, 2016)

Cox, Pamela, and Annabel Hobley, *Shopgirls* (London, 2015)

Crofts, Freeman Wills, *The 12.30 from Croydon* [1934] (London, 2016)

Cunningham, Ian, *A Reader's Guide to Writers' London* (London, 2001)

Cunningham, Michael, *The Hours* (London, 1998)

Curtis, James, *The Gilt Kid* [1936] (London, 2007)

—, *They Drive by Night* [1938] (London, 2008)

Davidson, Ian, *Voltaire: A Life* (London, 2012)

Day-Lewis, Cecil, *The Worm of Death* (London, 1961)

de Bernières, Louis, *Sunday Morning at the Centre of the World: A Play for Voices* (London, 2001)

de la Mare, Walter, *The Riddle* [1947], gutenberg.ca/ebooks

De Quincey, Thomas, *Autobiographic Sketches* (London, 1876)

Defoe, Daniel, *Moll Flanders* [1722] (London, 1921)

—, *A Tour through the Whole Island of Great Britain*, ed. Pat Rogers (Harmondsworth, 1971)

Delderfield, R. F., *The Dreaming Suburb* [1958] (London, 1976)

Dickens, Charles, *David Copperfield* (London, 1850)

—, *Dombey and Son* [1848] (London, 1921)

—, *Great Expectations* (London, 1861)

—, *The Lamplighter* [1838], ebook (London, 2003)

—, *Oliver Twist* [1838] (Oxford, 1936)

—, *Our Mutual Friend* [1865] (London, 1997)

—, *The Pickwick Papers* [1836] (London, 1993)

—, *Sketches by Boz* [1836] (London, 1995)

—, *A Tale of Two Cities* [1859] (London, 2003)

Donne, John, *Poems of John Donne*, vol. 1, ed. E. K. Chambers (London, 1896)

Dostoyevsky, Fyodor, *Notes from Underground* [1864] (New York, 1992)

Drabble, Margaret, *The Garrick Years* (London, 1964)

Dunn, Nell, *Up the Junction* [1963] (London, 2013)

Durrell, Lawrence, *The Black Book* [1938] (London, 2012)

Dyer, Geoff, *The Colour of Memory* (London, 1990)

Eclair, Jenny, *Camberwell Beauty* (London, 2012)

Eliot, T. S., *The Waste Land: A Facsimile and Transcript of the Original Drafts*, ed. Valerie Eliot (London, 2010)

Emecheta, Buchi, *In the Ditch* (London, 1979)

—, *Second-class Citizen* (London, 1974)

Evans, Diana, *26a* (London, 2005)

Evaristo, Bernadine, *Lara: 'The Family is Like Water'* (London, 2009)

—, *Mr Loverman* (London, 2013)

Ewart, Gavin, *Londoners* (London, 1964)

Falconer, Helen, *Primrose Hill* (London, 1999)

Fell Smith, Charlotte, *The Life of John Dee, 1527–1608* (London, 1909)

Fisher, Allen, *Gravity* (Cambridge, 2004)

Fishman, Robert, *Bourgeois Utopias* (London, 1989)

Fitzgerald, Penelope, *Offshore* [1979] (London, 2013)

Ford, Mark, *Thomas Hardy: Half a Londoner* (London, 2016)

Forster, E. M., *Collected Short Stories* (Harmondsworth, 1977)

—, *Marianne Thornton: 1797–1887, a Domestic Biography* [1956] (London, 2000)

Foster, R. F., *W. B. Yeats: A Life*, vol. 1: *The Apprentice Mage, 1865–1914* (Oxford, 1998)

Fowles, John, *The Collector* [1963] (London, 2004)

Foxe, John, *The Acts and Monuments of the Martyrs* (London, 1875)

Frayn, Michael, *Sweet Dreams* [1973], ebook (London, 2015)

—, *Towards the End of the Morning* (London, 1969)

Freud, Ernst, ed., *The Letters of Sigmund Freud* (New York, 1992)

Gaiman, Neil, *Neverwhere* [1996] (London, 2013)

Games, Stephen, *Betjeman's England* (London, 2009)

Gardam, Jane, *The People on Privilege Hill and Other Stories* (London, 2007)

Gibbons, Stella, *My American* [1939] (London, 2011)

—, *Westwood; or, The Gentle Powers* (London, 2011)

Gilchrist, Alexander, *The Life of William Blake* (New York, 1997)

Gillman, Alexander, *The Gillmans of Highgate* (London, 1895)

Gissing, George, *The Nether World* [1889] (London, 1982)

—, *In the Year of Jubilee* [1894] (London, 1994)

Gittings, Robert, *John Keats* (London, 1968)

Glinert, Ed, *Literary London: A Street by Street Exploration of the Capital's Literary Heritage* (London, 2007)

Goldsmith, Oliver, *The Miscellaneous Works of Oliver Goldsmith* (London, 1837)

Gordon, Richard, *Good Neighbours: Suburbia Observed* (London, 1976)

Gosse, Edmund, *Father and Son* (London, 1907)

Greene, Graham, *It's a Battlefield* [1934] (London, 2002)

—, *The End of the Affair* [1951] (London, 2001)

—, and Henry J. Donaghy, eds, *Conversations with Graham Greene* (Jackson, MS, 1992)

Griggs, Leslie, ed., *Unpublished Letters of S. T. Coleridge* (London, 1932)

Gunaratne, Guy, *In Our Mad and Furious City* (London, 2018)

Haddon, Mark, *The Curious Incident of the Dog in the Night-time* (London, 2003)

Hamilton, Patrick, *Twenty Thousand Streets Under the Sky* [1929–34] (London, 1987)

Hanson, Michele, *What the Grown-ups were Doing: An Odyssey through 1950s Suburbia* (London, 2013)

Hapgood, Lynne, *Margins of Desire: The Suburbs in Fiction and Culture, 1880–1925* (Manchester, 2009)

Hardy, Thomas, *The Works of Thomas Hardy: With an Introduction and Bibliography* (London, 1994)

Hawkins, Paula, *The Girl on the Train* (London, 2015)

Heller, Zoe, *Notes on a Scandal* (London, 2004)

Henri, Adrian, *Collected Poems, 1967–85* (London, 1986)

Herbert, A. P., *The House by the River* [1920] (London, 2001)

Higson, Charles, *Happy Now* (London, 1993)

Hollinghurst, Alan, *The Swimming-pool Library* (London, 1988)

Home, Stewart, *Come before Christ and Murder Love* (London, 1997)

—, *Red London* (London, 1994)

Hornby, Nick, *Fever Pitch* [1992] (Harmondsworth, 1998)

—, *High Fidelity* [1995] (London, 2000)

Howard, Keble, *The Smiths of Surbiton* (London, 1906)

Howitt, William, *The Northern Heights of London* (London, 1869)

Hughes, M. V., *A London Family, 1870–1890* (Oxford, 1946)

Hunt, Leigh, *Essays* (London, 1841)

Huxley, Aldous, *Brave New World* [1932] (London, 1972)

Isherwood, Christopher, *The Sixties, Diaries: 1960–1969* (New York, 2010)

Jacobson, Howard, *No More Mr Nice Guy* (London, 1999)

James, Alex, *Bit of a Blur: The Autobiography* (London, 2008)

James, Henry, *English Hours* [1905] (New York, 2011)

—, *London Stories and Other Writings* (London, 1989)

James, P. D., *Original Sin* (London, 1994)

Jefferies, Richard, *Nature near London* (London, 1905)

—, *The Story of My Heart* (London, 1901)

Jerome, Jerome K., *Three Men in a Boat* (London, 1889)

Johnson, B. S., *Alberto Angelo* [1964] (London, 2013)

—, *Christy Malry's Own Double-entry* (London, 1973)

Johnson, Pamela Hansford, *Important to Me* (London, 2012)

Johnson, Samuel, *Letters of Samuel Johnson, 1777–1781*
    (Princeton, NJ, 2014)

—, *The Major Works*, ed. Donald Greene (Oxford, 2008)

Judah, Ben, *This Is London* (London, 2016)

Judt, Tony, *The Memory Chalet* (London, 2011)

Keats, John, *The Letters of John Keats*, ed. Sidney Colvin
    (London, 1928)

Keiller, Patrick, *The View from the Train* (London, 2014)

Kelman, Stephen, *Pigeon English* (London, 2012)

Kelvin, Norman, *The Collected Letters of William Morris*, vol. II
    (Princeton, NJ, 1988)

Kennedy, A. L, *Serious Sweet* (London, 2016)

Kersh, Gerald, *Fowlers End* [1957] (London, 2001)

King, John, *Skinheads* (London, 2008)

Kops, Bernard, *The Dissent of Dominic Shapiro* (London, 1966)

—, *The World Is a Wedding* (London, 1963)

Kureishi, Hanif, *The Buddha of Suburbia* (London, 1990)

—, *Gabriel's Gift* (London, 2001)

Lahr, John, ed., *The Orton Diaries* (London, 1996)

Lamb, Charles, *The Letters of Charles Lamb*, ed. Thomas Noon
    Talfourd (London, 1837)

Lanchester, John, *Capital* [2012] (London, 2013)

—, *Mr Phillips* (London, 2000)

Larrabeiti, Michael de, *The Borrible Trilogy* (London, 2013)

Law, Michael John, *The Experience of Suburban Modernity:
    How Private Transport Changed Interwar London*
    (Manchester, 2014)

Lawrence, D. H., *The Letters of D. H. Lawrence*, vol. II: *1913–1916*,
    ed. George Zytaruk, revd James T. Boulton (Cambridge, 2002)

—, *The Mortal Coil and Other Stories* (Harmondsworth, 1971)

—, *The Rainbow* [1915] (Harmondsworth, 1979)

—, *The Woman Who Rode Away and Other Stories* (Cambridge, 2002) le Carré, John, *Tinker Tailor Soldier Spy* (London, 1974)

Levy, Andrea, *Small Island* (London, 2004)

Lewalksi, Barbara, K., *The Life of John Milton: A Critical Biography* (London, 2008)

Lewis, Norman, *The Happy Ant-heap and Other Pieces* (London, 1999)

Lexton, Maria, ed., *The Time Out Book of London Short Stories* (Harmondsworth, 1993)

Lindsay, Jack, *Rising Tide* (London, 1953)

Lodge, David, *Quite A Good Time to Be Born: A Memoir, 1935–1975* (London, 2015)

Lott, Tim, *The Scent of Dried Roses* [1996] (London, 2009)

—, *White City Blue* (London, 2000)

McCaffery, R. J., 'Coleridge!' Scoplaw.Blogs.com, accessed 16 September 2020

McCambridge, David, *The Journals of Claire Clairmont*, ed. Mary Kingston Stocking (Cambridge, MA, 1968)

McEwan, Ian, *The Innocent* (London, 1990)

—, *My Purple Scented Novel* (London, 2018)

Machen, Arthur, *'A Fragment of Life'*, ebook (2012)

—, *The Great God Pan and Other Horror Stories* (Oxford, 2018)

—, *The Islington Mystery*, ebook (2012)

MacInnes, Colin, *The Colin MacInnes Omnibus: His Three London Novels* (London, 2005)

Mackay, Charles, *Memoirs of Popular Delusions* (London, 1852)

Mackay, Shena, *Dunedin* [1991] (London, 2016)

Mackenzie, Compton, *Sinister Street* (London, 1915)

MacNeice, Louis, *Autumn Journal* [1939] (London, 2013)

Maddox, Brenda, *The Married Man: A Life of D. H. Lawrence* (London, 1994)

Malikani, Gautam, *Londonstani* (London, 2007)

Marsh, Richard, *The Beetle* [1897] (London, 2004)

Marshall, J., *The Life and Letters of Mary Wollstonecraft Shelley*, vol. 1 (London, 1970)

Maxwell, Gordon S., *The Fringe of London* (London, 1925)

Mayhew, Charles, *London Labour and the London Poor* (London, 1861)

Millar, Martin, *Lux the Poet* (London, 2009)

Miller, Betty, *Farewell Leicester Square* (London, 1941)

Mills, Magnus, *The Maintenance of Headway* (London, 2010)

Minton, Anna, *Ground Control* (London, 2009)

Moggach, Deborah, *Close to Home* (London, 1979)

Moorcock, Michael, *London Bone* (London, 2002)

Morris, William, *News from Nowhere* [1890] (London, 2003)

Morrison, Blake, *South of the River* (London, 2008)

Mortimer, John, *Rumpole and the Penge Bungalow Murders*
    (London, 2004)

Muir, Edwin, *An Autobiography* (London, 1955)

Mulrooney, Greta, *Araby* (London, 1998)

Mulvihill, Margaret, *Natural Selection* (London, 1985)

Murdoch, Iris, *Under the Net* [1954] (London, 2002)

Muthesius, Hermann, *The English House* (London, 1908)

Myerson, Julie, *Home: The Story of Everyone Who Ever Lived
    in Our House* (London, 2004)

Naipaul, V. S., *Mr Stone and the Knights Companion*
    (London, 1963)

Nairn, I. A., *Nairn's London* [1966] (London, 2014)

Neate, Patrick, *The London Pigeon Wars* (London, 2004)

Nesbit, E., *The Story of the Treasure Seekers* [1899] (London, 2008)

Newland, Courttia, *The Scholar: A West Side Story* (London, 2001)

Niffenegger, Audrey, *Her Fearful Symmetry* (London, 2010)

Olsen, Donald J., *The Growth of Victorian London*
    (Harmondsworth, 1979)

O'Neill, J. M., *Duffy Is Dead* (London, 1988)

Orwell, George, *The Collected Essays, Journalism and Letters
    of George Orwell: In Front of Your Nose, 1945–1950*
    (Harmondsworth, 1968)

—, *The Complete Novels* (London, 2000)

—, *Keep the Aspidistra Flying* [1936] (London, 2000)

Palin, Michael, *The Complete Diaries* (London, 2005)

Palmer, Samuel, *St Pancras; being Antiquarian, Topographical, and
    Biographical Memoranda, Relating to the Extensive Metropolitan
    Parish of St. Pancras, Middlesex; with Some Account of the Parish
    from its Foundation* (London, 1870)

Papadimitriou, Nick, *Scarp* (London, 2012)

Parker, Tony, *The People of Providence* [1983] (London, 2011)

Parks, Tim, *Tongues of Flame* (London, 1985)

Parsons, Tony, *Stories We Could Tell* (London, 2006)

Peacock, Thomas Love, *Nightmare Abbey and Crotchet Castle* (Harmondsworth, 1982)

Pepys, Samuel, *The Shorter Pepys*, ed. Robert Latham (Harmondsworth, 1987)

Petit, Chris, *The Hard Shoulder* (London, 2001)

Pinter, Harold, *The Caretaker* (London, 1964)

Plath, Sylvia, *Johnny Panic and the Bible of Dreams* (London, 1977)

Platt, Edward, *Leadville* (London, 2000)

Poe, Edgar Allan, *The Complete Tales and Poems of Edgar Allan Poe* (London, 1982)

Porter, Roy, *London: A Social History* (London, 1997)

Pritchett, V. S., *London Perceived* (London, 1962)

Pullinger, Kate, *When the Monster Dies* (London, 1990)

Pynchon, Thomas, *Mason & Dixon* (London, 1997)

Raban, Jonathan, *Soft City* (London, 1984)

—, 'My Own Private Metropolis', *Daily Telegraph*, 9 August 2008

Rankin, Robert, *The Brentford Trilogy* (London, 1988)

Rendell, Ruth, *The Vault* (London, 2011)

Repton, Humphrey, quoted in J. C. Loudon, *The Landscape Gardening and Landscape Architecture of the late Humphrey Repton* (Edinburgh, 1840)

Reynolds, Graham, ed., *Constable's England* (New York, 1983)

Rhys, Jean, *Voyage in the Dark* [1934] (London, 1967)

Riddell, Charlotte, *City and Suburb* (London, 1861)

Ridge, William Pett, *Mord Em'ly* [1898] (London, 1992)

—, *Nine to Six-thirty* (London, 1910)

—, *Outside the Radius* (London, 1899)

—, *Sixty-nine Birnam Road* (London, 1909)

Robb, Graham, *Rimbaud* (London, 2000)

Rubens, Bernice, *Our Father* (London, 1987)

Ruskin, John, *The Opening of the Crystal Palace Considered in Some of its Relations to the Prospects of Art* (London, 1854)

—, *Praeterita* (London, 1886)

Sala, G. A., *Daylight and Gaslight* (London, 1859)

Scott, M., ed., *The Katherine Mansfield Notebooks* (Minneapolis, MN, 1997)

Sebald, W. G., *Austerlitz* (London, 2001)

Self, Will, *The Book of Dave* (London, 2006)

—, *How the Dead Live* (London, 2000)

—, *Umbrella* (London, 2012)

Selvon, Sam, *Moses Ascending* (London, 2008)

Shamsie, Kamila, *Home Fire* (London, 2017)

Shan, Bullock, *Robert Thorne: The Story of a London Clerk* (London, 1907)

Sharp, William, *The Life of Robert Browning* [1890] (London, 2007)

Sherriff, R. C., *The Fortnight in September* [1931] (London, 2006)

—, *Greengates* (London, 1936)

Silverstone, Roger, ed., *Visions of Suburbia* (London, 1997)

Simpson, Helen, *Cockfosters* (London, 2015)

—, *Constitutional* (London, 2006)

Sinclair, Iain, *Downriver* [1991] (London, 2002)

—, *Hackney, That Red-rose Empire* (London, 2009)

—, *Lights Out for the Territory: Nine Excursions in the Secret History of London* [1997] (London, 2003)

—, *London Orbital* (London, 2002)

—, *London Overground: A Day's Walk around the Ginger Line* (London, 2015)

—, *Radon Daughters* (London, 1994)

Smith, Ali, *There but for the* (London, 2012)

Smith, Dodie, *101 Dalmatians* [1956] (London, 1989)

Smith, John Thomas, *A Book for a Rainy Day; or, Recollections of the Events of the Last Sixty-six Years* (London, 1845)

Smith, Stevie, *The Collected Poems of Stevie Smith*, ed. James MacGibbon (London, 1975)

—, *Me Again: Uncollected Writings* (London, 1981)

—, *Novel on Yellow Paper* [1936] (London, 2003)

Smith, Zadie, *White Teeth* (London, 2000)

—, *NW* (London, 2012)

Spender, Stephen, *World Within World* (London, 1951)

Steedman, Carolyn, *Landscape for a Good Woman: A Story of Two Lives* (London, 1986)

Stevenson, W. H., ed., *Blake: The Complete Poems* (London, 2007)

Stibbe, Nina, *Love, Nina* (London, 2013)

Stukeley, William, *The Family Memoirs of the Rev. William Stukeley*, vol. III (London, 1887)

Svevo, Italo, '*This England Is So Different . . .*': *Italo Svevo's London Writings* (London, 2003)

Swift, Graham, *The Light of Day* (London, 2003)

Swift, Jonathan, *The Works of Jonathan Swift, Containing Additional Letters, Tracts and Poems*, vol. XIII (London, 1824)

Symonds, John Addington, *Shelley* [1878] (Cambridge, 2011)

Symons, Julian, *The Blackheath Poisonings: A Victorian Murder Mystery* [1978] (London, 1992)

Taylor, Teddy, *Baron's Court, All Change* (London, 2011)

Tearne, Roma, *Brixton Beach* (London, 2009)

Tempest, Kate, *The Bricks that Built the Houses* (London, 2016)

Thackeray, William Makepeace, *The Book of Snobs and Travels in London* [1848] (London, 1903)

—, *Vanity Fair* [1848] (London, 1993)

Theroux, Paul, *The Family Arsenal* [1976] (London, 2010)

Thomas, Edward, *The Happy-go-lucky Morgans* (London, 1913)

Thomas, Leslie, *Tropic of Ruislip* [1974] (London, 1997)

Thomson, David, *In Camden Town* (London, 1983)

Thomson, James, *The Poetical Works of James Thomson* (London, 1897)

Thoresby, Robert, *The Diary of Robert Thoresby*, vol. II (London, 1830)

Thornbury, Walter, *Old and New London* (London, 1878)

Toksvig, Sandi, *Between the Stops* (London, 2019)

Tolley, Christopher, *Domestic Biography: The Legacy of Evangelicalism in Four Nineteenth-century Families* (Oxford, 1997)

Tomalin, Claire, *Charles Dickens* (London, 2012)

Twain, Mark, *Mark Twain, the Globetrotter*, ebook (2017)

Vine, Barbara, *King Solomon's Carpet* (London, 1991)

Walpole, Horace, *A Description of the Villa of Horace Walpole* [1784] (London, 1834)

—, *The Correspondence of Horace Walpole with George Montagu*, vol. I (London, 1837)

—, *The Letters of Horace Walpole, Earl Orford*, ed. Peter Cunningham, vol. II (London, 1861)

Walsh, John, *The Falling Angels: An Irish Romance* (London, 2000)

Walton, Isaak, *The Compleat Angler* [1653] (London, 1893)

Ward, Ned, *A Walk to Islington*, ebook [1699], accessed 26 April 2018

Waters, Sarah, *The Paying Guests* (London, 2014)

—, *Tipping the Velvet* (London, 1998)

Watson, S. J., *Before I Go to Sleep* (London, 2011)

Waugh, Evelyn, *A Little Learning: The First Volume of an Autobiography* (London, 1964)

—, *Vile Bodies* [1930] (London, 2000)

Weinreb, Ben, et al., *The London Encyclopaedia*, 3rd edn (London, 2008)

Wells, H. G., *Ann Veronica* [1909] (London, 2005)

—, *The Complete Short Stories of H. G. Wells* (London, 1987)

—, *The New Machiavelli* [1910] (London, 2005)

—, *Tono-Bungay* [1908] (London, 1994)

—, *The War of the Worlds* [1898] (London, 2005)

—, *When the Sleeper Wakes* [1910] (London, 1994)

Welsh, Irvine, *Trainspotting* [1993] (London, 2011)

Wheatle, Alex, *Brixton Rock* (London, 1999)

—, *East of Acre Lane* (London, 2006)

White, Jerry, ed., *London Stories* (London, 2014)

Whitehead, Andrew, ed., *London Fictions* (London, 2013)

Williams, Harry, *South London* (London, 1949)

Williams, Nigel, *The Wimbledon Poisoner* [1990] (London, 2013)

Wilmott, Peter, *The Evolution of a Community* (London, 1963)

Wilson, A. N., *My Name Is Legion* (London, 2004)

Wilson, Jacqueline, *Opal Plumstead* (London, 2014)

Wilson, Robert McLiam, *Ripley Bogle* (London, 1989)

Wodehouse, P. G., *Carry On, Jeeves* (London, 1925)

—, *Psmith in the City* (London, 2003)

Wolfreys, Julian, *The J. Hillis Miller Reader* (Stanford, CA, 2005)

Womersley, David, and Richard A. McCabe, eds, *Literary Milieux: Essays in Text and Context Presented to Howard Erskine-Hill* (Newark, DE, 2008)

Woolf, Virginia, *A Moment's Liberty: The Shorter Diary* (London, 2010)

—, *Selected Essays* (Oxford, 2008)

Wyndham, John, *The Day of the Triffids* [1951] (Harmondsworth, 1969)

Zephaniah, Benjamin, *Face* (London, 1999)

ACKNOWLEDGEMENTS

All my love to Gwen, Stella and Eliza, and Jessie too, for putting up with so much, yet again. Special thanks to everyone who worked so hard on this project at Reaktion Books. And cheers to Sebastian for the maps.

ILLUSTRATIONS

Maps designed and created by Sebastian Ballard.